juvenile
delinquency

juvenile delinquency

third edition

Ruth Shonle Cavan
and
Theodore N. Ferdinand

Northern Illinois University

J. B. Lippincott Company
Philadelphia New York Toronto

Copyright © 1975, 1969, 1962 by J. B. Lippincott Company

This book is fully protected by copyright and, with the exception of brief excerpts for review, no part of it may be reproduced in any form by print, photoprint, microfilm, or by any other means without the written permission of the publishers

ISBN-0-397-47320-6

Library of Congress Catalog Card Number 74-23101

Printed in the United States of America

1 3 5 7 9 10 8 6 4 2

Library of Congress Cataloging in Publication Data

Cavan, Ruth Shonle, 1896-
    Juvenile delinquency.

    Includes bibliographies and index.
    1. Juvenile delinquency.   I. Ferdinand, Theodore N., joint author.
II. Title.
HV9069.C35   1975   364.36   74-23101
ISBN 0-397-47320-6

preface

In this third edition of *Juvenile Delinquency* we have sought to accomplish several goals. We have attempted to relate the evidence of delinquency to four broad perspectives in sociological theory, providing thereby a framework in terms of which the student might more readily interpret the data of delinquency. We have integrated recent advances in the typological description of delinquency into our argument, and we have examined briefly psychological and social psychological interpretations of delinquency. Wherever possible we have also utilized in our discussion the most recent statistical summaries from state and federal agencies.

The rapidly changing panorama of the juvenile justice system has also been captured, as it were, in full flight. Both the juvenile court and the juvenile code are evolving in quantum leaps as a result of recent United States Supreme Court decisions affecting the disposition of juvenile cases and drastic shifts in the goals of juvenile corrections. We have described these changes in detail to give the student an appreciation of their scope and the directions they seem to be leading the juvenile justice system. Considerable attention has also been given to research describing and evaluating juvenile correctional institutions as well as to diversionary programs that pose both an alternative and a critique of juvenile institutions.

In spite of all these changes, the second edition of *Juvenile Delinquency* has not been entirely set aside. We have received numerous comments on the thoroughness, clarity, and balance of the last edition, and we have sought above all else to maintain those qualities in this edition. In short, we have attempted to integrate the best research and theorizing of the 1970's with the solid foundation provided by previous editions of this work.

Several colleagues deserve our sincere thanks for their generosity in time and intelligence. Pawel Horoszowski, John Rhoads, and A. Richard Heffron, our editor at J. B. Lippincott Company, all have offered a variety of suggestions regarding different sections of this revision. Jane Ferdinand also made numerous suggestions that contributed directly to the value of our work. Their comments all have helped in no small measure to make this revision better. Finally, one author, Theodore N. Ferdinand, has a long-standing debt to two former teachers: Robert Lowe and Theodore Newcomb. Each of these men in his own way made a contribution to this author's development as a scholar and a scientist, and both deserve to be recognized for their outstanding quality as teachers and as human beings.

Ruth Shonle Cavan
Theodore N. Ferdinand

January, 1975   DeKalb, Illinois

contents

facts and fallacies about juvenile delinquency

chapter 1

Juvenile delinquency occurs throughout the United States, affecting some children of all religious beliefs, every socio-economic class, and each ethnic group. No area, no group is immune.

Well-adjusted children are everyone's concern. Especially in a democracy, the public as well as the government is obligated to provide facilities for rearing children—all children—to lead happy and useful lives. In the United States, great sums are spent to provide for the education, health, recreation, and personal guidance of all children. For children whose parents cannot meet basic needs of food, clothing, and shelter, special provisions are made in governmental and private welfare programs. Skilled professionals specialize in keeping children mentally and physically well and train them for responsible adult life: obstetricians, pediatricians, child psychologists, teachers, religious educators, specialized nurses, and recreation and youth leaders of various kinds.

Parents themselves are deeply concerned. They regard rearing well-adjusted children as one of their major life projects. Many parents read books on child care, conscientiously join study groups, and anxiously consult specialists. Others are also concerned but rely more on traditional methods, common sense, and advice from relatives and neighbors.

Nevertheless, many children are unhealthy, poorly educated, maladjusted emotionally, or habituated to misbehavior. Common sense tells us not to

1

expect perfection of children or adults, but neither does it assent to routine acceptance of human imperfection.

This book is concerned with only one of many types of poor adjustment—juvenile delinquency.

What Is Juvenile Delinquency?

Officially, juvenile delinquency consists of misbehavior by children and adolescents that leads to referral to the juvenile court. In some states the specifics of such misbehavior are rather explicitly stated in the law; in other states the definition of delinquency is so vague and general that the dividing line between delinquency and normal misbehavior is largely a matter of public opinion, the opinion of the policeman who arrests the child, or the judgment of the juvenile court. This lack of precision and uniformity has led some cynics to say that juvenile delinquency is whatever the law says it is. It would be more exact to say that it is behavior which the people of a state and their leaders believe to be a threat to public safety or a hindrance to the best development of the child, and whose prohibition they have incorporated into law.

Specifically juvenile delinquency in different states ranges from the most serious crimes such as murder, burglary, or robbery, to irritating but trivial acts such as playing ball in the street, building a tree house in a public park, or obstructing traffic on a sidewalk. Fortunately, most delinquent acts are of the less serious variety. But there is always the fear on the part of adults that the trivial acts, if continued, may somehow lead to long-lasting or serious misconduct.

Delinquency of Juveniles Is Centuries Old

The legal concept of juvenile delinquency is new. The first legal definition was formulated and the first juvenile court was established in Illinois as recently as 1899. But the failure or inability of children and youth to live up to standards set by adults is age-old. The forbidden behavior of children and youth, along with the severe punishments dealt out, is included in the general criminal laws of different countries in different periods.

FOUR THOUSAND YEARS AGO

The oldest known code of laws, the Code of Hammurabi, dating from 2270 B.C., takes account of many types of misconduct, some specifically of youth. This Code records the laws of Babylon, which developed over many centuries. The laws regulate business transactions, property rights, personal relationships, rights of master and slave, and family relationships and responsibilities.

In the period of the Code, the husband was the patriarchal head of the family, charged with many responsibilities to his wife and children. In patriarchal societies rebellion against the father, even by adult sons, was not tolerated. Punishments were severe.

Item 195 in the Code of Hammurabi states: "If a son strike his father, one shall cut off his hands."[1] Since the age of the son who would be so severely punished is not specified, the law might have applied chiefly to adult sons. It should be noted that severe punishments run all through the Code of Hammurabi, including not only physical mutilations, but death for many offenses, sometimes specified as death by drowning or burning. The Code of Hammurabi also provided for the adoption of certain children, who were then expected to be loyal to the foster father. The Code provides: "If the son of a Ner-se-ga (palace official), or a sacred prostitute, say to a foster father or mother, 'Thou art not my father,' 'Thou art not my mother,' one shall cut out his tongue." Another provision states: "If the son of a Ner-se-ga, or a sacred prostitute, long for his father's house, and run away from his foster-father and foster-mother and go back to his father's house, one shall pluck out his eye."[2]

Another early indication of father-son difficulties that sounds surprisingly modern comes from the translation of clay tablets dated about 1750 B.C., which were excavated in Nippur, about a hundred miles south of present-day Bagdad, Iraq. The translation is of an essay written by a professor in one of the more noted Sumerian academies, exalting the values of formal education. Boys attended school from sunrise to sunset the year round, from early youth to young manhood. Industriousness was encouraged by generous use of corporal punishment. The essay is in the form of a father's admonitions to his indifferent son. The father instructs the son to attend school, stand with respect and fear before his professor, complete his assignments, and avoid wandering about the public square or standing idly in the streets. In short, the son is to be about the business of getting an education. The father upbraids his son for lack of industriousness, failure to support him, too great an interest in material wealth,

[1] Albert Kocourek and John H. Wigmore, *Source of Ancient and Primitive Law, Evolution of Law, Select Readings on the Origin and Development of Legal Institutions*, Little, Brown and Co., Boston, 1951, Vol. 1, p. 427. Even more severe punishments were sometimes used in other groups. Striking of either parent, cursing or disobeying, and rebelling against a parent were punishable by death, according to certain entries in the Bible.

[2] *Ibid., numbers* 192, 193 of the Code.

and refusal to follow his father's vocation. Many of the adjurations sound very familiar at the present time.[3]

During the early period of the Roman Republic the Roman father exercised almost unlimited authority over other family members, including his children. Under *patria potestas* he had the power of life or death over them; he could administer any degree of corporal punishment; he could command his children to marry or divorce as his whim dictated; he could place them in an adopted family; or he could sell them into slavery, if he wished.[4] There is no indication how often Roman fathers actually resorted to such severe measures, but by Roman law they could if they so desired.

Gradually, the severe punishments of the early laws were ameliorated, first in practice and later in amended and/or new laws. Among the Hebrews, for example, punishment by death was replaced by warnings and flogging. Finally, youth were divided into three groups, infant, prepubescent, and adolescent, with penalties increasing in severity as degree of maturity increased.[5]

DELINQUENCY IN EARLY EUROPEAN EXPERIENCE

Old English laws provided penalties for offenses committed by children. For example, under the laws of King Aethelstan, about 924–939 A.D., any thief over twelve years old received the punishment of death if he stole more than twelve pence. (This amount was later reduced to eight pence.) However, with the passage of time, the law was eased for children, and no one under sixteen years could be put to death unless he resisted or ran away.[6]

After the Norman Conquest, a difference in responsibility was recognized for children. Eventually children under seven years old were pardoned. But severe penalties were still imposed on older children and adolescents of the same age as present-day juvenile delinquents. For example, in reviewing early crimes committed by English children, for which they received the same punishments adults would have received, Blackstone, writing in the eighteenth century, refers to the following:

> *girl of thirteen, burned to death for killing her mistress;*
> *boy of ten, hanged for killing his companion;*

---

[3] Samuel Noah Kramer, "A Father and His Perverse Son," *National Probation and Parole Association Journal*, 3 (April, 1957), 169–173. The tablet from which the above translation is taken is in the University Museum in Philadelphia.

[4] Cf. Sir Henry Maine, *Ancient Law*, E. P. Dutton & Co., Inc., New York, 1960, p. 81.

[5] Frederick J. Ludwig, *Youth and the Law, Handbook on Laws Affecting Youth*, Foundation Press, Inc., Youth Council Bureau Project, Brooklyn, N. Y., 1955, pp. 12 ff.

[6] *Ibid.*, p. 15.

boy of eight, hanged for burning two barns;
boy of ten, executed for killing his bedfellow.[7]

Blackstone uses these cases simply as illustrations of the youthful age at which children were considered responsible for their actions. He does not indicate how frequently children committed murder or were executed, nor does he make a statement about less serious types of juvenile misbehavior.

That there were juvenile delinquents in the seventeenth and eighteenth centuries is evident from the founding of the Hospital of Saint Michael in Rome by Pope Clement XI, "for the correction and instruction of profligate youth, that they who when idle were injurious, may when taught become useful to the state."[8]

Other European countries followed this lead, the chief growth of reform schools coming in the early part of the nineteenth century, replacing to some extent physical punishments and imprisonment of juveniles in jail with adult criminals. At this time England had an increased problem of delinquency among city children, for whom it established Kingswood Reformatory for the confinement of the "hordes of unruly children who infested the streets of the new industrial towns" of England.[9] An English report in 1818 states that all information gathered "unites in demonstrating the lamentable fact, that juvenile delinquency has of late years increased to an unprecedented extent, and is still rapidly and progressively increasing; that the crimes committed by the youthful offenders are often of the worst description; and that an organized system for instruction in vice, and the encouragement of depravity is regularly maintained."[10]

Present concern about juvenile delinquency is but a continuation of parental and public anxiety beginning before written records. Many of the actual kinds of delinquency are the same now as thousands of years ago.

CENTURIES OF FAILURE

Undoubtedly the most disturbing fact about this survey of delinquency is that no society has mastered the technique of successfully initiating children

[7] Sir William Blackstone, *Commentaries on the Laws of England*, edited by Thomas M. Cooley, fourth edition edited by James DeWitt Andrews, Callaghan and Co., Chicago, 1899, Vol. 1, p. 1230.

[8] Cited in *Comparative Survey on Juvenile Delinquency*, Part I, *North America*, Division of Social Welfare, Department of Social Affairs, United Nations, Columbia University Press, New York (Sales Number 1952, IV, 13), p. 9.

[9] *Ibid.*, p. 10.

[10] Society for the Diffusion of Knowledge upon the Punishment of Death and the Improvement of Prison Discipline, London, *Report of the Committee of the Society for the Improvement of Prison Discipline and for the Reformation of Juvenile Offenders*, Bensley and Sons, London, 1818, p. 11.

into the expectations and demands of their society and thus avoiding the problem of delinquency. Today each society still struggles with the twin problems of the socialization of its children and the rehabilitation of the deviants.

Juvenile Delinquency in the United States

MAGNITUDE OF THE SITUATION

Each year over 1,800,000 arrests of persons under eighteen occur in the United States, and more than 1,125,000 juveniles appear before the nation's juvenile courts for non-traffic offenses; they equal 2.9 per cent of all children aged ten through seventeen—the "juvenile delinquency" years.[11] This percentage is for one year. During the entire eight years in which the juvenile court holds jurisdiction over them, the probability that a boy or girl will appear in court is considerably increased over the probability in any one year. In a longitudinal study of 9,945 Philadelphia boys, Wolfgang *et al.* reported that 3,475 or 35 per cent had at least one recorded police contact between the ages of ten and eighteen, and 1,862 or 19 per cent had more than one offense to their credit.[12] And for the nation as a whole it has been estimated that about one in every nine youths (one in every six males) will be referred to the juvenile court before his eighteenth birthday.[13] Morover, the problem is growing more serious each day. From 1960 to 1971 the total number of juveniles arrested more than doubled, increasing by 124.5 per cent, and the number of girl delinquents more than *tripled*, increasing by 229.2 per cent over the same period. Thus, in spite of the fact that the proportion of juveniles in the population has been declining since 1970, the percentage who engage in delinquency has continued to increase, with the result that more and more delinquents are arrested each year. In addition to the children who actually appear before the court, approximately the same number of minor offenders are handled directly by the police or through a police juvenile bureau without referral to the court. If these children are counted along with the court cases, the total is again increased.

MORE BOYS THAN GIRLS. It is generally true that for every one girl brought to the attention of the juvenile courts, there are three boys. Their arrests spread

[11] Since a detailed statistical analysis is given in Chapter 3, only the bare outlines of the statistical picture are given here.

[12] Marvin E. Wolfgang, Robert M. Figlio, and Thorsten Sellin, *Delinquency in a Birth Cohort*, University of Chicago Press, Chicago, 1972, pp. 65, 244.

[13] *Challenge of Crime in a Free Society*, President's Commission on Law Enforcement and the Administration of Justice, U. S. Government Printing Office, Washington, D. C., 1967, p. 55.

over a long list of offenses, mostly of a minor nature. Four per cent or more of boys are arrested for each of the following offenses in decreasing frequency: larceny, burglary, disorderly conduct, curfew and loitering law violations, runaway, vandalism, narcotics violations, auto theft, and liquor law violations (see Table 3, Chapter 3). Only five offenses account for more than 4 per cent of arrests of girls: runaway, larceny, disorderly conduct, curfew and loitering violations, and narcotics violations. Thefts involving material goods of considerable monetary value, murders, and serious vices occur occasionally, but they are rare.

COSTS OF DELINQUENCY. The most serious cost is the human one—the scarring effect on children apprehended by the police, brought before the courts, and sent to correctional institutions even though their offenses were not serious. To a child wavering between mild or occasional misbehavior and the more serious misconduct leading to adult criminality, the experience of arrest, trial, and correctional institution may catapult him into more serious delinquency. The child or adolescent who commits a major crime has often developed a serious character defect or emotional maladjustment that only the most skillful and lengthy treatment can change.

The financial cost is also high, with most of the payment for services coming directly from the taxpayer's pocket. The direct financial cost of public services required by delinquents—police, detention facilities, courts, and institutional care—is difficult to estimate, but it must be enormous when we consider that they handle up to 1,800,000 juveniles a year. Property losses due to delinquency are also sizable. In 1971 losses due to auto theft and larceny by juveniles came to about $374,700,000. When we add this figure to the cost of the juvenile criminal justice system in America, an estimate of a billion dollars per year as the cost of delinquency to the country cannot be far wrong.

Misconceptions About Causes of Delinquency

What causes any child to disobey, or any adult to cut a legal corner? The causes of nonconformity to rules and laws are many. Delinquency is simply a certain type of misbehavior that has been singled out for special attention. However, many people assume that all juvenile delinquency constitutes one kind of misconduct, due to one biological cause or growing out of one kind of life experience. Actually, the contributing factors to delinquency are as varied as the types of misbehavior grouped under this general term. Let us look at some of the supposed causes, each of which is in some way related indirectly to some type of delinquency, but no one of which is a direct cause.

Are Delinquents Feeble-minded—or Superior?

The answer is neither; they represent a cross section of the juvenile population. Feeble-minded children sometimes get into difficulties: they may wander from home, expose themselves in public without intent to offend anyone, or yield to violent emotions. Many such children are committed to schools for the feeble-minded where they can be given closer custody than at home. Seriously feeble-minded children would not be capable of the planning and cooperation needed to commit delinquencies. At the other extreme, brilliant children sometimes become delinquent. The commission of a delinquent act or a crime usually is not a matter of rational decision so much as a social activity carried out with others or an attempt to fulfill personal needs. Intelligence may come into the planning and execution of a crime; in fact, some of the crimes that shock the nation have been committed by young people of superior intelligence. But there is no undue tendency for brilliant children to commit crimes or to become delinquent. The motivation for delinquency and crime lies elsewhere than in high intelligence or lack of it. The manner in which a crime is committed may be related to intellectual ability. The long-established idea that most if not all delinquents and criminals are feeble-minded has been discarded. Now, one must consider whether the child has been discriminated against because of dullness or brilliance. One must look for the way in which his intelligence or lack of it has contributed to the manner in which the delinquency was committed. But a direct controlling connection between intelligence or lack of it and delinquency does not exist.

Are Most Delinquents Seriously Maladjusted Emotionally?

Authorities who are psychologically oriented tend to answer this question in the affirmative. The affirmative answer usually comes from clinicians, who have children referred to them showing evidence of emotional maladjustment, one evidence of which may be delinquent behavior. They rarely have association with the much larger number of delinquents who seem no more neurotic or psychotic than the average person. Here we must recognize that few people are so perfectly adjusted that they do not show some signs of tension, some rebellion to frustration, some anxieties. The important point is not whether a delinquent has some symptoms of neurosis or psychosis, but whether the conditions that underlie these symptoms are also the causes of delinquent behavior.

Criminologists who study delinquents in the community instead of the clinic are convinced that most delinquents are not seriously maladjusted emotionally. One estimate is that 25 per cent are somewhat disturbed emotionally.[14] The origin of delinquency in the other 75 per cent is assumed to lie in the social and cultural features of their communities.

ARE THE CHILDREN OF SOME RACES AND NATIONALITY GROUPS "NATURALLY" DELINQUENT?

Superficially, some racial and ethnic groups seem to have a monopoly on delinquency and crime, because their rates of arrest and court appearances are higher than the average. However, careful study of the problem points to a negative reply. High rates of arrest, court appearances, and commitments to prison seem to be more closely related to socio-economic circumstances than racial or ethnic membership. Edward Green compared the arrest rates of white and black inhabitants of Ypsilanti, Michigan, between 1942 and 1965, and he found that when the effects of socio-economic status and Southern origins are removed, "the arrest rates of the races tend toward parity and in several instances a higher rate for whites."[15] There is little doubt that crime and delinquency are more common in the ghetto than elsewhere, but these problems seem to be specific more to the area and its disorganized conditions than to the particular ethnic or racial group that happens to live there. As a ghetto group establishes itself or its children on a firm educational and economic basis and moves from lower class to middle class status, rates of delinquency decline. Delinquency thus is a symptom of a particular phase of adjustment among racial ethnic groups. For example, a little over a hundred years ago in New York City, the Irish, newly arrived, engaged in many fights and riots. The Irish have long since become integrated into the American pattern of conformity. Many nationality groups have experienced a similar pattern of delinquency and crime but later become assimilated into American life. The most recent example is that of the Puerto Rican migration, chiefly after World War II, into New York City. Not yet fully adjusted, the children of this group are accused of rampant delinquency. In time, they too will take their place in American social and cultural life.

[14] William C. Kvaraceus *et al.*, *Delinquent Behavior: Culture and the Individual*, National Education Association of the United States, Washington, D. C., 1959, p. 54. The estimate was made by Walter B. Miller, Harvard University, who was Director of the Roxbury Youth Project Research, Roxbury, Massachusetts.

[15] Edward Green, "Race, Social Status, and Criminal Arrest," *American Sociological Review*, 35 (June, 1970), 488–490.

Is the Family Responsible for Delinquency?

Basically, the family carries a heavy responsibility for the character and personality formation of every child. In general, each set of parents does the best it can. Few parents wish evil for their children. But many parents are unable to give their children the love and guidance they need; many are unable to introduce their children into the cultural mores or help them meet the social expectations of the larger community. When laymen or social agencies say "the family is responsible for delinquency," they are really begging the question. Parents whose children are drifting into delinquency or are actually delinquent are themselves in need of help.

The broken home with one or both parents absent has been scored as a cause of delinquency. It is true that delinquents come from broken homes in somewhat higher proportions than nondelinquents; but there is no sharp division. Many children from broken homes are nondelinquent, and many from unbroken homes are delinquent. At most, some types of broken homes indicate an unfavorable family life; but the important factor seems to be the quality of family life rather than the physical presence of both parents.

The employed mother has also been criticized as a factor in delinquency. A somewhat higher proportion of delinquent than nondelinquent children do have employed mothers. But to hold the employed mother responsible for delinquency is another blanket assumption which needs closer study. At an earlier period when most mothers worked from dire necessity, the home with an employed mother also was often the broken home and the poverty-stricken home. The employment of the mother often left the children without adequate supervision, but its greater significance for understanding delinquency was as a symptom of unfavorable family conditions, none of which alone created delinquency, but all of which precipitated an unfavorable family situation.

Today when the trend is toward widespread employment of mothers for many reasons other than necessity, the employment of the mother may connote a desire for greater family security, continued education of children, a better home, a summer vacation, or any one of a number of things thought to be of benefit to all members of the family.

Are Crime Comics to Blame?

The debate about the relation of crime comics and television murder scripts to delinquency has strong advocates on both sides. The situation repeats the debate of the 1920's about the effect of crime movies on children. One group asserts that crime pictures of any type serve as a catharsis for hostility usually repressed under social disapproval. When released through vicarious participation in violently portrayed incidents, the hostility becomes harmless.

Their opponents suggest that violence in the mass media not only provides convenient examples of violent behavior but also tends to legitimate its use. There have been few studies of the direct relationship between delinquency and violence in the mass media, but a pioneering effort in this area is the research performed by Herbert Blumer and Philip Hauser in the 1920's.[16] They concluded that movies about crime did not stimulate youth to attempt a life of crime. They were, however, preferred by a larger percentage of already delinquent children than of nondelinquent children. Some delinquent children stated that they had learned specific techniques for the commission of crimes from the crime motion pictures. Pictures of luxury and easily acquired wealth sometimes gave a rationalization for thievery, and both boys and girls were at times sexually aroused by certain torrid love scenes. But choice of pictures and the effect of the pictures were related to already developed interests and values.

More recently the National Commission on the Causes and Prevention of Violence has considered television as a cause of violence, and some of its conclusions are that violence on television tends to prompt violent outbursts on the part of viewers, particularly if the violence is portrayed as justified and if the viewers are *not* angry prior to viewing the violent program.[17] The Commission also reported that television is virtually saturated with violence —violent programs occupy on the average 81 per cent of available time—and that more than half of the poorer classes watch television four hours or more per day.[18] Of the general population, however, only about one-sixth watch that much. Thus, although movies and crime comics may not foster delinquency, television seems to contribute directly to the high level of violence in American society.

IS THE GANG RESPONSIBLE FOR DELINQUENCY?

Gangs of adolescent boys (occasionally of girls) are often accused of drawing boys into delinquency and of perpetuating delinquency and passing it on to younger boys. It is true that the lone delinquent is the exception. A number of studies indicate that most acts of delinquency are carried out by two or three boys. In their classic study of Chicago delinquency, Shaw and McKay found that 19 per cent of all offenders were isolates; 58 per cent of the offenses were carried out by two or three boys, 18 per cent by four or five

[16] Herbert Blumer and Philip M. Hauser, *Movies, Delinquency, and Crime*, Macmillan Co., New York, 1933.

[17] David L. Lange, Robert K. Baker, and Sandra J. Ball, *Mass Media and Violence*, U. S. Government Printing Office, Washington, D. C., 1969, p. 243.

[18] *Ibid.*, pp. 212, 327.

boys, and only 6 per cent by six or more boys.[19] More recently, however, Hirschi has pointed out that delinquents neither identify with their delinquent companions nor respect their opinions, and Klein has reported that only certain types of offenses tend to be group delinquencies, e.g., assault or auto theft, while other types, e.g., malicious mischief or incorrigibility, are committed most frequently in isolation.[20]

Although the group committing an offense is usually small, many boys belong to larger groups or sometimes to organized gangs. Few crimes necessitate more than a few participants, and a large number of boys intent on burglary, stealing a car, or destruction of property would soon become conspicuous and stand in danger of an arrest. The function of the larger group is to give approval for the delinquencies of small cliques or groups within the larger group. The clique may gain status within the larger group by daring delinquencies. The gang as such functions directly in delinquency primarily through fights between rival gangs, when the number of combatants increases the chance of success even though at the same time it may attract police attention. Its relationship to the most common kinds of delinquencies of youth is indirect.

The delinquencies of individual boys or girls have received less attention than group delinquencies and gang fights. It is suggested that the individual delinquent is likely to be a seriously maladjusted adolescent, whose misconduct has more relationship to his own emotional needs than to clique or gang approval.

Each of the above factors—mental capacity, emotional maladjustment, racial and ethnic affiliations, family conditions, crime comics, movies, and television, the juvenile gang—may have some relationship to delinquency. But none of these factors has a direct one-to-one relationship with any type of delinquency. The way in which these and other influences may be interwoven in the development of delinquent behavior is elaborated in later chapters.

Misconceptions About Prevention and Cure

The erroneous belief that factors such as those just discussed are primary, unitary causes of delinquency impedes progress toward the prevention of delinquency and the rehabilitation of the delinquent. Science has made prog-

[19] Clifford R. Shaw and Henry D. McKay, *Social Factors in Juvenile Delinquency*, National Commission on Law Observance and Enforcement, U. S. Government Printing Office, Washington, D. C., 1931, No. 13, Vol. 2, pp. 194–195.

[20] Travis Hirschi, *Causes of Delinquency*, University of California Press, Berkeley, 1969, Chapter VIII; and Malcolm W. Klein, *Street Gangs and Street Workers*, Prentice-Hall, Inc., Englewood Cliffs, N. J., 1971, p. 117.

ress since the time of the Code of Hammurabi in understanding motivations of behavior, but it has not yet accurately pinpointed the various processes by which the crazy-quilt of delinquency develops. Even with the best of present knowledge, prevention and rehabilitation are difficult, and progress toward more adequate methods is slow. Many people advocate sure-shot methods of prevention and cure, some of which have little validity, while others may have an indirect or partial usefulness.

SEVERITY VERSUS CODDLING

The trend in treatment of juvenile delinquents and adult criminals has been away from severe punishments. Nevertheless, one segment of public opinion urges severe physical punishments, imprisonment, and even capital punishment for homicide by juveniles. It is not clear whether the demand for severity emanates from honest convictions, fear because of the increase in juvenile court cases, desire in some cases for a cheap solution making little demand on the taxpayer, or an unconscious projection of all kinds of hatred and resentment against the delinquent. Parallel with the demand for severity is the stigmatization of therapy and re-education as coddling. Therapy and re-education are slow processes and perform no miracles. They are, however, in line with the best that we know of how children learn and are motivated to follow the social codes.

The severe physical punishments of the past put a stop neither to juvenile delinquency nor to adult crime. Several thousand years ago capital punishment by cruel methods, cutting off of fingers or hands, branding, or flogging, were common penalties. Some of these punishments continued into the nineteenth century. Imprisonment became the accepted method of punishment during the early 1800's. Isolation from society, few contacts and no communication between prisoners, and sometimes solitary confinement for years within the prison became standard treatment. Sometimes infractions of prison regulations were punished by whipping and other forms of physical abuse. As reform schools for children and youth were built, many of the same practices were followed. But still delinquency and crime did not stop.

Gradually, various forms of education and retraining for juveniles superseded the more severe methods. At first military drill and vocational training were the standbys. Since the 1920's emphasis has shifted to psychological and social rehabilitation, with the objectives of clearing up emotional twists and of teaching socially acceptable attitudes and habits. It cannot be said, however, that any of these methods has either rehabilitated delinquents or prevented future delinquency. The methods now are more humane than in the past, and they take account of each delinquent as an individual, seeking to reach the cause of his misbehavior. Therapy and re-education are not coddling. They demand effort on the part of the delinquent, the willingness to try to understand himself, and the readiness to live by the rules of society. These processes may be very difficult for the free-roving youth who has rejected the more stable social institutions to live by his individual impulses or by the rules of a small group of other boys. Intelligent discipline by the family, supported by other adults in charge of juveniles, and eventually self-discipline by the juveniles themselves are among the objectives of rehabilitation. These objectives are not accomplished by severe punishments, in fact, quite the opposite.

SHOULD PARENTS OF DELINQUENTS BE PUNISHED?

The erroneous belief that the family alone is responsible for delinquency has led some to demand that parents of delinquents be punished for not preventing the delinquent behavior.

Systematic punishment of parents has been tried in a few places. For ten years, Judge Paul W. Alexander of Toledo punished parents. Over a thousand cases of adults, half of them parents (mostly mothers), were heard by the court on the charge of contributing to delinquency. Three-fourths of the parents pleaded guilty or were found guilty. One out of four of those convicted served an average of almost a year in prison; the remainder received suspended sentences. A review of the practice, instigated by Judge Alexander himself, revealed that there was no evidence that delinquency had been curbed by punishment of the parents. Judge Alexander concluded that in the main punishment of parents was a form of revenge.[21]

Usually parents who are sentenced for contributing to the delinquency of their children have not done any specific thing to lead the children to delinquency. They have more often failed to rear their children to conform to laws and social rules. Their own inabilities or emotional problems are usually at the root of the failure. Nothing specific that they have done or not done to contribute to an act of delinquency can normally be pointed out to these helpless or hopeless parents.

The disastrous effects of punishing parents have often been pointed out. When the mother is imprisoned, the home is broken up and her children must be placed in institutions or foster homes or left to care for themselves. Typically, when she is released, she receives no help in reassembling her children and re-establishing her home. Meanwhile, the respect for her by neigh-

---

[21] Cited by Sol Rubin, *Crime and Juvenile Delinquency*, published for the National Probation and Parole Association by Oceana Publications, Inc., New York, 1958, pp. 34–35.

bors and children declines. Older children are given a crutch on which to lean in shifting responsibility for their conduct to their mother. If the father is the one imprisoned, the mother must go to work or the entire family must be supported by relief agencies.

It has been found also that once judges accept the idea that punishment of parents is valid, they tend to use it in many cases and relax their efforts to arrange for the rehabilitation of children or of the family as a whole.

Many who oppose punishment of parents do not deny the powerful influence of parents on the development of children's personalities and behavior, but do absolve them from blame for the delinquency. As an alternative to punishing parents, they propose aid to parents through education and counseling.[22]

CURFEWS ARE NO ANSWER

A curfew effective at an early evening hour is an attempt at an easy way to curb outward misbehavior without digging up the roots of the problem. Curfew ordinances, often setting nine o'clock as the deadline, are popular in many cities. Parents use the curfew as a threat to get their children home, and police feel that almost any youth on the streets after the designated hour should be questioned for loitering. The public in general assumes that parents should enforce the curfew on their children and be held responsible for misbehavior after that hour.

Curfews raise numerous problems. Police enforce them unevenly, and when they do approach teen-agers, they are often unable to tell whether the young people are above or below the age set by law. Parents also dislike having their nondelinquent children questioned by the police. Many programs at churches, schools, and community centers run past the usual curfew hour and crowds of youth are legitimately on the street late at night, but may be subjected to grilling by the police.

Probably more important is the fact that a curfew does not attack the causes of delinquency or provide anything constructive. A report made by the Connecticut State Juvenile Court, which was opposed to curfew laws, compares the enforcement of the laws to a state of siege signifying that a city's

---

[22] Irving Arthur Gladstone, "Spare the Rod and Spoil the Parent," *Federal Probation*, 19 (June, 1955), 37–41; Justine Wise Polier, "The Woodshed is No Answer," *Federal Probation*, 20 (September, 1956), 3–6; Polier; "Back to What Woodshed?" Pamphlet No. 232, Public Affairs Committee, New York, 1956. Mr. Gladstone is a school principal, and Judge Polier is a justice in the Domestic Relations Court of New York City. Both oppose punishment of parents.

youth programs are ineffective. The report points out that only about 2 per cent of children are in trouble and that 86 per cent of all delinquencies occur before nine o'clock, but the law is imposed on all youth, innocent and delinquent alike.[23]

Various writers point out that curfew laws do not stop delinquency. The normally nondelinquent youth does not wander aimlessly about the street, and the delinquency-bent youth finds ways to evade the law or openly disregard it. The negative approach of the curfew does not bring about needed changes in personality and behavior patterns.

RECREATION NEEDED BY ALL CHILDREN

Another easy answer to the problem of delinquency is to provide enough recreation for all children. The need of all children for recreation is now generally recognized, as is the fact that in cities the back yard, the vacant lot, the attic, and the open country are not available. Community centers, churches, schools, and public recreation departments have therefore accepted the responsibility of providing space, equipment, and leadership. Recreation may be used as a means of personality development and character training, but chiefly when children are organized into small groups which meet frequently with good leaders. Even then there is no absolute assurance that delinquency will be prevented or delinquents rehabilitated. The carry-over of the effect of the limited hours of recreation into the many hours of daily life spent in other situations is not complete.

Although interest in recreation as an antidote to delinquency continues high in America, most of the research into this question stems from the 1930's and 1940's. In general, these studies indicate that even though many delinquents or pre-delinquents can be attracted to recreational programs, they tend to be the least delinquent youths, they tend to avoid closely supervised programs, and they tend to spend only a very small portion of their time in these programs even when a strong effort to enlist their interest is made.[24] Overall there is serious question regarding the effectiveness of recreation programs in combating delinquency in view of their seasonal nature and the limited impact they have upon serious delinquents in a neighborhood.

[23] Frank L. Manella, "Curfew Laws," *National Probation and Parole Association Journal*, 4 (April, 1958), 165–166.

[24] Cf. Ethel Shanas and Catherine E. Dunning, *Recreation and Delinquency*, Chicago Recreation Commission, 1942; Frederic M. Thrasher, "The Boys' Club and Juvenile Delinquency," *American Journal of Sociology*, 42 (1936), pp. 66–80; and Ellery F. Reed, "How Effective are Group Work Agencies in Preventing Delinquency?" *The Social Review*, 22 (1948), pp. 340–348.

WHAT ABOUT SLUM CLEARANCE?

As with recreation, everyone is entitled to clean, well-equipped housing and neighborhood services, but they do not necessarily prevent or reduce delinquency. Some early assertions that there was a direct relationship between decline in delinquency and public housing overlooked the fact that often the people displaced from old slums when land was cleared did not return to the new housing. Higher rents and a different standard of living often brought in families whose children were not delinquency-oriented. In some projects, as soon as a child is detected in delinquency, the family is evicted. In these projects the delinquency rate is low, but the family has simply moved outside the project, and the delinquent child continues his activities. Nothing is solved.

Probably no social reform has failed its early promise more dismally than public housing for low income families. It has often been built so as to reinforce existing patterns of racial segregation; it has contributed to the continuing decline in dignity among lower income families; and it has seriously aggravated the problem of crime and delinquency in lower class neighborhoods.[25] Although improving the living conditions of low income families was and is a worthy goal, its failure lies mainly in its execution. Much public housing was constructed with a peculiar insensitivity to the effects of location and architecture upon social interaction, with the result that low income, often fatherless, families with large numbers of adolescents were crowded together in high-density settings where there were innumerable opportunities to engage in delinquencies in poorly supervised areas. It would be difficult to contrive a more criminogenic environment even with the best of sociological advice. The results are well known. Indeed, in some housing projects, conditions are so bad that the residents have all moved out and the only alternative is to abandon them and turn their sites to other uses.[26]

What is needed over and above new housing is a sense of pride and community identity, but these develop only with difficulty in low-rent projects where hundreds of families, previously unknown to each other and often inexperienced in urban living, suddenly come together in a compact housing project.

A community, when confronted with a perplexing problem like delinquency, often tries a shortcut instead of meeting its problem head-on. Many of the approaches already discussed stem from efforts to find easy shortcuts.

---

[25] Cf. Oscar Newman, *Architectural Design for Crime Prevention*, U. S. Government Printing Office, Washington, D. C., 1973, Chapters 4 and 5.

[26] The Pruitt-Igoe public housing project in St. Louis was finally closed in 1973 after its occupancy fell to about 20 per cent of capacity. It was constructed in 1955 at a cost of thirty-six million dollars. See *New York Times* (June 10, 1973), p. 41.

Some are based on wishful thinking (curfew for instance)—if only this easy solution would work. Some seem to be the result of hostility on the part of the public and an attempt to assign blame on someone (punishment of parents or severe treatment of delinquents). A few are catch-all solutions—some program is recognized as valuable in its own right and must therefore surely be a cure for delinquency (recreation, slum clearance, and adequate housing). When applicable at all, many of these programs touch only part of the problem. Delinquency is behavior, and like all behavior it is related on the one hand to inner needs and on the other to social groups and cultural ways of the groups of which the person is a member.

Delinquency Is Worldwide

This chapter began with the statement that juvenile delinquency is age-old. It concludes with data to point out that juvenile delinquency is also worldwide. The United States is not alone in its struggle to control delinquent behavior. Every civilized country has its own problems. It is not possible to compare rates because of different concepts of delinquency, different age limits, and differences in agencies handling delinquency. In a study of nineteen European countries, made under the United Nations, it was noted that all the countries had special institutions for long-term care of juvenile delinquents.[27] Even Iceland had one institution to accommodate fifteen boys between the ages of fourteen and eighteen. The United Nations also conducted a study in nine countries in the Middle East and Near East and in each found special recognition of youthful offenders in the general criminal code, although at the time of the study one country, Jordan, had passed special legislation regarding juvenile delinquents.[28] In Asia and the Far East, also, laws make special provisions for young offenders, again a recognition of delinquency and crime among youth.[29] Forms of punishment and institutions vary from country to country but are vivid evidence of the existence of juvenile delinquency.

[27] *The Prevention of Juvenile Delinquency in Selected European Countries*, Bureau of Social Affairs, Department of Economic and Social Affairs, United Nations, Columbia University Press, New York (Sales Number 1955, IV, 12), p. 35.

[28] *Comparative Study on Juvenile Delinquency*, Part V, *Middle East*, Division of Social Welfare, Department of Social Affairs, United Nations, Columbia University Press, New York (Sales Number 1953, VI, 17), p. 1. The countries covered were Egypt, Iran, Jordan, Lebanon, Saudi Arabia, Syria, Turkey, and Yemen.

[29] *Comparative Survey on Juvenile Delinquency*, Part IV, *Asia and the Far East*, Division of Social Welfare, Department of Social Affairs, United Nations, Columbia University Press, New York (Sales No. 1953, IV, 27), Chapter 1. The countries surveyed were Burma, Ceylon, India, Japan, Pakistan, the Philippines, and Thailand.

In all parts of the urbanized world, as in the United States, crime and delinquency are on the increase. Canada experienced almost a one-hundred-fold increase in convictions between 1901 and 1966.[30] In the 1960's crime grew about ten per cent per year in Great Britain and Northern Ireland.[31] In the Netherlands the theft of bicycles and motorcycles, which is a typical juvenile offense in that country, increased 170 per cent between 1957 and 1962.[32] In Poland the rate of juvenile offenses increased 3.5 times between 1960 and 1966.[33]

Among Asian countries, Japan has recently reported a rise in delinquency rates after a declining period.[34] In Malaysia, where delinquency had been comparatively rare, there were 2,000 convictions of juveniles in 1970.[35] In Thailand youth crime doubled between 1962 and 1964.[36] Reports of delinquency come from other parts of the world: Africa, South America, and Mexico.[37]

Other types of crime, troublesome in the United States, also afflict other nations. Drug abuse among young people is an international problem.[38] Although accurate statistics on drug abuse are difficult to assemble, prevention or treatment programs have been established in most major European

[30] *Report of the Canadian Committee on Corrections—Toward Unity: Criminal Justice and Corrections*, Ottawa, Queen's Printer, 1969.

[31] Note by the Secretary-General, *Crime Prevention and Control*, United Nations General Assembly, 27th Session, Agenda item 53, pp. 5–6.

[32] Dr. C. N. Peijster, "Automobile Theft by Minors," a paper presented at the Fifth International Criminological Congress, Montreal, September 1, 1965, p. 4.

[33] Stanislaw Walczak, "Niektóre problemy strategii w walce z przestępczościa," *Przeglad Penitencjarny*, No. 2, 26, 1970, p. 11.

[34] Government of Japan, *Summary of the White Paper on Crime—1971*, Ministry of Justice, February, 1972, pp. 31–54.

[35] *1970 Report on the World Situation*, United Nations, New York, 1971 (Sales No.: E.71.IV.13), p. 224.

[36] *Report of the Secretariat, Third United Nations Congress on the Prevention of Crime and the Treatment of Offenders, United Nations*, New York, 1967 Sales No.: 67.IV.1), p. 18.

[37] Note by the Secretary-General, *Crime Prevention and Control*, Lois B. deFleur, "Ecological Variables in the Cross-Cultural Study of Delinquency," *Social Forces*, 45 (June, 1967), 556–570; Ruth S. and Jordan T. Cavan, *Delinquency and Crime: Cross-Cultural Perspectives*, J. B. Lippincott Company, Philadelphia, 1968, Chapter 3.

[38] For example, Buikhuisen and Timmerman report that the number of drug users among secondary school children in the Netherlands increased from 11.2 per cent in 1969 to 20.3 per cent in 1971. Heavy users among this same population more than doubled in the same period, increasing from 2.5 per cent to 6.5 per cent. Cf. W. Buikhuisen and H. Timmerman, "Druggebruik onder Middelbare Scholieren," *Tijdschrift voor Criminologie* (September, 1970), pp. 173–181.

cities, including those in the Communist bloc, just as in the United States.[39]

Juvenile street groups are also a problem. Informal cliques of juveniles engage primarily in public nuisance activities like minor vandalism, petty theft, and other forms of mischief. Organized delinquent gangs after the pattern of Chicago, New York, or Philadelphia are rare in European countries, but when they exist, they are often equally vicious and destructive.[40]

Delinquency in Europe and Asia has changed with the times, as is also true in the United States. For instance, as automobiles increase in a given country, automobile thefts also increased.[41] Department stores with open shelves and self-service (only recently established in Europe) have spawned an increase in shoplifters. World War II with its many privations seemed to justify thefts of food and other necessities, to be followed later by thefts of luxuries. In England, the disorderliness of outlandishly dressed Teddy Boys of the 1960's has given way to robbing on the streets and in local stores.[42] Israel has noted a difference in delinquency by social class with middle class boys indulging in occasional minor delinquencies and lower class delinquents in more serious, persistent delinquency.[43]

Delinquency is not limited to urbanized countries nor to cities in developing countries, although it is typically an urban phenomenon.[44] Isolated, undisturbed tribes have little if any juvenile delinquency, although adult crime flares in these tribes in the form of murder or feuds, often triggered by personal quarrels. Children are under close but informal surveillance by their parents and other adult tribal members, and they are usually incorporated into formal tribal activities at an early age. Difficulties arise, however, when cities are established around some industry financed and managed very often by Americans or Europeans. The city attracts many youth who thereby escape close supervision and incorporation into tribal activities and who enter the city as detached individuals without skills for employment or memberships in a small controlling group.

[39] The dearth of statistics on drug abuse in Europe is rapidly being corrected by studies at a number of criminological institutes and centers in Rome, Stockholm, Groningen (the Netherlands), and elsewhere. Cf. Note by the Secretary-General, *Crime Prevention and Control*, for a discussion of preventive and treatment measures taken by foreign countries.

[40] Cavan and Cavan, *op. cit.*, Chapter 8.

[41] *Ibid.*

[42] Colin McGlashan, "The Making of a Mugger," *New Statesman*, 84 (October 13, 1972), 496–497.

[43] S. Shoham and M. Hovav, "Social Factors, Aspects of Treatment and Patterns of Criminal Careers among the B'nei Tovim," *Human Relations*, 19, No. 1, (1966), 47–56.

[44] Cavan and Cavan, *op. cit.*, pp. 220–232.

As an example, the Eskimos in Alaska and Northern Canada live in a wide range of social situations—from small tribal villages that move summer and winter to educated Eskimos living in cities according to Caucasian social customs.[45] Eskimos who are unable to find employment and move toward acculturation live precariously both economically and culturally. Adolescent boys and girls are drawn to the taverns, dance halls, and street corners, where they are freed from family control and open to exploitation. Stealing from strangers is not a crime in Eskimo tribal culture. But practiced in town, it, along with drunkenness and sexual activities, soon brings boys and girls alike to the attention of the police.

Mexico also has experienced the deleterious effect of urban life on families accustomed to tribal or simple village life in the hinterland of Mexico City.[46] From tight family control and a clear cultural definition of crime, families or individuals find themselves adrift when they migrate to Mexico City. Although they tend to live in related groups, often in slums, isolated by walls and, at night, by locked gates, the family is unable to maintain itself economically or to control the behavior of its adolescent girls and boys. Minor thefts, public rowdiness of boys, and sexual promiscuity of girls violate the mores of the village and the laws of the city but are regarded as survival techniques in the city. Organized delinquency and crime are also present but occur primarily among older youth and adults.

Although these cross-cultural examples reveal many of the same characteristics of delinquency as in the United States, direct comparisons cannot always be made. A study of delinquency in Cordoba, Argentina, that tested certain theories based on American delinquency showed that they were not relevant to delinquency in Cordoba.[47] In each society delinquent behavior grows out of social and cultural stress and deprivation peculiar to itself.

No Easy Way Out

Most children grow up to become responsible adults; most individual acts of delinquency do not lead to a delinquent personality or to professional adult criminality. The usual methods of child-rearing and discipline are probably adequate for the great mass of children. But the hard core of delinquents who set themselves apart from society and contribute heavily to adult criminality slip through the meshes of ordinary socialization techniques. For this group, no country has any sure way of preventing the development of the confirmed delinquent or of accomplishing rehabilitation.

45 *Ibid.*, Chapter 2.
46 *Ibid.*, Chapter 3.
47 leFleur, *op. cit.*

BIBLIOGRAPHY

CAVAN, RUTH SHONLE, AND CAVAN, JORDAN T., *Delinquency and Crime: Cross-Cultural Perspectives*, J. B. Lippincott Company, Philadelphia, 1968.

GIBBENS, T. C. N., ed., *Cultural Factors in Delinquency*, J. B. Lippincott Company, Philadelphia, 1966.

LANGE, DAVID L., ROBERT K. BAKER, AND SANDRA J. BALL, *Mass Media and Violence*, U. S. Government Printing Office, Washington, D. C., 1969.

LUDWIG, FREDERICK J., *Youth and the Law, Handbook of Laws Affecting Youth*, Foundation Press, Inc., Brooklyn, New York, 1955.

RUBIN, SOL, *Crime and Juvenile Delinquency*, Oceana Publications, Inc., New York, 1958, **Chapter 2.**

juvenile delinquency
defined

Juvenile delinquency refers to the failure of children and youth to meet certain obligations expected of them by the society in which they live.

Legal Definitions

The Children's Bureau, a federal agency, uses a legal definition of delinquency in its reports:

> Juvenile delinquency cases are those referred to courts for acts defined in the statutes of the State as the violation of a state law or municipal ordinance by children or youth of juvenile court age, or for conduct so seriously antisocial as to interfere with the rights of others or to menace the welfare of the delinquent himself or of the community. This broad definition of delinquency includes conduct which violates the law only when committed by children, e.g., truancy, ungovernable behavior, and running away.[1]

VARIETY OF LAWS

Each state, the District of Columbia, Puerto Rico, and the federal government have all passed laws defining the types of behavior that justify bring-

[1] *Juvenile Court Statistics 1971*, U.S. Department of Health, Education, and Welfare, DHEW Publication No. (SRS) 73-03452, Washington, D.C., 1972, p. 7.

ing a child or youth before a special juvenile court. Fifty-three varying legal definitions are based on the underlying principle of protection for the child and community. However, they vary in many details.[2]

The first juvenile delinquency law, passed by the State of Illinois in 1899, specifies many exact kinds of delinquency in addition to the offenses covered by the criminal laws. Many other states have also passed an omnibus type of law.

> "DELINQUENT CHILD" DEFINED. SEC. 1. Be it enacted by the People of the State of Illinois, represented in the General Assembly: That for the purposes of this Act a delinquent child is any male who while under the age of 17 years, or any female who while under the age of 18 years, violates any law of this State; or is incorrigible, or knowingly associates with thieves, vicious or immoral persons; or without just cause and without the consent of its parents, guardian, or custodian absents itself from its home or place of abode, or is growing up in idleness or crime; or knowingly frequents a house of ill repute; or knowingly frequents any policy shop or place where any gambling device is operated; or frequents any saloon or dramshop where intoxicating liquors are sold; or patronizes or visits any public pool room or bucket shop; or wanders about the streets in the night time without being on any lawful business or lawful occupation; or habitually wanders about any railroad yards or tracks or jumps or attempts to jump onto any moving train; or enters any car or engine without lawful authority; or uses vile, obscene, vulgar, or indecent language in any public place or about any school house; or is guilty of indecent or lascivious conduct.

The recent trend is to pass more general laws that list fewer specific offenses. In 1965, Illinois modified its original law as follows:

> ARTICLE 2, SECTION 2-2. DELINQUENT MINOR. Those who are delinquent include (a) any boy who prior to his 17th birthday or girl who prior to her 18th birthday has violated or attempted to violate, regardless of where the act occurred, any federal or state law or municipal ordinance; and (b) any minor who has violated a lawful court order under this Act.
> SECTION 2-3. MINOR OTHERWISE IN NEED OF SUPERVISION. Those otherwise in need of supervision include (a) any minor under 18 years of age who is beyond the control of his parents, guardian or

---

[2] Students who wish to learn about the specifics of a given state should consult the statutes for that state or a collection of laws, such as Wendell Huston, compiler, *Social Welfare Laws of the Forty-eight States*, Wendell Huston Co., Seattle, Washington, 98104. This publication is kept up to date through supplements.

other custodian; and (b) any minor subject to compulsory school attendance who is habitually truant from school.

The older omnibus type of law imposed many restrictions upon juveniles that were not applicable to adults. For example, the following list details some of the behaviors that were specifically forbidden to juveniles by the early juvenile statutes:

(Knowingly) associates with thieves, vicious or immoral persons
Absents self from home (without just cause) without consent
(Habitually) wanders about railroad yards or tracks
(Habitually) uses vile, obscene or vulgar language in public places
Wanders streets at night, not on lawful business
Patronizes public poolroom or bucket shop
Smokes cigarette (or uses tobacco in any form)
Uses intoxicating liquor
Is given to sexual irregularities.[3]

General laws are more readily adapted to change and to the idiosyncrasies of local areas and groups than are specific laws. The more specific the law, the more rapidly it becomes irrelevant. Opinions change as to what is undesirable behavior. Such behavior itself may change; for instance, the original Illinois law forbade certain behavior on or around railroad trains, but nothing was said about automobiles, which were few at the time the law was passed. Smoking, forbidden in some states, was formerly thought undesirable—even immoral—but is now a common practice among adults and older adolescents. Finally, what is regarded as undesirable in one region, one social class, or one ethnic group may be regarded as normal or even desirable in some other group.

LEGAL AGE OF DELINQUENT CHILDREN

Many states do not specify an age below which a child would not be considered capable of judging right and wrong conduct. When a lower age is specified, it is usually seven years; that is, below the age of seven a child would not be held responsible for his conduct, no matter what he did. His parents, however, might be held responsible for failure to supervise him.

The upper age limit for juvenile delinquency varies in different states from sixteen to twenty-one years. The most commonly used upper limit is the eighteenth birthday: on one day the boy is still seventeen years old, and mis-

[3] Rephrased from Frederick B. Sussman, *Law of Juvenile Delinquency*, Oceana Publications, 80 Fourth Avenue, New York, 1950, revised and updated by publisher's editorial staff, 1959, p. 21. Note that six of the nine offenses listed above were specifically mentioned by the 1899 Illinois statute.

conduct would bring him to the juvenile court as a juvenile delinquent; the next day he celebrates his eighteenth birthday, and misconduct would bring him to a court that handles adult criminal cases. However, after his eighteenth birthday, he would not be held in any court for misconduct of the type specified only in juvenile delinquency laws.

In recent years there has been a distinct tendency to lower the age of delinquency from eighteen to sixteen or seventeen. In 1957 eleven states set the dividing line between adult criminality and juvenile delinquency for both boys and girls at sixteen or seventeen, but in 1971 fourteen did.[4] The region with the lowest average age of delinquency is New England. Three of the six New England states use seventeen; two have established sixteen as the dividing line; and only Rhode Island has set eighteen as the age of adult responsibility. The Far Western states of Oregon, Washington, California, and Hawaii have the highest average age of delinquency, either eighteen or twenty-one, and the rest of the states range between sixteen and eighteen with the bulk of them selecting eighteen as the basic dividing line.[5]

Table 1 gives a summary of the ages below which a child would be classified as a juvenile delinquent. In some states the upper age limit is a year or

TABLE 1

Age below which boys and girls are under the jurisdiction of juvenile courts for delinquency in forty-one states, Puerto Rico, and the Virgin Islands

(Number of States)

AGE	SAME AGE FOR BOYS AND GIRLS	DIFFERENT AGE* BOYS	GIRLS
Below age 16	5	2	
Below age 17	9	1	
Below age 18	28		3
Below age 19			
Below age 20			
Below age 21	1		

Source: *Juvenile Court Statistics 1971*, U. S. Department of Health, Education, and Welfare, DHEW Publication No. (SRS) 73-03452, December 7, 1972, pp. 15-20.
 * The Supreme Courts of these three states recently declared different age limits for boys and girls unconstitutional.

[4] These conclusions were deduced by comparing Table 1 with a similar table in Ruth Shonle Cavan, *Juvenile Delinquency*, Second Edition, J. B. Lippincott Co., Philadelphia, 1962, p. 27.
 [5] Cf. *Juvenile Court Statistics 1971*, *op. cit.*, pp. 15-20.

two higher for girls than for boys. In general, however, the eighteenth birthday is the dividing line between juvenile and adult in the world of misconduct.

In a large number of states, children (usually of adolescent age) who have committed a very serious crime (for example, murder) must or may be tried in the criminal courts as would adults and are subject to adult penalties. New Mexico has a provision that if a boy or girl aged fourteen or over is charged with a felony and this adolescent is not a "fit subject for reform or rehabilitation," the juvenile court may transfer the case to the criminal court. Under the age of fourteen, however, the child, no matter how unpromising he might seem or how serious the crime he had committed, would still be considered a juvenile delinquent, subject to the juvenile court. In some other states, children of still younger ages may be tried in the adult criminal courts for serious crimes. In the late 1940's, a boy of twelve was tried in the Criminal Court of Cook County (Chicago), Illinois, for murdering a playmate, and about the same time in a western state another boy of twelve was sentenced to a long term in prison (for adults) for killing his sister.

Some states have passed laws for older adolescents, setting up special categories of misconduct and specialized courts. These provisions are intermediate between juvenile delinquencies and courts on the one hand and adult and criminal courts on the other.

OTHER OFFICIAL DEFINITIONS

Three official definitions other than the one cited from the Children's Bureau are also in common use. The most sweeping defines delinquent children as juveniles who have been arrested or picked up informally by the police. Many of these children are released or in some cities handled by special youth bureaus attached to the police department. About half are referred to the juvenile court; these are the children classified by the Children's Bureau as delinquents. Many of them are handled informally, without a written record of being adjudged a juvenile delinquent. Some people argue that only those adjudged delinquent should be classified as juvenile delinquents. Another and still more restricted group consists of children committed to correctional institutions. Research on delinquency may be based on any one or more of these definitions. In order of size they are arrests (largest number), referrals to court, informal or adjudicated cases (about equal in number), and institutionalized cases.

Whatever the classification, all have as their base the offenses specified in the juvenile delinquency law of the state. Deviation from this law, when it is detected and the child is either brought in by police or otherwise referred to the juvenile court, constitutes delinquency of an official type.

Nonlegal Definition of Delinquent Behavior

When attention is centered on legal processes, the legal definitions are applicable. But when one is concerned with tracing the development of delinquency or with its prevention and the rehabilitation of children with behavior problems, perhaps outside the legal procedures, a looser definition is required. For example, we might define any child who deviates from normal behavior so as to endanger himself, his social career, or the community as a juvenile delinquent.

Such a definition (as is true also of some of the more flexible legal definitions) immediately raises all kinds of questions. What is normal social behavior? Who decides whether the child is a menace to himself or his future interests? Who decides what constitutes a menace to the community? Many people make these decisions—parents themselves, teachers, ministers, youth leaders, and many others. In extreme instances, these people may notify the police or refer a child to the juvenile court. But they may also refer the child to a social agency which is less concerned about legal definitions than with the personal and social adjustment of the child in his particular social groups.

Interest in development and adjustment rather than legality also eliminates the age limitations. Misbehavior similar to legal delinquency may begin in the preschool period and may continue into later adolescence or early adulthood, when it may be abandoned or may lead into professional adult criminal behavior.

Public Intolerance as a Measure of Delinquency

The preceding section suggests that delinquent behavior is really part of a continuum ranging from extremely antisocial actions to extremely conforming behavior which elicits a variety of public responses ranging from outraged condemnation through mild disapproval to strong approval. This formulation has now largely replaced the older idea that good and bad, delinquency and conformity are sharply defined dichotomies. Figure 1 schematizes the concept. For purposes of discussion seven stages are recognized. The central stage, called D in the figure, represents the expected, "average" behavior of children. Average behavior conforms for the most part to the values of society, and even where there is some deviation it does not threaten or attack the values of society. The expectation is not for perfection but for overall conformity punctuated by minor deviations. Public opinion not only does not condemn the foibles of youth but views them with mild approval as indicative of ingenuity, independence, competitiveness, or aggressiveness.

Examples of class D behavior among children would be an occasional

FIGURE 1
Hypothetical Formulation of a Behavior Continuum

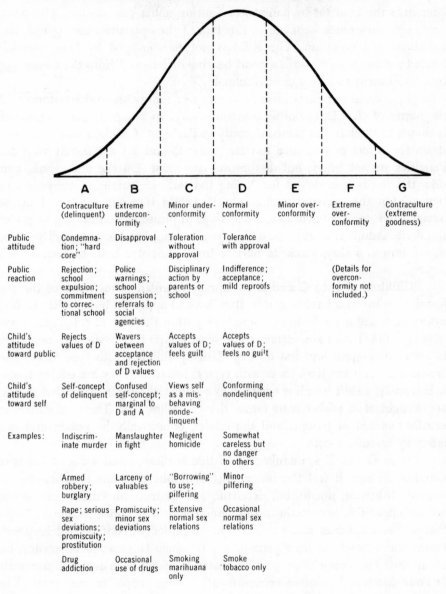

	A Contraculture (delinquent)	B Extreme underconformity	C Minor underconformity	D Normal conformity	E Minor overconformity	F Extreme overconformity	G Contraculture (extreme goodness)
Public attitude	Condemnation; "hard core"	Disapproval	Toleration without approval	Tolerance with approval			
Public reaction	Rejection; school expulsion; commitment to correctional school	Police warnings; school suspension; referrals to social agencies	Disciplinary action by parents or school	Indifference; acceptance; mild reproofs		(Details for overconformity not included.)	
Child's attitude toward public	Rejects values of D	Wavers between acceptance and rejection of D values	Accepts values of D; feels guilt	Accepts values of D; feels no guilt			
Child's attitude toward self	Self-concept of delinquent	Confused self-concept; marginal to D and A	Views self as a misbehaving nondelinquent	Conforming nondelinquent			
Examples:	Indiscriminate murder	Manslaughter in fight	Negligent homicide	Somewhat careless but no danger to others			
	Armed robbery; burglary	Larceny of valuables	"Borrowing" to use; pilfering	Minor pilfering			
	Rape; serious sex deviations; promiscuity; prostitution	Promiscuity; minor sex deviations	Extensive normal sex relations	Occasional normal sex relations			
	Drug addiction	Occasional use of drugs	Smoking marihuana only	Smoke tobacco only			

truancy, helping oneself to the fruit in someone's back yard, rowdyism after a spirited basketball game, mischief on Halloween, coming home somewhat later than the hour set by parents, or fighting under provocation. The public "puts up" with much behavior of this type. When penalties are applied, they are slight and short-run. The child is not handicapped by being officially labeled a delinquent through a court hearing or removed from the community by commitment to a correctional school.

Two variations from class D occur: one represents underconformity to the norms of class D, the other overconformity. In Figure 1, underconformity is shown to the left and overconformity to the right. Children and youth who strain the limits of tolerance too far (areas C and E) are merely tolerated. Penalties are not heavy, but disapproval is evident. On the underconforming side, the youth is criticized for "going too far," or "straining everyone's patience." On the overconforming side, the child is overly careful of his behavior. He is too conscientious, too anxious to please by conforming to perfect standards. Adults may approve of his "perfection," but his peers will probably regard him as a sissy, afraid to deviate from adult standards to even a slight degree.

Children in both C and E are usually regarded as members of the conforming group who have begun to stray beyond approved boundaries. In both cases efforts are made to bring them back within the area of tolerance. Those with type C behavior are restrained; those with type E behavior are encouraged to show more spirit and less docility. Usually children with type C behavior arouse more concern than those with type E behavior. They are edging toward delinquency, a shift which is regarded as a potential danger. Nevertheless, they are thought of as misbehaving rather than as delinquent. Their difficulties are usually handled by parents and the school, occasionally by police, and only rarely by juvenile courts.

Areas C and E are flanked by distinctly disapproved areas of behavior. Children in area B feel the full weight of public disapproval. They are frequently dishonest, untruthful, deceitful, and destructive. Parents and school are no longer able to restrain or discipline them. The police take over. Nevertheless, these children and youth are not regarded as confirmed delinquents. Police release many to their parents or refer them to some social agency, but often with the threat that another instance of misbehavior will mean the juvenile court and possible commitment. Young people in this area of behavior are therefore in an anomalous position. Disapproval pushes them toward affiliation with other delinquents; they are often socially ostracized and informally penalized. At the same time, the lot of the confirmed delinquent may still repel them.

On the side of the overly conforming youth, area F, disapproval also is expressed. Such epithets as "goody-good," and "teacher's pet" are freely used. These young people are not publicly penalized as are the underconforming youth, but they may be avoided by their more adventuresome peers and forced into social isolation.

Areas B and F are the ones where children tend to stabilize their self-conceptions as "average," "delinquent," or "better than other people." If children and youth whose behavior falls into areas B or F are not drawn back into the central areas of behavior, as many of them are, they tend to develop behavior of types A or G. Behavior becomes consistently under- or over-conforming, as the case may be. The delinquent child has become the "hard-core" or "real" delinquent who tends to make delinquency a central and important part of his life. The overconforming child has become "saintly," or "too good to be true." The attitude of the public toward these extreme groups is often to reject them. The delinquent child comes within the legal definition of delinquent and usually has a juvenile court hearing, followed by probation or commitment to a correctional school. The overconforming child is socially ostracized and at adolescence may voluntarily withdraw into some isolating religious group.

The discussion will now be concerned only with the delinquent child, although many of the same processes leading to delinquency seem applicable to the overconformer as well. The confirmed delinquent is not only rejected by the community at large, but in turn rejects the community. He tends to drop out of groups and institutions that expect his behavior to go no further than that permitted in the area of tolerance. He truants from school and quits school as early as possible. He refuses to enter community centers, churches, or public recreational areas or is ejected from them because of misbehavior. Sometimes he declares war on such institutions and enters them to riot or forces an entrance at night to wreck the inside of the buildings. With others of his kind he builds up a secluded social world, with its own peculiar scale of values, roles of activity, and levels of status. What the public thinks, what the area of tolerance in behavior permits, no longer matter greatly to him.[6]

This peculiar world of the confirmed delinquent or the older skilled criminal is popularly referred to as the underworld. Sociologists sometimes call it the delinquent subculture. It is, however, more than a subculture, a term

[6] David Matza has suggested that delinquents rarely if ever approach this degree of alienation from the dominant culture and its values. Instead of a delinquent subculture, which is totally alienated from the prevailing culture, he feels that they enter a subculture of delinquency, which shares many of the values and ideals of the dominant society. The emergence of racist inner-city gangs in many cities seems to belie this thesis, however. See David Matza, *Delinquency and Drift*, John Wiley & Sons, Inc., New York, 1964, Chapter 2.

that implies simply some marked differences from the general culture. The extreme of delinquency (or of overconformity) is not only different from but is opposed to the dominant culture as typified by area D. The term contraculture is more significant than subculture in pointing up the characteristics of the extremes of the continuum between excessive underconformity and excessive overconformity.[7]

Any contraculture has developed values and modes of behavior that are in conflict with the prevailing culture (see Figure 1, areas A and G as opposed to area D). These values and modes of behavior tend to be the opposite of those of the prevailing culture. They have, however, grown out of the tensions and conflicts which characterized the failure of some youth in areas B and F to come to adjustment with the expected or demanded behavior of area D.

Figure 1 shows a bell-shaped curve superimposed on the behavior continuum that runs from the confirmed delinquent to the confirmed overconformer. There is no firm evidence that the behavior continuum conforms to a normal distribution (indeed, it probably does not), but we do know that less than 1 per cent of all boys and girls between the ages of ten and seventeen are committed to a correctional school in any one year, and that only about 3 per cent face a nontraffic hearing in juvenile court (area A). Police take about another 3 per cent into custody but do not refer them to the court, and schools, social agencies, and outraged citizens bring pressure to bear on other misbehaving youth (in area B). A rough guess would place about 13 per cent in area B, and therefore, about two-thirds are in areas C, D, and E, if we assume similar proportions for areas F and G.

Several conclusions and observations can be made. The more serious a misbehavior is regarded by the public, the fewer are the children who indulge in that behavior. The younger the child, the more likely it is that his behavior will fall into areas D or C rather than A. Adolescents may spread out over the entire continuum in decreasing numbers from D to A, but they make up most of the delinquents in area A.

This formulation of delinquency as part of a continuum with public opinion defining the stages at any given place and time helps us to clear up a number of problems. For example, it helps to explain why the number of institutionalized delinquents has gone down in recent years while the number of adjudicated delinquents has skyrocketed. Public opinion regarding what is appropriate treatment for those in area A has changed dramatically since

[7] J. Milton Yinger, "Contraculture and Subculture," *American Sociological Review*, 25 (1960), 626–635.

the 1940's. Other applications of this formulation will be pointed out in subsequent chapters.

Who Is the Delinquent?

At what point along this continuum of behavior is anyone justified in labeling a boy or girl as a delinquent? The law labels any child as such who presumably has committed even one act of delinquency, however mild. The legal definition is inadequate, however, for the understanding of the child's position in his society, the tolerance or disapproval of the public, or the building up of a concept of delinquent personality. An essentially conforming child may commit a few acts of delinquency but still feel himself to be part of the central or D group, holding D values and feeling guilty when he deviates beyond the area of tolerance. The self-concept of the delinquent is a product of extreme deviation and especially of acceptance of a delinquent contraculture.

The misbehaving nondelinquent and the confirmed delinquent can be distinguished in several ways. Culturally, the misbehaving nondelinquent is socialized in the prevailing values of his large cultural group, that is, social class or ethnic group. He accepts the values of his culture but occasionally performs acts that are contrary to them. These acts are likely to be within the area of tolerance on the bell-shaped curve. The delinquent has for various reasons escaped such socialization. In time he tends to become socialized in a delinquent set of values and customs, referred to variously as the underworld, delinquent subculture, or delinquent contraculture. The delinquent contraculture not only differs from the general culture, but has values that are opposed to or destructive of those in the general culture.

Socially, the misbehaving nondelinquent retains his association with conforming groups such as family, school, church, and community center. He accepts the fact that authority is necessary, even though he may defy it at times. His intimate groups are conforming though at times misbehaving. In contrast, the delinquent person associates with other delinquent persons, who form his intimate or reference group. He seeks their good opinion, and he values status in the delinquent group more than in conforming groups. He often cuts himself off physically from conforming groups through truancy from school and home and avoidance of church and community center. He comes to regard as enemies the representatives of conforming institutions, such as teachers and police.

Psychologically, the misbehaving nondelinquent conceives of himself as conforming, honest, fair, and a member of the conforming community. He feels guilty when he misbehaves, even when he is not caught. In contrast, the delinquent person regards his acts as "right" and justifiable under the circumstances of his life. Although he would not label himself as a delinquent, he conceives of himself as tough, able to "outsmart" others, and justified in taking what he needs or wants with little regard for the rights of other people.

A relatively minor proportion of delinquents falls outside this formulation —the emotionally disturbed whose delinquency is a response to uncontrollable inner pressures. Disturbed children may be found within either the normal culture or the delinquent contraculture. If such a child is a member of a delinquent group he often fails to achieve high status because of his erratic and unreliable behavior. Some disturbed children are completely ungrouped, sometimes divorced from the values of both the dominant culture and the delinquent contraculture. Inner pressures may lead to a chain of compulsive acts or to violent outbursts. Other children tend to retreat into an unrealistic world of their own which they may share with others, as among some juvenile drug users.

It is evident that not all children who commit delinquent acts conceive of themselves as delinquent or have delinquent personalities in the sense that delinquency is a central part of their values or behavior. There are stages of delinquency. Also, it is evident that many cultural, social, and psychological factors contribute to the formation of a delinquent personality—so many and in such varying degrees and combinations that it is difficult to formulate a single theory of development which systematically takes them all into account. However, each of these factors can be discussed separately, and certain interrelationships can be found.

Use of Different Definitions

Whether one uses the strictly legal definition of delinquency or a looser definition of damaging misbehavior depends upon the purpose of the research or the practical programs. When police, court, and correctional procedures are the focus of attention, the legal definitions are pertinent. When emphasis is upon development of misbehavior, prevention, or readjustment, the wider definition in terms of deviation from expected social norms is more appropriate.

BIBLIOGRAPHY

CAVAN, RUTH SHONLE, "The Concepts of Tolerance and Contraculture as Applied to Delinquency," *Sociological Quarterly*, 2 (1961), 243–258.
————, ed. *Readings in Juvenile Delinquency*, Third Edition, J. B. Lippincott Company, Philadelphia, 1975, Section 1.

CLINARD, MARSHALL B., *Sociology of Deviant Behavior*, Fourth Edition, Holt, Rinehart & Winston, New York, 1973, Chapter 1.

HUSTON, WENDELL, compiler, *Social Welfare Laws of the Forty-eight States*, and supplements, Wendell Huston Company, Seattle, Washington. 1937.

MATZA, DAVID, *Delinquency and Drift*, John Wiley & Sons, Inc., New York, 1964, Chapter 2.

SUSSMAN, FREDERICK B., *Law of Juvenile Delinquency*, Oceana Publications, New York, 1959.

YINGER, J. MILTON, "Contraculture and Subculture," *American Sociological Review*, 25 (1960), 625-635.

the statistical measurement of delinquency

chapter 3

Many of our ideas about delinquency and the delinquent child are gained from statistical reports. The explicit figures of a statistical statement inspire confidence in the layman, who often accepts them uncritically. Nothing, however, is more misleading than statistics which are not understood and evaluated. This chapter presents the chief sources of statistics, what they include, and what they tell about delinquency. Patterns of delinquency especially typical of juveniles are also pointed out along with an indication as to why they are juvenile.

No nationwide statistics comparable to census reports on the population exist. The best estimates on a national basis come from the Federal Bureau of Investigation and the Children's Bureau. Studies in individual localities help to round out the picture.

Arrests of Juveniles

The most inclusive statement of children and adolescents who get into trouble comes from the Federal Bureau of Investigation in reports of the number of arrests made during a given year.

LIMITATIONS OF ARREST DATA

Police departments decide individually whether or not to cooperate with the Federal Bureau of Investigation in filling out the report blanks sent to them by the Bureau. No representative of the FBI makes visits to each police department to secure data corresponding to the door-to-door calls by representatives of the Census Bureau. Also, since the reporting is on a voluntary basis, the departments that cooperate do not constitute a carefully chosen representative sample of the population such as one would find in a carefully planned research project.

In its reports, the FBI carefully states the basis for each statistical table, which the reader must take into account in interpreting the tables. Large cities are more completely covered by reports than small ones. For example, the 1972 reports cover 98 per cent of the population in standard metropolitan statistical areas, 91 per cent in other cities, and 76 per cent in rural areas. Also some regions of the country respond more fully than others.[1]

The FBI reports are for arrests, and each arrest is counted. A person arrested three times counts as three arrests and not as one person who has been arrested three times. In 1972 nearly 1,800,000 arrests were made of persons under age eighteen. About half of these arrests were handled by individual law enforcement agencies without making a formal charge or referring the juvenile to juvenile court. The other half were referred to the juvenile court.

The classification of offenses is controlled by a list of offenses with definitions. This list includes some typically juvenile offenses (violation of curfew laws and running away) but does not include traffiic violations.

CRIME CLASSIFICATION[2]

1. *Criminal homicide.* (*a*) Murder and non-negligent manslaughter: all willful felonious homicides as distinguished from deaths caused by negligence. Excludes attempts to kill, assaults to kill, suicides, accidental deaths, or justifiable homicides. Justifiable homicides are limited to: (1) the killing of a person by a peace officer in line of duty; (2) the killing of a person in the act of committing a felony by a private citizen. (*b*) Manslaughter by negligence: any death which the police investigation establishes was primarily attributable to gross negligence of some individual other than the victim.
2. *Forcible rape.* Rape by force, assault to rape and attempted rape. Excludes statutory offenses (no force used—victim under age of consent).
3. *Robbery.* Stealing or taking anything of value from the person by force or violence or by putting in fear, such as strong-arm robbery, stickups, armed robbery, assault to rob, and attempt to rob.
4. *Aggravated assault.* Assault with intent to kill or for the purpose of inflict-

---

[1] Federal Bureau of Investigation, *Uniform Crime Reports for the United States,* 1972, U.S. Government Printing Office, Washington, D.C., 1973, p. 61.

[2] The following list is from *Ibid.*, pp. 58–59.

ing severe bodily injury by shooting, cutting, stabbing, maiming, poisoning, scalding, or by the use of acids, explosives, or other means. Excludes simple assault, assault and battery, fighting, etc.

5. *Burglary—breaking or entering.* Burglary, housebreaking, safecracking, or any unlawful entry to commit a felony or a theft, even though no force was used to gain entrance and attempts. Burglary followed by larceny is not counted again as larceny.

6. *Larceny—theft* (except auto theft). (*a*) Fifty dollars and over in value; (*b*) under $50 in value. Theft of bicycles, automobile accessories, shoplifting, pocket-picking, or any stealing of property or article of value which is not taken by force and violence or by fraud. Excludes embezzlement, "con" games, forgery, worthless checks, etc.

7. *Auto theft.* Stealing or driving away and abandoning a motor vehicle. Excludes taking for temporary use when actually returned by the taker or unauthorized use by those having lawful access to the vehicle.

8. *Other assaults.* Assaults and attempted assaults which are not of an aggravated nature.

9. *Arson.* Willful or malicious burning with or without intent to defraud. Includes attempts.

10. *Forgery and counterfeiting.* Making, altering, uttering or possessing, with intent to defraud, anything false which is made to appear true. Includes attempts.

11. *Fraud.* Fraudulent conversion and obtaining money or property by false pretenses. Includes bad checks except forgeries and counterfeiting.

12. *Embezzlement.* Misappropriation or misapplication of money or property entrusted to one's care, custody, or control.

13. *Stolen property; buying, receiving, possessing.* Buying, receiving, and possessing stolen property and attempts.

14. *Vandalism.* Willful or malicious destruction, injury, disfigurement or defacement of property without consent of the owner or person having custody or control.

15. *Weapons; carrying, possessing, etc.* All violations of regulations or statutes controlling the carrying, using, possessing, furnishing, and manufacturing of deadly weapons or silencers and attempts.

16. *Prostitution and commercialized vice.* Sex offenses of a commercialized nature and attempts, such as prostitution, keeping bawdy house, procuring or transporting women for immoral purposes.

17. *Sex offenses* (except forcible rape, prostitution, and commercialized vice). Statutory rape, offenses against chastity, common decency, morals, and the like. Includes attempts.

18. *Narcotic drug laws.* Offenses relating to narcotic drugs, such as unlawful possession, sale, or use. Excludes federal offenses.

19. *Gambling.* Promoting, permitting, or engaging in gambling.

20. *Offenses against the family and children.* Nonsupport, neglect, desertion, or abuse of family and children.

21. *Driving under the influence.* Driving or operating any motor vehicle while drunk or under the influence of liquor or narcotics.

22. *Liquor laws.* State or local liquor law violations, except "drunkenness" (class 23) and "driving under the influence" (class 21). Excludes federal violations.
23. *Drunkenness.* Drunkenness or intoxication.
24. *Disorderly conduct.* Breach of the peace.
25. *Vagrancy.* Vagabondage, begging, loitering, etc.
26. *All other offenses.* All violations of state or local laws except classes 1–25.
27. *Suspicion.* Arrests for no specific offense and released without formal charges being placed.
28. *Curfew and loitering laws (juveniles).* Offense relating to violation of local curfew or loitering ordinances where such laws exist.
29. *Runaway (juvenile).* Limited to juvenile taken into protective custody under provisions of local statutes as runaways.

JUVENILE ARRESTS IN THE TOTAL CRIME PICTURE

The participation of boys and girls in the total crime picture is high. Among all arrests in 1973, 26.4 per cent were of juveniles under eighteen. The percentage is 26.5 in cities, considerably higher in suburbs, 33.1; and much lower in rural areas, 20.1, as Table 2 shows.

Cities and suburbs run far ahead of rural areas in the percentages of all arrested persons committing serious crimes who are under eighteen. Serious crimes have been selected by the Federal Bureau of Investigation to form a Crime Index; the crimes included are criminal homicide, forcible rape, robbery,

TABLE 2

Arrests of persons under age eighteen as percentage of total arrests at all ages for each offense, for city, suburban, and rural areas, 1973

OFFENSE CHARGED	CITY	SUBURBAN	RURAL
Total arrests, all ages	5,458,702	1,718,877	416,500
Arrests under age 18	1,444,632	569,417	83,747
Per cent under age 18	26.5	33.1	20.1
Per cent for each offense			
Criminal homicide:			
(a) Murder and non-negligent manslaughter	11.1	7.4	7.7
(b) Manslaughter by negligence	14.2	14.6	8.4
Forcible rape	20.8	20.6	13.1
Robbery	34.6	30.2	18.1
Aggravated assault	17.7	18.6	7.0
Burglary—breaking or entering	54.2	56.9	47.1
Larceny—theft	49.0	52.2	35.4
Auto theft	57.1	59.1	50.9
Subtotal for above offenses	45.4	48.6	35.3

TABLE 2 *(continued)*

OFFENSE CHARGED	CITY	SUBURBAN	RURAL
Other assaults	19.5	22.3	8.4
Arson	61.5	67.5	30.9
Forgery and counterfeiting	11.9	10.4	10.9
Fraud	4.4	3.4	1.4
Embezzlement	8.7	7.2	5.1
Stolen property; buying, receiving, possessing	34.7	38.7	26.7
Vandalism	69.3	77.0	58.7
Weapons; carrying, possessing, etc.	16.1	21.0	11.0
Prostitution and commercialized vice	3.9	4.7	4.9
Sex offenses (except forcible rape and prostitution)	19.4	25.9	15.1
Narcotic drug laws	27.0	31.3	19.4
Gambling	2.9	4.8	2.1
Offenses against family and children	3.0	3.2	1.7
Driving under the influence	1.4	1.7	1.3
Liquor laws	40.0	49.1	41.6
Drunkenness	2.7	5.8	3.4
Disorderly conduct	22.4	30.7	13.1
Vagrancy	11.2	25.6	23.2
All other offenses (except traffic)	28.7	30.5	16.0
Suspicion	32.3	45.3	21.4
Curfew and loitering law violations	100.0	100.0	100.0
Runaways	100.0	100.0	100.0

Data: Federal Bureau of Investigation, *Uniform Crime Reports for the United States, 1973,* U.S. Government Printing Office, Washington, D.C., 1974.

City arrests are based on reports from 4,547 cities over 2,500 population with estimated population of 113,386,000, p. 139.

Suburban arrests are based on reports from 2,729 agencies, with estimated population of 54,067,000, p. 148.

Rural arrests are based on reports from 1,120 agencies, with estimated population of 17,529,000, p. 156.

aggravated assault, burglary, and auto theft. In cities and suburbs slightly less than half of the arrests for this group of crimes are of persons under eighteen; in rural areas slightly more than a third of all arrests for serious crimes are of juveniles. In city and suburban areas about half of the arrests for burglary, larceny, and auto theft, and in cities about a third of the arrests for robbery, are of juveniles. In rural areas juveniles play a less important part in the criminal problems of the area.

Among less serious crimes city, suburban, and rural arrests exhibit a common pattern for certain juvenile offenses. In all three areas, juvenile arrests account for better than 50 per cent of vandalism, and in cities and suburban

TABLE 3

Total juvenile arrest trends by sex, 1973

	(Males under Eighteen)			(Females under Eighteen)		
OFFENSE CHARGED	NUMBER ARRESTED	AS PER CENT OF ALL MALE ARRESTS	PER CENT COMMITTING EACH OFFENSE	NUMBER ARRESTED	AS PER CENT OF ALL FEMALE ARRESTS	PER CENT COMMITTING EACH OFFENSE
Total	1,274,978	24.5	100.0	355,744	37.6	100.0
Criminal homicide						
a. Murder and non-negligent manslaughter	1,315	11.2	0.1	127	6.1	0.04
b. Manslaughter by negligence	306	12.4	0.02	21	6.5	0.01
Forcible rape	3,632	19.7	0.3	—	—	0.7
Robbery	31,372	34.0	2.5	2,340	35.1	0.7
Aggravated assault	21,286	16.8	1.7	3,626	18.7	1.0
Burglary—breaking or entering	154,885	54.4	12.2	8,330	51.2	2.3
Larceny—theft	211,032	50.2	16.6	85,891	44.3	24.1
Auto theft	60,154	56.8	4.7	3,995	59.2	1.1
Subtotal for above offenses	484,382	45.6	38.0	104,330	42.4	29.3
Other assaults	41,347	18.0	3.2	10,420	28.7	2.9
Arson	5,645	60.0	0.4	539	45.7	0.2
Forgery and counterfeiting	3,239	11.1	0.3	1,224	11.5	0.3
Fraud	2,266	4.1	0.2	768	3.1	0.2
Embezzlement	333	8.3	0.03	82	6.5	0.02
Stolen property; buying, receiving, possessing	20,921	34.8	1.6	1,856	27.6	0.5
Vandalism	74,070	69.8	5.8	5,440	61.1	1.0
Weapons; carrying, possessing, etc.	17,040	16.6	1.3	962	10.8	0.3

TABLE 3 (continued)
Total juvenile arrest trends by sex, 1973

OFFENSE CHARGED	(Males under Eighteen)			(Females under Eighteen)		
	NUMBER ARRESTED	MALE ARRESTS AS PER CENT OF ALL	PER CENT COMMITTING EACH OFFENSE	NUMBER ARRESTED	AS PER CENT OF ALL FEMALE ARRESTS	PER CENT COMMITTING EACH OFFENSE
Prostitution and commercialized vice	444	4.1	0.03	1,293	4.1	0.4
Sex offenses (except forcible rape and prostitution)	8,287	19.1	0.6	1,198	32.9	0.3
Narcotic drug laws	98,753	25.0	7.7	21,864	32.8	6.2
Gambling	1,373	2.8	0.1	102	2.2	0.03
Offenses against family and children	622	1.7	0.05	257	6.9	0.07
Driving under the influence	7,976	1.4	0.6	610	1.4	0.2
Liquor laws	55,893	38.3	4.4	13,904	54.0	3.9
Drunkenness	28,526	2.7	2.2	4,706	5.7	1.3
Disorderly conduct	81,786	22.5	6.4	17,943	22.5	5.0
Vagrancy	4,739	15.1	0.4	1,090	6.4	0.3
All other offenses (except traffic)	169,553	24.8	13.3	51,268	40.8	14.4
Suspicion (not included in totals)	10,150	29.9	0.8	1,879	34.3	0.5
Curfew and loitering law violations	92,898	100.0	7.3	22,154	100.0	6.2
Runaways	74,885	100.0	5.9	93,734	100.0	26.4

Data: Federal Bureau of Investigation, *Uniform Crime Reports for the United States, 1973*, U.S. Government Printing Office, Washington, D.C., 1974, p. 132.

areas for more than 60 per cent of arson as well. They also constitute a substantial portion (though not a majority) of all arrests for such offenses as buying, receiving, possessing stolen property, sex offenses, narcotics violations, violations of liquor laws, and suspicion.

It is significant that arrests of juveniles for both narcotics violations and violations of liquor laws have risen sharply in recent years, reflecting broad changes in values and perspective among young people. In 1965 juveniles comprised only 11.6 and 27.0 per cent respectively of all arrests for these two offenses, but by 1973 these percentages had climbed to 26.3 and 43.5 respectively.[3] The high level of juvenile arrests for selling, receiving, or possessing stolen property no doubt reflects juveniles' heavy involvement in property offenses, many of which are ultimately solved by tracing stolen property to the offender.

We may conclude that there is not a completely distinctive pattern of crime for juveniles in cities, suburbs, and rural areas, but only minor variations in certain offenses. For example, the suburbs tend to have a disproportionately high percentage of juvenile arrests for arson, vandalism, narcotics violations, violations of liquor laws, and disorderly conduct. But they do not markedly exceed the other areas in larceny or in assaults. Most of the suburban offenses suggest a lack of discipline and rejection of the normal restraints that society places on personal conduct.

Rural juvenile arrests are lower than city or suburban arrests for almost all offenses.

Comparison of Arrests for Boys and Girls

BOYS ARE MORE ACTIVE IN CRIME THAN GIRLS. Among the 1973 arrests of juveniles under eighteen, 78.2 per cent were boys, for a ratio of about 3.6 boys for every girl. In Table 3 a comparison between boys and girls is shown, and it is noteworthy that except for prostitution and runaways there is no offense in which the number of girls exceeds that of boys.

Male Juvenile Arrests—It is apparent from Table 3 that boys under eighteen are arrested for more than 50 per cent of male arrests for burglary, larceny, auto theft, arson, and vandalism. Only rarely are boys involved in arrests for fraud, embezzlement, commercialized vice, gambling, offenses to family and children, drunkenness, and vagrancy. All arrests for curfew violation and running away are of persons under eighteen, since these laws do not apply to adults.

Female Juvenile Arrests—A remarkable similarity in arrests of boys and girls can be seen in Table 3. There are, however, some exceptions. Among all

[3] *Ibid.*, Table 31, p. 130; and *loc. cit.*, 1965, Table 22, p. 114.

female arrests for sex offenses, girls under eighteen account for 32.9 per cent; boys account for only 19.1 per cent of all male arrests for this offense, although the total number of sex offenses among boys far exceeds that for girls. Girls account for a larger proportion of female arrests than boys of male arrests for robbery, aggravated assault, auto theft, other assaults, forgery and counterfeiting, narcotics violations, offenses against family and children, violations of liquor laws, drunkenness, and suspicion. Clearly girls are a more important factor in female deviance than boys are in male deviance.

It is obvious from Table 3 that juveniles commit most if not all the offenses that adults do. Indeed, in many respects they are *the most important factor* in the total crime problem. For example, seventeen-year-olds exhibit a higher rate of violent crime than all but one age group (i.e., eighteen-year-olds), and youths 13 through 17 commit more than 40 per cent of all property offenses.[4]

What then are the offenses of juveniles? In terms of the part they play in the total crime picture they are burglary, larceny, auto theft, arson, and vandalism—all types of stealing or destruction of property.

MOST FREQUENT OFFENSES OF BOYS AND GIRLS. As can be seen in Table 3, the most frequent serious offense for both boys and girls as judged by arrests is larceny—16.6 and 24.1 per cent. Runaways account for 26.4 per cent of girls' offenses but only 5.9 of boys'. Other offenses are widely scattered and show no heavy concentration. Boys are much more prone than girls to commit burglary, auto theft, and vandalism. Girls are more likely to commit larceny, and to run away from home. Attention is called again to the fact that 3.6 boys are arrested for each girl and that for all offenses except runaways, prostitution, and commercialized vice boys exceed girls in numbers. Disorderly conduct and violation of curfew laws are found in about equal proportions among both male and female delinquents. The offenses, grouped into five large categories, are depicted in Figure 2.

Characteristics of Juvenile Crime

When these broad classes of crime are broken down into more specific kinds of violations, the picture of delinquency as distinct from adult crime becomes clearer. The types of stealing common among the young tend to be opportunistic and to require agility and daring. Larceny, for example, is often opportunistic. A boy sees an unguarded bicycle and takes it; a girl's attention

[4] *Ibid.*, Table 30, p. 128.

FIGURE 2

Types of Offenses of Boys and Girls Leading to Arrest. Data from Table 4

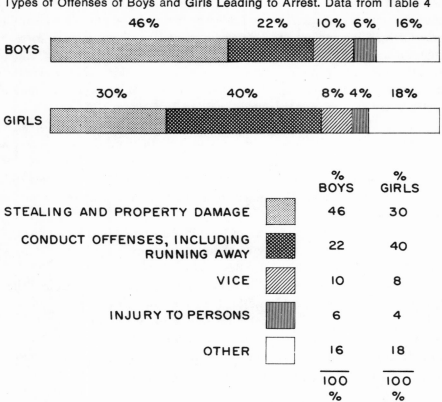

	% BOYS	% GIRLS
STEALING AND PROPERTY DAMAGE	46	30
CONDUCT OFFENSES, INCLUDING RUNNING AWAY	22	40
VICE	10	8
INJURY TO PERSONS	6	4
OTHER	16	18
	100 %	100 %

Data: Federal Bureau of Investigation, *Uniform Crime Reports for the United States, 1973,* U.S. Government Printing Office, Washington, D.C., 1974, p. 132.

is drawn to a piece of jewelry in a store with no salesperson near; she slips it into her purse and leaves.

The amateurish, pilfering type of shoplifting typical of the juvenile can be illustrated by the activities of seven boys ranging in age from thirteen to fifteen. Among other things, they had stolen a crowbar, hair tonic, playing cards, gloves, magazines, ice cream, candies, comic books, wallets, staplers, cigarettes, padlocks, gum, flashlights, batteries, cigarette cases, peanuts, shirts, film, a wall soap dispenser, and four quarters from a hair dryer. These articles were taken from two drug stores, two department stores, a sporting goods shop, an office supply store, and a pet shop.[5]

[5] Newspaper item, city of 125,000.

The peak years of arrests for burglary are during the teens. Many burglaries are committed by children under age fifteen. The number of arrests declines after age eighteen and becomes negligible after age forty. It may be that only the very daring and skilled remain, striking infrequently but obtaining large sums of money or valuable goods. These large undertakings require long periods of observation to determine the safest time to enter and entail elaborate plans of entry and exit. Such exploits are the work of professional criminals, not of children.

Children and teen-agers are usually small-scale burglars. Cases of juvenile delinquents are filled with episodes wherein two or three boys break a window or find an open transom in a small store or a gas station, enter, steal any available cash and small articles to be sold or used, and escape without detection. These boys are not professionals. Burglary is simply one of a number of illegal acts common to their way of life. Many live at home and use the money not for necessities but for luxuries and entertainment.

Although arrests for robbery are less common among juveniles than larceny, burglary, and auto theft, several types may be identified. Jack-rolling or theft from drunken adults carried out by one or two teen-agers involves little danger or possibility of identification, but nets only small sums of cash. Extortion of money from younger children under threat of a beating is another type of robbery.

Gang assault and robbery are carried out by a number of boys, with or without prior planning and selection of a victim in advance. In both New York and Chicago such crimes often occur in subway or elevated stations or on trains, where victims have little chance to escape, and police rarely are sufficiently numerous to guard stations and trains. An example is the holdup attack on a passenger in the Chicago subway by fourteen youths between the ages of fourteen and eighteen. The group had planned to attend a dance which they found on arrival had been cancelled. They took a subway to the center of the city and while walking through the subway tunnel to transfer to another line they decided to hold up someone on the train. Some of the boys blocked the exits from the train and others sat beside passengers to prevent them from coming to the victim's assistance. One boy then seized the man selected as a victim by the neck while another went through his pockets. When he resisted, a third youth hit him in the face; later he was also kicked in the face. The boys secured a wristwatch and $26.00. Their explanation was that it was "something to do" when they found the dance had been cancelled.[6]

Even though this assault and robbery was not planned in advance, the

[6] Reported in *Chicago Daily News*, September 23, 1960.

boys used techniques familiar to them and without doubt used on previous occasions.

Offenses not typical of youth are types of theft involving great skill or access to large sums of money, such as one would find in positions of trust, which juveniles do not hold: for example, forgery, counterfeiting, fraud, and embezzlement. Juveniles have few opportunities to commit such offenses, which, as adult crimes, may run into thousands or even millions of dollars.

Vandalism, typically a juvenile offense, is included under the general designation of malicious mischief or some other omnibus term when delinquent acts are classified. The exact amount of vandalism is therefore unknown, but limited studies and individual reports indicate that it is a specific and continuing type of delinquency. The following excerpt from a report of individual acts of vandalism indicates some of the more costly and extensive types.

Over the Memorial Day weekend, 1960, twenty-five Chicago schools received an estimated $50,000 worth of damage. Classrooms and offices were ransacked, a fire was set in a principal's office, windows were broken, and ink was splashed on walls and used to make crude drawings or write obscene phrases; in one school a radio, phonograph, and records were damaged. In some schools lunchroom refrigerators were broken into and food was thrown against walls and ceilings. Many schools not entered had windows broken from the outside.

The United States culture is fairly tolerant of a certain amount of vandalism, provided the damage has little money value. Adults grumble but seem to expect to clean up after youthful disorderliness and to stand the minor expenses involved in slight damage. Halloween is celebrated by an institutionalized form of vandalism which often threatens to get out of hand. Efforts are made to forestall such vandalism by offering instead parades, parties, and prizes for well-decorated store windows and substituting "treats" for "tricks."

Actual property damage is disparaged, but relatively little is done about the situation. Since most vandalism takes place after dark and around unguarded buildings or construction sites, the vandals are usually not caught. When they are, the children are unable and the parents either unable or unwilling to make restitution for large amounts of damage. Consequently, most companies and some householders carry insurance to cover such damage. Since the cost of repair and replacement is assured, the victims do not press for the discovery of the culprits.

Whether youthful vandals disproportionately represent any one social class or ethnic group is an unsettled question. The actual situation in which the boys find themselves, the dearth of outlets for energy or hostility, and the opportunities available in unguarded buildings with many windows may be determining factors.

Although rare at any age, assaults and murders are also committed occasionally by juveniles. A psychiatrist with wide experience among offenders states that most homicides by juveniles result from gang warfare and often are not premeditated.[7] However, when gangs do meet with intent to fight they carry knives, guns, clubs, belts with heavy buckles, car antennas, sharpened canes, and other weapons capable of causing death. Even with such an arsenal, neither gang intends to annihilate the enemy but hopes to surpass it in bravery and drive it back into its own territory. Actual murder may not be premeditated, but serious physical injury is often caused which may lead to death.

Assaults which may or may not cause death to the victim may be directed by small gangs against someone unknown to the gang but who by chance is at hand when the gang is aroused or bent on adventure. The victim may be of another race or a person in authority who has unsuccessfully attempted to control the behavior of the gang. If a woman is the victim, she may be raped before being injured or killed. These unplanned assaults and murders apparently are overt expressions of inner tensions or even momentary frustrations. The identity of the victim is incidental. In these cases the assault is not the first or only offense of the gang; it is part of a generally delinquent way of life.

Sometimes individuals plan robberies that get out of hand and result in murder. An illustrative case is that of a seventeen-year-old youth who planned a robbery on an elevated train platform in Chicago in order to get money to support his sixteen-year-old mistress and her baby. The victim fought back, and the boy stabbed him. The boy said later that he did not mean to kill his victim but had to stab him to get away. He had a delinquency record going back to his eighth year and had been in a correctional school.

Other individual assaults, often murderous, seem to be the explosion of deep emotions. They may be either planned or spontaneous. The victims may be parents, other family members, complete strangers with whom there is only a casual contact, or someone who has added to already existing tensions. The offender may have a previous record as an emotionally deprived or disturbed child—although not suspected of murderous impulses. He may previously have committed other kinds of delinquency. But sometimes he has seemed to be a normal—or even a model—youth.

Sometimes young children of ten or twelve commit such murders, but

[7] Melitta Schnideberg, "Child Murderers." Abstract of a paper read at the Fifteenth Annual Meeting of the American Society of Criminology, 1958, *Journal of Criminal Law, Criminology and Police Science*, 49 (1959), 569–570.

in general the offenders are in their middle or late teens. Often the child or youth displays little comprehension of the enormity of his act and no guilt or repentance. Although these individual murders cover a wide variety of types and details, it is often assumed that the offenders are emotionally disturbed or even psychotic. Psychiatrists who have studied child murderers hesitate to pinpoint the problem. Although their reactions are abnormal, they cannot be lumped under such a catchall term as "sick," psychopathic, or schizophrenic.[8]

OFFENSES INVOLVING ALCOHOL

Few youth of juvenile delinquency age are victims of alcoholism, which may be defined as "a chronic behavioral disorder manifested by repeated drinking of alcoholic beverages in excess of the dietary and social uses of the community and to an extent that interferes with the drinker's health or his social or economic functioning."[9] The offenses for which youth are arrested are violation of state or local liquor laws, driving while intoxicated, and drunkenness. Taken together, these three offenses account for 7.2 per cent of all arrests of males under eighteen made in 1973.[10]

Males under eighteen account for only a small percentage of arrests for drunkenness and drunken driving—2.7 and 1.4 per cent respectively. Arrests for both of these offenses increase rapidly after age twenty-one, when in many states the purchase of liquor becomes legal and therefore may be easily acquired, reaching a peak during the forties, after which there is a slight decline. Violation of liquor laws, however, is an offense of the young, with most arrests at ages seventeen through twenty, the period during which young people, especially boys, wish to participate in adult activities but are often restricted in the purchase of liquor. The violations become an offense not because of any innate viciousness of the activity but because of the arbitrary limitations set by law on the age when liquor may be purchased. Unlike murder or larceny, forbidden to all people, purchase of liquor is permitted to adults but is made a legal offense for youths.

Among adults, violation of liquor laws does not involve illegal purchase alone but many offenses by proprietors of liquor stores, such as not observing closing hours and other regulations, including nonsale to minors.

Drinking is much more widespread among youth than arrests indicate. A recent nationwide survey reveals that 43.9 per cent of American youth today

[8] *Ibid.*

[9] Mark Keller, "Alcoholism: Nature and Extent of the Problem," *Annals of the American Academy of Political and Social Science*, 315 (1958), 2.

[10] See Table 3, pp. 42–43.

regularly use alcohol and another 36.0 per cent use it occasionally.[11] Regional surveys of high school students show much the same pattern.[12] Drinking, however, does not inevitably lead to drunkenness, nor drunkenness to arrest. Public disturbances or fighting as a result of drunkenness often lead to arrests but the youth may be charged with disorderliness instead of being charged with drunkenness.

The concern about drinking among youth is not limited to the disorderly conduct which may follow but to a fear of future consequences in periodic drunkenness or eventually in alcoholism itself. Since the etiology of alcoholism has not been definitely established, it is difficult to make such assertions. Theories of the cause of alcoholism range from the presence of a biochemical defect to constitutional predisposition to personality problems rooted in childhood to environmental factors. Certainly among the many youth who drink, few will become alcoholics.

AGE AND SEX DIFFERENCES. The FBI reports show few arrests under age fifteen for violation of liquor laws and few under age sixteen for drunkenness. Driving while intoxicated is rare until ages eighteen and nineteen. In the juvenile period, offenses involving liquor therefore are located in adolescence and especially later adolescence.

For both boys and girls, drinking tends to be a social activity, carried out in a group, often in connection with other social activities. However, the pattern of drinking varies between boys and girls. Only about three-fourths as many high school girls as boys drink outside their own homes; and fewer girls drink to the point of feeling "high" or becoming intoxicated.[13] Both boys and girls most often had their first drink on special occasions, among family and friends, such as a wedding or birthday. Boys more than girls drank before parties. They more often had their first drink of hard liquor (as distinct from beer) in automobiles. These facts indicate that boys drink with other boys as well as with girls. Girls rarely drink with their own sex only.

CULTURAL INFLUENCES. In drinking, adolescents reflect the culture of their ethnic and social class groups. Ethnic groups who regard alcoholic beverages

[11] See Lloyd Johnston, *Drugs and American Youth*, Institute for Social Research, Ann Arbor, Michigan, 1973, Figure 2-7, p. 50.

[12] James F. Short, Jr., and F. Ivan Nye, "Extent of Unrecorded Juvenile Delinquency: Tentative Conclusions," *Journal of Criminal Law, Criminology and Police Science*, 49 (1958), 297–298; E. Jackson Baur and Marston M. McCluggage, "Drinking Patterns of Kansas High School Students," *Social Problems*, 5 (Spring, 1958), 317–326.

[13] Short and Nye, *op. cit.*; Baur and McCluggage, *op. cit.*

as food or as a condiment to meals teach their children to drink wine or beer as a normal part of food consumption; in these groups drunkenness tends to be rare. Jewish, Italian, and Chinese ethnic groups are examples.[14] However, if the pattern whereby drinking is integrated into the daily life and controlled by family and community is broken by exposure to other customs, the controlled type of drinking tends to break down. Also, if in the process of social adjustment, stresses become intense, drinking may increase.

Social classes also tend to have distinctive attitudes toward drinking. The middle and upper classes are relatively tolerant of youthful drinking, especially if done in moderation. Drinking beer, wine, or mixed drinks is common in the home usually with adult supervision. Drinking in restaurants or bars, however, is more rare primarily because of age restrictions on the sale of alcoholic beverages.

Drinking in the lower class differs according to the ethnic background of the group. When drinking is integrated into ceremonial and eating patterns, it may remain at a low level even in public places. When drinking has not been so integrated and especially when hard liquor rather than wine or beer is the chief beverage drunk, a certain amount of male drunkenness may be accepted as part of the lower class culture. The locale for drinking is likely to be the public tavern (in the past the saloon), patronized primarily by men.

In lower class communities where heavy drinking is tolerated by the mores, taverns do not hesitate to break laws and serve adolescents or sell bottled goods to them. Many of the taverns are also centers for gambling, prostitution, and obscene entertainment and are regarded as social recreational centers for the neighborhood. In small cities, also, taverns serve as social centers and illegally cater to youths who wish to drink.

In these lower class communities where drinking and drunkenness among adolescent males are accepted, adult males also drink heavily and thus set the pattern of drinking as a symbol of adulthood and masculinity.

DRINKING AND DELINQUENCY

Drinking seems less a cause of delinquent behavior than part of a pattern of behavior which has a variety of deviant facets. Drinking (and presumably drunkenness) is far more common in the past experiences of correctional school boys and girls than among high school students. The regional surveys

---

[14] Albert D. Ullman, Socio-cultural Backgrounds of Alcoholism," *Annals of the American Academy of Political and Social Science,* 315 (1958), 48–54; Harrison M. Trice and David J. Pittman, "Social Organization and Alcoholism: A Review of Significant Research since 1940," *Social Problems,* 5 (Spring, 1958), 294–307.

already cited showed that 89.7 per cent of western correctional school boys compared with 57.2 per cent of western high school boys bought or drank alcoholic beverages; 79.4 per cent of correctional school boys but only 29.5 of high school boys had bought or used it more than once or twice.[15] Among girls twice as high a percentage of correctional school girls as of high school girls (90.2 versus 44.5) had bought or used alcoholic beverages; among those who had used them more than once or twice the corresponding percentages were 80.5 and 17.6.

MOTIVATIONS FOR DRINKING BY YOUTH. It is probably impossible to assign all drinking to one motivation. For some youth it is an extension into public behavior of ethnic patterns of family drinking. For others, it is an attempt to prove manhood in the lower class world of the tavern. For still others, it is part of recreational life such as a dance or other type of party where added daring or gaiety seems called for. Some find in it a means to defy adult restrictions. Within limits, many adults are tolerant of drinking by older adolescents, usually at home or at private parties where there is some adult control. When drinking exceeds these limits, it usually occurs in a small closed group of adolescents in an automobile or gang hangout. The illegality of most adolescent drinking outside the confines of the family calls for a certain amount of circumspection and secrecy, except, perhaps, in the lower class, where the tavern, although a public place, actually serves as a private men's club.

RACE AND DELINQUENCY

In Table 4 the distribution of arrests of persons under 18 among the several races in America is given, and two conclusions immediately become apparent. First, white or black adolescents are responsible for virtually all (98.6 per cent) of the delinquency in the United States. Second, black teenagers are arrested about twice as often as we would expect on the basis of their proportion in the population, i.e., about 12 per cent.

A close examination of Table 4 further reveals that black youths are arrested more than all the rest for murder and non-negligent manslaughter, robbery, weapons-carrying, possessing, etc., prostitution and commercial vice, and gambling. This pattern of criminality among black teen-agers probably arises from the fact that in the North blacks for the most part are crowded into urban ghettos where juvenile gangs and vice abound. Black gangs are a

[15] Short and Nye, *op. cit.*

TABLE 4

Percentage distribution of juvenile arrests by race, 1973

OFFENSE CHARGED	RACE			TOTAL
	WHITE	NEGRO	OTHER	
Criminal homicide:				
a. Murder and non-negligent manslaughter	35.0	62.5	2.5	100.0
b. Manslaughter by negligence	79.3	16.8	3.9	100.0
Forcible rape	43.7	54.4	1.9	100.0
Robbery	30.4	68.5	1.1	100.0
Aggravated assault	52.6	46.1	1.4	100.1
Burglary; breaking or entering	70.0	28.6	1.2	99.8
Larceny; theft	70.5	28.2	1.3	100.0
Auto theft	68.8	29.1	2.0	99.9
Subtotal for above offenses	67.4	31.2	1.4	100.0
Other assaults	59.0	39.7	1.2	99.9
Arson	79.8	19.4	0.7	99.9
Forgery and counterfeiting	76.8	22.1	1.1	100.0
Fraud	74.9	24.5	0.7	100.1
Embezzlement	80.2	19.0	0.7	99.9
Stolen property; buying, receiving, possessing	66.3	32.7	1.0	100.0
Vandalism	85.0	14.1	0.9	100.0
Weapons; carrying, possessing, etc.	61.4	37.3	1.2	99.9
Prostitution and commercialized vice	40.0	58.9	1.2	100.1
Sex offenses (except forcible rape and prostitution)	66.9	31.7	1.4	100.0
Narcotic drug laws	89.1	10.0	0.9	100.0
Gambling	25.1	73.3	1.7	100.1
Offenses against family and children	88.9	9.1	2.0	100.0
Driving under the influence	92.8	4.8	2.4	100.0
Liquor laws	94.8	2.9	3.2	99.9
Drunkenness	87.7	7.4	5.0	100.1
Disorderly conduct	72.5	26.5	1.1	100.1
Vagrancy	70.3	25.9	3.8	100.0
All other offenses (except traffic)	76.3	22.5	1.1	99.9
Suspicion	77.2	22.3	0.4	99.9
Curfew and loitering law violations	68.7	30.0	1.4	100.1
Runaways	88.2	10.1	1.8	100.1
All offenses	75.2	23.3	1.4	99.9

Adapted from Federal Bureau of Investigation, *Uniform Crime Reports for the United States, 1973,* U. S. Government Printing Office, Washington, D.C., 1974, Table 34, p. 134.

prominent feature in most, if not all, major northern cities, and their contribution to violent crime is recorded almost daily in the nation's newspapers. These gangs, moreover, have contributed to the flow of deadly weapons into black neighborhoods with the result that virtually everyone, including teen-agers, has ready access to guns of one sort or another. Consequently, many quarrels that otherwise would have ended in shouting and shoving matches are now settled by deadly shootouts.

The victims of this deadly violence, of course, are nearly always other blacks. Up to the age of fifteen most victims of murder are white, but between the ages of fifteen and fifty-four black victims predominate.[16] Clearly, the target of black violent crime is most often other members of the black community.

Juvenile Court Cases

Juvenile cases that are not adjusted by police are referred to the juvenile court. Juvenile court statistics are published by the U.S. Department of Health, Education, and Welfare and are based on 2,019 cooperating courts selected to represent the United States as a whole, with regard to regional location, population density, percentage of nonwhite population, and rates of growth.[17] The cases consist of children of juvenile court age who are referred to the court by the police after arrest and in addition a smaller number of cases referred directly to the court by parents, social workers, schools, and other agencies. The figures do not refer to individual children, but to cases; each time a child is referred to the court on a new delinquency charge, a new case is counted. Thus a child with a serious behavior problem might contribute three or four cases in a single year.

The official estimate from the Department of Health, Education, and Welfare is that in 1971, 1,125,000 cases were handled in the nation's juvenile courts, representing 970,000 different children or 2.9 per cent of all children aged ten through seventeen; traffic cases were not included.

As was true for arrests, there are about three male court cases for every female case. Cities predominate in court cases as in arrests. The rate of delinquency cases (number of cases per 1,000 child population aged ten through seventeen) is twice as high in urban areas as in rural. "Semi-urban" cases fall between urban and rural rates (the three are 42.1, 37.9, and 20.7).

---

16 Federal Bureau of Investigation, loc. cit., 1972, Table 25, p. 118.

17 U.S. Department of Health, Education, and Welfare, Juvenile Court Statistics, 1971, December 7, 1972, p. 6. All juvenile court statistics in this chapter are from this publication.

Age Distribution of Arrested Juveniles

The juvenile delinquency age period is usually considered to be ten through seventeen, at which age in most states the boy or girl ceases to be a juvenile, so far as delinquency is concerned, and becomes an adult; if he is arrested his case is tried in an adult, not a juvenile, court. Many of the offenses of which he might be guilty as a juvenile no longer apply to him as an adult: for example, curfew violations or running away from home. At the lower end of the age range, few children are arrested below age thirteen. Police may pick them up, scold them, call in their parents, but not make a formal arrest.

Is Delinquency Increasing?

This is a controversial question because of the many factors that must be taken into account in determining whether increasing statistical trends indicate genuine increases in misbehavior. According to Figure 3 the number of delinquency cases increased sharply during World War II, declined in the immediate post-war years, and then began a rapid increase that, with slight temporary variations, continues. The trend in population figures for children aged ten to seventeen has followed a somewhat different trend and has not kept pace with the swelling volume of delinquency cases. Between 1957 and 1971 delinquency cases increased 156 per cent, while the child population increased only 49 per cent.

Caution should be used in interpreting these figures. They refer only to cases heard in juvenile courts. It is generally assumed that they indicate a genuine increase in acts of delinquency. However, to some extent at least, the increase might be the result of a change in police policy, in the number of cases referred to the court rather than handled directly by the police, or even in the number of arrests made, which might tend to increase the number of cases referred to the courts. A slight increase in delinquency rates, published in newspapers across the land, tends to frighten people and to create an outcry for greater vigilance by the police and more authoritative handling of cases. Thus the number of cases may be artificially built up without an actual or a proportionate increase in the number of delinquents. Also, it is not clear what the effect is on marginally delinquent youth when they feel that the public has turned against them and that the police are overly watchful. Do they tend to conform or does the air of suspicion push them over the edge into truculence and retaliation? Although we may question the increase in misbehavior, it is true that a greater proportion of children than formerly are being arrested and brought before the court.

FIGURE 3

Trend in Juvenile Court Delinquency Cases and Child Population 10-17
Years of Age, 1940-1966 (Semi-logarithmic Scale)

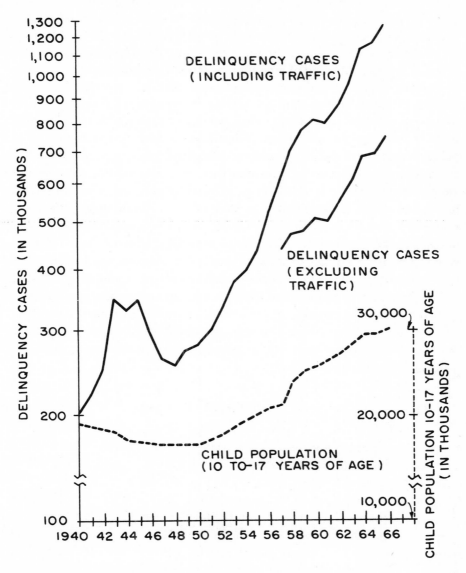

Data: *Juvenile Court Statistics, 1971*, p. 11.

Methods of Handling Cases by the Juvenile Court

The juvenile court has two chief methods of handling cases: judicial and nonjudicial. About half of the cases are handled nonjudicially by the judge or an appropriate court officer; these cases are not placed on the official court calendar, and no public record remains. The other half of the cases—typically the more seriously delinquent ones—are handled judicially: the case is placed on the official court calendar for adjudication by the judge, and court action is begun through the filing of a petition or other legal paper.

More than half of the nonjudicial cases result in a reprimand or in the release of the child without further hearing; a few children are placed on probation; almost none are committed to a public institution, although about one-tenth are referred to other types of institutions. Less than a fourth of the judicial cases are dismissed or adjusted without further hearing. About one-seventh are committed to an institution or agency, and most of the remainder are placed on probation, usually in their own homes. Thus, most delinquents brought to court attention remain in their own homes and neighborhoods, in association with their old friends, and subject to the same influences that led initially to their delinquency. The shock of court appearance and the supervision of probation officer or social agency is often insufficient to counterbalance delinquent influences, and many children appear again in court. Only about 7 per cent of those arrested are committed to juvenile institutions or agencies, and these children are away from home only about 8.4 months.[18] Delinquency, therefore, begins in the community and becomes a problem there, and more often than not, adjustment, if it occurs at all, must take place in the community.

Delinquent Behavior Not Officially Reported

Not all children who commit delinquent acts are included among the arrest or court cases. Some misbehavior even of a serious nature is not detected by responsible adults; some is detected, but not by the police, and is not referred to the police. Neighbors may adjust payment for property damage with the parents of the offending child; storekeepers may stop a young shoplifter as he leaves the store and relieve him of stolen articles; schools adjust many types of delinquent behavior occurring in and near school property. Many minor delinquencies are simply passed over by observers, even by the victims, as part of the process of growing up.

A complete cataloging of delinquency calls for inclusion of the unre-

---

18 *Statistics on Public Institutions for Delinquent Children*, 1970, Department of Health, Education, and Welfare, 1971, p. 6.

corded delinquency. The conception of delinquency changes to some extent with such inclusion. Delinquency, especially of minor types, is found to be very widespread throughout the community permeating all social classes.

UNREPORTED DELINQUENTS: NEW YORK

Attention was forcibly directed to the incomplete nature of official reports first in 1936, when Sophia Moses Robison published a report called *Can Delinquency Be Measured?*[19]

After a thorough study of reports on delinquent behavior from forty-three public and private agencies in New York City, she found that juvenile court records alone included only about two-thirds of known delinquents, not including chronic truants. Children under treatment at private agencies often came from upper-middle or upper class families, children erroneously believed to be immune to delinquent impulses. Many of these children were not included in court statistics.

Volume of Unreported Delinquency—Not only does the juvenile court miss a substantial portion of known delinquents; the police also fail to apprehend a large number of juveniles who commit delinquent acts. A study of 114 boys in the Cambridge-Somerville, Massachusetts, area recorded sixty-four acts of delinquency per boy over a five-year period, or more than one delinquency per month. These boys were from the lower and lower-middle class, and many had been referred to the study because they had shown signs of delinquent behavior. All had had some counseling over a five-year period from age eleven to age sixteen.[20]

Of the 114 boys, only thirteen had not committed an act that could be classified as legal delinquency. Of the remaining 101 boys, sixty-one were unofficially delinquent with no court record, and forty had court records. Table 5 shows a grouping of the 6,416 acts of delinquency attributed to the boys during the five-year period. The majority of the delinquencies are minor in nature. So trivial are many of them that they fall into segments C and D of the bell-shaped continuum of behavior presented in Chapter 2—in other words, they represent the normal deviations anticipated and tolerated by society.

COMPARISON OF HIGH SCHOOL AND CORRECTIONAL SCHOOL STUDENTS

Several studies have probed the backgrounds of high school or college students, socially accepted and playing the role of nondelinquents. In one study high school and correctional school students were compared as to fre-

[19] Published for the Welfare Council of New York City by Columbia University Press, New York, 1936.

[20] F. J. Murphy, M. M. Shirley, and H. L. Witmer, "The Incidence of Hidden Delinquency," *American Journal of Orthopsychiatry*, 16 (1946), 686–696.

TABLE 5

Recorded and Unrecorded Delinquencies of 101 Boys Over a Period of Time

DELINQUENCY	DELINQUENCIES NUMBER	DELINQUENCIES PERCENTAGE
Minor delinquency, such as truancy, petty theft, trespassing, running away, being stubborn, etc.	4,406	68
Violation of city ordinances, such as vending without a license, playing ball in streets, swimming or fishing in forbidden places, violating the curfew law, etc.	1,394	22
Serious offenses, such as burglary, larceny, assault, drunkenness, sex offenses, etc.	616	10
Total	6,416	100

Data: Fred J. Murphy, Mary M. Shirley, and Helen L. Witmer, "The Incidence of Hidden Delinquency," *American Journal of Orthopsychiatry*, 16 (1946), 686-696.

quency and seriousness of delinquent acts.[21]

Twenty-one items of legal delinquency were used as the basis for the study. The formal terms of the law were translated into language more understandable to adolescents. Thus robbery became "used force (strongarm methods) to get money from another person," and "incorrigibility" or "ungovernability" became "defied parents' authority." Questionnaires were anonymously filled out by high school students in three small western communities and by inmates in a western state training school for delinquents. It was not possible to secure arrest records for the high school students, therefore this group may have a few students who have been arrested or who are on probation; in fact, a few might have spent some time in a correctional school.

Every offense on the list presented to high school students, shown in Tables 6 and 7, was checked by some high school boys and girls, although often by only a few. A much higher percentage of the training school boys and girls checked offenses. The greater number of offenses by training school boys was particularly noticeable in stealing and fighting. Training school girls

[21] The present discussion is based on James F. Short, Jr. and F. Ivan Nye, "Extent of Unrecorded Juvenile Delinquency, Tentative Conclusions," *Journal of Criminal Law, Criminology and Police Science*, 49 (1958), 296–302. Other aspects of the complete study are found in Short, "A Report on the Incidence of Criminal Behavior, Arrests, and Convictions in Selected Groups," *Research Studies of the State College of Washington*, 22 (June, 1954), 110–118; Short and Nye, "Reported Behavior as a Criterion of Deviant Behavior," *Social Problems*, 5 (1957–58), 207–213; Short and Nye, "Scaling Delinquent Behavior," *American Sociological Review*, 22 (1957), 326–331. An earlier study by Porterfield compared admitted delinquencies of college students with offenses of juvenile court cases; every college student had committed one or more offenses, the average being 17.6 for men and 4.7 for women. See Austin L. Porterfield, *Youth in Trouble*, The Leo Potishman Foundation, Fort Worth, Texas, 1946, pp. 37–51.

TABLE 6

Reported Delinquent Behavior among Boys in High School and Correctional School

TYPE OF OFFENSE	PER CENT ADMITTING COMMISSION OF OFFENSE		PER CENT ADMITTING COMMISSION OF OFFENSE MORE THAN ONCE OR TWICE	
	HIGH SCHOOL	CORRECTIONAL SCHOOL	HIGH SCHOOL	CORRECTIONAL SCHOOL
Driven a car without a driver's license or permit	75.3	91.1	49.0	73.4
Skipped school	53.0	95.3	23.8	85.9
Had fist fight with one person	80.7	95.3	31.9	75.0
"Run away" from home	13.0	68.1	2.4	37.7
School probation or expulsion	11.3	67.8	2.9	31.3
Defied parents' authority	33.1	52.4	6.3	23.6
Driven too fast or recklessly	46.0	76.3	19.1	51.6
Taken little things (worth less than $2) that did not belong to you	60.6	91.8	12.9	65.1
Taken things of medium value ($2–$50)	15.8	91.0	3.8	61.4
Taken things of large value ($50)	5.0	90.8	2.1	47.7
Used force (strong-arm methods) to get money from another person	(6.3)*	67.7	(2.4)*	35.5
Taken part in "gang fights"	22.5	67.4	5.2	47.4
Taken a car for a ride without the owner's knowledge	14.8	75.2	4.0	53.4
Bought or drank beer, wine, or liquor (including drinking at home)	57.2	89.7	29.5	79.4
Bought or drank beer, wine, or liquor (outside your home)	(43.0)*	87.0	(21.1)*	75.0
Drank beer, wine, or liquor in your own home	(57.0)*	62.8	(24.1)*	31.9
Deliberate property damage	44.8	84.3	8.2	49.7
Used or sold narcotic drugs	2.2	23.1	1.6	12.6
Had sex relations with another person of the same sex (not masturbation)	8.8	10.9	2.9	3.1
Had sex relations with a person of the opposite sex	40.4	87.5	19.9	73.4
Gone hunting or fishing without a license (or violated other game laws)	62.7	66.7	23.5	44.8
Taken things you didn't want	22.5	56.8	3.1	26.8
"Beat up" on kids who hadn't done anything to you	13.9	48.7	2.8	26.2
Hurt someone to see them squirm	15.8	33.4	3.2	17.5

Data: James F. Short, Jr., and F. Ivan Nye, "Extent of Unrecorded Juvenile Delinquency," *Journal of Criminal Law, Criminology and Police Science*, Northwestern University School of Law, 49 (1958), 297.

* These questions were omitted from the schedule given to high school students in the western state. The percentages in parentheses are from a sample of midwest high school students.

TABLE 7

Reported Delinquent Behavior among Girls in High School and Correctional School

TYPE OF OFFENSE	PER CENT ADMITTING COMMISSION OF OFFENSE		PER CENT ADMITTING COMMISSION OF OFFENSE MORE THAN ONCE OR TWICE	
	HIGH SCHOOL	CORRECTIONAL SCHOOL	HIGH SCHOOL	CORRECTIONAL SCHOOL
Driven a car without a driver's license or permit	58.2	68.3	29.9	54.4
Skipped school	41.0	94.0	12.2	66.3
Had fist fight with one person	28.2	72.3	5.7	44.6
"Run away" from home	11.3	85.5	1.0	51.8
School probation or expulsion	3.7	63.4	0.2	29.3
Defied parents' authority	30.6	68.3	5.0	39.0
Driven too fast or recklessly	16.3	47.5	5.4	35.0
Taken little things (worth less than $2) that did not belong to you	30.0	77.8	3.5	48.1
Taken things of medium value ($2–$50)	3.9	58.0	0.6	29.6
Taken things of large value ($50)	1.3	30.4	0.9	10.1
Used force (strong-arm methods) to get money from another person	(1.3)*	36.7	(0.3)*	21.5
Taken part in "gang fights"	6.5	59.0	1.1	27.7
Taken a car for a ride without the owner's knowledge	4.5	36.6	0.6	20.7
Bought or drank beer, wine, or liquor (including drinking at home)	44.5	90.2	17.6	80.5
Bought or drank beer, wine, or liquor (outside your home)	(28.7)*	83.9	(10.8)*	75.3
Drank beer, wine, or liquor in your own home	(54.2)*	71.1	(16.4)*	42.2
Deliberate property damage	13.6	65.4	1.6	32.1
Used or sold narcotic drugs	0.5	36.9	0.3	23.8
Had sex relations with another person of the same sex (not masturbation)	3.6	25.0	0.5	12.5
Had sex relations with a person of the opposite sex	14.1	95.1	4.8	81.5
Gone hunting or fishing without a license (or violated other game laws)	20.3	27.5	3.9	21.3
Taken things you didn't want	3.6	43.0	0.6	13.9
"Beat up" on kids who hadn't done anything to you	3.1	37.8	0.9	18.3
Hurt someone to see them squirm	9.3	35.4	1.1	20.7

Data: James F. Short, Jr., and F. Ivan Nye, "Extent of Unrecorded Juvenile Delinquency," *Journal of Criminal Law, Criminology and Police Science*, Northwestern University School of Law, 49 (1958), 297.

* These questions were omitted from the schedule given to high school students in the western state. The percentages in parentheses are from a sample of midwest high school students.

exceeded high school girls in fighting and sex relations. The comparison of high school and training school youth is significant for repeated offenses. Relatively few high school youth repeated, compared to the number of repeaters among training school youth. In a more detailed analysis, the authors indicated that in their sample of students, a small percentage of both boys and girls exceeded the training school groups in delinquency, but that in general the boys and girls sent to the training school were more persistently and seriously delinquent than the high school students.

Many of the delinquencies seem to represent the minor acts of deviation tolerated by society. These would be represented by acts very common to both high school and correctional school students. These acts not being highly disapproved, high school students probably engaged in them with little feeling of guilt. Among correctional school students, they were probably incidental to other, more serious types of delinquency which brought them to court conviction. Among boys, deviations tolerated are driving a car without a license or permit, skipping school, having fist fights with one other person, taking things worth less than $2, buying or drinking beer, wine, or liquor, including drinking at home, and going fishing or hunting without a license. All these were checked by more than half of the high school boys and by still more correctional school boys. Correctional school boys had many more repetitions of these offenses than high school boys and in addition had more often committed more serious offenses found among only a few high school boys. Girls typically act delinquently less often than boys. Nevertheless 30 per cent or more of the high school girls had driven a car without a driver's license, skipped school, defied parents' authority, taken little things worth less than $2, and bought or drunk beer, or wine, including drinking at home. Higher percentages of correctional school girls had committed these offenses; in addition they often had more serious offenses on their records and a higher rate of recidivism.

Finally, in a careful study of 522 randomly selected adolescents in Flint, Michigan, Martin Gold found that only a small fraction of all delinquents were ever caught and booked by the police.[22] But he also discovered that the determining factor in whether a child was apprehended was his persistence. Those youngsters who repeated their delinquent behavior time after time were much more likely to be arrested than those who did not. Indeed, Gold indicates that police arrest data probably give a reasonably accurate picture of the level of *serious* delinquency in a community.

It would appear that minor offenses repeated only infrequently are within the normal range of behavior expected of most teen-agers. In addition, boys may escape serious penalties for a moderate amount of fighting and

[22] Martin Gold, "Undetected Delinquent Behavior," *Journal of Research in Crime and Delinquency*, 13, No. 1 (January, 1966), 27–46.

evading hunting and fishing laws; girls may show some defiance of parents' authority. But when these tolerated deviations are often repeated or are combined with other, more serious offenses, which threaten or injure other people or their property, youths may find themselves under arrest, in juvenile court, and committed to a correctional school.

In other words, the delinquency that comes to the court's attention is a combination of an immoderate amount of "normal" deviation and serious offenses which threaten or injure.

These studies throw new light on the earlier studies which seemed to show that many delinquent children were in some way escaping detection. Some serious offenders of course do escape detection, but, in general, it seems that many of the undetected offenders are actually acting within the area of tolerance for deviating behavior.

An Interpretation of the Statistical Studies

The percentages given in this chapter support the hypothesis of the bell-shaped continuum presented in Chapter 2. Although the studies of high school and college students seem to indicate that all students have at some time committed at least a minor act of delinquency, small percentages of youth were also found who were free or virtually free from delinquency—Sections E, F, and G of the curve. The high school students, with their small proportion of serious delinquencies and large proportions of tolerated misbehavior, represent Sections C and D. The arrested youth fit into Section B, and the court and correctional school cases into Section A.

BIBLIOGRAPHY

ANGELINO, HENRY, "Shoplifting: A Critical Review," *Midwest Sociologist*, 15 (Spring, 1953), 17–22.

CAMERON, MARY OWEN, *The Booster and Snitch, Department Store Shoplifting*, Free Press of Glencoe, Inc., New York, 1964.

CLINARD, MARSHALL B., AND ANDREW L. WADE, "Toward the Delineation of Vandalism as a Sub-type in Juvenile Delinquency," *Journal of Criminal Law, Criminology and Police Science*, 48 (1958), 493–499.

GOLD, MARTIN, "Undetected Delinquent Behavior," *Journal of Research in Crime and Delinquency*, 13 (January, 1966), 27–46.

MARTIN, JOHN M., *Juvenile Vandalism*, Charles C Thomas, Publisher, Springfield, Ill., 1961.

MURPHY, FRED J., MARY M. SHIRLEY, AND HELEN L. WITMER, "The Incidence of Hidden Delinquency," *American Journal of Orthopsychiatry*, 16 (1946), 686–696.

PORTERFIELD, AUSTIN L., *Youth in Trouble*, Leo Potishman Foundation, Fort Worth, Texas, 1946.

ROBISON, SOPHIA MOSES, *Can Delinquency Be Measured?* Columbia University Press, New York, 1936.

SCHWARTZ, EDWARD E., "A Community Experiment in the Measurement of Delinquency," *Yearbook 1945, National Probation Association*, New York, 1945, 157–182.

SHAW, CLIFFORD R., AND ASSOCIATES, *Brothers in Crime*, University of Chicago Press, Chicago, 1938.

————, *The Jack-Roller*, University of Chicago Press, Chicago, 1930.

SHORT, JAMES F., JR., "A Report on the Incidence of Criminal Behavior, Arrests, and Convictions in Selected Groups," *Research Studies of the State College of Washington*, 22 (June, 1954), 110–118.

————, AND F. IVAN NYE, "Extent of Unrecorded Juvenile Delinquency, Tentative Conclusions," *Journal of Criminal Law, Criminology and Police Science*, 49 (1958), 296–302.

————, "Reported Behavior as a Criterion of Deviant Behavior," *Social Problems*, 5 (Winter, 1957–1958), 207–213.

————, "Scaling Delinquent Behavior," *American Sociological Review*, 22 (1957), 326–331.

WATTENBERG, WILLIAM W., AND JAMES BALISTRIERI, "Automobile Theft: A 'Favored Group' Delinquency," *American Journal of Sociology*, 57 (1952), 575–579.

WEDEKIND, RICHARD, "Automobile Theft, The Thirteen Million Dollar Parasite," *Journal of Criminal Law, Criminology and Police Science*, 48 (1957), 443–446.

theories
of delinquency

The theoretical explanation of delinquency has developed very rapidly since 1955, when Albert K. Cohen published *Delinquent Boys*.[1] Although some of the ideas presented in Cohen's pioneering work are now outmoded, it nevertheless inspired an extensive examination of the problem in the 1950's and 1960's with the result that today delinquency theory is as well developed as any other area in all of sociology. In the next several chapters we shall examine several types of delinquency theory, describing both the blind alleys and the promising avenues of research that have been followed since Cohen's epochal work.

What Kind of Theory Is Needed?

All theories rest upon distinct perspectives, and to evaluate any particular theory adequately it is necessary to examine its basic assumptions as well as its conclusions regarding the natural world. In approaching delinquency theoretically, therefore, we shall begin by clarifying the assumptions upon which this discussion rests.

The perspective to be developed here assumes, first, that delinquent behavior consists of many different patterns reflecting a wide variety of circum-

---

[1] Albert K. Cohen, *Delinquent Boys*, Free Press of Glencoe, New York, 1955.

stances and forces. Some of these patterns may be explained in terms of a single theory. But not all of them can. Consequently, the great variety of delinquent behavior seems to demand more than one theoretical viewpoint to explain its many forms.

Second, we are assuming that each of the distinctive patterns of delinquency displays a cluster of *interrelated* characteristics. Even though chance and drift may characterize the careers of many delinquents, their *reactions* to this experience are focused and selective, and their delinquency falls into distinct patterns of characteristics.[2] Our theories must be geared to these patterns.

Third, we are assuming that delinquent behavior is inherently more complex than any single theory or group of theories can possibly anticipate. If there is an element of chance in the typical delinquent's career, theory cannot explain *ultimately* why any particular youngster becomes delinquent, because to some extent fate alone is responsible, i.e., he was in the wrong place at the wrong time. But to the degree that fate is a factor, any theory of behavior will inevitably fall short in explaining the twists and turns of an individual's social career. It may give a good accounting of the risks attached to any particular situation, but it cannot explain why circumstances come together as they do to shape individual experience.

With these assumptions, we can begin to describe the kind of theory that we will need to understand delinquency and the questions we can properly ask of it in our attempts to explain delinquent behavior. We will need a theoretical approach that is adequate to the full diversity of delinquent behavior. Not one that condenses it into a uniform white light, but one that refracts its variety into a spectrum of different hues and colors. Our theories should also deal with clusters of characteristics, and they should relate delinquent behavior to these clusters, not to individual traits. Finally, we should recognize that however efficient our theories may be in explaining existing patterns of delinquency, there will always be an elusive quality about individual behavior that ultimately resists explication.

Six Problem Areas for Delinquency Theory

Once we have established a general form for our theories of delinquency, we still must identify the kinds of questions we want the theories to resolve. There are six general problem areas regarding delinquency. First, we must

[2] Several theorists have suggested recently that the careers of delinquents unfold to some extent in terms of chance and happenstance. See, for example, David Matza, *Delinquency and Drift*, John Wiley & Sons, New York, 1964, Chapter 6; and Fred L. Strodtbeck and James F. Short, Jr., "Aleatory Risks versus Short-run Hedonism in Explanation of Gang Action," *Social Problems*, 12 (Fall, 1964), 127–140.

establish the constellations of attitudes, cognitive styles, motives, and emotions that stimulate delinquent behavior. Although there are attitudes and motives that do not result in distinctive patterns of behavior (e.g., daydreams, desires that cannot be satisfied, goals that cannot be fulfilled), it is also true that virtually all behavior—delinquent as well as nondelinquent— derives from a characteristic cluster of such personality attributes. Accordingly, the first question we must ask is, *What are the personality patterns that give organization and direction to delinquent behavior?*

Personality theory is best equipped to deal with this question, since it deals specifically with syndromes of psychological forces that organize behavior, but it is beyond the scope of this work to go into this theory very deeply.[3] Many sociologists feel some reluctance in employing psychological explanations of behavior, and two broad surveys have shown that there is little if any consistent association between personality traits and deviancy.[4] But the fact remains that there *is* a psychological dimension to behavior, and to ignore or reject it is to deprive ourselves of an important tool that in some cases is essential to an understanding of delinquency.

The second question we must ask regarding delinquent behavior deals with the formation of the personality patterns that underlie delinquent behavior. Not only must we know the structure of attitudes and motives associated with delinquency, but we must also know how these structures came into being. The second question, therefore, is: *What are the socializing pressures that create the personality patterns underlying delinquent behavior?* Since this question deals not only with psychological structures but also with social processes, social psychologists are probably best equipped to handle it.

But those who have been most interested in the socialization of delinquents have typically been psychiatrists who are not keenly aware of group processes and their influence on socialization, or sociologists who discount the influence of personality upon attitudes and motives. In the next chapter we shall explore these first two questions in a balanced fashion, considering both the psychological structures that lie behind delinquent behavior and the socializing processes that contribute to their development.

The third question focuses upon the social circumstances that thwart or facilitate delinquent behavior. Delinquency always unfolds in terms of the

[3] Good examples of the ways in which personality theory can be used to explain delinquency include Fritz Redl and David Wineman, *The Aggressive Child*, Free Press, New York, 1957; and Kate Friedlander, *The Psychoanalytic Approach to Juvenile Delinquency*, International Universities Press, New York, 1947.

[4] Cf. Gordon P. Waldo and Simon Dinitz, "Personality Attributes of the Criminal: An Analysis of Research Studies, 1950–1965," *Journal of Research in Crime and Delinquency*, 4 (July, 1967), 185–201; and Karl F. Schuessler and Donald R. Cressey, "Personality Characteristics of Criminals, *American Journal of Sociology*, 55 (March, 1950), 476–484.

social opportunities and obstacles confronting adolescents, and a full understanding of the problem depends upon our identifying these social circumstances with some precision. Our third question becomes, therefore, *What are the immediate social situations that shape and influence delinquent behavior?*

The influence of a particular situation, of course, is not always the same for all delinquents. One child's opportunity is another's obstacle, and so the course of a child's behavior depends basically upon the interplay between his own predispositions and his situation.[5] Hence, no simple relationship between concrete circumstances and delinquency should be expected, nor has one been found. For example, there is evidence that disturbed parent-child relationships often result in aggressive delinquency with one type of child but in mildly neurotic, nondelinquent behavior in another.[6] We shall explore this complicated question in greater detail in Chapters 7, 8, and 10.

Strictly speaking, this third question is not properly addressed to theory, since it depends upon an *interaction* of dissimilar patterns, i.e., personality syndromes and social situations. But it does provide a firm foundation for answering our fourth question, *What are the broad social processes that engender the social situations which shape delinquency?*

A number of authors draw a sharp distinction between the concrete circumstances of delinquency and the general principles that explain specific circumstances.[7] If seriously disturbed parent-child relationships are a factor in certain types of delinquency, we should also be concerned with the general patterns that such relationships reveal, because it is entirely likely that similar patterns in other contexts will have the same result. Thus, it may be that arbitrariness and brutality between teachers and pupils have much the same effect on children as parental arbitrariness and brutality. If we can discover the general principles that describe the relationship between delinquency and a variety of concrete situations, our understanding will be considerably enhanced. The specific circumstances of delinquency change drastically from one generation to the next, but the general principles explaining delinquency change much more slowly, if at all. For example, throughout the nineteenth

---

[5] There have been several attempts recently to systematize this approach to behavior. See Alan C. Acock and Melvin L. deFleur, "A Configurational Approach to Contingent Consistency in the Attitude-Behavior Relationship," *American Sociological Review*, 37 (December, 1972), 714–726; J. Milton Yinger, *Toward a Field Theory of Behavior*, McGraw-Hill, New York, 1965; and Theodore N. Ferdinand, *Typologies of Delinquency*, Random House, Inc., New York, 1966, Chapter 3.

[6] Cf. Sheldon and Eleanor Glueck, *Family Environment and Delinquency*, Houghton Mifflin Co., Boston, 1962, Chapter 14.

[7] See, for example, Edwin H. Sutherland and Donald R. Cressey, *Criminology, Ninth Edition*, J. B. Lippincott Co., Philadelphia, 1974, pp. 72–74.

century delinquency was found largely among European immigrants and first-generation Americans in the major cities of the Northeast and Midwest. Hence, delinquents tended to be Catholic, wretchedly poor, and white. Today, delinquency is still found among migrants to the great metropolitan centers of the nation, but *now* delinquents are more often Protestant, moderately poor, and black. The basic social processes underlying delinquency have probably changed very little in the last century and a half, but the specific circumstances and characteristics of delinquents have changed dramatically.

For this reason we must go behind the concrete situations and characteristics of delinquency and ferret out the underlying social processes that are ultimately responsible. In Chapter 6 we shall designate four such basic processes: social organization, social disorganization, cultural disorganization, and cultural deviance. And in our discussion of these four social processes, we shall weigh the significance of each in terms of an extensive and growing body of research describing the concrete situations of delinquents in America.

Our fifth theoretical concern focuses on the broader society and its influence on these four basic social processes. It poses the question, *How are these four basic processes affected by the organization of the surrounding society?* To resolve this problem we will consider two different types of societies—gemeinschaft and gesellschaft—and we shall estimate the distinctive manner with which each fosters or diminishes the basic social processes that are especially relevant to delinquency.[8] There is considerable evidence describing the varying patterns of delinquency found in different societies. This evidence provides many useful clues as to the ways in which distinctive societies foster delinquency among young people. A fuller understanding of the ways in which different types of societies encourage or suppress delinquency can throw our own experience with the problem into much sharper relief. It may be that delinquency in the United States derives ultimately from institutions and concepts of social order that stand at the very center of national life. To cope with the problem effectively, therefore, may require a degree of change in America that few Americans would find tolerable. It may also be that such a pessimistic diagnosis is not entirely warranted. But only a careful examination of delinquency in different types of societies can help us answer the question. In Chapter 6 we shall explore the issue further.

The last question that we might reasonably ask of theory is much more practical; it focuses upon the problems of treatment, prevention, and control. Given the nature of delinquency as revealed in our answers to the first five questions, we might reasonably ask, *Can we affect its level or characteristics*

[8] See Chapter 6 for a detailed discussion of these types of societies.

in any very significant way? Our answer in the chapter ahead (after lengthy discussion, of course) is yes, and consequently in Chapter 14 we examine critically the great variety of techniques and methods that have been utilized to control delinquency in the family, school, or community.

This discussion suggests two major conclusions regarding delinquency that are worth making explicit. First, the understanding and prevention of delinquency are intimately interrelated. It makes little sense to suggest remedial programs in the community if there is no understanding of the ways in which communities foster delinquency. In the absence of such knowledge society has tended to blame the delinquent for his misdeeds and focus its remedial efforts on him. We are beginning to understand, however, that delinquency arises not only because of basic problems in the children, but also because of difficulties in their social groups, particularly the family and school. It is hoped that the discussion advanced in succeeding chapters will clarify the manner in which communities create their own delinquency problems and provide intelligent guidance to community leaders in coping with it.

Our second conclusion is directed more specifically to the student of delinquency. It will become increasingly clear as we move ahead in this work that a multidisciplinary approach is required for a full understanding of delinquency in American society. Accordingly, those who hope one day to contribute to this understanding must themselves prepare broadly for the task. They must seek training in the disciplines most relevant to delinquency, i.e., psychology and sociology, and a familiarity with the law, human physiology, and social welfare would also be very useful. Thus, the student of delinquency must become expert in a wide range of disciplines, avoiding thereby the twin banes of modern education: specialization to the point of banality and generalization to the point of irrelevancy.

BIBLIOGRAPHY

CLOWARD, RICHARD A., AND LLOYD E. OHLIN, *Delinquency and Opportunity*, Free Press of Glencoe, New York, 1960, Chapter 2.

COHEN, ALBERT K., "Multiple Factor Approaches," from his *Juvenile Delinquency and the Social Structure*, Ph.D. Dissertation, Harvard University, 1951, pp. 5–13. Also reprinted in *The Sociology of Crime and Delinquency*, Second Edition, Marvin E. Wolfgang, *et al.*, eds., John Wiley & Sons, Inc., New York, 1970.

SUTHERLAND, EDWIN H., AND DONALD R. CRESSEY, *Criminology*, Ninth Edition, J. B. Lippincott Company, Philadelphia, 1974, Chapter 4.

socialization, personality, and delinquency

In the last chapter we saw that the most immediate problems in explaining delinquent behavior are the personality patterns that underlie delinquency and the socialization processes that are responsible for these patterns. In this chapter we shall examine both questions carefully.

A Controversy: The Socialization of Delinquents

The general question of how delinquents and criminals get that way has stirred much debate among criminologists. For psychologically oriented criminologists delinquency and criminality are the result of serious imbalances or conflicts in the personalities of individuals. For them delinquency is an eccentric pattern of behavior in which the delinquent is at odds with the values and mores of *his* groups. He is not only a delinquent (when he violates the law) but also a deviant in that he typically offends the moral sensibilities of those closest to him. Thus, from the psychological viewpoint the typical delinquent exhibits a contorted personality; his personal idiosyncrasies are largely responsible for his deviant or delinquent behavior; and he is alienated from those in his immediate social environment.

Sociologically oriented criminologists, however, see delinquent behavior as basically similar to nondelinquent behavior. It is an adaptive or even conforming response to social conditions and not eccentric or deviant at all. In fact delinquency is regarded by them as a reasonable adjustment to the kinds of stresses that confront young people in modern society. Anyone in a similar position might well respond in the same way.

Moreover, psychologists look for unusual, base motives to explain why delinquents behave as they do, whereas sociologists insist that delinquents are neither more base nor more blameworthy in their motives than thee or me. The two viewpoints, therefore, place delinquents at quite different levels of virtue, and beneath their assumptions regarding the sources of delinquency are a variety of ill-formed views regarding the social and moral worth of delinquent behavior. Naturally, each questions the assumptions and conclusions of the other and attempts to refute them.[1]

Nevertheless, both viewpoints are valid, at least partially, and in this section we shall explore each as an account of what delinquents are like and how they are socialized. When we have described the basic processes of socialization, we shall consider the personality types of delinquents and the pressures that contribute to their delinquency.

A PSYCHOLOGICAL INTERPRETATION

The psychologists that have made the most headway in explaining delinquency are concentrated largely in the psychoanalytic school. And in the variety of explanations offered, three general personality patterns can be readily identified as leading up to delinquency.[2] First, we have those children—we shall label them symptomatic delinquents—whose early sexual behavior is so vigorously punished by socializing adults that it is steadfastly repressed into the unconscious. These children generally display few unusual mannerisms before puberty, but when they mature into adolescence, their sexual needs mount to irrepressible proportions and overwhelm their inhibitions. Since the motives that were originally repressed in childhood continue to be abhorrent in adolescence, the direct satisfaction of their sexual needs is not possible. But the human mind is resourceful, and alternative techniques for gaining sexual satisfactions are discovered and developed.

These techniques may have an obvious sexual dimension as in voyeurism, or they may be apparently asexual as in pyromania or kleptomania, but they all have a common purpose: to relieve sexually based yearnings without calling

[1] See, for example, Michael Hakeem, "A Critique of the Psychiatric Approach to Crime and Correction," *Law and Contemporary Problems*, 23, No. 4 (1958), 672–702.

[2] See Theodore N. Ferdinand, *Typologies of Delinquency*, Random House, New York, 1966, pp. 176–201 for an extended discussion of these three paths to delinquency.

into play deeply feared patterns of sexual behavior.[3] The personalities of these youngsters are relatively stable otherwise, but the intensity of their unconscious sexual needs is so great that they periodically intrude upon consciousness in disguised form and provoke irrational, compulsive patterns of behavior.

Such children usually grow up in highly conventional families in which the parents hold very strict views regarding sexual behavior which they impose relentlessly upon their children. At the same time there is often a seductive undercurrent in which an unusually intense mother-son or father-daughter relationship stimulates the sexual fancies of the child.[4] Outwardly, however, the family appears quite conventional to the community.

The delinquent aberrations of such youngsters can be dangerous as in pyromania, or mildly annoying as in window-peeping, but their intent is generally not malicious, just idiosyncratic. They are often genuinely sorry for their misdeeds and consciously want to control their bizarre behavior, but it is rooted in unconscious needs which they do not understand and cannot cope with. Hence, they will return again and again to their particular form of delinquency until the anxieties upon which it is based are resolved in one fashion or another.

A second path that also culminates in delinquency, according to many psychoanalytic theorists, originates in the youngster's *conscious* motives and involves him in serious difficulty as he attempts to express them. Many children are exposed to such intense hostility in childhood that they develop aggressive motives out of all proportion to those of their peers, and as they grow into adolescence they become difficult and even dangerous to those around them. Such children undergo what Harry Stack Sullivan has called a malevolent transformation, i.e., they only feel and express hatred and maliciousness, and as they approach physical maturity, their destructiveness can become a serious problem. Because their delinquent behavior consists primarily of unprovoked, impulsive assaults against others, they have been described in the psychoanalytic literature as unsocialized aggressive children.[5]

A similar pattern, stemming from completely different circumstances,

---

[3] See Ernest Simmel, "Incendiarism," in *Searchlights on Delinquency*, K. R. Eissler, ed., International Universities Press, Inc., New York, 1949, pp. 90–101; or Otto Fenichel, *The Psychoanalytic Theory of Neurosis*, W. W. Norton, New York, 1945, pp. 341–349, 370–372. Not all forms of theft, arson, or window-peeping, however, can be explained in this fashion.

[4] See Simmel, *op. cit.*, pp. 92–93.

[5] Cf. Lester E. Hewitt and Richard L. Jenkins, *Fundamental Patterns of Maladjustment*, State Printer, Springfield, Ill., 1947, pp. 34–42.

involves the overindulged child.[6] Such children develop when one parent (usually the mother) establishes an extremely close relationship with the child at the expense of the other parent. The child (usually a son) never develops the inner controls that would permit him to accept opposition gracefully, and when faced with frustration or resistance in social relationships, he flies into a violent rage. When he enjoys the admiring approval of those around him, he is confident and congenial, but when others resist his purposes and reject his ideas, his fury lashes out like a lightning bolt, and he becomes dangerously angry. Since his egocentrism encourages him to exploit others, his life is punctuated with misunderstandings and soured relationships so that his behavior grows increasingly antisocial and vicious as he becomes alienated and disenchanted. Thus, in adolescence and beyond he can become dangerous to others in the community.

Such children typically come from families that are severely disorganized. Relations between the parents are seriously strained, often to the point of separation or divorce. The parents themselves often exhibit severe personal disturbances and use the child as a foil for their own pathologies.

These children, however, should not be regarded as simply mirroring the disorganization of their homes in their own behavior. Their behavior often goes far beyond the patterns established in the family. For example, in such families the mother typically surrounds the boy with solicitude and consideration to which he responds with venomous anger. If his motives were simply a reflection of his familial environment, he might be expected to exhibit kindness and affection toward his mother. Similarly, since his father plays an ineffectual, peripheral role, the boy might be expected to adopt a pattern of diffident restraint toward his father. Instead we see an attitude of contempt and belligerence.

The overindulged child illustrates a very important point in psychoanalytic theory: The family provides a social setting within which the personality develops, but the result depends basically upon the ways in which familial pressures impinge upon the child's personality structure. When the dynamic equilibrium of the personality is disturbed in just the right way, a relationship of affectionate consideration can give rise to motives of exploitative viciousness. From the standpoint of psychoanalytic theory the *structure* of the personality is every bit as important as the environment in fixing personality development, and it is an oversimplification to suggest that an in-

[6] See Margaret S. Mahler, "Les 'Enfants Terribles,'" in K. R. Eissler, ed., *op. cit.*, pp. 77–89; or David Levy, *Maternal Overprotection*, Columbia University Press, New York, 1943, pp. 159–199.

dividual's attitudes and motives will inevitably reflect the values and norms of his social groups—especially when delinquents are the focus.

A third pattern of difficulty that troubles many teen-agers is rooted in their ego functions and is reflected in the ineffective manner with which they manage interpersonal relationships.[7] Some youngsters are so plagued by self-doubt and feelings of inferiority that they experience extreme difficulty in organizing themselves to confront the many trials of adolescence. They may have a high level of native talent, but unless they can focus themselves effectively, their abilities will be dissipated in random, futile gestures. Such youngsters come to doubt their own sense of reality and moral value and often surrender to the drift of people and events around them. But drifting creates in its wake even greater fears and doubts which make a sense of self even more difficult to achieve.

The root problem here is impaired ego functioning, and a poor social adjustment is both a factor in and an outgrowth of the problem. These youngsters typically come from families that are still intact but that exhibit a great deal of intramural strife.[8] The children are subjected to contradictory standards, and they never develop a clear sense of the proper way to behave. The family is not pathological, but the parents are inconsistent, and there is a great deal of petty bickering on all sides.

The adolescents caught in this kind of vicious circle are often resentful toward adults and isolated from their peers, but their own fears and self-doubts usually inhibit any overt aggression toward those who are basically responsible for their plight. Rather, they express their resentment through petty acts of maliciousness or theft that inflict painful psychological wounds, but which in the long run merely compound their difficulties. Thus, in this case delinquency is an expression of inner confusions brought on by a contradictory and defeating social environment.

Our final pattern of delinquency can be most conveniently understood in terms of Erik Erikson's concept of the ego-identity.[9] All of us have more or less definite pictures of what kind of people we are, how we are attractive or unattractive, worthy or unworthy, and all these images taken together con-

---

[7] For example, see Fritz Redl and David Wineman, *The Aggressive Child*, Free Press, Glencoe, Ill., 1957, pp. 74–140.

[8] Cf. Sheldon and Eleanor Glueck, *Physique and Delinquency*, Harper & Row, New York, 1956, Chapters VIII and IX, for a discussion of the conflict-ridden family life of the neurotic (ectomorphic) delinquent.

[9] See Erik H. Erikson, "Identity and the Life Cycle," *Psychological Issues*, Vol. 1, Monograph 1, International Universities Press, Inc., New York, 1959, Chapter 3, for a concise statement of Erikson's theory of ego-identity.

stitute our self-concepts. The self-concept is developed through intense, close social relationships and inevitably takes on the coloring of the individual's immediate socio-cultural environment. Indeed, the organization of a self-concept depends largely upon the articulation of the individual's interests and talents with the values of his groups, and when a congenial blending of the two is achieved, the individual forms what Erikson calls an ego-identity.

According to Erikson, the ego-identity is the core of the individual's self-concept around which he structures his other attitudes and ideals, and it is based upon those of his personal qualities that coincide with the values of his immediate peers and win their approval. Thus, it provides a framework for organizing who he is, and he reflects this fact in the enthusiastic way in which he accepts the goals and values of his group. By means of his ego-identity the individual forms a bond with his immediate groups and in return gains a legitimated self-concept that is relevant to his social environment and that serves as a medium through which his group's values become his own.

For many reasons some individuals may find this articulation of personal feelings with group values difficult, and the result according to Erikson is often ego-diffusion.[10] Instead of self-confidence and a well defined purpose, such individuals display indecision, ambivalence, and confusion regarding their proper course in society. They exhibit, in other words, many of the characteristics of impaired ego functioning we have just examined.

The important point here, however, is that any kind of group, including a delinquent group, can serve as the basis of an adolescent's identity. And when adolescents form delinquent identities, they show all the qualities of other teen-agers with strong identities, except that their values and ideals are drawn from a delinquent subculture.[11]

A delinquent identity, however, raises special problems for the adolescents involved, because whatever approval it may kindle in their immediate peer groups, it inevitably raises strong opposition and resentment among more broadly based groups. Thus, a delinquent's identity needs powerful support from peers in order to persist in the face of widespread condemnation in the community.

As with most adolescents, the identities of delinquents are constantly developing and changing. As they move into new statuses and responsibilities in adulthood, their identities shift, and delinquent values no longer serve as the basis of their self-concept. But certain individuals find in delinquency a

[10] Cf. *ibid.*, pp. 88–94, 122–129.
[11] *Ibid.*, pp. 129–132.

meaningful expression of many deep-seated resentments and resist giving up this identity for one more consistent with an adult status in society.

Such delinquents typically exhibit a strong sense of unconscious guilt, an irrational hatred of men in authority, a heightened sensitivity to suggestions of weakness or inferiority, a sympathy for the underdog, and a fatalistic pessimism regarding their own destiny. They typically derive from families in which the father was a dominating figure, often abusing the mother and the children arbitrarily. In this kind of setting intense Oedipal rivalries arise in which the son develops a powerful resentment toward the father together with intense unconscious guilt. The son's guilt arises from the antagonism between his love and admiration of the father, which develops during infancy and early childhood, and his hatred of the father, which emerges during late childhood and adolescence.

It is easy to see why such individuals find delinquency so meaningful. It supports the expression of most of their basic sentiments while insulating them from criticism and their own guilt by legitimating their actions. This peculiar resonance creates an unusually strong delinquent identity and has prompted the label "crystallized delinquent."[12] They tend to follow the delinquent exploits of their peers, but their self-discipline and organization permit unusual levels of finesse and often a role of leadership. Their crystallized identity, moreover, usually means that delinquency for them is a stepping-stone to adult careers in crime.

With this description of the crystallized delinquent, we conclude our discussion of the psychological approach to socialization. We have attempted to be fair here, but any analytic approach to such a complex problem inevitably presents weaknesses as well as strengths, and it will be worthwhile to examine both. That psychoanalytic theory is highly relevant to delinquent behavior is suggested by the fact that many researchers from a variety of viewpoints have discovered delinquent types that correspond very closely to the personality patterns derived from psychoanalytic theory.[13] Whether psychoanalytic theory provides a valid diagnosis of the causes of each type in personality dynamics, or whether the treatments it prescribes are effective, are questions that can be legitimately raised.[14] But there can be little question that

[12] Ferdinand, *op. cit.*, pp. 190–193.

[13] Perhaps the best nonpsychoanalytic example is the research by Sheldon and Eleanor Glueck wherein the neurotic delinquent (ectomorph), the overindulged child (endomorph), and the unsocialized aggressive child (mesomorph) have been clearly identified. See Sheldon and Eleanor Glueck, *op. cit.*, Chapters XI, XII, and XIII.

[14] See, for example, Hans Eysenck, *Crime and Personality*, Houghton Mifflin Co., Boston, 1964, p. 142.

the personality patterns it describes actually do occur among delinquents.

But to say that psychoanalytic theory is relevant to delinquency is not to say that it is a *general* theory of delinquent behavior. The delinquents we have pictured here have several characteristics in common. Their behavior is essentially spontaneous in that it wells up from within the personality. It is not structured by social or moral understandings, and it often assumes a very primitive form. Unsocialized aggressive children, for example, lash out at those in their way with little thought to the injury they may cause or even the trouble they may create for themselves. If their behavior violates some customs or laws it is of little ultimate significance, since they cannot control what they do anyway. Their behavior is automatic with only minimal provocation from the immediate situation. Thus, psychoanalytic theory is most useful in describing primitive, unself-conscious patterns of behavior, and more complex forms—particularly those which depend upon shared values, reciprocal responsibilities, or self-conscious deliberations—are beyond its scope.

Moreover, it attempts to explain these primitive patterns of behavior in terms of extraordinary relationships with family members to the exclusion of broader social processes that not only often affect familial relationships but also contribute directly to the primitive patterns of behavior themselves. In sum, psychoanalytic theory would appear to be highly relevant to some types of delinquent behavior, but it is clearly not a complete explanation of the problem.

THE SOCIOLOGICAL VIEWPOINT

The socialization of delinquents is explained quite differently from the sociological standpoint. Writing in reaction to the limitations of psychoanalytic theory, E. H. Sutherland suggested that delinquency is a learned pattern of behavior not unlike other culturally defined forms and that in order to explain why it develops, we ought to focus on the organization of the delinquent's neighborhood or community instead of on his personality.[15] According to Sutherland's famous principle of differential association, "A person becomes delinquent because of an excess of definitions favorable to violation of law over definitions unfavorable to violation of law."[16] Thus, delinquency is learned by the juvenile when his peers present him with the techniques, values, and beliefs of delinquency, and he adopts them in his own behavior to the exclu-

---

[15] Edwin H. Sutherland and Donald R. Cressey, *Criminology*, Ninth Edition, J. B. Lippincott Co., Philadelphia, 1974, Chapter 4.

[16] *Ibid.*, p. 75.

sion of conventional techniques, values, and beliefs. Delinquency for Sutherland, therefore, is much like other social patterns: it persists because key reference groups in the community, i.e., teen-age cliques and gangs, endorse its values and transmit them to younger members of the community. The crucial question is not, How do juveniles become delinquent? because the answer is simple: Just like other people become lawyers, judges, or policemen. The question should be, How do delinquent gangs and cliques become established in the community? Sutherland says, therefore, that the solution to the problem is not to be found in the processes of socialization but rather in the processes of *differential social organization*, i.e., in the social processes that foster delinquent reference groups in certain communities but not in others.[17]

More recently sociologists have attempted to refine Sutherland's formulation by suggesting that certain reference groups play a more central role in forming an adolescent's values than others. Walter Reckless and his co-workers, for example, have suggested that "good" self-concepts tend to form in youths from supportive, cohesive families, and that such self-concepts in turn isolate them from delinquent values and teen-agers in neighborhoods where delinquency is a common, if not prevalent, pattern.[18] According to Reckless, a boy with a good self-concept has a relatively favorable opinion of himself and his family, and he tends to avoid companions and situations that might involve him in delinquent behavior. His good self-concept seems to insulate him from definitions that are favorable to law violations, and since his self-concept is an enduring feature of his personality, it continues to insulate him over a relatively long period and in a variety of social situations. Presumably a "bad" self-concept, i.e., one in which the self is seen as unworthy and ineffective, would function in the opposite fashion to throw bad boys into contact with definitions and people favorable to law violations over the long run.

But if an adolescent's self-concept plays a determining role in his selection of companions and experiences, an obvious question is, How do "bad" self-concepts develop? Many observers have assumed that it is seriously *deviant* or *delinquent behavior* which initially fosters a negative or delinquent self-

[17] *Ibid.*, Chapter 5.

[18] Walter C. Reckless, *The Crime Problem*, Third Edition, Appleton-Century-Crofts, Inc., New York, 1961, pp. 346–353. Recent research, however, suggests that a good self-concept insulates adolescents from delinquency *only* when it is buttressed by significant others who disapprove of delinquent behavior. Thus, the insulating power of a good self-concept is greater among those adolescents whose parents are emotionally supportive than among adolescents whose parents are not; it is greater among upper class blacks than among lower class blacks; and it is greater among white boys with no delinquent friends than among white boys with delinquent friends. See Gary F. Jensen, "Inner Containment and Delinquency," *Journal of Criminal Law and Criminology*, 64 (December, 1973), 464–470.

concept because it kindles ill will among those closest to the youngster and prompts in him a keen sense of his alienation and deviance.[19]

In recent years, however, some criminologists have offered an alternative explanation. These criminologists point out that many if not most adolescents indulge in various forms of deviance, and that if delinquent behavior is the first step in the process that ultimately produces a delinquent self-concept, many more adolescents than already do should regard themselves as delinquent. Lemert suggests, instead, that it is the act of labeling a child delinquent which often precipitates a delinquent self-concept and seriously antisocial behavior.[20]

When a youngster is accused of seriously deviant actions, he often reacts defensively with the result that his relationships with the accuser are seriously undermined, his feelings about himself are further impaired, and his behavior deteriorates dangerously. Thus, in the face of serious accusations by significant adults, a pattern of secondary deviation may emerge in which the youth counter aggresses against those responsible for his initial difficulty. Once this has happened, the child is well on his way to becoming a delinquent. Not only does he begin to have grave doubts about his own worthiness, but he also encounters with increasing frequency people who reinforce these doubts with their own suspicions.[21] Labeling a child delinquent, therefore, reorders his feelings and social experience and makes the emergence of a bad self-image almost inevitable. Thus, according to Lemert it is the labeling process itself that often transforms an ordinary adolescent into a "bad" boy.

Solomon Kobrin has taken this idea one step further by suggesting that the good and bad labels which the community attaches to its different members bear a close relationship to its values and ideals, i.e., to its civic identity.[22] The labeling process, therefore, is one of the means whereby community structure is imposed upon its members, and via the labeling process the community is able to perpetuate its images of good and evil among its

[19] See Edwin M. Lemert's criticism of Merton's analysis of anomie in "Social Structure, Social Control," *Anomie and Deviant Behavior*, Marshall B. Clinard, ed., Free Press of Glencoe, New York, 1964, pp. 83–97.

[20] See Howard S. Becker, "Introduction," *The Other Side*, Howard S. Becker, ed., Free Press of Glencoe, New York, 1964, pp. 1–6; or Edwin M. Lemert, "The Concept of Secondary Deviation," in *Human Deviance, Social Problems, and Social Control*, Second Edition, Edwin M. Lemert, ed., Prentice-Hall, Inc., Englewood Cliffs, N.J., 1972, pp. 62–92.

[21] Perhaps the best description of this process is contained in David Matza, *Becoming Deviant*, Prentice-Hall, Inc., Englewood Cliffs, N.J., 1969.

[22] Solomon Kobrin, "The Labeling Approach to Delinquency," unpublished paper presented at the Henry McKay Symposium, University of Chicago, Spring, 1972.

members. Thus, the youths who are labeled bad and become delinquent are living proof of the community's civic identity and its significance in the minds of the citizens.

When stated in this fashion the argument of the labeling theorists seems entirely reasonable. But the next step in their argument is much more controversial. If parents, teachers, the police, and the courts are essential to the creation of a delinquent self-concept, it is these adults who are primarily responsible for our delinquency problem. Although some parents, teachers, police, or judges may react in a balanced way to the childish antics of adolescents, all too often their response is out of proportion to the offense with the result that a child is sometimes labeled delinquent simply because a particular adult is extremely upset by the child's behavior. Thus, the labeling process is used by the complaining adult to throw guilt on the child in a dispute that often has two sides.[23] A teacher, for example, may brand a child as a behavioral problem and refer him to the school psychologist when he reacts to her narrow prejudice against his actions; a parent may refer his daughter to a juvenile officer when she resists his oppressive, unjust methods of punishment. Thus, the labeling process is sometimes used by erring adults as a way of covering up their mistakes and throwing the burden of their failure entirely on the juvenile. Howard S. Becker suggests that in these cases we would do better to study the motives and attitudes of those who label youngsters as delinquent instead of the "delinquents" themselves.[24]

It is a mistake, however, to assume that because some youngsters are unjustly labeled delinquents, the criminal justice system is the major cause of delinquency in the community. Those who have had a long and intimate experience with adjudicated delinquents are well aware of the fact that a rupture in the child-parent relationship often precedes an adolescent's appearance in juvenile court, and that adults occasionally accuse children unjustly of delinquency. Nevertheless, there is also a sizable number of adolescents who provoke their parents, teachers, neighbors, and peers beyond endurance. And in these cases the courts and the police are merely responding to complaints from those who know them (the adolescents) best in adjudicating them delinquents. In many cases, therefore, the adolescent repeatedly violates important

[23] The ways in which labels get stamped on juveniles in court is carefully explored by Robert M. Emerson in *Judging Delinquents*, Aldine Publishing Co., Chicago, 1969. See also Robert M. Emerson and Sheldon L. Messinger, "A Sociology of Trouble," a paper presented at the Annual Meetings of the Society for the Study of Social Problems, August, 1972, for an interesting account of the factors that swing the labeling process for or against the juvenile.

[24] Howard S. Becker, *Outsiders*, Free Press of Glencoe, New York, 1963.

norms in the community and thoroughly earns his label as a delinquent before he ever enters the court.[25]

The study of the agents of social control and their labeling functions will undoubtedly lead to greater insight into the ways in which labels become defined and how human failings affect the way they are applied. But studies of the labeling process should not displace studies of delinquents, because as often as not their contribution to their label is significant.

Up to now the several views we have considered have all assumed that the socialization of delinquents is essentially a deterministic process, that once the die is cast, the possibility of any other outcome is remote. But in recent years a number of authors have taken sharp issue with this view in criminology.

In 1964 David Matza suggested that the socialization of delinquents is largely haphazard with accident and circumstances playing a large part in the process.[26] According to Matza a series of pre-conditions must be fulfilled before a youngster can entertain the idea of delinquent behavior, and even then, a number of hurdles must be overcome before he can actually qualify as a bona fide delinquent.

The drift toward delinquency begins when the adolescent learns that there are a variety of rationalizations that can be used to neutralize his moral responsibility for his behavior. He can claim that he didn't intend to do it; and that he did it in self-defense; that he temporarily lost control of himself; or that it was an accident. His drift toward delinquency is accelerated when the juvenile learns to reject the authority of the juvenile courts. And it is completed when he is caught in a mood of fatalistic despair which prompts him to search out ways of making a significant impact on his environment. At each stage of the process, Matza points out, there are many opportunities for the pre-delinquent to turn from delinquency, and many obstacles to be overcome before he becomes a delinquent; for example, the pre-delinquent must acquire sufficient skills to avoid seeming ludicrous to his peers in his attempts at delinquency.

Fred Strodtbeck and James F. Short have developed a similar point of view in their concept of aleatory risks.[27] They suggest that delinquency often results not from a rational decision but from a convergence of circumstances

---

[25] Cf. Sethard Fisher, "Stigma and Deviant Careers in School," *Social Problems*, 20 (Summer, 1972), 78–83; and Jack D. Foster *et al.*, "From Delinquent Behavior to Official Delinquency," *Social Problems*, 20 (Fall, 1972), 202–209.

[26] See David Matza, *Delinquency and Drift*, John Wiley & Sons, Inc., New York, 1964, Chapters 3, 4, 5 and 6.

[27] Fred L. Strodtbeck and James F. Short, Jr., "Aleatory Risks versus Short-run Hedonism in Explanation of Gang Action," *Social Problems*, 12 (1964), 127–140.

which made delinquency the most convenient, if not the happiest, solution for the child. Pre-delinquents, according to Strodtbeck and Short, gravitate to situations that inherently carry a high risk of delinquent behavior. The boy who carries a gun for self-protection is placing himself in some jeopardy since merely carrying the weapon without a permit is a felony, and should he be provoked into using it against someone, another felony may result. When membership in a gang is added to these high-risk situations, the likelihood of delinquency is increased even further. Thus, many youngsters get deeply involved in delinquent behavior without ever consciously setting out to do so. The sweep of events and situations carries them along in such a way that delinquency is often the most convenient response.

Finally, Albert K. Cohen comes to much the same conclusion in his analysis of deviance.[28] Cohen maintains that deviance can best be understood as the result of an interactive process in which the deviant and a series of situations interact in such a way that deviant behavior becomes more and more likely. The deviant's prior actions, his present circumstances, and his dispositions all combine to limit the range of nondeviant actions open to him. At any given stage in the process there are many alternatives, and it is only by making the "proper" choice through a series of such encounters that deviant behavior results. Thus, Cohen also tends to view deviancy as a pattern of drift in which a deviant outcome depends basically upon the convergence of the right combination of circumstances with the right type of individual. In most cases, the circumstances and individual will not mesh and deviant behavior will not result.

It is clear, then, that modern criminologists tend to see luck and circumstance as playing an important part in the socialization of delinquents. In our study of delinquency it would be well to keep this insight in mind. Very few delinquents ever reached the juvenile court or the training school as a result of an unwavering urge to antisocial behavior. Many, if not most, were caught in a series of circumstances which made delinquency the easiest course at the moment, and as their choices were narrowed down by their growing experience with delinquency, the chances of their being arrested increased appreciably. Thus, the socialization of delinquents is to some extent, at least, a process of drift in which circumstances play a significant part.

By way of concluding this section, let us highlight the three general views advanced by sociologists to explain how delinquents get that way. First, we have the view suggested by Reckless that delinquency is understandable in

---

[28] Albert K. Cohen, *Deviance and Control*, Prentice-Hall, Inc., Englewood Cliffs, N.J., 1966, pp. 102–106.

terms of the social attitudes and self-concept of the offender. These qualities affect the youngsters involved pretty much in spite of the quality of their immediate social environment. Thus, delinquents are seen as possessing a definite inclination toward deviant behavior by virtue of firmly established attitudes regarding the self, with relatively little help from defeating circumstances or delinquent peers.

An alternative view advanced by David Matza and others holds that delinquency is largely an individual reaction to adverse circumstances. The youngster who constantly faces rejection or defeat adjusts by slowly relinquishing conventional values and adopting deviant ones. Peers hasten this process by suggesting delinquent techniques and rationalizations, but chronic, adverse experience is the basic force that pushes him ultimately to delinquency.

Finally, we have theorists like Edwin H. Sutherland who see delinquency as the result of normative pressures from the immediate social environment. The juvenile may have conventional inclinations as a result of a "good" self-concept, and he may encounter general approval among adults in the community, but if his nearest peers endorse delinquent values, there is every reason to believe that he will, too.

There are, then, three major dimensions to the problem of socialization. We must explain why individuals develop self-concepts that foster a persisting inclination toward deviancy. We must account for the effects of chronic rejection on the personality of adolescents and explain how they encourage deviant as opposed to conventional patterns of behavior. And we must explain why youngsters accept the values, techniques, and beliefs of delinquent groups and adopt them for their own. The theories presented here take us a long way toward solutions of these problems.

The Personality Patterns of Delinquents

Having examined the socialization processes that shape delinquents we are now in a position to ask what types of delinquents commonly result from these processes. What are the attitudinal and motivational patterns that seem to underlie delinquent behavior?

There are, of course, a great variety of psychological typologies that might be considered here, but in the interests of parsimony we shall discuss just one, that of Marguerite Warren and her co-workers. This typology was developed on the basis of long experience with delinquents both in the community and in institutions, and it is as comprehensive as any in the literature. For these reasons it was selected for careful examination here.

The theory itself is based upon a developmental concept of the human personality.[29] Just as the child matures physically and thereby gradually acquires the agility, stature, and strength essential to the role of the adolescent and ultimately the adult, so too the child's personality matures by acquiring functions and abilities that extend his emotional and psychological range. These developing capacities, furthermore, are integrated with his existing repertoire so that overall his psychological ability to cope with his environment gradually improves. Warren adapted this theory of personality growth to delinquency by postulating that any failure to develop the appropriate skills at a given stage would raise serious problems of interpersonal adjustment and could lead to delinquency.[30] Her typology distinguishes three broad levels of interpersonal maturity as relevant to delinquency.

The first includes those children who relate to their environment in a most primitive fashion. They do not form emotional bonds with those close to them, and they relate to others as if they were simply things. Since they have difficulty in imagining what others may think and feel in response to their actions, they are unable to anticipate the reactions of others and to adjust themselves accordingly. Thus, they are at the mercy of their own momentary needs and emotions, and they continue to behave in an impulsive fashion until cold necessity, i.e., physical restraint, intervenes. They have little self-control and little ability to organize themselves for future opportunities. Theirs is a world of unfeeling, unprincipled coercion. Within this broad category there are two sub-types: those who confront their environment with anger and aggression; and those who adapt to it passively by molding themselves to stark necessity as best they can. The former type bears a strong resemblance to the unsocialized aggressive child discussed earlier and is described by Warren as Asocial Aggressive. The latter is labeled Asocial Passive.

Warren's second broad class includes those delinquents who relate very shallowly with those around them, but who also recognize the hierarchical nature of their social environment and attempt to gain their ends by winning approval from those who stand high in the local hierarchy. They have matured sufficiently to recognize key power figures in their social environment, but they do not understand the moral or social restraints that limit their power, and accordingly their attempts to negotiate their social environment are often

[29] C. E. Sullivan, M. Q. Grant, and J. D. Grant, "The Development of Interpersonal Maturity: Applications to Delinquency," *Psychiatry* 20 (1957), 373–385.

[30] Marguerite Q. Warren, "Classification of Offenders as an Aid to Efficient Management and Effective Treatment," *Journal of Criminal Law, Criminology and Police Science*, 62 (1971), 239–258.

arbitrary or misdirected. Those above them are manipulated to satisfy their egocentric wants and those below are coerced with little concern for the normative restraints that apply in such relationships.

Included within this class are delinquents who seek to gain approval by conforming mechanically to those in power, the Immature Conformists; those who seek to gain approval by conforming mindlessly to the values of their delinquent peers, the Cultural Conformists; and those who side with no one but attempt to achieve their ends by manipulating those in power, the Manipulators. This latter type corresponds to the overindulged child discussed earlier.

The third category of delinquents, the neurotics, exhibit considerably more interpersonal maturity than the first two levels. Youngsters in this class have a keen awareness of their own inner life and a clear basis for assessing and reacting to the feelings of others. In addition they can form bonds of affection and are restrained in their actions toward others by an ability to empathize. They internalize conventional values and they evaluate themselves and others in terms of these values. Moreover, because they respond to the complexity of their world, they are more effective in adapting to moderately difficult problems both in the short and in the long run.

Nevertheless, they exhibit an overwhelming sense of their own guilt and worthlessness; they are resigned to playing a marginal, exploited role in life; and they are easily discouraged in their attempts to change themselves and their lives. That is to say, they exhibit many symptoms of ego impairment, as described earlier. The Anxious Neurotics at this level respond to interpersonal difficulties with extreme swings of mood and anxiety and typically flee situations that become too stressful. The Acting-out Neurotics, on the other hand, respond to stress with nervous outbursts of antisocial behavior often directed obliquely toward those who have contributed to their emotional discomfort.

Two additional types at this level differ from neurotics in that the source of their difficulties is rooted more in the environment than in the dynamics of their personalities. Nevertheless, their reactions to environmentally induced stresses are shaped more by their own personalities than by anything else. These types are classified in terms of the nature of the pressures that provoke their delinquency.

The youngsters who fall into delinquency as a result of dramatic changes in stress levels in their environment exhibit Stress Reactions.[31] Drastic changes

[31] Ted Palmer, a colleague of Marguerite Warren's, has recently offered a revision of Warren's original typology, replacing her Situational Emotional Reactions with the Stress Reactions and the Adjustment Reactions described here. Cf. Ted Palmer, "Non-Neurotic, Higher Maturity Delinquent Adolescents," Community Treatment Project Series: No. 3 (Winter, 1971), 6–19.

in their families produced by divorce, separation, abandonment, or death, or the demands made by new step-parents or foster families, can produce coping reactions which ultimately result in delinquency.

Another type of stress reaction arises from overwhelming challenges to personal validity. For example, being spurned by a girl friend, being turned down for an important job or for college, or being victimized by peers can produce a loss of control, and an irrational striking back in an attempt to vindicate himself or punish his tormentors.

A third type of reaction results when the adolescent is confronted with difficult, basic decisions for which he is not well prepared, e.g., marriage, the army, or college. He may react with a spree of delinquency as a way of delaying the final act of deciding and avoiding the attendant responsibility. He is reluctant to narrow his options by following an irrevocable course, and his acting out testifies to his fears and uncertainties regarding the course ahead. A final pattern of stress reaction stems from attempts to win acceptance from peers. Although the boy may have serious misgivings about their behavior, he goes along with them and their delinquency to gain approval.

Another broad pattern of adolescent difficulty stems basically from problems in adjustment and gives rise to a third general type at this level, Adjustment Reactions. Like stress reactions they can also arise in a number of ways. A common reaction among teen-agers to parental overprotectiveness or restrictiveness is rebellion, and if the confrontation hardens into closed-minded obstinancy on either part, the antagonism may escalate until the result is episodic delinquency. Another adjustment problem facing many youths today is that deriving from parental conflict. For a variety of reasons the quality of relations in the home may leave much to be desired, and the adolescent may react by exploiting differences between the parents or by withdrawing emotionally. The damaged parent-child relations may in turn provoke serious alienation of the child and acting out in the form of delinquency. Finally, many adolescents throw off a passive, compliant, agreeable posture vis-à-vis parents when they pass into puberty by adopting a more defiant, rebellious attitude. In this case it is a declaration of personal independence rather than a reaction to excessive parental control, but the result is often much the same, i.e., alienation and rejection on both sides. These problems do not always result in delinquency, but they do signal deep disturbances in the parent-adolescent relationship, and a common result of such disturbances is delinquency.

A final pattern at this level that is easily distinguished from the neurotics and the delinquents reacting to stress or adjustment problems is the Cultural Identifier. This youngster has organized his personality around a delinquent or contraculture scheme of values and achieved purpose and integrity as a result.

His conflict with the larger society provides meaning to his life, and he judges himself and others in terms of his inverted value system. He responds to like-minded others with affection and respect; he is self-disciplined and can handle difficult challenges with relative ease. On the other hand, he has contempt for those who lack self-discipline or moral courage. He is a delinquent only because his core values prescribe delinquency.

All in all, Warren and her co-workers distinguish ten types of delinquents in terms of three broad levels of interpersonal maturity. She reports that 46 per cent of the delinquents in her population of probationers are either Acting-out or Anxious Neurotics; another 26 per cent are Conformists; 14 per cent are Manipulators; less than 6 per cent are in the Asocial category; and the remainder, 9 per cent, are either Cultural Identifiers or Stress or Adjustment Reactions. It is important to note that more than half of the delinquents she studied are at the most mature level, i.e., in the neurotic category or higher. This fact augurs well for the possibility of treating delinquents—a question we shall return to later.

Warren suggests that her typology embraces most if not all the types described by other researchers, including those describing female delinquents. And for the most part her claims appear to be valid. It is not difficult to fit typologies worked out by other researchers into Warren's paradigm, and there is evidence that girl delinquents do, indeed, exhibit many if not all of these

TABLE 8

The Distribution of 400 Probationers Among Warren's
Ten Personality Types*

PERSONALITY TYPE	PER CENT OF POPULATION
Asocial Aggressive	less than 1
Asocial Passive	5
Immature Conformist	16
Cultural Conformist	10
Manipulator	14
Acting-out Neurotic	20
Anxious Neurotic	26
Stress and Adjustment Reactions	3
Cultural Identifier	6
Total	100

* Marguerite Q. Warren, "The Case for Differential Treatments of Delinquents," *The Annals,* 381 (January, 1969), p. 54.

personality patterns.[32] Moreover, Warren goes beyond many typologies in that she identifies a number of types that are largely ignored by others, e.g., the Asocial Passive type.

Nevertheless, she also describes two types that strictly speaking should not be included—the Stress and Adjustment Reactions—because their delinquency results from situational and not psychological pressures. And she ignores an important class of delinquents—those who act symptomatically in response to deep-seated, unconscious conflicts. The psychological literature contains ample evidence that delinquency is occasionally the result of powerful, unconscious urges bursting into consciousness in disguised form and affecting behavior.[33] Admittedly, cases of this type are relatively rare, but they are widely documented and deserve consideration in a psychological typology of delinquents. Finally, much research remains to be done regarding the socialization processes that lead up to these several personality types and the psychological processes that lie behind the behavior they exhibit. Beginnings have been made on both questions, but there is still a long way to go before they can be answered satisfactorily.[34]

CONCLUSION

In this chapter we have attempted to take a balanced view of several basic problems confronting those who would explain delinquent behavior. With the psychoanalytic criminologists we have assumed that it is important to identify the crucial effects that family members have upon the development of personality patterns commonly found among delinquents and to understand the psychodynamics underlying their behavior. With the sociological criminologists we have suggested it is important to recognize the contributions of "bad" self-concepts, existential circumstances, and normative pressures to the development of delinquents.

In the past, champions of these several views have not always been tolerant toward alternative positions, and they have been sometimes regarded as mutually contradictory. Nevertheless, it is entirely likely that several distinct

---

[32] See, for example, Clyde B. Vedder and Dora B. Somerville, *The Delinquent Girl,* Charles C Thomas, Springfield, Ill., 1970, for several case studies of female delinquents.

[33] See footnotes 3 and 6 above, for examples.

[34] In addition to the works by Warren already cited, see Ted Palmer, "Stages of Psycho-Social Development as Reflected in Two New Levels of Interpersonal Maturity," *Youth Authority Quarterly,* 22 (Fall, 1969).

processes affecting youngsters in quite distinct and even contrary ways exist side by side. Indeed, as we have seen, this condition is probably most often the case. Thus, it is hoped that the old chauvinistic debates between psychological and sociological criminologists regarding the appropriate viewpoint for the study of crime or delinquency are at an end so that the strengths and weaknesses of *both* viewpoints can be systematically appraised.

BIBLIOGRAPHY

HEWITT, LESTER E., AND RICHARD L. JENKINS, *Fundamental Patterns of Maladjustment*, Illinois State Printer, Springfield, Ill., 1947.

LEVY, DAVID, *Maternal Overprotection*, Columbia University Press, New York, 1948.

REDL, FRITZ, AND DAVID WINEMAN, *The Aggressive Child*, Free Press of Glencoe, New York, 1957.

WARREN, MARGUERITE Q., "Classification of Offenders as an Aid to Efficient Management and Effective Treatment," *Journal of Criminal Law, Criminology and Police Science*, Vol. 62 (1971), 239–258.

delinquency and societal processes

Having explored the personality patterns and socialization experiences of delinquents in the last chapter, we are now ready to examine the social aspect of delinquency. Once adolescents have begun to think and feel like delinquents, they still must adjust to the everyday situations they encounter. But these situations do not spring up in society haphazardly. Rather, they are shaped by pervasive, fundamental societal processes that influence society quite generally. In order to understand delinquent behavior, therefore, it is necessary to distinguish two distinct levels whereby social processes affect the problem. On the broadest level, we must identify the societal processes that shape the structure and flow of social interaction generally in society, and on a more specific level we must trace the influence of these broader forces upon the immediate situations of delinquents and show how they mold their behavior. In this chapter, then, we shall explore the former problem carefully, and in subsequent chapters we shall show how the family, school, and gang are in turn influenced by the broad societal processes to which we now turn.

We shall be concerned in this chapter with four basic processes that structure social life: social organization, social disorganization, cultural disorganization, and cultural deviance. Each of these affects the situations and circumstances of delinquency in a distinctive fashion and therefore must be examined individually. But all of them may be active at the same time in shaping any given community, often in opposition to one another, and to diagnose the root causes of delinquency in any given neighborhood it is important to identify the distinctive contribution of each.

Social Organization

Social organization refers to the manner in which a social group coordinates individual efforts toward group goals and ideals. Quite obviously, there are a variety of ways in which a system of roles might be organized to accomplish the purposes of the group, and each of these arrangements shapes in a distinctive fashion the behavior of the people involved. Hence, one of the basic societal processes shaping the life of a group is its social organization.

Although the specific variations which a group or community might exhibit are virtually infinite, two common ways in which communities tend to be organized have been described by Ferdinand Toennies as gemeinschaft and gesellschaft.[1] A gemeinschaft community, according to Toennies, is characterized by a rare concord of feeling and attitude, a pervasive rapport that enables its members to achieve an extraordinary degree of social unity. To be sure, these communities are often stratified in terms of political authority, economic resources, and social rank, but these strata serve only to bind the members more closely by heightening their sense of interdependence and formalizing their social and political obligations to one another. Because such societies are typically organized in terms of kinship ties, the dominant social form is status relationships.

In gesellschaft communities we find an entirely different pattern of organization. Instead of sympathy and concord, we find a spirit of individualistic competition. The members of such a community are typically preoccupied with their own interests and indifferent to the fate of others. The bond that holds them together is the market through which they exchange things of value. And because the market is the central institution of gesellschaft communities, the contract is the dominant social form in extrafamilial interaction.

These two types of communities are founded on sharply contrasting styles of social relationships, and accordingly they shape the activities of their members in quite different ways. For example, since status relationships tend to embrace the members of gemeinschaft communities during a major portion of their lives, the specific obligations of these relationships become an integral part of their personal feelings for one another. Those in lowly positions are

---

[1] These terms were first used by Ferdinand Toennies in *Community and Association*, Charles P. Loomis, trans., Routledge & Kegan Paul Ltd., London, 1955, First Book: First and Second Sections.

treated and feel inferior, whereas those in exalted positions act and feel superior. Nevertheless, because of the stability of these relationships, such a close rapport emerges at all levels that nuances of posture and accent are as important as words in communication.

The intimacy and stability of status relationships mean, further, that they provide an excellent medium for applying social controls throughout the community. Since there is close rapport among the members of these communities, they quickly detect forms of deviancy almost before they begin, and since strong bonds tie almost everyone to the group, punitive sanctions strike with telling effect upon the deviant. Such communities, therefore, are uniquely effective in detecting and suppressing almost all forms of deviancy.

Gesellschaft communities, however, are considerably less vigilant in this regard, principally because of contractual relationships. Contractual relations, which are the dominant social form in such groups, emerge primarily when individuals have a pressing need to exchange things of value but little social basis otherwise for effecting an exchange.[2] Thus, contractual relations emerge by default when no other social guidelines are available to govern relationships. Since they tend to unfold primarily among strangers, they are typically brief, formal, and closely circumscribed.

In the initial phase, the partners in a contractual relationship negotiate intensively to settle the terms of the relationship. When these have been agreed upon, the relationship moves into its second phase, in which each of the partners undertakes to complete his end of the contract.

During the first phase both candidates are free to pursue their interests as they see fit. They may accept or reject the proposals of any candidate, and they may define the contract in virtually any way they desire. As a result those who continuously engage in contractual relationships tend to develop a clear sense of their ability to shape their own experiences and careers. Moreover, since in the initial phase candidates are careful to show only those qualities that display their merits as candidates, they typically develop considerable skill at giving a good impression *and* at ferreting out the flaws and blemishes of others. Thus, an impersonal skeptical attitude toward surface appearances is common among those who are experienced at contractual relations. Finally, since each candidate is interested in fulfilling a rather narrow need, his interest in others extends only to those qualities which have a direct relevance to his needs of the moment. All candidates are judged in terms of the same criteria,

2 See Henry Maine, *Ancient Law*, E. P. Dutton and Co., Inc., New York, 1960, for an excellent explanation of the evolution of laws of contract in ancient society.

and the most promising one is selected. Those who are usually successful in such relationships derive thereby a sense of competence, but those who often fail tend to feel inadequate.

Contractual relations are ill-suited as a medium for applying social controls because they are episodic, impersonal, and formal. The episodic character of contractual relations means that those who regularly participate in them will never get to know their partners very well, and the formal, impersonal style they cultivate means that any relationships they do form will be only superficial and narrowly circumscribed. Thus, deviant behavior can become quite pronounced before those in contractual relationships can detect it, and even when they do, they cannot suppress it effectively because of their impersonal manner, i.e., punitive sanctions cause little shame or remorse where emotional ties are weak.

Gesellschaft communities, therefore, are particularly ineffective in mobilizing and applying informal social controls against embryonic forms of deviance because contractual relations tend to reduce the emotional and social accessibility of the members of these groups to one another. Gemeinschaft groups, on the other hand, encourage close, lasting bonds among their members via status relationships, and accordingly they apply informal social controls quickly and effectively whenever needed.

Gesellschaft societies, however, are not organized entirely in terms of contractual relations. Relatively stable families and neighborhood groups are found even in the most advanced societies. But in these societies the effectiveness of such status groups is considerably weakened by virtue of the fact that gesellschaft societies sponsor considerable mobility and a spirit of individualism, both of which undermine the intimacy and solidarity of status groups.

Since contractual relations are easily formed and dissolved, they encourage considerable fluidity in personal relationships, and the waxing and waning of market forces exerts strong pressures on members of gesellschaft societies to move to the farthest reaches of the market. Hence, in such societies there is a ceaseless movement of people which inevitably disturbs the stability of status groups like the family and the community. Moreover, the spirit of individualism, which contractual relations foster, encourages members of status groups to challenge the ideals of these groups and reject their moral authority.

For these several reasons gesellschaft communities or societies tend to show sharply higher levels of deviancy, including delinquency, than those organized after the gemeinschaft pattern. For example, in 1971 in the United States the rate of arrests in cities over 250,000 in population was 2.7 times that in rural areas, and for juveniles under eighteen the arrest rate in cities exceeded that of rural areas by a factor of 3.1.[3] Moreover, the fact that even in this emancipated age women and girls tend to spend more of their lives among such status groups as the family and neighborhood may also help to explain the fact that in 1971 the ratio of male to female arrests in the United States was 5.6 to 1, and for juveniles it was 3.5 to 1.[4]

Social organization, therefore, affects the level of deviance in society by its influence upon the ways in which informal social controls are applied and by its effect upon the prevailing ethos in society.

Other theorists have argued along similar lines. Emile Durkheim, for example, showed that suicide and homicide are powerfully shaped by the level of social integration in society.[5] High levels of social integration tend to produce high rates of altruistic suicide and homicide, but low levels of integration tend to be accompanied by little homicide and high rates of egoistic suicide.[6] Social dislocation and anomie, on the other hand, tend to encourage both anomic suicide and homicide.[7] Durkheim, therefore, argued that the levels of both suicide and homicide in society are affected by the manner in which society is organized.

Taking up where Durkheim left off, Andrew Henry and James Short attempted to explain the complex relationship between homicide and suicide by postulating that suicide is likely where external restraints are weak and homicide is likely where external restraints are strong.[8] They postulated that strong external restraints constitute a frustrating experience and prompt an aggressive response against those who are the source of the frustration. But where external restraints are weak, externally based frustration is minimal, and aggression is directed inward against the individual himself. Among the condi-

---

[3] Calculated from *Uniform Crime Reports for the United States, 1971*, U.S. Government Printing Office, Washington, D.C., 1972, Table 24, p. 116; Table 36, p. 133; Table 46, p. 148. Although a comparison of rural and urban arrest rates is risky because of variations in arresting policies in the police departments in the two areas, it is unlikely that the differences displayed can be attributed entirely to this factor.

[4] *Ibid.*, Table 32, p. 126.

[5] Emile Durkheim, *Suicide*, John A. Spaulding and George Simpson, trans., Free Press of Glencoe, New York, 1951, Book Three, Chapter 2.

[6] Altruistic suicide refers to suicide committed in behalf of the group, i.e., as a sacrifice to the goals and ideals of the group, as kamikaze pilots did during World War II. Egoistic suicide, on the other hand, refers to suicide committed as a result of weakened ties with one's groups. *Ibid*, Book Two, Chapters 2, 3, and 4.

[7] Anomic suicide occurs when the individual is confronted with a change in his social position that is intolerable, e.g., a divorce or a sudden loss of income. *Ibid.*, Book Two, Chapter 5.

[8] Andrew F. Henry and James F. Short, Jr., *Suicide and Homicide*, Free Press of Glencoe, New York, 1954, pp. 75, 82.

tions that influence the strength of external restraints are the individual's status, i.e., high status removes many external restraints, and his relational systems, i.e., strong relational systems immerse the individual in social relationships that forcefully control his behavior. Hence, those in weak relational systems or at high statuses should show high suicide rates and low homicide rates. Conversely, those in strong relational systems or at low statuses should show low suicide rates and high homicide rates.

To support their thesis, Henry and Short cited the pattern of suicide and homicide rates found among the following groups: whites have higher suicide rates than blacks, males show higher rates than females, upper income groups have higher rates than lower income groups, and Army officers show higher suicide rates than enlisted men.[9] All of the groups with higher suicide rates tend also to be higher status and, therefore, confront weaker external restraints. The higher suicide rates of the elderly compared with those of younger people, and of urban residents compared with rural residents, are explained by relatively weaker relational systems in both cases.[10] All the groups with low suicide rates (with the exception of females) also exhibit relatively high homicide rates, further confirming the hypothesis of a relationship between social organization and deviance.[11]

Travis Hirschi also examined the relationship between social organization and delinquency, and he established that delinquency is powerfully affected by the strength of the juvenile's attachments to his parents, his school, and his peers.[12] Where the attachments are close, delinquency is minimal, but where they are weak, delinquency is common. According to Hirschi, close attachments among the members of a community tend to inspire conventional beliefs and activities and a concern for the good opinion of others, all of which tend to diminish the likelihood of delinquent behavior.

All of these theorists suggest clearly that the organization of society has a pervasive impact upon its level of deviance by virtue of the effects it has upon the quality of social relations and acceptance of social values. Social organization as a process, however, cannot account for every question about deviance that we might legitimately raise. For example, as Durkheim clearly admits, it cannot explain why someone in a group with weak informal con-

[9] *Ibid.*, p. 70.

[10] *Ibid.*, p. 78.

[11] *Ibid.*, Chapter VI. And even in the case of females, the *proportion* of homicides among all offenses committed by females is higher than the comparable figures for males.

[12] Travis Hirschi, *Causes of Delinquency*, University of California Press, Berkeley, 1969, Chapters VI, VII, and VIII.

trols selects one kind of deviance instead of another.[13] Nor, for that matter, can social organization as a process throw much light on the forms of deviance that develop in a community where the roles are weakly integrated and the informal controls ineffective. It can only suggest that the levels of deviance will be high where social organization is attenuated, but it cannot indicate which forms of deviance will evolve, nor can it explain why individuals elect one form over another.

Social Disorganization

Social disorganization has been much more thoroughly studied by criminologists, and our understanding of delinquency as an outgrowth of social disorganization has advanced rather far. The first theorist to explore the problem systematically was Robert K. Merton in his pioneering paper, "Social Structure and Anomie."[14] Using Durkheim's concept of anomie as his point of departure, Merton attempted to fashion a theory of anomie which pinpointed social structural processes as the ultimate source of the problem.

Durkheim had suggested that anomie arises when the individual confronts a personal dislocation to which he cannot adjust, e.g., sudden unemployment or the death of a spouse. These situations are difficult to accept, because the individual's former statuses are undermined without any substitute roles or positions to take their place. The individual is thrust into the uncomfortable position of not knowing what to expect from others, i.e., into normlessness and anomie.

Durkheim's formulation of the problem seems to imply that anomie is often the result of personal misfortune, but Merton's contribution was to indicate that anomie can also result from basic flaws in the organization of society. Merton pointed out that the individual is thrust into anomie when the cultural goals of society are denied him even though he has scrupulously adhered to the institutionalized means whereby people ordinarily achieve those goals. Consider, for example, the student who studies tirelessly for his exams but receives only D's or F's for his trouble. He can react to his dilemma by selecting one of the following: innovation, which involves developing substitute means to desired cultural goals; retreatism, which involves a rejection of both the means and goals of society; and rebellion, which involves a substitu-

---

[13] Durkheim, *op. cit.*, p. 357.

[14] Robert K. Merton, "Social Structure and Anomie," *American Sociological Review*, 3 (October, 1938), 672–682.

tion of different means and goals for those proffered by society. All of these reactions illustrate quite clearly that the anomic individual searches for alternative means to achieve his goals, which can involve him in one form or another of deviant behavior. The important point here, however, is that Merton identified contradictions in the organization of society as a major source of anomie in advanced societies.

Using Merton's insight but not his terminology, Albert K. Cohen developed an explanation of delinquent gangs which highlights the social contradictions facing working class youths.[15] According to Cohen, working class children are rejected by their middle class peers and teachers because working class values often lead to inappropriate behavior in middle class schools. Cohen postulates that the resulting status frustration produces a reaction among working class boys against the values of the middle class and ultimately leads to working class delinquency. Thus, like Merton, Cohen holds that a discrepancy between culturally defined goals and the institutionalized means available to working class children provokes delinquent behavior and ultimately gangs.

Richard Cloward and Lloyd Ohlin, in turn, extended Merton's thesis by suggesting that one of the basic conditions fostering delinquency in America is the inaccessibility of legitimate opportunities in comparison with illegitimate opportunities for adolescents.[16] Many working and lower class youngsters are denied access to legitimate careers, while membership in delinquent gangs offers many advantages otherwise unavailable. The relative accessibility of these gangs, according to Cloward and Ohlin, explains much of the delinquency in working class and lower class neighborhoods.

These several theorists seem to be saying that frustration, anomie and delinquency tend to develop when the rules of society are designed so as to deny social rewards to those who conform to the normative structure and ordinarily would be rewarded for their conformity.[17] There is a basic contradiction in the very organization of society such that conforming behavior for some is actively discouraged. We shall use the term *social disorganization* to refer to this condition.

[15] Albert K. Cohen, *Delinquent Boys*, Free Press of Glencoe, New York, 1955, Chapters IV and V.

[16] Richard A. Cloward and Lloyd E. Ohlin, *Delinquency and Opportunity*, Free Press of Glencoe, New York, 1960, Chapter 6.

[17] In an otherwise excellent essay Albert Cohen proposed a somewhat different definition of social disorganization. He suggests that social disorganization exists when the constituted order of society is disrupted. This condition would seem to describe an *absence* of organization and not disorganization, where the flaw is rooted in the constituted order itself. See Albert K. Cohen, "The Study of Social Disorganization and Deviant Behavior," in *Sociology Today*, Robert K. Merton, *et al.*, eds., Basic Books, Inc., New York, 1959, p. 476.

To illustrate the concept, consider the case of the young black in many American communities. Early in life he is assured by his parents, teachers, and others that intelligence, self-denial, and prudence will result ultimately in social honor, a good job, and various material benefits. To the extent that racial prejudice exists in his community, however, he learns that the rewards of society are denied him no matter how carefully he prepares himself for a successful career. The community is disorganized because there are unwritten rules denying rewards to blacks which contradict the generally acknowledged rules prescribing how the rewards of society are to be distributed. Individuals caught in this condition tend to lose confidence in conventional beliefs and ultimately are forced into anomie. Initially they may be fully committed to the normative structure, but gradually as the full weight of their dilemma crushes in upon them, they drift away and into a pattern of deviancy.

A large amount of research has been done to assess this point of view regarding the causes of delinquency, and curiously much of it has failed to support the theory. For example, considerable attention has been paid to the question of whether social class is closely related to delinquency. We might expect that the strains of social disorganization bear down especially hard upon members of the lower class, since they receive fewer social rewards than any other class. The results, however, have been largely negative.

Nye, Short, and Olson examined this question via questionnaires given to 2,865 high school students in six western and midwestern small towns. They found no consistent relationship between class position and self-reported delinquent behavior.[18] Clark and Wenninger examined the same question among 1,154 adolescents living in three distinct communities in or near Chicago and in a farming area, and they found that delinquency is more closely associated with the cultural life of the community than with the youngster's social class in the community.[19] A lower class youngster in a community with little delinquency is less likely to be delinquent than a middle class youngster in a community where delinquency is a well-established pattern.

In an extensive study of delinquency in Richmond, California, Hirschi found "no important relationship between social class . . . and delinquency."[20] He did report that "a small group at the bottom of the class hierarchy whose children are more . . . delinquent, and, at the other extreme, we find that the

[18] F. Ivan Nye, James F. Short, and Virgil J. Olson, "Socio-economic Status and Delinquent Behavior," *American Journal of Sociology*, 63 (January, 1958), 381–389.

[19] John P. Clark and Eugene P. Wenninger, "Socio-economic Class and Area as Correlates of Illegal Behavior Among Juveniles," *American Sociological Review*, 27 (December, 1962), 826–834.

[20] Hirschi, *op. cit.*, p. 75.

sons of professionals and executives are consistently less . . . delinquent," but these differences were too small to regard as clear evidence for a relationship between social class and delinquency.[21] Dentler and Monroe administered a theft scale to 912 junior high schoolers in three communities in Kansas, and they found no relationship between the father's occupation or education and the son's delinquency.[22] Finally, although Reiss and Rhodes report that "the probability of being classified a serious, petty, or truancy offender is greater for blue-collar than white-collar boys" in a study of 9,238 white schoolboys in Tennessee, they also suggest that "the status structure of the school exercises a greater effect on delinquent behavior than does ascribed social status."[23]

The evidence that social class is related to delinquency is, therefore, very weak. Only three out of six studies, i.e., those by Hirschi, Clark and Wenniger, and Reiss and Rhodes, report any relationship at all between social class and delinquency. And in all three, other conditions in the immediate situation of the delinquents are found to be more powerful than class position in shaping their behavior. The best that can be said here is that there is probably a very broad association between delinquency and social class that can be easily over-ridden by more immediate conditions.

The absence of a strong relationship between social class and delin-quency might suggest a re-examination of social disorganization as an explana-tion of delinquency. It is our contention that however intriguing these results may be, they by no means destroy the value of this approach to delinquency. These studies have consistently compared the *father's* class position with the teen-ager's tendency to delinquent behavior. If they were truly testing social disorganization as a factor in delinquency, they should have measured the adolescent's social standing and compared it to his delinquent behavior. There is no good reason to expect a strong relationship between a father's anomie and a son's delinquency.

Several researchers have compared the youngster's *own* social position with his tendency to commit delinquent behavior, and the results in this case are more encouraging. Hirschi, for example, found that a teen-ager's position in school was closely related to the likelihood of his being delinquent.[24] Aca-demic aptitude, attitudes toward school and teachers, grades, and self-perceived

[21] *Ibid.*

[22] Robert A. Dentler and Lawrence J. Monroe, "Social Correlates of Early Adolescent Theft," *American Sociological Review*, 26 (October, 1961), 733–743.

[23] Albert J. Reiss, Jr. and Albert L. Rhodes, "The Distribution of Juvenile Delinquency in the Social Class Structure," *American Sociological Review*, 26 (October, 1961), 725.

[24] Hirschi, *op. cit.*, Chapter VIII.

ability all relate to delinquency in Hirschi's study, and these results led him to conclude that "academic incompetence [leads] to poor school performance to disliking of school to rejection of the school's authority to the commission of delinquent acts."[25] Stinchcombe also examined the relationship between social standing and rebellion among 1,600 high school students in a small California town.[26] He found that rebellion was *most* prevalent among lower-middle class boys who were under considerable pressure to succeed in school but who by virtue of poor grades were failing. Furthermore, when he examined the level of alienation among high school students, he found it highest among those students for whom school promised little or no post-high school benefit.[27] Thus, where the student's success in school is regarded as important but failure is his lot, or where school is not directly relevant to the student's post-high school plans, rebellion or alienation is most intense.

Polk and Schafer have also looked at this problem in a study of more than 800 high school students, and they report that scholastic success is an important factor in school adjustment and that "school adjustment shows a much higher relationship to delinquency than does social class."[28] They also report that success in interscholastic athletics tends to insulate blue-collar low achievers from delinquency. Apparently, success in at least one sphere of competition is necessary to bring the youngster into the social patterns of the school, but generalized failure leads to exclusion from student activities and often to delinquency. These several studies show very clearly that where conformity is ineffectual in gaining social rewards, deviance is a common result.

Another considerable body of research has focused on the theory of Cloward and Ohlin mentioned earlier that delinquency results from the relative availability of illegitimate opportunities in comparison with legitimate opportunities. The results, however, have not confirmed their expectations regarding the nature of delinquency.

James F. Short, Jr. and his co-workers examined this question thoroughly in their study of twenty-two delinquent gangs and nearly 600 boys in Chicago. They report that black children tend to perceive greater illegitimate opportunities than whites but that gang members regardless of race tend to see

25 *Ibid.*, p. 132. Hirschi regards these results as embarrassing to strain theory, i.e., social disorganization as an explanation of delinquency. But as we shall see, they confirm it.

26 Arthur L. Stinchcombe, *Rebellion in a High School*, Quadrangle Books, Chicago, 1964, Chapter 6.

27 *Ibid.*, Chapter 4.

28 Kenneth Polk and Walter E. Schafer, eds., *Schools and Delinquency*, Prentice-Hall, Inc., Englewood Cliffs, N.J., 1972, pp. 68, 99.

fewer legitimate opportunities than non-gang boys.[29] On the surface this finding might seem to confirm Cloward and Ohlin's thesis of a differential opportunity structure producing delinquency. But Short also reports that the perception of fewer legitimate opportunities is developed by gang members only *after* the youths have joined the gang![30] Thus, it would appear that the availability of illegitimate opportunities is *the* crucial factor and that the accessibility of legitimate opportunities is relatively unimportant. Finally, Reiss and Rhodes examined Cohen's thesis of working class status frustration, and although they found some status frustration among bottom status students, the frustration of these students derived from invidious comparisons with other bottom status children and not with middle status children as Cohen expected.[31]

Clearly, then, adolescents are highly sensitive to disorganization in their immediate environment and when conforming behavior is not rewarded, frustration, rebellion, and delinquency are common results. On the other hand, where social disorganization is more remote, e.g., in the situation of a father or in the adolescent's future, the impact is much less, though not absent entirely.

The studies summarized here also suggest some of the general forms actively producing social disorganization in society. Certainly racial, religious, and ethnic discrimination, where they exist, play a major part in denying earned rewards to significant portions of the conforming population.

A more general source of anomie among young people, however, is the competitive pattern imposed on virtually the entire school-aged population from childhood to early adulthood. The fact that most rewards in school are distributed through rigorous competition means that a small but significant portion of the student body is condemned to failure simply because they are less skillful than most of their peers in areas of major competition, i.e., in scholarship, athletics, or dating. Whatever members of this unfortunate minority do in school, they cannot ease the burden of repeated failure, and many of them simply drift out of prevailing patterns of behavior where they are regularly and consistently punished and into deviance.

On an even more general level, the market system has much the same

[29] Ramon J. Rivera and James F. Short, Jr., "Occupational Goals: A Comparative Analysis," in *Juvenile Gangs in Context*, Malcolm W. Klein, ed., Prentice-Hall, Inc., Englewood Cliffs, N.J., 1967, p. 83.

[30] James F. Short, Jr., Ramon Rivera, and Ray A. Tennyson, "Perceived Opportunities, Gang Membership and Delinquency," *American Sociological Review*, 30 (February, 1965), 56–67.

[31] Albert J. Reiss and A. Lewis Rhodes, "Status Deprivation and Delinquent Behavior," *The Sociological Quarterly*, 4 (Spring, 1963), 135–149.

effect upon the adult population insofar as it imposes a competitive stance among those seeking to establish contractual obligations in the market. Those who fail, moreover, experience the pangs of anomie every bit as intensely as those who are consistently denied cultural rewards because of racial, religious, or ethnic discrimination. And their kind of anomie is even more difficult to remedy because it is rooted in the very institutions upon which most modern industrial societies are founded, i.e., the market system. It would seem, therefore, that social disorganization among significant portions of the population is unavoidable among modern industrial societies.

Cultural Disorganization

Cultural disorganization, as the name implies, has some elements in common with social disorganization. As with social disorganization, cultural disorganization identifies contradictions in society as the root factor in delinquency. But cultural disorganization refers to value conflicts between groups in society and not to conflicts between rewards systems and opportunity structures.

The impact of cultural disorganization on the individual, however, is not unlike that of social disorganization. It tends to shatter the person's commitment to the norms of his group and, thereby, exposes him to anomie. With social disorganization the individual ultimately becomes convinced that conformity to society's values is futile, because recognition and rewards are unattainable, but with cultural disorganization he ultimately loses confidence in *his* group's values and ideals as a result of its confrontation with other groups.[32]

The best example of this process is the impact of white, Protestant cultural patterns on minority groups in the American society. The result is sometimes a sense of shame among members of these groups, a loss of parental authority over young people, and adolescent rebellion and deviance. Many studies of immigrant groups and delinquency were done in the early decades of this century, and they reported that American-born children of foreign-born parents, i.e., those youngsters exposed most sharply to cultural disorganization, tended to have the highest rates of delinquency.[33] Certainly the black family in America has also been affected drastically by cultural disorganization. Although other factors have also contributed to the problem, cultural disorganization has been a major factor undermining black pride and self-confidence.

[32] Thorsten Sellin, *Cultural Conflict and Crime*, Social Science Research Council, New York, 1938, pp. 63–70.
[33] See *Ibid.*, pp. 84–106.

Black leaders have recognized this fact and struggled against it in a variety of ways, e.g., with the slogans "black is beautiful" and "I *am* somebody."

Several studies provide evidence in support of this view. Bernard Lander, for example, found that those neighborhoods in Baltimore approaching a composition of 50 per cent white and 50 per cent black exhibited the highest levels of delinquency, and he concluded that anomie is greatest in such neighborhoods.[34] Some years later Wilson examined much the same thesis, and he also found that anomie was least for blacks where their percentage was greatest.[35] Anomie, therefore, is clearly related to cultural disorganization.

Cultural disorganization also influences delinquency in an entirely different fashion. As George Vold has pointed out, groups with sharply contradictory goals occasionally engage in open conflict and criminal activities against one another.[36] Any adolescents involved in such patterns of conflict would necessarily be committing delinquent acts. Racial, religious, or ethnic rivalries have generated intense conflicts in America since colonial times, and adolescents have participated in them eagerly whether they were race riots, anti-Catholic mobs, ghetto riots, or lynch mobs. The pluralistic character of American society, therefore, has contributed directly to its high level of inter-group conflict and thereby also to its high level of anomie and delinquency.

The market system of economic exchange, however, has also made a noteworthy contribution. Several theorists have commented on the fact that the market system tends to create two distinct classes with antagonistic interests: those who sell in the market and those who buy.[37] As long as both have roughly equal power, neither is exploited and the exchange process does not give rise to serious rivalries. But when one class gains an advantage and systematically exploits it at the expense of the other, serious conflict often results.

The disadvantaged class seeks to restore equality by adjusting the rules of the market so that parity in negotiating power is regained. These changes

[34] Bernard Lander, *Toward an Understanding of Juvenile Delinquency*, Columbia University Press, New York, 1954, pp. 62–65.

[35] Robert A. Wilson, "Anomie in the Ghetto: A Study of Neighborhood Type, Race, and Anomie," *American Journal of Sociology*, 77 (July, 1971), 66–68. Although Wilson also found that delinquency was highest in the ghetto, where anomie is least, it does not refute our thesis because he was not measuring the anomie of adolescents but of adults.

[36] See George Vold, *Theoretical Criminology*, Oxford University Press, New York, 1958, Chapter 11, pp. 214–219.

[37] See, for example, Toennies, *op. cit.*, pp. 87–115; H. H. Gerth and C. Wright Mills, eds., *From Max Weber*, Routledge & Kegan Paul Ltd., London, 1948, pp. 185–186; and Norbert Wiley, "America's Unique Class Politics: The Interplay of the Labor, Credit, and Commodity Markets," *American Sociological Review*, 32 (August, 1967), 529–541.

often generate violent conflicts and considerable crime on both sides. During the last half of the nineteenth century in America, labor-management disputes have regularly boiled over into violent confrontations, and the populist movement which sprang into life after the Civil War similarly had its origins in disparities in market power between the farmers, on the one hand, and the banks and railroads, on the other. To the extent that modern industrial societies are organized by the market system, therefore, antagonistic groups with a tendency to engage in open conflict will no doubt be a continuing feature of the social order.

In much the same vein Marxist theorists have long regarded capitalism as the principal source of class conflict in modern industrial societies. Ownership of the means of industrial production, i.e., factories and machine technology, confers upon the bourgeoisie an immense economic advantage which it uses systematically to depress the wages and raise the productivity of the working class. As the discrepancy in the standard of living of the two classes increases, the bourgeoisie increasingly resorts to the power of the state and the criminal justice system to preserve its economic and political privileges against the insistent claims of the poor. Thus from the Marxist viewpoint crime and delinquency are largely an expression of protest by members of the working class against the depressed living conditions that capitalism has forced upon them.

The solution to crime and delinquency, according to this perspective, lies in the expropriation of the means of production (peacefully if possible, violently if necessary) by the working class. Once private ownership of the means of production has been abolished and the bourgeoisie forced into the working class, the fruits of industrial production will be distributed equitably among all segments of the population. The lot of the working class will improve dramatically and there will be no further basis for class conflict or working class criminality.

The major difficulty with this point of view lies in its monolithic quality.[38] Marx's analysis of capitalism still stands as a monument to his genius, but when Marxist criminologists reject any other explanation of crime, they fly in the face of a vast amount of evidence. Socialist societies (e.g., the U.S.S.R.) still display serious crime and delinquency problems long after their

---

[38] See, for example, Alan Wolfe, "Political Repression and the Liberal Democratic State," *Monthly Review*, 23 (December, 1971), 18–38; and Richard Quinney, *Critique of Legal Order*, Little, Brown and Company, Boston, 1974. For a more balanced exposition of Marxist criminology see William J. Chambliss, "Functional and Conflict Theories of Crime," *An MSS Modular Publication*, Module 17 (1973), 1–23.

major industries have been nationalized, and they are no less ruthless in dealing with criminals than nonsocialist societies. Clearly, the nature of a society's economic system is not the only factor in its crime problem.

There are other processes that also generate conflict in society. Ralf Dahrendorf, for example, has pointed out that since industrial organizations are organized hierarchically with an elite group making policy for the rank and file, the interest goals of the two groups are opposed and occasionally open conflict results as they pursue their antagonistic interests.[39] Thus, insofar as industrial managers and others responsible for administering large bureaucratic organizations are insensitive to the values and needs of rank and file personnel, chronic conflict is likely to result. For these several reasons, then, cultural disorganization is likely to be a continuing problem in most industrial societies.

Cultural Deviance

In contrast to the approaches discussed thus far, culture deviance refers to patterns of deviance that are inspired by the cultural patterns of established groups in society. There are, of course, a variety of groups whose basic values and goals conflict with the laws of society, and they necessarily encourage crime or delinquency among their members. Organized crime, right-wing and left-wing extremist groups, and certain immigrant groups expect their members from time to time to behave in ways that violate the law, and insofar as juveniles are included among their membership, they encourage delinquency.[40]

These groups, however, do not constitute the bulk of the problem. There are also perfectly legitimate groups whose values do not directly conflict with the mores of society, but whose more zealous members find themselves committing delinquent acts as they ardently pursue the values of their groups. Almost any group in society, therefore, can generate crime or delinquency if its cultural themes are pursued too aggressively by its members.

The first theorist to draw attention to this fact was Walter B. Miller in his trailblazing essay, "Lower Class Culture as a Generating Milieu of Gang Delinquency." He suggested that six prominent concerns of lower class members tend to orient young males along a delinquent path.[41] Specifically, Miller

---

[39] Ralf Dahrendorf, *Class and Class Conflict in Industrial Society*, Stanford University Press, Stanford, 1959, Chapters VII and VIII.

[40] Harry M. Shulman, *Juvenile Delinquency*, Harper and Row, New York, 1961, pp. 219–223.

[41] Walter B. Miller, "Lower Class Culture as a Generating Milieu of Gang Delinquency," *The Journal of Social Issues*, 14 (Fall, 1958), 5–19.

postulated that a lower class preoccupation with trouble, toughness, smartness, excitement, fate, and autonomy tends to encourage delinquent behavior among adolescents especially as they seek to gain status and solidarity with other lower class boys. Thus, as a lower class boy establishes his toughness, demonstrates his shrewdness in outwitting others, is drawn to thrilling exploits, becomes resigned to the inevitability of trouble with the law, and struggles to maintain his autonomy vis-à-vis adults, there is every chance that he will be led into conflict with the law.

But if the lower class inclines its boys toward delinquency by virtue of the values it proffers them, the same can be said for other classes as well. For example, Ferdinand has suggested that upper-middle class youngsters are prompted to commit assaultive offenses by the emphasis in their class upon competitive validation of the self and in their peer groups upon physical dexterity, and they are implicitly urged to commit a variety of sexual offenses including forcible rape by intense competition among both boys and girls for the affections of the other.[42] Scott and Vaz suggest that the middle class youth culture contributes both opportunity and encouragement for much middle class delinquency and, therefore, is a major factor in the delinquency of that class.[43] And several authors have pointed out that the auto plays a central role in the culture of the upper-middle class adolescent, because it is a symbol of affluence and masculine agility, and it is indispensable to dating and sex play.[44]

In the upper-upper class Ferdinand postulates that a generalized indifference to materialistic values leads teen-agers to commit a variety of property offenses including theft and malicious destruction of property, and an upper-upper class rejection of puritanical values sometimes results in a variety of improprieties including sexual offenses, drug abuses, and alcoholic excesses.[45]

These speculations regarding the distinctive patterns of delinquency to be found in the several social classes have prompted a number of excellent studies into the question. Fannin and Clinard, for example, compared dimensions of the self among fifty middle and lower class delinquents.[46] They found

[42] Theodore N. Ferdinand, *Typologies of Delinquency*, Random House, New York, 1966, pp. 100–110.

[43] Joseph W. Scott and Edmund W. Vaz, "A Perspective on Middle-Class Delinquency," *Canadian Journal of Economics and Political Science*, 29 (August, 1963), 324–335.

[44] See Howard L. Meyerhoff and Barbra C. Meyerhoff, "Field Observations of Middle Class 'Gangs,'" *Social Forces*, 42 (March, 1964), 328–336; and Ferdinand, *op. cit.*, p. 106.

[45] Ferdinand, *op. cit.*, pp. 96–100.

[46] Leon F. Fannin and Marshall B. Clinard, "Differences in the Conception of Self as a Male Among Lower and Middle Class Delinquents," *Social Problems*, 13 (Fall, 1965), 205–214.

that lower class delinquents regarded themselves as tough, powerful, fierce, fearless, and dangerous to a greater extent than middle class delinquents did. These differences, moreover, carried over into behavior, because Fannin and Clinard report that their lower class boys were much quicker to fight than middle class boys, and they fought more viciously as well.[47]

Middle class delinquents thought of themselves, according to Fannin and Clinard, as more daring and adventuresome, and they tended to see courtship as a process of winning girls through sophistication and persuasion rather than through physical toughness and prowess, as many lower class boys viewed it.[48] In light of this difference in values between the two groups, it is curious that middle class delinquents also admit to committing forcible rape somewhat more frequently than lower class youngsters. Sixteen per cent of the boys from the middle class had committed rape, but only 12 per cent of the lower class boys had.[49]

Fannin and Clinard clearly support Miller's suggestion that lower class boys value toughness and Ferdinand's assertion that middle class boys emphasize agility and finesse more than strength in relationships with others. And their finding of a slightly higher frequency of forcible rape among middle class delinquents documents Ferdinand's expectation that sexual improprieties including rape will constitute a sizable problem among middle class delinquents. They also point out, however, that middle class delinquents are more adventuresome and daring than lower class boys, something Miller has specifically rejected.

Short and Strodtbeck focused their attention upon these same questions, and they found that their Chicago gang boys consistently endorsed the utility of toughness more highly than middle class boys.[50] But they also found *no* difference between lower class and middle class boys on this same dimension.[51] They further reported however, that gang boys and lower class boys consistently valued such middle class values as working for grades in school, reading good books, and saving money more highly than middle class boys. Lower class boys, on the other hand, endorsed hanging on the corner with friends and getting a steady job washing and greasing cars more strongly than middle

[47] *Ibid.*, pp. 211–212.

[48] *Ibid.*, pp. 212–213.

[49] *Ibid.*, p. 212.

[50] James F. Short, Jr. and Fred L. Strodtbeck, "Values and Gang Delinquency: A Study of Street-Corner Groups," in *Group Process and Gang Delinquency*, University of Chicago Press, Chicago, 1965, pp. 47–76.

[51] *Ibid.*, Table 36, p. 64.

class boys.[52] Thus, Short and Strodtbeck agree with Miller that there is a distinctive lower class culture, but they did not find that toughness is one of its more salient focal concerns.

Unlike these researchers, Vaz was interested in the middle and upper classes, and he reports that delinquency tends to be associated with involvement in the middle class youth culture.[53] In a related study of upper class delinquency Vaz compared adolescents at a private school in Canada with youngsters at a public school, and he found that private school students were more likely to have taken little things of value not belonging to them, to have remained out all night without their parents' permission, to have destroyed or damaged property, to have skipped school, and to have driven beyond the speed limit.[54] They also were more tolerant toward excessive use of alcohol than their public school counterparts, although their attitudes toward sexual indulgence, if anything, were more prudish than those of their public school counterparts.[55]

Finally, in a study of 589 middle class boys and girls, Wise reports that the most common offenses among both boys and girls in the middle class were noncoercive, nonviolent forms of delinquency and sexual or alcoholic indulgence.[56]

These several studies, then, seem to bear out the conclusions voiced earlier that the upper, middle, and lower classes support characteristic forms of delinquency. There is evidence that there is a distinctive lower class culture; that segments of the lower class do subscribe to the value of toughness; and that this value is reflected in the delinquency of lower class youths. But there is some question about the extent to which toughness is a reflection of the values of the gang *or* of the lower class. At the moment toughness appears to be more characteristic of delinquent gangs than of the lower class as a whole.

In the middle class finesse and sophistication are more highly valued than toughness, and sexual activity seems to be more highly prized among middle class youths than anywhere else. Peer groups and the youth culture are also major factors in defining and crystallizing delinquent behavior among

---

[52] *Ibid.*, pp. 59–65.

[53] Edmund W. Vaz, "Juvenile Delinquency in the Middle-Class Youth Culture," *Canadian Review of Sociology and Anthropology*, 2 (February, 1965), 52–70.

[54] Edmund W. Vaz, "Delinquency and the Youth Culture: Upper and Middle-Class Boys," *Journal of Criminal Law, Criminology and Police Science*, 60, No. 1 (March, 1969), 33–46.

[55] *Ibid.*, p. 41.

[56] Nancy Barton Wise, "Juvenile Delinquency Among Middle-Class Girls," in *Middle Class Juvenile Delinquency*, Edmund W. Vaz, ed., Harper & Row, New York, 1967, pp. 179–188.

middle class adolescents, although it is still unclear what pressures lead an adolescent into delinquency, once he has become firmly established in the youth culture. Does repeated failure in school push the child out of more conventional channels and into a quasi-delinquent youth culture, as in the lower class, or does the youth culture induce delinquency among middle class youths quite apart from difficulties at home or in school? The parallels and differences between working class gangs and the middle class youth culture deserve much more attention than they have received up to now.

Upper class teen-agers were distinctive in their casual attitudes toward property and its handling and in their acceptance of alcoholic indulgence. But it is interesting, in view of the suggestions offered by Ferdinand earlier, that upper class youngsters in Vaz' sample exhibited definite inhibitions regarding sexual misconduct. Their apparent inhibitions, however, may only reflect the relatively high interest in sexuality of middle class youngsters.

We have postulated in this section that deviance often reflects the prevailing values of established groups in society and that to explain the forms of delinquency found among various social classes we have only to turn to their cultural patterns. It is in this sense, then, that the cultural themes of social groups determine the nature of their delinquency problem.

CONCLUSION

These, then, are the four general approaches to understanding delinquency that are broadly mentioned in the criminological literature. Although they are occasionally described by their champions as if only one were valid and all the rest of little worth, it is our conviction that each of them provides valuable insights into distinctive aspects of delinquency in modern society.[57] To be sure, each point of view presents a different array of strengths and weaknesses.

For example, social organization theory points to conditions in society that buttress the defenses against deviance, whatever its forms. It can indicate which kinds of society are likely to exhibit large amounts of deviance and which very little, but it affords little insight into the forms of deviance, nor does it suggest how individuals assume a deviant demeanor.

Social and cultural disorganization, on the other hand, describe contradictions in the organization of society which inhibit conforming behavior and in many cases make deviance in some form the only reasonable path. These

---

[57] Cf. Travis Hirschi's comparison of the virtues of control theory with the deficiencies of strain theory and cultural deviance theory. Hirschi, *op. cit.*, Chapter II.

points of view describe forces in society that prompt deviant attitudes among the members of society, but they cannot indicate what forms their deviance will take, nor can they specify what reactions their deviance will provoke in society. Theories of cultural delinquency, however, do describe the forms that delinquency is likely to take among specific groups and classes, although they fail to point out *why* only some members adopt a delinquent pattern of behavior and not others.

Each point of view offers a different perspective upon the problem, and accordingly all should be regarded as complementary and not competitive. Indeed, in many communities delinquency results from all the conditions identified by the several points of view, and in order to understand the problem comprehensively it will be necessary to consider them all.

Indeed, Short's research into twenty-two gangs in inner-city Chicago mentioned earlier illustrates this point very nicely. Gang membership tended to dim the youngster's perception of legitimate opportunities, and Short regarded this finding as evidence against Cloward and Ohlin's thesis that blocked legitimate opportunities were a factor in the formation of delinquent gangs.[58] It is entirely likely, however, that blocked aspirations *were* a factor in the emergence of a broadly based impulse toward deviance among blacks and that once this impulse had given birth to a variety of deviant groups, including delinquent gangs, legitimate opportunities became relatively unimportant as a factor in delinquency, and the accessibility of delinquent gangs became of overriding importance.

In all likelihood, therefore, our explanations of delinquency in specific communities will need to marshal all four approaches to the problem to explain its various facets. Any other course seems likely to lead to oversimplifications and gaps in our understanding.

BIBLIOGRAPHY

CLARK, JOHN P., AND EUGENE P. WENNIGER, "Social-economic Class and Area as Correlates of Illegal Behavior Among Juveniles," *American Sociological Review*, 27 (December, 1962), 826–834.

CLOWARD, RICHARD A., AND LLOYD E. OHLI, *Delinquency and Opportunity*, Free Press of Glencoe, New York, 1960.

COHEN, ALBERT K., *Delinquent Boys*, Free Press of Glencoe, New York, 1955.

DURKHEIM, EMILE, *Suicide*, John A. Spaulding and George Simpson, trans., Free Press of Glencoe, New York, 1951.

FERDINAND, THEODORE N., *Typologies of Delinquency*, Random House, New York, 1966.

[58] See footnote 30, p. 104.

HENRY, ANDREW F., AND JAMES F. SHORT, JR., *Suicide and Homicide*, Free Press of Glencoe, New York, 1954.

HIRSCHI, TRAVIS, *Causes of Delinquency*, University of California Press, Berkeley, 1969.

LANDER, BERNARD, *Toward an Understanding of Juvenile Delinquency*, Columbia University Press, New York, 1954.

MERTON, ROBERT K., "Social Structure and Anomie," *American Sociological Review*, 3 (October, 1938), 672–682.

MILLER, WALTER B., "Lower Class Culture as a Generating Milieu of Gang Delinquency," *The Journal of Social Issues*, 14 (Fall, 1958), 5–19.

NYE, F. IVAN, JAMES F. SHORT, JR., AND VIRGIL J. OLSON, "Socio-economic Status and Delinquent Behavior," *American Journal of Sociology*, 63 (January, 1958), 381–389.

POLK, KENNETH, AND WALTER E. SCHAFER, eds., *Schools and Delinquency*, Prentice-Hall, Inc., Englewood Cliffs, N.J., 1972.

SHORT, JAMES F., JR., RAMON RIVERA, AND RAY A. TENNYSON, "Perceived Opportunities, Gang Membership and Delinquency," *American Sociological Review*, 30 (February, 1965), 56–67.

SHORT, JAMES F., JR., AND FRED L. STRODTBECK, *Group Process and Gang Delinquency*, University of Chicago Press, Chicago, 1965.

VAZ, EDMUND W., *Middle Class Juvenile Delinquency*, Harper & Row, New York, 1967.

gang delinquency and the isolated delinquent

Delinquency is largely a group phenomenon. Studies of the 1930's and 1940's have shown that from 70 to 85 per cent of boy delinquencies are committed by two or more boys, only 15 to 30 per cent by one boy alone.[1] The small clique is the most common delinquent pattern. Among delinquencies carried out by more than one boy, 65 to 70 per cent are the work of two or three boys. The remaining groups rarely include more than four boys. More recently Travis Hirschi reports that youngsters who admitted to two or more delinquencies also had the largest number of friends picked up by the police.[2] Delinquents clearly prefer the social and moral support of other delinquents as they set about delinquent behavior.

This ganging tendency, however, is most prominent among older delinquents. In a study of 102 delinquent boys in New York City from six to sixteen, Craig and Budd found that only 38 per cent of the delinquencies

---

[1] Clifford R. Shaw and Henry D. McKay, *Social Factors in Juvenile Delinquency,* A Study . . . for the National Commission on Law Observance and Enforcement, U.S. Government Printing Office, Washington, D.C., 1931, No. 13, Vol. 2, p. 195; William Healy and Augusta R. Bronner, *New Light on Delinquency and Its Treatment,* Yale University Press, New Haven, Connecticut, 1936, pp. 63–64; Sheldon and Eleanor Glueck, *One Thousand Juvenile Delinquents,* Harvard University Press, Cambridge, Massachusetts, 1934, pp. 94, 100; William C. Kvaraceus, *Juvenile Delinquency and the School,* World Book Company, Yonkers-on-Hudson, New York, 1945, p. 116.

[2] Travis Hirschi, *Causes of Delinquency,* University of California Press, Berkeley, 1969, pp. 98–100.

were committed with companions, whereas 62 per cent were committed while alone.[3] These figures are almost the opposite of earlier findings. This reversal can probably be accounted for by differences in ages or in types of delinquency between the earlier studies and this study. Among the 102 boys, among those aged thirteen and under, only 25 per cent had companions, whereas among those aged fourteen to sixteen, 48 per cent had companions. Boys over age sixteen are not included; it seems reasonable to conclude that the percentage with companions would be greater than for the mid-teen boys.

A breakdown by offense showed that 63 per cent of boys arrested for thefts (by far the most common juvenile offense) committed their theft with companions. Offenses with companions accounted for 37 per cent of property damage cases, including vandalism and malicious mischief; 31 per cent of assaults; 27 per cent of minor criminal offenses; and only 10 per cent of "juvenile offenses," for which an adult would not be an offender. More serious offenses were committed by companions in 91 per cent of such instances, compared to 28 per cent of minor offenses. Serious offenses were also more typical of older than younger boys, the offender was more likely to be adjudicated guilty by the juvenile court, and recidivism was more likely to occur. Gang fights, which would be companion or group offenses, are not included.

In summary, the study suggests both quantitative and qualitative differences between younger boys and mid-adolescents, with adolescents being more likely to commit more serious crimes, to repeat the crimes, and to have companions in the commission of offenses than younger boys.

The Clique and the Gang

Delinquent gangs may consist of loosely federated small cliques, of street clubs with informal natural leadership, or of organizations with an age hierarchy and specialized leadership.

Some gangs begin, perhaps in preadolescent years, with a closely linked clique of four or five boys. If another small clique develops in the area, the two may combine without losing their identity. More members may be needed for some particular sport. In time other small cliques are added, not through formal action but because of something they can add to the customary activities of the already established clique or cliques. Each clique tends to keep its

---

[3] These boys were part of the total sample used in a ten-year validation study of the Glueck Prediction Table. The boys consisted of thirteen Puerto Ricans, twenty-seven whites, and sixty-two blacks, all of whom lived in deteriorated, high-delinquency areas at the age of six. Maude M. Craig and Laila A. Budd, "The Juvenile Offender: Recidivism and Companions," *Crime and Delinquency*, 13, No. 2 (1967), 344–51.

leader but acknowledges a central leader when the entire group undertakes some enterprise.

As the group grows, the members may form small cliques of boys with special interests who nevertheless also wish to be part of a larger group. The cliques shift and angle for increased importance in the combined group, trying to place the clique leader in the top position and themselves in a favored status with reference to the other cliques.

The pair, triad, or small clique is the most common social form in delinquency whether the boys are members of a larger gang or not. Organized juvenile gangs rarely commit crimes as a unit. After all, few delinquencies can be carried out successfully by large groups because of the increased likelihood of discovery with an increase in number of boys. Outright fights, riots, or mass vandalism are almost the only delinquencies that can be more successfully carried out by a large group than a small one. In spite of flaming newspaper headlines, such delinquencies rarely occur; the usual delinquency is theft on a small scale. Drinking and sex parties are also sometimes carried out by an entire group or gang.

Table 9 shows for one disorganized Chicago neighborhood the division of delinquencies into those carried out by groups of delinquents and those committed by individuals or small cliques. Some forms of misbehavior are adaptable to both large and small groups and to the individual. But there is also a distinction among other delinquencies. Drinking and certain sex activities and fighting tend to be group activities. Both minor and major offenses involving property and annoyance or injury to other persons tend to be individual or clique offenses. The potentially most damaging of the large group or gang offenses is fighting.

The true function of membership by the delinquent in a large group is not for delinquency but for social and status functions. Delinquent and non-delinquent peer groups serve many of the same functions for their members, although the activities by which these functions are achieved may differ. Delinquency is one—but only one—way by which the delinquent gang carries on its activities and meets the personal needs of members.

Types of Gangs

Various attempts have been made to classify gangs. Yablonsky, using the general term collective structure, places gangs in a continuum according to their degree of cohesion, norms, and role definitions.[4] The least defined struc-

---

[4] Lewis Yablonsky, *The Violent Gang*, Penguin Books, Baltimore, 1966, p. 223.

TABLE 9

Number of Group Members Involved in Classified Types of Antisocial Behavior
During the Period from June 31, 1955 to December 31, 1955,
Newly Disorganized Area, Chicago

| | GROUP MEMBERS ENGAGING IN ANTISOCIAL BEHAVIOR | | | |
| | ALONE OR WITH LESS THAN HALF OF THE GROUP | | WITH HALF OR MORE OF THE GROUP | |
	N	%	N	%
Violations of city ordinances, including curfew laws, traffic laws, hopping streetcars, swimming in forbidden places, playing ball in streets, etc.	89	48.3	87	42.9
Minor offenses				
Against property, including truancy, trespassing, sneaking into movies, running away, petty stealing, minor defacing of property, etc.	62	33.7	—	—
Against persons, including abuse of younger children, marked annoyance of older persons outside of family or friendship circle, etc.	15	8.2	—	—
Drinking and sex within group	—	—	75	36.9
Fight against another group	—	—	41	20.2
Major offenses				
Against property including breaking and entering (burglary), larceny, major vandalism, etc.	15	8.2	—	—
Against persons, including strongarm or armed robbery, use of narcotics, knifing, forced sex relations, etc.	3	1.6	—	—
Total number of boys	184	100.0	203	100.0

Rearranged from Charles H. Shireman, *The Hyde Park Youth Project, May 1955–May 1958,* Welfare Council of Metropolitan Chicago, Chicago, undated, p. 129.

ture is the mob, including youth rioters and lynching mobs. Somewhat more structured is the near-group or violent gang. Most fully structured is the group consisting of social gangs and delinquent gangs. Cloward and Ohlin identify three types of subculture, suggesting three types of delinquent gangs: the criminal, which orients its members toward adult criminal careers; the conflict, which leads to violence; and the retreatist, organized around drug addiction.[5] Field workers, carrying on research among gangs, have generally found it difficult to locate gangs that fall exclusively into one or another pattern, although gangs may favor one or another pattern of behavior, that is, there are delinquent gangs that almost never engage in violence, and other gangs that engage from time to time in planned violence but also carry on other types of delinquency such as disorderly conduct, thefts, or sexual exploitation.

INFORMAL AMORPHOUS GANGS

The fluid, unstable quality of Chicago gangs was observed in the twenties by Thrasher.[6] He says that the "ganging process is a continuous flux and flow," with individual members joining and leaving and with more permanent breaks through conflict or arrest.

That fluidity still exists is shown by data from the 1960's produced by a research project in two high delinquency areas in Chicago.[7] In 1962, the staff of the project had contacts with thirty-five groups, all sufficiently aware of a group relationship to have names (Aristocrats, Dukes, Kool Gents, Top Boys, and so on). Fifteen months later, in 1963, the staff had contacts with forty-four groups, but only fifteen were continued by name from 1962. Twenty of the 1962 names had disappeared from the list and twenty-nine new names had appeared. A number of reasons account for the changes. Members of a group may leave the area: they or their families move, they enter military service, or (occasionally) some members are jailed. The remnants of groups may then merge with some other group, or they may combine under a new name. Other members may remain in the community but "outgrow" the group, finding a new orientation through marriage. Internal conflicts within a group may lead to its dissolution; members then join other groups. Sometimes a group simply decides to change its name. In the history of any one group, several of these reasons may operate. Members of these groups often do not

---

[5] Richard A. Cloward and Lloyd E. Ohlin, *Delinquency and Opportunity*, The Free Press of Glencoe, New York, 1960.

[6] Frederic M. Thrasher, *The Gang*, University of Chicago Press, Chicago, 1927, pp. 35–37.

[7] Hans W. Mattick and Nathan S. Caplan, *The Chicago Youth Development Project, Institute for Social Research*, University of Michigan, Ann Arbor, 1964, pp. 96, 104.

disappear from the community; the membership is simply reshuffled and the same boys reappear in different combinations, under new names.

The fluid type of gang has been referred to by Yablonsky as a near-group, more stable than the temporary mob but without the formal structure of a true group.[8]

According to the near-group theory, the gang builds up around a central core of five or six boys, who need the gang as a group within which to work out personal problems that might vary from one boy to another. There is no consensus as to goals; each boy is trying to meet individual needs. Additional boys have a loose affiliation with the gang, participating or not as any particular activity meets each boy's temporary needs. A still more remote ring of boys does not identify with the gang but on occasion may accompany a gang, for instance, on a fight, to enjoy the excitement. Thus there is no definite membership. In this loose affiliation, individual boys with many types of emotional needs may try to meet them without much responsibility for the group or its purposes.

Malcolm Klein has compared Yablonsky's rough division of the gang into core and fringe members with the actual structures of four Los Angeles gangs, and his research indicates the following conclusions:

1. Core and fringe members are about equal in numbers.
2. The social and economic characteristics of their families are almost identical.
3. Core members attend gang meetings more frequently and typically outnumber fringe members at these meetings.
4. In terms of number of recorded offenses, proportion of assaultive offenses, frequency of offenses, and length of delinquent career, core members are much more delinquent than fringe members.
5. Aggressive behavior is more heavily influenced by personal needs and weaknesses than by gang membership.
6. Gang leadership tends to be drawn from among those members who are not sociopathic or otherwise seriously psychologically disturbed.[9]

Other researchers have also challenged Yablonsky's conclusion that gang leaders are among the most sociopathic members in the gang. In a study of street gangs and clubs in Hyde Park, Chicago, only about 10 per cent of the members (not leaders alone) were found to be emotionally disturbed and were referred to a casework agency.[10]

---

[8] Lewis Yablonsky, "The Delinquent Gang as a Near-Group," *Social Problems*, 7 (Fall, 1959), 108–117.

[9] Malcolm Klein, *Street Gangs and Street Workers*, Prentice-Hall, Inc., Englewood Cliffs, N.J., 1971, pp. 70–92.

[10] Charles H. Shireman, *The Hyde Park Youth Project, May 1955–1958*, Welfare Council of Metropolitan Chicago, Chicago, undated, p. 147.

ORGANIZED CLUBS OR GANGS

Some gangs have as one purpose—but not the only one—maintenance of their status and protection of their home territory from intruding gangs. Some of these gangs fulfill the qualifications of near-groups, but others are more fully organized, and groups of older boys often reach a high point in organization. Nevertheless, group processes are informal and methods of obtaining new leaders are so unformulated that the gang may disintegrate if the leader moves away, is arrested and committed to a correctional school, or fails to meet his obligations. However, usually other boys are ready to step into the vacated position. Membership is handled by the simple method of testing out each new potential member.[11]

Some of the more definitely structured gangs have subsidiary gangs, arranged by age. Each sub-gang moves up step by step in status as the members grow older, with the oldest sub-group ready to replace the dominant gang as its members leave the gang for the armed forces, jobs, marriage—or sometimes prison. A typical organization is that of the "Outlaws," in which youth over nineteen hold the controlling position as Senior Outlaws. In lower levels are the Intermediates, aged seventeen to nineteen, Junior Outlaws, aged fifteen to seventeen, and Midget Outlaws, aged thirteen to fifteen. Some organized boys' gangs have an auxiliary of girls, in this instance, Outlawettes, aged fourteen to sixteen and Little Outlawettes, aged twelve to fourteen. All these segments rarely meet together, but they maintain a sibling relationship with each other, with older segments overseeing and controlling the activities of the younger, gradually passing on to them the attitudes, codes, and approved behavior patterns of the older group. They set the traditions and reputation of the gang. The younger groups emulate the older ones. The total assemblage or aggregate using a given name and feeling part of the same organization might total as many as fifty to seventy members.

Each age group numbers fifteen to twenty boys and is itself broken into cliques of three or four boys, each with its own leader. When the larger group acts as a unit, different boys act as leaders for different functions, such as athletics, a dance, or an intergang fight. In addition to the vertical organization, some gangs have a horizontal organization and a brother relationship with one or more other gangs whereby they do not fight each other but join together to attack or defend territory against an opposing gang. When members of

11 Walter B. Miller, "The Impact of a Community Group Work Program on Delinquent Corner Groups," *Social Service Review*, 31 (December, 1957), 390–406; Miller, "Lower Class Culture as a Generating Milieu of Gang Delinquency," *Journal of Social Issues*, 14 (April, 1958), 5–19; *Reaching the Fighting Gang*, New York City Youth Board, New York, 1960, Chapters 2 and 3. See also Klein, *op. cit.*, Chapter 3.

such gangs move to other communities, they may organize a new gang which then maintains a brother relationship with the original gang. A network of gangs may then project itself into several areas, not necessarily contiguous.

Conflict Gangs

This term is applied to gangs, one of whose calculated activities is physical fighting with other gangs. The fights are not sporadic and spontaneous such as often occur between boys over some difference of opinion or small slight. Such individual fights may occur between members of the same gang as well as between boys who are not gang members. Conflict does not necessarily serve the same purpose in all gangs.[12]

INDIVIDUAL AND GANG STATUS

Intergang skirmishes may take place at almost any time, but full-scale encounters are planned well in advance, either through clandestine messages to the gang to be attacked or with intergang arrangements of time, place, and weapons. Since fighting is always a potential activity, the fighting (or bopping) gangs tend to be well organized, with "war counselors" and appointed members to store and, as needed, distribute weapons which may range from clubs to guns.

The fights serve no utilitarian purpose but are a way to maintain certain values important to the gang. One is the maintenance of a certain territory or "turf" which the gang holds for itself, free of interference from competing gangs. The intangible value is to demonstrate courage (heart) and a reputation for daring. Occasions for fights are sometimes contrived in order to redemonstrate possession of these values. The gang that defends its turf or successfully encroaches upon another's has higher status than the defeated gang and is regarded with fear and admiration by nearby gangs. Within its own territory it receives the admiration of young boys who either aspire to become members or who are in younger, auxiliary groups.

A high degree of disorganization and lack of adult or institutional control are also a necessary condition for the development of gangs that so thoroughly violate the orderliness of a community.

[12] The discussion of conflict gangs is drawn from a number of sources, chiefly the two Miller sources, *op. cit.*; *Reaching the Fighting Gang*, *op. cit.*; Ira Henry Freeman, *Out of the Burning, the Story of Frenchy, A Boy Gang Leader*, Crown Publishers, Inc., New York, 1960; Irving Spergel, *Racketville, Slumtown, Haulberg*, University of Chicago Press, Chicago, 1964; James F. Short, Jr. and Fred L. Strodtbeck, *Group Process and Gang Delinquency*, University of Chicago Press, Chicago, 1965; and David Dawley, *A Nation of Lords*, Anchor Books, New York, 1973.

Tendency to Overemphasize the Conflict Gang

The dramatic quality of gang fights leads to a tendency to overemphasize their ferocity and frequency. An intensive study, averaging two years per gang, of seven of the "toughest" gangs in Boston pinpoints some of the attributes of their violent delinquencies.[13] Field workers recorded about 54,000 actions and sentiments relating to some sixty behavioral areas, of which about 1,600 or 3 per cent related to assaultive behavior. Among the sixty behavioral areas (for example, drinking behavior, sexual behavior, theft, and police-oriented behavior), assaultive behavior ranked ninth, with theft being the most common delinquency. Most of the assaultive behavior was in words, not deeds— i.e., threats. Moreover, the assaults were generally mild in nature, though disapproved by middle class norms. For example, there were thirty disapproved assault-oriented actions for every instance of arrestable assault and five instances of arrestable assault for every court appearance. Few of the assaults involved weapons. None of the gang members studied appeared in court on charges of either murder or manslaughter between the ages of seven and twenty-seven.

Assaults and fights were not uniformly found among the gangs studied. They were more frequent among males than females, among late teens (when manhood is finally established) than younger or older youth, and between gangs rather than individuals. Although all boys in the study were lower class, those most frequently oriented to assaultive behavior were of the lowest status among all the boys. To the extent that race made a difference, white boys were slightly more assaultive than black boys.

While fights were a fairly important gang activity, they did not dominate gang life. According to the study, many intergang fights that were carefully planned were as carefully avoided in ways to preserve gang honor. A champion from each side might represent the rival gangs in a "fair fight"; the police might be tipped off in advance; the gang might "reluctantly" agree to mediation by social workers.

At the same time we must not ignore the fact that conflict gangs exist today in many major cities and carry out serious violence against members of other gangs or nonmembers in their neighborhoods. In the 1950's they were a serious problem in many eastern cities, but during the 1960's their activities subsided noticeably. Since 1971, however, they have become troublesome again in cities like New York and Philadelphia. Between 1963 and 1970 there was an average of twenty-one gang killings per year in Philadelphia, but in 1971

---

[13] Walter B. Miller, "Violent Crimes in City Gangs," *Annals of the American Academy of Political and Social Science*, 364 (1966), 96–112.

and 1972 there were eighty-two and in New York, fifty-seven gang-related homicides were reported in 1972 alone.[14] Chicago has had a continuing problem with delinquent gangs at least since the 1920's, but conflict gangs did not emerge as a significant factor on the South and West Sides of Chicago until the late 1950's, where today they are still firmly established.

Much of the gang violence that seems to the public wanton and unnecessary is actually the means to achieve personal and ideological goals essential to the gang and its members. For many of them the gang is important in helping to "secure and defend their honor as males; to secure and defend the reputation of the local area and the honor of their women; to show that an affront to their pride and dignity demands retaliation."[15]

It must be cautioned, also, that gang members are not totally committed to delinquent values. The gang, in spite of its delinquency, functions in a community which is generally law-abiding. Members more often than not have parents who lean toward legal conformity although the pressures of life and the lower class culture may cause them to short-cut many corners. Children have been subjected to conforming values by the school and through the agencies of mass communication. Therefore they are likely to have mixed attitudes toward both conformity and deviancy, toward honesty and dishonesty, toward avoidance of injury to others and assault. Even though seriously delinquent at times, they often accept the values of the larger society as basic and their delinquent values as secondary, and they seek to rationalize or neutralize their delinquent behavior. They may do this in at least five ways:[16]

1. The delinquent may deny personal responsibility for his delinquent acts. Many delinquents are adept at picking up factors that have been found associated with delinquency and using them as excuses for their behavior—they place responsibility on a broken home, unloving parents, or bad companions. The delinquent persuades himself that these conditions caused him to be a delinquent and that he is not responsible.
2. The delinquent may define delinquency as only those actions that specifically harm some individual. He may define stealing a car for his own use as

14 *The New York Times*, June 11, 1973, pp. 30f, and July 2, 1973, pp. 1f, Second Part.

15 The author ends with this statement: "At root, the solution to the problem of gang violence lies in the discovery of a way of providing for men the means of attaining cherished objectives—personal honor, prestige, defense against perceived threats to one's homeland—without resort to violence. When men have found a solution to this problem [on a national basis], they will at the same time have solved the problem of violent crimes in city gangs." Miller, "Violent Crimes in City Gangs," p. 112.

16 Gresham M. Sykes and David Matza, "Techniques of Neutralization: A Theory of Delinquency," *American Sociological Review*, 22 (1957), 664–670.

borrowing; vandalism as harmless, since the person whose property is damaged can probably afford the loss; truancy as harming no one.

3. The delinquent may deny that the person injured or wronged is really a victim. He has simply been rightfully punished for what he has done to the delinquent. The attack on a person or group of lower status is justified because this person or group has not "stayed in his/its place." School vandalism is "all right" because the principal or teacher was unfair.

4. The delinquent may "condemn the condemners," that is, accuse the persons (or segment of society) who criticize or condemn him as being delinquent themselves, of showing spite, or of being corrupt or brutal. He thus seeks to excuse or justify his own misbehavior.

5. The pull toward loyalty to the gang may override the awareness of the values of the larger society. The gang is a group bound by emotional ties. The immediate personal rewards of conforming to this intimate group's values are greater than the more distant benefits of conforming to law or abstract principles of ethics. For the gang boy, these abstract principles are not represented by personal friends but only indirectly or in formal relationships with teachers, ministers, social workers, and so on.

In these ways the delinquent boy tries to solve the dilemma of ambivalent attitudes toward legal conformity. The fact that he becomes delinquent does not necessarily mean that he completely rejects legal standards or ethical values of society. He knows these standards, and has accepted and internalized some of them. But under the conditions of gang life he does not always follow them and seeks to ease or avoid in advance feelings of guilt by strong rationalizations for his conduct.

However, a few delinquent individuals and gangs move so far away from normal values that they become unresponsive to conventional groups.

Special Terms and Symbols

Many delinquent groups use special terms and symbols which set them apart from conventional society. Such terms and symbols are characteristic of many groups, from Scouts to men's lodges. They seem to serve a common purpose: to identify the members as belonging to a particular group, to give a feeling of superiority to outsiders, and to create prestige among certain other groups. In general people look with amusement or admiration on the symbolic apparatus of groups in their own subculture, but are inclined to regard with fear, abhorrence, or disgust the symbols of groups of other subcultures. For example, Scout uniforms are worn with pride by middle class boys and girls and regarded with approval by middle class adults. Many lower class boys and adults alike look on them with amusement and scorn. Likewise, the garb of many delinquent gangs is approved in lower class culture but regarded as a symbol of deviancy by middle class people.

The language and symbols of delinquent gangs throw light on gang values and activities.

GANG LANGUAGE

As is true of almost any group with the same background of interest and experience, gangs have developed a "little language" of their own which spreads generally throughout the delinquent contraculture. Similar specialized terminology is found in the professions, many occupations, the sports world, high schools, and the like.

Gangs do not refer to themselves as gangs, a word with unpleasant connotations to delinquent boys as to others. Their group is a club, a respectable word that implies that the gang does not regard itself as engaged in reprehensible activities.

Other special words reflect major interests. Some are given below with their meanings.

Names of gangs tend to have special significance. They may identify the territory that "belongs" to the gang; the name of a street, park, or area may be used. Other names attribute courage to the gang, for example, Warriors, Vikings, or Comanches; these also imply warlike qualities. Still others have a general connotation of danger: Cobras, Scorpions, Dragons, Tigers, or Daggers. Other names identify the gang with individuals or groups of high status, for example, Viceroys, Lords, Egyptian Kings, Dukes, and Gents. Ethnic names are sometimes used. Other names have no easily understood connotation but perhaps refer to special experiences of the gangs.[17]

The preoccupation of some conflict gangs with fighting and the fear of attack is shown by the wide variety of terms having to do with fighting.

1. Bopping club—a street-fighting gang; to bop—to fight
2. Burn—use of guns in a fight
3. Cool (a noun)—agreement not to fight
4. Fair fight—stylized, arranged fight without deadly weapons
5. To fall—to attack or raid another gang
6. Gangbang—a fight between gangs
7. Go down—embark on a fight or rumble
8. Humbugging—fighting

[17] The terminology has been assembled from Harrison E. Salisbury, *The Shook-up Generation*, Fawcett Publications, Inc., Greenwich, Connecticut, 1958; *Reaching the Fighting Gang*, New York City Youth Board, New York, 1960, especially pp. 295–296; and R. Lincoln Keiser, *The Vice Lords*, Holt, Rinehart and Winston, New York, 1969.

9. Hustling—seeking victims for financial gain
10. Jap—an attack
11. Piece—a gun
12. Rumble—an intergang fight
13. Steel—a knife
14. Turf—territory claimed by a gang; to mind our turf—to protect our territory
15. War counselor—the boy whose specialty is planning intergang fights
16. Wolf-packing—seeking victims to enhance one's reputation

Among delinquent gangs there is also an emphasis upon certain moral qualities in terms of which the members evaluate one another.

1. Brotherhood—the bond that unites gang members into close, meaningful relationships
2. A front—the techniques or line a gang member uses in the game
3. Game—an encounter in which the individual seeks to manipulate others to his own advantage
4. Heart—the ability to face hazardous situations without regard to personal safety
5. Punking out—the process of avoiding dangerous situations out of fear

Sex is another abiding interest which has its own terminology, some of which follows:

1. Deb—a girl
2. Fish—close dancing without moving the feet, sexually exciting

Status is extremely important and has its own vocabulary.

1. Chicken—a coward
2. Coolie—a boy who does not belong to a gang
3. Faggot—a boy who does not join a gang and is assumed to be a coward
4. Rep—reputation for heart
5. Sounding—insulting someone, sometimes leads to a fight

The lists could be greatly extended. Special forms of delinquency, such as illegal possession and sale of drugs and addiction, have their own specialized vocabularies.

Symbolic Dress

Gang unity is emphasized by some characteristic style of haircut or type of dress. Some gangs buy leather jackets and have their names inscribed on them. Girls who are friends or who form a kind of auxiliary may wear a similar jacket. In the southwest the pachuco or "zoot suit" has been popular with Mexican youth. A special kind of shirt or hat may characterize a gang. In like manner, many conventional groups have special uniforms, jackets, badges, or insignia.

Riots

A consideration of riots lies to a large extent outside the area of juvenile delinquency. The habitual pattern of juvenile violence is self-contained within the structure of juvenile gangs, with only sporadic attacks on outsiders. Physical destruction tends to be limited to vandalism of one or a few buildings, often schools that are a part of the delinquents' social world. A riot is a disorderly and often violent uprising of the populace in general, usually based on a situation of tension that affects a large segment of the population. Often a race or social class is the subject of the tension; in that case, the riot tends to be limited to the community where this population group lives or works.

Riots are primarily an activity of older teen-agers and young adults. The riot arrest records for sixteen cities showed the following age distribution: age fifteen to twenty-four, 52.5 per cent; age twenty-five to thirty-five, 28.3 per cent; age thirty-six to fifty, 15.6 per cent; and age fifty and over, 3.6 per cent.[18] A generalized description of the typical rioter in the riots of the 1960's states that he was a black male teen-ager or young adult, a lifelong resident of the city in which he rioted, a high school dropout—but somewhat better educated than nonrioters—and unemployed. He was not a hoodlum, habitual criminal, or riffraff. He was proud of his race and hostile to both middle class blacks and whites.[19]

The violence and damage of a riot goes beyond any of the violent episodes recorded for juvenile gangs. A riot typically includes fires, looting, sniping, large crowds, and use of police, National Guard, or federal forces in large numbers. The more serious riots last two or more days. In smaller riots there are no or only one or two deaths. In the larger riots, deaths are numerous. In the Detroit riot of 1967, forty-three persons were killed and 324 injured; in Newark, twenty-five were killed and 725 injured.[20] Looting and fires run property loss into the millions of dollars in the larger riots. These and the many smaller riots are not the work of juveniles.

Juveniles, however, are involved. An analysis has been made of the persons arrested in 1965 in connection with the Watts riot in Los Angeles.[21] Al-

---

[18] *Report of the National Advisory Commission on Civil Disorders*, Bantam Books, New York, 1968, p. 172. *Ibid.*, p. 111.

[19] These findings regarding the ghetto riots of the 1960's accord very well with recent research into nineteenth-century riots in Europe. Rudé, for example, reports that rioters in Great Britain in the last century were predominantly members of the established working class and not drifters or criminals. See George Rudé, *The Crowd in History*, John Wiley & Sons, Inc., New York, 1964, pp. 60–61, Chapter 13.

[20] *Ibid.*, pp. 115, 164.

[21] Los Angeles (County) Probation Department, *Riot Participation Study: Juvenile Offenders*, Research Report No. 26, Los Angeles, California, 1965.

though arrest records cannot be taken as a complete record of riot participants, they give some indication of the types of people involved. Of 3,927 people arrested, 556 or about 14 per cent were legally juveniles, that is, under eighteen. An analysis of the characteristics of these juveniles showed that the average juvenile participant was a black male, aged seventeen, who had been born in California and had lived in Los Angeles more than five years. He was in the ninth or tenth grade, not doing well in school, and indifferent to community-sponsored youth organizations. Typically, the juvenile's family had some problems, and the family income was less than $300 a month. Most of these juveniles were arrested for looting, within a mile of their homes. Most of them had no or only one prior probation referral or police contact; most were placed on probation by the court. The juveniles denied any real involvement in the riot. This evidence indicates that juveniles were a significant though by no means predominant or decisive group in the Watts riot. For the most part they were simply a cross section of the young males in the neighborhood.

Another study, based on interviews with people in nine riot-torn cities, stated that teen-agers tended to participate in cliques of two or three. Some were undoubtedly members of gangs, but the gangs did not operate as such in the riots. Gangs did not plan the riots, but after a riot had started groups of teen-agers on the spur of the moment might plan to loot a certain store.[22]

Newspaper stories and observations by nonrioters who witnessed rioting suggest that teen-agers joined the riots as they might have joined any other exciting event that might suddenly occur. Laughing, shouting, grabbing clothing from stores, or carryng away portable items such as television sets or radios were observed. Adults apparently took the lead and set the example. Comments, chiefly from adults, secured after the riot ended indicated no sense of guilt, but an attitude of evening the score against white store owners who, it was often asserted, had sold shoddy goods or charged high prices or both. Teenagers seemed to reflect the attitudes and behavior prevalent in the community at the time. They seem not to have originated or initiated the riots.

The above statements apply to the violent riots that occur in urban ghettos, built upon prior tension, and set off by some aggravating incident. Older teen-agers and youth have their own type of riots, such as those on college campuses or at vacation spots. These are planned and initiated by youth, but they do not as a rule include burning, extensive property damage, or looting. Often they are carried out by middle class youth in a general

[22] Saul Bernstein, *Alternatives to Violence, Alienated Youth and Riots, Race, and Poverty*, Association Press, New York, 1967, pp. 26–35.

or specific protest against institutional or conventional behavior expected of them.[23]

Delinquency by Individuals

Approximately 15 to 30 per cent of boys who come before the juvenile court have committed their delinquencies alone. The difference in percentages is probably due primarily to differences in definition of group and isolated delinquencies. At any rate, isolated delinquency is infrequent. Whether isolated delinquency also indicates an isolated individual is another question. It has already been shown that most delinquencies are committed by two or three boys. These boys as well as the individual delinquent may also be members of a gang. Their status in the gang may well depend upon the successful completion of a delinquency. They may, in fact, represent the gang and steal candy, cigarettes, alcoholic drinks, or equipment for the use of the gang.

Little has been done in studying the truly individual delinquent, who not only commits his delinquencies alone but who has little or no delinquent contacts. It is possible to do little more than speculate or offer isolated examples.

The isolated delinquent may be a social isolate, who either is unable to make friends or who prefers to work or play alone. Throughout society there are people who do not make close affiliations with groups. If such a person is motivated toward delinquency, he would tend to carry out his delinquency alone, just as he prefers to study alone, read instead of play with others, or have a hobby that does not require cooperation. It is normal for him to act as an individual and not as a member of a clique or gang.

The isolate may be maladjusted in some way and express his difficulties overtly in secret crimes that somehow symbolize his dissatisfactions. These crimes may become continuous, repetitive in type, and sometimes progressively more serious. His satisfaction is completely covert and does not depend upon group applause. However, the crimes do not solve his problem but only temporarily relieve tensions; as tensions increase again, another crime is in order. If the maladjustment is deep and serious, the crimes may be serious and lie outside the usual run of juvenile delinquencies. A Chicago case will illustrate. A young boy of middle class status became overly interested in sex and expressed this interest in symbolic ways, at one period through stealing and hiding women's underwear. In adolescence he found sexual satisfaction in breaking into apartments and finally was unable to resist the compulsion to

---

[23] See Thomas S. Smith, "Conventionalization and Control: An Examination of Adolescent Crowds," *American Journal of Sociology*, 74 (September, 1968), 172–183.

murder any woman whom he found, although he did not molest her sexually. Three murders were committed before the boy, then just past sixteen years of age, was located and identified.

Other instances of isolated delinquency may not symbolize long-standing maladjustment but be an explosive outburst of long-smoldering emotions. Children and youth as well as adults sometimes commit murder when the tension of inner emotional turmoil reaches the point when it can no longer be contained. The murder may be planned or impulsive; it may be a single episode or one of a series of murders quickly performed. The offender may then run away in fear but meekly surrender when police find him, his emotional tensions having been discharged. Less serious assaults may follow angry quarrels. Destruction of property may be a displacement of anger toward some person. When these emotions are not shared and when they come to a head quickly and are immediately expressed in violence, the delinquency is likely to be the act of one individual. At other times and in other ways, the offender may be a member of a group and share in group activities.

In another Chicago case, a boy of twelve murdered a younger companion who had threatened to report a theft from his mother by the older of the two boys. The young murderer had a lifelong history of unstable family life, absence of his father, and rejection by his mother. He was so poorly adjusted in school that he had been referred repeatedly to a clinic. Therapeutic treatment was recommended but never carried through by his mother. The killing of his companion was the climax to the twelve years of emotional turmoil. This boy lived in a lower-middle class neighborhood. He did not run with a gang and had few friends. He had been suspected in one or two minor thefts, committed alone, but was not regarded as a delinquent.

Individual acts of delinquency also occur when an individual wishes, through a hidden act of delinquency, to maintain or improve his position in some nondelinquent group. Thefts, juvenile or adult, often are motivated to obtain funds with which to improve an insecure position. The child may take money from his mother's purse or from a neighbor with which to buy candy or presents for other children, among whom he holds an insecure position.

The isolated delinquent is limited in the kinds of delinquency he can carry out and in the satisfactions obtained. A delinquency that requires teamwork is beyond him. For example, a typical group pattern for breaking into stores is for one boy to act as lookout, one to wait at the wheel of a car, and one or two to enter the store. The delinquency requires coordinated work and trust among the boys. The individual thief must somehow combine the activities of the three or four boys; he must bear the full burden of responsibility and guilt. However, he does not need to share the stolen articles with anyone, and he avoids the possibility of an accomplice's being arrested and revealing the names of his companions.

Isolated delinquency also lacks the recreational aspects of many types of group delinquency. An individual boy may steal a car, but much of the satisfaction is lost if he cannot display his prize to appreciative friends by offering them rides around the city. Similarly, burglary by a clique often has recreational aspects in the planning, risk, daring, and display of skill. Both the proceeds and the satisfaction of success are shared. Group vandalism also often takes on definite recreational features.

Individual delinquency runs through all social classes. Its relation to class subcultures has not been studied.

The Nondelinquent in the Delinquency Area

Even in areas of high delinquency rates, a minority of boys and many fewer girls than boys become seriously and persistently delinquent. Very little attention has been given to the reasons why some children do not become delinquent when many cultural and social pressures push children toward delinquency. Some light is gained from studies that compare delinquent and nondelinquent children.

ENVIRONMENTAL FACTORS

The comparison of delinquent children with an equal number of nondelinquent siblings, made by Healy and Bronner, emphasizes the importance of the different types of relationships that may exist between each child and his parents.[24] Even though outwardly the family appears to be the same for all the children, actually each child has his own special relationship with each parent. In general, in Healy's study the family background was not completely favorable: in 54 per cent of families there was serious disharmony between the parents and in only 30 per cent was the relationship between the parents distinctly harmonious. Nevertheless, even in the disharmonious families, some children were nondelinquent. The authors point to the need to consider the constitutional characteristics of each child and the relationship of each child to each parent. They state, ". . . for any single case any of the supposed influences have to be evaluated as they may or may not have affected the child's conduct. If this were not so, how does it happen that such a considerable pro-

[24] Healy and Bronner, *op. cit.*

portion of the children in these families do not become delinquent?"[25] One strong positive relationship may offset other negative relationships.

The material presented in Chapter 10, "The Family Setting of Delinquency," shows that nondelinquents more often than delinquents live in families that are unbroken, cohesive, warmly affectionate, and fair in discipline. The relationship with the mother is especially significant. Nevertheless, many delinquents come from homes with favorable family relationships and many nondelinquents come from homes with unfavorable ones. In the studies yielding these conclusions, it cannot be assumed that all children in the families represented by one delinquent member were delinquent, nor that all the siblings of the nondelinquent boys chosen for study were also nondelinquent. The favorable family conditions create a pressure toward nondelinquency; nevertheless, the specific family relationships for each child need to be taken into account, as Healy and Bronner pointed out.

The same reasoning applies to any given child's relationship with school or community. Individual clashes of personality and fortuitous experiences may be determining factors in the child's early turning toward delinquent or nondelinquent behavior. Even in those areas of a city where teachers find it most difficult to understand their students and where the traditional school program is least suited to the needs of students, some children find school a rewarding experience and continue until graduation. Friendly and understanding teachers, capable of teaching well, and curricula adapted to the needs of the children are positive forces against delinquency, but do not guarantee successful development of the child.

SELF-CONCEPTS

Based on the unique combination that each child has in temperament, family, peer group, school, and community relationships, he develops a self-concept as either delinquent or nondelinquent. This self-concept is the real key to the fully developed delinquent as well as the nondelinquent child.

The self-concept is social in origin, growing out of the child's perception of what others think about him. What they think varies greatly and is not always closely related to the child's behavior. Toward some children there are biased stereotyped attitudes—for example, the black is always shifty, the Jew is always grasping, the middle class person places material success above human values, and so on. Simply by being born into a certain biological or social group, a child may find a prejudiced self-concept thrust upon him. His

---

[25] Healy and Bronner, *op. cit.*, p. 33.

individual behavior is another factor that determines what others think of him and how they behave toward him.

In some communities that are highly unified in culture, the child may find a uniform set of attitudes toward him. He tends then to accept the self-concept offered to him, especially if it is a favorable one. Often, however, he finds that different people or different groups react differently to him. He has a choice of self-concepts and often wavers among them. This is the situation of the preadolescent school child who fluctuates between conformity and underconformity.

As the child finds certain self-concepts more rewarding to him, he tends to affiliate with the groups that approve of a given self-concept. It is often only in such a group that he is rewarded by approval and status. Other groups disapprove of him and project on him a different and unpleasant self-concept. This process goes on for both delinquent and nondelinquent children, until the preponderance of relationships of each is with groups that give him a self-satisfying self-concept. Those groups whose opinions become especially important are called reference groups.

ROLES

Self-concepts of all kinds are deeply influenced by social roles. The delinquent gang has a variety of roles, one of which each incoming member must assume if he is to become a functioning member of the group. Likewise, the nondelinquent finds roles waiting for him in various youth organizations and in school. The reactions of the group toward the member, his self-concept based on these reactions, and the roles he actually fills tend to fuse into one pattern that becomes highly satisfying to the member.

A person may have a number of self-concepts growing out of a number of different reference groups, each calling for different roles. For example, the good boy who conforms in school and who is active in church may also have a delinquent reference group. He does not have a consistent set of self-concepts. When the self-concepts merge into consistency, the person has a self-image or ego-identity that tends to become the standard by which he measures much of his behavior.[26] His groups also tend to become consistent, and he withdraws from groups that do not support the self-image. His roles are consistent with his self-image and with each other. With reference to delinquency, the extreme of this tendency is the underconforming contracultures.

[26] See Erik H. Erikson, "Identity and the Life Cycle," *Psychological Issues*, Vol. 1 (1959), especially Chapter 3.

The Development of Nondelinquent Self-concepts

In high delinquency areas it cannot be assumed that the nondelinquent is what one should expect, with the delinquent being the one whose behavior alone must be explained. So deep and pervasive are the pressures toward delinquency that the need arises to account for nondelinquency.

What "insulates" some—in fact, the majority—of boys in high delinquency areas from becoming delinquent? Especially, what accounts for consistently obedient boys, well adjusted in school and community? Reckless and Dinitz studied sixth-grade boys in Columbus, Ohio, to find answers to these questions.[27] Teachers of sixth-grade pupils in areas of highest delinquency rates were asked to classify the boys into three groups: those who they felt would never have trouble with police or courts, those who they felt sure would have, and ones about whom they were uncertain. Among these twelve-year-old boys, well below the peak delinquency age of sixteen, approximately half were classified as "good" and not headed for trouble, about 25 per cent as potential delinquents, and about 25 per cent as not showing clear tendencies in either direction.

The boys were given certain tests and questionnaires, and their mothers were also given tests and interviewed. Tests of delinquency tendencies and social responsibility confirmed the opinions of the teachers. Search of police and juvenile court records resulted in elimination of sixteen nondelinquent boys, since they had some type of record though never for a serious offense. The mothers or mother-substitutes of some boys could not be located. The final groups consisted of 125 "good" boys and 108 prospective delinquents, of whom 23 per cent already had records with police or court, some for serious offenses.

The data assembled revealed that the socio-economic status of nondelinquent and delinquency-prone boys was approximately the same. Home conditions differed, giving the usual picture of greater stability and cohesion and better parent-child relationships in the nondelinquent than in the potentially delinquent group. The researchers did not stop with this finding but probed deeper, with the following results:

1. Nondelinquents more often than delinquency-prone boys felt that their parents were concerned about them and were fair to them; they felt that their families were equal or superior to any other family. They also felt that family relationships were harmonious.

[27] This study has been discussed in a number of articles listed in the bibliography under the names of Reckless, Dinitz, or Scarpitti. It is briefly summarized in Walter C. Reckless, *The Crime Problem*, Appleton-Century Crofts, Inc., New York, 1960, pp. 346–353.

2. Parents of nondelinquent boys more often than parents of delinquency-prone boys supervised their sons, were interested in them, and felt that they were good boys and would never be in serious trouble with the police. They felt that their sons had selected good friends.
3. The nondelinquent boys regarded themselves as "good," did not believe they would ever have trouble with the police, and in fact avoided trouble at all costs. Few of their close friends had ever had any trouble with the police, and the boys said they would drop a friend who was headed for trouble.

In general, the delinquency-prone boys and their parents held views that were the opposite of the above.[28]

The conclusion drawn by Reckless and Dinitz is that the nondelinquent boys belonged to reference groups that defined them as good: family, school, peer groups. The boys not only played the role of good boy but had a self-image of themselves as good. Moreover, they were satisfied with their roles and their groups. They tended to avoid contacts and behavior that were not in accord with this self-image.

The next question that the researchers asked themselves was whether or not the self-image was well established at age twelve and would prevail during adolescence, when delinquency reached its height in the areas in which the boys lived. A follow-up study was made four years after the initial study when the average age of the boys was sixteen. Four of the previously nondelinquent boys had had encounters with the police, respectively for violation of curfew and drunkenness, malicious mischief, school truancy, and auto theft; only the last delinquency was referred by police to the juvenile court. The attitudes of the boys toward family, friends, and bad conduct remained almost identical with those held at age twelve. The self-image of being a good boy already established at age twelve held at age sixteen for 96 per cent of the boys.[29]

The Psychologically Disturbed Delinquent—Reckless makes the point that the good or poor self-image derived from significant reference groups does not apply to compulsive acting-out neurotics who become repeatedly involved in fire-setting, ritualistic stealing, exhibitionism, or peeping-tom activities. Other explanations must be sought for their often erratic behavior.

Many of these difficulties, however, have their origin in group contacts that have proved highly unsatisfactory or that have not socialized the child into a pattern of control, whether delinquent or nondelinquent.

[28] It should be noted that Hirschi found much the same pattern of relationships differentiating delinquents and nondelinquents. See Travis Hirschi, *op. cit.* Chapters 6 and 8.

[29] The follow-up group consisted of 103 boys; twenty-two of the original group could not be located.

The Critical Point in Juvenile Delinquency

From the point of view of adult crime, the most serious phase of juvenile delinquency does not come during the tumultuous period of adolescence, regardless of how much nuisance value the depredations of delinquency have for teachers, community, and the police. Only a minute proportion of delinquencies cause the loss of any large amount of property or serious injury or death to someone. The critical point in juvenile delinquency comes toward the end of the delinquency period when adolescents face the pattern of adult life. Will they become conventional citizens in the terms of their subculture, small-time criminals, individual professional criminals, or possibly members of highly organized criminal rackets or syndicates? The seeds for their choice are germinated during childhood and adolescence; but their choice also depends upon the easy availability of adult crime and contacts that may lead to association with adult criminals. The choice may not be deliberately made; boys may drift into adult criminal activities just as they drift into conventional jobs. They must have attitudes, however, that condone or support their choice and they must have criminal "job opportunities."

From the point of view of society, the probability of the lower class delinquent boy finding a "job opportunity" in crime is greater than the probability of the middle class boy. The middle class boy is more likely to be exposed to unethical or criminal practices after he becomes employed than when he is selecting an occupation, since many businessmen and corporations use questionable methods to avoid payment of taxes or to meet severe competition. The lower class delinquent therefore is more of a nuisance or threat to society during adolescence and more likely to be drawn into crime as an adult.

The gang boy is likely to build up attitudes and behavior that make him susceptible to adult criminal activities. The gang affords fertile ground for the growth of a delinquent contraculture. As the gang becomes detached from conventional lower class society it builds up its own delinquent codes and customs; its own systems of rewards and punishments; its own little social world. As gangs gain status and prestige in any particular area they attract other boys and quickly pass on to them the contraculture. Gangs that have an age-graded structure quite deliberately induct the younger boys into the codes, delinquent skills, and personal habits of the gang.

Boys identify themselves with the gang and do not respond to individual approaches from teachers or social workers. To leave the gang would often mean both social and emotional isolation for the boy, and would require a self-confidence and self-sufficiency that most of the boys do not have. For this reason social workers sometimes make an appeal to the entire gang, seeking to convert it into a club of the conventional athletic or social type.

The danger point to society from the gang as a whole comes at the point where the gang has cut itself off from acceptance of conventional ethical and moral values and has developed contravalues which not only differ from but are opposed to conventional values. Few gangs reach an extreme point in this process; those which do are almost immune to efforts to bring them back to acceptance of conventional values. In the delinquent contraculture, boys not only act in a delinquent manner but conceive of themselves as tough, hard, and superior to boys who endure the limitations of conformity, hard work, and the pursuit of future goals.

The emotionally disturbed adolescent may continue his delinquencies, falling as an adult into one of several types, the ne'er-do-well, the drunkard or drug addict, or the compulsive or violent criminal. What eventually becomes of him depends upon the tolerance of the community, the seriousness of his threat to society, and the availability of special facilities for treating him.

BIBLIOGRAPHY

BERNSTEIN, SAUL, *Alternatives to Violence, Alienated Youth and Riots, Race, and Poverty*, Association Press, New York, 1967.

CAVAN, RUTH SHONLE, ed., *Readings in Juvenile Delinquency, Third Edition*, J. B. Lippincott Company, Philadelphia, 1975.

CLOWARD, RICHARD A., AND LLOYD E. OHLIN, *Delinquency and Opportunity*, Free Press of Glencoe, Inc., New York, 1960.

COHEN, ALBERT K., *Delinquent Boys, The Culture of the Gang*, Free Press of Glencoe, Inc., New York, 1955.

CRAIG, MAUDE M., AND LAILA A. BUDD, "The Juvenile Offender: Recidivism and Companions," *Crime and Delinquency*, 13, No. 2 (1967), 344–351.

DAWLEY, DAVID, *A Nation of Lords*, Anchor Books, New York, 1973.

DINITZ, SIMON, WALTER C. RECKLESS, AND BARBARA KAY, "A Self Gradient among Potential Delinquents," *Journal of Criminal Law, Criminology and Police Science*, 49 (1958), 230–233.

Journal of Research in Crime and Delinquency, 4 (January, 1967), entire issue.

KEISER, R. LINCOLN, *The Vice Lords*, Holt, Rinehart and Winston, New York, 1969.

KLEIN, MALCOLM W., ed., *Juvenile Gangs in Context*, Prentice-Hall, Inc., Englewood Cliffs, N. J., 1967.

KLEIN, MALCOLM, *Street Gangs and Street Workers*, Prentice-Hall, Inc., Englewood Cliffs, N. J., 1971.

MILLER, WALTER B., "The Impact of a Community Group Work Program on Delinquent Corner Groups," *Social Service Review*, 31 (December 1957), 390–406.

————, "Lower Class Culture as a Generating Milieu of Gang Delinquency," *Journal of Social Issues*, 14, No. 3 (1958), 5–19.

————, "Violent Crimes in City Gangs," *Annals of the American Academy of Political and Social Science*, 364 (1966), 96–112.

Reaching the Fighting Gang, New York City Youth Board, New York, 1960.

RECKLESS, WALTER C., SIMON DINITZ, AND BARBARA KAY, "The Self-Component in Potential Delinquency and Potential Non-delinquency," *American Sociological Review*, 22 (1957), 566–570.

————, "Pioneering with Self-Concept as a Vulnerability Factor in Delinquency," *Journal of Criminal Law, Criminology and Police Science*, 58 (1967), 515–523.

————, AND ELLEN MURRAY, "Self Concept as an Insulator against Delinquency," *American Sociological Review*, 21 (1956), 744–746.

————, "The 'Good' Boy in a High Delinquency Area," *Journal of Criminal Law, Criminology and Police Science*, 48 (1957), 18–25.

Report of the National Advisory Commission on Civil Disorders, Bantam Books, New York, 1968.

Riot Participation Study: Juvenile Offenders, Los Angeles (County) Probation Department, Los Angeles, California, 1965.

SCARPITTI, FRANK R., ELLEN MURRAY, SIMON DINITZ, AND WALTER C. RECKLESS, "The 'Good' Boy in a High Delinquency Area: Four Years Later," *American Sociological Review*, 25 (1957), 555–558.

SHORT, JAMES F., JR., ed., *Gang Delinquency and Delinquent Subcultures*,

————, AND FRED L. STRODTBECK, *Group Process and Gang Delinquency*, University of Chicago Press, Chicago, 1965.

SPERGEL, IRVING, *Racketville, Slumtown, Haulburg*, University of Chicago Press, Chicago, 1964.

SYKES, GRESHAM M., AND DAVID MATZA, "Techniques of Neutralization: A Theory of Delinquency," *American Sociological Review*, 22 (1957), 644–670.

THRASHER, FREDERIC M., *The Gang*, University of Chicago Press, Chicago, 1927, revised 1963.

YABLONSKY, LEWIS, "The Delinquent Gang as a Near-Group," *Social Problems*, 7 (Fall, 1959), 108–117.

————, *The Violent Gang*, Penguin Books, Baltimore, 1966.

typologies
of delinquency

A great deal of interest has developed in recent years in typologies of delinquency. There is consensus now that there are many different types of delinquency, each with its own particular set of causal factors as well as its own distinctive cluster of characteristics. Criminologists are generally agreed that it is a mistake to treat the problem as if all delinquents were alike, and it is widely acknowledged that a valid, comprehensive typology is badly needed. But there is no consensus regarding the manner in which these typologies are to be constructed or the function they are to fulfill. And as the number of typologies has multiplied, the level of agreement has declined.

Some have attempted to build typologies based on empirical observation, but they have concerned themselves with only a narrow slice of all possible characteristics, and they have come up with a picture of delinquency that ignores certain important features of the problem. Gibbons, for example, defined nine behavioral patterns commonly found among delinquents—predatory gang delinquent; conflict gang delinquent; casual gang delinquent; casual delinquent, nongang member; automobile thief—joyrider; drug user—heroin; overly aggressive delinquent; female delinquent; and behavioral problem delinquent.[1] He described these nine patterns in terms of their interactional setting, self-concept, attitudes, role-career, social class, family background, peer group

[1] Don C. Gibbons, *Changing the Lawbreaker*, Prentice-Hall, Inc., Englewood Cliffs, N.J., 1965, Chapter 3.

associations, and contact with defining agencies.[2] Unfortunately, he neglected to mention any personality patterns that the different types exhibit, and missed, therefore, a crucial dimension of behavior. Emotional and motivational patterns are a central factor in behavior, and a complete description of behavior must focus on these characteristics as well as the social and social psychological ones mentioned by Gibbons.[3]

But sociologists are not the only ones guilty of using an overly narrow perspective in describing delinquency. Sheldon and Eleanor Glueck, the deans of American delinquency research, have proposed several typologies of delinquency based upon their comprehensive study of five hundred institutionalized delinquents. Nowhere, however, do the Gluecks describe the offense patterns exhibited by their several types. A survey of the characteristics of delinquents must certainly consider the kinds of offenses they commit, because the kinds of offenses are one of the key dimensions of their delinquency. Empirical typologies such as the Gluecks have proposed must be reasonably comprehensive if they are to serve adequately as a basis for theorizing about the nature and causes of delinquency.

Others have attempted to define a typology of delinquency by distilling the implications of social or psychological theories into succinct descriptions of distinctive delinquent patterns. Such theoretically based typologies have been described as ideal typologies (after Weber's ideal type), because they are basically conceptual in form and origin.[4] They are limited more by the restrictions of logic and theory than anything else. They make no pretence at describing all aspects of delinquent behavior, because theories about delinquency themselves necessarily are limited by the nature of their assumptions and their analytic level. Ideal typologies, therefore, are inevitably limited in scope. But since their function is not to describe delinquency, but rather to provide testable hypotheses regarding its nature, their limited scope is not a serious defect.

We have already considered two good examples of ideal typologies of

---

[2] *Ibid.*, Chapter 2.

[3] Gibbons explains his failure to focus on personality patterns of offenders by citing the fact that few personality patterns have been shown to be associated specifically with the delinquent behavioral patterns he identifies. See *ibid.*, pp. 61–73. He apparently ignores the fact that offenders with different kinds of personality patterns become involved in the delinquent roles he describes, just as different kinds of people become professors. In both cases the fact that there are no constant personality correlates of the role in question does not mean that personality factors do not affect the manner in which the incumbent enacts the role.

[4] See Theodore N. Ferdinand, *Typologies of Delinquency*, Random House, New York, 1966, Chapter 3; and Arthur Wood, "Ideal and Empirical Typologies for Research in Deviance and Control," *Sociology and Social Research*, 53 (January, 1969), 227–241.

delinquency. In Chapter 5 we described a typology of delinquency developed by Marguerite Warren and her co-workers on the basis of a psychological theory of interpersonal maturity. Included in her typology were ten patterns: Asocial Aggressive, Asocial Passive, Immature Conformist, Cultural Conformist, Manipulator, Acting out Neurotic, Anxious Neurotic, Stress Reactions, Adjustment Reactions, and Cultural Identifiers. Although this typology has been exhaustively studied and subsequently modified to reflect the results of careful research, it was initially a statement regarding the patterns of delinquency that were to be expected, if the theory of interpersonal maturity were correct.

In Chapter 6 we also considered briefly an ideal typology developed by Richard Cloward and Lloyd Ohlin on the basis of the sociological theory of anomie and Sutherland's theory of differential association.[5] Cloward and Ohlin suggested that three distinct delinquent subcultures should emerge based upon the ways in which individual adolescents interact with the opportunity structures of the community: criminal, conflict, and retreatist subcultures, each of which in turn gives rise to a delinquent gang with its own distinctive values and pattern of delinquency. Cloward and Ohlin's theory of delinquency does not pretend to explain all facets of delinquent behavior, and accordingly their typology of delinquent subcultures is far from comprehensive. But it does provide a succinct, testable statement about delinquency which was drawn from two extensive bodies of theory regarding deviancy, and as such it serves a very important purpose. It is to Cloward and Ohlin's credit that their typology inspired a large number of empirical studies of delinquency.

But as useful as their typology is in checking the value of certain theories, it is of little value in predicting how specific youngsters will act. It cannot explain their behavior, because we need to know their psychological predispositions in addition to their subcultural orientation to suggest how they will behave. But their typology does provide some insight into the causal factors behind three distinctive delinquent patterns, and because it is theoretically based, their recommendations for prevention or control go beyond the simplicities of common sense.

Cloward and Ohlin's typology of delinquency illustrates both the strengths and the weaknesses of ideal typologies. Because they are based on limited theoretical perspectives, they present a circumscribed analysis of delinquency. They can neither describe how delinquents actually behave, nor suggest

---

[5] Richard C. Cloward and Lloyd E. Ohlin, *Delinquency and Opportunity*, Free Press of Glencoe, New York, 1960.

their characteristics as implied by other theoretical viewpoints. But since they are theoretically based, they can provide considerable insight into the causes of delinquency, and they can yield suggestions regarding prevention and control that get to the heart of the matter.

We suggested earlier that there is little agreement regarding the functions that typologies of delinquency are to serve. We can now appreciate the mischief such confusion creates by returning again to Gibbons' typology.[6] There is much of value in Gibbons' typology, and we will cite his work elsewhere in support of our own analysis. We single his typology out at this point only for illustrative purposes.

His typology is obviously an empirical typology, since it is drawn more from empirical observation than from any specific theory of delinquency. But it is used primarily as a prescription for treating the several types it identifies. Without a systematic theory to identify and explain the factors behind delinquency, it is hard to see how any recommendations for treatment can be much more than common sense. Had Gibbons developed an ideal typology and based it more completely upon theory, his comments would carry more weight, but there is nothing in an empirical typology that implies how the patterns of delinquency it reveals can be changed.

For all their analytic power, however, the narrow focus of ideal typologies points up the need for a third kind of typology, one that retains the advantages of a theoretical foundation without the limited perspective that that implies. Such a typology of delinquency should reflect all the theories that are relevant to the problem, but at the same time it should fit them together so that they are applicable to the actions of specific delinquents. Such a typology (we might label it a synthetic typology because it blends together different viewpoints) should present the strengths of ideal and empirical typologies while avoiding their weaknesses.[7] We shall proffer the outline of a synthetic typology of delinquency at the conclusion of this chapter.

A Synthetic Typology of Delinquency

In order to construct a synthetic typology of delinquency, we must, first, deal with two questions: What are the ideal typologies that are relevant to delinquent behavior? and, What is the specific methodology for constructing synthetic typologies of behavior? Let us examine each question in detail.

[6] Gibbons, op. cit., Chapters 3 and 6.

[7] For a detailed description of synthetic typologies see Ferdinand, op. cit., pp. 55–70 and Chapter 6.

Sociological Typologies of Delinquency

There are, of course, a great variety of ideal typologies that are highly relevant to delinquency. But here we shall concern ourselves primarily with those which deal with the social side of delinquency.

It is difficult to organize sociological typologies of delinquency systematically because our theories of delinquency are largely of the middle range. They encompass only a few aspects of the social environment relevant to delinquency, and consequently there is very little commonality among the typologies they suggest. Nevertheless, three distinct kinds of sociological approaches to delinquency can be discerned: those which relate delinquency to broad societal or cultural pressures; those which relate it to individual offender roles; and those which relate it to gang roles. Each viewpoint singles out a significant segment of the delinquent's environment and tries to explain his behavior in terms of social processes deriving therefrom. Our task here is to describe each approach in detail, and to blend them all into a single typological statement regarding the social patterns of delinquency.

Sociologists have been interested in the relationship between deviancy and broad societal or cultural pressures since at least the time of Karl Marx. In a certain sense deviancy is a paradox to sociologists because it is difficult to explain how a society or a community that can muster immense, pervasive pressures to conformity could at the same time actively encourage significant amounts of deviancy with these same conforming pressures. If we ignore the obvious fact that there are bound to be eccentric individuals from time to time who have difficulty conforming to any but a very permissive code of behavior, it is difficult to explain deviancy purely in terms of social processes which are organized basically to produce conformity and *contain* deviancy.

SUBCULTURAL PATTERNS OF DELINQUENCY

One of the most successful attempts thus far, by Richard Cloward and Lloyd Ohlin, is that discussed briefly above. Let us examine their theory now in greater detail. They suggest basically that delinquency is encouraged when adolescents find it difficult to realize their ambitions via legitimate opportunities because of cultural and structural barriers which prevent most lower class members from achieving goals that members of higher classes realize almost routinely. Cloward and Ohlin hold that ". . . widespread tendencies toward delinquent practices in the lower class are modes of adaptation to structured strains and inconsistencies toward the social order."[8]

But structural strains are not enough to inspire delinquency on a broad

[8] Cloward and Ohlin, *op. cit.*, p. 106.

scale. There must be in addition positive pressures toward delinquency. Socio-cultural strains merely pose an adjustment problem; they do not provide a delinquent solution, which must come from other sources. Cloward and Ohlin propose that the push *toward* delinquency arises basically in illegitimate op-portunities which all communities provide in more or less degree.[9] In working class communities where there is a close integration between adults and young people, and between the criminal underworld and conventional segments of the community, many youngsters are acquainted early with a wide range of criminal activities, and a delinquent subculture specializing in criminal activi-ties tends to develop. In the absence of such subcultures and of legitimate opportunities, the community tends to evolve a conflict subculture, and illegit-imate opportunities in this area are relatively open to youngsters seeking a solution to their adjustment problems. Finally, Cloward and Ohlin suggest that those adolescents who are denied access to both legitimate and illegitimate opportunities will tend to evolve a retreatist subculture specializing in drugs. Thus, Cloward and Ohlin propose a threefold typology of delinquency which focuses essentially on the norms and values of delinquents and not upon their behavior.

Despite the care with which Cloward and Ohlin ground their typology of delinquency in theories of community organization and differential opportu-nity, two important gaps remain. Many lower class neighborhoods are well integrated and exhibit few if any established criminal groups in their midst. Thus, Cloward and Ohlin fail to indicate the type of subcultural delinquency that is likely to arise in many lower class communities, and, of course, they ignore the middle and upper classes altogether.

To fill these gaps we must turn to other theorists. As indicated in Chap-ter 6, Walter B. Miller proposes that delinquency arises in many lower class communities because it is a natural outgrowth of the focal concerns of lower class culture.[10] According to Miller, lower class males place great stress upon toughness and masculinity; conmanship; thrills, risk, and danger; autonomy; the importance of fate; and coping effectively with trouble. It is easy to see how a youngster who lived by this code might on occasion commit delinquent acts. Assaultive behavior, for example, and many forms of dangerous but thrilling behavior (which would include a variety of criminal acts) should be prominent in the typical lower class youngster's repertory of behavior.

Although Miller has considerable insight into the nature of lower class

[9] *Ibid.*, Chapters 5 and 6.

[10] Walter B. Miller, "Lower Class Culture as a Generating Milieu of Gang Delin-quency," *Journal of Social Issues*, 14 (Fall, 1958), 5–19.

delinquency, he nevertheless has failed to distinguish between working class and lower class focal concerns.[11] For example, the working class individual is more aggressive and independent than the typical lower class member; hence, an emphasis upon toughness, autonomy, and excitement is probably more typical of the former than of the latter. The lower class individual, however, is more interested in gaining his ends through guile and deception and in avoiding trouble; hence, the focal concerns of the lower class emphasize more the importance of conmanship and trouble. Naturally, these distinctions will be reflected in the patterns of delinquency found in the two classes, and accordingly it would appear that the fighting and criminal gangs mentioned by Cloward and Ohlin would tend to be working class but that the retreatist gang would tend to be lower in origin.[12]

A fourth variant, which Cloward and Ohlin fail to mention, but which is also an important pattern of delinquency, is the theft subculture described by Spergel.[13] According to Spergel the theft subculture is essentially a variation on a more general working class delinquent subculture in which a variety of delinquent acts, including several types of theft, is pursued. In contrast to the fighting and criminal subcultures, this pattern is notable for the mild character of its delinquency. Indeed, this theft subculture is so integrally a part of adolescent, working class life that it is difficult to separate the two.

Moving on to the middle and upper classes, as noted in Chapter 6, Ferdinand has proposed an aggressive-exploitative pattern of subcultural delinquency in the upper-middle class and a mischievous indulgent pattern in the upper-upper class.[14] Based upon an emphasis in the upper-middle class on competition through sexual adventures and athletic adroitness, he proposes that a variety of sexual deviancies and aggressive conflicts interlaced with more

---

[11] Several authors have commented on the character of lower class life. See, for example, Michael Harrington, *The Other America*, Macmillan, New York, 1963, pp. 133–137; and Michael Schwartz and George Henderson, "The Culture of Unemployment," in *Blue Collar World*, Arthur B. Shostak and William Gomberg, eds., Prentice-Hall, Inc., Englewood Cliffs, N.J., 1964, pp. 459–468.

For a description of the working class, see S. M. Miller and Frank Riessman, "The Working Class Subculture: A New View," *Social Problems*, 9 (1961), 86–97.

[12] See for example, the description of an addict subculture in Albert K. Cohen and James F. Short, Jr., "Research in Delinquent Subcultures," *Journal of Social Issues*, 14 (1958), 26–27. There are, of course, many addict gangs composed of middle class adolescents. But these gangs are not explainable simply in terms of middle class values.

[13] Irving Spergel, *Racketville, Slumtown, Haulburg*, University of Chicago Press, Chicago, 1964, Chapters II and III. For other studies of theft in gangs see Cohen and Short, *op. cit.*, pp. 27–28; and Walter B. Miller, "Theft Behavior in City Gangs," in *Juvenile Gangs in Context*, Malcolm M. Klein, ed., Prentice-Hall, Inc., Englewood Cliffs, N.J., 1967, pp. 25–37.

[14] Ferdinand, *op. cit.*, pp. 96–100.

conventional behavior will be typical of teen-agers in this class. Ordinarily, however, their delinquency will not be institutionalized in the form of delinquent gangs. And in the upper-upper class Ferdinand suggests that a mild pattern of drug and alcoholic abuse together with sexual indulgences and theft will occur among teen-agers on the basis of a quest for style and a rejection of an ascetic code of morality.

Essentially, then, we have identified six distinct patterns of subcultural delinquency based upon the organization of the community and the cultural forms of its several social classes: a lower class retreatist subculture; working class fighting, criminal, and theft subcultures; an upper-middle class aggressive-exploitative subculture; and an upper-upper class mischievous-indulgent subculture. These patterns of subcultural delinquency will form the framework of our social typology of delinquency.

DELINQUENT ROLES

Another aspect of delinquency that has received some attention among sociologists is the delinquent roles that are available to juveniles. Not only do social classes provide cultural support and encouragement for delinquent behavior, but so, too, do a number of specific roles which involve them directly in delinquent activity. To understand the behavior of some delinquents, therefore, it is necessary to consider these roles and their links with the broader social structure.

Gibbons' typology, which we have already examined, should be of some value here because in his typology he focuses on nine "role-types" that are often followed by delinquents.[15] Three of his role-types, however, are most relevant to a discussion of gang roles, i.e., predatory gang delinquent, conflict gang delinquent, and casual gang delinquent; and four others are delinquent patterns that are not role-defined at all, namely, the casual delinquent, nongang member; the overly aggressive delinquent; the female delinquent; and the behavioral problem delinquent. The latter four patterns are governed more by personal idiosyncrasies—as Gibbons himself clearly indicates—than by role prescriptions, and hence, should not be considered here.[16] Nevertheless, Gibbons does present two independent delinquent roles that we should examine: the drug user and the automobile thief. In addition to these we shall also describe five other delinquent roles: robbery, vandalism, shoplifting, burglary, and sex offenses.

DRUG USERS. The role of the drug user clearly illustrates how a delinquent

15 Gibbons, op. cit., pp. 75–100.
16 Ibid., pp. 85–88, 92–97.

role can draw the incumbent into more serious crimes, and quickly transform the nondelinquent into a delinquent with a strong criminal commitment. The basis of the drug user is found in a vast network of dealers and pushers who can and will supply virtually any kind of illicit narcotic at handsome profits. There are, therefore, very strong incentives urging drug pushers to involve young people in drug use, and this fact in combination with the avant garde spirit of the young today makes the drug user role a common one in America.

There are several features of the drug user's role that involve him inexorably in increasingly serious criminal acts. Drug use itself is illegal, and becoming a drug user necessarily involves the individual in criminal activity. But beyond this obvious fact drug use also develops a momentum that propels the individual to more serious patterns of drug use and into other types of criminality.[17] For example, the individual who begins with marijuana often makes connections with pushers who could also supply him with heroin and other addictive drugs, if he should want them. Indeed, it is not unusual for pushers to give free samples to show the potential user his "wares." Marijuana, of course, is not addictive and few users develop a compulsion for it. Moreover, there is no necessary progression from marijuana to hard drugs. But the fact remains that it is nearly as easy for a user to get heroin and other hard drugs as it is to get marijuana, and if he should become addicted to hard drugs, the deadly drama unfolds quite predictably.

As his habit matures, the drug user often finds that he needs an increasing supply and, therefore, more money. And if his habit outruns his income, he is obliged to turn to burglary, larceny, or pushing (or, if a girl, to prostitution) to augment his income and keep himself adequately supplied. Thus, the heavy drug user typically finds his role as a drug user conveying him onto other more serious criminal roles.

Not only does drug use throw the individual into contact with a variety of other criminals, but it also cuts him off from friends and relatives who might influence him toward other more legitimate roles.[18] Even if he should avoid arrest, he becomes secretive and suspicious of their motives toward him. He hides his addiction and resents their well-meaning efforts to steer him in other directions. He blocks them off, and as they become alarmed, he retreats even

---

[17] For an excellent description of this process, see Thomas M. Quinn, "The Impact of Law on the Heroin Distribution System, the Addict and the Community," Institute for Social Research, Fordham University, New York, 1971. See also James Inciardi, "Unreported Criminal Involvement of Narcotic Addicts," paper presented at the thirty-fourth annual meeting of the Southern Sociological Society, May, 1971; and John A. O'Donnell, "Narcotic Addiction and Crime," *Social Problems*, 13 (Spring, 1966), 374–85.

[18] See David Matza, *Becoming Deviant*, Prentice-Hall, Inc., Englewod Cliffs, N.J., 1969, for a graphic description of this process.

further. The drug user avoids, thereby, the threat of discovery but also all social influence that might divert him from his self-destructive path. Thus, being a drug user forces the individual into a situation where other types of serious delinquency become almost inevitable.

Drug abuse is clearly greatest in the more urban regions of the society.[19] For example, both in the West (particularly in California) and in the Northeast (particularly in lower New England and New York) marijuana use among recent high school graduates approaches 50 per cent, and the use of hallucinogens and amphetamines is also substantially higher in these two regions than in other areas of the country. In the South and the Midwest the use of drugs by high school graduates is only about half as common as in the two regions named above. Similarly, about 53 per cent of recent high school graduates in cities with population of 300,000 or more use marijuana to some extent, but in rural areas the rate is less than half as great—24 per cent. Thus, urbanicity and drug abuse seem to go hand in hand.

Adolescent Drug Users and Addicts—Addiction is defined as: "(1) an overpowering desire or need (compulsion) to continue taking the drug; (2) a tendency to increase the dose; (3) a psychological and sometimes a physical dependence on the effects of the drug."[20] When the user becomes dependent upon the drug, he must constantly increase the amount taken in order to achieve the same effect that resulted earlier from a small quantity. Thus he enters upon a spiral from which there is no easy release. But not all adolescent drug users become addicts. In areas of heavy usage knowledge and folklore about narcotic drugs is widespread. Many boys begin the use as an experiment in new experiences or as sharing of a social activity with others. They may never become addicts, but may confine the use of drugs to the weekends, when social activities are most prevalent. For example, a study of 305 members of eighteen New York gangs, known for their active participation in intergang fights, showed that ninety-four used heroin more or less regularly. Only 43 per cent of the heroin users, however, took the drug daily and thereby qualified as addicts. The other 57 per cent of users were casual or "weekend" users. They did not become dependent on the drug nor find it necessary to increase the dosage. Their usage was a social activity. The drugs available to adolescents have often been diluted to such an extent that they are not completely habit-

[19] Lloyd Johnson, *Drugs and American Youth*, Institute for Social Research, Ann Arbor, 1973, pp. 93–100.

[20] This is the definition agreed upon by the World Health Organization's Expert Committee on Drugs Liable to Produce Addiction, Report on the Second Session (1950) cited in Roma K. McNickle, "Drug Addiction," *Editorial Research Reports*, 1 (March 28, 1951), 223.

forming. Casual users therefore have a chance to decrease or stop the practice without suffering excruciating physical pains.[21]

Many adolescent users begin their experiment with drugs through smoking marijuana cigarettes (reefers), usually in company with a few friends. From this practice they may graduate to the use of heroin (horse), a drug that is a derivative of opium. Typically, the boy begins by sniffing the drug up his nose (snorting); he moves from this to injecting the drug subcutaneously (skin popping); and finally he injects it intravenously (shooting the main line). By this time he usually is an addict (hooked), or has "the habit."

Addiction and Boys' Gangs—The majority of boys in typical delinquent and fighting gangs are not addicts, although some may be weekend users of small amounts of drug. In general, gangs exert pressure against the use of drugs by their members, and users do not try to induce their brother-members to use drugs nor try to sell drugs to them. Any proselytizing that they do is with nonmembers. However, drug usage is often begun in a little group of friends.[22]

Gang members feel that the addict is unreliable. He cannot be depended upon to carry out his role and if arrested may easily be induced to confess gang exploits by withholding the drug. Since addicts often become involved in serious attempts to steal, they are more likely to be arrested than are other boys.

If the addict has previously had a place of leadership in the gang, he usually loses it as his addiction increases. Many users are not leaders, however. They may be fringe members, who may take drugs first in an effort to increase their prestige. The long-run effect is to lower it.

As addicts lose status in the gang and find their interests deviating from those of other members, they tend to form smaller cliques within the gang and eventually to withdraw, either because other members mature and branch out into adult pursuits or because they find themselves more comfortable among a group of addicts. In the clique they can share their beliefs and follow their practices without criticism or feelings of guilt.

The Outcome of Addiction—It is generally agreed by those who work with addicts that physical withdrawal of the drug is not the whole answer.

[21] Daniel M. Wilner, Eva Rosenfeld, Robert S. Lee, Donald L. Gerard, and Isidor Chein, "Heroin Use and Street Gangs," *Journal of Criminal Law, Criminology and Police Science*, 48 (1957), 399–409. The article is one of a series from a study sponsored by the National Institute of Mental Health.

[22] Isidor Chein, "Narcotics Use Among Juveniles," *Social Work*, 1 (April, 1956), 50–60.

Among adolescent boys, those who use it casually seem to be able to control their demand without becoming addicts who are constantly impelled to increase the amount taken. They may voluntarily seek admission to a hospital for treatment. If their gang has few addicts, their friends may attempt to help them give up the habit.

The true addicts are in a more dangerous situation. Their physical addiction is often complicated by deep-seated psychological problems, held in abeyance by the drug but reappearing when the drug is not used. The supposedly cured addict soon relapses into his former habits. Because of the dependence on the drug and its availability, addicts can rarely be cured while they remain in their own neighborhoods. They must be removed and hospitalized where they cannot secure the drug and where psychiatric as well as physical treatment can be provided.

Addicts who are not voluntarily admitted to special hospitals—that is, who are committed by the courts—do not readily respond to the opportunity for therapy. The drug has become a sure way to escape from frustrations and tensions; therapy seems uncertain and involves facing the problems they have been avoiding. Unless the therapist can secure the addict's cooperation, help him face and solve his problems, and achieve the maturity to face them alone after he leaves the hospital, he is not cured. The fact that he has had no drugs over a period of several months means nothing when he is released and returns to his old environment, friends, and problems. Among those who have had physical withdrawal alone, 90 per cent return to drug use.

The cooperative addict finds the hospital a place of refuge where his need for protection from stresses is met. He can gather strength within the hospital and learn to meet the low-level demands made there before he returns to independence and his old stresses. Even so, he may relapse and return several times before he can forego drugs.

The adolescent addict who is not cured faces a hapless future. He becomes more helpless in solving his problems and in holding a job. He turns to petty crime as an answer. He accepts intermittent jail sentences and the pains of quick drug withdrawal as an inevitable part of life. Sometimes repetition of these experiences forces him to admit his addiction and his low status in society in general. He may or may not seek a cure.

Patterns of Drug Use—There has been considerable research recently into the patterns of drug use among high school students and young adults, and these studies indicate that the large majority of teen-agers have never tried any drugs other than alcohol or cigarettes. In 1970 in a nation-wide sample of 1,700 high school youths, Johnson found that 79.3 per cent of the students had never used marijuana or any other drug, and more recently in a sample of 2,921 teen-agers in Illinois, Rivera *et al.* found that 78 per cent had never tried drugs.[23] Moreover, the percentage of young people who use drugs regularly is very small. For example, Johnson reported that only 9.5 per cent of his sample used marijuana more than once or twice a month, and Rivera *et al.* found that only 7 per cent of their sample reported more than an experimental use of drugs.

There is, however, a substantial increase in the use of marijuana immediately after high school, mainly due to entrance into the military or college.[24] Of those who were nonusers in high school, 21 per cent of those in the military had become drug users within a year after high school graduation, and 13 per cent had become users of hard drugs. In college comparable figures for those who had been nonusers in high school were 22 per cent and 8 per cent respectively. Those who entered employment after high school showed the least likelihood of becoming drug users. Only 11 per cent of nonusers in high school became drug users after going to work, and only 2 per cent became users of hard narcotics.

Membership in the contraculture also strongly affects the level of drug use. Those who disagreed with America's Vietnam policy in 1970, who were politically alienated, and who had a strong preference for hard rock music were also much more likely to use drugs than those who did not.[25] Although delinquency is also closely associated with drug use, there is very little overlap among delinquents and those in the contraculture. Apparently, the two groups constitute two distinct populations of drug users.

ROBBERY. Robbery is another form of delinquency that adolescents occasionally attempt. The juvenile robber, however, displays a distinctive pattern that quickly identifies him as an inexperienced apprentice in comparison with more advanced adult robbers.[26] The professional robber typically decides upon his target well in advance (usually a large store or office with sizable amounts of money readily available); he recruits a team of specialists to fulfill the various roles needed in a robbery of a large store; he identifies the protective devices utilized by the owners of the store and develops a plan to neutralize them; he gathers together the necessary weapons and automobiles; he surveys

---

[23] Johnson, *op. cit.*, p. 20; and Ramon J. Rivera, *et al.*, "Patterns of Delinquency," unpublished paper presented at the Annual Meetings of the Society for the Study of Social Problems, 1973, Table 10.

[24] Johnson, *op. cit.*, p. 158.

[25] *Ibid.*, Chapter 7.

[26] John Conklin, *Robbery and the Criminal Justice System*, J. B. Lippincott Co., Philadelphia, 1972, Chapters 4, 6, 7 and 8. See also Everett DeBaun, "The Heist: The Theory and Practice of Armed Robbery," *Harper's Magazine* (February, 1950), 69–77.

the traffic patterns near the target and maps his escape route, and he often goes through a dress rehearsal—all this before he actually sets out on the robbery.

The juvenile robber, on the other hand, makes little if any preparation. Typically, he decides simply to survey a street or park to see if a potential victim presents himself. If one does, he reacts accordingly. He rarely carries a weapon (he is subject to arrest if searched by a police officer), nor does he plan a specific escape route. Much of his action is opportunistic in that it is designed to exploit whatever circumstances present themselves, but he does little to arrange circumstances to his benefit as the professional robber almost always does. Because his victims are weak and ineffectual, he is rarely caught, but his loot is relatively small (rarely exceeding $100); his victims often put up some resistance; and he is forced to react violently, often injuring his victims in the process.

The police and courts tend to regard robbery as a very serious offense, and in spite of their amateur status juveniles are often severely dealt with by juvenile judges, particularly when their victims are seriously injured. Thus, since juvenile robbers stand a good chance of being arrested for their offense if they persist at it, it tends to result in their becoming further involved in the criminal justice system and further socialized into the subculture of delinquency.

THE AUTO THIEF. The auto thief is another role that many juveniles are attracted to. The auto has assumed a unique significance in American life, and its rich symbolic meanings are not lost on American adolescents. It is a symbol of social status; of masculine potency; of emancipation from parental control; and as such it exercises an extraordinary fascination for many adolescents and adults as well. In response to the magnetic appeal of a flashy sports-car not a few adolescents drive one away at the first opportunity.

Although many teen-age car thieves commit other types of delinquent acts, a sizable number specialize almost exclusively in auto theft.[27] These delinquents fall into a rather distinctive pattern.[28] They are less seriously anti-social, and they are generally better adjusted in school, in their families, and with their peers than other types of delinquents. They are likely to be white,

[27] See "Hearings before the Subcommittee to Investigate Juvenile Delinquency, Part 18, Auto Theft and Juvenile Delinquency," U.S. Government Printing Office, Washington, D.C., 1968, pp. 4014–4026.

[28] William W. Wattenberg and James Balistrieri, "Automobile Theft: A 'Favored Group' Delinquency," *American Journal of Sociology*, 57 (1952), 575–583, and Erwin Schepses, "Boys Who Steal Cars," *Federal Probation*, 25 (1961), 56–62.

and they come from a higher economic stratum than other delinquents—although the significance of these latter facts is far from clear.

It may be that higher-status adolescents respond more intensely to the symbolic temptations of the auto. But it may also be that lower status adolescents simply have less opportunity to learn how to drive and, therefore, are less inclined to steal a car.

Rivera *et al.* in the research reported earlier throw some light on this question.[29] They report that auto violations were strongly associated with small town residence in their study of 2,921 teen-agers in Illinois. For adolescents, regardless of sex or race, the smaller the city, the greater the likelihood of involvement in auto violations including auto theft and stripping and selling auto parts. It would seem that the auto plays a more central role in the life of the small town adolescent, and as a result auto thefts are more common there than in the metropolitan center.

The most serious implication of the role of the car thief for juveniles is the risk it contains for a high speed police chase in an unfamiliar car.[30] Not a few adolescents are killed every year in such chases, and even if the adolescent escapes being killed himself, he stands a good chance of killing someone else and being charged with involuntary manslaughter. Otherwise, the prospect of becoming involved in serious crimes is not great for the typical auto thief, since he is not drawn to other types of delinquents, and even in training schools he is likely to make a good adjustment and be discharged from aftercare without further serious difficulty.[31]

VANDALISM. Vandalism is a fourth type of role open to juvenile delinquents. It emerges typically among cliques of otherwise unoccupied boys and depends heavily upon the contagious support that suggestions of vandalism receive from such groups.[32] Vandalism, however, does not ordinarily throw youngsters into extensive contacts with other delinquents beyond those already known, unless they are caught and sent to a detention home or training school. Moreover, the role does not significantly intensify the juvenile's momentum along a delinquent path by escalating the seriousness of his delinquency. Indeed, the youngster himself usually does not regard his vandalism as extremely

[29] Rivera *et al.*, *loc. cit.*, Table 9.

[30] Some police departments have instructed their officers not to pursue stolen cars because of the danger to others.

[31] See Schepses, *op. cit.*, p. 60.

[32] Andrew L. Wade, "Social Processes in the Act of Juvenile Vandalism," in *Criminal Behavior Systems, a Typology*, Marshall B. Clinard and Richard Quinney, eds., Holt, Rinehard and Winston, Inc., New York, 1967, pp. 94–109.

antisocial, and he is often surprised at the resentment his high-jinks evoke when he is caught.

Although vandalism is not among the more serious forms of delinquency, the fact remains that adolescents can do an enormous amount of damage when on a rampage. For example, in a city of 125,000 three boys, aged thirteen, fifteen, and sixteen, in the course of one evening damaged ten cars in a parking lot by breaking antennae, windshield wipers, and rear view mirrors. They also turned over a set of swings in a school playground, broke a window in the schoolhouse and one in a cleaning plant, broke a fence, and tore down a sign. They were caught before they did more damage. This was apparently unplanned vandalism, done "just for fun."

In New York, during the first year after a new school was opened, 598 windows were broken, costing $2,680 to replace.

New construction work offers many opportunities for youthful vandals. A survey of its members by the National Association of Home Builders described the following instances of vandalism:[33]

In Detroit a boy drove a bulldozer into a new house, with damage amounting to $650. A youthful vandal threw $600 worth of sewer crock into an excavation, breaking all. Two children in Baltimore shoved in the walls of two cottages while the mortar between the cement blocks was still wet. Workmen had to chip the mortar off each block and rebuild the walls. In Syracuse, the evening before six new houses were to be on display to the public, young vandals broke forty windows, flooded basements, plugged up drains, split the doors, and pounded nails into the plaster. In White Plains, New York, boys poured gasoline into the rooms of a house nearing completion. The damage was more than $35,000.

SHOPLIFTING. Shoplifting by juveniles is another relatively innocuous delinquent role. It has become a common pattern among youthful members of the contraculture as an expression of their disdain for materialism and conventionality, and it is often carried out in groups of two or more.[34] Although drug use may frequently accompany extensive shoplifting among juveniles, it does not seem to be causally related to it. Shoplifting is not sufficiently remunerative to support any but the mildest patterns of drug use. Moreover, amateur shoplifters are easily discouraged by arrests, and they often avoid the role after their activities have been revealed to their parents.[35] For

[33] Elizabeth W. Robinson, "Let's Build Them Better," *National Association of Secondary School Principals*, 40 (September, 1956), 119–124.

[34] Joseph Howard, "Shoplifting Among College Students," unpublished Masters Thesis, Northern Illinois University, 1975.

[35] *Ibid.*

all these reasons, shoplifting in itself does not ordinarily increase a juvenile's delinquent tendencies, nor does it lead to extensive involvement with other delinquents. It is more a symptom of his alienation than a stepping-stone to more serious antisocial patterns.

BURGLARY. Burglary, however, carries more serious implications for juveniles. It is regarded as a more serious offense by the police and the courts, and it tends to result in more drastic actions by them. Like shoplifting it is usually carried out by more than one youngster, but they are quite inexperienced and ineffective with the result that sooner or later they are likely to be apprehended.[36] Juvenile burglars usually are looking for consumables, e.g., beer, cigarettes, food, and money, and not fencible items; they are generally crude in breaking in as well as in their search of the premises; they often leave telltale evidence at the scene; they will victimize people, e.g., employers, teachers, or relatives, who quickly turn suspicion in their direction; they select stores or homes that contain little of value; and they do not know how to disguise their activities while at the burglary site. All of these mistakes mean that burglary by juveniles is risky and that there is some likelihood that youngsters who persist in the pattern will ultimately be sent to an institution where they will come into close contact with other juveniles with greater experience and sophistication. Thus, burglary as a role tends to heighten the juvenile's delinquent tendencies.

SEX OFFENSES. With the sexual revolution and the liberation of women much sex behavior that was previously regarded as morally blameworthy and legally culpable is today viewed at most as questionable.[37] Petting and sex play among teen-agers were never legally proscribed, but today sexual intercourse among emotionally attached adolescents is accepted by most teen-agers and even by some parents.[38] Nevertheless, the criminal code still proscribes such behavior and much else as well.

Sexual intercourse among unmarried juveniles is legally prohibited if the girl is below the age of consent. Violations, if prosecuted, can result in a charge of statutory rape. Sexual intercourse involving force or the threat of force, i.e., forcible rape, is also prohibited. Statutory rape is rarely prosecuted, however, because it results in considerable humiliation for the victim and severe punishment for the offender, who after all is often a juvenile with no more sexual

[36] See Theodore N. Ferdinand, "Burglary in Auburn, Massachusetts," paper presented at the American Society of Criminology meetings in Puerto Rico, 1972.

[37] See Theodore N. Ferdinand, "Sex Behavior and the American Class Structure: A Mosaic," *The Annals of the American Academy of Political and Social Science*, 376 (March, 1968), 76–85, for an analysis of the factors behind these changes.

[38] Ira L. Reiss, *The Social Context of Premarital Sexual Permissiveness*, Holt, Rinehart and Winston, Inc., New York, 1967, Chapter 2.

sophistication than the victim. Most charges of statutory rape result when the girl becomes pregnant, and the parents (or a social agency) decide to prosecute the father.

Sexual misconduct including prostitution is not uncommon in delinquent girls, although more often than not their arrest record only indicates more mundane offenses, e.g., shoplifting. As society becomes more permissive and sexually aware, the vigilance of the police and the juvenile court regarding sex offenses seems to subside. A teen-age girl with a pattern of sexual promiscuity but no other symptoms of delinquency would probably be dealt with informally in the home. A sexually active girl with other indications of delinquency, e.g., drug use or shoplifting, would probably be dealt with formally with an arrest and adjudication as a delinquent. Sexual misconduct alone is not enough today to establish serious delinquency for girls in most juvenile courts.

Flagrant promiscuity and prostitution, however, are still regarded with concern by parents, police, and juvenile judges. As we have seen, many teenagers are driven to prostitution by drug addiction, but in the course of their career as a prostitute they are thrown into association with a great variety of other criminal types that only serve to draw them more deeply into a life of crime.[39] If they are experienced and have a pimp, he is often linked with other members of the underworld—blackmailers, robbers, and drug pushers—who sometimes involve girls in more serious crimes. Moreover, their clients are often involved in various types of criminality. The role of the prostitute is the door to a variety of other deviant and criminal activities, and many girls pass through that door.

Abnormal sexual behavior such as bestiality, homosexuality, or exhibitionism is also broadly prohibited by law, but it is much less common among juveniles and much less important as an aspect of their sexual misconduct. Occasionally, however, boys and girls do fall into a pattern of sexually abnormal behavior. Sometimes these activities indicate failure of an adolescent to develop normal heterosexual attitudes or to divert sexual impulses into acceptable activities. Thus, some older boys exhibit their genitals in public and especially before girls; some may sexually attack a small girl who is unable to resist. These boys are few in number and now are usually regarded as psychologically disturbed and not delinquent.

Sporadic incidents of homosexuality among adolescents of the same age also occur, often as part of the rather wide range of sexual experimentation

---

[39] See, for example, Diana Gray, "Turning Out: A Study of Teen-age Prostitution," *Urban Life and Culture*, 1 (January, 1973), 401–425.

that many adolescents carry out before they have settled into approved adult types of sexual expression. Masturbation, either individually or among boys in a group, may be placed in the same category, although it is much more widespread. These several aberrations, however, are usually dealt with via medical treatment and not through the criminal justice system. Hence, these kinds of offenses do not ordinarily result in serious further involvement with other delinquents.

THE JUVENILE OFFENDER AS A DISTINCTIVE TYPE. We have stressed here the distinctive qualities of several delinquent roles which juveniles sometimes follow and as a result subsequently find themselves conveyed by the role to other more serious kinds of delinquent activity. It is also true, however, that the juvenile brings to such roles a distinctive set of characteristics that distinguish him and the roles he adopts from adult offenders.

Generally speaking, the offender roles we have just described are affected by the youthful age of their incumbents in the following ways.

1. The younger the child, the more likely is his offense to be limited to the possibilities of his home, immediate neighborhood, school, and a few local institutions. In other situations his mere presence while unattended arouses suspicion.
2. The younger the child, the more he depends upon stealth and secrecy.
3. Adolescents tend to make use of brute physical force or to use weapons readily obtained from materials at hand: the homemade gun, the garrison belt with heavy buckle, the sharpened cane, the knife ordered through a mail-order catalog. Adult criminals may have a whole arsenal of guns, but many adult criminals avoid weapons and depend upon manual skill, dexterity of movement, or the psychological manipulation of a victim who voluntarily succumbs to his wily schemes.
4. The younger the offender, the more likely he is to combine fun and play with his offenses; the adult criminal tends to be serious and calculating in his movements.
5. The younger the offender, the less he plans and the more likely he is to seize upon a good opportunity for theft, vandalism, or a fight. The older criminal plans ahead, and the more important the crime, the longer and more carefully he plans.
6. The preteen offender is less likely to have companions than the adolescent offender.
7. The needs satisfied by crime differ with age, following the general developmental trend of human beings.

ROLES IN THE DELINQUENT GANG

We have already seen that there are a variety of delinquent gangs, each with its own peculiar values and delinquent specialty. It is also true that specific roles within the gangs carry important implications for the delinquent behavior of their members, quite apart from the particular orientation of the gang. It is necessary, therefore, to examine the impact of different kinds of gang roles upon the behavior of their incumbents.

As noted in Chapter 7, Malcolm Klein has identified two distinct roles in the typical gang: the core member and the fringe member.[40] According to Klein the core member participates more fully in gang activities and is more delinquent than the fringe member. There is also some evidence that his assaultive behavior reflects personal predispositions brought with him to the gang instead of the influence of the gang. Leadership within the gang is ordinarily drawn from among the core members, and according to Short and Strodtbeck, the leaders are particularly vulnerable to pressures from both within and without the gang.[41] In the process of establishing himself in a leadership position, a boy may be forced to affect very aggressive behavior toward other gang members, and by way of maintaining his leadership of the gang, he may be forced to instigate a variety of aggressive moves against other gangs. But when his position as leader is relatively secure, his aggressiveness noticeably subsides both internally and externally. Thus, the role of leader also faces the adolescent with pressures that markedly affect his aggressiveness and accordingly his delinquent behavior as well.

But if leaders are shaped in important ways by the social dynamics of their gangs so, too, are the scapegoats that also occasionally appear in such groups. The youngsters who fall into this role provide a nice counterpoint to the ideals endorsed by core members in that the scorn and abuse heaped upon them serve to highlight the virtues and achievements of those who occupy higher positions in the gang. Boys who fit into this role seem to have a great variety of physical, psychological, and social disabilities, and they typically exhibit a compelling need to relate their troubles to anyone who will listen— including unwary street club workers, according to Mattick and Caplan.[42] These authors describe gang members in this role as stake animals, because their dependence upon street workers often deflects the worker from effective relationships with other gang members. Although there is no solid evidence to support the assertion, it is entirely likely that such boys are on the fringe of

---

[40] Malcolm Klein, *Street Gangs and Street Workers*, Prentice Hall, Inc., Englewood Cliffs, N.J., 1971, pp. 70–93.

[41] James F. Short, Jr. and Fred L. Strodtbeck, "The Response of Gang Leaders to Status Threats: An Observation on Group Process and Delinquent Behavior," *American Journal of Sociology*, 68 (March, 1963), 571–579.

[42] Hans W. Mattick and Nathan S. Caplan, "Stake Animals, Loud Talking, and Leadership in Do-Nothing and Do-Something Situations," in *Juvenile Gangs in Context*, Malcolm W. Klein, ed., Prentice-Hall, Inc., Englewood Cliffs, N.J., 1967, pp. 106–119.

the gang and that their delinquency is considerably less than that of their more solidly established peers.

There are also a variety of gang roles that stem from the specialized focus of specific gangs. Fighting gangs often develop two types of leaders: those who provide leadership during periods of relative peace, and war counselors who assume leadership during confrontations. In retreatist gangs certain individuals develop reliable contacts with drug dealers and act as suppliers for the rest of the gang, and in criminal gangs certain youngsters assume the lead in shop-lifting, burglarizing, and robbing. The teen-agers who move into these kinds of specialized roles within gangs often display unique ability in their role, but the fact remains that it is the role itself that inspires much of their behavior in behalf of the gang. Without the gang their delinquency would be less frequent and less intense.

A Social Typology of Delinquency

We are now in a position to suggest a social typology of delinquency which reflects the influence of all the relevant social processes that are regarded as important in molding delinquent behavior.

We have described in this chapter six distinct subcultural patterns which suggest, where they do not directly encourage, a wide variety of delinquent behavior. Not all these subcultural patterns ordinarily inspire delinquent gangs, but some do—and we shall consider the impact of these gangs and their role structure upon the seven offender roles which have also been considered here. Those juveniles who become delinquent without the intervention of a gang shall also be considered but only insofar as their offender roles interact with the values of their subcultural pattern.

To begin there is little doubt that gangs which specialize in certain kinds of offenses will inevitably introduce most of their members to the roles of their specialty. For example, retreatist gangs inevitably involve their members in the drug user role; criminal gangs foster an expertise in the roles of burglary, auto theft, and often robbery. Theft gangs focus on simpler types of theft like shop-lifting, joyriding in stolen autos, and simple forms of burglary together with an occasional spree of vandalism, and fighting gangs concentrate mostly on assaults, which may on occasion spill over into robbery or murder, against rival gangs as well as innocent bystanders.

Moreover, after gang members become involved in gang-sponsored offender roles, it is clear that they tend to practice the roles more frequently than nongang offenders, they tend to persist at them longer, and they tend to commit more serious offenses in the role than nongang offenders. Thus, membership in a gang tends to heighten the level of delinquency reached by its members in a variety of ways.

Middle and upper class adolescents do not often form themselves into delinquent gangs, but they do form a variety of clubs and cliques in high school that have some of the same effects on them that gangs do on working or lower class youths. Middle class youths, for example, often form high school clubs in which one of the main criteria for admission is sexual attractiveness. For a variety of reasons which we have already considered, these clubs tend to encourage a frenetic competition among boys for sexual experience with the result that some of them commit sexual offenses of several types. In most cases these offenses are not prosecuted because no one is seriously harmed, but when a girl becomes pregnant or is seriously assaulted, the boy may find himself deeply involved in the sexual offender role and all that that implies.

In the upper class rather amorphous cliques tend to emerge among teen-agers which implicitly encourage a variety of delinquent acts including sexual offenses and drug abuse. But the young people involved almost never mature into well established offenders, since their parents generally intervene before their cases can move very far in the criminal justice system. Thus, although teen-agers in this class may commit a variety of delinquencies, they rarely occupy offenders' roles.

Toward a Synthetic Typology of Delinquency

As we have already seen, a synthetic typology should blend together the insights of all relevant typologies, and now that we have defined a sociological typology of delinquency in this chapter and a psychological typology in Chapter 5, we are in a position to offer a synthetic typology of delinquency. Before we get too far into the definition of such a typology, however, we must first consider briefly how it is to be accomplished.

Kurt Lewin has suggested a methodology, which he called field theory, whereby psychological patterns in the individual might be related to the social and physical circumstances of his immediate surroundings to predict the probable course of his behavior.[43] In field theory the individual is seen as assessing the positive and negative features of his immediate situation (defined, of course, in terms of the individual's conscious needs and fears) and behaving

---

[43] See Kurt Lewin, *Field Theory in Social Science*, Dorwin Cartwright, ed., Harper & Row, Inc., New York, 1951. For more recent attempts to apply field theory to specific social problems see J. Milton Yinger, *Toward a Field Theory of Behavior*, McGraw-Hill Book Co., New York, 1965, and Theodore N. Ferdinand, *Typologies of Delinquency*.

accordingly. Thus, according to field theory behavior depends as much on the environment and its composition as upon the individual and his predispositions. Moreover, although there may be some tendency for individuals with particular likes and dislikes to seek out environments where these likes and dislikes are complemented, there is no necessity that such a happy fit of need and opportunity occur. Indeed, it is probably rare that the individual finds an environment that even approximates his momentary desires in most respects.

In using field theory to define a synthetic typology of delinquency, we need only to compare the individual's delinquent predispositions as indicated by our psychological typology with the opportunities and obstacles implicit in the offender and gang roles included in our sociological typology. Since there is no necessary affinity of particular personality types for particular delinquent roles, we must assume that each personality type sooner or later will encounter each of the delinquent roles. Hence, a comprehensive synthetic typology derived from the ten personality types described in Chapter 5 and the four gang roles and seven offender roles described in this chapter would consist of 110 types, i.e., eleven roles for each personality pattern. In the interests of brevity, however, we shall outline the possibilities of such a typology by describing only the more salient types in which the juvenile's needs and inhibitions are nicely complemented by the opportunities and restrictions of his roles.

The best example of this blending of situation and personal need can be found in the Cultural Identifier in a criminal gang. The Cultural Identifier exhibits the disciplined organizing ability and sympathy with the underdog that leadership in delinquent gangs requires, and the activities of the criminal gang provide exactly the kind of social medium he needs to express his resentment toward the dominant socio-cultural groups in society. His particular motives and attitudes incline him toward other delinquents, and his unusual abilities propel him quickly to a leadership position where he can elaborate his views fully. Indeed, his leadership potential is so great that he can transform an informal adolescent clique into a full-scale delinquent gang rather easily. Moreover, there is some likelihood that he will interject an ideological theme into the gang. If he were black, he would tend toward militancy, and as the gang became more alienated through its delinquency, his militancy might lead to a shift from delinquency to revolutionary activity. If he were white and lower class, his militancy would probably be less. In the middle class where there are revolutionary political groups, his energies would probably be channeled into radical activity and out of delinquency altogether.

He would not find the retreatist gang of the lower-lower class inviting because of its resignation and defeatism. Nor would aggressive-exploitative cliques in the upper-middle class interest him because of their fraternity-like social patterns and their unthinking celebration of a bourgeois style of life. The mischievous-indulgent cliques of the upper-upper class might attract him, but he would encounter resistance as he moved them toward revolutionary activity and away from the petty offenses more typical of this subculture.

The Cultural Identifier might also be drawn to certain of the individual offender roles open to juveniles. Larceny and especially shoplifting have become routine practices among many members of the middle class contraculture, and he might regard these offenses as a chance to express his contempt for middle class culture. Vandalism and burglary might also be followed for much the same reason.

The Cultural Identifier would not be likely to get involved in auto theft (his contraculture identification would cancel any lingering admiration of the auto as a symbol in American society); and his sympathy for the underdog would preclude exploitative relationships with girls and, hence, most types of sex crimes. And, finally, the hazards of drug use and its endorsement of self-indulgence would preclude anything more than an occasional experimentation in this area.

The Cultural Identifier, therefore, has a number of paths open to him in which his personal motives and attitudes would find strong socio-cultural support. Depending upon his race and social class, some would lead him into serious delinquency; others into serious revolutionary activity; but none would carry him very far into conventional society.

Another personality type with leadership potential is the Manipulator. He has a certain charm socially, and he is a good judge of character in that he reads individual weaknesses well and knows how to play upon them. Moreover, he is not afraid to assert himself ruthlessly over others. But his relations with others tend to be shallow and exploitative and, in contrast to the Cultural Identifier, apolitical. Thus, in the absence of other strong candidates, the Manipulator has some of the qualities of a good leader, although his ruthless, egocentric tendencies would tend to weaken any bonds he might establish with other members of the gang. If a leadership role were denied him, he would fit reasonably well into the core segment of most gangs, although even there he would resist the discipline of the gang in favor of a more individualistic pattern.

The social context that would blend most congenially with his needs is the aggressive-exploitative clique of the upper-middle class. It offers ample opportunity to apply an exploitative, manipulative style in social interaction, and it yields rich sexual rewards to those who succeed. His inclinations blend so well with this cultural setting that both he and the setting would find considerable inspiration in the union, i.e., there is a good chance that through his imaginative probes, the culture of the exploitative-aggressive clique would achieve new levels of elaboration and finesse.

His influence in other types of social settings, however, would be more limited. His preference of manipulation to violent confrontation would limit his role in fighting gangs, and his egocentric nature would weaken his identification with the cultural patterns and membership of most other types of gangs.

As an individual he would also be drawn to a number of roles available to delinquents. For example, as a result of his fascination with the opposite sex he would probably commit sexual offenses on occasion; and the excitement of burglary or robbery might also prove attractive. But should his goals be frustrated in any direction assaultive offenses or vandalism could also be the result. On the other hand, the passive posture of the drug user would not appeal to him; and the petty crime of shoplifting would be beneath his considerable skills and lofty self-image.

The remaining personality types identified by Warren would probably not find such a close matching of their motivations with social roles and as a result all of them would tend to fall into core, fringe, or scapegoat roles in the gang; or they would avoid gang membership altogether.

The Asocial Aggressive type, for example, might prove a worthy member of a fighting gang, especially when engaged in serious confrontations with other gangs. He typically assaults frustrating situations or people, and his violent tendencies could be utilized effectively by such gangs. But he relates very primitively with others, and at best he would be an unpredictable and unreliable gang member. In most other types of delinquent groups, he would play only a marginal role.

The Asocial Aggressive type would also be vulnerable to most of the temptations afflicting the young today, and accordingly he could be counted upon to commit sexual offenses or become a drug user if the opportunity arose. Auto theft, larceny, and burglary, however, would mean little to him, and except as group activities, he would not be inclined to explore their possibilities.

The Asocial Passive type seems destined to play an isolate role in juvenile society, and his primitive personality seems to rule out any but the simplest delinquent roles, i.e., the thief or drug user role. Through the latter, he could become involved in a retreatist gang, but his passive, asocial personality would forbid any very intense social involvement even there.

The Immature Conformist and the Cultural Conformist would relate to a delinquent environment in much the same way. They eagerly seek the approval of their peers, and under the stimulation of group pressure, they would do virtually anything prompted by other gang members. They are uncritical of the gang or its activities, and they are uninhibited in pursuit of most, if not all, its criminal goals. The "banality of evil" describes their demeanor quite well.

Their childish identification with the gang and its values, however, is not based on a close resonance of personal motives with the gang's culture, and consequently their participation is largely stereotyped and unimaginative. Because of their shallow emotional involvement in the gang, they lack the vision and purpose essential to effective leadership, and consequently their role is usually at the rank and file level. Moreover, it makes little difference to them which kind of gang they ultimately join. They have little preference for one type over another—it is peer support they seek—and as long as their peers regard the gang as worth-while, they will, too.

As far as individual roles are concerned, they will tend toward those which require the least skill or finesse. Auto theft or burglary, for example, will often seem too difficult for these fellows, but shoplifting, sex crimes, vandalism, and drug use will not. They will not be particularly successful in any delinquencies they attempt, however, and as they filter through the courts, detention homes, and training schools of their area, they will quickly affiliate with the nearest clique or gang.

The neurotic delinquents, i.e., the Anxious Neurotic and the Acting-out Neurotic, are probably the most unhappy of all the types described here. They are singularly unprepared for life as a delinquent. They are so inhibited that in comparison with other delinquents, they appear timid; and in the face of a serious challenge, they typically retreat. Their imagination does not dwell upon exploitative or destructive projects, and their air of anxious distraction gives them the appearance of being foolish and indecisive. For all these reasons other delinquents tend to see them as unstable, lacking in purpose and courage, and contemptible. Thus, they tend to avoid other delinquents, and when they are tolerated, more often than not they fall into a scapegoat role.

Since other delinquents tend to heighten their misery, if possible they pursue more individualistic roles—often with younger or female peers. Auto theft is a common pursuit because it provides temporary solutions to many of their problems. It assuages their sense of inferiority with the prestige it commands among their peers; the flashy power of a new sports car compensates for their fearful manner; and it provides mobility with which to escape oppressive situations. Thus, auto theft is a common offense for these types of delinquents.

Larceny and drug abuse would also be common activities among neurotics for the companionship they provide and for the pain and indignation they provoke among oppressive parents. Vandalism might also be an occasional offense among Acting-out Neurotics in response to emotional wounds inflicted by parents or peers, but more aggressive crimes like robbery, burglary, or sex offenses would be less common.

Through their association with drug users and dealers, they might be drawn into a retreatist gang, or in the upper-upper class, neurotic delinquents might find congenial associates in a mischievous-indulgent clique. The cynicism and iconoclasm of such cliques would appeal to their own sense of resentment and reinforce their tendencies in this direction. But in other gang settings, they would find little peace and less honor.

Conclusion

In this chapter we have defined a social typology of delinquency based on a wide variety of sociological thinking regarding juvenile delinquency, and we have coordinated this typology with Marguerite Warren's typology of delinquent personality types as they relate to male delinquents. We have suggested how eight of her types (the Stress and Adjustment Reactions were omitted) would react to selected delinquent roles, and in so doing we established the outlines of a synthetic typology of delinquency. Much research remains to be done, but several advantages of the synthetic typology become immediately apparent. By blending together social and psychological qualities, it provides a more complete picture of the delinquent and his behavior than either of the ideal typologies from which it was derived. All typologies by their very nature ignore certain of the idiosyncratic qualities that make individuals distinctive, and in this sense they provide a simplified picture of their nature. But synthetic typologies miss less of each individual's distinctiveness, because they draw upon a greater variety of perspectives and theories.

Moreover, they bid fair to yield the soundest basis for diagnosing and prescribing remedies for the several types they describe. They are based ultimately upon theory—hence, they go beyond common sense in their diagnosis; and since they postulate an individual in interaction with his environment, they anticipate the effects of adverse conditions upon the types in question and provide thereby a more realistic picture of the outcome of various kinds of treatment. All in all, then, insofar as typologies are useful in the analysis or prevention of delinquency, it is clear that synthetic typologies fill the need more adequately than other kinds.

Bibliography

CLOWARD, RICHARD A., AND LLOYD E. OHLIN, *Delinquency and Opportunity*, Free Press of Glencoe, New York, 1960.

COHEN, ALBERT K., AND JAMES F. SHORT, JR., "Research in Delinquent Subculture," *Journal of Social Issues*, 14 (1958), 20–37.

CONKLIN, JOHN, *Robbery and the Criminal Justice System*, J. B. Lippincott Company, Philadelphia, 1972.

FERDINAND, THEODORE N., *Typologies of Delinquency*, Random House, New York, 1966.

JOHNSON, LLOYD, *Drugs and American Youth*, Institute for Social Research, Ann Arbor, 1973.

KLEIN, MALCOLM, *Street Gangs and Street Workers*, Prentice-Hall, Inc., Englewood Cliffs, N.J., 1971.

MATZA, DAVID, *Becoming Deviant*, Prentice-Hall, Inc., Englewood Cliffs, N.J, 1969.

MILLER, WALTER B., "Theft Behavior in City Gangs," in *Juvenile Gangs in Context*, Malcolm M. Klein, ed., Prentice-Hall, Inc., Englewood Cliffs, N.J., 1967.

———, "Lower Class Culture as a Generating Milieu of Gang Delinquency," *Journal of Social Issues*, 14 (1958), 5–19.

SHORT, JAMES F., AND FRED L. STRODTBECK, *Group Process and Gang Delinquency*, University of Chicago Press, Chicago, 1965.

SPERGEL, IRVING, *Racketville, Slumtown, Haulburg*, University of Chicago Press, Chicago, 1964.

WADE, ANDREW L., "Social Processes in the Act of Juvenile Vandalism," in *Criminal Behavior Systems, a Typology*, Marshall B. Clinard and Richard Quinney, eds., Holt, Rinehart and Winston, Inc., New York, 1967.

WATTENBERG, WILLIAM W., AND JAMES BALISTRIERI, "Automobile Theft: A 'Favored Group' Delinquency," *American Journal of Sociology*, 57 (1952), 575–583.

YINGER, J. MILTON, *Toward a Field Theory of Behavior*, McGraw-Hill Book Co., New York, 1965.

individual differences among delinquents chapter 9

Although all children tend to follow a roughly similar pattern in maturation in a given culture, the factor of individual differences cannot be overlooked. Children are known to differ in physique, rate of growth, mental ability, and temperament. They are also affected by the way in which they are treated by their mothers and those in close relationships with them during their early childhood. Often it is difficult to distinguish inborn traits and capacities from the social influences of early childhood. These individual differences and the organization of such qualities into behavioral patterns are important to understanding delinquency.

The Search for a Cause

For many years, criminologists have sought for one factor in the individual's body or mind which would directly account for delinquency and crime. Scientists and laymen alike have found it difficult to accept the fact that, basically, delinquents and nondelinquents, criminals and noncriminals are much alike in biological make-up and in their responses to social and cultural influences. As Lawson G. Lowrey, a psychiatrist, has written,

> . . . despite extensive research and many ingenious efforts to delimit them, there are no such entities as "delinquent" or "criminal" personalities. To be sure, there are delinquents and criminals, and,

naturally, each has a personality, normal or abnormal, but all attempts to establish a distinctive delinquent or criminal *type* have eventually come to naught.[1]

In spite of this and similar blunt statements denying the existence of criminal types, one attempt after another has been made to isolate particular physiological traits or personality types that can be definitely identified as criminal or, among children, as delinquent.

Caution must be exercised in evaluating attempts to link delinquency or crime with specific traits or factors. As we have seen, no theory can explain all facets of delinquency, and as we apply different kinds of theory it is as important to learn the limitations of each theory as it is to identify its specific insights into the problem.

Theories of a Biological Criminal Type

CRIMINAL AS A PRIMITIVE SAVAGE

The discoveries and interpretations of Charles Darwin, who published *The Descent of Man* in 1871, had a powerful influence on thinking about the causes of criminal behavior, first in Europe, and after 1890, in the United States. Darwin himself did not develop a theory of criminology, but his theory of the evolution of man from lower animal forms opened the way for several interesting criminological theories, since discarded scientifically, but traces of which remain in current theories. Darwin's theory led to the supposition that men could be aligned on a graduated scale, some being more animal-like in characteristics than others. Criminologists readily assumed that criminals were animal-like.

The leader in developing biological theories of criminal behavior was Cesare Lombroso, an Italian physician and psychiatrist (1835–1909).[2] Lombroso made the concept of incomplete evolutionary development the basis of an elaborate theory. This theory of atavism, or reversion to an early type of man, was widely accepted in the United States from about 1890 to 1910. American writers described the criminal as a savage in the midst of civilization,

---

[1] Lawson G. Lowrey, "Delinquent and Criminal Personalities," Chapter 26 in *Personality and the Behavior Disorders*, J. McV. Hunt, ed., Ronald Press Co., New York, 1944, Vol. 2, p. 794. This chapter gives an excellent survey of the many attempts to find a unitary cause of all crime, dating back to 1812.

[2] Arthur E. Fink, *Causes of Crime, Biological Theories in the United States, 1800–1915*, University of Pennsylvania Press, Philadelphia, 1938, p. 100.

who had been hurled back thousands of years; the juvenile delinquent was often stigmatized as "the child born centuries too late," who presumably would have been at home in an early type of savage society but did not fit into twentieth-century society.[3]

Lombroso and his followers believed that the brain of the criminal differed structurally—and therefore in the way it functioned—from the brains of noncriminals. Other scientists disagreed. Different scientists dissected and studied the brains of criminals who had died or been executed. The end of the controversy in the United States came around World War I with the abandonment of the idea that a criminal brain existed as a structural anomaly.

Lombroso thought that the criminal revealed his criminality in observable physical peculiarities and therefore could be spotted while still alive.[4] These peculiarities, the stigmata of criminal behavior, included the following characteristics: low, narrow forehead, large jaws and cheekbones, outstanding ears, hairiness, precocious wrinkles, predominance of left-handedness, prehensile foot, and an arm span greater than the individual's height. When it was pointed out to him that some of the anomalies could be developed in the lifetime of the individual, Lombroso added a new criminal type, the degenerate, who represented a degradation from the normal process of development, a condition considered to be hereditary. He still clung to the idea that the degenerate could be identified by physical traits, e.g., thin upper lip; large ears, jaw, and cheekbones; and a ferocious squint. Further objections led Lombroso to modify his theories to include in his classification occasional criminals, criminals by contracted habit, criminal madmen, and criminals of passion. But he continued to believe that the true or born criminal was central in the classification of criminals.

Another related theory held that the criminal was a person arrested in individual development. The discovery that the human fetus seemed in its development to pass through stages also traversed in the biological evolution of man led to the unjustified expansion of this theory to include the psychological and social development of children after birth. G. Stanley Hall, outstanding psychologist at Clark University, was especially fluent in expound-

---

[3] Cited from various writers by Fink, *ibid.*, pp. 100–101.

[4] Cesare Lombroso, *Crime, Its Causes and Remedies*, Little, Brown and Company, Boston, 1912. This translation gives Lombroso's modifications of his early theories, which are outlined in the introduction. For summaries of Lombroso's theories see Ruth Shonle Cavan, *Criminology*, Thomas Y. Crowell Company, New York, 1962, pp. 688–693; or George B. Vold, *Theoretical Criminology*, Oxford University Press, New York, 1958, Chapter 4.

ing this theory. It required only a simple extension of this theory to explain delinquency and crime as a case of arrested development of the child, corresponding to some early, untamed stage of development of the human race.[5] Studies were made of living delinquents and criminals to try to find some physical or mental evidence of arrested development.[6]

In time, more extensive and careful research undermined the theories of delinquent and criminal biological types. Some criminals did have biological or physical peculiarities, but the relation of these to crime could not be established. Perhaps the most effective dismissal of the biological theories was a study by Charles Goring comparing English criminals with noncriminals, which revealed that there was no special physical type of criminal.[7]

JUVENILE DELINQUENTS. The theories of Lombroso and his associates as they pertained to juvenile delinquents rather than adult criminals received a setback from a careful study made in the late 1930's at the Institute for Juvenile Research, Chicago. The subjects were 4,000 grade school boys in two socioeconomic areas with high rates of delinquency. The data assembled for each boy were based on a medical examination, a neurologic review, a series of sixty-three anthropometrical measurements and indices, and extensive social and morphological information. The boys were aged six to seventeen; they were studied in three racial-social groups, Caucasoid, Negroid, and Mexican. The boys classified as delinquent either had an official record of delinquency or were known by persons and agencies in the areas to engage in delinquent practices. Those who made the examinations had no knowledge as to which of the boys had a record of delinquency and which had not. In fact, the classification into delinquent and nondelinquent was not made until the testing and collection of information had been completed.[8]

No relation was found between Lombrosian-type stigmata and criminal and delinquent behavior. Among white boys, no significant physical differences were found between delinquents and nondelinquents. Among black boys, some differences existed in gross physical appearance. In general, the researchers concluded that, in the areas studied, delinquents had fewer of the so-called

[5] There is of course no proof that in its early stages of development the human race was savage and brutal. No record remains of those early prehistoric days beyond a few stone implements.

[6] Fink summarizes various of these studies, op. cit., Chapter 5.

[7] Charles Goring, Abridged Edition of the English Convict, His Majesty's Stationery Office, London, England, 1919. Discussion may be found in Cavan, op. cit., pp. 684–685, and Vold, op. cit., pp. 52–55.

[8] This unpublished study was made by representatives of four professions: B. Boshes, physician; Solomon Kobrin, sociologist; E. Reynolds, physical anthropologist; and S. Rosenbaum, statistician.

stigmata of crime than had the nondelinquents. The delinquents tended to be superior from a medical and neurological standpoint; intelligence did not differ between the two groups.

LATER PHYSICAL STUDIES OF CRIMINALS AND DELINQUENTS

The various refutations of Lombroso's theories did not refute the basic idea that criminals and delinquents are in some way organically deficient or at any rate different from the average run of people. If they can be proved different structurally, the theory contends, they must be different in ways of thinking, feeling, and acting. Such relationships are difficult if not impossible to establish, especially when gross physical features are equated with the complexities of delinquent or criminal behavior. But attempts are still made to establish such relationships.

One of the most elaborate studies was made in the 1930's by Ernest A. Hooton, in which elaborate physical measurements were made on 17,076 male prisoners and various groups of noncriminals.[9] Over a hundred measurements were used, including exact measurements of the head, forehead, nose, chin, shape of features, and classification of the abundance and color of hair. The men were also classified by stature and body build. No measurements of intellectual capacity or personality were made, and social or cultural factors were not considered. Hooton failed to find any stigmata of crime, but came to the conclusion that criminals were by heredity organically inferior and that crime resulted from the impact of environment on low-grade human organisms. Without further ado, he concluded that the only way to eliminate crime would be to "extirpate" all physically, mentally, and morally unfit persons, or to place them in complete segregation.

Upon publication of Hooton's study, controversy raged in book reviews and articles. A few writers supported Hooton's conclusions, but more sought to refute them, pointing out deficiencies in his selection of criminals and noncriminals for comparison and condemning his bland assumption that physical structure is an indication of psychological motivations and social adjustment. Hooton also overlooked the fact that his statistics showed that a much higher percentage of criminals and noncriminals had the same characteristics than had different ones. They did not fall into two distinct groups.

At present one reads little about Hooton's studies, which seem to have had little effect on most researchers or on preventive or treatment methods.

---

[9] Ernest A. Hooton, *The American Criminal: An Anthropological Study*, Harvard University Press, Cambridge, Massachusetts, 1939, three volumes. In more popular form the study was published as *Crime and the Man*, Harvard University Press, Cambridge, Massachusetts, 1939.

He serves, however, as a link to another body of research, dealing with the physical characteristics of juvenile delinquents.

BODY TYPES OF JUVENILE DELINQUENTS

Another approach to physical marks distinguishing delinquents has been made by William H. Sheldon through a theory of somatotypes or body types.[10] Sheldon's theory postulates three body types, each of which shades off in either direction into the two other types. Each body type has a related temperamental pattern. Each merging body type that is a combination of two clear-cut body types has a corresponding psychiatric type.[11] The various relationships are shown in Table 10.

Sheldon later applied his theory to delinquency, using as subjects 200 young men referred to Hayden Goodwill Inn, a Boston social agency, by courts,

TABLE 10

Body Types, Temperamental Types, and Psychiatric Types Postulated
by William H. Sheldon

BODY TYPE	TEMPERAMENTAL TYPE	PSYCHIATRIC TYPE
Endomorphic: predominance of digestive, assimilative function; person is fat	Viscerotonia, relaxed, gluttonous, loves comfort, sociability, craves affection	
Intermediate types between endomorphic and mesomorphic		Manic
Mesomorphic: predominance of bone and muscle; person is muscular, active	Somatotonia, vigorous, active	
Intermediate types between mesomorphic and ectomorphic		Paranoid
Ectomorphic: predominance of mental functions; person is thin	Cerebrotonia, inhibited, shrinks from contacts, self-conscious, feelings of inadequacy	
Intermediate types between ectomorphic and endomorphic		Heboid

[10] A predecessor with a similar theory was E. Kretschmer, whose book *Physique and Character* (Harcourt, Brace & World, New Yok, 1925) set forth a theory of three body types: pyknic, with a heavy thickset body; asthenic, with a thin, underdeveloped body; and athletic, with a well-developed, muscular body. Kretschmer was interested in trying to relate types of mental illness to body type.

[11] William H. Sheldon *et al.*, *The Varieties of Human Physique*, Harper & Row, Publishers, New York, 1942; William H. Sheldon, *The Varieties of Temperament*, Harper & Row, Publishers, New York, 1949.

parole officers, and others.[12] With a capacity of eighty boys, the agency had contacts with about 500 youths a year, varying from fifteen to twenty-one years of age. The boys were scored subjectively on a scale running from 0 to 10 in terms of the interference of various factors with adjustment. The factors were mental insufficiency, medical insufficiency, first-order and second-order psychopathy, alcoholism, homosexuality, and primary criminality. Only the last three would be treated legally as crime. Sheldon, however, used his score to indicate degree of criminality. He then classified the boys by somatotypes and related these to the assumed degree of criminality. His conclusion was that delinquency is mainly lodged in the germ plasm and should be weeded out by selective breeding.

Sheldon's conclusions were challenged by the criminologist, Edwin H. Sutherland, who reclassified Sheldon's 200 subjects on a more meaningful scale of delinquency and crime (running from those with no delinquency to gangsters engaged in major crimes). He found a slight tendency for mesomorphic and manic components to increase and ectomorphic and heboid components to decrease with increasing criminality. The differences between the seriously delinquent and the nondelinquent boys were not statistically significant.

Another attempt to fit Sheldon's somatotypes to delinquency was made by Sheldon and Eleanor Glueck in their massive comparison of 500 correctional school youths and 500 nondelinquents in the Boston area.[13] Considerable effort was made to select nondelinquent boys who not only matched the delinquents in residence in underprivileged area, age, ethnic origin, and intelligence rating, but who were virtually free of any delinquency, even of the most trivial kind. They succeeded to the extent that only 26 per cent of nondelinquents had records of such casual offenses as smoking, hopping trucks, once or twice taking small articles from stores, crap-shooting, sneaking into movies, and occasionally truanting from school. The other 74 per cent had not done even these things. The study therefore compares extremes—the most seriously delinquent with the most devout conformers. On the bell-shaped curve of continuity given in Chapter 2, class A was compared with classes F and G and a few of class E. The middle group of "normal" boys was omitted.

According to the Glueck study, as shown in Table 11, about 14 per cent

[12] William H. Sheldon, in collaboration with Emil M. Hartl and Eugene McDermott, *Varieties of Delinquent Youth*, Harper & Row, Publishers, New York, 1949. For a sociological evaluation by a criminologist, see Edwin H. Sutherland, "Critique of Sheldon's *Varieties of Delinquent Youth*," *American Sociological Review*, 16 (1951), 10–13.

[13] Sheldon and Eleanor Glueck, *Physique and Delinquency*, Harper & Row, Publishers, New York, 1956. A brief statement is contained in the Gluecks' *Unraveling Juvenile Delinquency*, Harvard University Press, Cambridge, Massachusetts, 1950, Chapter 15.

TABLE 11

Sheldon Body Types Applied to Delinquents and Nondelinquents, Percentage Distribution

	496 DELINQUENT BOYS		482 NONDELINQUENT BOYS	
Body types				
Endomorphic component dominance				
Extreme endomorphs	1.2		5.0	
Endomorphs	2.8		4.8	
Mesomorphic endomorphs	3.2		1.5	
Ectomorphic endomorphs	4.6		3.7	
Total endomorphs		11.8		15.0
Mesomorphic component dominance				
Extreme mesomorphs	23.2		7.1	
Mesomorphs	16.9		12.2	
Endomorphic mesomorphs	13.3		3.1	
Ectomorphic mesomorphs	6.7		8.3	
Total mesomorphs		60.1		30.7
Ectomorphic component dominance				
Extreme ectomorphs	1.8		14.5	
Ectomorphs	5.0		14.7	
Endomorphic ectomorphs	4.2		3.1	
Mesomorphic ectomorphs	3.4		7.3	
Total ectomorphs		14.4		39.6
No component dominance				
Balanced types	13.5		14.7	

Reprinted by permission of the publishers from Sheldon and Eleanor Glueck, *Unraveling Juvenile Delinquency*, Harvard University Press, Cambridge, Massachusetts, Copyright 1950 by the Commonwealth Fund, p. 193.

of both the delinquent and the nondelinquent boys had balanced types of personality: that is, none of the three body types dominated. The difference in the percentages of delinquent and nondelinquent endomorphs was very slight. However, the difference among mesomorphs was very large, with a ratio of two delinquents to one nondelinquent. Among ectomorphs the difference was still greater, but tended to the opposite direction, with one delinqunt to almost 2.7 nondelinquents. In general, it might be said that mesomorphs (active, muscular types) might be expected to be numerous among delinquent boys, since much adolescent delinquency takes the form of stealing (including burglary and auto thefts), vandalism, disorderly conduct, breaking curfew, and running away—all implying physical activity. It should be noted from the table that the highest proportion of delinquent mesomorphs were extreme mesomorphs.

In correlating other traits with body type, the Gluecks found that the meso-morphs who became delinquent often had traits not usually found with this body type—destructiveness, feelings of inadequacy, or emotional conflict. Ordi-narily, the mesomorphs are emotionally stable and not given to emotional conflicts. The conclusion is therefore drawn that when the mesomorph has traits disharmonious with his body type, the outcome is likely to be delin-quency. It is worth noting also that in general the vigorous, muscular meso-morph is quite likely to express his problems in overt action rather than to inhibit his emotions.

A different set of relationships was found for the ectomorphs who were the most dominant type among the nondelinquents but constituted only a small percentage of the delinquents. Although ectomorphs are sensitive, their inhibitions and feelings of inadequacy would generally prohibit the customary type of active adolescent delinquency. However, under the stress of environ-mental pressures, ectomorphs tend to become delinquent. This reaction is in line with their general sensitivity.

Thus the findings tend to indicate that mesomorphs are motivated toward delinquency by traits incompatible with their body type, that ectomorphs are more responsive to environmental situations, and that endomorphs and bal-anced types seem to have no special internal or external factors that distinguish them in tendency toward delinquency.

The Gluecks conclude that there is no delinquent personality or stable combination of traits that determines that a given individual will become de-linquent.

In all studies of physical or biological types, the overlap between the physical characteristics of delinquents and nondelinquents or criminals and noncriminals is very great. The analysis by the Gluecks, trying to determine why some boys of a given body type are delinquent and some not, shows that other factors, often social and cultural in nature, in addition to traits that are assumed to be innate, are markedly influential.

Theories of Mental Capacity and Delinquency

When psychological testing first developed, in the period preceding World War I, the differences in mental ability as shown by tests were seized upon by many scientists and laymen alike as the explanation for many types of behavior—delinquency and crime among them.[14] The neatly ranked scores

14 George B. Vold, *op. cit.*, Chapter 5, gives a brief summary of the changing findings and attitudes regarding intelligence test scores of criminals.

of the tests were taken at face value as indicators of the degree of innate ability. The effect on scores of schooling, family educational background, and degree of familiarity with the English language and American customs was not yet recognized, as it is today. Therefore any group—racial, foreign-born, economic —with low scores was branded as innately inferior to the group upon which the tests had been standardized, usually a middle class white urban group. If low test scores and delinquency were associated together in any group, it was assumed that inferior mental ability was the cause of the delinquency. The situation was further clouded by the fact that standards for giving, scoring, and interpreting the earlier tests were not yet well established, and many untrained people gave tests and drew individual conclusions.

EARLY STUDIES

Perhaps the most outspoken of those who believed that dullness and feeble-mindedness were the chief causes of delinquency and crime was Henry H. Goddard, Director of the Research Laboratory of the Training School for Feeble-Minded Girls and Boys at Vineland, New Jersey.[15] Goddard thought that criminals fell into two classes: those who committed crimes willfully or through neglect and carelessness and therefore were responsible for their acts; and those whose offenses were the result of some defect which removed full responsibility. He did not believe that criminality itself was inherited but that inherited low mental ability impaired judgment, self-control, and the ability to distinguish right from wrong. If the feeble-minded person was also nervous or impulsive he was almost sure to become a criminal. In one statement, Goddard asserted that low-grade mentality, much of it feeble-mindedness, is the greatest single cause of crime and also that "every feeble-minded person is a potential criminal."

Goddard was familiar with the various studies made of offenders in institutions, which showed from 10 to 80 per cent of the inmates to be of low mentality. He also traced the family histories of 327 families with children at the Vineland School.[16] Although his imprecise methods tended to load his findings in favor of crime in these families, he found that only 10 per cent of the families and 1 per cent of the individuals involved were criminal. He went to great efforts to counter the low percentage, since it refuted his earlier convictions.

[15] Henry H. Goddard, *Human Efficiency and Levels of Intelligence*, Princeton University Press, Princeton, New Jersey, 1920; *Feeble-Mindedness, Its Causes and Consequences*, Macmillan Company, New York, 1914.

[16] Goddard, *The Criminal Imbecile*, Macmillan Company, New York, 1915.

REFUTATION OF THE THEORY OF
FEEBLE-MINDEDNESS AS A CAUSE OF CRIME

The great divergence in the proportions of low mentality found in different but similar institutions and the increasing precision of tests threw doubt on some of the earlier statements of the close relationship of feeble-mindedness and crime. The issue was conclusively settled insofar as adult crime was concerned by a precise scientific study made by Carl Murchison just after World War I.[17] Murchison was Chief Psychological Examiner at Camp Sherman, Ohio, and therefore had access to the tests given to all draftees during World War I. He tested the prisoners at Ohio Penitentiary, at the invitation of the warden, and later was able to secure tests from men in nine or ten other prisons. He compared the scores of the prisoners with those of the soldiers, taking into account race, native or foreign birth, and region. The results unequivocally proved that prisoners and soldiers, men of much the same age, had essentially the same range of mental test scores, that the great majority of both classes fell into the average range, and that both groups had men of low and high mentality in about the same proportions. Murchison discusses many of the factors that might affect the scores of both soldiers and prisoners, many of which offset each other. Regardless of these factors, the evidence was overwhelming that adult male prisoners were a representative cross section of the population of the United States insofar as mental ability was concerned.

MENTAL ABILITY AND JUVENILE DELINQUENCY

The studies cited were made on adult criminals. While their findings undoubtedly apply also to juvenile delinquency insofar as any automatic relationship between feeble-mindedness and delinquency is concerned, the question of mental ability and delinquency needs further exploration.

There is little evidence among cases brought to juvenile court that low-grade, feeble-minded boys and girls are numerous. Many such children are protected and cared for at home, where, with kind treatment, they create no disturbance. Others, who cannot be cared for at home, are placed early in special institutions for the feeble-minded, either private or state, but usually the latter. In many states the juvenile court judge has jurisdiction over the commitment of feeble-minded children to special institutions as well as over delinquent children. The obviously feeble-minded child who is brought in on a delinquency charge can be committed to a special institution or school for training or custodial care rather than to a correctional school. Thus a cordon

---

[17] Carl Murchison, *Criminal Intelligence*, Clark University, Worcester, Massachusetts, 1926.

of protective care is thrown around the child of obviously low mentality, whether his difficulty is simply inability to adjust to the normal demands of society or consists of delinquent acts.

The crux of the problem of mental ability and delinquency, then, lies in the range from dull-normal to brilliant—the average run of childern found in any community. Several problems need to be examined, among them to determine whether comparable groups of delinquent and nondelinquent children have distributions of mental test scores that differ significantly. Since it is known that scores vary according to the amount of education and cultural background, a fair comparison can be made only when delinquents and non-delinquents are matched on such factors.

Identity of background is provided in the comparison of delinquent children made by Healy and Bronner with the brother or sister closest in age. Race, ethnic, and general family background were identical. The intelligence quotients of the two groups showed very little difference. The delinquents had fourteen children with I.Q. above 110 (superior), the nondelinquents eighteen; in the middle or average range of 90–110, the delinquents had eighty-four children, the nondelinquents seventy-six; below 90, in the dull and feeble-minded ranges, the delinquents had seven and the nondelinquents eleven. Seriously feeble-minded were not included in the study.[18] The authors further state that I.Q. was not related to the length of time for treatment required to help the delinquents.

A California study compared 300 children referred to a child-guidance clinic in a rural county with 300 schoolchildren, matched for community of residence, sex and age.[19] The mean I.Q. of the delinquents was 86.7, and of the control group of nondelinquents, 89.3. In another study of 500 consecutive cases of delinquents, the average I.Q. of the delinquents was 92.5. This I.Q. was compared with that of the 3,000 schoolchildren upon whom the Stanford-Binet test had been standardized. The schoolchildren had an average I.Q. of 101.8; they came from a better educational and social background than the delinquent children. The first comparison given between 300 delinquent and 300 nondelinquent children was based on children from similar backgrounds.

Another problem is the relation of mental ability to the type of delinquency. Merrill found that, regardless of I.Q., the most frequent delinquency

---

[18] William Healy and Augusta F. Bronner, *New Light on Delinquency and Its Treatment*, Yale University Press, New Haven, Connecticut, 1936, pp. 75–76, 162, 190, 198.

[19] Maud A. Merrill, *Problems of Child Delinquency*, Houghton Mifflin Company, Boston, 1947, p. 338.

was stealing.[20] Children brought to the clinic because of forgery, defiance of parents, and malicious mischief tended to have better-than-average I.Q.'s. Those referred for sexual misconduct, truancy, vagrancy, and assault tended to have I.Q.'s below average. However, the differences were slight.

Still another problem related to intelligence is the amount of recidivism. Does the intelligent child learn more readily than the dull child that delinquency may bring unpleasant results and that he must control his behavior? Or does he devise more clever ways to avoid detections? Merrill found no significant difference in the distribution of I.Q. scores between single offenders and recidivists.[21] Others who have studied the same problem differ in their findings; some studies indicate a lower I.Q. among recidivists, while others show no difference.

Merrill concludes that intelligence level as measured by tests has little relation to the choice of a criminal career or its persistence. Intelligence may play a significant role in some delinquency, but it is not an isolated factor; the total personality is involved.

CLASSES OF CHILDREN WHO TYPICALLY TEST LOW

It is now known that almost all intelligence tests do not test "pure" native ability, but test ability as it is strained through informal and formal education, ability to understand and communicate in English, and motivation. In general, children whose parents have a low level of education and who have been unable to give their children an extensive vocabulary, a background of culture, and an interest in reading tend to test lower than children whose parents have given their children such benefits. Children who test low are found among lower class families and among certain foreign-born groups. If these children are compared with children of American middle class background, the scores of the two groups will overlap, for there are dull and bright children in both, but the average scores for the deprived group will be lower than those for the American middle class group.

Certain lower class and foreign-culture groups contain within their ways of life attitudes and customs that accustom their children to certain types of behavior which are accepted as normal in the group, but are considered delinquent by other groups in the larger community. Since intelligence test scores for the entire group may tend to run low, it is easy to make the mistake of attributing the delinquency to low mentality rather than to the cultural way of life of the group.

[20] *Ibid.*, pp. 173–174.
[21] *Ibid.*, p. 117. Other studies are cited.

Indirect Effect of Physical and Mental
Deviations on Delinquency

Inherited physical and mental differences exist, but they do not set one segment of the population aside as potential delinquents and criminals. They cannot, however, be dismissed without consideration of the part they play in the development of children. The roles offered to children are adapted to the normal, average child. Even slight deviations (such as lefthandedness) call for special adjustments on the part of the child. The child who is either very dull or very brilliant, feeble, crippled, muscular if a girl, or pretty if a boy, does not fit into the pattern of expected physical development for customary social roles. Moreover, the lack of adjustment usually increases as the child grows older. When he fails to make normal progress in development or is unable to accept the role offered, he is hindered by that failure as well as by the original handicap. He tends to move further and further out of step with the normal group.

It does not follow that he becomes delinquent, but he is very likely to feel left out and inadequate. On the other hand, sometimes the handicap presents a problem which he is determined to solve, especially if he receives some interested help from adults in forming a constructive attitude toward the handicap. Many fall into a middle group, accepting their handicap realistically and feeling neither inferior nor determined to excel at any cost.

The dull-normal child may react in similar ways: he may feel inferior or accept his status realistically or make an effort to excel in some line. The brilliant child often feels different and may regret or try to hide his brilliance when it seems to set him apart from other children. Occasionally he may use his brilliance in some clever delinquency or in trying to devise "the perfect crime."

Which of these directions adjustment will take seems to depend upon the way in which the child is treated by children and adults about him and the help that he is given in finding a satisfactory role. Physical or mental deviation itself does not cause delinquency, but if the child is rejected from normal groups and excluded from normal roles, delinquency may be one of the alternative choices open to him.

Theories of Delinquent Personalities

As theories linking delinquency and crime with mental defectiveness faded out and clinical psychology and psychiatry came to prominence, the neverending search for a single cause of delinquency shifted to personality disorders. Some psychiatrists have asserted that all delinquents are neurotics. Others have classified delinquents into several different types. When great care is taken in interviewing or when standardized tests are used, the results usually show that half or more of the delinquents do not have pathological or maladjusted personalities.

SYNDROMES OF DELINQUENT BEHAVIOR

One type of classification has been devised by Lester E. Hewitt and Richard L. Jenkins, a psychiatrist with experience in child guidance programs. The classification is based upon the records of 500 children referred to the Michigan Child Guidance Institute, 78 per cent of whom were boys. By statistical methods, syndromes or clusters of related traits were discovered; each syndrome was considered to be symptomatic of a fundamental pattern of maladjustment. With the cases classified into types by syndromes, environmental factors associated with each type were sought. The type of maladjustment and the environmental situation were regarded as closely related and exerting reciprocal influence.

Hewitt and Jenkins discovered three syndromes, described below. Taken together, they comprised only 195 (39 per cent) of the 500 cases. The remaining 305 cases (61 per cent) did not fit into the syndromes. These cases, even though they account for almost two-thirds of the total, were not discussed; presumably they did not have maladjusted personalities, although they had been referred to the Michigan Child Guidance Institute.[22]

TYPE 1. UNSOCIALIZED AGGRESSIVE BEHAVIOR SYNDROME. The child is defiantly aggressive toward others, disregards their rights, and lacks a feeling of responsibility in interpersonal relations. The six items found associated in this syndrome were assaultive tendencies, initiatory fighting, cruelty, open defiance of authority, malicious mischief, and inadequate guilt feelings.

These children usually came from deteriorated homes, often in the country or on the edge of some town. Their parents had little education. The children often were unwanted, probably illegitimate. They felt rejected. The relationship between the parents usually was poor.

The children tended to steal, to lie, and to treat others very badly. They could not get along with other children. Many were the "lone wolf" type.

Fifty-two cases (10.4 per cent) fell into this syndrome.

TYPE 2. SOCIALIZED DELINQUENCY BEHAVIOR SYNDROME. Seven traits were

---

[22] Lester E. Hewitt and Richard L. Jenkins, *Fundamental Patterns of Maladjustment: The Dynamics of Their Origin*, State Printer, Springfield, Illinois, 1946. See also Jenkins, "A Psychiatric View of Personality Structure in Children," Yearbook 1944. *National Probation Association*, New York, 1943; Jenkins and Hewitt, "Types of Personality Structure Encountered in Child Guidance Clinics," *American Journal of Orthopsychiatry*, 14 (1944), 84–94.

used to form this syndrome, three of which (including one of the first three) had to be present for a child to be placed in this classification: association with undesirable companions, gang activities, cooperative stealing, furtive stealing, habitual truancy, running away from home overnight, and staying out late at night.

Children with this syndrome usually lived in deteriorated inner-city areas with a tradition of delinquent behavior among children. They usually were typical gang members, loyal to the standards of the gang but not socialized into the standards of the larger community. The child was aggressive, a bully, and hostile to groups other than his gang. This type of delinquent has been called the pseudo-social type, adjusted to his own gang and its culture but unadjusted to conventional social life.

Seventy cases (14 per cent) fell into this syndrome.

TYPE 3. OVERINHIBITED BEHAVIOR SYNDROME PATTERN. The associated traits are seclusiveness, shyness, apathy, worrying, sensitiveness, and submissiveness.

The home background of the children in this classification was better than that of those in the other two syndromes, but the atmosphere was repressive. The mother might be ill. The child might have some physical defect. The child felt insecure at home. He tended to hide behind a shell of inhibition, but suffered from inner conflicts.

This child was more neurotic than delinquent. Overt symptoms were tics, nail-biting, and disturbances of sleep.

Seventy-three cases (14.6 per cent) fell into this syndrome.

The Hewitt-Jenkins classification differs from many of the others in that it does not imply that traits associated with delinquency are hereditary. The social environment in which the child has been reared is a dominant factor in personality formation, although this does not rule out the possibility of individual differences that might affect the interaction between child and environment.

DELINQUENCY AND EGO CONTROL

A somewhat different classification was made by Albert J. Reiss, Jr., a sociologist, of 1,110 white male juvenile delinquents who were probationers of the Cook County Juvenile Court (Chicago).[23] The classification was made by psychiatric social workers and, in extreme or doubtful cases, by psychiatrists.

The percentage found to have integrated personalities is significant—65.7 per cent. The delinquent person in this group, according to Reiss, in all proba-

[23] Albert J. Reiss, Jr., "Social Correlates of Psychological Types of Delinquency," *American Sociological Review*, 17 (1952), 710–718.

bility will become a mature independent adult. Whether the adult will be delinquent or nondelinquent is not stated.

A second type identified by the psychiatrists, amounting to 22.1 per cent, consisted of delinquents with relatively weak ego controls[24] who are described as very insecure persons with low self-esteem or as highly aggressive and hostile persons. Usually they suffer from internal conflicts and show symptoms of marked anxiety.

The third type in Reiss's series consisted of the group (12.2 per cent) with defective superegos. These delinquents have no internalized or personally accepted social values; they do not submit to the controls of middle class society. They do not have a well-developed conscience and, when they misbehave, have little sense of guilt. Boys of this type usually identify with an adolescent delinquent gang which rejects middle class norms.

Although this classification bears some resemblance to that of Hewitt and Jenkins, the two series of types are not comparable. What seems important is that both studies, using somewhat different methods of isolating maladjusted personalities, report that the majority (65.7 and 61.0 per cent) of the cases exhibited no unusual personality defects.

A weakness of both studies is that no comparable study of nondelinquent children was made. Might not nondelinquents also show somewhat the same percentage of maladjusted personalities? If so, delinquency could not be attributed directly to the maladjustment, but to other factors in the environment. This suggestion seems reasonable in view of the high percentage of delinquency among children whose personalities were not maladjusted. For two-thirds of the children some explanation other than maladjusted personality has to be assumed.

PATHOLOGICAL CHARACTERISTICS OF
DELINQUENT AND NONDELINQUENT CHILDREN

A comparison of pathological characteristics of delinquent and nondelinquent children is provided in the Glueck study of 500 correctional school

---

[24] Ego is the term used by Freud and adopted by psychologists and psychiatrists to refer to the active, practical part of the personality which guides the person in his day-by-day adjustment to the realities of his life. It provides the balance between the id (the basic urges, primitive impulses, often described as selfish, destructive, evil) and the superego (conscience), which sets forth the values and ideals for behavior. A weak ego is one that cannot maintain the balance between self-centered unsocial impulses and ideal standards. The unsocial impulses tend to predominate, and the person seeks immediate gratification for them regardless of social disapproval. If the behavior is inhibited, the person suffers from internal conflicts and exhibits neurotic symptoms.—Joseph Jastrow, *Freud, His Dream and Sex Theories*, Pocket Books, Inc., New York, 1932, pp. 86–92.

TABLE 12

Percentage of Delinquents and Nondelinquents with Different Types of Pathology

DESCRIPTION		DELINQUENTS		NONDELINQUENTS
No conspicuous pathology		48.6		55.7
Asocial, "primitive," poorly adjusted, unstable		16.9		5.9
Organic disturbances of the central nervous system		0.8		0.2
Psychotic trends, or divorce from reality		0.4		1.6
Neuroticism, causing the person to suffer more than average insecurity and anxiety and to develop protective devices that are not culturally approved and that lead to conflicts difficult to solve		24.6		35.8
Marked neuroticism, interferes with efficient adaptation	3.2		5.1	
Mild, does not prevent efficient adaptation	16.3		23.2	
Trends not classifiable as above	5.1		7.5	
Psychopathy, superficial personal relations, less severe than psychosis but more severe than neuroticism		7.3		0.4
Undifferentiated pathology		1.4		0.4
Total		100.0		100.0
Number of cases		496		495

$x^2 = 77.85$; $P < .01$

Reprinted by permission of the publisher from Sheldon and Eleanor Glueck, *Unraveling Juvenile Delinquency*, Harvard University Press, Cambridge, Massachusetts, Copyright 1950 by the Commonwealth Fund, Table on p. 239 and accompanying explanations. In Chapter 18 the Gluecks also give individual tables for forty-two Rorschach tests, comparing the individual characteristics of delinquents and nondelinquents. To the extent that they are applicable, they support Table 12, which is in part based upon them.

and 500 nondelinquent boys matched for residential area, age, ethnic origin, and intelligence rating.[25] The results are shown in Table 12.

An important factor is that almost half of the delinquents and only slightly more than half of the nondelinquents had no conspicuous mental pathology. Stated in reverse, 51.4 per cent of delinquents and 44.3 per cent of nondelinquents were found to have some type of pathology; the excess of

[25] Glueck and Glueck, *Unraveling Juvenile Delinquency, op. cit.,* p. 239.

delinquents over nondelinquents with pathological traits is only 7.1 per cent. According to this table, then, delinquent behavior cannot be attributed directly to maladjustment or to mental or emotional disturbances except, possibly, in 7.1 per cent of the cases.

Some comparisons of the specific pathologies help to throw light on delinquency. In both groups, the more serious pathologies (organic disturbances, psychotic trends) occur only rarely, and in both neuroticism is common, with mild kinds of neurotic reactions predominating.

Some interesting differences appear. Almost three times as many delinquents as nondelinquents were found to be asocial, "primitive," poorly adjusted, and unstable. Also, psychopathy, often associated with aggression, was more common among delinquents, although infrequent in both groups. Combining the two types, some 24 per cent of the delinquents, compared with 6 per cent of the nondelinquents, had tendencies toward aggressive behavior.

Neuroticism, curiously, is distinctly more common among nondelinquents; 35.8 per cent of nondelinquents showed some degree of neurotic symptoms but only 24.6 per cent of the delinquents. This difference in favor of the delinquents may indicate that a high degree of inner control, which may also result in mild forms of neurosis, is essential in children if they are to avoid serious delinquency. The absence of such controls conversely may place them in some jeopardy of delinquency.

Although this research failed to find any single personality pattern that inevitably brought about delinquency, it did identify several patterns that under the right conditions predisposed children to delinquency.

XYY CHROMOSOMES AND DEVIANCE

Although serious consideration of physiological factors as causes of delinquency ceased after the Gluecks, recently a body of evidence has emerged to the effect that men with an anomalous pattern in their sex chromosomes are also likely to be convicted of serious crimes.[26] Men with XYY chromosomes occur in hospitals for the criminally insane about twenty times more frequently than they do in the general population.[27] In comparison with normal men, such men tend to be unusually tall; less intelligent; and to display especially severe cases of acne; and in comparison with other prisoners they exhibit fewer violent crimes against the person; they begin their criminal careers unusually

[26] See Ernest B. Hook, "Behavioral Implications of the Human XYY Genotype," *Science*, 179 (January 12, 1973), 139–150 for a review of this evidence.

[27] *Ibid.*, p. 140.

early in life; they are especially resistive to therapy in the hospital; and their parental families are remarkably free from evidence of criminal behavior.[28] The evidence is reasonably conclusive, then, that men with the XYY chromosomes exhibit a tendency to follow criminal careers and as a result wind up in hospitals for the criminally insane somewhat more often than we might expect from their distribution in the population at large. Nevertheless, only about 2 or 3 per cent of those in such hospitals exhibit the XYY anomaly. Thus, only a tiny fraction of all criminals are at all affected by this factor.

Individual Differences in the Socio-cultural Setting

All in all, then, we have failed in this chapter to isolate a single physiological or psychological pattern that inevitably produces delinquency in children. To be sure certain personality types and physiological patterns expose the individual to greater risk than others, but even in these cases much also depends upon the socio-cultural pressures he encounters as well. In short delinquency seems to develop as the result of a great many social, psychological, and even physiological factors combining in often unique ways to produce individual delinquents, and consequently the search for *general* factors in delinquency has in the past and will probably continue in the future to come up empty-handed.

BIBLIOGRAPHY

CAVAN, RUTH SHONLE, ed., *Readings in Delinquency*, Third Edition, J. B. Lippincott Company, Philadelphia, 1975.

FINK, ARTHUR E., *Causes of Crime, Biological Theories in the United States, 1800–1915*, University of Pennsylvania Press, Philadelphia, 1938.

FOX, RICHARD G., "The XYY Offender: A Modern Myth?" *Journal of Criminal Law, Criminology and Police Science*, 62 (1971), 59–73.

GLUECK, SHELDON, AND GLUECK, ELEANOR, *Physique and Delinquency*, Harper & Row, Publishers, New York, 1956.

———, *Unraveling Juvenile Delinquency*, Harvard University Press, Cambridge, Massachusetts, 1950.

GODDARD, HENRY H., *The Criminal Imbecile*, Macmillan Company, New York, 1915.

———, *Feeble-Mindedness, Its Cause and Consequences*, Macmillan Company, New York, 1914.

———, *Human Efficiency and Levels of Intelligence*, Princeton University Press, Princeton, New Jersey, 1920.

[28] Richard G. Fox, "The XYY Offender: A Modern Myth?" *Journal of Criminal Law, Criminology and Police Science*, 62 (1971), 64. See also Brian C. Baker, "XYY Chromosome Syndrome and the Law," *Criminologica*, 7 (February, 1970), 13–18.

GORING, CHARLES, *Abridged Edition of the English Convict*, His Majesty's Stationery Office, London, England, 1919.

HEWITT, LESTER E., AND RICHARD L. JENKINS, *Fundamental Patterns of Maladjustment: The Dynamics of Their Origin*, State Printer, Springfield, Illinois, 1946.

HOOK, ERNEST B., "Behavioral Implications of the Human XYY Genotype," *Science*, 179 (January 12, 1973), 139–150.

HOOTON, ERNEST A., *Crime and the Man*, Harvard University Press, Cambridge, Massachusetts, 1939.

JENKINS, RICHARD L., "A Psychiatric View of Personality Structure in Children," Yearbook 1943, *National Probation Association*, New York, 1943.

———, AND LESTER E. HEWITT, "Types of Personality Structure Encountered in Child Guidance Clinics," *American Journal of Orthopsychiatry*, 14 (1944), 84–94.

LOWREY, LAWSON G., "Delinquent and Criminal Personalities," Chapter 26 in *Personality and the Behavior Disorders*, J. McV. Hunt, ed., Vol. 2, Ronald Press Company, New York, 1944.

MURCHISON, CARL, *Criminal Intelligence*, Clark University, Worcester, Massachusetts, 1926.

REISS, ALBERT J., JR., "Social Correlates of Psychological Types of Delinquency," *American Sociological Review*, 17 (1952), 710–718.

SHELDON, WILLIAM H., *The Varieties of Temperament*, Harper & Row, Publishers, New York, 1949.

———, *et al.*, *The Varieties of Human Physique*, Harper & Row, Publishers, New York, 1942.

———, with collaboration of Emil M. Hartl and Eugene McDermott, *Varieties of Delinquent Youth*, Harper & Row, Publishers, New York, 1949.

VOLD, GEORGE B., *Theoretical Criminology*, Oxford University Press, New York, 1958.

the family setting
of delinquency

The family is the primary socializing group in society. Not only does it establish the child's basic personality, but it also introduces him to the mores and values of the larger culture. Thus, in a variety of ways the family sets the direction for the individual's development in later life. It is his springboard into adulthood and the broader society.

Since the family is so crucial to the social and personal growth of the individual, it is not surprising that it also looms significantly in the backgrounds of many delinquents. For this reason we must explore the intricate relationships between the family and delinquency.

Identification with Parents

Children learn attitudes and secure personal emotional satisfactions primarily from people whom they admire and wish to emulate as models—in other words, from persons with whom they can identify. Whether a child can or cannot identify with a particular person depends in large measure on how he is treated by that person. Thus the young child's relationship to his parents is very largely a matter of how the parents feel and act toward the child. The externals of a family situation, such as a broken home or poverty, are important primarily as they affect the relationship between parents and children. In some families, for example, a divorce actually means an improvement in parent-child relations. Where the parents have drawn the child into their quarrels or have used him to embarrass or hurt one another, removing this situation by a separation or divorce can lead to an improvement in the child's relations with his mother or father. Dissolving the marriage has a variety of effects on all involved, but we should not assume that *all* of them are destructive to the child's personal and social growth.

SOURCES OF INFORMATION

The dynamics of parent-child relationships are understood mainly through the analysis of individual cases that come to the attention of psychiatrists and clinical psychologists. A child, delinquent or otherwise, who seems to be emotionally disturbed may be brought to a private practitioner or child guidance clinic. Since only obviously disturbed children are brought for diagnosis and treatment, their cases cannot provide a completely adequate basis for understanding the role of the family in delinquency. Many of these children are not delinquent, and many, many delinquent children never appear in such settings. While clinical observations can provide insights into the dynamics of family relations, they cannot yield a full picture of the ways in which parent-child relationships contribute to delinquency.

Comparative statistical studies of delinquent and nondelinquent children with reference to family background are another source of information. These studies do not explore the dynamics of the family relationships but show the prevalence of certain family conditions among delinquents as compared with nondelinquents.[1]

THE MOTHER'S ATTITUDE TOWARD THE BOY

In discussions of parent-child relationships, the attitude of the mother toward her children is often regarded as most significant. The warm, loving mother is the one with whom the child can identify and from whom he receives a sense of worth and self-confidence. The rejecting mother not only does not secure the child's identification but creates in him a sense of unworthiness and resentment.

A commonly held view is that virtually all delinquency is an indication of early parental neglect or rejection. The statistical data to be presented throw doubt upon such sweeping assertions. The great importance of family relation-

[1] Typical of clinical studies are those in the bibliography by Bettelheim, Eissler and Federn, Gardner, Healy, Jenkins, and Redl and Wineman. Typical of the comparative statistical studies are Axelrad, Glueck and Glueck, McCord and McCord, Monahan, Nye, and Reiss. The discussion draws from both of these lists as well as from a variety of other sources.

ships cannot be doubted, and such parental attitudes as neglect, indifference, hostility, and rejection are closely associated with delinquent behavior. However, by every measure of family relationships used in comparative statistical studies, a large percentage of the delinquents—often more than half—have good parental relationships. Conversely, at least a minority of nondelinquents come from homes with unfavorable emotional relationships. A complete contrast in family relationships does not differentiate delinquents from nondelinquents.

Nevertheless, many studies have shown that delinquents tend to have poorer relations with their parents than nondelinquents. Travis Hirschi reports that the child who is only weakly attached to his parents is more likely to be delinquent, regardless of his peer relationships.[2] And the Gluecks have shown that almost twice as many nondelinquent boys as delinquent boys had warmly affectionate mothers (see Figure 4). The mothers of delinquent boys tended to be overprotective, indifferent, or, in a limited number of instances, hostile or rejective.

FIGURE 4

Affection of Mother for Boy Among Five Hundred Delinquent and
Five Hundred Nondelinquent Boys

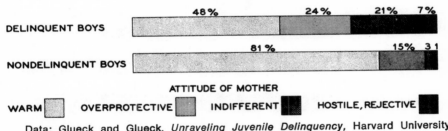

Data: Glueck and Glueck, *Unraveling Juvenile Delinquency*, Harvard University Press.

The record of adult criminality of men is also related to their boyhood family relationships, as shown by a study based on records of family relationships for 253 boys whose average age was eleven years. Sixteen years later a restudy was made with the original group classified into two groups on the basis of whether or not as adults they had been convicted of some crime. For each of many types of family relationships the percentage of criminal and noncriminal sons was computed. The analysis clearly answers this question: In a

[2] Travis Hirschi, *Causes of Delinquency*, University of California Press, Berkeley, 1969, Chapter VI.

family of a certain type what are the chances that at least one adult criminal son will be produced?[3]

Neglecting mothers were most likely to have an adult criminal son; nearly three-fourths of the neglecting mothers fell into this group, as Figure 5 shows. Approximately half of the passive, absent, or cruel mothers had a criminal son. Overprotective mothers were more likely to have noncriminal than criminal sons. The record for loving mothers was especially significant inasmuch as the kind of love made a vast difference. As many loving, neurotic mothers as cruel mothers had criminal sons. As would be expected, loving normal mothers had the best record, but even in this group a fourth had criminal sons. The sons referred to are only those who were included in the study project. Some of the mothers with a criminal son no doubt had other sons who may have been

[3] William and Joan McCord, *Origins of Crime*, Columbia University Press, New York, 1959. A report on the original study of the boys is found in Edwin Powers and Helen Witmer, *An Experiment in the Prevention of Delinquency: The Cambridge-Somerville Study*, Columbia University Press, New York, 1951.

FIGURE 5
Types of Mother in Relation to Criminal and Noncriminal Sons

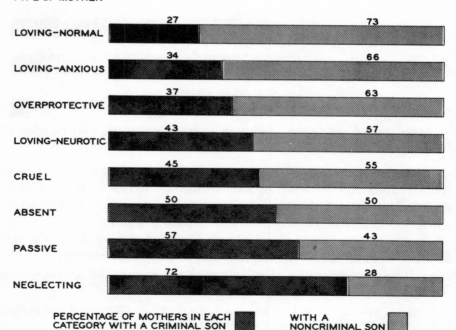

Data: McCord and McCord, *Origins of Crime*, Columbia University Press.

exemplary in their behavior. It would then be necessary to assume that their attitude toward sons who later became criminals differed from their attitude toward conforming sons.

Tables from the Gluecks' study suggest an emotional conflict in the minds of many boys, but more especially of delinquent boys.[4] Two thirds of the delinquents (and 90 per cent of the nondelinquents) were closely attached to their mothers. However, only 22 per cent of the delinquents (but 71 per cent of nondelinquents) felt that their mothers were deeply concerned for their welfare and went to great trouble to provide training and discipline; 59 and 28 per cent respectively felt the parents were well-meaning but did not provide helpful training; 19 and 1 per cent respectively felt their mothers were little concerned for them and were selfish, prejudiced, or rejective. Thus the delinquent boys' emotional attachment to the mother seemed to conflict with their feeling that she was not deeply concerned for their welfare, and this conflict was much greater among delinquent than nondelinquent boys.

The data presented above together with a vast amount of other data from the two studies cited seem to show an association between deviation and either actual or felt rejection by the mother. Whatever the dynamics involved, boys who felt that their mothers were rejecting, neglectful, or indifferent more frequently became delinquent or criminal than did boys who felt sure of their mothers' love and concern. The difference is a matter of degree, however, as the delinquent and nondelinquent boys are far from falling into two groups, the first with rejecting mothers and the second with loving mothers.

The Father's Attitude Toward the Boy

As was true for the mother's attitudes, paternal attitudes of indifference, hostility, neglect, and rejection were more often found among parents of delinquent than nondelinquent boys (Figure 6). Warm, cordial, and friendly feelings on the part of the father were associated with nondelinquency more often than with delinquency on the part of the son. However, for every type of attitude, a large overlap existed between delinquent and nondelinquent boys.

Adverse attitudes were not all on the father's side. Among the Glueck cases, only half as many delinquent as nondelinquent boys were attached to the father (32.5 per cent versus 65.1 per cent).[5] Delinquent more often than nondelinquent boys were indifferent or hostile to their fathers or were noncommittal. The percentage of boys who were attached to the father was much

---

[4] Sheldon and Eleanor Glueck, *Unraveling Juvenile Delinquency*, Harvard University Press, Cambridge, Massachusetts, 1950, pp. 127–129.

[5] *Ibid.*, p. 126.

FIGURE 6

Affection of Father for Boy Among Five Hundred Delinquent and Five Hundred Nondelinquent Boys

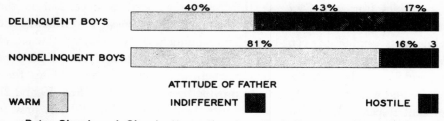

Data: Glueck and Glueck, *Unraveling Juvenile Delinquency*, Harvard University Press.

lower among both delinquents and nondelinquents than the percentages attached to the mother. This finding supports the theory that the mother is the most significant figure for the child, even into the early adolescent period.

About one-fifth of the delinquent boys compared with two-thirds of the nondelinquent boys in the Glueck study felt that their fathers had provided them with training and were deeply concerned.[6] Fully one-third of delinquents felt the father's attitude toward their welfare was poor, but only one in twenty of the nondelinquents shared this feeling.

DISCIPLINE BY PARENTS

Both the McCord and the Glueck studies showed that few boys, delinquent or otherwise, had parents who consistently mistreated them in the name of discipline. This finding does not mean that most parents of delinquents were kind and loving in discipline, although such discipline was found in the families of many nondelinquents. Relatively few parents of delinquents were kindly and consistent in discipline. Either erratic or lax discipline characterized most fathers and mothers of delinquents but was also found to some extent among parents of nondeviants.

THE FAVORABLE HOME

The data cited so far help to outline the type of home conducive to the development of delinquency and one that favors nondelinquent behavior. The McCords conclude from their findings, only a few of which are cited here, that the home most likely to produce adult criminals is the quarrelsome home with neglecting parents and lax discipline. Conversely, the cohesive, love-oriented home is least likely to produce adult criminals. When one parent is loving and

[6] *Ibid.*, p. 129.

the other rejecting, the love of the one helps to offset the neglect or harshness of the other. The loving mother is of special significance in socializing her sons to conforming behavior. While these findings apply to adult criminality, the somewhat similar findings of the Gluecks suggest that they also apply to delinquency. In favorable homes, boys feel accepted and loved; they are drawn to their parents as models worthy to be followed.

PARENTAL MODELS

The loving relationship between parents and child is one side of the coin of identification. The other side is the kind of model presented by parents to their children.

Hirschi concluded that criminal as well as noncriminal parents tend to uphold the mores of society, because his data indicate that intimacy in parent-child relations and *not* cultural orientation of the parents is closely related to delinquency.[7] Similarly, according to the McCords, parents consistently condemned criminality in their sons when it appeared. Apparently, however, parental admonitions are not enough. More significant is the behavior of the parents, especially when relations between the parents and son are rejecting.[8] Studies by the Gluecks and by the McCords show that many delinquents and criminals have had criminal or disorganized parents as models.

The Gluecks graded the homes of delinquents and nondelinquents as good, fair, or poor on the basis of the presence or absence of immorality, drunkenness, criminality, and unwholesome ideals. The great preponderance of poor standards in the homes of delinquents is shown in Figure 7.

[7] Hirschi, *op. cit.*, pp. 94–97.

[8] See Joan and William McCord, "The Effects of Parental Role Model on Criminality," *Journal of Social Issues*, 14, No. 3 (1958), 66–75.

FIGURE 7
Home Conduct Standards for Five Hundred Delinquent and Five Hundred Nondelinquent Boys

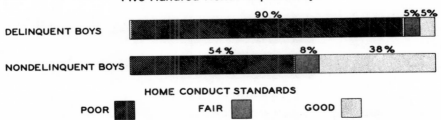

Data: Glueck and Glueck, *Unraveling Juvenile Delinquency*, Harvard University Press.

The fact that over half of nondelinquents also came from homes with poor standards raises several points. Since both groups came from lower class backgrounds, one would expect some deviations from what are essentially middle class standards. But it is necessary to recall that the nondelinquents had an almost perfect record of behavior, lacking even the minor delinquencies tolerated by the public. Why was the conduct of these boys so excessively conforming, when over half came from homes with some immorality, drunkenness, criminality, or unwholesome ideals?

Several clues may point to an explanation. One is the higher proportion of nondelinquent than of delinquent boys who were neurotic (Chapter 9). Some of the nondelinquent boys may have reacted to the poor home situation through neurotic anxieties instead of through overt acts of delinquency. Another suggestion comes from Figure 8, which shows the percentages of boys who felt their fathers were worthy of emulation. In contrast to the very high percentage of homes with poor parental standards (based, it is true, on both parents), few boys felt that their fathers were completely unworthy of emulation. Perhaps they were moved by loyalty to their fathers regardless of conduct. But it is also possible that the conditions that led the researchers to classify the homes as poor did not seem very much out of the ordinary from the lower class point of view of the boys. A third clue comes from the McCords, who found that when the father and mother were both deviant, the association with adult criminality was very high.[9] When one parent was deviant and the other not, the association was less close. The love of one parent, especially of the mother, tended to offset deviation in the other parent.

[9] McCord and McCord, *Origin of Crime*, pp. 93–116.

FIGURE 8

Emulation of Father Among Five Hundred Delinquent and Five Hundred Nondelinquent Boys

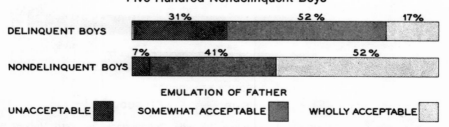

Data: Glueck and Glueck, *Unraveling Juvenile Delinquency*, Harvard University Press.

The Delinquent Girl and Family Relationships

As we indicate in Chapter 11, disturbed family relationships are much more prominent in the background of girl delinquents than boy delinquents. It might appear, therefore, that somehow the family is more important to the girl's social development than the boy's. And, indeed, many studies indicate that as compared with boys, a higher percentage of girl delinquents quarreled with their parents, felt "picked on" at home, disliked the father, and were hostile to the mother and especially to the stepmother if there was one.[10]

But there is good reason to suspect that much of the differences in this regard between boy and girl delinquents reflect mainly differences in "mix" and not basic differences between family relationships and girl or boy delinquents. For example, when we compare boy and girl delinquents who have committed similar offenses, these differences all but disappear.[11] Moreover, if girls were particularly affected by disturbances in the family, we would expect that *in absolute numbers* more girls than boys would become delinquent with this pattern prominently in their backgrounds. But such is not the case. To be sure, when we compare boy and girl delinquents from families in which the parents have deserted or divorced, the ratio (3.59 to 1) is much less than that between boy and girl delinquents whose families are still intact (8.97 to 1).[12] But the differences between boy and girl delinquents in their family relationships most probably results from the fact that so many more boys with good family relationships become delinquent and not because girls are basically more affected by family disturbances.

Broken Homes and Their Implications

Broken homes have been blamed for many years as the source of delinquent behavior. Older studies have little value, however, since the rates of broken homes among delinquents usually were not compared with corresponding rates among comparable groups of nondelinquents. Other studies grouped all types of broken homes together, whether from death, desertion, or divorce, disregarding the distinctive psychological reactions to each type of break. Others took no account of the social-class or ethnic attitudes toward broken

[10] William W. Wattenberg, "Differences between Girl and Boy 'Repeaters,'" *Journal of Educational Psychology*, 47 (1956), 137–146; Wattenberg, "Girl Repeaters," *National Probation and Parole Association Journal*, 3 (1957), 48–53; Wattenberg, "Recidivism among Girls," *Journal of Abnormal and Social Psychology*, 50 (1955), 405–406.

[11] H. Ashley Weeks, "Male and Female Broken Home Rates by Type of Delinquency," *American Sociological Review*, 5 (August, 1940), 601–609.

[12] Computed from Thomas P. Monahan, "Family Status and the Delinquent Child: A Reappraisal and Some New Findings," *Social Forces*, 35 (March, 1957), Table 1.

homes and the possibility that in some groups, intermittently broken homes might be accepted as near-normal. More recent studies go beyond the rates to explore the implications of different types of broken homes for the personality development and behavior of the child. As with many other topics, many studies of broken homes are confined to boys.

Broken Homes Among Delinquents and Nondelinquents

When control groups of nondelinquents are used, the control groups show a persistent but moderate excess of unbroken homes. Table 13 shows the percentages of delinquent and nondelinquent children living with both own parents in different parts of the country over a period of time ranging from the 1920's to the 1940's.

Contrary to popular assumptions, half or more of the delinquents live with their own parents. For this group, the broken home is not a distinctive factor in delinquency. The difference between delinquents and nondelinquents ranges from 6 to 24 per cent in the studies cited in Table 13. However, the percentages are based on delinquent children brought to court attention. They often have brothers and sisters, living in the same broken homes, who are not delinquent. Healy and Bronner, in their study of 153 boy and girl delinquents, found that 65.5 per cent came from homes with both parents present, 34.5 from various types of broken homes.[13] These delinquents came from 133 differ-

---

[13] William Healy and Augusta F. Bronner, *New Light on Delinquency and Its Treatment*, Yale University Press, New Haven, Connecticut, 1936, p. 35.

TABLE 13

Percentage of Delinquents and Nondelinquents Living with Own Parents

TYPE OF DELINQUENT CASES	NUMBER OF DELINQUENT CASES	SEX	PERCENTAGE LIVING WITH OWN PARENTS	
			DELIN-QUENTS	CONTROL GROUP
*Juvenile court cases, Chicago	1,675	Boys	57.5	63.9
†Juvenile court cases, California	300	Boys and girls	49.3	73.3
‡Correctional school, Massachusetts	500	Boys	50.2	71.2

    * Clifford R. Shaw and Henry D. McKay, *Social Factors in Juvenile Delinquency*, A Study . . . for the National Commission on Law Observance and Enforcement, No. 13, volume 2, U. S. Government Printing Office, Washington, D. C., 1931, p. 274.

    † Maud A. Merrill, *Problems of Child Delinquency*, Houghton Mifflin Company, Boston, 1947, p. 66.

    ‡ Sheldon and Eleanor Glueck, *Unraveling Juvenile Delinquency*, Harvard University Press, Cambridge, Massachusetts, 1950, pp. 88–89.

ent families that had produced a total of 194 delinquent children among a total of 461 old enough to become delinquent. Among all the children, 42 per cent were delinquent and 58 per cent nondelinquent. In other words, the broken home that produces one or several delinquents does not necessarily produce only delinquents.

The mere fact of the absence of one or both parents is less significant than the relationships that exist in the family among whatever family members are present. The absence of one or both parents reduces the probability of adequate relationships but does not necessarily destroy all significant relationships. The preceding section of this chapter brought out the importance of a loving relationship, fair discipline, and adequate parental models and the fact that one loving, nondeviant parent may offset the effect of a rejecting or deviant parent. Broken or unbroken, these relationships are significant. The type of break is important in terms of the different kinds of interference that it makes in good interpersonal relationships within the family.

Age of Delinquents

Preteen-age boys come from broken homes in greater proportion than adolescent boys, according to the Chicago study by Shaw and McKay.[14] At age ten almost twice the proportion of delinquent boys as of schoolboys (control group) came from broken homes. At ages fifteen to seventeen, the proportions of delinquents and schoolboys from broken homes were almost equal. Comparisons for girls are not available. The conclusion might be drawn that at the earlier ages boys are still more in need of identification with their parents and more dependent on them for affection and satisfaction of needs than are adolescents.

Sex and Broken Homes

Studies including both boys and girls show that fewer delinquent girls than boys live with both parents and that more come from broken homes. A third to a half of all delinquent girls live with both parents, compared with half to three-fourths of the delinquent boys. A Philadelphia study (Table 14) of court cases from 1949 to 1954 showed that 72.4 per cent of all white boy first offenders lived with both parents, compared with only 48.4 per cent of the girls.[15] As we have already noted, however, the marked difference in family stability between delinquent boys and girls probably reflects the fact that many

[14] Clifford R. Shaw and Henry D. McKay, *Social Factors in Juvenile Delinquency*, A Study . . . for the National Commission on Law Observance and Enforcement, U. S. Government Printing Office, Washington, D. C., 1931, No. 13, Vol. 2, p. 277.

[15] Monahan, *op. cit.*, pp. 250–258.

TABLE 14

Family Status of Delinquent First Offenders Disposed of in Municipal (Juvenile) Court, Philadelphia, 1949–1954

(Percentage Distribution)

A. WITH WHOM CHILD LIVED	WHITES		BLACKS	
	BOYS	GIRLS	BOYS	GIRLS
Both of own parents	72.4	48.4	47.2	27.3
Mother only	15.5	26.1	35.2	46.7
Mother and stepfather	4.2	7.0	2.8	2.7
Father only	2.6	4.6	3.8	5.2
Father and stepmother	1.3	3.1	1.4	2.0
Adoptive parents	0.1	0.3	*	0.1
Other family home	3.9	10.5	9.6	16.0
†Institution	(0.4)	(0.9)	(0.1)	(0.1)
Total	100.0	100.0	100.0	100.0
Number of cases	11,236	1,984	8,706	2,736
B. MARITAL STATUS OF PARENTS				
Own parents living together	73.1	49.7	47.8	27.9
Parents unmarried	1.6	4.1	10.7	20.3
Mother dead	2.9	6.3	4.8	7.5
Father dead	7.7	11.0	9.8	10.4
Both parents dead	0.5	1.6	1.7	2.1
Father deserted mother	0.7	1.7	2.3	3.6
Mother deserted father	0.2	1.8	0.2	0.3
Both parents deserted	0.1	0.1	0.2	*
Parents living apart	7.9	14.0	20.1	25.4
Parents divorced	5.3	10.7	2.4	2.5
Total	100.0	100.0	100.0	100.0
Number of cases	11,244	1,906	8,643	2,717

Thomas P. Monahan, "Family Status and the Delinquent Child: A Reappraisal and Some New Findings," *Social Forces,* 35 (1957), 250–258.

* Less than 0.05 per cent.

† Not included in 100 per cent.

more boys become delinquent for reasons unrelated to the family and not that young girls are especially vulnerable to family instability.

TYPES OF BROKEN HOMES

The most common type of truncated family that remains after a break is the mother and children, according to a Philadelphia study (Table 14-A). The delinquent boy or girl, if not living with both parents, is likely to live with the mother. The mother-child combination might be the result of separation, desertion, divorce, death, or failure to marry at all. Whatever may have gone before, at the time of delinquency the incomplete family nucleus is the mother and her children.

Broken homes are essentially ones in which the mother has not remarried (or never was married). Fathers and stepfathers very infrequently play a role. Stepmothers are also a rarity. The infrequent variant types of father only, stepfather (for whites), or stepmother include a higher percentage of girl than of boy delinquents.

Neither the broken home nor the mother-child home is found only among delinquents, although every type of broken home is more characteristic of the delinquent than the nondelinquent group, according to the Glueck study of lower class white boys (Table 15). Among the types of broken homes the mother-child combination far outranks other types among nondelinquents as among delinquents.

Difference Between White and Black Delinquents

The diversification of types of broken homes for blacks follows in general the pattern for whites, with one glaring exception. For both boys and girls the percentage of delinquents who live with both parents is only a little more than half the percentage of white delinquents who live with both parents. Table 14-A

TABLE 15

Living Arrangements of Five Hundred Delinquent and
Five Hundred Nondelinquent Boys

(Percentage Distribution)

WITH WHOM BOY LIVED	DELINQUENT BOYS	NONDELINQUENT BOYS
Both his own parents	50.2	71.2
One own parent (the mother four times as often as the father among delinquents, three times as often among nondelinquents)	34.6	19.8
One own parent and one stepparent	8.0	4.4
Two stepparents, foster parents, other relatives, brothers and sisters	7.2	4.6
Total	100.0	100.0
Number of cases	500	500

Reprinted by permission of the publisher from Sheldon and Eleanor Glueck, *Unraveling Juvenile Delinquency*, Harvard University Press, Cambridge, Mass., Copyright 1950 by the Commonwealth Fund, pp. 88–89.

shows that only 47.2 percent of the black boys as compared with 72.4 per cent of the white boys live with both parents; the unusually low percentage of 27.3 of the black girls as compared with 48.4 per cent of the white girls live with both parents. Complementing this difference is the large proportion of black boys and girls who live with the mother only—roughly twice the proportion for whites. Black children less often have stepfathers and more often live in other people's homes than do white children.

The key to this situation is the high percentage of unmarried mothers in the black group. Five or six times as many black delinquents as white have unmarried parents. Fathers more often desert mothers, and there are many more cases of separation of parents. (However, white delinquents' parents more often are divorced than black delinquents'.)

The greater proportion of unmarried, deserted, and separated parents among blacks is not confined to delinquents. It is a general condition among lower class blacks both in the South and in the North. For the total population 33 per cent of all black children under age eighteen live in families headed by someone other than the married father and mother; the corresponding percentage for white children is only 7.[16] Even when a couple does head the household, the union may be unstable, as is shown by a study of 2,253 households in Atlanta, Georgia. In 12 per cent of the marital unions, both the man and the woman were temporarily living together; 38 per cent were common-law marriages without legality but with more permanence than the temporary union; 50 per cent were licensed marriages. The lower the social-class level, the more often were the unions of the impermanent or nonlegal type.[17] A Chicago study also shows the prevalence of black families with female heads in the lower class—twice as high a proportion as in the black upper class.[18]

In many lower class neighborhoods, the family headed by the mother or grandmother is the normal type. Black men seem to have retained some of the role they had during slavery, when their masters rather than they were responsible for the support of their families. Black mothers, accustomed to work during the slave period, continue the dual role of employed woman and mother. Many black lower class households consist of a grandmother, mother, and dependent children. Continuity, stability, and authority are in female hands.

[16] *Ibid.*

[17] Mozell C. Hill, "Research on the Negro Family," *Marriage and Family Living*, 19 (February, 1957), 29.

[18] E. Franklin Frazier, *The Negro Family in Chicago*, University of Chicago Press, Chicago, 1932.

Into these maternal households, men come, either as husbands or companions, but feel free to desert periodically or permanently. The term serial monogamy has been applied to this situation.[19]

IMPLICATIONS OF THE MOTHER-CHILD HOME

An important implication concerns the normal differences in roles played by the father and mother throughout American culture but especially in some lower class subcultures. Usually the mother is the parent to whom the child first becomes attached, and, unless she rejects the child, she continues to exert an affectionate, understanding, and sometimes yielding influence on the child. The father usually is a more dominating figure with whom the child may come in conflict and who may react to the child more aggressively and punitively than the mother.

Data already presented from the McCord and Glueck studies show that the mother is a warmer and more loving figure in the child's experience than the father and that this is true for both delinquents and nondelinquents. Absence of the father from the home therefore removes the parent who is most likely to be hostile and disliked. But it also removes a basic source of control and discipline in the family. Thus, a fatherless family may exhibit less quarreling and less disorganization, but it probably also is a family in which the children enjoy more freedom from parental guidance and control. Where the mother is burdened with serious personal problems and is unable to support or nurture her children or to supervise them, delinquency in both boys and girls is a strong likelihood.

In general, then, a broken home is almost always one in which the remaining parent, usually the mother, is unable to exercise the same degree of control as when the family was intact. But the effect of the break upon the basic stability of the family depends a good deal upon the source of disorder and disorganization in the family. Where the mother was a basic source of bitterness and rancor, the absence of the father may spell even greater difficulties for the children. But if the father was a disturbing factor, his absence probably means greater cohesion and stability in mother-child relationships. A broken home, therefore, is not always a disorganized, destructive environment

---

[19] St. Clair Drake and Horace R. Cayton, *Black Metropolis: A Study of Negro Life in a Northern City*, Harcourt, Brace & World, New York, 1945, pp. 582–599; Walter B. Miller, "Implications of Urban Lower-Class Culture for Social Work," *Social Service Review*, 33 (September, 1959), 219–236. Miller's discussion is not limited to blacks but is especially applicable to them.

for children. Relative to what it was with both parents present, it may sometimes represent a distinct improvement.[20]

Another handicap, especially for boys, is the absence from the home of a masculine model. The father usually passes on to his sons the self-concept and role of the adult man in his subculture and to his daughters the conception that they should have of men in the subculture. When the father is not present, any one of a number of outcomes is possible. The boy may continue to model himself after his mother, developing a somewhat feminine self-concept and seeking a feminized masculine role, such as cook or some other service position. He may turn to some other adult male for a model, or he may find an adolescent version of the adult role through a delinquent gang.[21]

Two sub-types of mother-child families are distinguishable: the family in which the parents married, with some anticipation of permanency, and the marriage then disintegrated through some form of separation with or without divorce; and the family in which a marriage never took place or disintegrated before a definite family pattern had developed, to be followed by a kind of serial monogamy, usually illegal but with more permanence than casual promiscuity. The effects of the two types on children are probably not identical.

1. Some form of separation removes the legally married father from the home two to three times as often as death (Table 14-B). Conflict between the parents often precedes a separation, and bitterness may follow it. The way in which the mother speaks of the father affects the attitude that children have for the father. Studies of nondelinquent children aged six to ten years, separated from their father by military service, throw light on the relation between the mother's spoken attitudes toward the father and the child's conceptions of the father.[22] When the mother always spoke of the absent father in derogatory terms, the child's fantasies pictured the father as fearful and aggressive. The opposite was true when the mother always spoke favorably of the father. It seems probable that in many cases of permanent separation of parents, the mother may deride her husband to her children. The child then is not only deprived of a daily father model but would not have in memory a favorable model.

---

[20] This line of reasoning may explain why lower class black nondelinquents tend to come from fatherless families slightly more often than lower class black delinquents. In such families the father may represent a disorganizing influence; whereas in the fatherless black family, the mother is better able to govern her children effectively. See Ray A. Tennyson, "Family Structure and Delinquent Behavior," in *Juvenile Gangs in Context*, Malcolm W. Klein, ed., Prentice-Hall Inc., Englewood Cliffs, N.J., 1967, Table 5.

[21] Miller, *op. cit.*

[22] George R. Bach, "Father Fantasies and Father Typing in Father-Separated Children," *Child Development*, 17 (1946), 63–80.

In the much more rare case of a mother-child home resulting from the death of the father, there is less probability of bitterness and often a tendency for the remnants of the family to work together.

The addition of a stepparent, although infrequent (Table 14-A), often necessitates a difficult adjustment, whether or not the child is already delinquent, or it may contribute to the beginning of delinquency.[23] Usually the stepparent is a stepfather who may seek to exert authority over a stepchild without the compensating affection and need-satisfaction usually extended by the child's own father, whose authority is thus tempered. Stepfather and stepchild may mutually dislike and reject each other. On the other hand, if the stepfather develops affection for the child and if the child finds in him a trustworthy father model, the relationship may be helpful to the child and a preventive of delinquency.

The child may develop considerable hostility that he projects on weaker and less threatening figures than the stepfather. Or he may simply step out of the family and avoid home as much as possible. Typically, he steps into the street life of his neighborhood, which rarely offers an adequate substitute for a normal family relationship.

2. The second sub-type of mother-child family is the one in which a legal or otherwise stable union was never effected between father and mother. This type of family has been termed a "female-based" family by a sociologist who has worked intensively with lower class delinquent boys.[24] This family is especially commonplace among lower class blacks. Among blacks and whites, values, attitudes, and roles develop that are an outgrowth of this particular type of family and that affect the personality and behavior of children.[25] This family is not a breakdown of the more conventional American family, but a unique type, accepted in certain lower class subcultures and perpetuated from one generation to the next. The mother assumes the responsibility of rearing her children and the expense of maintaining the home, often with help from relief agencies.

One result of the fluidity of relationships between men and women is the high rate of illegitimacy, especially among blacks.[26] Black illegitimacy occurs much more often in lower class than in middle or upper class levels, according

[23] Charles E. Bowerman and Donald P. Irish, "Some Relationships of Step-Children to Their Parents," *Marriage and Family Living*, 24 (1962), 113–121.

[24] Miller, *op. cit.*

[25] *Ibid.*

[26] *Statistical Abstract of the United States, 1967*, U.S. Government Printing Office, Washington, D.C., 1967, p. 51.

to Chicago studies.[27] Deplored by the middle and upper classes, illegitimacy has little stigma in the lower class black family for either mother or child. The problems that arise are the result not of social stigma, but of inadequate care and the lack of a father to teach both sons and daughters responsible adult roles.

The illegitimate boy has a choice of roles. He may well repeat the role of his father or later male associates of his mother—the ne'er-do-well or the drifter. This role easily includes a variety of delinquencies for the boy and minor crimes for the adult.

When the boy does not blindly accept the role of irresponsibility, he may pattern himself after his mother in a modified feminine role, as suggested above.

A third possibility is the repudiation in adolescence of the feminine role and along with it "goodness" as a feminine trait. The boy then attempts to be tough and "bad," modeling himself after tough men in the neighborhood and affiliating with a gang of boys who are equally in the pursuit of masculine toughness.[28] Delinquencies follow as part of the technique of learning a tough masculine role adapted to lower class culture and lower class manual occupations.

The illegitimate adolescent girl, following the pattern of her mother and other adult female relatives, may find herself accused of sexual promiscuity, or she may drift away from her family and enter prostitution, a following condemned by her own family and class as well as by the middle class. If she becomes a streetwalker, she is liable to arrest and perhaps commitment to a correctional school.

The Disintegrated Family

The small percentage of children who live outside the family group may be bereft of any intimate continuing relationship with an affectionate adult with whom to identify. Such deprived children differ from rejected children in that often they have literally had almost no opportunity for an emotional identification with any adult. Nondelinquent institutional children, paired with children in foster homes and studied at various ages between three and twelve years of age, were found to be generally impoverished mentally—they had poor memories, experienced difficulty in grasping general concepts, were unorganized in responses to present situations, and were handicapped in planning ahead.[29]

[27] Frazier, *op. cit.*, p. 189; Drake and Cayton, *op. cit.*, p. 604.

[28] Miller, *op. cit.*

[29] William Goldfarb, "Psychological Privation in Infancy and Subsequent Adjustment," *American Journal of Orthopsychiatry*, 15 (1940), 247–255.

Although their physical needs were well met and they were not harshly treated, their emotional needs were not satisfied. The children tended to be placid and conforming. However, when released from this situation and placed in foster homes, they became hyperactive and uncontrollable, and their behavior was characterized by tantrums, fights with other children, and running away. Their behavior was impulsive, that is, not oriented toward a goal. In early years in school they were unmanageable and impulsive, and, when blocked, showed some hostility. In the foster home and elsewhere they demanded a continuous display of affection, seemed never to be satiated, but were unable to give affection in return. The rejected child, on the other hand, has usually spent some time with his parents and has some identification with them, which stimulates him to respond and to organize his activities.

Redl and Wineman, in their discussion of *Children Who Hate*, describe a boy of eight who fits rather well the pattern of the deprived child.[30]

> Larry was born in a charitable institution where he remained for two years. His mother, unmarried, visited him only occasionally. From the time he was two years old, he was transferred from one foster home to another. When he was six he went to live with his mother, who had married. The mother was unable to offer Larry a warm relationship. The stepfather was an alcoholic, brutal and bullying. Larry was severely mistreated physically by the stepfather, being beaten, kicked, thrown into a drainage ditch, and locked into a shed for hours at a time. Larry entered the residential school for aggressive delinquent boys, of which Redl was the director, shy, detached, and afraid of adults. As he adjusted to the school he became demanding, "commanding" someone to bring him articles that were not available. He was ridiculed by the other boys in the school and often made the scapegoat of their remarks and actions. He resented anything that he regarded as a favor done by a counselor to some other boy or as a slight to himself. His reaction was to refuse to listen to explanations and to scream his demands.

The other boys in the school (there were five most of the time) seemed to fall somewhere between deprivation and rejection, or to exhibit a combination. All were unable to control their impulses, unresponsive to counselors, and at times uncontrollable in behavior. Their past records included stealing, running away, and attempting to injure siblings.

Many such homeless children are shifted at short intervals from one place to another. The Gluecks found that 50.4 per cent of their 500 delinquent boys

[30] Abstracted from Fritz Redl and David Wineman, *Children Who Hate*, Free Press of Glencoe, Inc., New York, 1951, pp. 55–56, 113, 121.

had had one or more changes of family setting, compared with only 10 per cent of the nondelinquent group who had not lived consistently in one household. Of the delinquents, 19.6 per cent had made one or two changes, 16.9 per cent three to five changes, and 13.9 per cent six or more changes.[31] Black delinquents have an even higher proportion than white delinquents from shattered homes.[32] In a New York state correctional school, among white boys the same proportion (50 per cent) as in the Glueck study had lived continuously in one family. The black boys had a very different history of family stability. Only one-fifth had continuously lived in one family, and 17 per cent had lived in four or more different types of families. Under these conditions of constant change, many boys must necessarily fail to establish a permanent satisfying relationship with any adult.

Poverty and Employment of Parents

Poverty, unemployed fathers, and employed mothers have often been held accountable for juvenile delinquency. Since the Social Security Act was passed in 1935, the sharp edge of dire poverty has been blunted by such provisions as Aid to Dependent Children and Unemployment Insurance. Nevertheless much variation in economic status remains, even within the lower class.

POVERTY

In their study of 500 delinquents and 500 nondelinquents, the Gluecks matched the two groups on a number of economic items. The usual occupation of the fathers was almost identical, with 68.4 per cent of the fathers of delinquents and 62.5 per cent of the fathers of nondelinquents doing unskilled and semiskilled work.[33] However, the usual economic status of the families of delinquents was far below that of nondelinquents. Almost none of either group were in comfortable economic circumstances and two-fifths of both groups were sporadically dependent. Here the resemblance stopped. Twice as many nondelinquents as delinquents were from families with marginal comfort: 41.0 per cent versus 20.0 per cent. In the lowest group, usually dependent, were 36.2 per cent of the delinquents but only 14.6 per cent of the nondelinquents.

[31] Glueck and Glueck, *op. cit.*, p. 121.

[32] Sydney Axelrad, "Negro and White Male Institutionalized Delinquents," *American Journal of Sociology*, 57 (1952), 569–574.

[33] Glueck and Glueck, *op. cit.*, pp. 104, 106.

Boys from the low income group are also much more likely to repeat their delinquencies than are delinquent boys from comfortable or even marginal families. Figure 9 shows that among boys on probation in Cook County (Chicago), Illinois, the proportion who became recidivists increased as family economic status declined, with twice as high a proportion from the dependent level recidivating as from the comfortable level. Therefore, the conditions faced by the boy in the low income family seem not only to permit or encourage delinquency but to lead to continued offenses.

The question immediately arises as to why low income is conducive to delinquency among boys. Reiss, who compiled the data for Figure 9, suggests that economic deprivation may lead the boy to feel insecure and to doubt whether the economic system will provide for him in the future. Losing confidence in society, he loses his respect for the approval of society. He would therefore be able to justify his delinquencies and avert a sense of guilt.

EMPLOYMENT OF THE MOTHER

Traditionally the employed mother is as much a deviant from social customs and good family policy as the unemployed father. The ideal was the mother who devoted herself to the task of homemaking and rearing children. The mother who sought work usually did so because the family needed additional income for necessary expenses. She often was the mother without a husband in the home, or the wife of an unemployable or intermittently employed man. Economic need is still a motivation for employment of mothers; however, the percentage of mothers who are employed is increasing markedly

FIGURE 9

Economic Status of Families of Delinquents and of Recidivists, Cook County, Illinois

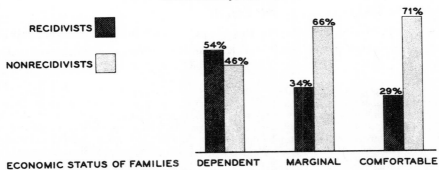

Data: A. J. Reiss, Jr., "Delinquency as the Failure of Personal and Social Controls," *American Sociological Review,* 16 (1951), 200.

and no longer represents dire economic need.[34] Employment often is a symbol of aspiration and of upward social mobility and as such may be an integrative and stabilizing influence.

The Glueck study shows only a moderate difference between the delinquents and nondelinquents, with both groups having more than half of the mothers at home (53.0 and 67.0 per cent respectively).[35] Approximately a fifth of the mothers of both groups had regular employment outside the home. More mothers of delinquents than of nondelinquents had occasional employment—26.6 per cent and 14.7 per cent. Within the delinquent group, mothers who worked tended somewhat more often than housewives to have husbands who were emotionally disturbed, had poor work habits, and were not supporting the family adequately.[36] Parents tended to be incompatible in the group with employed mothers, and the family lacked cohesion. Some of these situations were more acute in families in which the mother was occasionally employed than in those in which she worked regularly. Sons of employed mothers had less supervision and more freedom away from home than sons of housewives. However, many differences are not extreme and many of the sons of housewives also faced unfavorable situations in the home.

It seems difficult if not impossible to isolate the effect that employment of the mother has on delinquent behavior. Employment of the mother is part of a general family pattern involving an inadequate or disturbed father, low economic level, and lack of family cohesion, all of which are independently related to delinquent behavior. They are probably all closely interrelated. Together they create a disjointed family situation which fails to give the boy (and probably even more the girl) firm identification with loving and admired parents.

The Delinquency-prone Family

From the studies cited in this chapter and other less extensive studies much too numerous to be quoted, it is possible to draw some conclusions about

[34] The percentage of mothers with children under eighteen who were employed increased from about 20 per cent in 1948 to 49.4 per cent in 1971; the percentage of mothers of children under six who were employed increased from about 13 per cent in 1948 to 29.6 per cent in 1971. See *Children in a Changing World*, published and distributed by the White House Conference on Children and Youth, 1960, p. 10; and "Marital and Family Characteristics of Workers, March 1971," Special Labor Force Report Summary, U.S. Department of Labor, Table 2.

[35] Glueck and Glueck, *op. cit.*, p. 112.

[36] Sheldon and Eleanor Glueck, "Working Mothers and Delinquency," *Mental Hygiene*, 41 (July, 1957), 327–352.

the delinquency-prone family. In comparison with families of nondelinquent boys, delinquency-prone families as a group have a greater proportion of rejecting or harsh parents, parents who impress their sons as indifferent to their welfare, parents who are erratic or lax in discipline, or who offer little for the sons to admire or emulate. Delinquency-prone families are more likely than other families to be broken (for some delinquents there is no family at all), with the female-based family a common type in some groups. The delinquency-prone family frequently is financially dependent on outside assistance or public relief; when the mother is employed it is usually at occasional jobs. There is evidence that an accumulation of unfavorable factors increases the likelihood that the boy will become delinquent and also that he will become a recidivist. However, some unfavorable factors can be balanced against favorable ones—for example, the effect of the harsh father may be neutralized by the loving mother. Thus families differ as to the number and combination of favorable and unfavorable factors.

Within a family, proneness to delinquency differs from one child to another. Each child has his own personal relationship with his parents. One child in a family may be loved, another rejected; one child may be favored by the mother, another by the father. The ordinal position and the sex of a child may be factors. Moreover, children differ in physical and temperamental qualities. The strong boy may be treated differently than the handicapped boy, the bright child differently than the dull child, within the same family.

From this complicated web of family relationships each child acquires his first concept of himself, his first set of values, his first roles. If he is given a conception of himself as worthy, conforming, and good and acquires values that are aligned with those of the larger society and an opportunity to act out corresponding roles, he is not likely to become permanently delinquent, although he may as a child vacillate between good and bad behavior within the limits of tolerance for a child of his age and sex. The child who is rejected, who conceives himself as unworthy, who acquires a delinquent set of values or only a confusion of values, and who develops nonconforming or confusing roles to play is much more likely to become a delinquent.

Virtually all the material in this chapter is confined to the lower class, and it refers to children who have been sufficiently delinquent to become court cases, correctional school inmates, or adult criminals. Most of the data refer to boys. The moderately vacillating child, the middle class delinquent, and the girl delinquent have not yet been adequately studied in their family setting. Additional research is urgently needed since it cannot be assumed that the discussion in this chapter applies to these groups in the same way or to the same degree as to the seriously delinquent lower class boy.

BIBLIOGRAPHY

AXELRAD, SIDNEY, "Negro and White Male Institutionalized Delinquents," *American Journal of Sociology*, 57 (1952), 569–574.

BETTELHEIM, BRUNO, *Truants from Life, The Rehabilitation of Emotionally Disturbed Children*, Free Press of Glencoe, Inc., New York, 1955.

CAVAN, RUTH SHONLE, editor, *Readings in Juvenile Delinquency*, Third Edition, J. B. Lippincott Company, Philadelphia, 1975.

DRAKE, ST. CLAIR, AND HORACE R. CAYTON, *Black Metropolis: A Study of Negro Life in a Northern City*, Harcourt, Brace & World, New York, 1945.

EISSLER, K. R., AND PAUL FEDERN, editors, *Searchlights on Delinquency, New Psychoanalytic Studies*, International Universities Press, Inc., New York, 1949.

FRAZIER, E. FRANKLIN, *The Negro Family in Chicago*, University of Chicago Press, Chicago, 1932.

GARDNER, GEORGE E., "Separation of the Parents and the Emotional Life of the Child," *Mental Hygiene*, 40 (1956), 53–64.

GLUECK, SHELDON, AND GLUECK, ELEANOR, *Family Environment and Delinquency*, Boston, Houghton, Mifflin Company, Boston, 1962.

———, *Unraveling Juvenile Delinquency*, Harvard University Press, Cambridge, Massachusetts, 1950, Chapters 8–11.

———, "Working Mothers and Delinquency," *Mental Hygiene*, 41 (1957), 327–352.

GOLDFARB, WILLIAM, "Psychological Privation in Infancy and Subsequent Adjustment," *American Journal of Orthopsychiatry*, 15 (1940), 247–255.

HEALY, WILLIAM, AND AUGUSTA F. BRONNER, *New Light on Delinquency and Its Treatment*, Yale University Press, New Haven, Connecticut, 1936.

JENKINS, RICHARD L., *Breaking the Patterns of Defeat*, J. B. Lippincott Company, Philadelphia, 1954.

McCORD, JOAN, AND McCORD, WILLIAM, "The Effects of Parental Role Model on Criminality," *Journal of Social Issues*, 14, No. 3 (1958), 66–75.

———, *Origins of Crime. A New Evaluation of the Cambridge-Somerville Youth Study*, Columbia University Press, New York, 1959.

MONAHAN, THOMAS P., "Broken Homes by Age of Delinquent Children," *Journal of Social Psychology*, 51 (1960), 387–397.

———, "Family Status and the Delinquent Child: A Reappraisal and Some New Findings," *Social Forces*, 35 (1957), 250–258.

———, "The Trend in Broken Homes among Delinquent Children," *Marriage and Family Living*, 19 (1957), 362–365.

NYE, F. IVAN, *Family Relationships and Delinquent Behavior*, John Wiley & Sons, Inc., New York, 1958.

PARSONS, TALCOTT, "Certain Primary Sources and Patterns of Aggression in the Social Structure of the Western World," *Psychiatry*, 10 (1947), 167–181.

REDL, FRITZ, AND DAVID WINEMAN, *Children Who Hate*, Free Press of Glencoe, Inc., New York, 1951.

REISS, ALBERT J., JR., "Delinquency as the Failure of Personal and Social Controls," *American Sociological Review*, 16 (1951), 196–208.

Rosen, Lawrence, "The Broken Home and Male Delinquency," in *The Sociology of Crime and Delinquency*, Marvin Wolfgang *et al.*, eds., John Wiley & Sons, Inc., New York, 1970, pp. 489–495.

Shaw, Clifford R., and Henry D. McKay, *Social Factors in Juvenile Delinquency*, A Study . . . for the National Commission on Law Observance and Enforcement, Number 13, Volume 2, U. S. Government Printing Office, Washington, D. C., 1931, Chapters 9 and 10.

delinquency of girls   chapter 11

The delinquency of girls is of a different kind from the delinquency of boys. Although delinquency in both sexes inevitably reflects the ways in which personality patterns and goals interact with social expectations, boys and girls differ somewhat in their personality patterns as well as in the standards they must uphold, so that their behavior in general and their delinquent activities in particular follow distinctive paths. Superimposed upon these differences, moreover, are common problems arising out of similarities in their situation, e.g., adolescence. Thus, delinquency in girls is shaped by the peculiarities of the feminine status in society as well as by all the other difficulties that adolescents fall prey to, with the result that girl delinquency resembles boy delinquency in certain particulars but on the whole presents a pattern distinctly its own.

Characteristics of Girl Delinquency

As was pointed out in Chapter 1, about three boys appear before juvenile courts for every one girl. Although police juvenile officers are more likely to release young girls than boys without a court hearing, or to refer the girl directly to a social agency, this differential treatment accounts for only part of the differences in court cases. Even in socially disorganized areas, girls do not have free run of the community to the same extent as boys; family control is greater for girls; social expectations differ.

TYPES OF DELINQUENCY

These differences in the roles of boys and girls in the family and the community are reflected in the types of delinquency characteristic of boys and girls. The delinquencies of boys are overt and aggressive, in the form of burglary, larceny, vandalism, and disorderly conduct. Girls exhibit very low rates in these types of offenses, but much higher rates of runaway, truancy, and incorrigibility. To some extent these differences reflect basic differences in sex role, but not entirely. Boys commit more delinquencies in all categories (see Table 16), but the difference between the sexes is least in incorrigibility and general rebelliousness. Thus, the disproportionately large number of male delinquents arises primarily because of the large volume of male violent offenses.

The pattern of violent offenses so prominent in boy delinquency is quite consistent with the emphasis upon active confrontation in the male role. But boys and girls who are incorrigible are probably not behaving that way because of their sex role but rather because they have encountered serious strains in relating to important adults in their social world. Thus, since sex role has less to do with this type of delinquent behavior, we find boys and girls being incorrigible in more nearly the same numbers.

TABLE 16

Offenses of Adolescents Committed to Illinois Juvenile Institutions in 1972*

	BOYS		GIRLS		TOTAL	
OFFENSE CATEGORY	N	%	N	%	N	%
1. Larceny and nonviolent theft	292	26.0	22	17.6	314	25.2
2. Violent theft, personal violence and property damage	464	41.3	22	17.6	486	38.9
3. Sexual offenses	40	3.6	1	0.8	41	3.3
4. Incorrigibility and general delinquency	209	18.6	76	60.8	285	22.8
5. Antisocial conduct	116	10.3	4	3.2	120	9.6
6. Technical or unspecified	2	0.2	—	—	2	0.2
Total	1,123	100.0	125	100.0	1,248	100.0

* These figures were compiled from "Semi-Annual Statistical Summary, Juvenile Division" (January 1, 1972–June 30, 1972 and July 1, 1972–December 31, 1972), Division of Research and Long Range Planning, Illinois Department of Corrections, p. 17. Although these figures reflect most directly the policies of judges in sending adolescents to institutions, they also give us an approximation of the offenses that boys and girls commit to get to institutions. Drug offenders do not appear here because they are committed for the most part to drug rehabilitation centers.

EARLY BEGINNINGS OF DELINQUENCY

Little girls as well as little boys begin delinquent behavior in early childhood. Police pick up both boys and girls as young as six or seven years, although they do not usually refer them to the juvenile court at these early ages. Delinquency for both boys and girls reaches its highest point during adolescence; girl's cases especially tend to be concentrated at ages thirteen and over.

This concentration is related to changes in the type of delinquency as girls pass from childhood into adolescence. A Detroit study shows that girls below the age of twelve were guilty primarily of stealing small objects, usually through shoplifting—the same offense for which little boys are usually picked up.[1] In early adolescence girls were referred to the police primarily for incorrigibility, truancy from home, and some sex offenses. In mid-adolescence, girls were most frequently charged with sex offenses and disorderly conduct, with some continuation of incorrigibility and truancy from home. Boys in the meantime had shifted from petty thievery to more serious kinds of stealing and some instances of assault.

DEARTH OF STUDIES OF DELINQUENT GIRLS

Aside from statistical reports few studies have been made of delinquent girls. Nearly all of the major studies, e.g., those performed by the Gluecks or by Hirschi, have focused upon boys.[2] Moreover, those studies which are available have been unsystematic and limited in their theoretical underpinnings so that our knowledge of girl delinquency is weak and fragmentary in comparison with what is known about male delinquency.

Several reasons may be suggested for the greater emphasis on studying the delinquent behavior of boys. The recurrent frequency of male delinquency generates a greater source of social disorganization. In addition, many juvenile delinquents continue their misconduct and become the adult criminals of the next decade. Since adult male criminals exceed adult female criminals eight to one (more than double the ratio for juvenile delinquents), the assumption is that boys are more likely to continue into adult criminality than are girls. Moreover, the offenses of boys attack some of our most cherished values, since

---

[1] William W. Wattenberg and Frank Saunders, "Sex Differences among Juvenile Offenders," *Sociology and Social Research*, 39 (1954), 24–31; Wattenberg, "Differences Between Girl and Boy Repeaters," *Journal of Educational Psychology*, 47 (March, 1956), 137–146.

[2] In 1934, Sheldon and Eleanor Glueck published *Five Hundred Delinquent Women* (Alfred A. Knopf, New York), which dealt with women who had been in the Massachusetts Reformatory for Women. However, none of their many studies has been on delinquent girls. See also Travis Hirschi, *Causes of Delinquency*, University of California Press, Berkeley, 1969.

they usually involve destruction or theft of someone else's property. Girls' offenses primarily tend to harm themselves and are often outgrown as the girls reach a level of maturity where they are no longer in school or under the authority of parents. Minor sex offenses (promiscuity) are often curbed by marriage.

Actually, a valid point could be made that girl delinquency is a more serious problem than boy delinquency. If girls carry their problems into marriage, their lack of adjustment may affect the rearing of their children, sons as well as daughters. The chapter on the family emphasizes the influence that mothers have on the conduct of their sons. One way to curb the delinquency of boys might be to give more attention to the delinquency of girls.

Social Backgrounds of Delinquent Girls

One of the early studies of Chicago, which established the location of high-delinquency areas, included an ecological map of the residences of delinquent girls who had appeared before the juvenile court during 1917–1923. The distribution of rates resembles that for boy delinquents. The highest rates were in certain areas adjacent to the central business district, populated primarily by newly arrived immigrant groups; high rates also extended into a concentrated black slum area. The rates declined toward the periphery of the city as local communities increased in socio-economic status. When rates for boys and girls are compared by square-mile areas, a great similarity is evident; in general, areas with high boy rates also have high girl rates, so much so, in fact, that the correlation between the two series of rates is 0.79.[3] Studies made in the 1920's and 1930's of other cities—Cincinnati, Seattle, Minneapolis, St. Paul— show the similarity between the geographic distribution of rates for boys and girls.[4] For only one of these cities, Cincinnati, is the correlation between the boys' and the girls' series of rates given. It is .95, showing an even closer correspondence of high and low rate areas for boys and girls than was shown for Chicago.

In general, delinquency among girls flourishes in the same lower class and especially culturally disorganized and socially deprived areas that contribute to the delinquency of boys. These are also the same areas that produce large amounts of adult criminality as well.

[3] Clifford R. Shaw and associates, *Delinquency Areas*, University of Chicago Press, Chicago, 1929, pp. 137–160.

[4] Clifford R. Shaw and Henry D. McKay, *Juvenile Delinquency and Urban Areas*, University of Chicago Press, 1942, pp. 250, 363, 419, citing studies made by Norman S. Hayner and Calvin F. Schmid.

Although the correlation between rates for different areas is very high, it is not complete. In each city a few areas noted for high rates for boys have low rates for girls, or vice versa. Cultural and social factors may account for such differences.

The Labeling Process and Girl Delinquents[5]

As girls grow older and their misdemeanors become broadly known in the community, they may become labeled as "bad girls," problem girls, or simply as incorrigibles. The conventional expectation for girls is obedience at home and school, spending nights at home, and abstinence from full sexual relations. Many girls do not fit into this pattern, and they become involved in a cluster of related offenses. Typical are truancy, running away from home, shoplifting, using drugs, and casual sex relations with men in return for food, money, and a place to stay. When an arrest follows, the charge could be any one of several violations: running away, incorrigibility, or sexual offenses, although the latter is relatively rare. The girl is usually returned to her home town and placed in a detention home until her case is heard in court. Although such cases are rarely if ever reported in the newspapers, news of the girl's escapade spreads quickly and her label as a delinquent is quickly acquired.

A typical response in this situation is resentment and defiance toward her accusers, and as her relations in the community worsen, she is soon cut off from anyone who might persuade her to behave differently. Thus, the "bad girl" continues to be bad, to run away from disapproval, and even to escalate her misconduct. Her tarnished reputation, i.e., her label, simply hastened the whole process.[6]

Types of Delinquency by Social Class

The influence of social class and ethnic subcultures on delinquency has been demonstrated for boys; such influence is also evident in girl delinquency. Since the subcultural values and customs for girls differ from those for boys, the direction of pressure also differs.

[5] See a general discussion of labeling in Chapter 5.

[6] The labeling process is very similar to a self-fulfilling prophecy in which a prediction of an event serves to produce the event. See William D. Payne, "Negative Labels, Passageways and Prisons," *Crime and Delinquency*, 19 (January, 1973), 33–40; and Frederic L. Faust, "Delinquency Labeling, Its Consequences and Implications," *Crime and Delinquency*, 19 (January, 1973), 41–48.

MIDDLE CLASS GIRLS

Although middle class girls approach equality with boys in many respects, certain restrictions are made which affect actual misconduct and define what is allowed. In general, middle class girls are permitted somewhat less freedom by their parents and teachers than boys. Although broad changes are underway, it is still probably true that teen-aged girls are expected to adhere to a code of behavior that is more restricted, especially regarding sexual behavior, than are boys. Underlying this code for the girl is the necessity of making a good marriage in early adulthood.

The girl who is not respected, who is suspected of using drugs, who is thought to be promiscuous, or who becomes pregnant before marriage loses much of her desirability as a marriage partner. To be sure many young couples experiment sexually before marriage, but the typical middle class high school girl is expected to wait at least until college when serious courtship usually begins. The whole focus of social conditioning, therefore, for the teen-aged middle class girl is toward obedience to parents, restrictions of activities, and conformity to the mores, especially the sexual mores.[7]

The middle class girl does not feel strong pressure to assert herself competitively in preparation for future money-making. Most middle class girls expect the husband to be the main support of the family, the dominant one in making decisions, and the protector against the harshness of the outside world. They may plan to work before they have children or after the children are in school, but they regard their income as secondary to that of the husband.

The middle class girl learns this social pattern from her parents and often accepts her mother as model. Whereas the middle class boy is surrounded by feminine models throughout his childhood and must resist their influence in adolescence to achieve masculinity, the girl does not ordinarily undergo such a wrenching shift in identity.[8] If she accepts her mother's teachings and patterns her conduct accordingly, she moves smoothly from childhood through adolescence into adulthood, retaining her mother as model throughout.

But, as we have indicated, the cultural restrictions placed upon middle class girls are being relaxed today with the result that many parents are confused regarding how closely they *should* supervise their teen-aged daughters. This confusion, in turn, sets the stage for bitter parent-daughter disputes. If

[7] Ira L. Reiss, *Premarital Sexual Standards in America*, Free Press of Glencoe, Inc., New York, 1960. This book examines in detail the various shades of meaning given to different types of premarital sex relations, especially in the middle class.

[8] See Albert K. Cohen, *Delinquent Boys*, Free Press of Glencoe, Inc., New York, 1955, pp. 162–169.

the girl is too advanced in her behavior for her parents, or if they hold the reins too tightly, she may be tempted to defy them and remain out all night, date boys of whom they do not approve, or become a partner with some boy in a round of automobile-drugs-alcohol-sex escapades. If she associates her women teachers with her mother, she may defy them also. She is very likely to feel rejected and, in fact, may be rejected because of her behavior.

She will probably be rejected by other middle class girls who adhere more closely to the middle class code, and in her loneliness she may seek friends among other rejected girls, or she may turn to boys for meaning and a sense of importance. Her boyfriends, however, will not be those ordinarily approved of by her parents or teachers. Lacking both love and self-confidence, she grasps eagerly for the attention of boys. Heavy petting and sometimes sex relations on a casual and permissive basis follow. She may not be widely promiscuous, but her relationships with boys are not based upon mutual affection or a sense of responsibility to one another, and the result is often simply a compounding of her problems with her parents, teachers, and more conventional peers.[9]

The girl who has reached this point is violating middle class mores and delinquency laws at several points. She is considered "ungovernable" by her parents and teachers, and legally she is a sexual offender. Her violations of the code are likely not to extend to public disorderliness and may be known only in her school, to her parents, and to a limited group of other adolescents. Middle class adults are less likely to look upon her as a delinquent than as a misguided, troubled, maladjusted adolescent who needs help. She is quite likely to be referred to a child guidance clinic or a private psychiatrist. Even if parents in desperation refer her to the juvenile court as incorrigible or she is caught by police in some escapade, she is very likely to be handled informally or referred to a social agency rather than to receive a formal hearing in the juvenile court.

Considerable effort is expended to bring the middle class girl delinquent back into the framework of the subculture, to restore her respectability, and to improve her potential to be marriageable.

LOWER CLASS GIRLS

The cultural expectation for lower class girls, as for middle class girls, is sexual abstinence until marriage, but the situation of the lower class family is somewhat different—e.g., its social status is lower and its claims to respectability are more tenuous. Hence, minor deviations from social expectations are less

---

[9] See Gisela Konopka, *The Adolescent Girl in Conflict*, Prentice-Hall, Inc., Englewood Cliffs, N.J., 1966, especially Chapters 3, 5, and 6.

damaging socially and more common than in the middle class. Although lower class girls are expected to adhere to much the same standards regarding sexual conduct as middle class girls, the resultant scandal when they yield is much less, and accordingly sexual indulgence is relatively common for both boys and girls.[10] If kept to reasonable levels, however, this fact does not seriously hurt her chances for marriage nor irreparably damage her reputation in the eyes of her peers.

But if the girl makes sexual liaisons a central part of her life, becomes publicly conspicuous in securing partners, and seems on the road to prostitution, she is more likely to be arrested. Often sexual relations are only one part of a wider pattern of related delinquent activities. For example, a girl is in conflict with her parents and teachers; she runs away from home to another city or to a different part of her own city if it is large. She is immediately faced with the need for money. Since she is still of school age she cannot find work. She may then solve the problem of money for a room, food, and other necessities by permitting herself to be picked up by men whom she meets around taverns. Some shoplifting or petty larceny supplies a supplement. In time she is very likely to be arrested. In many cities it is routine for such a girl to be given a physical examination which will reveal whether she has had intercourse, is pregnant, or has a venereal disease. She may then be charged with being a sexual offender, although her illegal sexual activities are simply part of a wider pattern of misbehaviors, all of which, incidentally, are an effort to solve personal problems.

The hazards of unrestrained sexual relations are considerable for young girls. Not only does she encounter a number of people who have very little regard for her physical or social welfare, she also runs a serious risk of contracting venereal disease. In retracing networks of syphilitic infection, public health agencies sometimes uncover extensive chains of contacts, including anywhere from forty to 600 persons. Not infrequently girls of thirteen to sixteen have contacts with men who have become infected from older professional prostitutes; these young girls then pass the infection along to others in the course of promiscuous sex relations. Contacts may be made in youth clubs, taverns, or restaurants which serve as teen-age hangouts; the place of intercourse often is an automobile. Young girls often are introduced by a mutual friend to the

---

[10] See Alfred C. Kinsey et al., *Sexual Behavior in the Human Female*, W. B. Saunders, Philadelphia, 1953, Table 80, p. 337 and Table 115, p. 440; Alfred C. Kinsey et al., *Sexual Behavior in the Human Male*, W. B. Saunders, Philadelphia, 1948, Table 85, p. 348. See also Theodore N. Ferdinand, "Sex Behavior and the American Class Structure: A Mosaic," *Annals of the American Academy of Political and Social Science*, 376 (March, 1968), 82–84.

youth with whom they later have intercourse; or they become acquainted informally in the hangouts. In a network of related contacts involving forty-seven persons, the following teen-age girls were involved:[11]

Betty, a girl of sixteen, unmarried, rarely frequented bars; parents separated, mother an alcoholic. Eventually became pregnant by a married man, Boris, who infected her.

Helen, aged fourteen, sister of Betty, who introduced her to Boris, with whom she had intercourse. She had had trouble with the police and was a habitual truant. She also had intercourse with a twenty-nine-year-old man met at a bar, and with a thirty-year-old man.

Ellen, aged eighteen, with an eight-month-old illegitimate daughter. Her mother was dead and her father lived in another state; she lived with a married sister. She was known as a "problem child." She contracted syphilis from Boris and passed it on to another man.

Gilda, aged nineteen, married but separated from her husband; she had sexual relations with Boris and other men.

Marian, aged thirteen, an eighth-grade student who was a habitual truant. She contracted syphilis from a man who had contracted it from Ellen.

Lorraine, aged seventeen, contracted syphilis from her husband, who had contracted it from his mother-in-law, who had contacts with Boris.

In a network of eighty-three persons, half of the girls involved were under nineteen years old, half of the men under twenty-four. One of the youngest, Zeena, aged twelve, came from a broken home. She was a habitual truant, and bragged about having syphilis. She hung around a drive-in where soft drinks and sandwiches were served. She had had sex relations with eight men. Three other teen-age girls named six, twelve, and twenty-two male contacts. Descriptions of other and larger infectious networks are similar, usually with approximately half the girls being in their teens.

While still of juvenile delinquency age, few girls are professional prostitutes in the sense that they demand and receive payment for intercourse. Their sex relations tend to be casual venturesome experiences for pleasure or popularity or in imitation of slightly older girls who permit sex relations. However, as they become known as easy marks among boys and men, they drift toward prostitution.

---

[11] *Venereal Disease in Children and Youth*, U. S. Department of Health, Education, and Welfare, Public Health Service, Bureau of State Services Communicable Disease Center, Atlanta, Georgia (undated, statistics cover 1959), pp. 15–24.

Variations in Lower Class Values for Girls

The values and customs of some ethnic subcultures may differ from those just described. For example, among Italian ethnic groups virginity at marriage is highly valued for girls. Among families that follow the ethnic traditions, girls are closely supervised. Compact self-contained communities may show a surprising difference in the delinquency rates of boys and girls. In a midwest city of moderate size, in lower class Italian neighborhoods the most disorganized of the neighborhoods had no more girl delinquents than neighborhoods with a higher degree of stability. The rate for boys in the highly disorganized area was double the rate in the more stable areas. Inquiry revealed that it was part of the value system of the Italian-born parents that the girls should be carefully protected but that the boys should gain their entrance into manhood through greater freedom, which in the American city often led into delinquency.[12]

In a study of the Italian community in an eastern city the same emphasis on supervision and chastity of girls is brought out.[13] Young Italian men, free to follow their personal inclinations in sexual matters, tended to seek sexual partners outside the Italian community, and respected the Italian mores that frowned upon pair-dating. When the time came to marry, they turned to the protected Italian girls for wives.

Somewhat the reverse of this cultural attitude is found in the lower class black or Latin community, in which sexual promiscuity of girls is accepted casually, both by the girl's family and by young men in the community.[14]

Changing Adolescent Values

In the restless decade of the 1960's both boys and girls found new ways to evade family and community restrictions and to search for new life styles for themselves. Many young teen-agers followed the movement of older adolescents in leaving home, accepting the label of hippies or social dropouts, and entering into short-lived communes.[15] With no definite plan except to get

[12] Unpublished study made by Ruth Shonle Cavan in the 1930's when the Italian colony was still intact.

[13] William Foote Whyte, "A Slum Sex Code," *American Journal of Sociology*, 49 (1943), 24–31.

[14] Cf. Hylan Lewis, *Blackways of Kent*, University of North Carolina Press, Chapel Hill, 1955, pp. 82–93; and Oscar Lewis, *La Vida*, Random House, Inc., New York, 1966.

[15] Clifford J. English, "Leaving Home: A Typology of Runaways," *Society*, 10 (July-August, 1973), 22–24; Abraham Miller, "On the Road: Hitchhiking on the Highway," *Society*, 10 (July-August, 1973), 14–21; and Lewis Yablonsky, *The Hippie Trip*, Western Publishing Co., Racine, 1968.

away from conventional life and no means of support, they drifted from place to place or settled in metropolitan havens where alienated youth found tolerance for their freedom of behavior. A similar pattern of wandering, especially by boys, was common during the depression years of the early 1930's.[16] Its recurrence in recent years differs in that apparently more girls today are "taking to the road." Shoplifting, panhandling, drug use, and sexual freedom among groups are characteristic. Gradually parents, welfare agencies, and police have grown somewhat tolerant, though still basically disapproving.[17] Parents try to keep some contact with their wandering children and when they are located, send them money. Social agencies in some cities have opened runaway centers, which give not only shelter but medical care (especially for venereal diseases and hepatitis) and counseling. Unless some serious crime is committed this conduct is gradually being accepted as a social or personal aberration rather than as delinquency or criminality.

Among later teen-agers and some younger ones, boys and girls are living together in semipermanence, without marriage commitments, and temporary liaisons are also increasing. Such arrangements are facilitated by the availability of contraceptive pills and abortions which remove one of the inconvenient results of illicit sexual intercourse—unwanted pregnancy.[18] Although sex relations among unmarried couples have occurred widely since the beginning of civilization, the present pattern of behavior differs somewhat in that (1) it reaches more broadly into the middle class than before, and (2) it is practiced openly with the rental of apartments by couples, joint bank accounts, and ownership of cars.[19] This behavior violates various laws of long duration designed to limit sexual behavior to marriage (with tolerance, however, for prostitution). So long as there is no public disturbance and parents and other adults do not complain, police tend to shut their eyes to these private arrangements.

The above examples of changing adolescent values and behavior exem-

---

[16] Thomas Minnehan, *Boy and Girl Tramps of America*, Farrar and Rinehart, New York, 1934.

[17] Robert R. Bell, "Parent-Child Conflict in Sexual Values," *Journal of Social Issues*, 22 (April, 1966), 34–44.

[18] Miriam Birdwhistell, "Adolescents and the Pill Culture," *The Family Coordinator*, 17 (1968), 27–32.

[19] Phillips Cutright, "The Teenage Sexual Revolution and the Myth of an Abstinent Past," *Family Planning Perspectives*, 4 (January, 1972), 24–31; Nancy B. Greene and T. C. Esselstyn, "The Beyond Control Girl," *Juvenile Justice, Journal of the National Council of Court Judges*, 23 (November, 1972), 13–19; Marian D. Hall, "Understanding Sex Behavior," *Mental Hygiene*, 50 (July, 1966), 371–73; and Eleanor D. Macklin, "Heterosexual Cohabitation among Unmarried University Students," *The Family Coordinator*, 21 (October, 1972), 463–472.

plify the current difficulty in defining delinquency, especially for girls. When is a runaway or sexually active adolescent girl to be defined—labeled—as delinquent; when is she a teen-ager seeking a period of freedom—a *wanderjahr;* and when is she experimenting with sex as a preliminary to marriage? When is she to be left alone to create her own life style, when referred to a clinic as in need of counseling or therapy, and when to be arrested, adjudged delinquent, and perhaps sent to a training school for delinquent girls? Clearly the mere engagement in behavior that has conventionally been defined as delinquent is not an adequate cause for arrest.

Group Associations

A higher percentage of girl delinquents than of boy delinquents are without definite group or gang association: 86 versus 67 per cent, according to a Detroit study of police cases.[20] In general they are less well-adjusted socially, and they display greater personality disturbance than boys.[21] The greater prominence of poor social and psychological adjustment among girl delinquents may arise from the fact that relatively few avenues to delinquency are open to girls. Many otherwise normal boys become delinquent because of peer group pressures, but such is less often the case with girls. Thus, few girls become delinquent who do not also exhibit serious and chronic disturbances in their relationships at home or at school. Since there is no reason to anticipate sharp sex differences in this respect, about the same number of boys probably also become delinquent for these same reasons. The overall differences between boy and girl delinquents, therefore, emerge primarily because there are so many more well-adjusted adolescents among male delinquents than among female delinquents.

PEER GROUPS AND DELINQUENCY

Small cliques and groups of girls may make their forays into night life a joint project. The girls offer protection to each other and exert mutual control; they lessen the chance that some man will try to pick up a girl without her willingness. They may meet a group of boys in a tavern or dance hall and drink, talk, and dance together. Depending upon the interests of the girls, at the end of the evening they may leave as a mutually protective group, or they may pair off with boys or men to continue into petting and sexual activities. The profes-

[20] Wattenberg and Saunders, *op. cit.*

[21] See Starke R. Hathaway and Elio D. Monachesi, *Analyzing and Predicting Juvenile Delinquency with the MMPI,* University of Minnesota Press, Minneapolis, 1953, Table 3, p. 46.

sional streetwalker usually operates alone; her objective is to make money, and her reputation is measured against that of other prostitutes and not against the conventional standards of morality. Even the promiscuous teen-age girl is not "selling herself" for money; she wishes to avoid the designation of prostitute. She is looking for fun, excitement, entertainment, perhaps small gifts. She still hopes to preserve her reputation and eventually to marry. The clique or group of girls aids her to achieve these objectives.

Aggressive gangs of girls are rare. When they do occur they often represent attempts by those involved to mimic the activities of gangs of boys in the immediate neighborhood. Isolated incidents involving a gang of girls are reported periodically in the newspapers. One such incident involved an attack on two girls, aged thirteen and fifteen, by a band of eight teen-aged girls, known to hang out on a corner in the area. The attacking girls were dressed in blue jeans and were smoking cigarettes. They engaged the two girls, not delinquent nor members of their group, in an argument and then followed the two as they tried to evade their attentions. They first flicked ashes in the girls' faces and threatened to poke the cigarettes in their eyes, then pushed the girls around and flung one into the gutter, injuring her. The other escaped and ran for help. The attackers were not immediately caught, nor was the reason for the attack known.

Relation of Girls to Boys' Delinquent Gangs

Among preadolescents, a girl or two may be admitted to a boys' gang on equal terms. She is usually an active tomboyish type who can equal the boys in physical strength and daring. With adolescence, when boys and girls become aware of sex differences and become interested in those of the opposite sex, the girls are likely to drop out of the gang. While in, they participate in the boys' activities.[22]

Adolescent girls may become adjuncts of boys' gangs, individually or in groups, but are not accepted on a basis of equality. Girls who are the "steady dates" of members, especially of leaders, are tolerated on the fringe of the gang. Groups of girls may become subordinate auxiliaries of gangs, supplying dating partners for dances, sexual partners in a discreet way, or a protective front for the boys during times of active intergang fighting. Girls may carry the boys' weapons before and after a gang fight; if police interfere, no weapons are found on the boys. Police hesitate to search the girls, since only policewomen may search girls or women.

[22] Frederic M. Thrasher in his book *The Gang* (University of Chicago Press, Chicago, 1927, pp. 225–227) describes such a gang; it was an oddity rather than the customary thing.

Gangs of older youths who engage in robberies of stores or taverns often depend upon a girl to enter the place several times previous to the burglary to take note of windows, doors, where the cash is kept, and so on. The girl does not participate in the actual break-in and hence cannot be connected with the crime, although later she may share directly or indirectly in the proceeds.

The organization of girls' gangs may be on an age basis, if the boys are so organized. They adopt a name derived from the gang's name, but indicating a lower status, perhaps by the adding of "-ette" to the gang's name, indicating smallness. In other gangs, the girls' groups are called debutantes, pointing up their social function. If the boys wear a distinctive jacket or cap, the girls wear a similar one to indicate their relationship. Although the girls' groups are as a whole subordinate to the boys' gangs, each girls' group is internally organized with its own leaders. It seems, however, to have few activities independently of the boys' gang, and its chief function is to cater to some need or desire of the gang. The gangs thus accept the lower class concept, especially dominant in some ethnic groups, that the male is dominant, the female subordinate.

Individual girls who date delinquent boys often benefit indirectly from the delinquencies. The theft of an automobile may be for the purpose of taking a girl out for an evening; the stolen jewelry may include a gift for the girl; the money stolen or secured from the sale of stolen property may provide for an evening's entertainment or for gifts. The girl may or may not be aware of the delinquencies; if she is, she may find the boy attractive because of his daring; or she may simply ignore the origin of the money or gifts. She benefits from the boy's delinquencies but she is not legally responsible.

In summing up delinquencies of girls, we may conclude that the sex exploits and incorrigibility for which girls are arrested are only part of a more inclusive pattern of delinquent activities which sometimes includes relationships with delinquent boys. At the same time, a large proportion of girls who are arrested seem not to have group affiliations.

A Problem of Interpersonal Relations

Girl delinquents resemble boy delinquents in age distribution, concentration in lower socio-economic areas, and a background of disorganized family life. Delinquent boys seem to be struggling to reach masculine values of success and status through various competitive devices such as outwitting police, showing superior courage, and finding a way to gain money without hard work. The delinquent girl is concerned with evading unpleasant interpersonal relationships at home and establishing successful relationships with boys, often defined in terms of sexual attraction. The confirmed delinquent boy moves into adult crime usually for financial gain, the confirmed delinquent girl moves into prostitution and minor forms of stealing, or into a common-law or legal marriage where her support may come from the criminal activities of her husband.

BIBLIOGRAPHY

BELL, ROBERT R., "Parent-Child Conflict in Sexual Values," *Journal of Social Issues*, 22 (April, 1966), 34–44.

BIRDWHISTELL, MIRIAM, "Adolescents and the Pill Culture," *The Family Co-ordinator*, 17 (1968), 27–44.

COHEN, ALBERT K., *Delinquent Boys, The Culture of the Gang*, Free Press of Glencoe, Inc., New York, 1955, pp. 137–147.

CUTRIGHT, PHILLIPS, "The Teenage Sexual Revolution and the Myth of an Abstinent Past," *Family Planning Perspectives*, 4 (January, 1972), 24–31.

ENGLISH, CLIFFORD J., "Leaving Home: A Typology of Runaways," *Society*, 10 (July-August, 1973), 22–24.

FAUST, FREDERIC L., "Delinquency Labeling, Its Consequences and Implications," *Crime and Delinquency*, 19 (January, 1973), 41–48.

FELICE, MARIANNE, AND DAVID R. OFFORD, "Girl Delinquency . . . A Review," *Corrective Psychiatry and Journal of Social Therapy*, 7, No. 2 (1971), 18–33.

GALVIN, JAMES, "Some Dynamics of Delinquent Girls," *Journal of Nervous and Mental Diseases*, 123 (1956), 292–295.

GLUECK, SHELDON, AND GLUECK, ELEANOR, *Five Hundred Delinquent Women*, Alfred A. Knopf, New York, 1934, pp. 34–42, 147–152.

GREENE, NANCY B., AND T. C. ESSELSTYN, "The Beyond Control Girl," *Juvenile Justice, Journal of the National Council of Court Judges*, 23 (November, 1972), 13–19.

GREENWALD, HAROLD, *The Call Girl: A Social and Psychoanalytic Study*, Ballantine Books, New York, 1958.

HALL, MARIAN D., "Understanding Sex Behavior," *Mental Hygiene*, 50 (July, 1966), 371–373.

HATHAWAY, STARKE R., AND ELIO D. MONACHESI, *Analyzing and Predicting Juvenile Delinquency*, University of Minnesota Press, Minneapolis, 1953.

KONOPKA, GISELA, *Adolescent Girl in Conflict*, Prentice-Hall, Inc., Englewood Cliffs, N. J., 1966.

LYNN, D. B., "A Note on Sex Differences in the Development of Masculine and Feminine Identification," *Psychological Bulletin*, 66 (1959), 126–135.

MACKLIN, ELEANOR D., "Heterosexual Cohabitation among Unmarried University Students," *The Family Coordinator*, 21 (October, 1972), 463–472.

MILLER, ABRAHAM, "On the Road: Hitchhiking on the Highway," *Society*, 10 (July-August, 1973), 14–21.

MINNEHAN, THOMAS, *Boy and Girl Tramps of America*, Farrar and Rinehart, New York, 1934.

PAYNE, WILLIAM D., "Negative Labels, Passageways and Prisons," *Crime and Delinquency*, 19 (January, 1973), 33–40.

SCHOEPPE, AILEEN, "Sex Differences in Adolescent Socialization," *Journal of Social Psychology*, 38 (1953), 175–185.

WATTENBERG, WILLIAM W., "Differences between Girl and Boy 'Repeaters'," *Journal of Educational Psychology*, 47 (1956), 137–146.

———, "Girl Repeaters," *National Probation and Parole Association Journal*, 3 (1957), 48–53.

———, "Recidivism among Girls," *Journal of Abnormal and Social Psychology*, 50 (1955), 405–406.

———, AND FRANK SAUNDERS, "Sex Differences among Juvenile Offenders," *Sociology and Social Research*, 39 (1954), 24–31.

YABLONSKY, LEWIS, *The Hippie Trip*, Western Publishing Company, Racine, 1968.

the life histories
of four delinquents

The four case summaries given in this chapter illustrate two basic ideas: the ways in which various factors associated with delinquency combine, often fortuitously, to foster delinquency; and the process by which minor delinquencies of early childhood develop into the serious delinquencies of later adolescence and (in three cases) into the criminal behavior of adults.

The cases show two different clusters of factors. One case is of a boy deprived of close relationships in either a family or a peer group. He was set afloat in society without roots, preparation for employment, or a sense of social responsibility. Fortuitous circumstances had familiarized him with the use of firearms. Childhood attempts to solve certain problems by stealing found their adult counterpart in armed robbery. Another case depicts a boy with normal working class family relationships, whose moral standards and habits were developed in close ties first with semidelinquent street-corner boys and later with adult criminals. As an adult he was a career criminal of moderate success. The third case concerns a typical gang boy, the influence of whose peer group far outweighed the influence of his family. Of above-average intelligence, he was eventually able to identify with adults who understood his problems and who were able to provide a way of life, status, and prestige that did not depend upon membership in a fighting gang.

The fourth case describes a girl whose middle class but impoverished family fell apart when her parents were divorced. Without strong parental ties or close peer attachments, she became an introverted teen-ager who dreamed of a literary career but found solace only in a succession of temporary relationships. Seeking to win approval, she followed a pattern common among rootless girls of shoplifting, promiscuous sex, and finally prostitution, all complicated by drug addiction.

All these cases are summaries of actual case histories supplemented in one case by a careful study of agency records covering the entire life of the child. The accounts are factual, although the identities of the persons involved have been disguised.[1]

The cases are not presented as typical of delinquency in general or of a certain type of delinquency. They were selected for very simple reasons. A limited number of detailed cases of delinquents is in print; unpublished cases are often fragmentary, slanted toward one or another theory, or not available for publication because of their confidential nature. These four published cases were readily available in rather complete form. Moreover, in each case the history of the child is carried on into adulthood, thus giving a complete longitudinal picture through the childhood years into a firmly fixed adult mode of life.

The Delinquent Deprived of Family or Peer Group Identification

The deprived child is one who has never had an opportunity to live intimately within a family group. Hence he fails to secure identification with parents. Learning of values and approved norms comes through the process of identification with the parents or other adults. Their values and norms are accepted by the child as right; thus the basis of his conscience is formed. The deprived child does not go through this process. Sometimes an attachment to some adult other than the parent—a relative, minister, teacher, youth leader, or neighbor—acts as a partial substitute, but some children lack even this partial identification. The second source of identification usually is the peer group, which offers its version of values and norms. They may be congruent with or opposed to the adult values and norms. In either case, the child is incorporated into the peer group and has the security of acceptance by his fellow members. When a child lacks both family and peer group, he picks up the pattern of his

---

[1] Other case studies prepared by professionals are also in print. These were not used for a number of reasons. Some represent a past period; others do not carry the case beyond adolescence; still others are strongly slanted toward one or another theoretical interpretation. For the purpose of illustration, the unadorned accounts by journalists seemed most appropriate and provided opportunity for selection of a variety of factors associated with delinquency without strong emphasis on any one theory. The bibliography at the end of this chapter lists other published case studies.

life in hit-or-miss fashion without much regard to the values and expectations of other people.

Identification with an intimate group serves another function in addition to development of values and norms. It gives the child a sense of worth. The child without close attachments often feels that he is no good and unwanted by anyone. Moreover, he has no opportunity to learn how to build up a close friendship or love relationship with anyone.

The deprived child is rootless. He drifts into and out of situations with little planning. He is concerned with his own impulses and needs; his behavior is unrestrained by consideration for others. He may be openly hostile or simply bewildered and ineffectual.

It does not follow that such a child necessarily becomes delinquent, but the usual restraints imposed by conscience and group controls are lacking. Fortuitous circumstances may cause the child to become delinquent. If his needs are met through his delinquency, he may continue in it. He does not feel moral or social qualms or responsibilities.

The case that follows traces the experiences of a deprived child from birth to his imprisonment at age twenty. His story illustrates the conditions of the deprived child who has never lived in one family long enough to build up close identifications with parent-substitutes. He usually lived in foster homes in middle class neighborhoods where his position as a foster child set him apart from other children who lived with their own parents. He was taunted by other children and hence failed to build up associations with a peer group. Thus deprived of both adult and peer primary associations, he failed to develop a clear concept of his own identity or role. He also failed to absorb the moral values of society but lived in terms of immediate individual impulses and needs.

Robert Brown was born in a hospital in New York City to a young woman who was not married to his father.[2] His mother took him home with her and for two years seemingly supported him by working as a waitress. She left him alone or with neighbors while she was at work. When he was two years old she became ill and asked for help from the Federation of Protestant Welfare Agencies. They suggested a foster home or a day nursery while she recuperated, but his mother did not follow through on either suggestion. Six months later in December, the Society for the Prevention of Cruelty to Children investigated a complaint and found Robert and his mother in an un-

---

[2] Summarized from Croswell Bowen. *They Went Wrong*, McGraw-Hill Book Company, New York, 1954, pp. 30–96. The account is based on study of agency records that began with the boy's birth, evidence brought out at the trial, and interviews with the boy and others. Comments in brackets are those of the authors of this textbook; they emphasize factors that have been discussed in preceding chapters as significant in the development of delinquent behavior.

heated furnished room. The SPCC filed a complaint in Children's Court, charging Robert's mother with neglect of child. Robert was placed in the SPCC's child shelter, and the judge ordered an investigation. The Department of Welfare reported that Robert's mother was unable to support him, and the judge placed Robert in the care of the Department of Welfare for placement in a foster home. Robert never saw or heard from his mother again.

Robert's mother was born in England and at the age of twelve came to the United States with her father and four brothers and sisters. She attended high school for two years, was married at the age of seventeen, and had a son. Five years later she deserted her husband and son. Two years later, Robert was born, an illegitimate child.

Robert remained in the care of the Department of Welfare for about three weeks after the court took him from his mother, at which time he was accepted by the New York Foundling Hospital for care. This is a Catholic agency, chosen because Robert's mother was Catholic. Robert remained at the hospital for three weeks until he was placed in a foster home.

In the twelve years between the ages of four and sixteen, Robert lived in five foster homes and one orphanage. A general pattern developed in each foster home placement. At first he made a good impression, and the relationship with the foster mother tended to be friendly, even close. This period was followed by one of dissension or conflict with the foster mother. The mother gradually became estranged from him and finally requested his removal. Each new foster home entailed a change of school; in addition, he was sometimes shifted from public to parochial school or vice versa. Usually, he adjusted well at first in school. Then he would begin to have trouble with teachers and pupils. Almost from the time he first entered school, he stole small sums at home and school. A brief summary of each placement shows the developing pattern.

1. The Foundling Hospital, which retained supervision throughout his childhood, first placed him in the Korowski home where there were three children of the parents and two other boarding children. The family lived in Jamaica, near New York. The parents became fond of Robert, and he sometimes returned to visit them after he left.

The initial good adjustment lasted until after he entered school at the age of six. There children were curious as to why his name was Brown rather than Korowski. He began to wonder about his parents. Also other children seemed to come from families with more money to spend than his foster parents had. He began to steal money from the teacher's desk that had been collected for milk. He bought candy to distribute to other children. He teased other children and was mildly disorderly in the classroom. Both teacher and foster mother criticized him to the visitor from the Foundling Hospital with the boy present. The teacher asked other children to report his misdeeds before him.

He was transferred to a parochial school, but the stealing continued. He was again criticized before other children.

At this point, at the age of eight, he was given a psychiatric examination. His intelligence quotient was found to be 109, and he appeared to react normally.

2. The Foundling Hospital decided to try a different foster home. He was in the second home only a few weeks when he contracted diphtheria and spent several weeks in a hospital. While he was there, another child was placed in the foster home.

3. Upon release he entered his third foster home with the Dolsons, who lived on Long Island. Mr. Dolson was a municipal clerk in New York. At first Robert seemed to fit into the family, although he disliked Mr. Dolson from the beginning. When he picked up a toy pistol belonging to the Dolson's son, Mr. Dolson laughed and said jokingly, "I see he's never going to be any good." Robert, already in some doubt about his status, blamed himself because he was no good; according to his later statements, he felt that this was because he didn't have a mother.

He asked Mrs. Dolson about his mother but she was unable to tell him anything; the visitor likewise could not help him. His concern about his parents was a dominant theme. He came to dislike Mrs. Dolson and was extremely jealous of her son, two years his senior. He was destructive of articles of which Mrs. Dolson was fond, and it seemed to her he did everything he could to hurt her feelings. Mrs. Dolson for her part denied him simple pleasures that neighborhood children enjoyed.

Robert attended a parochial school in the area, where again the children taunted him because his name differed from that of his foster parents. He shoved them around and stole money from them. He was transferred to a public school, where he adjusted well at first but in a few months seemed nervous and was not studying. Stealing at school continued; one time he stole from neighbors.

4. After four years at the Dolsons, Robert at the age of twelve was placed in his fourth foster home. He and Mrs. Dolson parted without any show of regret on either side. He remained only one year with the Snows. They accepted him as one of their own children, of whom they had two. Neighbors also accepted him, and he was invited to children's parties. He had an allowance;

Mr. Snow found him a small job and then supplemented his earnings so that he could have a bicycle. Mr. Snow also took him to see a priest and he became an altar boy. He was adjusting well in school.

The end of this happy situation came four months after placement when a boy at school stood before a glass paneled door and said to Robert, "We don't allow orphans in here." He slammed the door, whereupon Robert crashed into the door, breaking the glass.

He began to steal again, at home and from a neighbor. He was persistent in questioning Mrs. Snow about his mother, but she was unable to tell him anything.

When Robert entered high school, Mrs. Snow took him to the city to see a psychiatrist, an experience that Robert enjoyed. His stealing had increased. He angered a grocer by stealing a pie and a little later was picked up by the police on a complaint that he had stolen money from a house. He admitted the theft, after having first accounted for the money to Mrs. Snow by saying he earned it caddying on the golf course. He used part of the money to treat children to rides on a merry-go-round.

5. The Foundling Hospital resumed care of Robert, and he was placed in his fifth foster home. Robert stayed with Mrs. Hubert, a widow, for about a year, when she decided to go to work in a factory.

6. Robert was now fourteen, an age when foster home placement is extremely difficult. The hospital therefore placed him in a Catholic orphanage about twenty-five miles from the city. He was not received by the other boys as well as had been expected he would be—since they, too, were orphans, he had expected immediate friendliness. Other boys were friendly to the nuns, but this repelled him. He ran away several times, refused to study, and as he approached the age of sixteen requested release to fend for himself. This request was granted, although he still remained under the nominal custody of the Department of Welfare.

At the orphanage he made one contact that seemed meaningful to him and that continued off and on until the time of his imprisonment. This was with Father Bernard Donachie, a young man preparing for the priesthood who, with other seminary students, took troublesome boys on picnics or to the movies. Father Donachie offered the boy friendship and understanding, which were accepted. He and the boy had long talks, and Robert later regarded him as his only real friend. Father Donachie was appalled at the lack of emotional depth or conception of moral values that Robert possessed.

[Comment by authors: Robert's response to Father Donachie was normal for his age. In midteens if not earlier boys tend to emulate some man and to break their attachments to their mothers. Robert apparently had not had a close attachment to any foster father, with the possible exception of Mr. Snow. His attachment to Father Donachie was thus especially significant, but a normal one to make. Robert had lacked a strong attachment to any woman. He seemed unable to accept the friendliness of any foster mother—and the mothers were drawn to him at first—because of his anxiety over his mother which seemed to stand in the way of the usual identification that a small boy would develop for an affectionate foster mother. At the orphanage he was beyond the age to find the nuns satisfactory mother-substitutes. In other words, he had completely missed the emotional development as well as the moral training that might have come from an early identification with his mother, normally followed by identification with his father. Regardless of the material comforts in all the homes, Robert was deprived of the essentials for good personality development.]

With Robert's release from the orphanage, another phase of his life began, the most prominent feature of which was his rootlessness and his utter lack of ability to accept the responsibilities of work. For a time he changed rooms and jobs every few weeks, unable to earn more than a minimum wage as he lacked training and adequate education. He began to steal and for a time traveled around the East. Once he was arrested for vagrancy but released when it was learned he was still a charge of the Department of Welfare. He tried in vain to find his mother; he sought information about her from social agencies that had had contact with her, but they either could not or would not tell him as much as he wished to know. He had a brief friendship with a girl from a respectable family, whose father, Mr. Harris, continued to aid him through various escapades.

Finally, by changing the date of his birth on his certificate of baptism, he enlisted in the marines. Soon he was associating with a marine who spent his time drinking and fighting. He deserted, after stealing a revolver, and returned to New York. With no job and no money, he began to steal, sometimes alone, sometimes with some other young man. At gun point, they held up people in taverns or on the street, in random fashion without preliminary planning. In one night Robert and a friend secured $225 and three wristwatches. He was arrested the same night and was sentenced to Elmira Reformatory, where he spent two years, including periods of up to thirty-nine days in solitary confinement for misbehavior.

Released on parole, he was almost immediately involved in more armed holdups. He either could not stay with a job or could not find one. He lied to his parole officer and stopped seeing him. His lies were discovered, and a search was made to return him to the reformatory. However, he was not found. He was now associating with other young criminals hanging around the Times

Square area. He rented a small apartment and was generous with food and drink for various young people he met. He was especially fond of two waitresses who had rooms in the building. He paid his expenses by armed holdups, carried out alone, that netted him about $75 each.

He had no feeling of guilt about the holdups. His only remorse seemed to be that he had betrayed the friendship of Mr. Harris, who had tried to help him in his struggles. He resolved this pang of guilt by sending Mr. Harris a false report that he had a job and would see him soon.

His final armed robbery was little different from preceding ones except that in the course of it he killed a man without provocation. He held up a small hotel at night, taking $175 and herding three employees into a rear office. He demanded that they open a cabinet that he thought was a safe containing more money. They were unable to do this, and Robert threatened to kill one. He maintained later that he did not intend to kill anyone, but his finger slipped, and one man was instantly killed. Robert fled and returned to his apartment in a state of agitation. He told one of his girl friends what had happened. She told a friend with whom Robert had had a quarrel, although the girl did not know this. The man apparently tipped off the police, and Robert was arrested without resistance.

Robert was tried with three able attorneys appointed by the court to defend him. During the time when he was in jail awaiting trial he was visited by the Monsignor who was head of the Foundling Hospital and by Father Donachie, who had befriended him when he lived in the orphanage. Not one of his foster parents or friends came to see him.

Three psychiatrists examined Robert and brought in three different reports. Dr. Frederic Wertham gave Robert a Rorschach test, the interpretation of which showed that Robert was disturbed mentally and was subject to periods of intellectual confusion. He functioned in an immature explosive manner, had deep fears, felt rejected, and was arrested in emotional development at a level before the normal one of puberty. Dr. Wertham felt that Robert was dominated by a fixation on the mother image, shown in his desire to travel as symbolizing his search for his mother and his daydreaming about her. With this preoccupation he had failed to develop emotional warmth or normal social relationships. Dr. Wertham also thought his violence stemmed from the comic books that he had read as a child.[3]

Dr. Wertham diagnosed Robert as having a schizoid psychopathic per-

[3] Dr. Wertham is noted for his belief that comic books are a major influence in the commission of violent crimes by youth. See his *Seduction of the Innocent*, Holt, Rinehart & Winston, New York, 1953. Many psychiatrists do not share this view.

sonality with obsessive and paranoid features; the stress was so acute that Robert was legally insane at the time of the killing, that is, he could not detect right from wrong.

Robert was also examined by Dr. Perry Lichtenstein, a psychiatrist attached to the staff of the district (prosecuting) attorney. His report was mainly a refutation of Dr. Wertham's report. He did not find that the murder was explosive, nor that Robert had a mother complex that affected his sense of right and wrong. He was not legally insane.

A third psychiatrist, Dr. Leo Orenstein, chief of the psychiatric clinic of the Court of General Sessions, also examined Robert. He characterized Robert as immature and poorly adjusted, with deep-seated feelings of insecurity, based on his childhood experiences. He had an attitude of indifference toward social and conventional demands and dramatized his aggressive behavior as an outcome of his difficulty in finding security. Because of his insecure childhood, he had failed to sublimate his infantile aggressive impulses and projected them on society. Robert was not psychotic or legally insane. He was classified as of average intelligence, with an aggressive personality.

Robert's own explanation was that he needed money; he could earn very little and he wanted some comforts and luxuries. He wanted to have a good time. He regarded robbery as a way to "earn" money and prided himself on not robbing drunks or swindling people by selling fake jewelry. He resented the fact that the newspapers called him a "killer." He wanted to find his mother but did not believe that caused him to steal; he did not think comic books were a cause.

Robert confessed to second degree murder and was given a sentence of forty-five years to life in prison.

[Comments: Robert's many moves during childhood from one foster home to another and the partial acceptance by each foster mother, followed by rejection, left him without identification with a mother (later with a father). He therefore did not receive the normal socialization that children in a stable family group usually receive. When he was finally without the supervision of the orphanage, he had no ties to an intimate group that would judge his behavior.

The taunting by schoolmates had interfered with the development of peer group associations. In the middle class areas in which he lived, these associations would probably have been nondelinquent. He did not associate with delinquents as a child or young adolescent. He was socially isolated. His later contact with the Harris girl was shortlived; his contacts with the two waitresses were superficial. He seemed unable to make any deep friendships with people of his own age. His attempts to make friends as a child were through buying candy for other children. As a young adult he continued this method, buying food and whiskey and inviting acquaintances to his apartment.

His progress in stealing follows normal developmental stages: first, pennies at school, then larger sums from houses when he found an easy opportunity, then articles from stores. After he became familiar with firearms in the marines, he began to steal at gunpoint. He did not plan his crimes well in advance; he continued to operate on an opportunistic basis. He did not belong to a group of skilled criminals. He was an amateur throughout.

Robert represents one type of juvenile delinquent, who has never quite been assimilated into any primary group and who seeks through thefts a way to meet needs that more conventional people satisfy through social relationships and through earning money.]

From Delinquent Child to Career Criminal

This second case illustrates the developmental character of delinquent and criminal behavior. It traces the progression from little-boy escapades for fun and food, to opportunistic or partially planned thefts of money as a sideline to normal family and school life, to a noncriminal occupation which collapsed under the weight of criminal acts, and finally to an adult career as a skilled thief.

Eugene was not the victim of tragic circumstances. He came from a working class family; he was not neglected or mistreated. He did not live in an area with a high rate of delinquency. He was not a member of a thoroughly delinquent gang and did not as a young adolescent associate with adult criminals. But he and his pals found many opportunities to get money and other things they wanted without working for them. Apparently they were never effectively halted in their drift toward crime. Neither family nor school set conventional goals for Eugene toward which he might work. They did not succeed in implanting in him strong moral standards. As a youth he acted impulsively, looking for a quick return for his efforts. Crime offered more opportunities to get what he wanted than the type of work he was prepared to do. Later, stealing became his occupation and guided his activities.

The case traces Eugene's life from childhood until he reached the age of forty-five. At that time he "retired" from his criminal career, not because of any inner reformation but because he feared one more arrest and conviction might send him to prison for the rest of his life.

Eugene's crimes were primarily in the field of theft; the list consisted of various types of thefts and other crimes related to theft. It included petty larceny, grand larceny, burglary and possession of burglar's tools, safe-blowing, robbery, armed robbery, automobile theft, transporting stolen automobiles across a state line, bootlegging, receiving stolen property, arson, assault and assault with intent to kill, carrying concealed weapons, frequenting and operating a gambling place, vagrancy, bribery, perjury, subornation of perjury, jury tampering, conspiracy, and being a fugitive from justice. As a boy, this man of crime was a run-of-the-mill juvenile delinquent.

Eugene was born to working class parents who lived in a small Chicago suburb[4] His father, a machinist, was regularly employed. Family relationships were satisfactory; other children in the family (two girls) turned out well. Even after he had become heavily involved in crime, Eugene maintained friendly intermittent contacts with his family. Since he rarely carried out a serious crime in the suburb, they were unaware of the extent of his activities.

Eugene's school relationships were superficial and not wholly satisfactory. He attended regularly but studied only enough to get by. When he entered high school, he became aware that some children came from wealthy families; others, like Eugene, were of working class origin. Eugene was sensitive to the differences; the wealthy children had many more privileges and their own circle of friends. Their future was planned for them by their parents. Eugene felt unwelcome among them. He had no future plans and little motivation to remain in school. After one year of high school he ran away at the age of fifteen and succeeded in enlisting in the navy.

Eugene's childhood friends were five or six boys with backgrounds similar to his own, who found their recreation on the streets. They stole from fruit carts, partly for the fruit, but partly for the fun involved in being chased by the vendor. They made forays into nearby orchards for fruit to eat. They made friends with the driver of a bakery wagon and soon learned who the customers were. They then would order cake at the store and charge it to a customer. No one stopped them; they regarded these activities as normal and felt no sense of guilt.

With adolescence their activities expanded. They would wait on the station platform of the elevated railway until a train pulled in. Then just as it pulled out, they would reach through an open window and grab a purse that some woman had lying loosely in her lap. The train proceeded to the next sta-

---

[4] John Bartlow Martin, *My Life in Crime*, Harper & Row, Publishers, New York, 1952. Martin is a responsible journalist who specializes in serious articles and books on crime. The present book is the life story of a criminal, whom Martin calls Eugene, as he told it to Martin.

tion; the boys hastily left the platform. They spent the money at an amusement park. They carried off candy cases from elevated stations, locked and unattended at night, and ate the candy. They were never caught in these escapades.

During Eugene's years in the navy, the pattern of his future life was set. He had already learned that many things can be achieved without work. Also, he was now thrown with young adults and soon found some who were exploiting their assignments for their own profit. Some officers were not averse to making extra money. He paid an officer $50 to get him assigned to a job that would not involve drilling, which Eugene regarded as hard work. He became a night watchman with a key to the warehouse which he was expected to inspect for any fires. Soon he was spending a minimum of time on his job, bribing his way past the guard, and carrying bundles of goods from the warehouse to dispose of them through friends he had made at a nearby restaurant. Stolen blankets, pea coats, socks, sweaters, and other articles brought him a tidy income, much of which he lost in crap games. Eventually he was discovered; he lost his job in the warehouse and was sentenced to thirty days at hard labor.

Later he was assigned to a hospital ship on the West Coast. His shore leaves introduced him to the world of vice. His free time was spent with professional prostitutes, among whom he found a ready market for narcotic drugs stolen from the ship. He was caught participating in the burglary of a safe on shipboard and was sentenced to prison for two years and given a dishonorable discharge. In nine months he was released on parole. In prison he made contacts with older professional criminals and on release went to a hotel in San Francisco about which he had learned while in prison. This hotel was the hangout of experienced criminals, each with his own special type of crime. Eugene paid one of them $50 to introduce him to the crime of armed robbery. Eugene's share was several hundred dollars, soon spent on prostitutes. He began to travel about the country, riding freight trains, committing burglaries, getting arrested, bribing his way out of trouble when he could and spending short periods in jail when he could not. Eugene was now eighteen, just at the upper age of classification as a juvenile delinquent. He returned home, where he lived for a while. He worked but continued to burglarize and eventually was caught. His parents, thinking this was his first experience in stealing, secured a lawyer for him. He was placed on probation, which turned out to be very superficial and no impediment to continued stealing.

He transferred his activities to Chicago where he was affiliated with first one group of criminals and then another. He made no pretense of working. He never became integrated into organized crime but remained a burglar, working alone or with one or two associates. He moved from one part of the country to another, since a string of burglaries in one city might end in arrest. He never married, but lived from time to time with first one woman, then another, leaving each when he felt it expedient to move on. He never became involved in community affairs. He was always ready to move on at a moment's notice.

Several times he was convicted of stealing and spent several terms in state and federal prisons, including returns for violation of parole.

He stole and spent immediately some $18,000 to $20,000 a year. In his total career as a criminal covering a span of about twenty-five years, including the time spent in prisons, he estimated that he had stolen money and goods worth a half million dollars, on which he had realized about $150,000, all spent as he got it. (The yearly average from his amount is less than his figure given above of $18,000 to $20,000 per year, which might have represented his best years.)

Long years in prison did not reform him. He never felt a sense of remorse or guilt. He did regret that he had not become a member of some organized criminal group, where he might have made more money and avoided arrests and convictions through political fix. Imprisonment caused him to change his occupation from criminal to a legal job, since he feared that another conviction would send him to prison for life. He was never able to secure a job of importance because he could not risk investigation of his past life. He dared seek only mediocre jobs, none of which paid more than a living wage.

[A comparison of Eugene's story with other published biographies or autobiographies of thieves indicates that it probably is rather typical of what happens to professional thieves. His childhood and adolescence seem fairly typical of the working class. Everyday activities include stealing of a minor nature that is common to the street life of lower class urban areas, whether in the inner city or in industrial suburbs. The boys "pick up" the ways of stealing as they may also pick up the techniques of playing ball in a vacant lot. The stealing, as the ball-playing, is all part of a boy's life, expected, tolerated.

Sometime during adolescence the boy's activities become predominantly either criminal or noncriminal. He does not necessarily make a decision to become a criminal. Usually he drops out of school, which seems to have no meaning for him. He associates with other dropouts. He may find a job but drop it because it too has no interest or meaning for him. Sometimes the job opens ways for stealing. Especially if he is not caught and the rewards are high, crime makes more and more appeal to him. He finds himself more at home in the hangouts of criminals than in the clubs of the more conventional boys.

The final step is the acceptance of a criminal philosophy of life, with various rationalizations that protect the criminal from a sense of remorse or guilt. Common rationalizations of thieves are that thievery is a form of work, since it requires planning, specific skills, and personal risk. The thief may pride himself on stealing only from the rich, never from the poor. If he does not carry a gun, he takes pride in this fact and justifies his behavior by comparison with that of criminals who threaten people with guns or physical force.

The acceptance of a philosophy of crime apparently begins in childhood, partly because the rationalizations are part of the street culture and partly because no conventional agency has built up an opposing concept of what is good to insulate the boy against the impact of the philosophy of the delinquent and criminal world.]

A Gang Boy Who Redefines His Concept and Role

In certain disorganized areas of cities where conventional and law-enforcement agencies are inactive or weak, boys' gangs develop that not only prey on householders and businessmen but are in conflict with each other. Families are unable to compete with the pull of the gangs. Indigenous agencies and businesses, manned by residents of the area, often are tolerant of the delinquency of youth. To them, as to the boys, social agencies, school attendance officers, and the police often seem to interfere with their lives and to cause trouble. They tend not to seek help from these sources.

Not all gang boys grow up to be ne'er-do-wells or criminals. Many find places in conventional jobs. A few extricate themselves completely not only from their gang but also from the area that breeds gangs and crime.

The present case is of a black boy in a lower class neighborhood in Brooklyn, a boy beyond the control of his parents, steeped in the delinquency of the streets, and leader of his gang. The description of his gang life can be duplicated many times in other published accounts. The case is important in that it shows the process by which the boy, separated from his gang, is led to change his self-conception and to seek a new, conventional role. The boy had an intelligence quotient of 160, which placed him far above the average in ability. His intelligence however did not save him from gang life nor did it cause him to reason logically that legal pursuits are any better than criminal ones. It did make it possible, however, for him to take a long leap from a lower class area through college and graduate school into a respected professional middle class occupation.

Frenchy, as the boy is called in the book about him, was the son of

Jamaican blacks who had migrated to New York.[5] His mother was from a middle class family, whose proudest achievement was their cooperation in helping Frenchy's uncle secure a medical education. This uncle was constantly held up to Frenchy as the model after whom he should pattern his life. Only in late adolescence did this model come to have personal meaning for him.

Frenchy's father was a working man, lower in social status than the mother's family; her marriage to him had been disapproved but her contacts with her family remained close. The father worked steadily, except for periods of illness or unavoidable unemployment. The father followed the life of the lower class man of the area, playing policy, gambling a little, and drinking a little but not to the extent that his job or family status was damaged. When Frenchy was a small child, it was a matter of pride that his mother did not work outside the home. Later, such employment became necessary during a long period of illness on the part of the father, when the family sank to a poverty level. Later, the family was able to move to a somewhat better neighborhood than the typical slum where Frenchy began his life.

Frenchy's relationship with his mother was close; she was loving and sympathetic, although she strongly disapproved of his delinquencies. His one regret seemed to be the pain that he gave her, yet the feeling was never strong enough to prevent his continued misbehavior. He and his father were antagonistic. The father was inclined to be authoritarian and to punish Frenchy for any trouble by severe beatings.

At school Frenchy found the work easy to do, so easy in fact that he was bored. He had the highest grades in his class. He misbehaved in school in ways annoying to the teacher; he drummed on his desk like a bongoman and sang calypso songs. Once he hit a teacher.

After his mother began to work, Frenchy spent all his free time with the neighborhood gang. After the family moved, he continued to return to the old neighborhood to be with them. At first he was simply a little boy hanging on the fringe, admiring the older boys. Later he was admitted to the activities and was head of a unit of the Bishops gang. By the time he was thirteen, his unit had broken away to form an independent gang, called the Deacons, of which he was the leader.

The activities of the gang were typical of street gangs—hanging around a meeting place, working a little at odd jobs, stealing a little, indulging in sex activities with girls who permitted it, experimenting with marijuana, and occa-

[5] Ira Henry Freeman, *Out of the Burning*, Crown Publishers, New York, 1960. Freeman is a journalist who has made black boys' gangs a field for special study. The history of Frenchy is the story, in fictional form, of one boy's experiences.

sionally planning and executing brief but violent fights with a rival gang, sometimes with the use of guns.

By the time Frenchy was fourteen, he had been before the Children's Court thirteen times, all but the last time being released to his parents, who by the time he was out of elementary school had no control over him. On the thirteenth appearance in Court, Frenchy was committed to the Warwick State Training School for boys, at Warwick, with the approval of his parents.

He had expected his parents to plead for his release as they had done previously; their refusal was an admission of their defeat, but to Frenchy it was evidence of their rejection of him.

Frenchy had been proud of his police record, which gave him status with the street gangs, but he had many misgivings about the training school. Terrible tales of mistreatment and beatings came back to the gangs from boys who had been there. To Frenchy's surprise there was no mistreatment as such, although the headmasters of the cottages on occasion might subdue a refractory boy by physical force.

Frenchy at first had many difficulties in accepting the orderliness and restraints of institutional life. He had still more difficulty in realizing that the school might have anything of value for him. He faced one crisis when the Superintendent refused to grant him a home furlough because he felt sure Frenchy would immediately swing back into his old gang. He was assigned to a job as assistant to the librarian, a situation where his potential academic ability could find some expression.

In time, Frenchy adjusted sufficiently that he and another boy were enrolled at the public high school in the city of Warwick. They were the first training-school boys to have this privilege. Frenchy was able to rise to the trust placed in him. He worked hard, entered successfully into extracurricular activities, and did not try to run away. He continued to live at the training school, commuting daily to the high school.

[This was probably the first time in his life that Frenchy had looked to a conventional institution and to law-abiding individuals for status and prestige. Several factors seem to be involved. His contacts with his gang had been effectively severed by distance and absence. To his surprise, he had found that he was not treated like a junior public enemy at the training school, an attitude he had come to accept as typical of school officials and police. He respected the authority of the officers who maintained order, apparently in much the same way that he had respected the leaders of his gang when he was an underling in membership. In his experience, leaders enforced their authority, by physical force if necessary. In addition, he appreciated the understanding extended to him, especially by the Superintendent, A. Alfred Cohen. He had also found his superior in the library to be friendly and encouraging. He was not treated as an outlaw; he was given an opportunity to gain prestige along new lines. At the public high school, he and the other training-school student apparently were something of a novelty. They were part of an experiment to determine whether delinquent boys could adjust in the community. Everyone wanted and expected them to succeed. He was no longer an outcast. Frenchy found it more difficult but as satisfying to meet these conventional expectations as he previously had found it to meet the expectations of his gang.]

Frenchy was finally released on parole at his own earnest request and somewhat against the best judgment of Mr. Cohen who was not sure his degree of rehabilitation had strengthened him enough to resist the pull of his gang, once he had returned to the old situation. His release placed on him a personal obligation not to disappoint Mr. Cohen; he now took his model of behavior from a member of the conventional community and not from a gang leader.

Frenchy had many problems on parole. He did not re-enter the gang, in spite of their disgust over his refusal. His new goal was to complete high school. Because of his record, fourteen high schools refused to admit him before he found one that would accept him. He was able to weather this overt rejection by conventional society. Finding work was not easy, and he wavered between working for small wages and stealing. He settled into work. He graduated from high school a few months before he was seventeen with an average grade of B. By now, college seemed desirable and possible. He enrolled in evening courses, continuing to work during the day. Family approval was now a strong supporting factor. Even his father, who had previously "washed his hands" of him, was proud of him.

[Not every boy who is sent to training school achieves a success story, even on a lower academic level than was true for Frenchy. What happened to Frenchy, however, was essentially what happens in the transition of a boy from complete identification with a delinquent gang to conventional life. The separation from his gang was a crucial factor; the boys were no longer at hand to admire him or to give him an outlet through delinquency. He might simply have found substitute friends of the same type at the training school. However, the association with the librarian followed by his enrollment in a school of well-behaved adolescents gave substitute intimate contacts unconnected with delinquency. Frenchy wanted prestige, success, and a role of leadership. He found them in legitimate ways.

Had Frenchy been allowed to remain in his own home and in contact with his gang, it seems probable that he would have become more deeply involved in stealing and gang violence, until it would have been impossible for him to abandon such activities. In a few years he would have been beyond juvenile court age and a serious crime would have sent him to prison. Prison is an excellent place for a budding criminal to make contacts with more experienced criminals. Frenchy, who, at the time his life story was published, had graduated from college and held a responsible professional position, might simply have become one more added to the criminal population.]

The Decline and Fall of a Disorganized Girl

Delinquency among girls differs from that of boys. Although parental neglect and mistreatment create serious pressures for boys and girls alike, their reactions to these pressures differ significantly. For example, delinquency in girls often emerges incidentally as they attempt to cope with their disturbed emotions and troubled home situations. Moreover, it rarely takes the form of a violent assault upon the environment as is sometimes the case with boys. For these reasons the delinquent girl typically presents the rather pathetic picture of a youngster caught in a web of destructive interpersonal relationships from which there is no satisfactory escape. And her delinquency must be seen as largely a futile protest against the isolation and humility of her condition. Such is the case of Janet Clark. Her story traces her early reactions to a disorganized home, her search for meaningful peer relationships, and her final submergence in drugs in early adulthood.

Janet Clark had a compelling need to write an autobiography, and to this end she related her life story to a social scientist who taped their conversations. After Janet's premature death, the taped material was edited and published by Helen MacGill Hughes, and the account presented here is derived from that case study.[6]

Janet's recollection of her early family life is based upon her somewhat jumbled memories and what she later learned from older relatives. The family itself lived in a middle class neighborhood and consisted of Janet, her parents, a grandfather, an aunt and uncle, a cousin, and a woman who cared for Janet, all living in one apartment. Janet felt that she had had warm relationships in this medley of persons, although she remembers tension but no quarreling between her parents. At the same time, she felt unwanted by her mother. Later in life Janet learned that her mother had attempted an abortion, prompting her conclusion that "I was the result of an abortion that did not succeed."

Janet's mother, a nurse, worked hard and long and was often tired and

[6] Helen MacGill Hughes, ed., *The Fantastic Lodge, the Autobiography of a Girl Drug Addict*, Houghton Mifflin, Boston, 1961.

irritable. Her father was more attentive; he played with her as with a toy to be laid aside at will; but he was irresponsible and unemployed. Janet was five when her parents were divorced.

Janet went to live with her aunt and uncle, and their daughter, May, who was several years older than Janet and the object of much favorable attention. Janet was soon relegated to second place. She occasionally visited her father until he died a few years after the divorce. Her mother alternately sent her boxes of candy and toys and neglected her. Her aunt and uncle often quarreled. Thus at the age of five Janet had moved from a warm but disorganized family into an equally disorganized family where warmth was lacking. She had nightmares, sucked her thumb, and wet the bed. Her model was her teacher and her outlet was writing endlessly.

When Janet was eleven or twelve she returned to her mother—only to find that her dreams of living with a loving mother could not come true. Her mother's duties as a nurse extended through the evening and required the employment of a woman to stay with Janet. By high school Janet was on her own. Her greatest satisfaction was in school. She was however unable to gain acceptance from a group of girls to whom she was attracted.

To this point in midadolescence she had not been involved in any delinquent or markedly deviant behavior. Her great but unsatisfied desires were to have a close relationship with her mother and to be accepted into a peer group of girls. She had neither and, looking back, described herself as introverted.

She found friends in a group of boys who hung out in a park—boys from neighborhood families. Play was rough, there was a bit of drinking, and as the only girl she was the object of early aggressive sex play. Sometime later she began to concentrate on a somewhat older man, had her first full sex experience, and found herself pregnant. Her mother and close relatives were horrified but protected her; the baby was given up for adoption. In the meantime she had dropped out of high school but continued in evening courses.

She had a close girl friend, Lil. They visited bars together, met and discarded men, and managed to shield each other from unwanted male attention. She met the members of a jazz orchestra that played in one of the bars and a new phase of her life began. The attentions of the musicians gave her a feeling of importance; they also introduced her to marijuana. She and Lil became deeply involved with both the musicians and marijuana.

Meanwhile, Janet's mother with whom she lived went from man to man. According to Janet she was like a child, supporting herself and Janet, but lonely and discouraged. Both she and Janet dated black musicians and eventually her mother married a black.

Janet's musician friends introduced her to the use of heroin. She had now completely cut herself off from conventional middle class life, and spent entire nights going from bar to bar, staying at hotels with her male friends, rarely going home, and still more rarely letting her mother know where she was staying. Nevertheless, she managed to work and attend college part-time. However, toward the end of one semester she dropped out of college, left her job, and "lived" on pot.

Apparently in an attempt to regularize her life, Janet married Bernard, a trombone player. Her relatives attended the wedding and her mother paid for the honeymoon. Janet began to work and Bernard worked off and on. To increase her income Janet began to steal on the job, but to outward appearances, they were a conventional married couple. Janet failed to make a good sexual adjustment with Bernard, however, and soon they separated. Janet returned to Lil, the round of bars, casual sexual partners, and the constant use of marijuana.

[Comment: Had Janet and her husband been able to work out their personal difficulties, Janet might have moved more fully into conventional life. But she was unable to achieve this, and the security that marriage might have brought was denied her.]

Two important events, however, brought Janet a momentary measure of stability. Her aunt arranged psychiatric treatments for her and over a continued period of time she maintained a cooperative relationship with the psychiatrist, as he tried to work toward a solution of her drug problem, without however sufficient effort on Janet's part to break off completely from her habit. The second event was her attachment to Bob, a musician, who introduced Janet to heroin, to which she was soon addicted.

The relationship between Janet and Bob moved far beyond simple sexual contacts which she had already had with a succession of other men. They loved and depended on each other, but were unable to marry as Janet had never divorced Bernard. Jobless and moneyless, Janet and Bob became drug pushers. They lived precariously in hotels or in Janet's mother's apartment. Their contacts were limited almost entirely to other addicts. Neither was completely independent from his parents, who scolded and pleaded but never rejected them. Bob intermittently had work in a jazz orchestra; but at best he was only a fringe member of musicians' groups. He and Janet were accepted for what they were: addicts who needed help just to survive. They seemed to have a marginal position with both their parents and the musicians.

After they began to push drugs, it was almost inevitable that Janet and Bob would be arrested and given short jail terms that forced drug withdrawal but cured nothing. Janet became less and less able to control her conduct. If she found a job she could not bring herself to go to work; she could not force herself to keep appointments with her psychiatrist. She was only in her early twenties.

[At this point, her autobiography ends. A postscript by the sociologist who taped her accounts gives a summary of her concluding years.]

Janet continued on a downhill road. In desperation over his own condition Bob left, removing the one person to whom she was attached. She alternated between living with her mother and in a rooming house.

She found some acceptance in an intellectual but tolerant neighborhood. Shoplifting, prostitution, bribing police to avoid arrest, and continued use of drugs all became routine. She spent much of her time in local hangouts. She became a physical wreck, gaunt and unkempt. Several times she made abortive attempts at suicide, but only when she was sure she would be rescued in time. Finally she voluntarily entered a state hospital in a last attempt to straighten out her life. The hospital was experimenting with an open policy and a degree of patient self-government. Certain categories of patients (among them Janet) could come and go. She was thus able to continue her drug habit and added quantities of barbiturates to heroin. Somewhat stabilized she began to think again of finding a publisher for her autobiography.

One night at the hospital she took a large dose of sleeping pills and went to sleep on a couch in one of the main lounges of the hospital. Attendants who saw her thought she was in a natural sleep and did not disturb her. By morning she was dead. Thus at the age of twenty-eight, her downhill life came to an end.

[Janet's inability to solve her problems as she saw them began early in life. She was deprived during childhood of a close relationship with her mother and later she was refused membership in an intellectual peer group. Gradually she lowered her concept of herself as a middle class, young intellectual and accepted membership in, first, a group of lower class free-roving boys and, later, with the only girl friend she mentions, in jazz musician groups. Eventually she found a close, loving relationship with one of the musicians, which ended when he felt unable to free himself from drug addiction so long as he maintained a close relationship with Janet. Janet continued to be dependent on her mother and an aunt as well as on the psychiatric treatment provided by the aunt. She thus became marginal both to the bohemianism of the jazz musicians and to her middle class family.

She had been pulled into the use of drugs through her need for acceptance by some group—which was more or less by happenstance the jazz musicians. Even with the support of her lover and psychiatric treatment, she was unable to face life without drugs. After her lover left her, only drugs remained, and she rapidly deteriorated.

Her delinquent and criminal behavior was not the result of a criminal personality, but rather a derivative of her general inability to govern herself and her life satisfactorily which in turn led ultimately to her dependence on drugs and her self-destruction.]

BIBLIOGRAPHY

BOWEN, CROSWELL, *They Went Wrong*, McGraw-Hill Book Company, New York, 1954.

FREEMAN, IRA HENRY, *Out of the Burning*, Crown Publishers, New York, 1960.

FREEMAN, LUCY, *"Before I Kill More—,"* Crown Publishers, New York, 1955. (The reference to Kennedy, Foster, *et al.* concerns the same case.)

"Girl Delinquent, Age Sixteen," *Harper's Magazine*, 164 (1932), 551–559.

HUGHES, HELEN MACGILL, ed., *The Fantastic Lodge, the Autobiography of a Girl Drug Addict*, Houghton Mifflin Company, Boston, 1961.

KENNEDY, FOSTER, HARRY HOFFMAN, AND WILLIAM H. HAINES, "Psychiatric Study of William Heirens," *Journal of Criminal Law and Criminology*, 38 (1947), 311–341.

MARTIN, JOHN BARTLOW, "End of a Boy's Life," *McCall's Magazine*, 75 (July, 1948), pp. 25 ff. Reproduced also in Barron, M. L., *The Juvenile in Delinquent Society*, Alfred A. Knopf, New York, 1954, pp. 3–10. (This account of the life of a boy aged twelve who killed a younger boy ends with his first trial and his commitment to prison for twenty-two years. His case was appealed to the state supreme court, and the decision was reversed on the ground that the boy was too immature to understand the significance of the guilty plea that he had made. In his second trial he was found not guilty on the ground that he was emotionally disturbed at the time of the murder and therefore unable to tell right from wrong. He was placed under the care of a guardian and sent to a private school for problem boys.)

———, *My Life of Crime*, Harper & Row, Publishers, New York, 1952.

SHAW, CLIFFORD R., *The Jack Roller*, University of Chicago Press, Chicago, 1930. (This and the following books by Shaw are famous among the life stories of juvenile delinquents. The autobiographical portions are in the boys' own words. Sociological, and in some instances psychological and psychiatric, analyses are included.)

———, *et al.*, *Brothers in Crime*, University of Chicago Press, Chicago, 1938.

———, in collaboration with M. E. Moore, *The Natural History of a Delinquent Career*, University of Chicago Press, Chicago, 1931.

WERTHAM, FREDRIC, *Dark Legend: A Study in Murder*, Duell, Sloan and Pearce, New York, 1941.

schools, delinquency, and employment

Juvenile delinquency is related to the public schools in three ways: serious misconduct in and around schools; truancy, both as a delinquency itself and as the open door to other kinds of delinquency; and the day-long idleness of boys and girls who drop out of school before graduation and find it difficult to become incorporated into conventional adult activities, such as steady employment. An examination of these three situations finds the schools in a paradoxical position of fighting a losing battle against misconduct and temporary or permanent absenteeism, and at the same time providing opportunities for prevention and control of delinquency.[1]

Place of Public Schools in Society

From approximately age six to sixteen, boys and girls are expected to be in regular school attendance during about nine months of each year. Thus, virtually all adolescents encounter school over an extended period, and the school is the first social institution to have broad responsibilities over children. Inevitably, therefore, the school receives a very broad range of children, includ-

[1] For a detailed and critical discussion of the school in relation to delinquency, see Walter E. Schafer and Kenneth Polk, "Delinquency and the Schools," *Task Force Report: Juvenile Delinquency and Youth Crime*, President's Commission on Law Enforcement and Administration of Justice, U. S. Government Printing Office, Washington, D. C., 1967, pp. 222–277.

ing not a few who are ill-prepared to accept the social patterns of the school. It is not surprising that the school is both a magnet for childish mischief and a major factor in the delinquency of children.

The Social Organization of Schools

Schools, like all formal groups, have evolved a structure of roles and a code of rules that permit them to accomplish their mission of educating children with effectiveness and dispatch. It could be argued that alternate ways of organizing schools should be tried so as to enhance their effectiveness, but the fact remains that *some* organization is necessary. Generally speaking, this organization imposes a distinctive style of behavior upon both pupils and teachers, which in the main prescribes a role of docile passivity for pupils and a role of active direction for teachers. Thus, children who are active, fun-loving, and involved with one another are asked to curb their childish delights for the serious activity of their education. Moreover, as classes get larger and the teachers more impersonal in high school, they are expected to control themselves even when the teacher is unable to supervise them closely. Thus, for many children the school represents an alien institution imposing a foreign ethic but without the authority or even the ability to enforce it.

Most youngsters make the best of this situation. They develop close relationships with those around them, and they accept the role they are forced into. But others find few immediate rewards for their trouble, and school represents for them time wasted away from the real world. Still others, however, resent the regimen of the school, its demands for punctuality, civility, and passive obedience, and they challenge directly its authority. We shall examine the reasons why some children confront the school in this fashion and find themselves moving into a path of defiance that all too often develops ultimately into full-scale delinquency.

Goals of Education

Back of this situation lies the purpose for which public schools were first organized in the later part of the eighteenth century, i.e., to create a responsible, literate citizenry, able to read both the Bible and the laws. At least some education for all children became the goal. This goal is supported by laws in all states that specify the age when a youth may legally withdraw from school. Most states had passed such laws by 1900, the last state in 1918. Since then, many states have lengthened the compulsory attendance period and tightened attendance laws.[2] The goal of public education for all children has been approached so far as elementary school education is concerned; high school education has been less well received, although the proportion of teen-agers graduating from high school has constantly risen.

Opposed to this goal is the fact that public schools actually have appealed to and set up curricula primarily for a limited portion of children headed for ever further training and education. These children come from middle class families who anticipate higher education for their children. They come to school with enough cultural background and interest in learning to ease their adjustment to school and motivate them to fit into the learning pattern.

CONTEMPORARY TYPES OF PUPILS

In addition to middle class children, favored by public schools, there are many lower class pupils of all types of backgrounds. In large cities, some schools cater primarily to one social class or one ethnic or racial group, because of the voluntary tendency of people of like culture or skin color to live in little colonies within the city. Other school districts cut across ethnic or racial boundaries and bring together incompatible or antagonistic groups of pupils.

The problem also includes the marked difference between teachers and pupils in social class affiliation. One estimate is that 3 per cent of public school pupils are upper class, 38 per cent middle class, and 58 per cent lower class.[3] Teachers are predominantly middle class. Moreover, teachers are steeped in middle class traditions of educational methods and values. Methods of evaluating the pupil's ability are based largely on intelligence tests standardized on middle class children, tending to discriminate against lower class children. The adequate child by these tests tends to be the middle class child. Public schools tend to emphasize middle class standards and values, suited to the tested intelligence of the typical pupils of an earlier period. The values of the lower class and varied ethnic groups, whose children now fill many schoolrooms, are largely unknown and when known deprecated.

The lack of harmony between school curricula and teachers' attitudes on the one hand and the values and customs of lower class parents and their children, on the other, often becomes apparent when the child first enters school. The lack of coordination is especially destructive when the child comes from a foreign-culture family and is unable to speak English easily or at all.

[2] W. H. Burton, "Education and Social Class in the United States," *Harvard Educational Review*, 23, No. 4 (Fall, 1953), 243–256. The author is on the faculty of the Graduate School of Education, Harvard University.

[3] *Ibid.*

Unless special classes are organized to teach such children English, they are hopelessly handicapped. When parents have little education in their own culture, the children find it all but impossible to maintain the level of work believed suitable for their age and year of school attendance. Many become academically retarded. Reading retardation is especially significant in their lack of progress, since success in most subjects depends upon reading speed and comprehension. Many children therefore suffer from occupying a low status in the eyes of the teacher and of more successful children. They may accept this evaluation and become passive and resigned; or they may rebel against their status.

Many lower class parents and children come to regard school, especially high school, as unrelated to the values and life needs of the lower class. It is of value to the child to be able to fend for himself physically and to begin to earn money as soon as possible to help his parents and take care of his own expenses. Even those parents who desire better things for their children than they themselves have had, do not look beyond manual skills, such as those of a craftsman or a machine operator.[4] Most of the parents are themselves unskilled or semiskilled workers. They have only grade-school education and their highest and often unfulfilled aspiration for their children is high school or trade school. Many, in fact, would be content to have their children leave school in the early teens if this were legally possible. The parents are not only unable to prepare their children for successful school adjustment, but often tacitly or openly encourage rebellion, truancy, or early withdrawal.

The above discussion should not blind the reader to two facts: some middle class children do not adjust well to school; and approximately half of the lower class children graduate from high school and a small number attend college. Nevertheless, the problem of poor school adjustment centers in lower class children.[5]

Misconduct in and around the School

Gradually schools have assumed more and more responsibilities for the conduct and welfare of pupils within the school. To the basic purpose of education, many schools have added medical and dental examinations, balanced lunches, vocational and psychiatric counseling, and vocational training. They have also developed special curricula and classes for handicapped children, and

[4] James S. Davie, "Social Class Factors and School Attendance," *Harvard Educational Review*, 23, No. 3 (Summer, 1953), 175–185.

[5] *Ibid.*; W. Lloyd Warner, Robert J. Havighurst, and Martin B. Loeb, *Who Shall Be Educated?* Harper & Row, Publishers, New York, 1944, pp. 52–53.

they have assumed broad policing functions for disruptive children. Only when the disruptions reach an advanced level does the school admit defeat and call for police aid.

Misconduct varies from the infrequent use of narcotics to an almost universal impertinence, according to a survey of teachers' opinions in urban junior and senior high schools.[6] More than 90 per cent of schools had chronic experience with the following types of misbehavior: impertinence and discourtesy to teachers; failure to do homework and other assignments; use of profane or obscene language; cheating on tests and homework; lying of a serious type; stealing objects of small value; obscene scribbling in lavatories; and unorganized fighting. It seems probable that none of these would qualify as delinquency in a legal sense, although they would be disruptive to the role of the teacher or the process of teaching.

Destruction of property was reported from 96 per cent of the urban schools. As the discussion on vandalism in Chapter 8 showed, schools often are the targets of youthful vandalism. Only one additional example will be given. In the year ending June 30, 1964, schools in the District of Columbia suffered the loss of 27,689 window panes, 8,382 more than in the previous year. The Superintendent commented that the $300,000 required to replace the windows could buy 100,000 books or build a swimming pool.[7]

Truancy, found in 94 per cent of the urban schools, is discussed in a later section of this chapter.

Serious types of misbehavior that might well bring the student into juvenile court were much less frequent in urban schools. These were, in order of decreasing occurrence, stealing of a serious nature, sex offenses, drinking intoxicants, gang fighting, carrying switchblade knives, guns and so forth, physical violence against teachers, and use of narcotics.

In the survey of teachers' opinions, school neighborhoods were classified by the teachers according to industrial or residential usage of land, living conditions, and income. When teachers' reports on classroom behavior were classified by living conditions, the results shown in Table 17 were discovered. Misconduct increased steadily as living conditions declined. Classroom misbehavior was reported twice as often in classrooms in essentially industrial neighborhoods as in totally residential neighborhoods. Income level was less closely related to classroom behavior; it seems probable that teachers were less able to estimate the family income than to judge the living conditions or industrial-residential

---

[6] *Teacher Opinion on Pupil Behavior, 1955–1956*, Research Bulletin, Vol. 34, No. 2, April, 1956, National Education Association of the United States, Washington, D. C., p. 59.

[7] Note in *Federal Probation*, 28 (1964), p. 79.

TABLE 17

Percentage of Teachers Reporting Troublemaking and Physical Striking In Their
Classroom, According to Living Conditions of School Neighborhoods

LIVING CONDITIONS IN SCHOOL NEIGHBORHOOD	PER CENT OF TEACHERS REPORTING THAT 10 PER CENT OR MORE OF THEIR PUPILS WERE REAL TROUBLEMAKERS	PER CENT OF TEACHERS REPORTING SOMEONE IN THEIR SCHOOL HAD BEEN STRUCK BY A PUPIL IN THE PRECEDING TWELVE MONTHS
Very good	2.7	7.8
Above average	2.4	9.3
About average	4.4	*
Below average	9.1	20.3
Very bad (slum area)	32.9	48.0

Teacher Opinion on Pupil Behavior, 1955–56, Research Bulletin, Vol. 34, No. 2, April, 1956, National Education Association of the United States, Washington, D. C. Column 2 is unpublished data obtained in connection with Table 25, p. 78 of the Bulletin; column 3 is from p. 78. Used with permission.
    * Percentage not given.

ratio. Specific types of misbehavior are not classified by type of school neighborhood. Other sources, however, show that the serious delinquencies and acts of violence are more frequent in schools in slum neighborhoods than in better residential neighborhoods (that is, in lower class than middle class). It is important to note, however, that even in slum neighborhoods, many children are not troublemakers. According to Table 17, only a third of teachers in slum areas regarded 1 per cent or more of their pupils as real troublemakers and slightly less than half reported physical violence in their schools (not simply classrooms) during a twelve month period.

METHODS OF DEALING WITH MISCONDUCT

Whether the misbehavior originates in family, neighborhood, or school, the classroom teacher has the problem of dealing with the misbehaving pupil, often finding himself (or more likely herself in the elementary school) faced not only with violations of school rules but also of laws which he is nevertheless expected to handle without recourse to the police. The teacher is often in a helpless condition; the influx of unwilling pupils increases the disciplinary problem, especially as the teen years approach when pupils reach adult stature and dare open defiance. With problems increased, teachers have been shorn of their earlier stern, even harsh means of discipline.[8] In "the good old days," rules

[8] John Manning, "Discipline in the Good Old Days," *Phi Delta Kappan*, 41 (December, 1959), 94–99.

were strict and sternly enforced by corporal punishment before an audience of peers or by other forms of physical distress, such as confinement in some dark corner or standing on one foot placed within a wooden shoe containing a sharp peg. A pupil might be forced to hold out a heavy object at arm's length or to stoop over touching a peg in the floor, with limbs held rigidly erect. Girls as a rule were less severely punished than boys—perhaps their misdemeanors were less serious. It should be noted that in the "good old days," pupils did not attend school for as many years as at present, and it seems probable that most of the corporal punishment was dealt out to children rather than to adolescents.

Today, some 86 per cent of elementary school teachers and 30 per cent of junior high school teachers may administer corporal punishment. However, theories of permissiveness, personality development, and motivation tend to preclude corporal or other types of painful or humiliating punishment. Teachers are aware of what they may not do to enforce discipline but feel that they have few positive measures to substitute for the older physical punishments. The admonition that they should make the classwork sufficiently interesting to hold the attention and motivate the best efforts of the pupils often is not realistic in terms of the school curriculum, overcrowding, and types of pupils. A Chicago case illustrates the teacher's dilemma.

The teacher, Mrs. T., after eight years of successful elementary school teaching, found herself faced with serious disciplinary problems. Her case was heard by the Board of Education, which voted, although not unanimously, to dismiss her from the school system. In defense of her inability to maintain discipline, she and other school personnel listed some of the things a teacher might not do either because of definite rules or because of objections of the principal. They could not assign homework as a penalty; keep children after school as they were then exposed to street hazards after the crossing guards had left their posts; keep a child out of a class he especially enjoyed; ask parents to come to the school for an interview, as experience had shown nothing was gained; grasp a pupil by the wrist or arm to escort him to his seat since the child might later exaggerate the amount of force used; or isolate him from other pupils, as this tended to stigmatize the child. Although principals were expected to give teachers suggestions and to come to their aid in severe disciplinary cases, not all principals gave positive and firm help.[9]

School boards and principals dislike to admit that they cannot maintain discipline and that occasional serious delinquencies or crimes occur in and around schools, sometimes of a type that would immediately command police attention if they occurred elsewhere. These would include serious thefts, major

9 *Chicago Daily News*, March 22 and 24, 1960.

vandalism, physical attacks of various sorts; they might also include the re-taliatory counterattacks of men teachers or principals on impudent adolescent boys, especially in states that legally forbid corporal punishment.

Misbehavior in schools is not an isolated activity on the part of students. Many school troublemakers are also home and community troublemakers. These boys and girls are likely sooner or later to be arrested; they may have to be absent from school for a few hours to attend a court hearing or longer to carry out a period of detention in a state correctional school. They may return to school on probation after the hearing or on parole after release from the correctional school. If they have not reached the age for legal withdrawal from school they are expected to be in school attendance regardless of their out-of-school record or clash with police. Each such absence intensifies the school problem if for no other reason than that the pupil, often already retarded, falls still further behind the class. Moreover, he usually is degraded in the eyes of the teacher, middle class pupils, and upwardly mobile lower class pupils. Among other poorly adjusted, semidelinquent or delinquent pupils his status may increase with his added experience with court and correctional schools. The school, which must receive him back, bears much of the burden of his read-justment.

Truancy

School absenteeism falls into a number of types: children lawfully absent because of illness; those unlawfully absent with the knowledge or connivance of the parents, for example, to care for younger children or to work even though legally under age for employment; and children unlawfully absent from school without the knowledge of their parents. The last type is truancy in the strict sense of the word. An occasional truancy is not regarded as serious, but continued truancy may bring both school and legal penalties.

The amount of truancy varies from city to city and within a city from one school to another. A New York City report states that every day about one child in ten is absent, but only about 18 per cent of the absentees are truants.[10] It is customary in most cities for schools to deal with truants through their own avenues of investigation and discipline. Although habitual truancy is no longer sufficient grounds for an adjudication of delinquency, chronic truants often are involved in criminal behavior that *is* grounds for delinquency. Hence,

---

[10] *Children Absent from School*, Citizen's Committee on Children of New York City, 1949; Alfred J. Kahn, "Who Are Our Truants?" *Federal Probation*, 15 (March, 1951), 35–40. Professor Kahn, with the New York School of Social Work, is also consultant for the Citizen's Committee on Children of New York City.

they are likely to come to the attention of both the police and the juvenile court.

CHARACTERISTICS OF TRUANTS

Habitual truancy is primarily an adolescent phenomenon, occurring most frequently during the ages of fourteen to sixteen, the peak ages for delinquency. It begins, however, as early as the first grade; it decreases sharply after the terminal age for compulsory school attendance is reached. Approximately 60 per cent of truants are boys.[11]

Details about the truant closely resemble details about the school troublemaker and in fact about juvenile delinquents in general. A study in San Francisco showed that the median I.Q. for truants was 95, with a range from 43 to 163, compared with a median of approximately 100 for all students.[12] Despite the small difference, the truants were academically poorly adjusted. Although 5 per cent of truants were accelerated and 25 per cent were in the appropriate grade, 70 per cent were retarded at least one semester. Retardation of two or more years was found for 15 per cent of truants but only 1 per cent of all students.

Many of San Francisco truants tended to be school troublemakers, as judged from the fact that a third had grades of D or F in school citizenship; two-thirds, however, rated C or better. Thirty per cent of the truants had no other recorded symptom of poor adjustment than the truancy itself. Whatever motivated the habitual truancy was not readily evident to the agencies handling the truant. In 70 per cent of the cases, other difficulties were noted, such as illness, running away, stealing, nervousness, deviant sex acts, and fighting.

TYPES OF TRUANTS

A loose classification of San Francisco truants, made from the records, resulted in the following distribution of types:

In 50 per cent of the cases, situational factors were prominent, such as a lack of clothing, the parents kept the child at home, the school was too difficult, or the child was not interested or accepted by other pupils.

In 30 per cent of the cases, the pupil was withdrawn, depressed, ill, daydreamy, and failed in school although he was capable.

In 20 per cent of the cases, the pupil was aggressive and apparently tru-

---

[11] *Children Absent from School, op. cit.;* John L. Roberts, "Factors Associated with Truancy," *Personnel and Guidance Journal,* 34 (1956), 431–36.

[12] Roberts, *op. cit.,* The truants comprised a sample of 175 from the Bureau of Attendance, sixty-six from the Child Guidance Service, and ninety-seven from the Juvenile Court, all from the San Francisco Unified School District.

anted to get even with the world; his record indicated defiance, fighting, cruelty, and stealing.

No single pattern of dissatisfaction is dominant in the cases. In an individual case of habitual truancy, only a study of that case would reveal whether the child was escaping from an intolerably frustrating or humiliating school situation, from rejection by other children, or from inner turmoil originating outside the school. Further, the truant might find those activities which he could carry out away from school more desirable to him than those in the school.

SOCIAL CLASS AND TRUANCY

The San Francisco study found that half of the truants came from families on public assistance, which suggests lower class placement at least economically.

TRUANCY AND DELINQUENCY

Habitual truancy is no longer considered as delinquent behavior in many states, but it does throw the adolescent into a variety of situations that sharply increase the likelihood of his being delinquent. His retardation is increased by chronic absences; his poor adjustment and dissatisfaction with school increase, and truancy may seem all the more attractive. The pupil is caught in a vicious circle. When truanting, the pupil usually must remain more or less in hiding. The store where he typically hangs out after school may not welcome him during school hours; community centers and recreation areas are not organized to operate during school hours for school pupils and again, the presence of a pupil would bring inquiries and perhaps lead to a report to the school. Most would hesitate to go home. The truants—several together perhaps—are forced to hide in a "clubhouse," along the railroad tracks, or in an empty building somewhere. Truancy per se does not inevitably lead to delinquency. But the high percentage of truants among delinquents probably indicates a tendency common to both, i.e., an inability to fit into an orderly, regulated pattern of life.

THE TRUANT'S FUTURE

The association of truancy with delinquent behavior and later adult crime is shown by a follow-up study of individuals brought before the Juvenile Court of Cook County (Chicago) on truancy proceedings in 1930.[13] So far as was

[13] Henry D. McKay, "Report on the Criminal Careers of Male Delinquents in Chicago," *Task Force Report: Juvenile Delinquency and Youth Crime*, President's Commission on Law Enforcement and the Administration of Justice, U. S. Government Printing Office, Washington, D. C., 1967, p. 112.

possible from official records the adult experience with crime (that is, after age seventeen) was tabulated. Of the court truants of 1930, 58.2 per cent had been arrested as adults, 45.3 per cent had been convicted, and 31.9 per cent committed to penal institutions. When their experience as juveniles (under age eighteen) was added, 71.3 per cent of all juvenile court truants had records of violations of law. These figures do not imply that truancy causes later delinquency or adult crime. But persistent truancy may be taken as an indicator of a larger pattern of delinquency and a portent of adult crime in almost three-fourths of truancy court cases.

Early Withdrawal from School

Most states have laws requiring school attendance until age sixteen. Some pupils virtually leave at a younger age through habitual, long-continued periods of truancy. If the truant teen-ager leaves home, as sometimes happens, or if parents are uncooperative, the attendance officer may not locate the truant for weeks or months. If a pupil has been especially troublesome in school and seems impervious to all attempts to help him, he may be allowed to drop out with tacit approval of teacher and principal. Most dropouts, however, are at, or past, the legal age limit but have not completed high school. Unlike habitual truants, they are not delinquent by definition. They do not need to hide. They are old enough to go to work.

Dropping out at a time when a greater percentage of young people are graduating from high school and entering college creates concern on the part of educators, many of whom believe that the schools are failing a segment of the population. The specialist in delinquency problems has a different interest. Early dropouts find it difficult to get and hold jobs, especially jobs that will provide them with money to buy the clothing and afford them the amusement they want. And in the absence of more constructive activities, it is feared that they often turn to delinquency.

Some recent research throws considerable light on the complex relationship between delinquency and dropping out. In a comprehensive investigation of 2,617 adolescents in California schools, Elliott and Voss found that in the years just preceding their leaving school, the dropouts' delinquency rate rose sharply.[14] After they dropped out of school, however, it fell even more rapidly. The conclusion is inescapable that school poses a serious adjustment problem for many juveniles and that dropping out provides a convenient way

[14] Delbert S. Elliott and Harwin L. Voss, *Delinquency and Dropout*, Lexington Books, Lexington, Mass., 1974, Chap. 5.

of avoiding it. Naturally, leaving school early implies a variety of difficulties in its own right, which we have already noted, but leaving school means to many teenagers an escape from a stressful, humiliating situation. Forcing a child to remain in such a situation may be even more harmful in the long run than permitting this relatively simple solution to a painful problem.

FREQUENCY AND SOCIAL CLASS

The number of pupils who drop out before graduation from high school shows the extent of the problem. Approximately half of the pupils who are in fifth grade (prior to the age for legally leaving school) do not complete high school.[15] States vary greatly in dropout rates. In 1954, Wisconsin had the best record with a loss of only 200 per 1,000 pupils between fifth grade and graduation; Georgia, with the worst rate, lost 770.

Within an individual city, the percentage of dropouts is not evenly distributed among all schools or all communities. The percentage increases sharply as social-class level or socio-economic status declines. For example, a study of 3,736 youths in New Haven showed that in the upper-upper class areas 98.2 per cent of adolescents aged sixteen and seventeen were in school.[16] The percentage dropped to 57.4 per cent of attendance by youths in the lower-lower class areas.

Studies using other measures of social class or socio-economic level show the same trend. Various studies show that 72 to 84 per cent of dropouts are from lower-income families.[17] When occupation is used as the measure, professional, managerial, clerical, and sales groups contribute many less than their share of dropouts; farmers, skilled laborers, and homemakers have an average proportion of dropouts; unskilled laborers and especially unemployed, retired, or unclassified groups contribute two to three times their share.[18] Dropouts are also likely to have poorly educated parents.

CHARACTERISTICS OF DROPOUTS

A study of 10,000 dropouts prior to graduation in cities of 30,000 to 350,000 population in seven different areas of the country, made by the United States Department of Labor, helps to pinpoint the type of student who drops out.[19] In all cities, the legal age for leaving school was sixteen years; neverthe-

[15] R. A. and L. M. Tesseneer, "Review of the Literature on School Dropouts," *Secondary School Principals Bulletin*, 42 (1958), 141–153.

[16] Davie, *op. cit.*

[17] Tesseneer, *op. cit.*

[18] Joseph C. Bledsoe, "An Investigation of Six Correlates of Students Withdrawal from High School," *Journal of Educational Research*, 53 (September, 1959), 3–6.

[19] Seymour L. Wolfbein, "Transition from School to Work: A Study of the School Leaver," *Personnel and Guidance Journal*, 38 (1959), 98–105.

less, 10 per cent of dropouts were under this age, having left because of ill health, marriage (of girls), and the like. Thirty-four per cent of the dropouts left school at the legal age of sixteen, 27 per cent remained an additional year, 17 per cent dropped out at age seventeen, and 12 percent at age nineteen or older.

Age is not a clear indication of the amount of schooling received: 31 per cent had only eighth grade education or less; 30 per cent ninth grade; and 39 per cent tenth or eleventh grade. Slightly over half were two or more years behind the proper placement for their age, and another third one year or more retarded. Only 15 per cent were in their proper grade. Many had attended school enough years to have graduated but because of retardation were far behind the boys and girls with whom they first started school. Part of the answer is in mental ability as shown by the Otis Mental Ability Group Test: 46 per cent of dropouts as compared with 21 per cent of graduates rated below 90 (below normal) I.Q.; 48 per cent compared with 63 per cent had scores between 90 and 109 (normal); and 6 per cent as compared with 16 per cent had I.Q. scores of 110 or higher (superior). However, many dropouts have the ability to graduate.

Assigning reasons for leaving school is a difficult task. School records state the reason as seen by the administration; pupils themselves give very similar reasons. Some have to do with the school situation: the pupil either is unable to do the work or he sees no relationship between school work and his major needs or what he foresees as his occupational future; the pupil is unable to achieve satisfactory interpersonal relationships with the teacher or with other pupils—he is not popular or he feels left out of things. But there are also pulls from the outside: the pupil wants or needs money or his family expects him to begin to earn; military service catches up with some of the older boys; girls want to marry. Thus the pupil balances his dissatisfactions with school against his anticipated satisfactions if he drops out of school.[20] If school has meaning for him personally or in terms of future occupation or further education, he tends to remain in school, even though his mental ability is rather low; if school has less meaning than the things he can find or hopes to find outside, he tends to leave school, often when he has the mental ability to graduate.

Although the dropout rate is high for both boys and girls, boys are

20 *Ibid.*; *Retention in High Schools in Large Cities*, Bulletin No. 15, 1957, U. S. Department of Health, Education, and Welfare, U. S. Office of Education, 1957; Joel B. Montague, "Social Status and Adjustment in School," *Clearing House*, 27 (September, 1952), 19–24; S. J. Caravello, "The Drop-out Problem," *High School Journal*, 41 (1959), 335–340.

slightly more inclined than girls to leave school before graduation.[21] Among those who drop out, girls fare better than do boys.[22] About a fourth of the girls soon marry, thus accomplishing one of the major life goals of most girls. Those who go to work find jobs as clerical workers, saleswomen, and waitresses. If they have taken business courses, their opportunities for good job placement are improved. Almost two-fifths of the boys find unskilled jobs, as they have no definite vocational training. High school graduates tend to find better-paying jobs and to remain in them longer than the dropouts, who tend to have an irregular work record during their first period after leaving school. Many occupations now require high school graduation and the dropout finds himself in a low-wage, dead-end job. The boy's dream of a large income, smart clothing, a car, a girl to entertain, and eventually marriage must be reduced to fit reality. When the boy is unable to make this adjustment and especially if he becomes unemployed, he often is a candidate for an idle street-corner group, a delinquent gang, or for personal debilitation.

Before the pupil drops out of school he often has been one of the troublesome pupils in school and/or a habitual truant. Dropping out for many students is simply the last step of a process that began soon after they entered, growing out of poor school adjustment academically and often socially and out of failure of family and community to give support to continuance in school. Actual ability of the student may be less important than the family and community factors.

The School's Responsibility

To what extent is the school directly or indirectly responsible for delinquency? To what extent can the school reduce troublesomeness, habitual truancy, and early withdrawal?

INDIRECT RESPONSIBILITY

No general statement can be made that schools are directly responsible for delinquent behavior. Occasionally inept methods of teaching or the resentment of a teacher may contribute directly to individual cases of delinquency. Primarily, principals and teachers—those in direct relationships with children —are handicapped by deficiencies which they cannot control. Some of these are as follows:

[21] Bledsoe, op. cit.; Retention in High Schools in Large Cities.
[22] Wolfbein, op. cit; Caravello, op. cit.

1. Laws that require attendance of virtually all children except the most seriously handicapped between fixed ages, usually six to sixteen.
2. Failure of many school boards and of city or county governmental units to provide special education for misfits, whether mental, physical, or social.
3. Overcrowding of schools, with large numbers of pupils per teacher, or with half-day sessions and no provision for filling the released time of pupils.
4. Poorly prepared teachers, especially during the 1950's and 1960's when the demand for teachers exceeded the supply of well-trained applicants.
5. Over the years, gradual assumption by schools of more and more responsibility for various functions and the corresponding public attitude that most of the child's development—physical, personality, and academic—rests with the schools. The public tends to expect schools to handle all types of children, whether or not they have special facilities for dealing with those not able to benefit by the existing kind of education.
6. The widely accepted attitude by principals, teachers, and public that the schools should push children up the socio-economic ladder, whether or not the children wish or are able to make the ascent.

Serious questions have arisen as to whether the schools have overreached reasonable boundaries of responsibility. Should other agencies provide special programs for the misfits, leaving to the schools the function of education in the narrower sense of academic and vocational training for children prepared to benefit by it? In larger cities, especially, school systems have made numerous approaches to the problem of nonacademic needs of students.

Special Programs of Schools

Special programs for schools usually are not couched in terms of delinquency prevention but in positive terms of better academic and personal development. Nevertheless, they often prevent delinquency. They help children adjust or relieve the classroom physically of troublesome children.

SCHOOL COUNSELORS OR SOCIAL WORKERS

School counseling services have been added to a number of schools. Teachers may refer individual children to the service, where staff members analyze the child's difficulties, interpret his problems to the teacher, and often visit the child's home. The counselor assigned to the case may continue some relationship with the child in school, but as a rule, refers a family in need of expert help to an appropriate community agency. If the child has serious personality problems, an attempt is made to have the family arrange for psychiatric treatment outside the school. The counselor then interprets, helps to adjust school problems, and acts as a liaison among school, family, and community agencies.

There have been attempts from time to time to bring a broad range of social services for problem children into the school itself. But recent research indicates that whatever the general benefits of such a program, it has little preventive effect upon delinquency. Tait and Hodges evaluated a project in which a wide range of social and psychiatric services was made available to the children of a Washington, D.C. elementary school, and they found that "the treated group had no fewer, and possibly more, delinquents than the untreated group."[23] They concluded that the proper function of social service staff in the school should be diagnostic and not treatment.[24]

SPECIAL CLASSES AND SCHOOLS

Some cities have established special ungraded classes in some schools, or entire special schools for children who do not adapt to the usual school program.[25] The pupils in special classes and schools often represent a potpourri of problems: withdrawn children, emotionally unstable children, aggressively active children, habitual truants, and others. Usually attention can be given to children as individuals, especially if classes are small and the services of various specialists are provided. One rule of the effective special class or school is an individual approach to catch the attention and interest of the pupil and then build on that interest to meet some of the specific needs of the child. The ideal end objective is to adjust the child and return him to his regular school in condition to fit into the classroom. In some situations, however, the special class simply becomes a catch-all for misbehaving children; its function then is to remove the child from a classroom and permit other pupils to do their work, although the special program may not be of much benefit to the troublemaker himself.

Chicago has long had a system of special schools. The Montefiori school (established in 1929 as part of the public school system) and the Moseley school receive boys in a day-school program which operates throughout the year. One branch of each of these schools is for girls. The Chicago Home for Girls, a branch of Montefiori, operates ten months of the year for girls who need to be removed from their own or foster homes, and the Chicago Parental Home is a year-round residential school for boys. Other units of the public school system are operated throughout the year in the detention home, the

[23] C. Downing Tait, Jr. and Emory F. Hodges, Jr., *Delinquents, Their Families, and the Community*, Charles C Thomas, Springfield, Illinois, 1962, pp. 143–144.

[24] *Ibid.*, pp. 139–141.

[25] William C. Kvaraceus and William E. Ulrich, *Delinquent Behavior, Principles and Practices*, National Education Association, Washington, D. C., 1959, Chapter 6, "Providing Help through Special Classes," describes both special classes and special schools.

House of Correction, and the Cook County jail. The public school system also maintains twelve adjustment rooms in elementary schools for boys under twelve years of age.[26]

New York City opened special classes in some elementary schools in 1940 for potential delinquents. In 1947, special schools known as "600 schools" were established, consisting of ten institutional schools, two remand (detention) centers, ten day schools, and six annexes to institutional organizations. Only one of the schools is for girls. The pupils include children who are troublemakers, delinquent, emotionally disturbed, and psychotic. Most pupils have had some court experience. One function of the schools is to remove the children from regular classrooms where their behavior prevents learning by themselves and others, and to rehabilitate them when possible for return to the regular schools.[27]

Other large cities have similar special classes and schools. Most of them remain more or less experimental, still discovering what services are needed and what results can be expected.

SPECIAL PROGRAMS FOR RETENTION OF STUDENTS

Many students who lose interest in school and become chronic truants or early dropouts are not emotionally maladjusted. From working class backgrounds, they anticipate entering some form of manual or skilled employment. If they have not been able to secure vocational training of a practical nature, school may easily seem unnecessary and superfluous. If such boys drop out of school and do not find jobs, they often tend to drift into delinquent behavior. An expansion of practical and vocational types of education to fit these boys specifically for the jobs they may reasonably hope to fill would undoubtedly reduce early dropping out and also place them in a position to work at jobs with better remuneration than they often secure.

Another special type of training suggested for lower class pupils has been to prepare them in general for law-abiding lower class life.[28] This point of view recognizes, first, the differences in values and objectives of the middle and lower class, and, second, the fact that many lower class youth probably will not be upwardly mobile and, therefore, should be prepared for lower class life as a worthwhile level of society. Respect for lower class values would ease the

26 Kvaraceus and Ulrich, *op. cit.*, pp. 215–219; Edward H. Stullken, "Chicago's Special School for Social Adjustment," *Federal Probation*, 20 (March, 1956), 31–36.

27 Kvaraceus and Ulrich, *op. cit.*, pp. 182–183.

28 William C. Kvaraceus and associates, *Delinquent Behavior, Culture and the Individual*, National Education Association of the United States, Washington, D. C., 1959, pp. 62–75.

adjustment of the youth who wishes to rise but cannot for any one of a number of reasons, and who often finds delinquency an outlet for his feelings. This point of view seems to run counter to the usual school emphasis on middle class values as superior to lower class values and to the pressure on students to move if possible toward middle class status. An adoption of this approach should be made with caution, in order not to create a permanent lower "caste," and to keep the way of upward mobility open for students desiring and able to move upward in accordance with the traditional American ideal.

Employment as Delinquency-Preventive

Since many lower class youth become chronic truants and early school dropouts, the suggestion has been made that the age for compulsory education and for a work permit should be lowered. The boy or girl would then be able to leave school early in the teens and go to work. Heated arguments between the advocates of continued schooling and of early employment have found their way into print.

EARLY EMPLOYMENT

A juvenile court judge has assailed the school and child labor laws as the chief cause for adolescent idleness, especially by youth not interested in attending school.[29] Other statements emphasize the fact that in our culture work gives prestige and carries the adolescent on into adult status.[30]

There are powerful arguments on both sides of the issue. Early dropouts find it more difficult to find and hold well-paying jobs than the high school graduates.[31] Unemployment is much more common among the dropouts.

In addition, the trend of business and industry is away from unskilled labor and toward greater use of machines, whose operation requires maturity and specialized training. In discussing job placement, one guidance counselor has called attention to the fact that in seventy-one occupations with labor shortages the minimum educational requirement is four years of education at the high school level.[32] Undisciplined delinquents and early dropouts are not eli-

[29] William C. Long, "Let's Put Our Idle Teen-agers to Work," *American Magazine*, October, 1955. For views on both sides see "An Open Letter to Judge Long," *American Child*, 38 (March, 1956), 1–2; "Two Views on Child Labor Laws," *American Child*, 37 (May, 1955), 4; "Are the Child Labor Laws to Blame?" *American Child*, 40 (May, 1958), entire issue.

[30] "Federation Employment and Guidance Service," *Special Youth Board Project Report*, New York, mimeographed, April 21, 1958, p. 2.

[31] Wolfbein, *op. cit.*

[32] Caravello, *op. cit.*

gible for good jobs. They may find their way into unskilled, dead-end jobs or drift from one job to another. Whether the kind of work they can enter is delinquency-preventive is open to question, especially for the boy who has unrealistically dreamed of a glamorous job.

On the other hand, there is a good chance that dropouts who are forced to return to school will become seriously delinquent. Moreover, it is probably true that work gives prestige more readily in middle class than in lower class types of occupations. In a study of the attitudes men hold toward their jobs, a number of men were asked what they would do if they inherited sufficient money to stop work. The skilled and unskilled workers showed a much greater willingness to work than men in prestige jobs.[33] When asked whether they would continue in their same jobs if they inherited money but wished to continue to work, 61 per cent of the middle class but only 34 per cent of the total working group said that they would continue in the same job; only 16 per cent of unskilled workers would want to continue in their category.

Early school dropouts come primarily from the unskilled class or from families in which the father is unemployed or retired. Unprepared to do more than their dissatisfied fathers do, it is questionable to what extent work would build up their feeling of worth and status or provide money to fulfill their ambitions.

INTEGRATION OF SCHOOL AND EMPLOYMENT

A halfway program has been suggested whereby students work and attend school, with the job integrated into the school program.

In various communities organizations have taken the initiative in screening youth in or out of schools and finding jobs for them. The organization may act as a liaison between an employer who is solicited for job openings for youth, the school counselor who recommends students, and the recommended student who wishes to work. The work may be part-time during the school year or for a portion of the summer. The response of the employed youth is very good: they like to work, and they spend their money wisely.[34] But the value of such programs for delinquency prevention is in considerable doubt. Robert J. Havighurst directed a project in which 200 socially and educationally maladjusted boys from Kansas City were enrolled in a work-study program which provided ". . . half days of classroom work geared to their abilities, . . . needs, interests, and personal orientations and half days of supervised work

[33] Nancy C. Morse and Robert S. Weiss, "The Function and Meaning of Work," *American Sociological Review*, 20 (1955), 191–198.
[34] *Youth and Work*, National Child Labor Committee, New York, 5 (October, 1958).

experience. . . . The findings indicate . . . that only about one-fourth of the boys profited from the Work-Study Program. Thus, this study . . . failed to demonstrate that supervised work experience, even under relatively controlled conditions, could be useful in materially reducing delinquency. . . ."[35]

Educators Redefine the Problem of Delinquency

In the 1960's, schools began to redefine the problem of delinquency as part of a larger problem of unadjusted youth who, under certain circumstances, turned to delinquency as a way of satisfying unmet needs. Some educators termed these young people alienated.

> We call them 'alienated" because they do not accept the ways of living and achieving that are standard in our society. As younger children they probably accepted the standard ideas of right and wrong, complied with school regulations and tried to succeed, but the combined and repeated frustrations of failure in school and mistreatment at home have turned them either into members of delinquent subgroups or into defeated, apathetic individuals.[36]

The authors of the above statement estimate that in a normal cross section of youth in small cities, 15 per cent are alienated and in large cities perhaps as many as 30 or 40 per cent. A part of these only would be delinquent.

Attention has shifted from trying to prevent delinquent behavior per se or rehabilitating already delinquent youth to providing youth with means to develop as far as they are able and guiding them into paths of achievement in conventional society. The theory that underlies these efforts is based on Merton's schema of alternate means of reaching desired goals and on Cloward and Ohlin's application of this schema to delinquent behavior. This application has already been discussed in Chapter 6, with its emphasis on contrasting legitimate and illegal avenues to achievement.

COMPENSATORY EDUCATION

Recognition that the traditional education oriented to middle class students, many of whom anticipate attending college, is not adequate for the needs of lower class students has led to a vast proliferation of special types of programs. Many come under the general heading of compensatory education,

---

[35] Winton M. Ahlstrom and Robert J. Havighurst, *400 Losers*, Jossey-Bass Inc., San Francisco, 1971, p. 5.

[36] Robert J. Havighurst, Bernice L. Neugarten, and Jacqueline M. Falk, *Society and Education, A Book of Readings*, Allyn and Bacon, Boston, 1967, p. 265.

defined as "a type of education which should help socially disadvantaged students without reducing the quality of education for those who are progressing satisfactorily under existing educational conditions."[37]

Special programs that might be grouped under compensatory education are not aimed directly at the delinquent or potential delinquent. They are planned for the development of any deprived youth. Ideally, if such children are helped to achieve educational and social goals, they will be less likely to find a haven in delinquent peer groups—they will be able to reach success goals through legitimate means.

The programs run all the way from preparing young children for entrance into kindergarten or first grade, such as the Head-Start programs, to those planned for upper elementary, junior, and senior high school, such as Higher Horizons and Upward Bound. Job Corps programs catch the youth who needs training for a vocation. These programs are financed by private grants or various forms of governmental aid. They are still in an experimental stage and firm evaluations are not completed in terms of their stated purposes or as a preventive of delinquency.

BIBLIOGRAPHY

AHLSTROM, WINTON M., AND ROBERT J. HAVIGHURST, *400 Losers*, Jossey-Bass Inc., San Francisco, 1971.

BLOOM, BENJAMIN S., ALLISON DAVIS, AND ROBERT HESS, *Compensatory Education for Cultural Deprivation*, Holt, Rinehart, & Winston, New York, 1965.

CARAVELLO, S. J., "The Drop-out Problem," *High School Journal*, 41 (1959), 335–340.

CAVAN, RUTH SHONLE, ed., *Readings in Juvenile Delinquency*, Third Edition, J. B. Lippincott Company, Philadelphia, 1975, Section 4.

COHEN, ELI E., AND LILA ROSENBAUM, "Will Relaxing Child Labor Laws Help Prevent Delinquency?" *Federal Probation*, 23 (March, 1959), 44–47.

ELLIOTT, DELBERT S., AND HARWIN L. VOSS, *Delinquency and Dropout*, Lexington Books, Lexington, Mass., 1974.

"From School to Work," U. S. Department of Labor, Bureau of Labor Statistics, Washington, D. C., 1960.

KVARACEUS, WILLIAM C., *Dynamics of Delinquency*, Charles E. Merrill Books, Columbus, Ohio, 1966, Part 4.

————, WALTER B. MILLER, AND COLLABORATORS, *Delinquent Behavior, Culture and the Individual*, National Education Association, Washington, D. C., 1959.

————, WILLIAM E. ULRICH, AND COLLABORATORS, *Delinquent Behavior Prin-*

[37] Benjamin S. Bloom, Allison Davis, and Robert Hess, *Compensatory Education for Cultural Deprivation*, Holt, Rinehart, & Winston, New York, 1965, p. 6.

ciples and Practices, National Education Association, Washington, D. C., 1959.

President's Commission on Law Enforcement and Administration of Justice, *Task Force Report: Juvenile Delinquency and Youth Crime*, U. S. Government Printing Office, Washington, D. C., 1967, Appendices E, M and N.

Retention in High Schools in Large Cities, Bulletin 1957, No. 15, U. S. Department of Health, Education, and Welfare, U. S. Office of Education, Washington, D. C., 1957.

ROBERTS, JOHN L., "Factors Associated with Truancy," *Personnel and Guidance Journal*, 34 (1956), 431–436.

SAMUELS, GERTRUDE, "Visit to a '600' School," *New York Times Magazine* (March, 1958), 12, 57–58.

"School and Delinquency," *Crime and Delinquency*, 7 (July, 1961), entire issue.

"Social Class Structure and American Education," *Harvard Educational Review*, 23 (Summer, 1953) and 23 (Fall, 1953), entire issues.

SPENCE, RALPH B., *Reducing Juvenile Delinquency*, New York State Youth Commission, Albany, New York, revised 1955.

STULLKEN, EDWARD H., "Chicago's Special School for Social Adjustment," *Federal Probation*, 20 (March, 1956), 31–36.

———, "The Schools and the Delinquency Problem," *Journal of Criminal Law, Criminology and Police Science*, 43 (1953), 563–577.

TAIT, C. DOWNING, JR., AND EMORY F. HODGES, JR., *Delinquents, Their Families, and the Community*, Charles C Thomas, Springfield, Ill., 1962.

"Teacher Opinion on Pupil Behavior, 1955–1956," *Research Bulletin of the National Education Association*, 34 (April, 1956), 51–107.

TESSENEER, R. A., AND TESSENEER, L. M., "Review of the Literature on School Dropouts," *The Bulletin* of the National Association of Secondary School Principals, 42 (May, 1958), 141–153.

WATTENBERG, WILLIAM W., ed., *Social Deviancy among Youth*, National Society for the Study of Education, Yearbook No. 65, Part 1, University of Chicago Press, Chicago, 1966.

WOLFBEIN, SEYMOUR L., "Transition from School to Work: A Study of the School Leaver," *Personnel and Guidance Journal*, 38 (1959), 98–105.

controlling juvenile delinquency   chapter 14

Controlling delinquency effectively means mounting successful campaigns in three distinct sectors: those adolescents who have already fallen into a delinquent pattern of behavior must be encouraged to follow more acceptable paths; those youngsters who are not yet delinquent but seem headed toward delinquency must be reoriented; and the conditions in the family and community that contribute to delinquency must be corrected or eliminated. The control of delinquency, therefore, depends ultimately on our ability to rehabilitate adjudicated delinquents; to treat pre-delinquents; and to reform the communities of America so that they stop producing delinquents. A failure in any sector inevitably undermines efforts in the other two, but unfortunately we have not been broadly successful in accomplishing any of them. It should come as no surprise, therefore, that delinquency today is a more serious problem than it was in the 1920's and 30's when the nation first awoke to the scope of its delinquency problem and began to do something about it.

In this chapter we shall concern ourselves with the remedies that have been proposed over the years to correct criminogenic features in the community and family and with the techniques that have been devised to reorient pre-delinquents along more constructive paths. In subsequent chapters we shall turn to the adjudicated delinquent and the failures that have attended virtually all attempts to salvage him from a career in delinquency and crime. Special attention will be given to the reasons for our generalized failure to find the key to delinquency control. Has it been a matter of faulty methods or technique? Of deficient theories? We shall confront these questions as we consider the various attempts to control delinquency in the following pages.

Delinquency Prevention

Preventing delinquency depends on our ability to identify the basic conditions in the social fabric that contribute to delinquency, and in Chapter 6 we described four societal processes that affect the level of crime and delinquency in the community: social organization, social disorganization, cultural disorganization, and cultural deviance. We also identified several distinctive types of delinquency in the form of both roles and subcultural patterns in Chapter 8. Thus, we are in a good position to indicate the kinds of conditions in the community that foster delinquency and the steps that should be taken to relieve these conditions.

SOCIAL INTEGRATION AND DELINQUENCY

Social organization is relevant to delinquency because it establishes the intimacy and stability of social relations in the community. Other things being equal, the more stable and the more personal relationships are, the less deviancy including delinquency there will be. In order to prevent delinquency, therefore, we should encourage greater social integration and interdependence among the members of the community. By so doing we will improve the ability of the community to guide its young people into constructive roles in the community as well as its ability to discover and reorient those adolescents who are moving toward delinquency.

These were exactly the aims of the Area Projects established and developed by Clifford R. Shaw in Chicago in the 1930's. The assumption behind these projects was that delinquency is ". . . principally a product of the breakdown of the machinery of spontaneous social control."[1] To correct this deficiency in the community, Shaw proposed that the members of the community be enlisted in an area-wide organization devoted to an urgent community goal. In spite of the fact that these neighborhoods were deeply disorganized, the projects were successful in gaining the support of local residents, because community people were systematically involved in their operations and given leadership posts in many cases. They were also relatively successful in involving all

[1] Solomon Kobrin, "The Chicago Area Project—A 25-year Assessment," *Annals of the American Academy of Political and Social Science*, 322 (March, 1959), 22.

segments of the community including those citizens with delinquent or criminal records. By using the Area Projects to open up new avenues of interaction among adults and adolescents, it was hoped that adolescents would be brought more fully into the social patterns of the community and diverted thereby from antisocial behaviors and delinquency.

According to Witmer and Tufts, this hope was largely realized.[2] Between 1930 and 1942 delinquency declined in three out of four communities where Area Projects had been established, and in one neighborhood forty out of forty-one parolees completed their paroles without being recommitted to an institution. Thus, in Chicago, at least, Area Projects seem to have reinforced the social structure of the community and to have improved its ability to influence the behavior of its members and especially of its young people.

As Martin points out, however, not all communities are disorganized in the same fashion as the Chicago neighborhoods, and Area Projects would probably have little beneficial effect in such communities.[3] Stable, ethnic, working class communities often exhibit little of the social disintegration of inner-city lower class neighborhoods, and attempts to bolster their social integration in this fashion would be ill-advised.

But the community is not the only group whose social integration has a bearing on delinquency. The family, too, must gain the interest and affection of its younger members if it is to steer them toward fulfilling roles in adulthood. And where it has failed—where the parents have little interest in their children and less influence over them—that is where delinquency is likely to appear. Accordingly, considerable attention has been given by social workers and family therapists to a variety of problems that impair parent-child relationships. One such program was organized at the Henry Street Settlement House in New York City for families with pre-delinquent children in a high delinquency area.[4] Five groups of parents were formed under the auspices of the Settlement House in which discussions focusing upon their children were regularly held. Through the varied perspectives that such discussions revealed, parents were encouraged to exert more control over their children where they had been too relaxed and to be more tolerant where they had been too restric-

[2] H. L. Witmer and E. Tufts, *The Effectiveness of Delinquency Prevention Programs*, Children's Bureau, U.S. Department of Health, Education, and Welfare, Publication 350, U.S. Government Printing Office, Washington, D.C., 1954, p. 16.

[3] John Martin, "Three Approaches of Delinquency Prevention: A Critique," *Crime and Delinquency*, 7 (January, 1961), 16–24.

[4] Ruth S. Tefferteller, "Delinquency Prevention Through Revitalizing Parent-Child Relations," *Annals of the American Academy of Political and Social Science*, 322 (March, 1959), 69–78.

tive. Moreover, closer relations among the parents developed through the discussion groups with the result that as a body they all became more effective in curbing the antisocial behavior of their children. Most attempts at dealing with delinquency in the family have enlisted clinical services and concentrated upon serious personal pathology. But the Henry Street Settlement program suggests that fashioning strong bonds between neighbors with pre-delinquent children can also have positive effects.

SOCIAL DISORGANIZATION AND DELINQUENCY

Eliminating social disorganization particularly as it applies to inner-city residents was one of the primary goals of President Lyndon B. Johnson's administration in the 1960's. Massive manpower programs designed to provide job training for inner-city people, social welfare programs to care for their social ills, and educational programs to start their children toward meaningful lives and careers were established with a view to providing those who wanted to lift themselves out of poverty a way of doing so. These programs were not focused essentially upon adolescents nor were they designed to eliminate delinquency, but one of the beneficial results, it was hoped, would be a reduction of crime and delinquency in the inner city. Unfortunately, the urban riots of the late 1960's and the turmoil surrounding the Vietnam War aborted these programs and contributed to the election of Richard M. Nixon in 1968, who promptly set about redesigning or dismantling many of Johnson's Great Society programs. Thus, it is difficult to say whether Johnson's War on Poverty would have succeeded had it been allowed to develop to completion, but there is general agreement that the impact of the War on Poverty on delinquency was negligible.[5]

Several studies of attempts to divert seriously delinquent youths from delinquency via carefully designed work and educational programs have been made, and they all report failure. For example, the Neighborhood Youth Corps (NYC) was established in 1964 to provide counseling, remedial education, and supervised work to young people between the ages of sixteen and twenty-one from impoverished families. Gerald R. Robin studied 247 enrollees in Cincinnati, and in comparison with 119 youths who had applied but were not enrolled in NYC, he found that ". . . there is no evidence that NYC participation reduced delinquency among its enrollees while they were working in the program."[6] He repeated this study in Detroit and found again in com-

---

[5] A balanced evaluation of overall impact of Johnson's Great Society programs is contained in the entire issue of *Public Interest*, No. 34, (Winter, 1974).

[6] Gerald R. Robin, "Anti-Poverty Programs and Delinquency," *Journal of Criminal Law, Criminology and Police Science*, 60 (1969), 327.

paring 500 NYC enrollees with 124 controls that "The gross effects in Detroit . . . are the same as those in Cincinnati, revealing no effect of program participation on reducing or preventing delinquency.[7]

James Hackler evaluated a similar program in Seattle in which ninety-six boys participated in a work-study program. In comparing those boys who took part with sixty boys who did not, Hackler found that ". . . though the differences were small, the controls changed more than any other group. Tests of significance do not show any meaningful differences between work and control groups."[8]

Another area of considerable difficulty for many adolescents, as pointed out in Chapter 6, is their school experience. When they encounter repeated failure in their attempts to relate to their peers and teachers, delinquency is a common result. Attempts at remedying these difficulties have focused upon bringing the curricula and the teachers closer to the pupils, thereby making both more meaningful and acceptable.[9] The overall impact of these programs, however, is still largely unknown, because assessments of them have been few and far between. But one experimental program was carefully evaluated by C. R. Jeffrey and I. A. Jeffrey in Washington, D. C.[10] Fifty inner-city adolescents between sixteen and twenty-one were enrolled for three years in an educational program in which they were paid up to $40 per week to study, pass high school equivalency tests, and carry out regular tasks at an educational center. Altogether 167 youths participated in the programs, but only forty-two remained to the end, and only thirteen ultimately passed their high school equivalency tests. The Jefferys reported no relationship between progress in the program and passing the high school equivalencies.

All in all, the effort to prevent delinquency by easing the strain of social disorganization in the adolescent's immediate environment, i.e., by providing him jobs, job training, or educational tutoring, does not seem to have had much beneficial effect. There are a variety of reasons for this disappointing result. First, although social disorganization may be pervasive in the inner city and a key factor in the genesis of delinquency there, once gangs have emerged and established a structural basis for subcultural delinquency, it is not enough

[7] *Ibid.*, p. 330.

[8] James C. Hackler, "Boys, Blisters, and Behavior—the Impact of a Work Program in an Urban Central Area," *Journal of Research in Crime and Delinquency*, 3 (July, 1966), 155–164.

[9] *Task Force Report: Juvenile Delinquency and Youth Crime*, The President's Commission on Law Enforcement and Administration of Justice, U. S. Government Printing Office, Washington, D. C., 1967, pp. 278–304.

[10] C. R. and I. A. Jeffrey, "Dropouts and Delinquency: An Experimental Program in Behavior Change," *Education and Urban Society*, 1 (1969), 325–336.

to present gang members with the skills to find useful, satisfying jobs. Youngsters deeply involved in gang activities are no more likely to respond to such efforts than are adults who are deeply involved in organized crime.

Another reason these projects have been less successful than originally hoped lies in the fact that they have often attempted to work with the most problematic children, i.e., those who were early dropouts from school, or those who have had the most serious delinquent records. Those who are already hard-core delinquents have often had a long experience of failure in a variety of institutions from public schools to correctional institutions. To expect to compensate for this lengthy history of defeat and the resultant cynicism and fatalism with a few months (or even years) of training, even with the most skillful and well-meaning of instructors, may be naive. Perhaps the job of removing the effects of social disorganization in a community is more difficult than we had originally imagined.

Disorganization in the family where the parents are confused, inconsistent, or consistently unjust with their children is also a major factor in delinquency, as we have seen in Chapter 10. Serious conflict between parents and children or among the parents themselves is often a precursor to delinquency, and accordingly a variety of approaches in dealing with such conflicts has been attempted. Traditionally, social workers, psychologists, and home economists have all been enlisted by communities in coping with chronic problem families on an individual basis.

In the Netherlands, however, a different approach to chronic problem families has been developed.[11] Shortly after World War I the Dutch established a network of "re-education centers" where families can be sent that have demonstrated a chronic inability to deal with their children or cope with their financial or social responsibilities. By the late 1950's this network had grown to include twelve camps located in rural areas in Holland and serving about 200 families. The camps themselves include in their staffs social workers, home economists, and other specialists who are available on a moment's notice to help resident families cope with their problems. The aim is to bring professional assistance to troubled families on a concerted and regular basis so that ultimately they can become more self-reliant. Naturally, the assistance is geared to particular problems in the family, but where problems have centered on the children, the policy has been to avoid separating the child from the family if at all possible. There is some evidence that this is a wise practice,

[11] Described in C. Downing Tait, Jr. and Emory F. Hodges, Jr., *Delinquents, Their Families, and the Community*, Charles C Thomas, Springfield, Illinois, 1962, pp. 128–133.

since foster-home placement does not seem to be a good substitute for the child's own family, even when it is beset with severe difficulties.[12]

CULTURAL DISORGANIZATION

Since the large Italian or Jewish ghettos have all but disappeared in America's major cities, criminologists have largely lost interest in cultural disorganization as an explanation of delinquency. But the fact remains that today there is still a large and growing migration of poor blacks and whites from the rural South into most of America's great cities. These latter-day migrants are at least as ill-prepared for metropolitan life as the Sicilian or Russian immigrants who came to Chicago or New York in the late nineteenth century, and the need is at least as great today for programs and institutions that can assist them in becoming acculturated to the social patterns of the city.

Perhaps the most active agencies in helping recent migrants adapt to the city are those which served in the same capacity eighty to one hundred years ago when European immigrants were their principal clientele—i.e., settlement houses. Today they still provide a great variety of useful services for recent migrants to the city, e.g., legal advice, social and financial counseling, cultural programs, consumers' co-ops. Many of these settlement houses are still located at their original sites because, although the racial or ethnic identity of their clientele may have changed, the lower class neighborhoods are still at their doorsteps.

PREVENTING CULTURAL DEVIANCE

Among the most pressing problems facing many major American cities is that of coping with the delinquent gangs which have sprung up in black and Latino inner-city neighborhoods and all but dominate social life in these neighborhoods. These gangs are responsible for a significant volume of both crime and delinquency; they are active in distributing a wide variety of deadly weapons throughout the inner city; and they have recently begun to take a direct role in supplying narcotics to residents of the inner city. In many ways, therefore, these gangs directly contribute to the crime problem and the serious deterioration of social life in inner-city black and Latino communities. It is probably no exaggeration to suggest that until we learn how to deal effectively with these gangs, we will not be effective in preventing either crime or delinquency in our major cities.

[12] Joan and William McCord and Emily Thurber, "The Effects of Foster-Home Placement in the Prevention of Adult Antisocial Behavior," *Social Service Review*, 34 (December, 1960), 415–420.

But the problem is more difficult than many have appreciated up to now. It is not simply a question of reaching gang members and making them aware of the opportunities for rewarding careers in legitimate activities, because these same gang members are also part of a well-organized structure which insists that they involve themselves from time to time in seriously antisocial actions regardless of their own preferences. It would be like asking a soldier in organized crime to give up his lucrative rackets in favor of a career as a truck driver. The whole momentum of the organization as well as the penalties entailed in quitting are so great as to make the proposal ludicrous. Thus, until we learn how to cope with the delinquent gangs and their influence on individual members, we will make little headway in dealing with delinquency in the inner city.

One extraordinary effort to cope with street gangs was launched as part of the Johnson administration's Great Society programs in 1967.[13] In November of that year two street gangs that had long been warring with each other on the Lower East Side of New York City declared a truce and joined in a variety of constructive programs. They began a number of self-help projects which testified to both their organizing ability and their ability to lead adolescents in prosocial as well as antisocial directions. The next year a nationwide organization of gang leaders was formed, Youth Organizations United, with funding from both the federal government and private foundations which eventually totaled nearly $300,000. Its mission was to stimulate gang leaders in major metropolitan centers to develop self-help enterprises similar to those organized in New York City. At about the same time two gangs in Chicago, the Blackstone Rangers (better known today as the Black P Stone Nation) and the East Side Disciples were granted $927,341 from the Office of Economic Opportunity for a training and employment program. The Vice Lords on Chicago's West Side received smaller grants from the Rockefeller Foundation and other private foundations for a variety of enterprises, e.g., an ice cream parlor, a management training institute, a street academy for high school dropouts, and a teen center. The aim of these projects was to help gang leaders develop a range of business and social agencies which in the end would provide meaningful, rewarding activities for gang members and make street delinquency unnecessary.

Unfortunately these goals were never realized, and when serious irregularities were discovered in the finances of the programs run by the Black P Stone Nation, the whole program collapsed under a barrage of criticism. It was

[13] An interesting description of the manner in which the federal government sought to woo gang leaders to constructive pursuits is contained in Richard W. Poston, *The Gang and the Establishment*, Harper & Row, Publishers, New York, 1971.

an interesting experiment in building alternatives to delinquency in the nation's major cities, but it seriously underestimated the complexity of the task. If a better administrative effort had been made, it might have succeeded. But as it unfolded it was clear that the sole administrative control was funding. Apparently it was hoped that money alone would divert the gang leaders from antisocial activity. But it was not enough, and several gang leaders were sent to prison for their part in the fiasco.

A more carefully designed program for reaching gang members and changing their orientation was the detached worker programs established in many major cities in the 1950's.[14] Since gang members were especially reluctant to approach social workers in their offices for help or counseling, it was felt that social workers should go to the streets and contact gang members in *their* setting. Not every social worker is prepared to move into the streets and work successfully with delinquents. Generally it requires younger, emotionally stable individuals who also have a peculiar knack for building rapport with lower class, often black, youngsters. Once the street worker has gained the confidence of gang members, he attempts to shift the gang toward socially acceptable activities by providing an exciting variety of services and organized activities for the gang. He may be most successful with the younger members, but regardless of where his influence is greatest, he often finds that insofar as he is successful with some gang members, he also threatens the political base of other key members in the group. Thus, street work requires a keen ability to appraise politically delicate situations and to adjust one's behavior appropriately. Many street workers have had the requisite finesse, but a few have been assaulted and even murdered by the very youths they were attempting to help.

There have been several careful evaluations of the effectiveness of detached workers in diverting gangs from delinquency, and the verdict is that street workers, if anything, seem to *stimulate* delinquency among the gangs they serve. Walter Miller evaluated a project in Boston in which seven gangs were provided street workers for up to thirty-four months.[15] Miller assessed the impact of these workers by comparing seven gangs that were provided workers with five other gangs that had only fleeting contact with street workers. He found that court appearances among the gangs with workers decreased

---

[14] There are several valuable descriptions of street workers and their methods. See Irving Spergel, *Street Gang Work: Theory and Practice*, Addison-Wesley Publishing Co., Reading, Mass., 1966; and Frank J. Carney, Hans W. Mattick, and John D. Callaway, *Action in the Streets*, Association Press, New York, 1969.

[15] Walter B. Miller, "The Impact of a 'Total-Community' Delinquency Control Project," *Social Problems*, 10 (Fall, 1962), 168–191.

slightly, i.e., 5.8 per cent over the course of the program. But when compared with the groups that had had no workers, there was little difference in the volume or pattern of their court appearances. Miller also examined illegal acts and disapproved behaviors of the seven gangs with workers and found only slight declines in both types of behavior. He concluded "all measures of violative behavior . . . provide consistent support for a finding of 'negligible impact.' "[16]

More recently Malcolm Klein evaluated a similar project, the Group Guidance Project in Los Angeles, in whch four black gangs with close to 800 members were provided a corps of ten detached workers over a period of four years. In what is, perhaps, the most thorough of such evaluations Klein found that instead of reducing delinquency among gang members, the Group Guidance Project actually was responsible for a significant increase.[17] Further, these increases were primarily in offenses committed with companions and among the younger members. After carefully weighing the results Klein concluded that the Group Guidance Project and the exciting activities it organized for the gangs contributed directly to their cohesiveness and their attractiveness to prospective members, and therefore, to their ability to guide individual members into delinquency.

In an ingenious test of this conclusion Klein and his colleagues mounted a two-year program in 1966 in which the street workers were instructed to work to *reduce* the solidarity of a Mexican-American gang of about 140 members in Ladino Hills in Los Angeles. They were successful in reducing cohesiveness dramatically and in stopping recruitment altogether. The number of juvenile arrests of gang members declined during the life of the project by 35 per cent. But since the number of gang members was also shrinking, the delinquency rate among gang members showed no change. As Klein points out ". . . one can at least take heart that the dramatic increase in delinquency rates during the earlier project was not repeated in the Ladino Hills Project."[18]

It appears, then, that detached worker programs have failed in the past because they have inaugurated attractive activities among groups with seriously delinquent leaders. Insofar as they have attempted to change the behavior of this delinquent cadre, detached workers have uniformly failed. But where they have sought to undermine the solidarity of the gang and its ability

[16] *Ibid.*, p. 187.

[17] Malcolm Klein, "Gang Cohesiveness, Delinquency, and a Street Work Program," *Journal of Research in Crime and Delinquency*, 6 (July, 1969), 135–166.

[18] Malcolm Klein, *Street Gangs and Street Workers*, Prentice-Hall, Inc., Englewood Cliffs, N. J., 1971, p. 303.

to attract recruits, they have succeeded. The lesson for future detached worker programs is clear.

Unfortunately, however, the solution to gang delinquency itself has not yet been discovered. It is apparent that established gangs cannot be reoriented simply by exposing them to the benign influence of federal bureaucrats and youthful detached workers. Perhaps a more concerted effort to deal with children's problems in their families, neighborhoods, and schools is necessary in conjunction with efforts to cope with the gang. It may be, however, that the solution to gang delinquency depends upon social and political resources far beyond the capacity of existing public agencies to muster. Gang delinquency is a reaction to the disintegration of social life in the inner city. Until we discover how to shore up the indigenous familial and communal structures of the inner city, we are probably going to have delinquent gangs.

Our inability to cope with delinquency, however, is not confined just to the problem of gang delinquency. Our discussion thus far has uncovered *no* broadly effective solutions to any of the societal conditions that foster delinquency. As we have indicated, part of the difficulty consists of our inability to muster sufficient resources to cope with the extent of the problem. But part of our problem also derives from the fact that solutions have often been proposed before an adequate diagnosis of the problem had been achieved.[19]

Delinquency in profoundly disorganized inner-city neighborhoods has been combatted with settlement houses; delinquents in well-established, working class neighborhoods have been provided with work-study programs; and fighting gangs have been provided with community action programs. It is conceivable that a more intelligent analysis of the specific forms of delinquency at hand coupled with a more refined prescription as to their remedy might have produced more impressive results than we have achieved up to now. For example, if the basic problem in a community is a widespread demoralization among the adults, as in many inner-city neighborhoods, it probably does little good to approach the delinquents in the area with a detached worker program. Area projects to provide a sense of cohesiveness and momentum and manpower training programs to relieve the sense of futility would probably have more lasting effect upon the problem of delinquency. But in relatively well-established neighborhoods where the basic problem is a widespread loss of meaningful interaction between adults and adolescents, some variation of the detached worker program to undermine gang solidarity would probably achieve greater overall results. Our failure to find the key (or keys) to delinquency

[19] Cf. John Martin, *op. cit.*

prevention indicates that we have not been adroit in using our understanding of the causes of delinquency to suggest *appropriate* remedies to the various forms that delinquency takes. When we become more skilled in this regard, our programs may also become more effective.

Treatment of Delinquents

Just as we have had only limited success in preventing delinquency, we have largely failed to find a broadly effective therapy for delinquents or pre-delinquents. There have been several studies of a variety of treatment techniques, and almost all of them report little or no success in changing delinquents or pre-delinquents via psychological treatment. Our task here is to document these failures, and to determine why they have failed.

The methods of psychological treatment can be usefully divided into four distinct categories, depending upon the intensity of the patient-therapist relationship and the depth of analysis involved in the treatment.[20] Counseling is the simplest on both counts and involves for the most part the analysis of interpersonal problems and giving advice based upon the adult's greater experience and longer viewpoint. Parents, teachers, probation officers, and others need little training to provide counseling, but effective counseling requires more than simple common sense and experience in life. It requires the ability to see the problem from the child's standpoint and to recognize when one's own experience is *not* relevant to the situation at hand. Many adults mistakenly assume that their own experience twenty or twenty-five years ago as an adolescent provides an infallible guide for young people today. All too often, however, the situation at hand bears little relationship to the counselor's own experience, and to assume uncritically that it is a good basis for resolving present difficulties is foolish if not irresponsible. Effective counseling depends on the individual's ability to see the essence of the problem clearly, to appreciate it from the child's perspective, to explain the problem to him in terms he can grasp, and to propose a solution that is effective and at the same time acceptable. Not every counselor has all these qualities—and not all counseling is useful.

Interpretive therapy requires more extensive training, but it also requires many of the prosaic qualities of effective counseling as well. Interpretive therapy seeks to discover troublesome routines of interaction with siblings, parents, peers, and others so that they can be subjected to conscious control

---

[20] Cf. Harry M. Shulman, *Juvenile Delinquency in American Society,* Harper & Row, Publishers, New York, 1961, pp. 636–640.

and corrected. Social interaction among parents and children, for example, can fall into very destructive ruts which no one actually desires but which all are helpless to control because they consist largely of unconscious, habitual reactions to long-standing irritants. As destructive habits of action and reaction begin to dominate relations between a parent and a child, they can poison the whole relationship. Interpretive therapy is especially useful in resolving these destructive patterns, because it is relatively simple to identify them and focus the patient's attention upon them. Once all parties are aware of their mutually defeating habits of interaction the development of more constructive modes is an easy step.

Relationship therapy, on the other hand, is designed to help the neurotic patient who is so emotionally ambivalent and personally shaken that he has real difficulty in managing his own affairs. Like Hamlet, he is unsure of the proper course to follow, and as a result his life assumes a disorganized, chaotic drift. His ineptness, moreover, stimulates considerable hostility among those around him, and he often has low self-esteem and feels depressed. Relationship therapy is designed to provide such patients with someone who is supportive, who is emotionally warm and appreciative, so that they can relieve their feelings of resentment toward their critics and begin to reknit the frayed strands of their emotions into an effective, organized personality. In relationship therapy the patient is expected to regain control over himself, his career, and his environment, and to become a positive individual again.

Psychoanalysis seeks to uncover repressed urges in the unconscious that are distorting the patient's behavior, and by bringing these urges to awareness rob them of their power and subject them to conscious control. Because it involves an analysis of the unconscious, psychoanalytic therapy requires long training and great care. Patients unconsciously use many artful defenses to avoid dredging up their most painful feelings and images; to interpret these unconscious images, once they have been identified, requires both experience and expertise. Psychoanalytic therapy, designed for those with deep-seated emotional conflicts, often requires lengthy periods of treatment.

EVALUATIONS OF PSYCHOTHERAPY

Although these several types of therapy have been used in treating delinquents, not all of them have been evaluated by means of carefully controlled experiments. Perhaps the most carefully conducted evaluation of psychotherapy as a method of treating pre-delinquents is that carried out by Powers and Witmer of the Cambridge-Somerville Youth Study in Massachusetts.[21] In

21 Edwin Powers and Helen Witmer, *An Experiment in the Prevention of Delinquency*, Columbia University Press, New York, 1950.

1935, 325 eleven-year-old boys were nominated by their teachers, police, welfare agencies, or churches as "difficult" or "average" children, and each was subsequently provided a counselor who acted as academic tutor, social worker, relationship therapist, or counselor, as the situation required. Another group of 325 boys was matched on personality and family situation and given no treatment other than that ordinarily afforded youngsters in need by the community. After five years the project came to an end and the results were analyzed.

There was little evidence that the counseling had had any general, positive effect.[22] The treatment group as a whole had slightly fewer court convictions by the time they had reached adulthood than the control group, but more treatment boys were convicted than their control group counterparts. When the intensity of the relationship between counselor and boy was examined, however, it was found that those who were seen every week by their counselor had fewer convictions than those who were seen less frequently. Moreover, when the sex of the counselor was taken into account, female counselors were found to be more effective with adolescent boys than male counselors. Thus, intensive relationship therapy carried on by female counselors may have some positive effect upon adolescent pre-delinquents, but as a method for treating pre-delinquents generally it has not been found effective.

A similar study was carried out by the New York City Youth Board in 1952–1953. Using the Glueck Prediction Table the researchers examined 223 boys in the New York City school system and concluded that twenty-one were pre-delinquent. They provided a range of psychiatric and social work services to the pre-delinquents but with little positive effect.[23] After ten years the treatment group of pre-delinquents was no less delinquent than the control group.

In the face of these discouraging results, the treatment of delinquents and pre-delinquents since World War II has taken a different tack. Prior to World War II most of the emphasis was upon treating individual adolescents—or at most, their families. Under the impetus of this emphasis upon individual treatment child guidance clinics were established, first in Chicago in 1909 under William I. Healy, and later throughout the nation. By the late 1950's there were about 650 psychiatric clinics in the United States, mostly in the large cities. Initially their aim was to provide therapy for problem children in

[22] Joan and William McCord, "A Follow-up Report on the Cambridge-Somerville Youth Study," *Annals of the American Academy of Political and Social Science*, 322 (March, 1959), 89–96.

[23] Reported in Jackson Toby, "An Evaluation of Early Identification and Intensive Treatment Programs for Predelinquents," *Social Problems*, 13 (Fall, 1965), p. 168.

the community, but gradually they began to serve more as diagnostic centers where problem children could be referred by the courts or the schools.[24]

As it became apparent after World War II that traditional forms of psychotherapy were of little value in treating delinquents or pre-delinquents, a different approach, group therapy, gained many supporters. Group therapy was initially developed by S. R. Slavson during the 1930's, and after World War II it was eagerly seized upon by many therapists and agencies as a useful way of treating delinquents.

FORMATION OF GROUPS

Group therapy is often used as a last resort in treatment of delinquency-prone children, after individual therapy has been carried on for a year or more without beneficial results. Typically, a child-guidance clinic will sort out such children and form them into small groups of eight or ten children each. Except among very young children, boys and girls are separated. Children's case histories are carefully reviewed by a staff committee before the therapy group is formed. Children having different problems are included in one group, but not in hit-or-miss fashion. If a number of the children are shy, for example, a moderately aggressive member may be added to the group. Although many children can enter such groups with relative ease, psychotic children and extremely aggressive children tend to disrupt the groups, and severely neurotic children tend to withdraw and avoid involvement. The groups meet at a regular time and place, usually once or twice a week, with a trained leader.

OBJECTIVE AND METHOD. The objective is not to weld the children into a permanent group nor to encourage them to meet outside the appointed time and place. The leader is fully as concerned with the therapy of each individual boy as was the psychiatrist or social worker whose treatment often precedes the entrance of the child into group therapy. The group situation has advantages over individual casework for certain children. In successful casework, the child must achieve a personal relationship with the caseworker, marked by trust, confidence, and respect. Some children cannot do this because of the nature of their problem; for example, the basic problem may be distrust and fear of an authoritative parent, and the child associates all adults in a position of leadership, such as the teacher or case worker, with that parent. Or the child may be so aggressive that he cannot conform to the expectations of an office interview. In the therapy group, the child may ignore the leader for many meetings. In a group, his reticence is less noticeable and he

---

[24] See James E. Teele and Sol Levine, "The Acceptance of Emotionally Disturbed Children by Psychiatric Agencies," in *Controlling Delinquents*, Stanton Wheeler, ed., John Wiley & Sons, New York, 1968, pp. 103–126.

feels less conspicuous than when confined in an interview with the case worker.

Among children his own age, with problems similar to or different from his own, the child begins to realize that he is not the only child with problems. The atmosphere of the group is permissive since there is no set program to be carried out (as in normal organized groups or clubs). He also can express his feelings freely, short of injury to himself or others. Therapy usually must continue for many months. Gradually, the child loses some of his fear of the leader, his timidity with other children, or conversely, his aggressiveness toward equipment, children, and leader. Often individual therapy is carried on simultaneously with both the child and his mother.

With young children, the room provided for the meeting usually is equipped with sturdy toys, games, and simple tools. With older children and adolescents, therapy goes on primarily through free discussion in which the leader plays a minimum role and offers no reprimand regardless of what is said. The members slowly begin to express verbally their resentments, to compare experiences, and to develop an interactive therapy in criticizing each other and in offering suggestions as to how one individual may handle a specific problem. Gradually, the leader is admitted to the discussion and may judiciously guide or help the youths to round out their discussions of their own problems.

The leader usually has training as a psychiatric social worker. He must be aware of each child's difficulties and note carefully the changes which occur. These are recorded in notes after the meeting. His attitude during the sessions is passive and neutral. He does not permit himself to be used by the children. The child who has found he had to comply explicitly at home in order to get along with his parents soon finds that he is always treated in friendly fashion by the leader, whether or not he is docile and obedient. The child who feels he must do favors for adults is not encouraged along this line, but is told he may do some special thing if he wishes. Thus the leader is warm and friendly but does not cater to the children's needs or to his own through the children.

BENEFITS OF GROUP THERAPY. The benefits of group therapy (not confined to therapy with delinquents) as reported in 300 articles yield the following list of nine most often reported mechanisms that take place:[25]

1. Acceptance by the group: the member acquires a warm comfortable feeling toward other members.
2. Altruism: in time the members wish to do something for others.
3. Universalization: the member realizes that he is not alone in his problems.

[25] Raymond J. Corsini and Bina Rosenberg, "Mechanisms of Group Psychotherapy: Process and Dynamics," *Journal of Abnormal and Social Psychology*, 51 (November, 1955), 406–411.

4. Intellectualization: he gains insight through acquiring knowledge in the group.
5. Reality testing: the group situation is permissive and nonthreatening; the member may try out expression of attitudes or behavior without fear of reprisals.
6. Transference: the member achieves a strong emotional attachment to the leader, to separate members of the group, or to the group as a whole. Eventually, in the course of therapy he will free himself of his dependence.
7. Interaction of whatever type seems to be beneficial.
8. Spectator therapy: each member gains in some way from listening to and observing himself and others.
9. Ventilation: the member releases pent-up feelings or expression of ideas usually not expressed in other situations.

In successful group therapy, the child eventually recognizes that he no longer needs the contact with the group. A typical pattern seems to be an initial distrust of the group with irregular attendance, then dependence on the group and regular attendance, followed by ability to adjust in his family and in the normal community and gradual withdrawal from the group.

There have been several attempts to evaluate the impact of group therapy upon pre-delinquents and delinquents, but the only carefully controlled study found little evidence of its effectiveness.[26] Girls with severe personal or emotional problems were nominated by the teachers at Girls Vocational High School in New York City for participation in a program of group therapy and social casework run by a social agency. Altogether 189 girls were selected randomly from the nominated population and assigned to the treatment program. When it was concluded, the girls who had participated were compared with those who had received no special help, and on a variety of measures little if any differences were found between the two groups. There were some weak trends that were encouraging, e.g., treatment girls were less truant, but for the most part these were not sufficiently strong to say definitely that the treatment program as a whole or group therapy in particular was responsible.

In addition there have been several attempts to establish the value of group therapy as a treatment technique, but for several reasons they have not succeeded. Perhaps the best publicized of these is the experiment at Highfields, New Jersey, a state correctional facility. In a mansion that was originally a private estate, a small group of adolescents was provided a short but intensive regimen of work in the day and group meetings at night. After release the Highfields boys showed a distinctly better adjustment than boys sent to the state training school, but the two populations were not perfectly comparable.

[26] Henry J. Meyer, Edgar F. Borgatta, and Wyatt C. Jones, *Girls at Vocational High: An Experiment in Social Work Intervention*, Russell Sage Foundation, New York, 1965.

The Highfields boys were not selected randomly and the two groups no doubt differed on several important dimensions quite apart from their different treatment settings. It is impossible to conclude that the better post-parole adjustment shown by the Highfields boys was due to their group treatment at Highfields.

Why Has Treatment Failed?

We have evaluated a wide range of therapeutic methods and we have been unable to find convincing evidence that psychotherapy in any of its several forms is effective in diverting adolescents from delinquency. But we cannot simply leave the matter at that. We must ask, Why has psychotherapy failed? There are a number of reasons.

PREDICTING DELINQUENCY. In any treatment program it is essential that youngsters who are ultimately going to become delinquent be identified as early as possible. The more advanced the child is toward delinquency, the more firmly embedded the motives and perspectives of delinquency are in his personality, and the more difficult it is to change him. Thus, early identification of pre-delinquents is an important step in using psychotherapy to prevent delinquency.

But predicting delinquency among six- or seven-year-old children is far from an exact science. It faces many difficulties that make a high degree of accuracy almost impossible, and inaccuracy in predicting delinquency, of course, inevitably undermines any therapeutic program. It dilutes the pre-delinquents for whom the therapy is intended with nondelinquents who essentially do not need the treatment with the result that the number of successes is diminished. This problem was probably a factor in the poor results found in the Cambridge-Somerville Youth Study. Average boys were included in the treatment population along with difficult boys. Presumably the average boys had less need of counseling and showed less change than the difficult boys. But insofar as average boys appeared in both the treatment and the control groups, the differential effects of any therapy on the treatment group would thereby be diminished. Clearly, inaccuracy in predicting delinquency jeopardizes any therapeutic program designed to prevent delinquency among pre-delinquents.

How accurate are the most highly developed instruments for predicting delinquency? The Glueck Social Prediction Table has been the focus of a concerted research effort to fashion a reliable, accurate prediction instrument, and is undoubtedly the best instrument currently available. On the basis of their research reported in *Unraveling Juvenile Delinquency* the Gluecks developed three scales to predict future delinquency among currently nondelinquent children. Only one of the scales has been subjected to continued research.

The Glueck Social Prediction Table is composed of five family relationships, each of which was found to differentiate markedly between the correctional school and the nondelinquent control group of boys whom the Gluecks studied. The accumulation of several or of all five unfavorable relationships in the experience of some boys was very highly associated with delinquency, while the accumulation of favorable aspects was very highly associated with nondelinquency. Each item was assigned scores in proportion to the frequency with which it was found in the delinquent group. Table 18 gives the five relationships, the types, and the weights. Theoretically the scores could run from a low (nondelinquent) score of 116.7 to a high (delinquent) score of 414.7. Both

TABLE 18

Glueck Social Prediction Table

SOCIAL FACTORS	WEIGHTED SCORE
1. Discipline of boy by father	
Overstrict or erratic	72.5
Lax	59.8
Firm but kindly	9.3
2. Supervision of boy by mother	
Unsuitable	83.2
Fair	57.5
Suitable	9.9
3. Affection of father for son	
Indifferent or hostile	75.9
Warm (including over-protective)	33.8
4. Affection of mother for boy	
Indifferent or hostile	86.2
Warm (including over-protective)	43.1
5. Cohesiveness of family	
Unintegrated	96.9
Some elements of cohesion	61.3
Cohesive	20.6

Sheldon and Eleanor T. Glueck, "Early Detection of Future Delinquents," *Journal of Criminal Law, Criminology and Police Science*, Northwestern University School of Law, 47 (1956), 175. The weighted score is the percentage of the total of delinquent and nondelinquent boys in each subcategory who were delinquent.

delinquents and nondelinquents run the limit from high to low, but with decided bulking of the two groups at opposite ends of the range of scores. The middle scores (200 to 299) are the least predictive, but include approximately a third of each group. If the scale were given to young children, with the idea of selecting potential delinquents for special preventive treatment, children with scores in this middle range could not be placed with any confidence in either the potentially delinquent or the potentially nondelinquent classification.

In 1952–1953, the Glueck Prediction Table was given to boys in the first grade of two New York public schools as the first step in testing the predictive value of the table.[27] There has been a continuous analysis of the results of this experiment, with the New York City Youth Board and the Gluecks consistently claiming a high degree of accuracy for the Glueck Prediction Table.[28]

Nevertheless, there have been several criticisms of their claims. Jackson Toby has pointed out that any prediction instrument which depends so heavily on the dimensions of family interaction cannot fail to misclassify children whose family relationships may be in the normal range but whose peer associations in adolescence are found mainly among delinquents.[29] Nor can any prediction instrument including the Gluecks' anticipate essentially fortuitous events that basically alter the child's socio-cultural environment. For example, a move by the family into a different neighborhood can fundamentally change a child's chances of becoming delinquent. Some of these unpredictable events may be associated with the quality of parent-child relationships but not to the extent that they can be safely ignored in predicting delinquency in adolescence for six- or seven-year-olds.

What does research reveal about the accuracy of the Glueck Prediction Table? The best results have been obtained using a revision of the five factor table originally proposed.[30] Since many pre-delinquents come from homes in which there is no father, it was decided to drop all questions regarding the father and to use instead three factors assessing the boy's supervision by the mother, the boy's discipline by the mother, and the cohesiveness of the family. The results of predictions based upon the revised three factor table are presented in Table

[27] *Delinquency Prediction, A Progress Report, 1952–1956: An Experiment in Validation of the Gluecks' Prediction Scale*, New York City, 1957.

[28] Maude M. Craig, "Application of the Glueck Social Prediction Table on an Ethnic Basis," *Crime and Delinquency*, 11 (1965), 175–185; and Eleanor T. Glueck, "Efforts to Identify Delinquents," *Federal Probation*, 24 (June, 1960), 49–56.

[29] Jackson Toby, "An Evaluation of Early Identification and Intensive Treatment Program for Predelinquents," *Social Problems*, 13 (Fall, 1965), 160–175.

[30] See Maude M. Craig and Selma J. Glick, "Ten Years' Experience with the Glueck Social Prediction Table," *Crime and Delinquency*, 9 (July, 1963), 249–261.

19. Altogether there were seven false negatives, i.e., seven boys were predicted for nondelinquency but in fact became delinquent, and four false positives, i.e., four children who were predicted as delinquent failed to become delinquent, out of 220 predictions. In other words the success rate was 209 out of 220, or 95 per cent. There was also a substantial number of children whose scores fell in the middle range for whom predictions were not possible, but disregarding them, let us examine the consequences of the errors that were made in 5 per cent of the cases.

Every error tends to reduce the effectiveness of any remedial program, but the effect of false positives is quite different from that of false negatives. False positives include those children for whom delinquency was predicted but who remained nondelinquent. Such children would necessarily be subjected to remedial programs along with the rest, but to the extent that they were in the program, it would be a waste of their time and the program's resources. Table 19 reveals that false positives constituted four out of twenty-seven delinquency predictions, or 15 per cent. Thus, their presence in the treatment group would result in a waste of 15 per cent of the resources of the remedial program.

The most difficult problem with remedial programs, however, is persuading skeptical parents of the need for their children to participate in treatment programs for pre-delinquents. Parents are often unwilling to accept such predictions about their children for obvious reasons, and if they are wrong three times in twenty, many parents may reason that the program unnecessarily stigmatizes their child as pre-delinquent. Thus, a moderately large percentage of false positives undermines the credibility of any remedial program and wastes its resources by spreading them over an unnecessarily large population.

It is possible to reduce the number of false positives by increasing the

TABLE 19

The Outcome of Delinquency Predictions Based Upon the Glueck
Revised Three Factor Table*

PREDICTION	OUTCOME		
	DELINQUENT	NONDELINQUENT	TOTAL
Delinquency	23	4	27
Even chance (no prediction)	9	10	19
Nondelinquency	7	186	193
Total	39	200	239

* Adapted from Maude M. Craig and Selma J. Glick, "Ten Years' Experience with the Glueck Social Prediction Table," *Crime and Delinquency*, 9 (July, 1963), Table 7.

cutoff point and predicting delinquency only for those whose scores are extremely high. In so doing, however, false negatives, i.e., those children who are predicted incorrectly as nondelinquent, are inevitably increased.

Increasing the number of false negatives in this fashion, however, contains its own disadvantages. As Stanfield and Maher point out, false negatives are exceedingly costly in that they include adolescents who are allowed to become delinquent and all that that implies in personal anguish and material loss with little or nothing done to prevent it.[31] In Table 19, the number of false negatives was 44 per cent of all those youngsters who ultimately became delinquent. Thus, if the Glueck Social Prediction Table were used in conjunction with a treatment program, fully 15 per cent of those in the program would not need it, and 44 per cent of those who did need it, would not receive it.[32]

OTHER PROBLEMS. Another reason that treatment programs thus far have not been successful derives from the fact that a substantial number of delinquents and pre-delinquents who appear ripe candidates for psychotherapy in reality need some other type of attention. Many adolescents become delinquent not because of psychologically based urges but because of other, often socially derived, pressures. Obviously, a gang member cannot be diverted from delinquency by psychotherapy as long as his membership in the gang remains intact, particularly if his membership is not closely related to psychological needs. Thus, the lack of results in applying psychotherapy to pre-delinquents probably derives to some extent from the fact that it has often been applied inappropriately to those who are headed toward delinquency for other than psychological reasons.

But even if a child's delinquency does reflect psychologically based urges, psychotherapy is often difficult for the child to accept because it casts him in a role that is intensely uncomfortable. As a patient receiving treatment, he expects the therapist to analyze his personality, identify the roots of his pathology, and remove it much as a surgeon removes a malignant tumor. But many delinquents and pre-delinquents cannot spontaneously adopt an attitude of passive acceptance toward adults who they believe want to change them

[31] Robert E. Stanfield and Brendan Maher, "Clinical and Actuarial Predictions of Juvenile Delinquency," in *Controlling Delinquents*, Stanton Wheeler, ed., John Wiley & Sons, New York, 1968, pp. 245–270.

[32] According to Wolfgang, Figlio, and Sellin, however, it might make sense to offer treatment programs specifically for those few boys (18 per cent of all delinquents) who repeatedly violate the law, because they account for fully 52 per cent of all delinquencies. In their case the Glueck Three Factor Prediction Table could be very useful, because it is highly likely that children who were later to become chronic delinquents would score at the top of the range where few errors in prediction are made. See Marvin E. Wolfgang, Robert Figlio, and Thorsten Sellin, *Delinquency in a Birth Cohort*, University of Chicago Press, Chicago, 1972, Chapter 6.

beyond recognition with techniques that are subtle and mysterious. The epithet *head shrinker* reflects the fears that many feel when confronted with a psychotherapist. Many adolescents including a great many pre-delinquents find it difficult to cooperate with any type of individual therapy, and the therapist's task as a result is rendered that much more difficult.[33] Group therapy, of course, avoids this difficulty, because the bulk of therapeutic interaction is carried on in the group with peers, but individual therapy is exceedingly difficult to initiate because it forces the child into an awkward position vis-à-vis the therapist.

CONCLUSION

We have surveyed attempts to prevent delinquency via community restructuring and via several types of psychotherapy, and the best that can be said at this point is that only a few preventive efforts have been shown to be effective. There is some evidence that Area Projects reduce delinquency (although delinquency remains a serious problem in at least one community that has had an Area Project for nearly forty years); detached worker programs may be useful in curbing delinquent gangs if they focus on undermining gang cohesiveness; and relationship therapy may have some value when practiced intensively by a female therapist with an adolescent clientele. On the whole, however, the results of this survey are discouraging. Most programs for preventing delinquency were outright failures, and the rest were only partially successful.

But all is not lost. Much of our inability to prevent delinquency undoubtedly stems from the fact that we naively attempted to apply our remedies before we knew precisely what kind of delinquency we were trying to prevent. Social scientists can no more dispense with a careful diagnosis in attempting to cope with delinquency than physicians can in curing disease. In the absence of careful diagnoses, however, remedies have been applied in mass fashion. The Cambridge-Somerville Youth Study is a good example. The boys who were given counseling and relationship therapy included many average (i.e., not difficult) children and also, no doubt, many boys whose "difficulty" was not based upon any type of psychological disorder. Inevitably, therefore, a careful assessment of the treatment program that was given these boys found little overall impact on the experimental group. Knowing what we know now, it would have been amazing had Witmer and Powers found anything else.

---

[33] See Hyman S. Lippman, "Difficulties Encountered in the Psychiatric Treatment of Chronic Juvenile Delinquents," in *Searchlights in Delinquency*, K. R. Eissler, ed., International Universities Press, New York, 1949, pp. 156–164.

When we begin matching our treatment techniques more artfully with the needs of the adolescents we are treating, we may find more encouraging results.

We have also pointed out that carrying out a careful evaluation of treatment programs depends upon our finding more effective methods of predicting delinquency. As things stand now a large portion of those who should receive some kind of treatment are not identified as pre-delinquent; and a significant number of those who are identified as such are not in fact pre-delinquents. With such inaccurate predictions it would be difficult to justify any treatment program, no matter how effective it was when applied to the *appropriate* populations.

All in all, then, the negative results described in this chapter may not be as discouraging as at first glance they seem. The only reasonable conclusion regarding treatment programs for pre-delinquents at this point is that they have not been adequately tested. The negative results indicate not ineffective treatment methods but rather ineffective application of these methods and faulty evaluations. The issue, in other words, is still in doubt.

BIBLIOGRAPHY

CRAIG, MAUDE M., "Application of the Glueck Social Prediction Table on an Ethnic Basis," *Crime and Delinquency*, 11 (1965), 175–185.

————, AND SELMA J. GLICK, "Ten Years' Experience with the Glueck Social Prediction Table," *Crime and Delinquency*, 9 (July, 1963), 249–261.

GLUECK, ELEANOR T., "Efforts to Identify Delinquents," *Federal Probation*, 24 (June, 1960), 49–56.

HACKLER, JAMES C., "Boys, Blisters, and Behavior—The Impact of a Work Program in an Urban Central Area," *Journal of Research in Crime and Delinquency*, 3 (July, 1966), 155–164.

JEFFERY, C. R., AND I. A. JEFFERY, "Dropouts and Delinquency: An Experimental Program in Behavior Change," *Education and Urban Society*, 1 (1969), 325–336.

KLEIN, MALCOLM, "Gang Cohesiveness, Delinquency, and a Street Work Program," *Journal of Research in Crime and Delinquency*, 6 (July, 1969), 135–166.

————, *Street Gangs and Street Workers*, Prentice-Hall, Inc., Englewood Cliffs, N. J., 1971.

KOBRIN, SOLOMON, "The Chicago Area Project—A 25-Year Assessment," *Annals of the American Academy of Political and Social Science*, 322 (March, 1959), 19–29.

MARTIN, JOHN, "Three Approaches of Delinquency Prevention: A Critique," *Crime and Delinquency*, 7 (January, 1961), 16–24.

McCORD, JOAN, AND WILLIAM McCORD, "A Follow-up Report on the Cambridge-Somerville Youth Study," *Annals of the American Academy of Political and Social Science*, 322 (March, 1959), 89–96.

MEYER, HENRY J., EDGAR F. BORGATTA, AND WYATT C. JONES, *Girls at Vocational High: An Experiment in Social Work Intervention*, Russell Sage Foundation, New York, 1965.

MILLER, WALTER B., "The Impact of a 'Total-Community' Delinquency Control Project," *Social Problems*, 10 (Fall, 1962), 168–191.

POSTON, RICHARD W., *The Gang and the Establishment*, Harper & Row, Publishers, New York, 1971.

POWERS, EDWIN, AND HELEN WITMER, *An Experiment in the Prevention of Delinquency*, Columbia University Press, New York, 1950.

President's Commission on Law Enforcement and Administration of Justice, *Task Force Report: Juvenile Delinquency and Youth Crime*, U.S. Government Printing Office, Washington, D. C., 1967.

ROBIN, GERALD R., "Anti-Poverty Programs and Delinquency," *Journal of Criminal Law, Criminology, and Police Science*, 60 (1969), 323–331.

SPERGEL, IRVING, *Street Gang Work: Theory and Practice*, Addison-Wesley Publishing Co., Reading, Mass., 1966.

STANFIELD, ROBERT E., AND BRENDAN MAHER, "Clinical and Actuarial Predictions of Juvenile Delinquency," in *Controlling Delinquents*, Stanton Wheeler, ed., John Wiley & Sons, New York, 1968.

TAIT, C. DOWNING, JR., AND EMORY F. HODGES, JR., *Delinquents, Their Families and the Community*, Charles C Thomas, Springfield, Ill., 1962.

TEELE, JAMES E., AND SOL LEVINE, "The Acceptance of Emotionally Disturbed Children by Psychiatric Agencies," in *Controlling Delinquents*, Stanton Wheeler, ed., John Wiley & Sons, New York, 1968.

TOBY, JACKSON, "An Evaluation of Early Identification and Intensive Treatment Programs for Predelinquents," *Social Problems*, 13 (Fall, 1965), 160–175.

WITMER, H. L., AND E. TUFTS, *The Effectiveness of Delinquency Prevention Programs*, Children's Bureau, U. S. Department of Health, Education, and Welfare, Publication 350, U. S. Government Printing Office, Washington, D. C., 1954.

background of present legal handling of juvenile delinquents

chapter 15

A misbehaving child may be neglected or handled informally by police and various institutions such as the school without being designated as a juvenile delinquent. If his behavior passes the toleration point of the community or he commits a serious offense and the police take him into custody, his misconduct becomes a matter of record. At this point he officially acquires a record as a juvenile delinquent (although it may be confidential) and enters upon a sequence of events prescribed by law or developed by practice. Not all children follow through the entire sequence. Depending upon the seriousness of the misconduct, the provisions for supervision, and the childs' own response, the child may be permitted to leave the sequence at various points.

Sequence of Practices

The complete sequence or process, if followed through from beginning to end, begins when the police arrest a child and ends with his discharge from parole after he has been confined in a correctional school. The steps are given below in outline form.

1. Police intercept a child in misconduct, respond to a complaint about a child, or on investigation find evidence that a child has been involved in certain misconduct. The child is taken to the police station. Depending upon the organization of police services and the policy of the police and of the juvenile court, the child is reprimanded and released, or turned over

to the police juvenile bureau (if there is one), or referred to a social agency or to the juvenile court.

2. If the child is referred to a fully developed juvenile court, his case is reviewed by an intake department. Certain children are released; others are referred to social agencies for treatment, and some are held for a hearing before the juvenile court judge. A minority of children reach court attention through direct referral by parents, school officials, or others without reference to the police. The court hearing and subsequent procedures are the same as when the police refer a child.

3. If an interval of time must elapse before the hearing, the child may be released to his parents or held in detention in jail or a special juvenile detention center.

4. When the judge hears the case, he has information available not only on the offense but also on the child and his family, assembled by social workers or probation officers attached to the court. If the hearing stretches out over several days, the child may continue to live at home or be held in the detention center.

5. The child may be dismissed with a warning to him and his parents.

6. The child may be placed on probation, under supervision of the probation officer or of some agency in the community. He usually continues to live at home, attend school, and follow a normal round of activities.

7. If his home is unsuitable for him, he may be placed in a foster home (if a younger child) or in an institution for dependent children (if he is an older child and his offense is minor).

8. If he has committed a serious offense or is a frequent recidivist, he may be committed to a state correctional school for a period of time.

9. When he is released from the school, he is usually placed under the supervision of a parole officer.

10. Eventually he is discharged from probation or parole.

11. In some states, if his offense is a serious adult-type crime, he may be tried in the adult criminal court. Somewhat the same procedure is followed but in a more formal manner; if he is found guilty he may be imprisoned for many years. In extreme cases, an older adolescent may be given a death sentence, although this rarely happens.

Ideally, except in the case of criminal court procedures, the child is shielded from exposure to adult criminals and is spared a formal criminal trial. Emphasis is placed on discovering why the child has become delinquent and on mapping a plan of action that will prevent future delinquencies. In practice, of course, the ideal is not always reached.

Development of the Juvenile Court

THE JUVENILE DELINQUENCY CONCEPT
Until 1899, except in a minor way, all children except the very young

were subject to the same laws and procedures as adults. In general, the United States followed the English tradition in legal matters. In English common law, children under age seven were not held accountable for criminal acts. From age eight to fourteen, children could be held responsible if it could be shown that they were sufficiently intelligent to understand the nature and consequences of their misdeeds and if they could distinguish between right and wrong. Such children could be subjected to the same type of trial and punishment as adult criminals, even to infliction of the death penalty in extreme cases. Blackstone, writing in 1795, refers to several earlier cases in which children of ten to thirteen years of age were subjected to execution for murder or other wanton crimes. Occasional similar cases of capital punishment are found in the history of the United States; for example, in New Jersey in 1828 a thirteen-year-old boy was hanged for an offense committed when he was twelve.[1]

The English common law dealt in a protective manner with other classes of children, in contrast to its treatment of delinquent children. As *parens patriae* (father of his country), the King was responsible for the care of children; this care he delegated to the Court of Chancery, whose objective was the common welfare. This court was founded on the idea of equity; it was able to act in a more flexible manner than was possible under the rigid legal rules of the common law. The original purpose of chancery wardship of children was directed primarily toward protection of the property interest of wealthy children.

Two precedents then existed for the modern concept of juvenile delinquency: first, that children under a certain age were not responsible for criminal acts; second, that some children were in need of protection by the courts. The concept of juvenile delinquency merged these two approaches. The age of non- or limited responsibility was raised from seven to sixteen or eighteen; and the delinquent was placed in the same position of care by a court of chancery as were dependent and neglected children. This move eliminated most criminal trials for children and led to the development of the juvenile court and a series of auxiliary institutions and practices to implement the purpose of protection and care, chief among them being detention centers, children's clinics, probation and parole services, and special correctional or training schools.

JUVENILE COURTS IN THE UNITED STATES

The first juvenile court in the world was established in 1899 in Cook County (Chicago), Illinois. The court had control over three categories of children—dependent, neglected, and delinquent. The delinquent child had

[1] Cited by Frederick B. Sussman, *Juvenile Delinquency*, Oceana Publications, New York, revised, 1959, p. 12.

ceased to be a criminal and had the status of a child in need of care, protection, and discipline directed toward rehabilitation. As with the other two categories of children, he became a ward of the state.

Although the juvenile court as a formal institution did not appear until 1899, various steps had been taken to soften the harshness of the laws as applied to juveniles, or to remove them entirely from the criminal courts. For example, Massachusetts enacted a statute in 1869 providing that an agent of the state board of charity should attend trials of juveniles, investigate their cases, protect their interests, and make suitable recommendations to the judge. Special trials for children's cases were provided in laws of 1870, 1872, and 1877. New York, Indiana, and Rhode Island followed the lead of Massachusetts. The juvenile court is the culmination of a long-term trend.

Laws providing for juvenile courts were not immediately enacted in all states. The last state to enact the necessary legislation was Wyoming in 1945. Juvenile courts are of various types in the different states and, within a given state, range from the simple situation in a rural county where the judge of some adult court sits as juvenile court judge as needed, to the highly complex system of related institutions constituting the juvenile court and its allied services in a populous urban county.

Juvenile Courts in Other Countries

Other countries, especially England and European countries, have also shown marked concern about the treatment of juvenile delinquents. England established juvenile courts through the Children Act of 1908, and Belgium and France through legislation of 1912. The Scandinavian countries have developed child welfare boards to handle delinquent as well as neglected and dependent children. Norway established such boards by the Child Welfare Act of 1896; Sweden and Denmark shortly thereafter provided for similar boards. These countries continue the use of child welfare boards and feel no need for special juvenile courts. The Middle Eastern countries have moved more slowly into the juvenile court movement, with the exception of Egypt, which set up its first juvenile court in 1905 and today has courts in both Cairo and Alexandria. In the Far East, countries formerly under the influence of, or attached to, Great Britain or the United States tend to have juvenile courts following the pattern of the dominant country. Pakistan has one juvenile court, which has functioned in Karachi since 1938. In India, various Children Acts were passed in different areas during the 1920's, giving rise to a limited number of juvenile courts. Japan's family courts, which handle all juvenile cases, date from the post-World War II period and are modeled after those of the United States.

Juvenile courts are gaining acceptance throughout the world. Except in some cases of very serious crimes, they protect children from a criminal court trial and relieve them of full responsibility for minor and some serious offenses. As will appear later, however, many court problems remain to be solved.

Development of Probation

Probation, now widely used, had its origin before the establishment of juvenile courts. Massachusetts established the first probation system without age restrictions in 1880, soon to be followed by Illinois, New York, and Indiana.[2]

Development of Juvenile Training Schools

The development of special correctional or training schools for juveniles long preceded the coming of the juvenile court. This movement was part of the general trend that eventually brought the juvenile court into existence— a trend recognizing the immaturity of children and youth, and the right of delinquents to special training. In both England and the United States, training schools were a development of the nineteenth century.

EARLY INSTITUTIONS

In Europe, a few now famous schools were established much earlier. An early school was the Hospital (home) of Saint Michael in Rome, founded in 1704 by Pope Clement XI. Here orphan as well as delinquent boys and infirm old people were housed. Hard work, silence, and solitude were the methods of corrective discipline by which delinquents were to be converted into upright youth.

Another development in England and Europe was the house of correction or workhouse beginning as early as the latter part of the sixteenth century. These institutions received a motley lot of unfortunates, vagrants, beggars, vendors unable to secure licenses, and petty criminals of all ages. Although the first ones were established in England and Amsterdam, the most famous was in Ghent, Belgium. In 1773 Hippolyte Vilain, burgomaster of Ghent, founded the workhouse as a response to the hordes of vagrants who wandered over Europe. Unlike most institutions of its day, the Ghent workhouse segregated prisoners according to seriousness of their misbehavior, sex, and age. One part of the institution was reserved for children. Hard work, complete obedience, and the learning of a trade were emphasized.

2 *Ibid.*, p. 13.

Schools of the Nineteenth Century

In the early nineteenth century, institutions specifically for delinquent children, separate from those for adults, were developed in England, Europe, and the United States. The first concern was for the homeless, uncared-for children wandering the city streets, sleeping in gutters and alleys, and living by their wits. Some were orphans, some deserted by their parents, some runaways from other cities. By our present classification they were neglected, dependent, and delinquent. The first institutions for their care were founded by wealthy philanthropic individuals or organizations dedicated to the care of children. In England, voluntary groups established correctional schools to which courts could send young criminals. They would be granted a pardon upon condition of placing themselves under the care of a charitable institution until they were "reformed." Following this step, they would be sent to the Colonies. The Reformatory Schools Act of 1854 enabled courts to commit offenders under sixteen to a reformatory, after serving a period of not less than fourteen days in prison. Gradually the government assumed more and more responsibility for support and management of correctional institutions. In Acts of 1857 and 1866, industrial schools were established for children under fourteen needing care and protection, and for legal offenders under twelve.[3] Nevertheless, many children under sixteen and some as young as ten were in prison. European countries were also beginning to separate children from adults.

In the United States the first break with the older policy of imprisoning children and youths with adult offenders came in 1825 when the Society for the Reformation of Juvenile Delinquents succeeded with state assistance in opening the New York City House of Refuge. A vacated barracks for soldiers was first used. The purpose of this institution was to care for and educate children apprehended by the police as minor offenders or vagrants, children often picked up on the streets and typically sentenced to six months in the penitentiary.

The House of Refuge received much the same public acclaim that the juvenile court received seventy-five years later. Clearly it marked a forward step in that children were segregated from adult offenders and provided with a special program of training. The state gave some support and later assumed entire responsibility for the House. Its location was moved several times and, more than a hundred years after its founding, it ceased to exist as a separate entity and was merged with the New York State Vocational Institution at West Coxsackie, a state training school for boys.

[3] Lionel W. Fox, *The English Prison and Borstal Systems*, Routledge and Kegan Paul, Ltd., London, England, 1952, pp. 327–328.

In 1826 a similar institution was founded in Boston, and in 1828 another in Philadelphia, both as the result of efforts by private organizations. By 1850 the trend for state-supported training schools was well established, and state after state established such schools. State-supported schools now far outnumber private schools.

These schools, which preceded the creation of the juvenile court, represented a growing concern that delinquent (often also destitute) children should not mingle with adult criminals in prisons and that some effort should be made to train them.[4] Children were still tried in adult courts and were subject to the same kind of sentences given to adults. Many, especially serious offenders, were still confined in prison.

The early institutions were prison-like in structure. However, in England and Europe experiments were being carried out with separation of delinquent children into small units within the institution, to create groups somewhat modeled after families. The first cottage type training schools in the United States were the girls' institution at Lancaster, Massachusetts, opened in 1854, and the boys' institution at Lancaster, Ohio, in 1858. The cottage system is now the customary type of training school.

Lack of Central Administration

In the United States the various legal agencies dealing with a delinquent suffer from a high degree of decentralization and lack of coordination. Each stage of the process from arrest to eventual freedom is under the control of a different administrative set-up. Consensus of policy may not exist at all; coordination of activities usually comes about only on a voluntary basis and may degenerate into conflict.

The city child is dealt with by municipal police operating under a municipal officer or body. Outside the city, the county sheriff has charge of law enforcement and is accountable to the county government. At times the state police arrest a delinquent. Lines between the jurisdiction of these police bodies are not always clear; moreover, the delinquent may have passed from one jurisdiction to another. If a serious crime has been committed by a juvenile, the city, county, and state police may each have some connection with the case and compete for the "honor" of handling it.

The juvenile court is usually operated on a city or county basis, but is not related administratively to the city or county police. The judge is usually

---

[4] For a critical analysis of the dominant motives behind the attempt to isolate juvenile delinquents from adult institutions and courts, see Anthony M. Platt, *The Child Savers*, University of Chicago Press, Chicago, 1969.

elected and operates more or less independently under the state law, or he may be part of a federation or council of judges. The probation officer is usually a subordinate of the judge.

The correctional school to which the judge commits a delinquent may be administered by a private board of directors or by a state group, such as a welfare or correctional department. When the child is released and placed on parole, the parole officer usually is attached to a state department.

All these agencies and institutions operate under state laws, which have been enacted individually for each agency or institution at different times. Moreover, each level of government lower than the state—county and munici-pal—makes its own regulations which are legal so long as they do not contra-dict general state laws. County and city need not coordinate their regulations, and in fact within either county or city, confusion may reign between different agencies.

Whoever is in charge of each correctional agency supervising the child— the police chief, the judge, the chief probation or parole officer, the director of a correctional school—makes policies and sets practices for the operation of his specific agency. Coordination may be worked out on this level for smooth operation of the cumbersome, disjointed machinery. Agreements may be made between police and juvenile court judge as to which types of cases police will handle independently and those to be referred to the juvenile court. The judge may have understandings with the various agencies to which he may commit the care of delinquents as to the kind of delinquent each agency can best handle. Nevertheless there are many misunderstandings and actual conflicts. The individual child may be passed smoothly and with a minimum of delay from one agency to another, or he may be shuttled back and forth between agencies which seem less concerned with the child than with their own autonomy.

Lack of a Standard Pattern

When municipal, county, and state agencies dealing with delinquency are considered in toto, literally thousands of different laws, policies, and prac-tices are revealed. Some are very good; some are deplorable. Not only are there fifty states (and Puerto Rico, the Virgin Islands, the District of Columbia, and the federal government), each with individual sets of laws and systems of agencies, but in addition, there are the regulations and ordinances of more than 3,000 counties, and 16,000 municipalities. Even within one state there is no uniformity of excellence among counties or cities. Moreover, it is vir-tually impossible to achieve uniformity of laws, regulations, ordinances, and agency systems by legal means.

For a number of years attempts have been made, with constant pressure and a measure of success, to induce cities, counties, and states individually to accept and enact into law or put into practice standard laws or practices devised by national or federal bodies. Significantly active have been the Children's Bureau of the federal government and the National Council on Crime and Delinquency (formerly the National Probation and Parole Association) which, independently or in cooperation, have published many reports and standard practices. The United Nations is taking world leadership in establishing standard policies and practices through a World Congress for Prevention of Crime and Treatment of Offenders held once every five years and attendant conferences and publications. These standards set goals toward which individual nations may work.

Special Terminology

In the effort to differentiate legal procedures for juveniles from those for adults, a special terminology has developed. The intent was to remove from the child the stigma attached to criminal terminology; unfortunately, the new terms now have become stigmatized. Since this terminology will be used in the chapters to follow, the words and phrases are given for future reference in the list that follows, including full definitions and their equivalence in terms used in adult legal procedures:

JUVENILE TERM	ADULT TERM
Adjudication: decision by the judge that the child has committed delinquent acts.	*Conviction of guilt*
Aftercare: supervision given to a child for a limited period of time after he is released from the training school but still under the control of the school or of the juvenile court.	*Parole*
Commitment: decision by the judge that the child should be sent to a training school.	*Sentence to imprisonment*
Detention: holding a child, usually prior to trial, in close physical custody in jail or whenever possible in a special juvenile detention center.	*Holding in jail*
Hearing: the presentation of evidence to the juvenile court judge, his consideration of it, and his decision on disposition of the case.	*Trial*

JUVENILE TERM	ADULT TERM
Petition: document stating the alleged delinquent acts of the child, filed with the juvenile court.	*Accusation or indictment*
Probation: supervision of a delinquent child after the court hearing but without commitment to a training school.	*Probation, with the same meaning*
Take into custody: act of the police in securing the physical custody of a child engaged in delinquency; avoids the stigma of the word arrest.	*Arrest*

BIBLIOGRAPHY

ABBOTT, GRACE, *The Child and the State,* University of Chicago Press, Chicago, 1938.

FOX, LIONEL W., *The English Prison and Borstal Systems,* Routledge and Kegan Paul, Limited, London, England, 1952, Chapter 9 and Appendix B.

NYQUIST, OLA, "How Sweden Handles Its Juvenile and Youth Offenders," *Federal Probation,* 20 (March, 1956), 36–42.

PLATT, ANTHONY M., *The Child Savers,* University of Chicago Press, Chicago, 1969.

SELLIN, THORSTEN, "Sweden's Substitute for the Juvenile Court," *Annals of the American Academy of Political and Social Science,* 261 (1949), 137–149.

WINES, ENOCH C., *State of Prisons,* Cambridge University Press, Cambridge, England, 1880.

police contacts chapter **16**

The juvenile court is always hailed as the most significant of the agencies that deal with delinquents, and it undoubtedly is in setting policies and making decisions on the disposition of children responsible for serious delinquencies. The police, however, have contacts with many more misbehaving and delinquent children than does the juvenile court. Of all children picked up or arrested by the police, only one-half are referred to the juvenile court. The other half are handled independently by the police; moreover, the police decide which children they will handle and how. In addition to dealing with delinquents, police have many informal encounters with children on the streets and in places where children loiter. Here they exercise general supervision as part of their function of maintaining order and protecting younger children from harm. The police exercise an extraordinary degree of authority quite independently of the juvenile court. Especially among young and minor delinquents, the police department is the one official agency that the child sees. It is extremely important, therefore, that police understand and exercise well this vast power that they have.

As long as misbehaving children were regarded simply as small-sized criminals, the police function toward them was very much the same as toward adult criminals, to repress misbehavior and crime when they saw it occurring and to bring offending children and adults alike to the police station with whatever force was necessary. The conception of children as immature and still developing personalities and of juvenile delinquents as not fully responsible for their acts has gradually led to new conceptions of police functions where children and youth of juvenile delinquency age are concerned.[1]

Law Enforcement

A basic function of all police is to enforce laws. This function may involve interfering with a crime that is in process, stepping in to prevent a crime that seems to be brewing, or making routine inspections of places, such as taverns or dance halls, operating under special regulations. Foot patrolmen, motorcycle police, and squad car units carry on these activities day and night without regard to the age of persons who may be involved. The constant surveillance is one of the chief ways in which order is maintained and delinquency and crime reduced in amount and seriousness.

Regulatory activities are protective as well as preventive. Many cases heard in court are for offenses of adults against children. Police action to prevent sale of liquor to minors, sale of narcotics to children, loitering of girls in questionable restaurants or taverns, or sexual approaches of men to young girls or boys is protective in that it reduces the dangers to children. It is preventive also inasmuch as children who participate often are violating juvenile delinquency laws. If police supervision reduces or eliminates the illegal acts of adults, delinquency in these areas of behavior is also reduced or eliminated.

When juveniles are involved in delinquent or criminal acts, the police are empowered to interfere. The drunken youth, the girl loitering on the streets late at night, boys found trying the locks on doors or windows, rowdiness, and fighting all call for police action. Complaints received by the police department of delinquent activity also require police action.

What the policeman does with the child or youth of juvenile delinquency age is partly a matter of discretion. In most instances he warns the child on the spot, or he may take the child to the police station, call in the parents immediately, and warn both parents and child. Usually no record is made of these on-the-spot adjustments. They far outnumber the instances in which a record is made.

These encounters may seem trivial; however, they are important for the future behavior of the child and his relationship with the police. If the policeman on the beat has warned a child and the child repeats his misbehavior, the time will come when the policeman will take more direct action. If he is

---

[1] For a complete discussion, see John P. Kenney and Dan G. Pursuit, *Police Work with Juveniles*, Charles C Thomas, Publisher, Springfield, Illinois, 1965.

finally taken into custody by the police, we might expect that the child would be referred immediately to the juvenile court. However, preliminary screening is often carried out by the police. The police thus make the first decision as to what will be done with the child.

SCREENING AND REFERRALS BY POLICE

INVESTIGATION. Agreement is general that the police should investigate the facts of the offense thoroughly; otherwise children may be falsely accused of delinquent or criminal behavior.[2] Sufficient social information about the child and his background is also needed by police in order to determine whether to return the child to his family, refer him to a health, welfare, educational, or recreational agency, or refer him to the juvenile court, which assumes responsibility for whatever further investigation is needed. The Children's Bureau suggests that a total investigation by the police might include the following:

1. Facts of the offense, including all details necessary to sustain a petition in court.
2. Record of any previous police action.
3. Record of any previous court or social agency action.
4. Attitudes of the child, his parents, and the complainant in the offense, toward the act.
5. Adjustment of the child in home, school, and community.[3]

While making this investigation, police may release the child to his parents or hold him at the police station. Opinion is divided as to how long the police are justified in holding a child while they investigate. The opinion of the committee that set up the Standard Juvenile Court Act was that it should not be more than two or three hours.[4] However, police may not be able to complete their investigation in this time.

To protect the child, the Standard Juvenile Court Act recommends that a child should not be held longer than twenty-four hours, excluding Sundays and holidays, unless a petition alleging delinquent behavior has been filed with

[2] *Police Services for Juveniles*, Children's Bureau Publication No. 344, U. S. Government Printing Office, Washington, D. C., 1954, pp. 7–10. The report incorporates the deliberations, range of opinion, and consensus of a conference of about fifty leading police officials and representatives of related fields, held in East Lansing, Michigan, August 3–4, 1953, under the sponsorship of the Children's Bureau and the International Association of Chiefs of Police.

[3] *Ibid.*, p. 10.

[4] Richard A. Myren and Lynn D. Swanson, *Police Work with Children*, Children's Bureau Publication, U. S. Government Printing Office, Washington, D. C., 1962, pp. 39–57. *Standard Juvenile Court Act*, sixth edition, National Probation and Parole Association, New York, 1959, pp. 37–43.

the juvenile court. When a special detention center is available, the child should be held there instead of in the jail.

RELEASE OF CHILD AND VOLUNTARY SUPERVISION. First, minor offenses, contrite attitude on the part of the child, adequate parents, and good social adjustment tend to facilitate release of the child to his parents without court hearing and legal disposition. Police sometimes exercise an unauthorized "voluntary" supervision over the child. Although the police maintain that the parents voluntarily accept this supervision, critics of the practice point out that the police represent authority and parents are afraid not to agree to the plan. Police also sometimes collect money from the child or his parents in order to make restitution for damage done by the child.

A conference of chiefs of police and representatives of related services revealed three points of view on these practices. One group felt that these informal methods of supervision and adjustment by police are justified by the effect they may have on the child's behavior. A second group thought the police should expand their regular police functions into the supervisory field only if the community was lacking in other facilities for this work. Other justifications for police supervision were that some parents will not seek casework with community agencies, children eventually realize that the police are not punitive but are continuously aware of their conduct, and that some police are trained to offer treatment.

A third group was opposed to all types of voluntary supervision by police. Arguments against such supervision were that the police were overstepping their authority and acting as prosecutor and judge as well as investigator, that the supervision was not voluntarily accepted by child and parents, that few police are trained to do casework, that police supervision duplicates services provided by other agencies, and that personnel must be increased with increased cost to the taxpayer.[5]

Under the circumstances, each police department, with or without consultation with the juvenile court, devises its own policy.

REFERRAL OF CHILD BY POLICE TO SOCIAL AGENCIES. When the child is referred to a social agency, he is also released to his parents. The referral is on a voluntary basis, that is, the police do not have legal authority to demand a referral. They can, however, bring considerable pressure to bear on parents, especially if the alternative seems to be referral to the juvenile court. Children so referred usually have exhibited somewhat serious misconduct but are not "hard core" delinquents with a long-established pattern of delinquency. Some-

5 *Ibid.*, pp. 24–27.

times the trouble seems to lie within the family itself, and referral may lead to readjustment of the entire family relationship.

Referrals depend upon the availability of appropriate social agencies in the community and their readiness to accept the cases. They also depend upon the ability of the parents to comprehend what a social agency may be able to do to help them and their child. Especially among newcomers to the city, services offered by social agencies may not be understood. Parents may be afraid or suspicious of them.

REFERRALS TO JUVENILE COURT. Usually, referral to the juvenile court is reserved for the one-half of delinquents taken into custody who have the most serious and persistent offenses. The conference of chiefs of police (East Lansing, 1953) agreed on the following reasons as justifying referral:

1. The particular offense committed by the child is of a serious nature.
2. The child is known or has in the past been known to the juvenile court.
3. The child has a record of repeated delinquency extending over a period of time.
4. The child or his parents have shown themselves unable or unwilling to cooperate with agencies of a nonauthoritative (social agency) character.
5. Casework with the child by a nonauthoritative agency has failed in the past.
6. Treatment services needed by the child can be obtained only through the court and its probation department.
7. The child denies the offense and the officer believes judicial determination is called for, and there is sufficient evidence to warrant referral or the officer believes that the child and his family are in need of aid.
8. There is apparent need for treatment.[6]

Agreement is general among police, court officials, and social workers that screening must take place before cases come to the attention of the juvenile court. Otherwise, in most cities the court would be so crowded with minor cases that a long delay would follow referral of the child. The basic question, however, is, How do the police carry out their screening responsibilities? Are they performed responsibly and intelligently, or are decisions to arrest or simply warn juveniles made on the spur of the moment? What factors affect the discretion exercised by police officers as they encounter suspected juvenile delinquents?

POLICE DISCRETION IN HANDLING JUVENILES

Considerable research has gone into the question of police handling of juveniles, and these findings indicate that six factors generally affect what the policeman does.

6 *Ibid.*, p. 20.

Perhaps the most important factor is the nature of the offense itself.[7] As expected, the more serious juvenile offenders ordinarily are given more severe dispositions by the police than minor offenders. The child's demeanor, however, is also a clear determinant of police dispositions.[8] When he is contrite and respectful, he is usually regarded as "salvageable" and given a less severe disposition than when defiant or unrepentant. There is, however, an interesting interaction between the seriousness of his offense, his demeanor, and his disposition. It is common for a juvenile who has been accused of a serious offense to be especially respectful and cooperative with the police, but generally to no avail. The seriousness of the offense outweighs the quality of his demeanor with the result that serious offenders are generally given severe dispositions regardless of their attitude toward the officer.[9]

Other factors that also enter into the question are the juvenile's prior arrest record and the quality of his family life.[10] These characteristics are more difficult for an arresting officer to determine, but if he is familiar with the youth's background because of previous contacts, these too are taken into account. Where the child has a record of prior delinquencies, or where he is on poor terms with his parents, or where the parents themselves are poor models for the child, the patrolman will more readily take the child into custody.

There is also considerable interest in race as a factor in the disposition of juveniles. Many blacks (and others as well) are convinced that many, if not most, police officers are prejudiced against blacks and that black suspects including juveniles are treated more harshly than others.[11] These questions have been carefully researched, and although the evidence regarding police attitudes toward blacks is reasonably clear, the evidence that the police give black juveniles more harsh dispositions is *not* clear. Black and Reiss, for example, in a survey of the Boston, Chicago, and Washington, D. C. police departments, report that 72 per cent of white patrolmen expressed prejudiced attitudes

[7] Nathan Goldman, *The Differential Selection of Juvenile Offenders for Court Appearance*, National Council on Crime and Delinquency, New York, 1963, Chapter IV.

[8] Irving Piliavin and Scott Briar, "Police Encounters with Juveniles," *American Journal of Sociology*, 70 (September, 1964), 210–212.

[9] Donald J. Black and Albert J. Reiss, Jr., "Police Control of Juveniles," *American Sociological Review*, 35 (February, 1970), 74.

[10] Theodore N. Ferdinand and Elmer G. Luchterhand, "Inner-City Youth, the Police, the Juvenile Court, and Justice," *Social Problems*, 17 (Spring, 1970), 520–521; and A. W. McEachern and Riva Bauzer, "Factors Related to Dispositions in Juvenile Police Contacts," in *Juvenile Gangs in Context*, Malcolm W. Klein, ed., Prentice-Hall, Inc., Englewood Cliffs, N. J., 1967, pp. 148–160.

[11] Cf. Harlan Hahn, "Cops and Rioters: Ghetto Perceptions of Social Conflict," *American Behavioral Scientist*, 13, Nos. 5, 6 (1970), 761–779.

toward black people at one time or another.[12] Piliavin and Briar similarly found that two-thirds of the officers they interviewed in one department openly expressed prejudice against blacks.[13]

But do prejudiced attitudes translate into unfair treatment of blacks by the police? The evidence is not compelling. Ferdinand and Luchterhand found that white police officers tended to use different criteria in handling white and black juveniles.[14] With black juveniles the police were oriented most to the child's attitudes toward authority and to the structure of his family, whereas with the white juveniles the police were influenced most heavily by the offense. But several other authors have reported little or no difference in police dispositions of white and black juveniles, especially when seriousness of offense and family structure are held constant.[15] It would seem, therefore, in the absence of consistent evidence to the contrary that the police do not generally allow their attitudes toward minority groups to interfere with an impartial administration of the law.

But how are we to account for widespread resentment felt toward the police among members of the black community? No one doubts that much of the law enforcement effort in large cities falls on the black community or that blacks in most major cities are arrested more frequently than their numbers alone would warrant (see Table 4 in Chapter 3). Moreover, it is inevitable, unfortunately, that a certain portion of those arrested by the police are entirely innocent. This is true in white as well as black communities. But with the larger number of arrests in the black community, the number of mistakes is greater with the result that a substantial percentage of the black population experiences "mistakes" or at least hears about them close at hand. Such a small portion of the broader white community are arrested that fewer mistakes are made and few whites ever become aware of them. Thus, whites in our larger cities feel that the police are doing a relatively good job whereas blacks feel that they are concentrating their effort on the black community and making many mistakes. Both are no doubt accurate descriptions of police behavior. But when you put these facts together with the fact that most police are white, the

[12] Donald J. Black and Albert J. Reiss, Jr., "Patterns of Behavior in Police and Citizen Transactions," *President's Commission on Law Enforcement and Administration of Justice,* Vol. 2, U. S. Government Printing Office, Washington, D. C., 1967, p. 135.

[13] Piliavin and Briar, *op. cit.,* p. 213.

[14] Ferdinand and Luchterhand, *op. cit.,* p. 520.

[15] Cf. Black and Reiss, "Police Control of Juveniles," p. 76; McEachern and Bauzer, *op. cit.;* and Norman L. Weiner and Charles V. Willie, "Decisions by Juvenile Officers," *American Journal of Sociology,* 77 (September, 1971), 199–210. See also Lawrence Rosen, "Policemen's View and Treatment of Blacks: A Review of the Systematic Evidence," in *Through Different Eyes,* Peter Rose, Stanley Rothman, and William Wilson, eds., Oxford University Press, New York, 1973, pp. 257–290.

conclusion that the police discriminate against the black community becomes almost irresistible to black people, even though most researchers have been unable to discover solid evidence of it.

Many of these same questions might also be raised regarding the disposition of female delinquents. Is there any evidence of bias against female delinquents by the police? The research here is less systematic, but the evidence suggests that sex *does* affect the arresting officer's disposition of juvenile cases. McEachern and Bauzer gathered information on 1,117 delinquent incidents in Los Angeles County, and their results indicate that female delinquents are more likely to be referred to juvenile court when the offense is minor (and presumably the sanctions imposed by the court are minor), but when the offense is serious, male offenders are referred disproportionately more often.[16] The police in Los Angeles County apparently seek to shield girls who commit serious crimes from the full impact in the courts of their misdeeds.[17] Thus, with regard to sex, bias does seem to affect dispositions made by the police, but in favor of girls who commit serious offenses.

Organization of Police Work with Juvenile Delinquents

Police work with delinquents is usually organized in three ways.

1. Especially in small cities, the regular force is the only one available for all types of police work.

2. In some cities in addition to the regular force there are special youth police or youth squads, attached to the investigative branch of the police department. These youth police supplement the regular police, taking over as much of the work of apprehension of delinquents and investigation of delinquency as is possible. However, the regular policeman on the beat would still interfere in an act of delinquency or crime if he were present and the youth police were not.

3. Juvenile control unit. Most of the large cities in the United States have their youth police organized into an independent department or juvenile control unit called by some such name as crime prevention bureau, juvenile bureau, youth aid division, or juvenile division. Duties of the juvenile control units vary from city to city, but are likely to include some of the following: investigation of juvenile gangs; utilizing information developed by other police units relevant to delinquents; patrolling known juvenile hangouts where conditions are harmful to children; maintaining records of juvenile cases; and

[16] McEachern and Bauzer, *op. cit.*, Table 3.

[17] Goldman reported much the same protective attitude toward all juveniles by one-third of the officers he interviewed. See Goldman, *op. cit.*, p. 101.

planning and coordinating a delinquency prevention program.[18] Some units routinely investigate certain types of situations inimical to children, such as family neglect or abuse, employment of minors, immoral vocations, admission of minors to improper places, possession or sale of obscene literature to children, bicycle thefts, offenses committed on school property, sex offenses involving juveniles except forcible rape, and gang fighting among juveniles.

Some juvenile control units have experimented with case studies and treatment, notably the Juvenile Aid Bureau of the New York City police department, during the early part of its experience. This function has now been stopped. It is generally agreed that police should not undertake social casework or individual rehabilitation.[19] For these services trained caseworkers are needed. The latter group defined the duties of police as patrol, investigation, and public education. The police should carry investigation to the point where the child is released as not in need of further aid or where he is referred to a social agency or the juvenile court.

SPECIAL YOUTH POLICE IN OTHER COUNTRIES

The trend toward special police for youth is not confined to the United States. Since 1926, with increasing emphasis, the need for police specially selected and trained to work with children and youth has been discussed in the General Assemblies and included in reports of the International Criminal Police Organization—Interpol. The First United Nations Congress on the Prevention of Crime and the Treatment of Offenders, held in Geneva in 1955, strongly urged the creation of special police services for juveniles on the part of nations not already providing such services.[20]

Industrialized nations more often have specialized police than do nations still essentially in an agrarian and handicraft stage of development. In the latter, special police may be found in one or two industrialized cities. In general, until large industrialized cities develop, delinquency tends to be infrequent and to be controlled through strong family organization. As in the United States, family organization tends to weaken or collapse in large cities, and delinquency becomes a public problem.

Periodic surveys by the United Nations report no special police units to deal with juveniles throughout much of Africa, the Middle East, and Southern

[18] Myren and Swanson, *op. cit.*, p. 39.

[19] *Ibid.*, p. 8; Alexander Aldrich, "The Police Role in Social Investigation," *The Legal Aid Review*, 57 (Fall, 1959), 14–19.

[20] *Special Police Departments for the Prevention of Juvenile Delinquency*, submitted by the International Criminal Police Organization—Interpol, General Secretariat, Paris, to the Second United Nations Congress for the Prevention of Crime and the Treatment of Offenders, London, August, 1960.

Asia.[21] In Japan and several major Asian cities, e.g., Manila, Bangkok, or Rangoon, however, juvenile police receive special training in working with children.[22] European countries for the most part either have specially trained police to work with delinquents, or the regular police officers are aware of special problems and often work closely with various child welfare committees. The impression given by the various surveys is an awakening awareness of juvenile delinquency as a public problem and a slow approach to special police services. In some countries services are well developed. As in the United States, large cities are more likely to have special services than small cities or rural areas.

Probably because much of it is new, police work with children does not fall into a standardized pattern. A few illustrations of police work with juveniles show the variety of approaches.[23]

In Federal Germany the chief police group that is active in delinquency prevention and control is the women's criminal investigation department (W. P. K., Weibliche Kriminalpolizei), first established in 1930 and now operating in all the states of the federation. In addition, all states except the Saar have young people's advisers (jugendsachbearbiter) attached to the police forces; given special training, these advisers deal with offenses committed by adolescents aged fourteen to eighteen.

Since 1947, Vienna, Austria, has had a special department to deal with juveniles (Jugendpolizei) at the federal police headquarters. A specially trained officer, wherever possible a woman, attached to each of the local federal police departments deals with cases involving juveniles. The Vienna federal police established a youth hostel (Jugendheim) in 1950 so that children in immediate physical or moral danger and suspects could be held until a decision was made to send them either to welfare centers or to the juvenile court detention center. About 600 children per year spend some time in this hostel.

In Japan, the National Police Agency in Tokyo has organized a Juvenile Sub-Section in the Crime Prevention Section. Each of seven regional police bureaus has a Juvenile Safety Section. All the police stations in the country have special juvenile branches, first established in 1949. Police cooperate with special public movements against delinquency, such as the month-long yearly campaigns organized by the Central and Prefectural Juvenile Deliberation

[21] *Comparative Survey on Juvenile Delinquency, Part V, Middle East,* ST/SOA/SD/ 1/Add. 4, United Nations, Department of Social Affairs, Division of Social Welfare, New York, 1953, p. 8.

[22] *Comparative Survey on Juvenile Delinquency, Part IV, Asia and the Far East,* ST/ SOA/SD/1/Add. 3, United Nations, Department of Social Affairs, Division of Social Welfare, New York, 1953, pp. 18–20.

[23] *Special Police Departments for the Prevention of Juvenile Delinquency, loc. cit.*

Councils, and the work of the various guidance centers. These centers are credited with aiding the police in detecting both delinquents and predelinquents.

England has no special juvenile officers or unit; however, policewomen, who are a normal part of the police departments all over the country, make a special point of trying to spot pre-delinquents. All children are a special concern of all police, who decide individually whether merely to caution a misbehaving child or to take formal action. Liverpool, a city of 800,000, has developed a plan to control delinquency which has been hailed as a great success. The Crime Prevention Branch of the police appointed a police juvenile liaison officer for each section of the city. The fifteen liaison officers work primarily with first offenders and are responsible for all criminal, social, and moral cases involving children under eighteen. They work with parents and coordinate the work done by various community and social agencies. In 1957 a special unit of policewomen was formed to work with girls up to the age of seventeen who seemed likely to become prostitutes.

Selection, Training, and Special Practices of Police for Juveniles

SELECTION

Despite the fact that there is broad agreement that juvenile officers must have unusual abilities both in asesssing the character of juveniles and in adjusting to their needs, the fact remains that an assignment as a juvenile officer is not regarded as desirable in many police departments.[24] Dealing with juveniles is seen as relatively undemanding and less important than other types of police work, and consequently, many juvenile officers feel stigmatized as a result of their specialization with delinquents. But if great care is not taken in selecting juvenile officers, great harm can result from the effects of inept handling of juvenile cases. Both the community and the police have much to lose if this task is left to those who are least experienced or least capable.

Women are often recruited to work with children. Policewomen are usually given special responsibility in dealing with all preadolescent children, both boys and girls, and with adolescent girls. For the preadolescents much of their work is protective; they visit places where children may be exploited or permitted to break laws, and they are especially on the lookout for sexual approaches to young children. Much of their work with older girls also revolves

---

[24] See, for example, James Q. Wilson, "The Police and the Delinquent in Two Cities," in *Controlling Delinquents*, Stanton Wheeler, ed., John Wiley & Sons, Inc., New York, 1968, p. 22.

around sexual exploitation or a drift toward prostitution. Men police officers usually work with adolescent boys, who often commit serious delinquencies or crimes necessitating arrest rather than warnings and preventive supervision.

There is no general agreement as to whether the officers working with juveniles should be selected from the already operating police force of a city or should be especially selected for youth work. Since they are police officers, a compromise position is that they should be specially recruited for youth work but should be assigned for six months to regular police work before being assigned to youth work. In this way they would be familiar with police problems and also trained sufficiently for reassignment to other than youth units if necessary.[25]

Three qualifications emphasized by the International Criminal Police Organization—Interpol for youth police—are that they should be "volunteers," that is, eager for this type of work; they should be young and in good physical condition; and they should be mentally and morally well-balanced. Otherwise, their effect on youth may be deleterious rather than beneficial.[26]

TRAINING

Since the regular police, even in cities with special youth officers, have many contacts with children and youth, all police should have some training both in laws concerning children and in how to approach and handle misbehaving or criminal children and youth. Special youth officers require additional, intensive training. This training may be on an in-service basis, although only the largest police departments as a rule have such programs. For smaller cities, regional training programs are better, drawing upon professionals outside the department for teachers, such as judges, trained probation officers, social workers, lawyers, professors in local colleges or universities, and others with training that qualifies them to participate in such a training program. The Children's Bureau makes the following suggestions for subjects to be covered:

1. Philosophy of police work with juveniles.
2. Laws pertaining to juveniles.
3. Conditioning factors in juvenile delinquency.
4. Duties of a juvenile control unit.
5. Intra-departmental relationship between the juvenile control unit and other police units and personnel.
6. Interviewing.
7. Screening process.

[25] *Police Services for Juveniles, loc. cit.,* pp. 40–41.

[26] *Special Police Departments for the Prevention of Juvenile Delinquency, loc. cit.,* p. 45.

8. Dispositions.
9. Knowledge and use of community resources.
10. Records.
11. Developing good relationships with related agencies and the public.
12. Preventing delinquency through community organization.[27]

A number of colleges and universities sponsor institutes on juvenile law enforcement running from two days to ten weeks, and leading either to a certificate or to college credit. A few universities have special degree programs in criminology or police administration which sometimes include individual courses applicable to youth police work. The social-work program is also applicable to some phases, as are courses in sociology and psychology. Standards for training are still in flux, but agreement is general that special training is needed.

Special Practices

In line with a rehabilitative philosophy and the avoidance of stigmatizing a child or youth as delinquent, certain special practices have developed. Usually members of the special youth police unit do not wear uniforms. It is regarded as especially important that they should not when calling at a child's home or school to interview him, his parents, or his teachers. The officer would, of course, identify himself as a member of the police force, but his civilian clothing would shield the family from curious neighbors. Also some children or families might regard the uniform as a symbol of force and be reluctant to cooperate from fear. The automobile in which the youth police officer rides should not carry an identifying symbol for the same reasons.

Police are agreed that complete records should be kept when a complaint has been received, an investigation made, or a child taken into custody. This record should be confidential and should be opened only to persons with a legitimate concern about a case. Otherwise children may be harmed by widespread knowledge of some minor offense or, as a law-abiding adult, be prevented from securing work because of a "police record." There is less general agreement about keeping records of children with whom the police have had informal contacts only. On one side, some argue that such records reveal harmful community conditions or provide light in case of later more serious delinquency. Others call attention to the only occasional value of such records, the amount of time involved in making them, and the later harmful effect they may have if they become public.[28]

---

27 *Police Services for Juveniles,* loc. cit., pp. 42–43.
28 *Ibid.,* pp. 27–29.

There are also conflicting opinions regarding photographing and finger-printing juveniles. In some states laws forbid these methods of identification; in states where they are permitted, individual police departments may have a policy opposing them. Such methods are contrary to general juvenile court principles, since they may later become part of general files which are checked by prospective employers at a time when the former misbehaving juvenile has become an upright adult. However, those who favor photographing and finger-printing point to their usefulness as means of identification.

A middle course is suggested by the Children's Bureau: to fingerprint only on authorization of the juvenile court; to limit fingerprinting to children suspected of committing such acts (felonies in adults) as robbery, rape, homicide, manslaughter, or major acts of burglary, to children with a long history of delinquency, and to runaways who refuse to reveal their identity. If a child is found not guilty of the act of which he was accused, the prints should be returned to the court for destruction. If fingerprints are filed in local, state, or federal bureaus they should be filed as civil identifications only.[29]

These and similar special practices are all designed to protect the child from stigmatization in his own eyes or among friends and neighbors. If he can be treated as an erring child or youth, subject to regaining or achieving conformity, the chances of rehabilitation are much greater than if he is officially or publicly designated a delinquent.

Expansion of Police Functions to Preventive Programs

Much inspection and patrol work that police do is preventive in that it probes situations harmful to children or checks the activities of children before they reach the point of actual lawbreaking. In some cities police have gone further and established clubs and recreational programs designed to prevent delinquency. In such situations police officers are assigned to operate these projects, to serve as youth leaders, or to raise money by solicitation; civilians may also be employed.

POLICE CLUBS ABROAD

Sponsorship of recreation and clubs is not limited to the United States. The police of many other countries have also expanded their preventive work into the recreational area. Clubs are reported in Australia, Belgium, Burma, Canada, Denmark, India, and Sweden. Usually the clubs are found only in major cities. Mannheim, Germany, initiated police-sponsored dance halls, an

[29] Myren and Swanson, *op. cit.*, pp. 84–89. *Police Services for Juveniles, op. cit.*, pp. 29–31.

activity that has spread to other German cities. In these halls young people from sixteen to twenty-five may come to dance. Only nonalcoholic drinks are served. In England, especially in London, the police operate youth clubs. In addition, thirty-seven cities in England and Wales operate "attendance centres" under the 1948 Criminal Justice Act. They are run by volunteer police officers in their spare time. The courts may send offenders aged twelve to twenty-one to these centers for a maximum of three hours a day. They receive physical training, courses in handicrafts, and lectures on good citizenship. For some of the boys, the activities in the centers prepare them for entrance into various youth organizations.[30]

EVALUATION OF RECREATIONAL PROGRAMS

It is difficult to evaluate the programs sponsored or operated by police departments. As preventives to delinquency, they are subject to the general criticism of recreational programs discussed in Chapter 14. On the other hand, there is general consensus that well-planned, supervised recreation is a constructive experience for all children and youth. There is some doubt as to how appealing the programs are to already delinquent adolescents.

Younger children and active adolescents often find them attractive. The extent to which they may prevent delinquency is almost impossible to measure.

Special criticisms have been directed toward many of the programs operated by police.[31] The charge is made that police are not trained for recreational or club leadership, that needed programs should be operated by professional recreational organizations. Another charge is that assigning police to recreational projects weakens the department as a whole and that these police would be more effective if engaged in their regular role. Police counter with the charge that recreational facilities are inadequate in many areas and they are simply filling a need not met by recreational agencies and that the contacts with youth generally improve the relationship between police and youth and make police work more effective.

OTHER PREVENTIVE ACTIVITIES

Police both in the United States and abroad engage in a variety of other activities not strictly in line with traditional police functions designed to prevent delinquency. These include lectures to school classes or assemblies and to parent-teacher groups; radio and television programs focused on delin-

---

[30] *Special Police Departments for the Prevention of Juvenile Delinquency, loc. cit.*

[31] Mary Holman, *The Police Officer and the Child*, Charles C Thomas, Publisher, Springfield, Ill., 1962.

quency prevention and the work of the police; teaching traffic safety to youth; and encouraging youth to visit police stations and to come for advice.

The efforts of police at delinquency prevention follow the pattern found in the community as a whole. Not being sure how to prevent delinquency, they try numerous approaches, many of which are undoubtedly constructive in nature although unproven as to their effectiveness in actually decreasing delinquency. They testify to the great interest in delinquency prevention that has become part of the concern of police departments across the country and to their readiness to accept the juvenile court philosophy of prevention and rehabilitation as a substitute for the outmoded philosophy of force and punishment.

Coordination of Police and Other Agencies

Many agencies in a community have a stake in delinquency prevention and control: the police, the juvenile court, the schools, and social agencies. Moreover, since the police tend to take a distinctive view regarding the causes and remedies of delinquency, there is plenty of room for misunderstandings and conflict between the police and other agencies that deal with children.

RELATIONSHIP WITH THE JUVENILE COURT

The degree of authority undertaken by the police in dismissing children or in referring them to other agencies may be a point of conflict. Some screening and diverting of children from the court is needed. The question is, Which agency is best qualified to do it? In some cities most preadolescent children and minor adolescent offenders are handled by the police delinquency control unit. At the other extreme, all children taken into custody by the police are immediately taken to the juvenile detention center where the probation officers attached to the juvenile court assume responsibility for the screening. One point to be considered is the division of labor between police and the probation branch of the court. Which children can be adequately screened by police, with or without special training for juvenile work? Which children require the more specialized services of a probation officer before decision is made as to release, referral to a casework agency for treatment, or referral to the juvenile court? Another question concerns the adequacy of training of the probation officers. Questions of screening are related to the training of police and court staff and especially to a policy agreed upon by police and court. Too much assumption of authority by the police may mean that many children in need of special services slip out into the community again. Or, children without basic delinquency trends are needlessly referred to the court, where they are screened out without a court hearing.

Police sometimes do not understand the philosophy and practices of the juvenile court. In an eastern city, police felt that when they had taken a child into custody and escorted him to the juvenile court in the core city, the child should be institutionalized and therefore removed from the suburb.[32] The judge placed a large number of children on probation; the sentiment of the police was that the child was back in the suburb before they had had time to return. They therefore instituted an illegal form of probation, instructing the child to report to them at regular intervals and requiring their parents to see that this was done. The parents did not know that this action by the police was illegal.

RELATIONSHIP BETWEEN POLICE AND PRIVATE SOCIAL AGENCIES

Whereas the court and its staff must accept the children referred by the police and make some decision about the case, the private social agency is not under this compulsion. A given agency may provide only a special type of service which may be limited to children of some specific race, religion, or nationality. It may have an overload of cases and simply place the name of a child on the waiting list, in order not to jeopardize the work already in progress. The staff may have an interview with a child, look into the background situation, and dismiss the child as one the agency cannot hope to help. Police must work within these limitations in referring children. It is necessary for them to know the limitations and policies of each agency and to establish workable relationships with each one.

When police attempt to do casework, even through specialized units, they often are severely criticized by social agencies, whose trained staff assert that the police are first police, and second, social workers. The police social workers are actually, or in the minds of clients, backed by the authority of the police department. Most social workers react negatively to the idea of such authority and feel that casework can be done successfully only when the client comes voluntarily. This point of view has been attacked recently through the philosophy of "aggressive casework," in which social workers make the initial approach to a family or child in need of treatment of some sort.

COOPERATION WITH SCHOOLS

Since schools serve as agencies of delinquency control, a division of labor

---

[32] See Stanton Wheeler et al., "Agents of Delinquency Control: A Comparative Analysis," in Controlling Delinquents, op. cit., pp. 45–50.

needs to be established between the police department and the school administration. Truancy is a case in point. Schools typically expect to handle truants up to a certain point, but truancy is prohibited in many state laws on delinquency, and beyond a certain point, schools rely on juvenile courts to enforce the school attendance law. Where this point lies, however, is open to question. Police and schools also need to define the boundary around a school building that separates police supervision from school supervision of children, both for their protection and for delinquency control. Residents in the neighborhood also need to understand the kind of misbehavior by children on the way to and from school which should be reported to the school or to the police. Other decisions need to be made jointly on the use of school records by police in the course of an investigation, as to when the police may approach a suspected delinquent in school and for what large gatherings police should be on hand for regulation and control of traffic and behavior. None of these overlapping areas needs to involve conflict; all need clarification.

BIBLIOGRAPHY

BLACK, DONALD J., AND ALBERT J. REISS, JR., "Police Control of Juveniles," *American Sociological Review*, 35 (February, 1970), 63–77.

CAVAN, RUTH SHONLE, editor, *Readings in Juvenile Delinquency*, Third Edition, J. B. Lippincott Company, Philadelphia, 1975, Section 7.

FERDINAND, THEODORE N., AND ELMER G. LUCHTERHAND, "Inner-City Youth, the Police, the Juvenile Court, and Justice," *Social Problems*, 17 (Spring, 1970), 510–526.

GOLDMAN, NATHAN, *The Differential Selection of Juvenile Offenders for Court Appearance*, National Council on Crime and Delinquency, New York, 1963.

GREENBLATT, BERNARD, *Staff and Training for Juvenile Law Enforcement in Urban Police Departments*, Children's Bureau Publication No. 13, U. S. Government Printing Office, Washington, D. C., 1960.

HOLMAN, MARY, *The Police Officer and the Child*, Charles C Thomas, Publisher, Springfield, Illinois, 1962.

KENNEY, JOHN P., AND DAN G. PURSUIT, *Police Work with Juveniles*, Charles C Thomas, Publisher, Springfield, Illinois, 1965.

MYREN, RICHARD A., AND LYNN D. SWANSON, *Police Work with Children*, Children's Bureau Publication, U. S. Government Printing Office, Washington, D. C., 1962.

PILIAVIN, IRVING, AND SCOTT BRIAR, "Police Encounters with Juveniles," *American Journal of Sociology*, 70 (1964), 206–214.

ROSEN, LAWRENCE, "Policemen's View and Treatment of Blacks: A Review of the Systematic Evidence," in *Through Different Eyes*, Peter Rose, Stanley Rothman, and William Wilson, eds., Oxford University Press, New York, 1973.

Russell, Bernard, *Current Training Needs in the Field of Juvenile Delinquency*, Children's Bureau Publication No. 8, U. S. Government Printing Office, Washington, D. C., 1960.

Weiner, Norman L., and Charles V. Willie, "Decisions by Juvenile Officers," *American Journal of Sociology*, 77 (September, 1971), 199–210.

Wheeler, Stanton, ed., *Controlling Delinquents*, John Wiley & Sons, Inc., New York, 1968.

detention of delinquent children and youth chapter 17

Detention of delinquents refers to keeping them in restrictive custody twenty-four hours a day when necessary during the process of investigating an offense, during any waiting period prior to the court hearing, and after the hearing but prior to being sent to a correctional institution, if they are committed to one.[1] Detention is not supposed to be a punishment. A child is not "sentenced" to detention as he may be to a correctional school. Detention is a form of holding a child prior to a court hearing or between a hearing and transfer to a correctional school.

Limited Need for Detention

Not all children are or need to be detained in custody. Approximately two-thirds of children referred to the juvenile court are released to the custody of their parents or to a responsible adult. The other third are detained, at least overnight and some for much longer periods prior to their court hearing. When children are released, their parents are responsible for bringing them to the court hearing, which may not be held until some days or weeks after the child is first taken into custody by the police or referred to the court without police action by parents, teachers, or others.

[1] For a comprehensive survey of detention, see "Correction in the United States," *Crime and Delinquency*, 13 (1967), 1–38.

Some children, however, cannot safely be placed in the hands of their parents and permitted the freedom of the community. If the child has been dangerously aggressive with threats or actions, he may be detained for the safety of others. If the parents or others are hostile toward the child because of his misdeeds, the child may be detained for his own safety. The delinquent who is known as a runaway or who has made suicide threats is also likely to be detained. The emotionally disturbed child may be detained for close psychiatric study. Runaways from other places who are picked up by the police often must be kept in safe custody until they can be returned to their homes or to police or to a welfare agency in their communities.

The decision to place a child referred to the court in detention rests with an intake officer, usually a probation officer, who functions under policies set up by the juvenile court judge. The decision is part of the total intake process of the juvenile court, which is described in Chapter 19.

Except in several states where a regional system of detention prevails, juvenile detention is handled on a county basis. The number of children in need of detention is closely related to the number of delinquent children in a county and, therefore, indirectly to the population of the county. Rural counties may have only one or two children per year who must be placed in detention; counties with small cities may detain several hundred while large cities detain thousands. The period of detention is short—from a few days to a few weeks. Therefore, at any one time during the year, only a few children are detained. It was estimated in 1969 that 488,800, or about 36 per cent of all juveniles arrested, were placed in detention facilities; however on any given day the number detained was only 13,600.[2]

The small number of children who need detention at any one time, combined with the custom of providing detention on a county basis, poses one of the major problems of creating suitable detention facilities for children.

It is now widely accepted that children should be separated from adult offenders and boys from girls. When possible younger children are also separated from older children and delinquents from dependent and lost children, thus facilitating specialized programs and control. These stipulations for good detention demand special quarters, even though they may not be fully used at any given time. Best detention practices also call for something more than physical safekeeping of the child. Especially for children who must remain in detention for several weeks while investigation or special studies are being made, a normal round of activities is needed as well as counseling in order to

[2] National Advisory Commission on Criminal Justice Standards and Goals, *Corrections*, U. S. Government Printing Office, Washington, D. C., 1973, pp. 257–258.

avoid demoralization of the child and to begin to lay the groundwork for re-habilitation that may be carried on after release in the community or in a training school, if the child is committed to one. These provisions necessitate suitable space beyond that occupied by sleeping quarters, such as indoor and outdoor recreational areas, dining area to avoid eating meals in the sleeping rooms, school-room, and interviewing room. A specialized staff is required to operate the program, in addition to the maintenance staff that takes care of the physical plant. These standards can be met only in special detention centers limited to children, constructed (or remodeled from some other structure) for the purpose.

Few counties need or can afford special detention centers. Approximately 85 per cent of all counties—about 2,550—have populations of less than 50,000 and hence, few delinquents in need of detention.[3] Slightly more than 400 counties have a population in excess of 100,000; and only these could reasonably be expected to support special detention quarters for delinquent children. The financial strain would be grave for many of the less populous counties in this group. Many of these counties make no special provision, and others use makeshift arrangements. In general, only the larger counties have specially constructed juvenile detention quarters.

From this situation two main questions arise: What means of detention do the counties with small population use? To what extent do the populous counties provide adequate detention quarters and program?

Detention Without Special Juvenile Detention Centers

A variety of places for detention is used by counties without special centers. Within the facilities available, many attempt to provide comfortable quarters. If an adjacent county has a juvenile detention center, arrangements may be made to pay this county for detention of the few children in need of it. A nearby state correctional school may accept children for detention. A dwelling house may have detention screens or bars placed over the windows of certain rooms and locks provided for room doors, perhaps in the home of a couple willing to assume supervision. A few rooms in some institution, as an old people's county home, may be screened or barred and used. Sometimes a few rooms in the courthouse or some other public building are similarly reinforced. These methods provide for the physical custody of children, but too often in barren jail-like rooms and without any provision for exercise or schooling, much less counseling.

[3] Sherwood Norman, *Detention Practice*, National Probation and Parole Association, New York, 1960, p. 165.

DETENTION IN JAILS

More often than any of the above, the county jail is used when there is no special juvenile detention center, even though the effect of jail detention is almost certainly harmful to the child.

The traditional place of detention for children and adults alike is the city or county jail. The practice dates from the period prior to juvenile court legislation when delinquents and criminals of all ages were thrust into a common jail to await trial, to serve a sentence as punishment, or to await transfer to a prison or, in earlier days, infliction of some form of physical punishment. With the establishment of juvenile courts, it became evident that the protective care and rehabilitation with which the juvenile courts were charged was vitiated by imprisonment in jails. Gradually makeshift centers were used and in time specially designed juvenile detention centers were constructed.

Nevertheless, it is estimated that each year from 75,000 to 100,000 children of juvenile court age are housed for some period of time in county jails, almost invariably without special accommodations for children.[4] Others may be detained in city jails for short periods.

CONDITION OF JAILS. Jails are operated by a municipal government under the administration of the city police department or by the county government under the direction of the county sheriff. As a class, jails are the most backward and neglected of all detention, correctional, and penal institutions. They have been called a public nuisance, a human garbage can, and the Black Hole of Calcutta, American style. A typical jail is a series of small-barred cells, resembling cages in a zoo, at best equipped with a narrow cot, with or without mattress, a flush toilet, and a washbowl with running water; although the washbowl is often lacking, and one toilet may serve a number of cells. Meals are served in the cells. Exercise space is usually lacking, as are activities of any kind. Prisoners, even before their guilt is proven, often simply sit or stand in the cell day after day. Some jails have a day room in which prisoners may mill around, with the stronger ones sometimes abusing the weaker and smaller ones. The jail may be kept well painted and clean, or not, depending upon the local situation. Many jails are so old that even an attempt at cleanliness and sanitation is only partly successful.

There are in the United States slightly more than 4,000 jails ranging from New York City's prison-like Tombs to the three cell lock-up found in

---

[4] National Council on Crime and Delinquency, *Directory of Juvenile Detention Centers in the United States*, National Council on Crime and Delinquency, New York, 1968, p. iii.

many village police departments.[5] Many of them are old (in 1970 one-fourth of all jails were more than fifty years old) and most of them are small.[6] But paradoxically it is the large, modern jails in metropolitan centers where the problems of over-crowding, racial conflict, and staff brutality are most common. Fortunately, children are more likely to be detained in the smaller jails than in cavernous city jails where the problems are most intense, since most if not all large cities have special detention facilities for children.

From time to time a state surveys its jails, and annually the Federal Bureau of Prisons surveys some 500 to 800 jails in order to designate those suitable for the detention of federal prisoners awaiting trial.[7]

Each year the Bureau drops from the list jails that rated poor the year before and adds some additional jails. Year after year, almost no jails are rated excellent, about half rate as good, about a third as fair and 6 or 7 per cent as poor.[8] These ratings are made in terms of suitability for adults, not children. In spite of this dismal picture, the federal inspectors note some improvement over the years, chiefly in food and medical care when needed by the inmates. Idleness remains the chief jail problem. Adults are rarely provided with any employment (even when serving sentences which may run to a year or more), and provisions for recreation, education for youths, and religious programs almost never exist aside from a weekly religious service.

In addition to these drawbacks, personnel in charge of the jail are almost universally untrained and often elected or appointed on a political basis rather than for their aptitude or preparation for jail administration.

UNSUITABILITY FOR CHILDREN. Especially from the point of view of children detained, little or no provision is made for segregating children from older offenders, ranging from the chronic alcoholic to the skilled thief or occasional murderer among males, and from shoplifters to prostitutes among females. When some attempt is made to separate children from adults, the result may be virtually complete isolation for the one or two children who may be in the small jail at any one time. Also, lack of supervision makes it possible for older children to torment or abuse younger ones. Certainly most jails, small or large,

---

[5] Law Enforcement Assistance Administration, National Jail Census, 1970: A Report on the Nation's Local Jails and Types of Inmates, U. S. Government Printing Office, Washington, D. C., 1970, pp. 6–7.

[6] Ibid., p. 4.

[7] See, for example, Hans W. Mattick and Ronald P. Sweet, Illinois Jails—Challenge and Opportunity for the 1970's, Center for Studies in Criminal Justice, University of Chicago, Chicago, 1970.

[8] Federal Prisons, 1953, United States Department of Justice, Bureau of Prisons, 1954, pp. 44–48.

offer little or no opportunity for exercise, recreation, or schooling for children, and make no provision for counseling. For these several reasons some children detained in jails will do almost anything to gain their release including suicide.

ATTEMPTS TO IMPROVE. The Federal Bureau of Prisons has no authority over jails, not even the ones in which federal prisoners are housed. It does, however, offer several types of training to jail personnel: a correspondence course for jail employees; short training courses given by the Bureau's jail inspectors; and conferences, often in cooperation with other agencies. The training is aimed at the improvement of jails in general and not in converting them into children's institutions. So far as children are concerned, the slow trend is to move them from jails into special detention centers adapted to their needs and equipped to lay the foundation for rehabilitation.

Juvenile Detention Centers

Improving detention centers for juveniles has been a long-standing objective for many in the field of delinquency, and in recent years it has been a specific concern of at least three federal bodies: the National Advisory Commission on Criminal Justice Standards and Goals, the President's Commission on Law Enforcement and Administration of Justice, and the Children's Bureau.[9]

REGIONAL DETENTION HOMES

Juvenile detention homes to serve a number of sparsely populated counties are recommended as the best substitution for jail detention and other inadequate types of detention in these areas. In several states, counties have been authorized to cooperate on building a detention home, but with one exception, nowhere have counties taken advantage of this permissive legislation. Either no one takes the leadership, or administrative tangles cannot be straightened out. In lieu of such permissive arrangements, state initiative is advocated, with the state establishing and operating regional detention homes to serve a number of counties. State and counties could combine in the financing. The plan seems especially feasible in states that have regional juvenile courts. By 1967 fourteen states had assumed responsibility at least in part for juvenile deten-

[9] See National Advisory Commission on Criminal Justice Standards and Goals, *Corrections*, Chapter 8; President's Commission on Law Enforcement and Administration of Justice, *Task Force Report: Corrections*, U. S. Government Printing Office, Washington, D. C., 1967, Chapter 2; and Edgar W. Brewer, *Detention Planning*, Publication No. 381, Children's Bureau, Washington, D. C., 1960, pp. 9–10. Most of the discussion on detention homes is based on these three publications.

tion, but of these only Connecticut, Delaware, Vermont, and Puerto Rico had assumed complete responsibility for administering juvenile detention facilities. In addition Georgia, New Hampshire, Massachusetts, Maryland, and Rhode Island operate regional detention facilities to supplement existing local facilities, and Virginia and Utah encourage regional facilities by reimbursing counties that undertake their construction. Not all of the facilities administered or sponsored by these states come up to minimum standards, but certainly regionalization and state administration represent steps toward more adequate programs, more professional staff, and more humane care for detained juveniles.

County Juvenile Detention Centers

Most detention centers or homes are found in populous counties with large cities. In 1967, 242 such centers served as many counties, although not all met present standards for construction and staffing.[10] Many counties are at the stage where they are discarding remodeled or outmoded detention homes and embarking on new buildings.

To aid in planning, the National Probation and Parole Association has published plans for different types of juvenile detention homes. In general, they group the centers into four types.[11]

1. The family-type home. Planned for a maximum of eight boys and girls, in separate sleeping quarters but with common areas for activities, the building also provides living quarters for a resident couple and sleeping rooms for people needed to relieve them. Security features consist of the fenced or walled recreation area, and stainless steel detention screens inside the glass panes at the windows prevent runaways or the breaking of the glass.

Such homes are most suitable for young and cooperative delinquent children. The small number of children virtually precludes a specialized staff, such as a recreation leader, teachers, or counselors. Dependence must be placed on the services of other agencies or on temporary appointments depending upon the needs of whatever children are in the home at any given time.

Family-type homes rarely provide the degree of security or the specialized supervision and services needed for overly aggressive or disturbed adolescents, who often are confined to the county jail in lieu of any other place of high security. The family home therefore only partially solves the problem of suitable

---

10 "Correction in the United States," p. 17.

11 *Standards and Guides for the Detention of Children and Youth,* National Probation and Parole Association, New York, 1958, Part 4.

detention. Moreover, it is found most often in sparsely settled counties where there is only intermittent need for juvenile detention, but in the long run such counties would provide better detention services by working with other counties for a regional home that could provide a greater variety of facilities for different types of children and a specialized staff.

2. The single-unit detention home. This type of center is designed for fifteen to twenty boys and girls, with separate sleeping quarters but common living areas. The usual design has a central section with a reception area in front and a service area in the rear. On either side extends a wing for sleeping rooms (one wing for boys, the other for girls.) Toward the center of the building are dining, living, recreational, and school areas.

3. The multi-unit home. This home duplicates many of the features of the single unit home, with a number of units for fifteen (or possibly twenty) children each. Separate units can be used for different age groups, and one unit is often reserved for disturbed children. Units may be semi-detached buildings of one story (popular in California) or built with several stories (more suitable for large cities).

4. Decentralized units. When a city finds it necessary to have more than a hundred children in detention at one time, it is advisable to have several district detention homes located close to probation offices serving the same district.[12] Certain professional members of the staff such as doctors and psychiatrists could serve several district centers.

Recommended plans emphasize attractiveness and comfort of the building and provision for a normal round of activities. At the same time, the building is intended for custody and hence should be escape proof, with stainless steel detention screens over all windows, tamper proof protection of light and ventilator panels as well as of all ducts, and locked outer doors. This makes it possible for staff and children to concentrate on program activities without anxiety. Supervision is necessary at all times; to this end, corridors should not have turns that cut off the view of a supervisor. The sleeping rooms and other rooms should have heavy tempered glass panels in the doors. Activities rooms should have safety glass panels built into the walls. Many other provisions are necessary in construction to prevent attempts at escape, to prevent the securing of some object which a youth may use as a weapon, and to forestall suicide. A temporary isolation room (or possibly in large centers more than one) is needed, into which a boy or girl may be placed if he is drunk or fighting when first brought in or later becomes so unruly that he cannot remain with others.

---

[12] Recently the National Advisory Commission on Criminal Justice Standards and Goals has recommended a maximum size of thirty residents! See *Corrections*, p. 269.

Realities of Detention

Although there is continuing pressure from federal and state agencies to improve detention facilities, the truth of the matter is that too many detention centers offer very little constructive care for detained juveniles. A 1967 survey by the National Council on Crime and Delinquency of conditions in detention homes revealed that 28 per cent did not provide regular medical care for their inmates and that 58 per cent did not provide casework service![13] Eighty-six per cent of detention homes in the United States required at most only a high school education for group supervisors, and 37 per cent were willing to accept a superintendent with no college training. In 61 per cent of the agencies no in-service training was provided, and the beginning salary of 74 per cent of the group supervisors was $5,000 or less. Superintendents received a beginning salary of $9,000 or less in 73 per cent of the centers. These figures illustrate that in the vast majority of detention centers, the staff is poorly trained and that no provision is made for bringing professional skills and insight to them as they gain experience on the job.

Moreover, the decision to detain a child is often placed in the hands of the police (twenty-one states do not require a judicial review of such decisions) with the result that many children are detained who could be safely returned to their families. A survey of juvenile detention in New York City found that 43 per cent of the children detained overnight or longer were ultimately released without a court hearing, and of the remaining 57 per cent, half were released to their parents without adjudication.[14] Clearly, by detaining so many children that do not need detention, New York City needlessly compounds its own budgetary problems, while at the same time it contributes unnecessarily to the anguish of most of the children it detains.

Large bureaucratic agencies can bring professional care to juveniles in detention, but they become so enmeshed in procedures and guidelines that an uncaring impersonality often becomes pervasive. Smaller facilities can, if staffed with carefully selected personnel, bring more personal concern to their responsibilities, but such staff often lack the expertise necessary to deal effectively with the more difficult cases. Is it any wonder, then, that many of the tragedies involving children today occur in jails or detention facilities? In 1965 four teen-age boys were asphyxiated in an Arizona jail when they were left unattended for eleven hours, and in Indiana a thirteen-year-old boy hanged himself after being detained for a week in jail. Next to his body was the note,

[13] Reported in President's Commission on Law Enforcement and Administration of Justice, *op. cit.*, pp. 121–129. All of data reported here are from this survey.

[14] *Ibid.*, p. 128.

"I don't belong anywhere." The solution to the problems of detention homes in many if not most cases is immediate return of the child to the community.

Length of Detention Period

Counties vary greatly as to the average length of time that children remain in detention centers. A survey of detention centers shows that the average period of detention in 1967 was eighteen days.[15] The period of detention should be controlled by the length of time required to prepare the case for the court hearing. Ten days to two weeks is the length of detention recommended by the National Probation and Parole Association.[16] Only in exceptional cases should the social investigation preceding the court hearing require more than this length of time. Children detained for two or three days might well have been released when first apprehended, since this period is scarcely adquate for a social investigation and is simply a disturbing experience to the child. Children who are detained longer than two weeks usually suffer a lowering of morale because of the separation from their family and friends, anxiety as to how the juvenile court judge will decide their case, and general dislike of confinement. Occasionally children must be detained longer than two weeks to permit a more thorough investigation or study, perhaps by a psychiatric clinic.

Children are detained longer than necessary for a variety of reasons. The juvenile court judge or the detention personnel may feel that in detention the child is "safe" from further trouble and also will be on hand for the court hearing. Detention may also arise from the unvoiced feeling that the child deserves some punishment, which he may not get after the court hearing. Both of the above practices are in violation of the purpose of detention, which is simply to detain a child until the hearing when he cannot safely be released to his parents or some other responsible adult.

Detention sometimes drags on simply because no terminal date has been set. A judge participating in the formulation of a standard juvenile court act recommended that the juvenile court judge should order detention for a limited period, the exact number of days to depend upon his estimate of the time needed to prepare each case for a hearing.[17] For example, an order of detention not exceeding one or ten days, as the case might be, should replace an order of detention until further order of the court. Such an order would signify that the probation officer was to make the social investigation promptly. If it be-

---

[15] "Correction in the United States," p. 34.

[16] Norman, *op. cit.*, pp. 220–221.

[17] *Standard Juvenile Court Act*, Sixth Edition, National Probation and Parole Association, New York, 1959, p. 42.

came apparent that the child did not require detention, he could be released before the end of the specified period; the detention could not be extended, however, without another order from the judge.

Detention is also sometimes prolonged because the training school to which a child has been committed is so overcrowded that it refuses to accept another child until some child in the school has been released. Thus, although the policy of the juvenile court is to transfer the child to the training school as soon as commitment is made, the child may have to be retained in the detention home. Since the detention home is under county supervision and the training school under state supervision, a coordinated policy may be difficult to establish. The mingling of committed children with those who are still awaiting hearings and who may be released on probation is not good for either group, but it is especially detrimental to the juveniles involved if their transfer to an institution is delayed for several days or even weeks. Although training schools have their own problems, the horrors of uncertainty are probably more destructive to committed juveniles than actuality.

Staff and Services

The staff of a detention center is usually large and is related to the program. A basic staff is required for operation of the center, regardless of the number of children in residence. In addition, trained people are needed for specialized functions and counseling, each with a limited number of children. The National Probation and Parole Association lists eight services as necessary for any detention center.[18]

1. Administrative, including secretarial, bookkeeping, and telephone services, community relationships, and staff development and supervision.
2. Health services providing for medical and dental examinations and care.
3. Casework services with the children, with reports to the probation office and court on each child's needs and potentialities.
4. Clinical services including psychological testing, psychiatric diagnoses as needed, and assistance to the staff in handling children.
5. Group work services, such as recreational and creative activities and daily living activities.
6. School, since many children are of school attendance age, and also to help structure the child's day. The Board of Education typically supplies teachers, who must adjust their teaching to each child's customary placement in school so that they may return to school when released.
7. Religious activities.

18 *Standards and Guides for the Detention of Children and Youth*, pp. 34–35.

8. Institutional services, such as housekeeping, laundry, food services, and maintenance of buildings and grounds.

This array is perhaps the ideal. In small centers, one person may be assigned several of these functions. Volunteers and community service groups may also contribute to the program, for example, religious services and recreation. In large centers, each service may represent a separate department. In any case, the services must be coordinated. The highly professional services are the most difficult to supply, especially in small communities. Part-time services of professionals in the community (medical, dental) may be used as needed.

The problem of staff is heightened by the necessity to duplicate certain services to provide three eight-hour shifts to cover the around-the-clock care and supervision that the children must have. Five staff members are required to staff one post around the clock when provision is made for sick leave, holidays, vacations, and weekends.

Illustrations of Detention Facilities and Programs

How detention homes operate can best be shown by descriptions of specific homes. The first is of a home with a capacity of fourteen children, the second of a large institution for 650 children. With essentially the same objectives, different methods of reaching these objectives are used. The small home depends upon supplementing staff with part-time services from professional people in the community and excellent use of volunteers. The small number of children in the home at any one time automatically provides small-group contacts and contacts between adults and children. In the large detention center, highly specialized full-time staff is possible; small-group contacts and personal relationships between adults and children are attained by living and activity units of twenty children each.

A SMALL DETENTION HOME

Parkview Home, South Bend, Indiana, serves a county of 232,000 population.[19] Built in 1953, it replaced the county jail as the place of detention. It has accommodations for fourteen children, primarily in single rooms, but including one dormitory for three boys. Boys and girls occupy separate wings but share a large living-dining area, a gymnasium, and activity rooms. The superintendent has a four-room apartment. Usually about nine children are in resi-

[19] Based on Norman, *op. cit.*, pp. 49–50, 59, 71–72, 126, and 186, and information supplied by Superintendent Ralph D. Rogers of the Home. The Home was constructed following a survey by the National Probation and Parole Association.

dence for an average of six days each. Four out of five boys and girls are adolescents between the ages of fourteen and seventeen inclusive.

Upon admission, each child is examined by a staff member for external evidence of injury or disease, and his temperature is taken. Within twelve hours, a physician makes a general examination. The physician supervises medical care of sick children in the Home; seriously ill children are transferred to a hospital. Parents pay for this care if they are able; otherwise, payment comes from the county.

Boys and girls share in many activities, always under supervision, such as group discussions that are held daily and various types of recreation. Other activities are carried out separately, as is customary in ordinary school programs. Boys and girls have separate gym periods and usually separate outdoor recreation. The staff feels that the joint activities reduce exaggerated interest in the other sex and avoid the infatuations that somtimes arise when boys and girls share the same detention home but have few contacts.

Religious counseling is provided by a minister from the community when the child's parents have not arranged for their own pastor to visit the child. The minister also confers with the superintendent regarding his impressions of the child. A one-hour interdenominational program is conducted each Sunday morning; Catholic children may attend mass at the local church, under the care of a Catholic layman. In addition, two Protestant church groups hold their services in the Home on alternate Sunday afternoons, with the children in the Home participating.

In addition to a staff of eight people (full-time or the equivalent in part-time services), the Home has a well-developed service of volunteers to supplement and enrich the program without staggering costs for additional staff. Volunteers also provide children with a contact with the world outside the Home and remind children that many people are interested in their welfare. Depending upon their interests and talents, volunteers do such things as run movie shows, join the boys in the gym, give art lessons, teach simple crafts, lead in singing, and help girls with cooking, sewing, and personal grooming. Students from the Department of Physical Education at the University of Notre Dame contribute to the program by volunteering their learning and talents to the recreational program. The following schedule gives the volunteer services for one week:

Monday, 2:00–4:30   Art class conducted by an artist for all children.
Tuesday, 7:00–9:00 P.M.   Recreational program with assistance of a sociology major from Indiana University Extension Center.
Wednesday, 2:00–4:00   On alternate Wednesdays representatives from the

Red Cross direct the children in helping with various Red Cross projects; for example, the children help assemble a Red Cross newsletter or arrange small boxes with various items for distribution overseas.

Thursday, 3:00–4:30   A sewing class for girls is conducted by a volunteer. The Home furnishes the materials, and girls make blouses, skirts, and pajamas for their use while in the Home.

7:00–8:00 P.M.   The men from St. Anthony's Church show movies for the children at the Home.

Friday, 3:00–4:30   Sewing class as outlined above.

8:00–9:00 P.M.   A retired scoutmaster conducts a handicraft class for boys.

Saturday, 1:00–3:00   Outside recreational activities with the volunteer help of Notre Dame physical education majors.

3:00–4:00   On alternate Saturdays a youth group from the Gospel Center Church hold their services at the Home, with children participating.

Sunday, 9:30–10:30   A minister, supplied by the Council of Churches of St. Joseph County, comes to the Home to hold Sunday School for the children.

4:00–5:00   A youth group from the Calvary Temple hold their services at the Home with children participating. This group comes on alternate Sundays.

Parkview Home has one lack, provision for a certified teacher to conduct classes. For most children the period of detention is short and does not entail much loss of school attendance. The children spend an hour each morning and each afternoon in classes conducted by the superintendent, his assistant, and volunteers. These periods consist of informal classroom activities, stressing reading, writing, and arithmetic, since a large proportion of the children lack ability in the three R's.

Each child's day from 7:30 A.M. to 9 P.M. is completely filled with scheduled activities, except from 3:00 to 4:30 when the children have a rest period in their rooms, during which they may read, write to their parents, or do schoolwork. They help prepare the meals, keep the building clean on an assigned schedule, have indoor and outdoor recreation, carry out the two hours of classroom work already described, and have time for personal grooming. In the evenings the children may have visitors, view TV in separate groups for boys and girls, or have organized play in the gym.

Included in the detention home is a room for court hearings which are held once a week or oftener if necessary.

A Large Detention Home

The Los Angeles County Juvenile Hall serves an area of some six million people.[20] Established first in 1906 and since expanded several times, it now occupies eighteen buildings spread over twenty acres. The institution has wide lawns and recreation areas and is enclosed by a high wall. The Hall is equipped to care for 650 boys and girls, the majority of whom are between the ages of fourteen and seventeen inclusive. During recent years Juvenile Hall has been greatly overcrowded with the population rising far byond the maximum capacity. One reason is that the rapid growth of population in Los Angeles County has overcrowded all institutions dealing with delinquent children— the detention home, courts, and training schools. Children must first wait in the Hall until their cases can be investigated and heard in the court; then another wait often follows until there are vacancies in the training school. Therefore the Hall is not only overcrowded, but the average length of stay is thirty days.

Juvenile Hall is administered by the Los Angeles County Probation Department. The staff is organized into four divisions, Medical-Psychiatric, Boys' Care and Training, Girls' Care and Training, and General Services. A large staff of 517 full-time (or equivalent) persons, including thirty teachers assigned by the public schools, is required to operate this large detention home.

Children are housed in groups of twenty. In the newer buildings each living unit has sixteen individual sleeping rooms and a four-bed dormitory. (Older buildings have larger dormitories.) Girls and boys are housed in separate areas, and the program is not coeducational.[21]

The group of twenty stays together all day, in school, at meals, during recreation, and in attendance on Sunday at religious services, always under the supervision of the same counselors. The large number of children makes it possible to group children according to age, physical development, and special types of problems. Thus in spite of the large size of the institution, children have the advantages of small group association and attention of familiar adults.

Children remain longer than is usually customary in detention centers—

20 Norman, *op. cit.*, pp. 67–68, 99–100, 106, 123–124, 136–137, 154–155, and 217–218, and correspondence with Superintendent David Bogen.

21 In regard to a specific question regarding coeducational activities, the Superintendent stated that the staff felt that "the hazard of undesirable relationships resulting from having boys and girls from various parts of our large metropolitan community become acquainted during the time when they are under the emotional stress of being detained for delinquent behavior, would outweigh the benefits they might derive from coeducational activities in the detention home. It appears that coeducational activities have been used to advantage in the detention homes of smaller communities without any serious adverse sequels."

an average of thirty days. The number of children and the long stay make possible various special services and necessitate a more elaborate program than many detention centers require where children are held an average of a week or two.

Medical care is in the hands of three full-time physicians, two half-time dentists, and thirty-eight registered nurses. The medical unit includes an infirmary for boys and one for girls, each adequate for nineteen patients, examining rooms, two dental offices, physicians' offices, and a dispensary. The medical staff also provides psychiatric and medical examinations for children under care of the juvenile court who are not resident in Juvenile Hall.

Separate schools with numerous classrooms and an auditorium-gymnasium in each are provided for boys and girls. Each school has its own outdoor playgrounds. The county superintendent of schools operates these schools as "special" schools. The program consists of academic subjects and a variety of other subjects suited to the interests of boys or girls. Emphasis is placed on developing favorable attitudes and interest in learning. An effort is made to help boys and girls who are detained for long periods to keep up with their schoolwork. The school is in session throughout the year, except for vacation periods at Christmas, Easter, and the beginning and end of the summer term.

A library with approximately 2,000 volumes and numerous magazines is maintained. Use of the library is coordinated with the school. Boys and girls may also take out books and magazines to read in their living units.

Recreational activities are fitted around the school program, with all-day recreation planned for weekends and during school vacations. Active recreation is carried on both outdoors and in the gymnasium. Quiet recreation centers in the living units which are equipped (through gifts) with radios and television sets. Table games, handicrafts, and reading are among the types of recreation. As with other activities, the living unit of twenty boys or girls shares recreation. Occasionally two or more units are brought together for games or other recreational activities.

A chapel provides the setting for separate religious services for boys and girls for each major religious group. Classes in religion are held in the living units on Sunday, and religious counseling is available during the week for children who wish it. The clergymen who have charge of these services come from outside religious groups and are not on the regular staff of the Hall.

A psychiatric clinic has operated in the detention home since 1928. The staff includes fifteen (part-time) psychiatrists, six psychologists, and five psychiatric social workers. The staff studies about 180 children per month (approximately 15 per cent of the total number of new cases appearing before the juvenile court). Other services include consultation with Juvenile Hall staff provided by a psychiatrist who visits the various living units during the week to see children who present exceptional problems; consultation with probation officers in regard to individual cases; and in-service training for staff. The clinic also provides training for psychiatric residents.

Detention of Juvenile Serious Offenders

A special problem of detention is posed by youth of juvenile court age who commit certain serious offenses. In all states except three some provision is made in the law whereby the criminal court may take jurisdiction over certain children in lieu of the juvenile court. The provisions are not uniform from state to state but in general pertain under specific conditions to children accused of crimes for which a sentence of death or life imprisonment may be imposed, or in some states all crimes for which a penitentiary sentence may be given. Sometimes a minimum age, usually between thirteen and sixteen, is imposed below which the criminal court cannot take jurisdiction. Sometimes the juvenile court initiates transfer to the criminal court, and sometimes the criminal court has the power to select cases it wishes to try. Whatever the provisions, a small trickle of boys and girls within the ages ordinarily assigned to juvenile court jurisdiction find their way to the adult criminal courts.

Once it has been decided that a child will be tried in the criminal court, he is no longer eligible for the detention home but is transferred to the county jail, where he is held for a criminal trial, on an adult basis. Since the philosophy of speedy disposal of cases, common in the juvenile court, does not apply to jail, the youthful suspect may remain in jail for many months.

In 1960, a fourteen-year-old Chicago boy accused of killing a five-year-old girl (which he denied) remained in jail four and a half months before trial. He was found guilty and sentenced to fourteen years in prison. His attorney moved for a new trial, a request which if granted could lead to many more months in a jail cell waiting for the time of the second trial.

In the later 1940's, a twelve-year-old Chicago boy spent a period of eighteen months in the Cook County jail waiting for a murder trial and retrial. He was in no way mistreated, but, in order to segregate him from adults waiting trial, he was kept in virtual isolation, having contacts with only a few prison officials.

Most children held in the Cook County jail are older than these two, have committed some type of theft, and remain in jail for only a short period of time. According to a study of 319 boys and girls held in the Cook County jail at some time during the years 1938–1942, two-thirds were aged sixteen, and only seventeen were as young as fourteen years.[22] Almost half were detained for less than a month, 42 per cent from one month up to six months, and 12 per cent from six months to more than a year.

The continued use of jail detention and trial in the criminal court indicates either a distrust of the juvenile court or a failure to provide the juvenile court with facilities to deal with older serious offenders. The situation is better, however, than in 1898, the year before the juvenile court law was passed; in that year 575 children were held in the Cook County jail, compared to an average of 106 per year for 1938–1942. The rate of detention was much higher in 1898, inasmuch as the population of Cook County was much smaller then than in 1940.

The situation in Cook County is not an isolated instance. Across the country many other children whose cases will be tried in criminal court are detained in jails for varying periods of time. After trial, some serve their sentences in the same jails in which they were detained; typically a jail sentence does not exceed one year.

BIBLIOGRAPHY

BREWER, EDGAR W., *Detention Planning*, Publication No. 381, Children's Bureau, Washington, D. C., 1960.

"Correction in the United States," *Crime and Delinquency*, 13 (1967), 1–38.

Law Enforcement Assistance Administration, *National Jail Census, 1970: A Report on the Nation's Local Jails and Types of Inmates*, U. S. Government Printing Office, Washington, D. C., 1970.

National Advisory Commission on Criminal Justice Standards and Goals, *Corrections*, U. S. Government Printing Office, Washington, D. C., 1973.

National Council on Crime and Delinquency, *Directory of Juvenile Detention Centers in the United States*, National Council on Crime and Delinquency, New York, 1968.

NORMAN, SHERWOOD, "Detention Intake," *Crime Prevention through Treatment*, 1952 Yearbook, National Probation and Parole Association, New York, 1952, pp. 140–155.

———, *Detention Practice*, National Probation and Parole Association, New York, 1960.

———, "Juvenile Detention," *National Probation and Parole Association Journal*, 3 (1957), 392–403.

———, "New Goals for Juvenile Detention," *Federal Probation*, 13 (December, 1949), 29–35.

———, AND JOHN B. COSTELLO, "Juvenile Detention and Training Institu-

---

22 Fred Gross, *Detention and Prosecution of Children*, John Howard Association, Chicago, Illinois, 1946, pp. 33, 72.

tions," Chapter 22 in *Contemporary Correction,* Paul W. Tappan, ed., McGraw-Hill Book Company, Inc., New York, 1951.

President's Commission on Law Enforcement and Administration of Justice, *Task Force Report: Corrections,* U. S. Government Printing Office, Washington, D. C., 1967.

Standards and Guides for the Detention of Children and Youth, National Probation and Parole Association, New York, 1958, Second Edition, 1961.

the juvenile court: jurisdiction and organization

The juvenile court is the special court devised to remove children from the jurisdiction of criminal courts, which are dominated by a philosophy of punitive justice. In the criminal court an accused person is given a formal trial to prove his guilt or innocence of a specific criminal act; traditionally he has been held responsible for this act, and conviction has been followed by punishment prescribed by law for the specific crime. In removing children from the jurisdiction of the criminal court, the law swept away both the punitive philosophy and the method of trial and punishment so far as children were concerned. A new philosophy was stated—the child was regarded as immature and hence not wholly responsible for his acts; he was entitled to protection and retraining or rehabilitation. The court was to act as a wise parent who would plan for the total welfare of the child rather than punish him for one specific act. Such a drastic shift in philosophy called for new personnel, new procedures in the courtroom, and different methods of treating the offender. Much confusion and many conflicts resulted from the transition from old to new. Not all of these have been resolved.

The Due Process Versus Treatment Dilemma of the Juvenile Court

The juvenile court is balanced precariously on a tightrope between its responsibility to mete out justice to juveniles accused of violations of law, and its responsibility to provide humane treatment for juveniles in trouble. There are many contradictions inherent in its dual responsibilities, and in recent years the juvenile court has wavered between them, uncertain as to which to pursue: justice or treatment for juveniles.[1]

The tradition that courts are to determine the basic question of guilt or innocence and to mete out punishments according to the gravity of the offense is a long one and cannot be easily swept aside. But as we have séen the juvenile court explicitly abandoned this tradition in favor of one which asserted that the juvenile court ought to use its authority primarily in behalf of the juvenile to insure his becoming a useful, productive citizen. A treatment philosophy became dominant, but with the gift of hindsight we can now see that in abandoning the due process tradition of the criminal court, the juvenile court had also abandoned its responsibility to serve justice as well.

In the name of treatment juveniles were subjected to essentially the same punishments as adult defendants—probation, imprisonment, or parole—but with one major difference. The punishments meted out to juveniles were *not* graduated according to their offense. Rather, they were formulated primarily in terms of the juveniles' overall social and psychological condition. Thus, in many cases juveniles were imprisoned for offenses that would bring only probation or a minor fine to adult offenders in criminal court. For example, in June, 1964, Gerald Gault was adjudicated a delinquent at the age of fifteen and committed to the Arizona State Industrial School for Boys for the remainder of his minority, i.e., for six years, for making an obscene telephone call—an offense for which an adult would probably receive a fine of $50 or imprisonment for not more than sixty days. Similarly, a study of juvenile courts in nineteen of the thirty largest cities in the United States found that children referred to the court for juvenile offenses (running away, truancy, incorrigibility, or disobedience) were more likely to be committed to an institution than those who were referred for felony or misdemeanor offenses.[2] Clearly, a treatment philosophy is no guarantee that juveniles will receive justice at the hands of the juvenile court. Quite the reverse, since an emphasis upon treatment dulls the court's concern for guilt or innocence and undermines its sense of propor-

[1] See H. Warren Dunham, "The Juvenile Court: Contradictory Orientations in Processing Offenders," *Law and Contemporary Problems*, 23 (Summer, 1958), 508–527.

[2] Paul Lerman, "Beyond Gault: Injustice and the Child," in *Delinquency and Social Policy*, Paul Lerman, ed., Praeger Publishers, New York, 1970, pp. 242–243.

tion between offense and disposition.[3] A disposition that is ideal from the standpoint of treatment might easily be the worst possible one from the standpoint of justice.

As if these problems were not enough, by the 1950's scandal after scandal in the nation's training schools came to light. As a result many were convinced that delinquents were receiving not treatment but punishment in them.[4] Thus, at the hands of juvenile courts juveniles were receiving neither a just disposition *nor* effective treatment. And by 1960 pressure was already strong to revise the philosophy and procedures of the court.[5] In that year delegates to the Second United Nations Congress on the Prevention of Crime and the Treatment of Offenders recommended:

> (a) That the meaning of the term *juvenile delinquency* should be restricted as far as possible to violations of the criminal law, and (b) that even for protection, specific offenses which would penalize small irregularities or maladjusted behavior of minors, but for which adults would not be prosecuted, should not be created.[6]

The United Nations delegates would turn over to schools and social agencies the prevention and solution of such behavior problems as truancy and incorrigibility since they are not comparable to crime as traditionally understood.

Shortly thereafter several states initiated far-reaching revisions of their juvenile code. In 1963 New York enacted the Family Court Act which distinguished between a juvenile delinquent and a person in need of supervision (PINS). The aim was to reserve most of the legal authority of the court for delinquents; for example, only delinquents could be arrested, detained, or committed to an institution. The legal authority of the court over PINS was

[3] C. S. Lewis was among the first to point out the full implications of a humanitarian policy toward offenders in his "The Humanitarian Theory of Punishment," *Res Judicatae*, 6 (1953), 224–230, also reprinted in *The Criminal in the Arms of the Law*, Leon Radzinowicz and Marvin Wolfgang, eds., Basic Books, Inc., New York, 1971, pp. 43–48.

[4] One of the best exposés of the terrible conditions in training schools during this period is Albert Deutsch, *Our Rejected Children*, Little-Brown, Boston, 1950.

[5] A pioneer in the effort to revise the procedures of the juvenile court was Paul Tappan. His essay, "Treatment Without Trial," *Social Forces*, 24 (March, 1946), 306–311, is still one of the best statements cataloging the deficiencies of the juvenile court from the standpoint of due process.

[6] Charles V. Morris, "Worldwide Concern with Crime," *Federal Probation*, 24 (December, 1960), 21–30. The United Nations Congress on the Prevention of Crime and the Treatment of Offenders is the world organ for setting standards. Countries participating in the Congress are not obligated to accept the standards, which, however, represent the consensus of opinion of the nations of the world.

sharply reduced, although its treatment responsibilities for PINS remained intact. In 1966 Illinois passed a similar statute (the Juvenile Court Act) which designated children who have difficulty in adjusting to a juvenile status, as minors in need of supervision (MINS), and as in New York reserved most of the coercive authority of the juvenile court for juveniles who had actually committed criminal offenses. Thus, one response to the Due Process-Treatment dilemma was to differentiate delinquent children from dependent or neglected children and from children experiencing serious adjustment problems at home or in school, and to restrict the authority of the court to detain or imprison primarily to the former category. The juvenile courts' treatment responsibilities were not repealed, but its coercive authority to limit freedom was restricted to delinquents. Dependent or neglected children and MINS or PINS were still under the court's authority, but they could not be legally detained or imprisoned.

An alternative response was pursued in California and a number of other states. In 1961 a new Juvenile Court Law was enacted in California which restored to juveniles certain due process rights routinely available to adult defendants in criminal court. For example, juveniles accused of an offense were provided legal counsel, if they could not afford their own, and the burden of proof was placed upon the state to prove its case against the juvenile. The question of guilt or innocence once again assumed critical significance, and due process requirements began to overshadow the court's treatment functions. Moreover, the treatment functions of the court were shifted to other agencies in the state, the California Youth Authority, or the probation system.

Finally, in 1966 the Supreme Court served notice that it could no longer ignore the problems of the juvenile court. In *Kent v. United States* (1966) it ruled that juveniles facing a waiver to criminal court were entitled to a hearing, the assistance of counsel, access to the court's social records, and a statement of the judge's reasons for waiving the case. This decision applied only to juveniles in District of Columbia courts, but in 1967 the Court ruled that many facets of due process could no longer be denied juveniles in any court—federal, state, or local. *In re Gault* (1967) (the same Gerald Gault mentioned earlier) held that a juvenile must be given a specific notice of charges in sufficient time to prepare a defense; that he is entitled to employ counsel for his defense, or if he is unable to employ counsel, to have counsel appointed in his behalf; that he enjoys all the protections against self-incrimination enjoyed by adults; and that he has the right to confront his accusers and cross-examine witnesses. In a later decision (*In re Winship*) in 1970 the Court ruled that the state must prove the fact of delinquency beyond a reasonable doubt. Juveniles are still not routinely permitted appeals of rulings in the juvenile court, but it is clear that these several decisions in the Supreme Court guaranteed a substantial degree of due process to juveniles.

The Supreme Court, however, was not ready to abandon the traditional concept of the juvenile court altogether, and in *McKeiver v. Pennsylvania* (1971) it ruled that juveniles accused of delinquency did not automatically enjoy the right to a trial by jury. The web of due process was woven rather tightly around the juvenile court, but not so tightly as to eliminate its treatment functions completely. Nevertheless, it is clear from these rulings that dispensing justice is the primary responsibility of the juvenile court today and that its treatment functions must be accommodated to the former where the two conflict.

Thoroughgoing reforms of social institutions often arouse considerable resistance, and the introduction of due process into the juvenile court is no exception. Lemert studied these changes as they occurred in California's juvenile courts, and he documented the emergence of pressure groups composed of probation officers, judges, and police opposed to the enactment of the original legislation and, after it was passed, to its implementation.[7] Moreover, after the reforms had been in effect for four years, he reports that 24 per cent of the probation officers felt the juvenile's lawyer served no useful purpose in the hearing and that another 28 per cent felt his main contribution was to make the parents and the children feel better. Nevertheless, it is clear from other evidence collected by Lemert that the reforms were having an effect on the dispositions of juveniles in California. When an attorney was present, the case was dismissed 2.7 times more often than when the juvenile appeared without counsel, and without an attorney a juvenile was 3.7 times more likely to be taken from his own home and placed in a foster home.[8]

Not only did attorneys significantly alter the course of juvenile hearings in California, but they also were often drawn into the planning of the juvenile's disposition as well. Thus, an unanticipated result of these reforms was the involvement of lawyers as resource persons in working out a viable solution to the juvenile's difficulties.

As reform took hold in the nation's juvenile courts, however, it soon became clear that it could be a long time before all juveniles coming before juvenile courts enjoyed the rights guaranteed them by the Supreme Court. A study of 229 boys committed to Pikeville State Training School in Tennessee between 1966 and 1970 revealed that 79 per cent of the boys had been com-

[7] Edwin M. Lemert, *Social Action and Legal Change*, Aldine Publishing Co., Chicago, 1970, Chapter 5.

[8] *Ibid.*, p. 192.

mitted without the benefit of counsel.[9] In the period after Gault, i.e., after May 15, 1967, 83 per cent had been committed without an attorney. Similarly, in a study of the juvenile courts in three cities in the post-Gault period, Lefstein, Stapleton, and Teitelbaum report that the right to counsel, the privilege against self-incrimination, and the right to confront one's accusers were all honored more in the breach than in the observance in two out of the three courts.[10]

Although the juvenile court has changed radically since 1960, it is likely that change is not yet complete. Despite substantial changes in the juvenile code, many, if not most, courts still conduct hearings and make dispositions according to the old, informal procedures of the past. But in the absence of a right to appeal, dispositions made in defiance of due process requirements are difficult to reverse by those juveniles affected. It would seem, therefore, that the right to appeal improper rulings is an essential element in the child's defense of his constitutional rights. Otherwise those judges who choose to ignore recent changes in the juvenile code governing delinquency suffer no particular sanction for their defiance.

Organization of Juvenile and Related Courts

The fully developed juvenile court is essentially an urban institution. Just as juvenile detention homes are impossible for sparsely populated counties, so are fully staffed juvenile courts beyond the financial resources of such areas. Only in counties with large cities are all or most of the provisions for a fully operating juvenile court achieved.

COUNTY AND REGIONAL COURTS

Most juvenile courts are organized on a county basis, as are other courts, detention homes, and many welfare agencies. However, in specific instances the area served is the city, a judicial district larger than the county, or a special region within the state. Connecticut, Hawaii, New York, Rhode Island, and Utah have organized their juvenile courts on a state basis, administered and financed by the state. Connecticut has three districts, each with a full-time judge; Rhode Island has two full-time judges who handle all juvenile delinquency cases for the state; and Utah has a juvenile court judge in each of six districts, three of whom are on a full-time basis. When a judge handles a district, he

---

[9] Michael H. Langley, H. Ray Graves, and Betty Norris, "The Juvenile Court and Individualized Treatment," *Crime and Delinquency*, 18 (January, 1972), 87.

[10] Norman Lefstein, Vaughn Stapleton, and Lee Teitelbaum, "In Search of Juvenile Justice—Gault and Its Implementation," *Law and Society Review*, 3 (May, 1969), 491–537.

usually travels from one county to another on a regular schedule, holding court in each county. The state-administered court with a limited number of judges is especially advantageous to sparsely populated states or areas within states, since it permits judges to devote themselves exclusively to children's cases and encourages them to develop specialized experience in children's needs and treatment possibilities.

RELATION TO OTHER COURTS

Juvenile courts may be independent of other types of courts. Such independent courts are especially suitable to large cities where the number of cases necessitates the full services of a judge. Another arrangement, especially found in sparsely settled counties, is for the court to be a part or function of another court such as the circuit, district, or probate court, which hears civil cases; and when the judge hears juvenile cases, his court becomes for the time being a juvenile court. In other systems, the juvenile court is one unit within a court of general jurisdiction, to which a judge may be assigned permanently or on a rotating basis. The latter arrangement involves periodic change and tends to prevent development of professional interest in juvenile court work on the part of the judge. Still another system merges the juvenile court work with that of other courts concerning children and families to create an integrated family court.

FAMILY COURTS

Some juvenile courts cover types of cases other than the customary three of delinquency, neglect, and dependency. For example, in some states cases of adults who have committed offenses against children may be tried in juvenile court. A family court goes beyond this; it has jurisdiction over all types of cases involving children or other family members where laws have been violated, necessitating legal action. The focus is on intrafamily relationships, especially those that affect children. The Standard Family Court Act recommends the inclusion of the following situations and offenses in the family court act:[11]

1. For children, exclusive original jurisdiction should extend over children who have violated federal, state, or local laws or municipal ordinances; whose environment is injurious to their welfare; whose behavior is injurious to their

[11] *Standard Family Court Act*, prepared by the Committee on the Standard Family Court Act of the National Probation and Parole Association in cooperation with the National Council of Juvenile Court Judges and the U. S. Children's Bureau, National Probation and Parole Association, New York, 1959. More recently the National Advisory Commission on Criminal Justice Standards and Goals has made a similar recommendation. See National Advisory Commission on Criminal Justice Standards and Goals, *Corrections*, U. S. Government Printing Office, Washington, D. C., 1973, pp. 293–295.

own or others' welfare; who are beyond the control of parents or custodians; or who are neglected or abandoned by their parents or custodians. The family court should also have the authority to determine the custody of any child or appoint a guardian; arrange for adoption; terminate the legal parent-child relationship; give judicial consent to the marriage, employment, or enlistment of a child when such consent is required by law; and arrange treatment or commitment of a mentally defective or mentally ill minor.

2. For adults, exclusive original jurisdiction to try a parent, guardian, or custodian for any offense against a child; to try an adult charged with deserting, abandoning, or failing to support any person in violation of law, or charged with committing an offense, other than a felony, against a member of his family; to handle proceedings for support, alimony, divorce, separation, annulment, and paternity of a child born out of wedlock; and for commitment of an adult alleged to be mentally defective or mentally ill.

In offenses for which an adult is entitled to a trial by jury and demands it, the juvenile court judge may certify him for criminal proceedings in the appropriate court.

A number of arguments can be advanced in favor of family courts:

1. The philosophy of the family court is similar to that of the juvenile court, to regard the family as a group or unit and deal with it as such, just as the juvenile court treats "the whole child." At present when a family is in difficulty, one court may hear divorce proceedings, another may deal with failure of the husband to support his family, another with abuse by one member of the family, and another with delinquency or neglect of children. Policies in the different courts may differ radically. The family is fragmented, each member being treated as an individual who has committed some offense. The family court would enable the judge to see the family as a whole and consider what was for the benefit of the family and its individual members.

2. The social, probation, and clinic services now used by the juvenile court could be brought into service for all family problems. When social services are now used in different courts dealing with family problems, they represent a duplication and added expense. Many courts having jurisdiction over some aspects of family matters do not have social services.

3. The same approach would be used as in the juvenile court, with legal safeguards but a socialized approach.

Objections center upon the vested interests of different courts and lawyers, whose function is usually minimized in a socialized court; a possible increase in cost to provide adequate social services; and a possible inadequacy of the socialized approach to handle problems that arise.

It seems probable that in the course of time, greater provision will be made for family courts, and a unified, socialized handling of family problems, within a framework of legal safeguards.

YOUTH COURTS

A youth court involves the extension of the juvenile court philosophy and methods to the next age group above the juvenile court age, that is, up to age twenty-one. Few such courts exist, and those which do are part of the criminal court system. But justification for them exists, especially in states where juvenile court jurisdiction ends with age sixteen or seventeen. The commission of serious delinquencies and felonies increases in later adolescence and often constitutes a serious threat to the community. Nevertheless, many boys and girls between sixteen or eighteen and twenty-one are not yet settled into an adult pattern—they are not yet anchored into life by jobs and marriage. Some, of course, will always resist such conformity, but for many others the possibilities of rehabilitation would be greater with a humane than with a punitive approach. In a sense, the youth court is a "last chance" before the criminal court is allowed to take its course and the deviant youth is classified as a criminal.

Some of the special youth courts in operation are limited in their jurisdiction to misdemeanors—that is, minor offenses, the penalty for which would be a fine or less than a year's imprisonment. The criminal courts still receive older adolescents who have committed serious crimes or felonies.

An example of a youth court is Youth Court of Chicago (formerly known as Boys' Court), established in 1914 and operating as one of the complex of specialized courts that comprise the Municipal Court of Chicago. The court has jurisdiction over boys between the ages of seventeen and twenty-one and operates under the criminal code that governs adults. The case of a boy is tried under conventional legal procedures with the purpose of determining whether the boy is guilty. If he is not, his case is dismissed; the boy may be given suggestions for securing help if he seems to need counseling or other help.

When a boy has been found guilty, the judge has a choice of dispositions. The boy may be committed to an adult penal institution, usually the municipal House of Correction or the county jail; placed on probation under the probation department; placed under the supervision of a private family casework agency, usually for six months with possible renewal; or recommended for psychiatric treatment. When the case is referred to an agency, it is continued for the requisite period of time and then at the end of the period comes back to the court for a renewal of continuance or a final disposition. If the boy has made adequate progress, he is dismissed; if not, one of the other possible dispositions may be used. The continuance gives an opportunity for social work but does not free the boy from the control of the court. Most of the offenses for which boys come to Youth Court are minor in nature; through the court, many of the boys are given an opportunity for rehabilitation without imprisonment.

Girls over juvenile court age do not have a special court in Chicago. If they are guilty of minor offenses, they may be tried in the Women's Court, which handles all law violations of women over sixteen except felonies and traffic violations. Many of the problems have to do with irregular sex relations, prostitution, or minor thefts. The Social Service Department of the Municipal Court aids in investigation of these young women, many of whom are referred to cooperating private social agencies.

Philadelphia also has youth courts within the Municipal Court to handle youth of both sexes aged eighteen to twenty. Cases are limited to misdemeanors.

New York City has several different types of youth courts which do not cover all types of cases nor all portions of the city. Unlike the youth courts of Chicago and Philadelphia, which operate under the criminal law, the youth courts of New York are organized under special Wayward Minor statutes, first passed in 1923 and later amended from time to time. The statutes give to both criminal courts and Children's (juvenile) Courts jurisdiction over youth between the ages of sixteen and twenty-one who are habitually addicted to the use of liquor or drugs, who habitually associate with undesirable persons or prostitutes, who are willfully disobedient to the reasonable and lawful commands of parents or guardian, or who are morally depraved or in danger of becoming depraved.[12] Serious offenses and felonies are not covered by the statute.

Under this Act, an adolescents' court was established in Brooklyn in 1935 for boys; it is part of the City Magistrates' Court. In the Borough of Queens, an adolescent court was established in 1936 as part of the Felony Court. With jurisdiction over the whole of New York City, the Wayward Minors' Court for girls, known as "Girls' Term," operates as part of the Women's Court.

In 1943 the Youthful Offender Act provided for a Youth Part to the criminal courts of New York, applicable to youth between the ages of sixteen and nineteen who have committed crimes not punishable by death or life imprisonment.[13]

The various youth courts, although they fall into the classification of

12 John Otto Reinemann, "The Expansion of the Juvenile Court Idea," *Federal Probation*, 13 (September, 1949), 34–40, reprinted in Clyde B. Vedder, *The Juvenile Offender, Perspective and Readings*, Doubleday and Company, Garden City, New York, 1954, pp. 280–288.

13 Frederick J. Ludwig, *Youth and the Law, Handbook on Laws Affecting Youth*, Foundation Press, Brooklyn, New York, 1955, Chapters 8 and 9.

adult courts, tend to use techniques similar to those of the juvenile court, with social investigations, a liberal use of probation, and emphasis on rehabilitation. In some cases it is also possible for a charge of a serious crime to be reduced to a misdemeanor for youth who seem adaptable to rehabilitation. The youth courts may be considered as an extension of the juvenile court point of view and methods into youth or young adulthood.

It is not mandatory that all youth should be tried in the youth courts in the various cities. Therefore some youth, even though their offenses are minor, are tried in the criminal courts.

The Juvenile Court and the Criminal Court

Children who have violated federal, state, or local laws formerly were tried in criminal courts. Their removal to juvenile court jurisdiction has caused uneasiness among legislators and lawyers who fear that criminal law is being flaunted and that juvenile courts are too easy or "soft" for "young criminals." Criminal court judges often do not like to give up their vested interests in trying criminal cases, and some prosecuting attorneys see the successful conviction of a youthful criminal as a spectacular chance to make a name for themselves. For these and other reasons in many states, the line between criminal and juvenile jurisdiction is not clearly drawn, or the two jurisdictions overlap for older adolescents. The controversy applies only to serious offenses that would be felonies if committed by adults. The minor violations that are not illegal if done by adults are firmly lodged in the juvenile courts; the criminal court has no interest in these offenses. As a result minor juvenile offenders, e.g., MINS or PINS, routinely receive the rehabilitative services provided by the juvenile court, but seriously delinquent children are often deprived of it.

In only three states, Oklahoma, Virginia, and New Hampshire, does the juvenile court have original exclusive jurisdiction for all offenses of all children within the juvenile delinquency age limits. In thirty-eight states, juvenile and criminal courts have overlapping or concurrent jurisdiction, sometimes for children of all ages, sometimes only for older adolescents. In some of these states, the juvenile court may waive its jurisdiction and transfer the child to the criminal court; in others officers of the criminal court may make the decision and take a case away from the juvenile court.

The juvenile judge should have the authority to transfer a case to the criminal court, provided that the child is sixteen years of age or older and that the offense would be a serious felony if committed by an adult. This recommendation is to provide for older adolescents who could not be adequately confined in the typical training school or who are thought not to be amenable to the treatment provisions and facilities of the juvenile court. The National Council of Juvenile Court Judges would prefer age fourteen as the dividing line between exclusive juvenile court jurisdiction and authority to transfer to the criminal court in order to include the rare cases of a child of fourteen or fifteen who might be already well steeped in criminal attitudes and behavior.[14] Whether the age limit is fourteen or sixteen, the cases requiring transfer to the criminal court are few in number and a very small proportion of all juvenile court cases.

EXCLUSIVE JURISDICTION TO CRIMINAL COURT

In twenty-three states the criminal courts have exclusive jurisdiction over some offenses, that is, they must be tried in the criminal courts regardless of the opinion or wish of the juvenile court. Almost without exception these offenses are punishable by long prison terms or execution when committed by adults. When the criminal court assumes jurisdiction, the child becomes subject to the penalties provided by law for adults. The children are no longer juvenile delinquents but juvenile criminals.

In fifteen of the twenty-three states giving exclusive jurisdiction over some offenses to the criminal courts, the criminal courts also have concurrent or overlapping jurisdiction with the juvenile courts in regard to less serious offenses. In these states the criminal courts may easily be more dominant in the handling of juvenile delinquents than the juvenile courts.

AGE OF CRIMINAL COURT JURISDICTION

As a rule, criminal courts may assume jurisdiction, even for the most serious offenses, only over children who have reached a certain age, whereas the juvenile court has jurisdiction over children usually beginning with the age of seven (or shortly thereafter). In two states the youngest age at which a child may be tried in the criminal court is ten; in two states, twelve; in four states, fourteen; in two states, fifteen; in nine states, sixteen; and in one state, seventeen. It should be recalled that in a few states, sixteen is the upper age for all juvenile court cases, after which all offenders are tried in the criminal court.

In actual practice, some young adolescents or even preadolescents are tried in criminal courts, found guilty, and sentenced to penal institutions. On the other hand, criminal judges are not insensitive to the possibility of injustice, especially to young adolescents who are not generally delinquent but may have committed one serious crime. Certain practices are permitted by

---

[14] *Standard Juvenile Court Act*, Sixth Edition, National Probation and Parole Association, New York, 1959, p. 33.

law or have developed administratively to ameliorate the harshness that other-wise might result. When there is concurrent jurisdiction, the criminal court may waive its right and agree that the child should be tried in the juvenile court. In other instances in which a youth comes under the jurisdiction of the criminal court, he may be placed on probation, given a suspended sentence during good behavior, or have his case continued. The charge may be held in abeyance without a trial; or the charge may be reduced from a felony to a misdemeanor, for example from assault to disorderly conduct, with a different pattern of trial and punishment.

CHILDREN IN STATE AND FEDERAL PRISONS

Each year in many states a large number of juveniles are admitted to state and federal prisons after conviction for felonies in criminal courts. In 1960, the last date for which reports on commitments by age were published, 11,838 persons under age twenty were committed to adult prisons.[15] They equalled 17.1 per cent of all commitments to prison for that year, but they were less than 1 per cent of all children tried in juvenile courts. Their most frequent offenses were burglary, larceny, robbery, and auto theft. The median length of sentence was less than for any other age group—about four and a half years.

Most of these young people in prison are in their late teens; however there are a few records of boys and girls in their early teens being sentenced to prison for long terms, usually for homicide. Since there are too few in any one prison for a special youth rehabilitative program, they are either thrown into contact with older prisoners, often steeped in crime, or they lead a sadly isolated life as the prison staff attempts to shield them from such contacts.

Judge of the Juvenile Court

The central figure in the juvenile court team is the juvenile court judge. He is almost invariably a lawyer by training, prepared to handle cases where a point of law is at stake, but with no training in child psychology or family sociology. For making decisions regarding a child's treatment and rehabilitation, he is no better prepared than the engineer, the architect, the dentist, or the doctor, or any other intelligent educated person. He is professionally prepared only to establish that a case legally comes within the jurisdiction of the juvenile court, to apply legal safeguards, to interpret the law, and to protect

---

[15] *National Prisoner Statistics, Characteristics of State Prisoners, 1960,* United States Department of Justice, Federal Bureau of Prisons, Washington, D. C., 1965, pp. 6, 24, 54.

the child from illegal disposition of his case. It is important that the judge should have sound legal training, but more than this is needed. The original conception of the juvenile court judge was that he should combine the best qualities of a wise, compassionate, but just parent. All too often, no doubt, actual judges fall short of this ideal, but thanks to several studies of juvenile judges, we now have a broad picture of what kind of people they tend to be.

According to a study of 1,564 judges sponsored by the National Council of Juvenile Court Judges in 1963, they are in the latter stages of their careers (average age was fifty-three); most of them have received law degrees (71 per cent); but a surprisingly large portion (48 per cent) never graduated from college.[16] Nearly 75 per cent were elected to their judgeship, and 62 per cent had been elected to different offices previously. Of those who were full-time judges only a few (28 per cent) spent more than one-quarter of their time in juvenile court. In comparison with lawyers, they place a high value on helping others, they favor participative leadership rather than directive leadership, and they reject punishment as an effective motivator of people.[17] Obviously, politics is an important part of their lives, and we can probably infer from these studies that most juvenile judges were elevated to the bench initially, at least, because of their political (and not their judicial) skills. Unfortunately, political effectiveness is no guarantee that a judge will also be effective in resolving the difficulties of juveniles that come before him.

Another difficulty is that only in large cities does the juvenile court judge devote all his time to the juvenile court. In smaller cities he is primarily a judge in a court handling civil affairs or minor criminal cases and only on occasion acts as a juvenile court judge. His mind-set and probably greatest interest are in his other court duties. Only occasionally is such a judge able to play his dual role with advantage for the children who come to the juvenile court.

Difficulties exist also in some cities where the juvenile court is one of a number of specialized courts in the court system. The judges are usually organized under the leadership of one judge, who assigns the judges to the respective courts. Some of the courts are heartily disliked by the judges, either because of the type of cases brought before them or because they do not serve as a stepping-stone to higher status in the judicial system or open the way to political office. To relieve this situation, judges are often rotated through the specialized courts, serving perhaps a year in each one. In many cases the juvenile court is the least desirable of the courts. It does not give status, it does not

16 Shirley D. McCune and D. L. Skoler, "Juvenile Court Judges in the United States —Part I: A National Profile," *Crime and Delinquency*, 11 (April, 1962), 121–131.

17 Regis H. Walther and Shirley D. McCune, "Juvenile Court Judges in the United States—Working Styles and Characteristics," *loc. cit.*, 14 (October, 1965), 384–393.

permit a display of legal acumen in handling a difficult case. The judges accept their term as a necessary but disliked part of their duties. The result is that few of the judges become expert in handling children's cases, nor are they motivated to acquire the knowledge of human nature needed by the juvenile court judge.

The usual tenure in office of a judge is a few years; then the judge must seek re-election. The settlement of difficult and widely publicized cases or conviction of criminal cases catches the public eye and increases the probability of re-election. The juvenile court judge may have handled difficult cases and may have set numbers of children on the road to rehabilitation. But the cases are not made public. Notorious cases of young delinquents more often than not are tried in criminal courts and add to the public's knowledge of the criminal court judge. The full-time juvenile court judge must be the anonymous official who works because of genuine interest in children and not because he regards his court record alone as the best means to re-election or to advancement into higher judicial positions or political life.

Some of the difficulties are overcome for smaller communities when a number of counties are grouped together to make possible a full-time juvenile court judge. Regional juvenile court judges are often appointed by state officials; they are therefore not handicapped by the specter of losing an election if they do not make a public showing of trying spectacular cases. In Utah, juvenile court judges are appointed by the Public Welfare Commission, for four-year terms. Usually those selected are affiliated with the political party in power. Although good judges may be selected in this way (and apparently have been in Utah), more assurance of high qualifications in all appointments would be given if judges were appointed from lists established by merit system evaluations, with reappointment when the judge's work had been satisfactory.[18]

Services to Supplement the Work of the Judge

Since the responsibilities of the judge are many and varied, supplementary services in large cities are part of the equipment of the juvenile court.

REFEREE

In many states the judge may appoint a referee to assist him. The referee usually hears cases and makes recommendations to the judge about the disposition of the case. The court is not compelled to accept the recommendation;

[18] *Concerning the Administration of Juvenile Courts*, Biennial Report of the Director of Bureau of Services for Children, State Department of Public Welfare, Salt Lake City, Utah, 1953–1956, p. 8.

he may change or reject it. However, since the referee often handles uncomplicated cases, his recommendations are likely to be accepted by the judge. The referee needs either legal training or a sound knowledge of law. In some courts the referee is a woman who handles girls' cases.

PROBATION STAFF

The probation staff, at its best, is composed of professional social workers. However, this standard is not always reached. The appointment of probation officers typically rests with the judge. The staff at its worst consists of people who have helped the judge secure enough votes to be elected; they may have neither training nor personal qualifications for the work. If the judge loses an election, the probation staff appointed by him is expected to resign so that the incoming judge may make his own appointments. Under these conditions, the best trained social workers regard probation work as professionally undesirable. Only when qualifications are established and appointments taken from the judge and placed under some form of civil service with permanent tenure can a well-qualified staff be secured. Sometimes an intermediate stage is reached in which a committee of leading citizens, including members interested in education and welfare, is appointed by the court to recommend or screen candidates for probation work; from the list presented, the judge makes his appointments. With a change of judge, the incoming judge will still be entitled to make new appointments.

A recent survey found that most probation departments in the United States fell short of the ideal arrangements described above.[19] Out of 235 agencies surveyed, only 47 per cent reported that probation officers received civil service appointments or their equivalent. A college degree was required by 74 per cent, and the modal beginning salary was $5,001 to $6,000. In-service training was provided in 48 per cent of the departments. The median caseload in the 235 departments was seventy-one to eighty probationers per officer, and 50 per cent of the agencies provide intake and referral services in addition to caseload supervision. Generally speaking, the larger the city, the more adequate the probation supervision provided, but it is clear from these figures that probation officers all too often are poorly educated and minimally paid for the enormous caseloads they must supervise.

[19] President's Commission on Law Enforcement and Administration of Justice, *Task Force Report: Corrections*, U. S. Government Printing Office, Washington, D. C., 1967, pp. 136–141.

Bibliography

CALDWELL, R. G., "The Juvenile Court: Its Development and Some Major Problems," *Journal of Criminal Law, Criminology and Police Science*, 51 (1961), 493–511.

CAVAN, RUTH SHONLE, editor, *Readings in Juvenile Delinquency*, Third Edition, J. B. Lippincott Company, Philadelphia, 1975.

DUNHAM, H. WARREN, "The Juvenile Court: Contradictory Orientations in Processing Offenders," *Law and Contemporary Problems*, 23 (1958), 508–527.

KRUEGER, GLADYS M., *Survey of Probation Officers, 1959*, Children's Bureau Report No. 15, U. S. Government Printing Office, Washington, D. C.

LEMERT, EDWIN M., *Social Action and Legal Change*, Aldine Publishing Co., Chicago, 1970.

LERMAN, PAUL, "Beyond Gault: Injustices and the Child," in *Delinquency and Social Policy*, Paul Lerman, ed., Praeger Publishers, New York, 1970.

LEWIS, C. S., "The Humanitarian Theory of Punishment, *Res Judicatae*, 6 (1953), 224–230.

National Advisory Commission on Criminal Justice Standards and Goals, *Corrections*, U. S. Government Printing Office, Washington, D. C., 1973.

NEIGHER, ALAN, "The Gault Decision: Due Process and the Juvenile Courts," *Federal Probation*, 31 (December, 1967), 8–18.

President's Commission on Law Enforcement and Administration of Justice, *Task Force Report: Corrections*, U. S. Government Printing Office, Washington, D. C., 1967, pp. 130–141.

ROSENHEIM, MARGARET K., editor, *Justice for the Child—The Juvenile Court in Transition*, Free Press, New York, 1962.

SHERIDAN, WILLIAM H., *Standards for Juvenile and Family Courts*, Children's Bureau Publication No. 437, U. S. Government Printing Office, Washington, D. C., 1966.

Standard Family Court Act, National Probation and Parole Association, New York, 1959; also printed in *National Probation and Parole Association Journal*, 5 (1959), 99–160.

Standard Juvenile Court Act, sixth edition, National Probation and Parole Association, New York, 1959.

Standards for Specialized Courts Dealing with Children, U. S. Government Printing Office, Washington, D. C., 1954.

TAPPAN, PAUL W., "The Adolescent in Court," *Journal of Criminal Law*, 37 (1946), 216–230.

———, "Children and Youth in the Criminal Court," *Annals of the American Academy of Political and Social Science*, 261 (1949), 128–136.

———, *Delinquent Girls in Court*, Columbia University Press, New York, 1947.

———, "Treatment Without Trial," *Social Forces*, 24 (1946), 306–311.

Task Force Report: Juvenile Delinquency and Youth Crime, President's Commission on Law Enforcement and Administration of Justice, U. S. Government Printing Office, Washington, D. C., 1967, Appendices B, C, and D.

functions of the
juvenile court
and probation office chapter 19

The function of the juvenile court is to investigate all cases referred to it that come within its jurisdiction and decide upon the best plan for the delinquent's immediate future, in terms of community welfare and the delinquent's own rehabilitation. Rehabilitation may be carried out under the immediate supervision of the court or through probation, or may be delegated to some other agency.

Intake and Classification of Cases

Children are referred to the juvenile court by other agencies or by individuals. The court itself does not send representatives into the community to discover which children are delinquent. The court's work begins when a child is brought to the detention facility or when a complaint is made against the child.

SOURCES OF REFERRAL

Although the police dispose of slightly more than half of all juvenile arrests via station adjustments, it is still true that more children come to the attention of the juvenile court through the police than in any other way.[1]

[1] Thomas P. Monahan, "National Data on Police Dispositions of Juvenile Offenders," *Police*, 14 (1969), 36–45.

Most of these arrests, however, result from citizen complaints to the police, about 78 per cent; and only a small minority, about 22 per cent, arise directly as a result of police initiative.[2]

Some children are referred by parents, teachers, social workers, and others. Parents and teachers are likely to refer children because they are incorrigible or beyond their control. Schools may refer destructive or disorderly students or persistent truants, although most schools handle truancy as an institutional problem without referral to the juvenile court. Police refer children for community delinquencies, such as disorderliness in public places, vandalism, theft, and fighting.

INTAKE

Intake refers to the preliminary steps taken to determine whether the child comes under the jurisdiction of the court and requires a court hearing. The term is commonly used in social work for the initial interview that a prospective client has when he comes to the social agency to ask for help. In this interview, the social worker in charge of intake determines whether the person's problems are ones that the agency can handle, and makes an appointment when the person may talk with one of the caseworkers who will then handle the case.

In the juvenile court the purpose is the same but the procedure may be more formal. The intake procedure usually is handled by a probation officer and constitutes one of the specific functions of probation officers. In a large court, a special intake department or intake officer may specialize in this phase of the court procedure. In smaller courts, one probation officer may handle intake along with other duties. If there is no probation officer, the judge makes the decision.

SCREENING OF CASES

In juvenile courts with a sufficient number of cases to have a well-developed staff, probation officers supplement the complaint made by police or others when they refer a child to court. They make a preliminary investigation to determine whether the child's case comes within the jurisdiction of the court and whether a petition should be filed against the child.

Usually some children who are referred have problems that do not come under the legal jurisdiction of the court. The officer in charge of intake does not simply turn these cases aside, but refers them to some community or social

---

[2] Donald J. Black and Albert J. Reiss, Jr., "Police Control of Juveniles," *American Sociological Review*, 35 (February, 1970), 66.

work agency that offers the help needed. This procedure is a voluntary gesture of help and is not backed up by the authority of the court.

Cases that come under court jurisdiction fall into two categories: unofficial and official. In the first type, if a petition does not seem necessary and the complainant does not insist upon one, the probation officer works out an informal and voluntary plan with the parents and the child. The judge may review these cases in whatever degree he thinks necessary, but typically this stage of the proceedings lies in the hands of probation officers or other social workers provided for the juvenile court.

The term unofficial case is loosely defined to include several types. In some instances it refers to cases where delinquency has been alleged but not proven or adjudicated; the judge makes some type of adjustment informally, perhaps by talking with parents and child or referring the parents to some social agency. The term is also applied to cases in which the probation officer feels that the child needs social casework but that legal action is not needed. Also the term may be used for cases that have formally come before the court but in which the delinquency is too trivial to demand court action. In general, in unofficial cases a formal complaint or petition is not filed and the case is not entered on the juvenile court calendar for a formal hearing, but some action is taken by judge, referee, or probation officer to adjust the case. Presumably all would come within the official jurisdiction of the court. Legally, there is no compulsion on the child or his parents to conform to the recommendations made to them. However, if the child's behavior does not improve and he is again referred to the court, the next step normally would be an official hearing.

The third or official group of cases consists of those under the jurisdiction of the court which seem to need further investigation and a firm treatment plan. These are the official cases which receive a court hearing, and they include children who ultimately will be adjudicated as delinquent as well as those who will be found MINS or PINS (about one-quarter of official cases).

COMPLAINTS AND PETITIONS

A written complaint on a standard form is made by the police or by the agency or individual that refers the child to the court. Only for the third group is a petition filed. The petition does not allege that a delinquent act has been committed, but usually opens with such a phrase as "In the interest of ——, a child under —— years of age." The specific behavior that brings the child under the jurisdiction of the court is given, as well as the names and addresses of the parents or guardian. This petition is then filed, and the case is scheduled for a court hearing.

Procedures vary somewhat at this point. A preliminary investigation by the probation officer may be necessary in addition to the police investigation to determine whether there is sufficient evidence to proceed with the case. In some courts the probation officer makes the decision; in others the judge holds a preliminary hearing and makes the decision himself. If the case is continued, a social investigation is made by the probation officer, and a court hearing is set as soon as conveniently possible. Parents are advised in writing of the specific nature of the complaint and summoned to appear with the child at the hearing.

Social Investigation

The second task of the probation officer is the social investigation. This investigation is more thorough and extensive than the police investigation, which has been limited to establishing the facts of the delinquency. The social investigation secures background data on the child to help the judge understand the case and decide what should be done about it.

In assembling data for the report, the probation officer may use a number of sources. If the county has a social service exchange, listing the names of all people who have sought aid from all types of agencies and the names of the agencies, the probation officer may start with this agency. If the child or his family has had contacts with other agencies, they are asked to contribute helpful information. Other sources of information are schools, the church that the family attends, community or recreational centers where the child has said he goes, employers of the older child or possibly his parents, and others acquainted with the child. Police records are also consulted. The investigation expands beyond the child's delinquencies to include the total round of his life and that of his parents. Much of the investigation is carried on by telephone.

The above describes the ideal situation. Often the probation officer is so rushed with duties and cases that the investigation is superficial. Also, probation officers untrained in the techniques of social case investigation are less likely to uncover the more subtle aspects than those who are trained. With the untrained investigator the report may be simply a statement of agency contacts, school performance, and neighborhood gossip.

When the report is drawn up for the judge's use, it usually contains suggestions or recommendations by the probation officer for the disposition of the child. For adequate recommendations, the probation officer needs to be thoroughly familiar with the facilities of the community as well as with legal provisions and restrictions. Community facilities include mental health clinics, residential institutions for pre-delinquent or mildly delinquent children, community and youth centers, recreational facilities, churches, and various types of schools and school programs. Formal knowledge of the facilities and programs is not sufficient. The probation officer should also know the attitudes of these agencies toward working with delinquent children—some agencies do not want them, regarding the delinquent child as the bad apple who may contaminate otherwise good apples.

During the social investigation, the services of a court clinic or community mental health and medical clinics may be sought for diagnosis and recommendations.

The Court Hearing

The court hearing is the equivalent of the trial in a civil or criminal court. Unlike a trial, it may assume the nature of a conference under chairmanship of the judge. It is not simply a conference, however, for the final decision is not made by majority vote but by the judge, with the authority of his position behind him.

ATTENDANCE AT THE HEARING

Unlike other trials, a juvenile court hearing is not an open, public meeting that anyone may attend. The minimum attendance at the hearing includes, beside the judge (or referee), the probation officer, the parents or guardian of the child, and the child and his counsel. In some courts, a court reporter is present to make an exact record of everything that is said; if the case is appealed, this record is transcribed, but not otherwise. Since few cases are appealed, many judges do not regard a court reporter as necessary. The parents or guardian are entitled to employ legal counsel and sometimes they do so. In some courts, the prosecuting attorney may have a representative present, but this is not customary.

Other persons who may be present are individuals interested in the child's welfare, especially if they are in a position to help the child, such as a minister, school social worker or principal, or representative of a social agency. Their presence is regarded as desirable, especially if they give the child a feeling of friendliness and can actually aid in the child's rehabilitation. They may also add to the reassurance of parents, who may feel wholly at the mercy of a judge whom they perhaps have never seen before and whose powers they do not understand.

PUBLICITY

From time to time the question of publicity for juvenile court hearings becomes an issue. Secrecy of court proceedings has always been opposed in the United States, since it may open the way for exploitation of or injustice to the accused person, perhaps in the interest of other persons who would stand to lose or gain in prestige, power, or finances, according to the outcome of a trial.[3] The question with reference to juvenile court hearings does not revolve around absolute secrecy so much as around who should be eligible to attend hearings and how much of the case should be made public. Specifically, should newspaper reporters be admitted?[4] State laws may permit or refuse permission to reporters to attend hearings on delinquency. Judges also may use their discretion within the laws. A survey made in 1966 of practices in 207 juvenile courts in cities of 100,000 and over showed that 32 per cent of the courts never permitted representatives of the press to be present at delinquency hearings, 40 per cent sometimes gave permission, and 28 per cent always. However, in half of the 207 courts limitations were placed on the reporting.[5] Judges have wide discretion about the admission of newspaper representatives and vary to some extent in their policy as to which if any hearing they may attend. In general, when news is given out, judges and newspapers have followed the policy of not publishing the names of delinquents or other identifying data.

It is argued that the public is entitled to receive all the news through all means of information—newspapers, radio, television, and motion pictures. Less than full coverage gives an incomplete and unrealistic view of the world. The newspapers or other media are the only ones capable of deciding which news should be printed, and they may be trusted to judge wisely and to set their own standards collectively or individually. Such news will arouse public interest and lead to eradication of delinquency and its causes.

Opposed to this argument is the doubtful beneficial result of the publication of stories on individual cases. Public demands for dramatic stories of individual delinquents or criminals often indicate a morbid interest, a need for vicarious participation in crime, or a hidden desire for punishment. Constructive movements do not grow out of these interests. Newspapers and other news media have done a valuable service in excellent feature or documentary

[3] Secrecy has bred brutality and resulted in false confessions when police have illegally detained adult suspects or have secretly used brutal methods to extort confessions. The brutality that comes to light from time to time in correctional schools or prisons is largely the result of the secrecy that surrounds what goes on within these institutions.

[4] For a general discussion, see Gilbert Geis, "Identifying Delinquents in the Press," *Federal Probation*, 29 (December, 1965), 44–49; "Publicity and Juvenile Court Proceedings," *National Probation and Parole Association Journal*, 4 (1958), 333–355.

[5] President's Commission on Law Enforcement and the Administration of Justice, *Task Force Report: Juvenile Delinquency and Youth Crime*, U. S. Government Printing Office, Washington, D. C., 1967, p. 82.

stories which give a well-rounded conception of factors causing delinquency or of treatment methods. Such stories do not endanger the rights or the welfare of any particular child.

Another argument that favors publicity is that the juvenile court needs a watchdog to protect public and individual interests and that the best watchdog is the press.

It is true that some newspapers by persistent campaigns carried on over long periods of time have shocked the public into realization of disastrous situations in slums, prisons, and correctional schools. These are situations whose remedy requires legislation and public money. If the juvenile court needs a watchdog to protect family and child, this service could be better rendered by a committee of responsible citizens who would not necessarily feel that individual cases should be made public, but who could judge of unmet needs and bring them either to the public or to the proper authorities, as would seem wise.

Another argument for publicity is plainly punitive in origin: "punks," "hoodlums," young "gangsters" should have their names held up to scorn and should receive public condemnation. It is asserted that the knowledge that their names would be printed would act as a deterrent.

Opposed is the fact that few studies have been made of the effect of publicity on the individual delinquency-prone youth. In general, making a public spectacle of a criminal has not stopped crime and has had some very ill effects on public sentiment. The National Council on Crime and Delinquency investigated the claim of a Helena, Montana judge that the release of names of juvenile delinquents to newspapers had been followed by a 49 per cent decrease in juvenile crime over a period of five years. Actually the investigation showed an increase in the number of arrests between 1962 and 1963 from 69 to 90, or 30.4 per cent.[6]

Among juveniles, publicity has sometimes boomeranged and far from humiliating the delinquent has given him a sense of importance as a public figure and has raised his status among other juveniles.

In any case, rehabilitation—never easy to accomplish—becomes more difficult. The less publicity an individual case has, the better is the chance to bring the delinquent back into conformity and to protect him in the future from either delayed hero worship or a stigma that he cannot cast off. Rehabilitation does not go on in the glare of publicity but through personal relationships of the delinquent with adult nondelinquents and when needed through specialized casework or clinic services.

[6] Geis, *op. cit.*, pp. 46–47; *Guides for Juvenile Court Judges on News Media Relations.* National Council on Crime and Delinquency, New York, 1965.

Another unfortunate aspect of full publicity is that it spreads the mantle of guilt over the delinquent's entire family, and perhaps his neighborhood. Parents, younger brothers and sisters, and other members of the family are held up to scorn, and for years their name may be associated with a particular crime. In one well-publicized juvenile crime, the family legally changed its name and moved to another city to escape from the stigma and to protect younger children in the family.

ADJUDICATION

In order that the judge may act legally, it must be determined that the child did actually commit a delinquent act. Unless there has been a preliminary hearing, the first item of the official hearing is the presentation of evidence in the presence of the child and his parents. The policeman who made the first investigation may present his facts. A complainant may state his reasons for filing a complaint or petition against the child. The probation officer may review facts as he found them. The child will be asked whether he behaved as these people have said. In most cases, children admit their delinquencies. When they do not or protest that they are innocent, they or their parents have the right to present opposing evidence. If it becomes clear that the child did not commit the delinquent act, he is dismissed. Otherwise, he is adjudicated a delinquent, or a minor in need of supervision (MINS), and a decree of this finding is placed on the child's record.

REVIEW OF THE SOCIAL INVESTIGATION

At this point, persons who have been called to the hearing simply to give evidence on the child's behavior may be asked to withdraw, except of course the probation officer. When it has been established that the child comes under the jurisdiction of the court, the hearing shifts emphasis from proof of misbehavior to review of the child's social situation and disposition of the case. At its best it may resemble a case conference of a social agency; at its worst an authoritarian and punitive judge berates the child and imposes penalties and punishment upon him.

The judge may have read the report of the social investigation made by the probation officer prior to the hearing, or he may see it for the first time at the hearing. The first, of course, is preferable. In any case, the competent judge usually reviews pertinent points with the parents and child, trying to give them some understanding of, and insight into, the background of the child's delinquency.

Disposition of the Case

The judge has a number of choices as to the disposition of cases that come under the jurisdiction of the court.

Judicial or Nonjudicial Handling (Formerly Referred to as Official or Unofficial)

The first, made by the judge or probation officer assigned to intake, is whether to handle the case judicially or nonjudicially. Within a given state as well as over the country as a whole the percentage of cases handled nonjudicially runs from none to as many as 96 per cent. These wide differences reflect the varying philosophies and policies of the local judges and, no doubt, also the different kinds of dispositions available under the two methods of handling cases. Certainly the differences are no indication of the proportion of serious cases occurring in each county. They represent very clearly the great authority vested in the judge. In a given county almost all the children may receive the stigma of being officially declared delinquent; in a similar county, almost all are protected from the stigma.

Choice of Disposition

The judge may choose from a number of dispositions. More than half of all nonjudicial cases are dismissed, adjusted informally through discussion or referral, or held open without further hearing. The most common disposition for judicial cases is probation, and throughout the country the percentage receiving probation is rising.

Probation is preferable when it is consistent with the best interests of both the child and the community, because it avoids labeling the child as a committed delinquent, it does not throw him into close contact with large numbers of other delinquents (which institutionalizing him would), and it costs about one-tenth the expense of institutionalization. The swing to probation was begun in the 1950's when a three-year project in Saginaw County, Michigan, to expand the use of probation in adult felony cases resulted in a drop of prison commitments from 34 per cent to 17 per cent of all felony cases and reduced the rate of probation revocation as well from 32 per cent to 17 per cent.[7]

It gathered momentum in 1961 when an experimental project was begun in northern California in which nonassaultive youths committed to the Cali-

---

[7] John B. Martin, "The Saginaw Project," *Crime and Delinquency*, 6 (1960), 357–364.

fornia Youth Authority, instead of being assigned to an institution, were sent to a Community Treatment Project (CTP) in which they were exposed to a variety of treatment programs including intensive counseling and group homes.[8] The youths were classified in terms of the interpersonal maturity typology described in Chapter 5, and the results indicate that in many cases, placement with CTP was very beneficial.[9] Youths classified as neurotic who had received a traditional disposition, i.e., who had been sent to an institution and subsequently paroled, were arrested on parole nearly three times as often as neurotic delinquents who were paroled after attending CTP. Moreover, the beneficial effects of CTP apparently continued long after discharge from parole. Those neurotic youths who had received a traditional commitment to an institution followed by parole had been convicted of 19 per cent more crimes within four years after receiving a favorable discharge than a comparable group of CTP graduates. Thus, for a substantial portion of the youthful offender population (neurotics constituted nearly 50 per cent of youths assigned to CTP), a disposition which left the child in the community was superior to commitment to an institution.[10]

By these same measures the remaining types, i.e., power-oriented youths and passive conformists, did less well in CTP programs than those who had received more traditional kinds of dispositions. Clearly, community placement is not better for every type of juvenile that comes before the courts.

Encouraged by the success of the Community Treatment Project, California inaugurated a probation subsidy program in 1966 whereby counties were reimbursed by the state for expenses involved in diverting juveniles from the California Youth Authority (CYA) to their own probation services. By July 1, 1971 substantial headway had been achieved. Juvenile commitments to CYA had been reduced by 41 per cent, and several other states were considering a similar system for encouraging the use of probation.[11]

We have seen that about 80 per cent of adults on probation make a satisfactory adjustment. With juveniles the figure is between 75 and 80 per

---

[8] Ted B. Palmer, "California's Community Treatment Program for Delinquent Adolescents," *Journal of Research in Crime and Delinquency*, 8 (January, 1971), 74–92.

[9] Ted B. Palmer, "The Youth Authority's Community Treatment Project," *Federal Probation*, 8 (March) 1974, 1–14.

[10] Both the interpersonal maturity typology and the claims of success made by the directors of CTP have come under considerable criticism. See Jerome Baker and Doris S. Heyman, "A Critical Appraisal of the California Differential Treatment Typology of Adolescent Offenders," *Criminology*, 10 (May, 1972), 3–58, and Paul Lerman, "Evaluative Studies of Institutions for Delinquents," *Social Work*, 13 (July, 1968), 55–64.

[11] Department of Youth Authority, *Annual Report, 1971*, Sacramento, California, 1972, p. 33.

cent. Moreover, it is estimated that as many as 90 per cent of all delinquents in court for the first time can be safely placed on probation, and as high as 50 to 75 per cent of those appearing in court for the second or third time.[12] Thus, there is still a long way to go before we have fully exploited probation in dealing with juveniles.

REASONS FOR DIFFERENT TYPES OF DISPOSITION

Each judge makes his own decision as to disposition. The probation officer or a clinic may make recommendations, but the judge is under no compulsion to follow them if he thinks something else may work better. Parents may make appeals, and the child may make requests, but these too are subject to the judge's authority. The personal element is a very profound factor.

In general young children, first offenders, and minor offenders are likely to be placed on probation. The child with a stable and intact family, or who is accompanied to court by an interested and responsible minister, recreation leader, or other adult willing to help, may be granted probation.

The recidivist who has perhaps failed to amend his conduct under previous probation, the serious offender, and the older offender are more likely to be committed to a training school. The child from a broken and perhaps completely disintegrated home is often sent to the training school, especially if no one comes forward to befriend him and give him care. The young child in this situation may be thought of as neglected more than delinquent, even though his behavior is troublesome, and may be placed in a foster home or an institutional home for such children, but not as a rule in the training school. (A few unfortunate children of this type are committed to correctional schools.)

Some judges find it difficult to understand the motives, aspirations, and frustrations of a child from another social class. Most judges are middle class; most juvenile delinquents who come before the court are lower class children. The differences in values of the two classes have already been discussed at length. Behavior that seems normal and advantageous to the lower class child— or his parents—may seem delinquent to the judge. Even when the lower class child commits a delinquency that his own class condemns, the middle class judge may not understand how the lower class situation nevertheless led the child into the delinquent act. Commitment is likely to follow.

Some judges are punitive in their attitude toward delinquency. They may hold a personal philosophy of vengeance, or, if they serve part of the time as criminal judges, they may be unable to shake off the punitive philosophy of

12 Austin H. MacCormick, "The Community and the Correctional Process," *Focus*, 27 (May, 1948), 88.

the criminal court and assume the rehabilitative attitudes appropriate for the juvenile court judge. The urge to punish may be especially strong when the judge faces a child of another race or social class, who is to him an unintelligible alien. Such judges tend to commit children to correctional schools.

Most judges, however, accept the general philosophy in the United States that children should not be sent to training schools except as a last resort. The small percentage of delinquents committed to training schools confirms this statement. Harsh treatment and brutality in some schools tend to overshadow the rehabilitative treatment of other schools. In addition, the fear always exists that the mildly delinquent child will become more delinquent from association with more thoroughly delinquent children in the school. He may come to think of himself as a delinquent—an outcast—and carry this attitude back to his home, school, and community when he is released. But in his own peer group he may achieve status and importance because he has "done time" in a training school, associated with older "big shots," and learned new ways to "get by." Because of these hazards, many juvenile court judges hesitate to commit a child.

The judge has no set rules to guide him, as has the judge in a criminal court whose decision, if not already made for him by the jury, must fall within legal limits that set the range of punishment for each crime. In theory at least, the juvenile court judge's concern is not punishment per se but the welfare and future development of the child and the safety of the community. Each case is an individual one, and each disposition should be made in terms of the needs of the individual child and the welfare of the community. The responsibility of the judge is considerable, and for this reason he needs personal qualities of a high order as well as a knowledge of law. He also needs the assistance of well-trained probation officers and a well-staffed clinic.

Probation

The child placed on probation remains in the community, usually in his own home, and carries on the normal activities of a child of his age and sex. Although there may be a slight stigma to being on probation, it does not condemn a child as a delinquent, as commitment to a correctional school does. The purposes of probation according to a California study are as follows:

1. In accordance with the scope of the Welfare and Institutions Code of the state of California, to make plans for and to readjust delinquent, dependent, and neglected children by:
   (a) Helping the child recognize and understand his needs and

problems and develop personal resources to meet them;
(b) Assisting parents to understand their children and give them guidance;
(c) Coordinating appropriate community services for the benefit of the family.
2. To protect children from harmful community influences, including unfit parents and other adults, and to help them develop resistance to the impact of these influences.
3. To protect the welfare of the community through reduction or elimination of delinquent behavior.[13]

The Probation Plan

Whatever the local conception is of the purpose of probation for the child, it begins with a plan agreed upon by the judge and the probation officer. This plan takes into account the social investigation, the child himself, his parents, and community facilities.

The judge may place certain obligations upon the child and his parents. In general the conditions include obedience of the child to his parents, regular attendance at school, being at home at an early hour in the evening, and avoiding disreputable companions and places. In addition, the judge may make special stipulations. Depending upon the acumen of the judge, such stipulations may or may not be helpful. If they are beyond the powers of the child or his parents to accomplish, they hinder adjustment. Such was the requirement that one judge laid on a child of mediocre intelligence that he must make grades of B. Another judge forbade earnest but helpless parents to whip a teen-age daughter but gave no help on how they should help her control her behavior. Other stipulations may lead toward rehabilitation, for example, that a moody or explosive child should be taken to a guidance clinic or that a restless child should explore the possibilities of a community center.

Judges differ greatly in their attitudes toward financial obligations. The Advisory Council of Judges of the National Probation and Parole Association states that fines and financial restitution for damages should be imposed only when they can be made part of the plan of treatment for the delinquent.[14] In either case, the amount should be small enough for the child to be able to earn most of it himself, without imposing an overwhelming burden on his parents. In cases of major vandalism or serious personal injury it is virtually

---

[13] Gertrude M. Hengerer, "Organizing Probation Services," *Reappraising Crime Treatment*, 1953 Yearbook, National Probation and Parole Association, New York, 1954, pp. 45–59.

[14] *Guides for Juvenile Court Judges*, National Probation and Parole Association, New York, 1957, pp. 80–82; Joseph L. Thimm, "The Juvenile Court and Restitution," *Crime and Delinquency*, 6 (1960), 279–286.

beyond the capacity of children to earn any appreciable proportion of the cost. Even small amounts pose difficulties for children still in school. Money payment as fine or restitution may cause the child to feel that such a payment cancels his poor behavior. It may actually interfere with his rehabilitation and development of a feeling of personal responsibility. However, if the amounts are small and help to impress on the child the wrong he has done to some other person, the payments may contribute to his rehabilitation.

The question of who is to pay for damage to property or for hospital and medical bills in case of personal injury is a serious one, since the injured person may not be in a position to pay the expense. Laws differ in various states as to whether fines can be used in juvenile court and the degree to which parents can be held responsible for damage caused by minor children. In addition many states today have victim compensation laws which provide payments to the victims of violent crime whether by juveniles or adults.

IMPLEMENTATION OF PROBATION PLANS. The task of interpreting the conditions of probation to the parents and the child, and of helping them implement the tasks assigned them, falls to the probation officer. If the parents have been instructed to secure certain community services, the probation officer acts as the go-between. The officer also explains that from time to time he will wish to see the child and perhaps the parents, at home, at his office, or in some other convenient meeting place.

The induction of the child and parents into probation is made most smoothly when the probation officer who made the social investigation will also supervise the probation. He is already familiar with the child's situation and at least some of his problems and has made initial contacts with the family.

Any program of redirection or rehabilitation requires time. Theoretically, in many states the child's wardship may extend until his twenty-first birthday. In practice, the judge sets a probation term of six to twelve months. On recommendation of the probation officer and following a review of the case by the judge, this term may be shortened and the case closed. On the other hand it may be extended, or it may be terminated and the child committed to a correctional school. Thus the probation period has considerable fluidity, depending upon the improvement or deterioration of the child's attitudes and behavior.

Many probation officers, especially if they have had training in social casework, view their function in wide terms, extending far beyond simply helping the child abide by court orders. Their goal is not only to bring the child's overt behavior into line but also to rebuild the child's personality.

To carry on casework the probation officer needs not only professional training but also a limited caseload. Fifty children as a caseload is recommended by the Children's Bureau, with a reduction to twenty-five if the officer also makes social investigations. It seems doubtful whether many probation officers are able to keep their caseloads to this number. In 1966 a survey of juvenile courts throughout the fifty states and Puerto Rico found that the median caseload was in the seventy-one to eighty range.[15]

TIME SCHEDULE OF PROBATION OFFICERS. A California study included a detailed analysis of the time schedule of probation work in Los Angeles County.[16] Interviewing, the key to casework, absorbed a third of the time. It was not distributed evenly over all individuals in the caseload. New cases, and especially those involving a serious delinquency, required as much as ten or fifteen hours for the social investigation. Cases of recidivists were also time-consuming. On the other hand, minor offenses required little time for investigation.

Supervision of children already on probation was minimal for at least half the cases. Supervision interviews often lasted only ten or fifteen minutes, time for a few questions and a warning. Other children did not require service, for example, those established in satisfactory foster homes or children awaiting return to another city. However, some children needed more service than they received; recommendations for special medical or clinical care sometimes were not carried out by parents; or the children were known to be continuing in delinquency. These children needed the time that the probation officer did not have to devote to them. It often seemed that routine office matters could not wait, but services to children could be delayed.

The large amount of time spent in travel was for investigations and home interviews; transporting children to court, to clinics, to a new foster home, to a correctional institution; or for returning a runaway child to his home or bringing back a runaway to the local community. In a city where the geographic area served by a given probation officer may be small, travel time may be limited, but in rural areas it may consume many hours. In the California study, probation officers in compact areas in the city of Los Angeles averaged 200 miles a month, but in rural areas mileage might run to 1,500 or even 2,000 miles per month.

The California study raises the question of the importance and necessity of some of the travel and some of the desk work when both cause a reduction in interviewing time and, hence, in casework services.

Other cities face many of the same problems as Los Angeles. In New York City the same crowding out of time for intensive counseling by other obliga-

15 President's Commission on Law Enforcement and Administration of Justice, *Task Force Report: Corrections*, U. S. Government Printing Office, Washington, D. C., 1967, p. 140.

16 Hengerer, *op. cit.*, p. 51.

tions occurs, and travel time is increased by a policy of assigning children to probation officers of the same religion; the officer, therefore, often has a widely scattered distribution of cases, with several officers of different religious backgrounds covering the same area. The probation officer has to be in the courtroom when one of his cases is called; while he knows the day upon which the case would come up, he might not know the hour since some preceding cases require little time and some a long period. In one New York City court, facilities for calling the probation officer from his office to the courtroom are inadequate with the result that the officer has to wait in the courtroom or adjacent corridor for his case to be called. Sixty to ninety minutes are regarded as routine, with some waits of two or three hours.[17]

Close contacts with probationers are difficult to maintain, partly because of lack of time and partly because arranging meetings with the children is extremely difficult. One officer arranged to interview his boys in a library where he had a comfortable room for the purpose.[18] He planned to see them twice a month. Thirty boys would be notified when to come; about twenty would appear. In three hours these boys were interviewed, an average of nine minutes each. Some boys had longer interviews, compensated for by very brief contacts with others. The interviews tended to become a matter of routine inquiry, about school, recreation, home, and church. Interviews held in the regular office of the probation officer were often far from satisfactory, with many interruptions and lack of privacy.

Visits to the boys' homes were also scheduled, but, since they were unannounced, the officer found no one home in approximately half the cases. Officers who are especially interested in their work sometimes make calls after the working day has ended in order to catch employed parents at home. No extra compensation is allowed the officer, although evening hours at his office are paid for.

Even well-trained and dedicated probation officers find themselves seriously handicapped by the multiplicity of duties and the drain on their time through travel, waiting for cases to be called, and fruitless house calls.

AUTHORITARIAN ASPECTS OF PROBATION

A widely held tenet of casework is that the client must come voluntarily to the agency and be able to reach good rapport with the caseworker. The caseworker must be permissive and nonauthoritarian. Casework agencies some-

---

[17] Alfred J. Kahn, *A Court for Children, A Study of the New York City's Children's Court*, Columbia University Press, New York, 1953, Chapter 7.

[18] *Ibid.*

times do not like to accept children referred by juvenile courts because the child may feel he is compelled to come. Many trained caseworkers do not like to accept positions as probation officers because they must work within the confines of legal and court conditions of probation.

The real danger in this authoritarian situation is not that there are legal boundaries—there always are—but that the probation officer may use his position and relation to the court to threaten the child with another court hearing or commitment to an institution. In order to help the child and his parents in more than a superficial manner, the probation officer must gain their trust and confidence. It is not necessary, possible, or desirable for him to set aside the responsibilities of his position. He is charged not only with helping the child but with preserving the safety and welfare of the community. At times the latter function takes precedence over the former. The child and his parents should never be permitted to look upon the probation officer as their ally in evading their responsibilities. They need to trust him as a representative of orderliness and legality who stands ready to help them in the areas where they have failed to restrain their behavior to fit into the community's expectations and demands.

The child and his parents should understand from the beginning both the position of the probation officer and the legal consequences that will surely follow if they do not or cannot conform. This knowledge is not a threat but reality. The probation officer should stand ready to help them learn how to conform, but not to protect and condone if they fail. He may have to report the child to the court or recommend institutionalization, psychiatric treatment, or transfer to a special school. The child and his parents should know from the beginning that there are possibilities from which the probation officer cannot shield the child, but that he will do all he can to help the child marshal his social and psychological strengths to live in a normal way in the community. If more specialized treatment or institutional confinement becomes necessary it is part of the function of the probation officer to try to give some understanding of why such a step is necessary and the benefit that may result. He does not abandon the child or family if events turn out for the worst rather than the best.

Working with Probationers in Groups

The several advantages of probation over other types of dispositions has encouraged many innovators to propose variations upon the traditional format which in the main enable broader control of the probationers' activities without committing them directly to an institution. No one has been more systematic in this regard than LaMar T. Empey and his associates. In 1956 Empey began a program for habitual offenders fifteen to seventeen years of age at Provo, Utah, in which the major emphasis was upon refocusing the peer group's values and goals via guided group interaction.[19] It was reasoned that since the most effective agent of change among juveniles is the peer group, the best way to reform delinquents is to induct them into prosocial peer groups in which the emphasis is upon constructive, conforming behavior. Boys were expected to attend school and to carry out work assignments, and any failure to do so was brought to the attention of their groups for correction. A similar program was launched in 1964 in Los Angeles.[20] In both cases systematic research was carried out both upon the impact of program on staff and students and upon students' adjustment in the community after release. Although both programs achieved enviable success levels, e.g., at Provo 84 per cent of those who completed the program had not been arrested six months after their release and at Los Angeles 73 per cent of the graduates had not been arrested a year later, neither program was markedly superior to a control group of delinquents who had received more traditional types of dispositions.[21] Empey explained the failure of these experiments by noting that in Provo the probationers against whom the experimental group had been compared underwent an extraordinary increase in success from 55 per cent to 77 per cent (although a 77 per cent success rate is not unusual among delinquents on probation) and that in Los Angeles the experimental program might have been more efficient if it had classified the delinquents into types of offenders and assigned them to an appropriate treatment program.[22]

GROUP THERAPY WITH PROBATIONERS AND THEIR PARENTS. Another use of group therapy in Los Angeles County has a dual purpose—boys meet in one group, and, at the same time, their parents meet with other leaders in another group.[23] Each group has two leaders, a probation officer and a professional consultant, all of whom confer together after each meeting. The groups are formed at the time a boy is placed on probation (groups of girls have not been organized), with about nine boys in a group. Ideally both parents should at-

[19] LaMar T. Empey and Jerome Rabow, "The Provo Experiment in Delinquent Rehabilitation," *American Sociological Review*, 26 (October, 1961), 679–696.

[20] LaMar T. Empey and Steven G. Lubeck, *The Silverlake Experiment*, Aldine Publishing Co., Chicago, 1971.

[21] LaMar T. Empey, "The Provo Experiment: Research and Findings," in *Combatting Social Problems: Techniques of Intervention*, Harry Gold and Frank R. Scarpitti, eds., Holt, Rinehart and Winston, Inc., New York, 1967, pp. 395–404; and Empey and Lubeck, *op. cit.*, p. 256.

[22] Empey, *op. cit.*, p. 403; and Empey and Lubeck, *op. cit.*, p. 274.

[23] Robert H. Geertsma, "Group Therapy with Juvenile Probationers and Their Parents," *Federal Probation*, 24 (March, 1960), 46–52.

tend, but in practice only the father usually attends. The scheme depends upon regular attendance not only of the boy but of at least one parent.

As with the groups of boys described in the preceding section, highly aggressive, schizophrenic, or regressed boys and those with other severe emotional disturbances are banned since they impede rather than enhance the therapy for other members and gain little for themselves. The boys tend to be run-of-the-mine active delinquents, able to express themselves within the normal range of personality variation.

The boys are encouraged to express themselves freely but within the context of their behavior problems. The leaders guide and limit the discussion when necessary, in order to make it as constructive as possible and to prevent verbal brawls. Gradually the boys think through their problems and become aware of different interpretations given to their acts by adults, especially adults in a position of authority.

Meanwhile, the parents are helped to examine their own problems and their relationship to their children and to the community. They are helped to distinguish their marital problems from problems that originate with their children. If they can understand and directly approach their own problems, they are less likely to "take out" their feelings or project blame on their children. They may thus come to see that they are in part responsible for their children's delinquency and need to solve their own problems in order indirectly to help their children. Another value to the family is that they gain a more realistic and less fearful view of probation, as a helping rather than a punitive procedure.

CAMPS FOR PROBATIONERS

Both California and Michigan have established camps for probationers who otherwise would have been committed to correctional institutions. The youths remain at the camps as probationers unless they cannot adjust in camp, when they are returned to the court for further action. The boy's probation officer, who has previously made the social investigation, retains contact with the boy while he is in camp, and supervises him for some months after his release from camp.

Los Angeles County maintains two reception camps, one for boys aged thirteen to fifteen and the other for boys aged sixteen to eighteen.[24] After a period of time in the reception center where the boy's capacities are evaluated and he is prepared for the camp, the boys are transferred to their permanent quarters. The County operates four junior probation camps for the younger boys, all oriented toward school. In addition to the conventional subjects, the

[24] Bernard Kogon, "Probation Camps," *Federal Probation*, 22 (September, 1958), 34–40.

flexible program includes such activities as woodshop, ceramics, painting, and photography. In some way the boy is given an opportunity to feel a sense of accomplishment. In addition, each boy works for two hours per day.

Older boys are placed in three forestry camps, with the program oriented toward work, with counseling, recreation, and school in the evening.

Through the camp program and a feeling of success in it, and in more subtle ways, as well as in the direct observation of the removal from camp of boys who do not adjust, the boys slowly grasp the idea that good behavior "pays off." The term in camp is indeterminate, but usually lasts from six to nine months. The true test of the program comes, of course, after the boy has returned to his family and customary community environment.[25]

As with the other group-therapy programs discussed, boys who have a long record of delinquent behavior perhaps with previous commitment to a correctional school or who are emotionally maladjusted do not adjust to the camp nor benefit from it. Physically weak or handicapped boys cannot stand up to the physical stresses of camp life. The boys must be of average intelligence or better. Since the camps are unwalled the boys must be sufficiently settled not to walk away.

How Successful is Probation?

The success of any rehabilitation measure is difficult to assess because there is little agreement regarding the definition of success. Do we regard anyone who has avoided commitment to a penal institution as a success? Or do we use a much more stringent criterion: satisfactory community adjustment? Do we use six months as the trial period, or do we extend it to five years? Do we include only those who graduate from the rehabilitation program, or do we include all who enter it including those who are subsequently removed for disciplinary reasons? Since there is no agreement, success in probation has been measured in a variety of ways. Nevertheless, enough information is now available to give us a good estimate of its value as a rehabilitative technique.

The best evidence regarding probation is provided by Scarpitti and Stephenson.[26] They followed 1,210 male delinquents in New Jersey for up to

25 An evaluation of a camp for youthful offenders on probation found broad changes in attitude among the probationers but only a weak relationship between these changes and adjustment in the community after release. See Theodore N. Ferdinand, "An Evaluation of Milieu Therapy and Vocational Training as Methods for the Rehabilitation of Youthful Offenders," *Journal of Criminal Law, Criminology and Police Science* 53 (March, 1962), 49–54.

26 Frank R. Scarpitti and Richard M. Stephenson, "A Study of Probation Effectiveness," *Journal of Criminal Law, Criminology and Police Science*, 59 (September, 1968), 361–369.

four years following their discharge from one of four programs: probation; assignment to a nonresidential group center where guided group interaction and regular work duties were the principal rehabilitative techniques used; assignment to a residential group center with a very similar program; and commitment to the state reformatory at Annandale.

In terms of their personal qualities and social backgrounds, the probationers presented a much more prosocial appearance as a group than the boys given other dispositions, with those committed to Annandale exhibiting the strongest antisocial orientation. Naturally, the more prosocial the boys admitted to a program are, the greater its likelihood of showing a high success rate. Since the probationers were already prosocial, they showed only slight change in attitude during their period of probation. The delinquents in group centers showed the greatest positive change in attitude (mainly an increase in ego-strength and a reduction in anxiety), and the changes exhibited by the reformatory boys during their confinement were largely negative (e.g., a marked increase in hostility). There was no measure of failure at Annandale, but the failure rates of both the probationers while on probation and the boys at the group centers were all similar, between 23 and 28 per cent. Using recidivism as another criterion of failure, i.e., appearance before the juvenile court followed by a punitive disposition, only 15 per cent of the probationers but 48 and 41 per cent of the boys at group centers and 55 per cent of the reformatory boys failed after discharge from their programs.

Since probationers were already much more conforming in attitude and behavior than the other three groups of delinquents, their lower failure rate could be reasonably attributed to this factor and not to probation as such. To rule out this inference, samples of boys from all four groups were matched in terms of their delinquent history, race, and socio-economic status. When these four groups were compared, probationers still showed a lower failure rate: only 21 per cent recidivated, whereas group center boys failed at rates of 45 and 49 per cent, and 56 per cent of the Annandale boys failed after discharge. By all counts probation seems to afford the best opportunity for a young delinquent to reorient himself and avoid subsequent difficulty.

Scarpitti and Stephenson also warn, however, that those boys who failed while on probation presented a distinctly negative picture. They were markedly different in terms of personality characteristics and social background from other probationers, and their recidivism rate was much higher than failures in other programs. Probation seems to be highly effective, but only if it is granted to those who are least delinquent. If a mistake is made, the result is likely to be failure for the child and further delinquency.

An obvious question at this point is, Couldn't probation with all its advantages be extended to seriously delinquent youths by limiting the caseloads of probation officers, thus giving them time to provide intensive supervision to only a few juveniles who present more serious difficulties? Unfortunately, the problem is not so simple as the question implies. According to recent research into the question, many if not most probationers complete probation successfully without any significant assistance from their probation officers.[27] They succeed not because they were granted probation but because of their own prosocial qualities. There is no evidence that intensive supervision would have any positive effect on probationers with less promising attitudes. Quite the reverse seems likely, since recent studies suggest that much of the probation officer's time is spent with his most difficult cases and that providing him with a smaller caseload results in little if any reduction in the failure rate of his probationers.[28] Once again, we see that an adroit matching of the juvenile with a program relevant to his needs is likely to be much more effective in the long run than simply assigning everyone to the same program no matter what his personal characteristics or the qualities of the program.

BIBLIOGRAPHY

EMPEY, LAMAR T., AND JEROME RABOW, "The Provo Experiment in Delinquent Rehabilitation," *American Sociological Review*, 26 (October, 1961), 679–696.

———, AND STEVEN G. LUBECK, *The Silverlake Experiment*, Aldine Publishing Company, Chicago, 1971.

GEERTSMA, ROBERT H., "Group Therapy with Juvenile Probationers and Their Parents," *Federal Probation*, 24 (March, 1960), 45–52.

GEIS, GILBERT, "Identifying Delinquents in the Press," *Federal Probation*, 29 (December, 1965), 44–49.

Guides for Juvenile Court Judges, National Probation and Parole Association, New York, 1957.

Guides for Juvenile Court Judges on News Media Relations, National Council on Crime and Delinquency, New York, 1965.

KAHN, ALFRED J., *A Court for Children, A Study of the New York City Children's Court*, Columbia University Press, New York, 1953.

PALMER, TED B., California's Community Treatment Program for Delinquent Adolescents," *Journal of Research in Crime and Delinquency*, 8 (January, 1971), 74–92.

———, "The Youth Authority's Community Treatment Project," *Federal Probation*, 38 (March, 1974), 1–14.

[27] R. F. Sparks, "The Effectiveness of Probation: A Review," in *Crime and Justice: The Criminal in Confinement*, Leon Radzinowicz and Marvin E. Wolfgang, eds., Basic Books, Inc., New York, 1971, Vol. III, pp. 211–218.

[28] *Ibid.*, pp. 214–215.

President's Commission on Law Enforcement and Administration of Justice, *Task Force Report: Corrections*, U. S. Government Printing Office, Washington, D. C., 1967, pp. 133–141.

SCARPITTI, FRANK R., AND RICHARD M. STEPHENSON, "A Study of Probation Effectiveness," *Journal of Criminal Law, Criminology and Police Science*, 59 (September, 1968), 361–369.

SPARKS, R. F., "The Effectiveness of Probation: A Review," in *Crime and Justice: The Criminal in Confinement*, Leon Radzinowicz and Marvin E. Wolfgang, eds., Basic Books, Inc., New York, 1971, Vol. III, pp. 211–218.

THIMM, JOSEPH L., "The Juvenile Court and Restitution," *Crime and Delinquency*, 6 (1960), 279–286.

institutions
for delinquents

When Winston Churchill suggested that a civilization could be measured by the quality of its penal institutions, he meant much more than that the ultimate test of a society's humanitarian impulse lies in the treatment it affords its criminals. Crime and punishment tap the wellsprings of society, its cultural center, and in this sense its prisons stand as a symbolic reminder of the meaning of such root concepts as conformity and deviance. But because crime and punishment reflect the cultural core of society, they also arouse extraordinary anxiety among the citizens of a changing, disorganized, pluralistic society. Since there is far from perfect agreement on the meaning of deviance, there is sharp disagreement on the nature of crime and its punishment. And any changes in the definition of crime or in the severity of punishment are likely to excite both firm support and outraged denunciation.[1] The issue of imprisoning juveniles in training schools is perhaps more hotly debated than any other in the whole field of criminology.[2]

The belief is growing today that the imprisonment of delinquents is

[1] See Walter B. Miller, "Ideology and Criminal Justice Policy: Some Current Issues," *Journal of Criminal Law and Criminology*, 64 (June, 1973), 141–162, for the ways in which criminologists on the right and on the left typically view these issues.

[2] See Charles R. Tittle, "Prisons and Rehabilitation: The Inevitability of Disfavor," *Social Problems*, 21 (1974), 385–395, for an analytic discussion of the issue.

morally and pragmatically bankrupt.[3] It forces juveniles who are innocent in the eyes of the juvenile court (they are not legally responsible for their actions) to undergo punishments as psychologically and physically painful as any that adult inmates must experience, which nevertheless only enhance the likelihood of their becoming delinquent again. Imprisonment of juveniles, therefore, is legally questionable, morally wrong, and practically speaking expensive and ineffective. Those who would entirely eliminate large-scale training schools for juveniles are gathering strength, and at least two states, Kentucky (in 1971) and Massachusetts (in 1972) have closed all such institutions. Other states (Florida and Illinois) have closed major institutions, while maintaining the rest at a reduced size.

The debate surrounding these changes has been furious with the critics complaining that community-based treatment centers (see Chapter 21) inundate the state with uncontrollable delinquents and encourage further crime by reducing to nothingness the punishment that delinquents suffer.[4] The evidence either way is ambiguous and the debate is likely to continue into the foreseeable future with the major industrial states progressively turning to small, community-based centers for treating delinquents and the more rural states continuing for the present to utilize more traditional types of punishment.

The function of juvenile institutions as beacons refracting its own definitions of conformity and deviance back upon society can also be discerned in the names and programs of the early institutions established for juveniles.[5] In colonial America there was little need for institutions serving juveniles. Wayward children were dealt with informally in the family and community, and serious crimes by children were handled in the courts much as adult criminality was. But after the Revolution the growing urbanization of American life together with the influx of immigrants changed all that. Many communities spawned ghettos filled with immigrants in which crime and deviancy of various types were common features. Juvenile gangs flourished in these early ghettos, and drifters and criminals from all along the eastern seaboard used them as

---

[3] Dr. Jerome Miller of the Illinois Department of Children and Family Services and formerly Commissioner of Youth Services in Massachusetts has led the attack against training schools in Massachusetts and throughout the nation.

[4] See Brian Vachon, "Hey man, what did you learn in reform school? Well, uh, like how to disconnect a burglar alarm," *Saturday Review of Education*, 38 (October, 1972), 69–76; and Liz Roman Gallese, "Reforming Reform," *Wall Street Journal*, June 12, 1972, p. 1. A more systematic review of the struggle to eliminate state training schools can be found in Lloyd E. Ohlin, *et al.*, "Radical Correctional Reform: A Case Study of the Massachusetts Youth Correctional System," *Harvard Educational Review*, 44 (February, 1974), 74–111.

[5] Our comments about early juvenile institutions are based largely on Robert M. Mennel, *Thorns and Thistles*, University Press of New England, Hanover, N. H., 1973.

havens from the law.[6] Moreover, troops of homeless children and adults began to appear in the major cities with the result that early in the nineteenth century institutions for neglected and homeless children as well as delinquent children were built in Boston, New York, and Philadelphia.

Shortly after the turn of the century the Boston Female Asylum, the New York Orphan Asylum, and the Boston Asylum and Farm School for Indigent Boys were established for homeless children, and in the 1820's Houses of Refuge were opened in New York (1825), Boston (1826), and Philadelphia (1828) for the care of juvenile delinquents.[7]

These early institutions were founded for the most part by private philanthropists who hoped to redeem young people in danger of being corrupted by city life. They saw the remedy for delinquency in a thoroughgoing regimen of religious instruction, school, and work. In their eyes evil was a constant companion tempting man to perdition, and it had to be overcome by cultivating man's higher nature through education and religion and by filling his hours with work. In this context work was not seen so much as an avenue to a social position and a meaningful career but as a convenient bulwark against worldly temptation. While in the institution the children were subjected to stern discipline, and the most common form of discharge was under an apprenticeship to an adult, who more often than not was a stranger to the child.

Akin to the effort to redeem children through an emphasis upon religion and work was the placing-out system in which children from the slums of New York and Boston were sent to farm families as far away as Michigan and Illinois.[8] If the city and its temptations were a major factor in delinquency, an obvious solution was to remove delinquents to rural areas where wholesome family life and close neighborliness were still the custom. Placing-out was utilized heavily by the Children's Aid Society of New York City in the 1850's, and it was practiced in other cities during the same period as well. It was seen as an alternative to institutionalizing juveniles, but it was based on much the same view of delinquency and its cure.

By the 1840's, however, industrialization was already well developed in the Northeast, and in its wake the conceptions of virtue and crime shifted perceptibly. Crime was no longer simply the result of a moral struggle in which the individual was responsible for his misdeeds. It was increasingly regarded as a deterministic process in which faulty heredity had doomed the individual to an inferior, if not criminal, status in society, and its ultimate solution was

[6] Cf. Herbert Asbury, *The Gangs of New York*, Alfred A. Knopf, New York, 1927.

[7] Mennel, *op. cit.*, pp. 1–13.

[8] *Ibid.*, pp. 35–44.

to be found in careful scientific studies of the phenomenon.[9] Nevertheless, delinquents still had to be cared for, and the several states set about building state reform schools. In 1847 Massachusetts built the State Reform School for Boys at Westborough and in 1856 the State Industrial School for Girls at Lancaster. Soon New York (1849) and Maine (1853) followed Massachusetts' lead, and in 1857 Ohio established the Ohio Reform or Farm School. By 1900 thirty-six states had similar institutions.

Although delinquents were no longer seen as morally culpable, conditions in these institutions, if anything, deteriorated. There were numerous reports of violence against staff members, arson against buildings, and brutality against children.[10] The program still emphasized work—not to avoid temptation, but to make a profit. Contract labor became commonplace in juvenile institutions and many of them made a significant contribution toward their own expenses.[11] Before the Civil War many of the institutions in populous states had been filled to capacity and more, and all too soon they began to resemble the prisons of adult criminals more than "reform" schools for children.[12]

By the end of the nineteenth century, however, the forces for change were gathering. Several attempts to establish more humane settings for delinquents were introduced. In 1890 William R. George established a camp for dependent and delinquent children at Freeville, New York which provided a considerable degree of self-government to its "citizens."[13] He named it the George Junior Republic, and before long institutions with similar philosophies and programs had opened throughout the country. In Great Britain Sir Evelyn Ruggles-Brise opened the first Borstal institution at Borstal, Kent for youthful offenders in 1900. It was patterned after Elmira Reformatory, which Zebulon Brockway had established in 1877, and it sought to humanize imprisonment by breaking down the barriers between staff and inmates and by instilling a philosophy of rewarding achievement instead of punishing failure.

The science of psychology was also beginning to make significant headway in the study of the mind, and its proponents quickly interested themselves in abnormal and delinquent behavior. They were interested in delinquency not as the stigmata of a biologically inferior individual but as the outgrowth of an anguished mind. In 1899, as we saw in Chapter 15, a juvenile legal code singled out juveniles for particular treatment in Illinois, and about this same time

9 *Ibid.*, Chapter 3.
10 *Ibid.*, pp. 55–62, 107–110.
11 *Ibid.*, pp. 59–62.
12 *Ibid.*, pp. 57–58.
13 *Ibid.*, pp. 116–120.

psychiatrists and psychologists in the United States and Europe became interested in their distinctive psychological characteristics as well. In 1909 the Juvenile Psychopathic Clinic was founded in Chicago with Dr. William Healy as its director, and by World War I similar clinics for the study of delinquents were opened in Massachusetts, Ohio, and Michigan. In Europe August Aichorn was developing a psychoanalytic theory of delinquency and in 1918 he opened an institution for delinquents near Vienna.

During the 1930's and 1940's several private institutions for delinquents were established in which various forms of psychotherapy were practiced to rid the child of delinquency. Bruno Bettelheim became director of the Sonia Shankman Orthogenic School in Chicago in 1944, and Fritz Redl founded Pioneer House in Detroit in 1946. There were few systematic evaluations of these early attempts to cure delinquency through psychotherapy, and little evidence that they were effective. But as America became an affluent, bureaucratic society, it no longer regarded delinquents as degraded and beyond hope. Instead they were pictured as the victims of intemperate parents and intolerant communities, and instead of treating them like little criminals in prison, it seemed more appropriate to treat them like patients in hospitals. In the 1950's and 1960's state institutions for juveniles came under considerable pressure to develop more effective methods for helping delinquents, and a variety of new techniques was introduced, e.g., milieu therapy, transactional analysis, and positive peer culture. Institutions that had resisted change for nearly a century suddenly were obliged to transform their philosophy, purpose, and structure in the early 1960's.

Many state training schools began to shift from punitive custodial programs to more humane treatment programs. In 1969 the Federal Bureau of Prisons opened the Robert F. Kennedy Youth Center at Morgantown, West Virginia, and its skillfully designed therapeutic and training programs emerged as models for the rest of the nation. Soon several states had developed institutions with similar programs of their own.

With the profound demoralization of America following the Vietnam War, however, many observers began to question the usefulness of juvenile institutions generally, and in the absence of sound evidence to the contrary many penologists, judges, and others concluded that they were inherently ineffective both as treatment centers and as custodial institutions. Confidence in institutions generally waned and the treatment of juvenile delinquents was turned back to the community (as during the colonial period) in the form of group homes, halfway houses, temporary shelters, and in an even greater use of probation (see Chapter 21).

It is clear that the treatment of juvenile delinquents is a very sensitive indicator of the changing public mood. However much we may seek to base the treatment of delinquents on sound scientific principles, in the last analysis it is public opinion that will chart the focus and structure of such programs. Development in technique and understanding depends not simply on artful research but also on finesse in shaping the public image of promising programs. Skill in public relations is becoming almost as necessary for directors of juvenile treatment programs as skill in therapeutic programming.

The Utilization of Juvenile Institutions

On June 30, 1971, 35,931 children were being detained in 192 training schools scattered throughout the United States, and another 2,486 juveniles were held temporarily in seventeen reception or diagnostic centers.[14] On that same date 7,074 children were living in ninety-six group homes, halfway houses, or shelters. Thus, despite the general disenchantment with large institutions, about 84 per cent of the juveniles being detained for relatively long periods were still being held in training schools which contained on average 184 inmates. The average length of stay in these institutions was 8.7 months. There were 106 training schools for boys, fifty-one for girls, and thirty-five for both boys and girls. Coed institutions, however, generally kept the boys and girls segregated except in school and in other closely supervised situations. Males outnumberd females in all institutions 3.5 to 1.

Although the utilization of training schools has declined in recent years, in 1971 16 per cent of them held more children than they were designed for, and another 62 per cent were at or near their capacity. Only 21 per cent were operating at less than 70 per cent of capacity. Sixty-one per cent were designed to hold 150 children or more and 21 per cent had a capacity of 300 or more.[15] Eighty-eight per cent of the training schools offered both vocational and academic educational programs, and over 90 per cent made use of both individual and group counseling. Well over 90 per cent offered their inmates recreation in the form of radios, movies, TV, libraries, gymnasia, or athletic fields, and 81 per cent provided infirmaries for their health care.

These institutions were administered by 24,037 full-time personnel with an average of 1.5 children per staff member. Only 145 psychologists or psychi-

---

[14] The statistics in this section were abstracted from National Criminal Justice Information and Statistics Service, *Children in Custody*, U. S. Government Printing Office, Washington, D. C., 1974, pp. 1–19, unless otherwise indicated.

[15] The maximum size for training schools recommended by the President's Commission on Law Enforcement and Administration of Justice was 150. See *Task Force Report: Corrections*, U. S. Government Printing Office, 1967, Washington, D. C., p. 212.

atrists were serving the 35,931 children, but there were also 966 social workers, 3,173 teachers, and 9,845 cottage staff members. These institutions cost $248,234,000 to operate in 1971, or $6,775 per child.

THE TRAINING SCHOOL PROGRAM

A training school is a custodial residential school for children, usually operated by the state. It receives delinquent children committed to it by the courts, primarily juvenile courts. Occasionally it is used also for other children in need of care, such as children awaiting trial, or feebleminded, neglected, or dependent children. In general, however, it is limited to delinquent children. In distinction from detention homes, the training school is designed for long-term care, that is, the period of time children remain is not measured in days or weeks, as in the detention home, but in months or years.

In addition to the minimum function of maintaining custody over the children and thus segregating them from the community, the training school has the full-time care of the children and must provide housing, food, education, recreation, religious training, adult supervision, and medical and dental care for them. The responsibilities of parents are superseded by those of the school and state. In addition, the school has the function of trying to change the delinquent attitudes and habits of the children so that when they leave they will not get into further trouble with police or courts and at best will have better balanced personalities and constructive attitudes. The formulation of training school functions and the methods used to achieve them differ from school to school and, as we have seen, have changed several times since training schools were first established.

THE CHILDREN COMMITTED. The committed child has been rejected by the community and temporarily exiled. Sometimes the parents, in despair, urge the judge to commit their child, thus explicitly rejecting him. The child tends to look upon commitment as a form of imprisonment and enters the institution in a hostile, fearful frame of mind. A few children from seriously deprived backgrounds soon learn, however, that the institution offers food, recreation, and protection from many of the hazards of street life. For some therefore it offers a haven from the dangers and uncertainties of their own communities. After an initial period of trial and error most children learn to adjust to institutional life, but a few do not. For a variety of reasons they cannot accept the close supervision of the school or association with other delinquents and they demonstrate their resistance in a number of ways including running away. Children committed to training schools then are not all of one type. They are individual personalities who react in many different ways to the institution and its regimen.

Offenses—The range of offenses of committed children does not differ from that which brings children to the attention of the court, but the concentration of offenses in certain categories does differ. In juvenile court about 75 per cent of the judicial cases involved adult offenses, but nearly 99 per cent of the children in training schools were adjudicated delinquents, i.e., convicted of adult offenses. The rest were being held pending court action, awaiting transfer, or were dependent and neglected children.

The Experienced Delinquent—We have already commented on the vast amount of unrecorded delinquency (see Chapter 3). The offense for which a juvenile is ultimately committed to an institution typically reflects only a small portion of his delinquent activity. Indeed, it is usually the last in a long series of offenses—the one that broke the camel's back. In fiscal year 1971, 61 per cent of the 67,558 children admitted to training schools were committed for the first time, 8 per cent had been there before, another 18 per cent were committed for parole violations, and nearly 8 per cent were transferred there, usually from a reception and diagnostic center. A large majority of those who had never been to a training school before had an extensive delinquent history before commitment. A study of the juveniles committed for the first time to Texas training schools in 1970–71 revealed that 75 per cent of the boys and 55 per cent of the girls had had a formal court record prior to the misbehavior that led to their commitment.[16]

I.Q. Scores and School Failure—A number of state reports give extensive information on the mental abilities of children in training schools. For example, the Boys Training School at Kearney, Nebraska admitted and tested 409 boys between July 1, 1969 and June 30, 1971. Sixteen per cent were in the above normal range, i.e., an I.Q. of 110 or above; 53 per cent were in the normal range, i.e., between 90 and 109; and 31 per cent were below normal, i.e., lower than 90.[17] Admittedly, children in training schools are not highly motivated to do well on I.Q. tests, and so these figures undoubtedly underestimate the I.Q. levels of the boys involved. Nevertheless, in a large, randomly selected population of children, about 60 per cent fall in the normal range and 20 per cent fall above and below this level. The Boys Training School admitted nearly twice as many boys with below normal I.Q. scores as with above normal I.Q. scores.

Much the same story is revealed when we examine the educational level of training school children. Of the 309 children admitted to institutions in Iowa in fiscal year 1971, 47 per cent were at or above their grade level for their

---

[16] Texas Youth Council, *Annual Report, 1971*, Austin, Texas, 1972, Table 9, p. 80.

[17] Mimeographed report, no title, no date.

age.[18] But 33 per cent were at least one year behind, and 10 per cent were three or more grades behind. These patterns in both I.Q. level and school failure are repeated in other training schools throughout the United States, although the specific figures may vary somewhat from state to state.

Intelligence test scores and failure in school bear some relationship to one another, but without speculating on the precise relationship, we nevertheless see here the limits within which the training school must shape its program if it is to help the children it receives.

Age—The legal ages for commitment to training schools cover a wide range. The upper limit for commitment is the upper age of juvenile court jurisdiction. In many states, however, youth may be retained in the school until age twenty-one, provided they have been committed for a delinquent act that occurred before the upper age of juvenile court jurisdiction. The lower age limit varies greatly. Many states have no minimum age below which juveniles may not be committed to an institution, and in 1971 39 per cent of those serving boys contained children under twelve years of age.[19] Seventeen per cent of the training schools serving girls held children under the age of twelve. A few states, e.g., Illinois, have no minimum age for adjudicating a child a delinquent but restrict the commitment of delinquents to institutions to those thirteen and over. Nearly half (48 per cent) of the institutions for boys contained no children younger than twelve, and another 14 per cent contained no one under fifteen. Since the upper age limit of the legal definition of delinquency is at least sixteen in most states, most training schools have children sixteen years old and older. The oldest resident in 89 per cent of the boys' training schools was at least sixteen, and the oldest female resident in 93 per cent of the girls' training schools was sixteen or older. The bulk of children in training schools therefore fall between the ages of twelve and sixteen. Some states maintain separate schools for younger adolescents and older adolescents with appropriate adjustments in their programs, especially in education and work.

Health—In many training schools each child is given a thorough physical examination upon entrance, and an effort is made not only to treat obvious illnesses but to upgrade the child's general standard of health and to give care. Testing and treatment for venereal disease and tuberculous conditions are routine, not only for the health of the child but to prevent infection of others in the school. Some schools immunize all students against polio, diphtheria, whooping cough, and tetanus and vaccinate all against smallpox. Glasses are

[18] Iowa Department of Social Services, *Annual Report, 1971*, Des Moines, Iowa, 1972, Table 12, p. 34.

[19] *Children in Custody*, Tables 9 and 10, p. 12.

supplied when needed. One school which admits approximately 160 students each year and has a total residence group of 350 students gives a complete dental examination upon entrance, supplies whatever dental work is needed, and meets dental needs as they arise later. In a period of two years, 1,200 fillings were put in, fifteen dentures were supplied, and other dental work was done for the students.

Mental health is also a problem among a small minority of boys and girls. Many states lack special hospitals for treating seriously disturbed children, and those which have them are often reluctant to treat delinquent children in them. The great majority of children in training schools are not disturbed to the point of not being able to adjust minimally, but the few who are deeply disturbed not only fail to benefit from the program but are generally disruptive as well. Thus many if not most training schools encounter a few children with deep emotional disturbances who are clearly beyond their capacity to help.

Family Background—The evidence is unequivocal.[20] More training school children come from broken homes than is true for delinquents in general or for nondelinquent children. Even in the smaller training schools with a limited number of children, the variety of broken and incomplete homes is very great, each suggesting different problems in the child's background. In one training school with 129 boys, parents were living together in 40 per cent of the cases, while the remaining 60 per cent were unevenly distributed into the following twelve types: parents separated, parents divorced, mother deserted, father deserted, mother insane, stepfather in the home, stepmother in the home, father dead, mother dead, father in prison, foster parents, child illegitimate (not stated where he lived). Other lists include children with adoptive parents or a background of residence in institutional homes.

When economic or occupational background of parents is given, the number receiving public assistance or who are unemployed or working at unskilled labor is large. Information on parental deficiencies indicates a high percentage of alcoholic parents or ones who are criminally inclined. All these factors have already been shown in earlier chapters to be more highly associated with delinquent than with nondelinquent children. Training school children are more likely than other delinquent children to have parents who have been unable to meet the stresses of life.

What the Training School Has to Cope with—Training school boys and girls are not the savages nor the mental defectives that they are sometimes painted to be, but neither are they a cross section of public school children.

[20] See, for example, Sheldon and Eleanor Glueck, *Unraveling Juvenile Delinquency,* Harvard University Press, Cambridge, 1950, Chapter VIII.

They are children handicapped with a variety of social and personal disabilities that do not yield easily to treatment techniques routinely applied in institutions.

A typical training school boy might look something like this:[21] He had a long history of delinquency prior to commitment to the training school. He was first arrested at 13.4 years; he has used marijuana and dangerous drugs; he had at least three arrests and one commitment before being committed to the training school this time; and nearly all of his friends were delinquents. Although he was in at least the tenth grade at commitment, he was reading at the eighth-grade level; he was involved in school misbehavior on a regular basis; and his attitude toward school was indifferent or worse. He had an I.Q. of 92 and no evidence of serious psychological disturbance. His family was relatively poor; neither parent had graduated from high school; and they were separated.

PROGRAM OF TRAINING AND TREATMENT. The impact of training and treatment is to some extent related to the period of time spent in the institution. Training schools vary greatly as to the length of time that they retain children before release. In a few schools the median length of stay is less than six months; in a few others eighteen or more months. The median for all schools, however, is 8.7 months. Each school has its own formal program; these programs are similar in many ways but vary according to the degree to which methods have shifted from punishment to treatment.

Reception-Orientation—A state with a number of training schools operating under one state agency may have a special reception and diagnostic center, usually of recent origin. Boys and girls are received at this center directly from the court and remain a matter of weeks. A psychologist gives tests to determine intelligence, proper school placement, degree of maturity, social attitudes, aptitudes, and other facts valuable in planning a program for the child. A complete physical examination is given not only to rule out infectious diseases but to reveal strengths and weaknesses and any handicaps that may be remedied. A psychiatrist may interview all children or only those apparently in need of special therapeutic treatment. A report from the court may come with the child, covering his social background; otherwise, a social worker investigates this area. The chaplain usually talks with the child. The child's behavior is also observed during the period in the reception center, and he is given some help in orienting himself to institutional life and its restrictions and possibilities. A complete report is drawn up. A case conference on each child results in a summary of his needs and abilities, and a program is outlined for him.

---

[21] This portrait was abstracted from California Youth Authority, *Annual Report, 1970*, Sacramento, California, p. 26.

In many states, the reception-orientation process is carried out in the school itself, where one building or a suite of rooms may be set aside in which each child can be studied, usually on a less extensive basis than outlined above, and a plan made for him before he is assigned to his cottage, classes, work, and so on. In small institutions, the procedure may be very limited and informal. The superintendent, chaplain, school principal, and perhaps a few other members of the personnel talk with the child, advise him on acceptable behavior, and assign him to his cottage and activities. Often there is very little choice of living quarters or activities. Many small institutions have little or none of the psychological or social work services found in larger institutions.

Education—The activities in a typical training school fall into several well-defined areas, all designed to fill the student's time as well as to retrain or rehabilitate him. Younger children, especially, spend a large part of their time in school. As a rule, training schools do not attempt an exact duplication of the public school program, although they provide for academic training. By testing or experience, students are placed in groups where they can do the work or are allowed to work along an individual plan under the supervision of the teacher. In many training schools, an effort is made to give the student an experience of success at whatever level he can manage. At the same time, academic education cannot be overlooked, since within a year most boys and girls will return to their homes and must re-enter public school.

Students who seem totally unsuited to an academic program are given training in simple skills, not necessarily with vocational intent. For example, boys with limited scholastic aptitude may be relieved of their academic responsibilities and assigned to various types of work on the grounds. Many training schools still operate farms—a carry-over from the nineteenth century when a rural environment was regarded as wholesome. Boys spend considerable time doing farm work under supervision. Since they are usually city boys this work cannot be thought of as vocational in purpose; it does, however, give the experience of steady occupation under supervision and often opens the way for a friendly relationship between boys and farm supervisors.

Training schools also have some specific vocational training that is oriented toward the time of release. For the boys such things as woodworking, machine shop, shoe repairing, painting, printing, auto mechanics, and electrical work are popular. The objective is not to turn out skilled craftsmen but to give some orientation to an occupation. Girls are usually given experience in housekeeping through the operation of their cottage. In some training schools, girls may learn the entire routine of the beauty parlor and, if they are successful, secure a state license to practice as a beautician, with no indication on the license as to where the training was received.

Some schools expand training by arranging for employment in some nearby community, under careful supervision.

Recreation and Social Life—Another round of activities comes under the heading of recreation. For both boys and girls much of this is of the active type, carried on outdoors in warm weather. Boys may have a highly developed system of athletics, sometimes playing against community teams. Marching bands are also popular. Such activities encourage the coordination of personal effort with team goals and a spirit of teamwork—something many boys lack when they enter such schools. Girls may also play team games but are less likely to enter into any serious or outside competition.

Informal activities cover a wide range, including reading and hobbies which may be carried on alone, club activities, motion pictures shown in the school, group singing, and many other recreational activities normal to the age and sex of the students.

Some schools make an effort to involve students in community activities off the grounds; their success depends in part upon the willingness of the community to participate and the degree to which the boys and girls are able to adjust to community expectations of good behavior.

Many schools permit visits home, perhaps for a long weekend, with a longer visit at Christmas or in the summer. The student travels by himself, or his parents are encouraged to call for him and return him. He must, of course, have a home or other assigned place to visit. These visits have a number of therapeutic advantages: they maintain the inclusion of the child in his family and neighborhood; they provide an opportunity for meetings with interested adults such as a school principal, minister, or social worker; and they test the student's ability to avoid getting into trouble back in the old environment and to assume personal responsibility for his own return. On the whole, these visits work out well, with only a few students failing to return or causing trouble during the visit.[22]

Coeducational Activities—The few training schools with both boys and girls in the same institutions, though usually in well-separated cottages, may plan a limited number of joint activities. Some school classes may be shared as well as a limited number of parties, dances, and programs of various sorts, all closely supervised. Free time is not spent together, nor is dating allowed.

A few training schools for girls attempt to arrange an occasional party to

[22] The superintendent of one training school for boys with emphasis on rehabilitation told one of the authors that the impact of their training was sufficient to carry the boy over a short period of a few days or a week, but often the changes accomplished during a few months in the training school were not ingrained deeply enough to offset the pull back to old companions and old delinquent activities when the boy was permanently released from the institution.

which boys or young men from some club or church group in a nearby town are invited. Since the young men must be appealed to from a philanthropic motive, the gatherings lack spontaneity. Natural pair interests are discouraged from developing since there is no opportunity for dating.

Several motives underlie the efforts to have some mixed activities. The customary interest of youth in the other sex is given some satisfaction, and an opportunity is given to teach some of the social graces to boys and girls (especially) who have been all too accustomed to promiscuous sex relations.

Religious Instruction—All schools provide some religious instruction, ranging from a service on Sunday, when a local minister comes to the training school, to the work of a full-time chaplain. Large schools near urban centers with a mixture of boys or girls of different religious backgrounds engage on a part- or full-time basis the services of ministers of the major religions—the Protestant minister, the Catholic priest, the Jewish rabbi. Schools provide chapels which either are reserved primarily for religious services or are multipurpose rooms with the religious paintings or altar concealed by a curtain when the room is used for motion pictures, entertainments, or even athletics. Each religion provides its own equipment for worship.

LIVING ARRANGEMENTS. The hours not spent in organized programs of education, work, and recreation are spent in the living quarters. In most training schools, every effort is made to provide comfortable quarters with as much similarity to normal family living as is possible under the conditions of large numbers of children, of overcrowded buildings, and of enforcement of strict rules to prevent mass disorderliness and running away.

Training Schools for Girls—Training schools for girls usually provide several residential houses if the number of girls makes this economical. Up to thirty girls may be in one house or cottage, as it is usually called. Each girl may have her own room, or small dormitory rooms may be used. The rooms are simply but comfortably furnished, usually with a cot, chest of drawers, chair, and small table. Girls are encouraged to make their rooms attractive by embroidering pillow covers or scarves for the chest. They may have photographs of close relatives.

Many schools pride themselves on providing individual styles of clothing, although these fall within a narrow range of choice in style and material. When uniforms are used, an effort often is made to introduce variety and color. In a southern school, each color indicates a different group of girls or different type of occupation. Blue uniforms are worn to work and after school. Raspberry colored uniforms are worn by the girls who are serving in the dining room, with a change to kelly green for Sundays and special occasions. Chartreuse uniforms are worn by the girls chosen by an instructor to take care of her room and clothing—a position of honor signifying that the girl is trustworthy. White is worn on Sunday morning, with a change to skirt and sweater (color of the girl's choice) for church services. Girls in the isolation cottage wear green for work and yellow for leisure-time activities. A variety of colors are worn by the girls when in school—aqua, rose, moss green, gold, tomato red, pink, mint green, and wine. The uniforms are made at the school. Although a group of girls wears the same color of uniform, each girl has her own individual garments. The color aids supervisors in placing a girl in her proper classification.

The training school cottage typically has a living room, dining room, and kitchen, and sometimes a simple recreation room in the basement. Girls are assigned to different tasks in the course of their stay, working at all the routines and skills of homemaking. In a typical dining room, the girls eat at small tables for four or six girls, with supervisory staff at another table in the same room. An effort is made to teach the girls good manners in dining and quiet comportment at the table. The living room is fully furnished in simple style; sometimes framed pictures painted by the girls are hung on the walls. A radio and television set are typical equipment. The recreation room in the basement may have simple sports equipment or may simply be a room to work off energy. In one training school, girls could roller skate in the basement.

All activities are carried out on a time schedule under supervision. Girls are not allowed to come and go at will. Each girl or small group of girls must be in a certain part of the house at a given time. They all arise at the same time, have a stated number of minutes in which to dress, a certain time when all put their rooms in order, a time to eat, and so on. All retire to their rooms at the same early hour of the evening, and at a given moment lights are turned off from an outside control box.

Attendants are assigned to supervise specific areas. An attendant is in charge at night, not only to prevent misconduct or escape attempts but for security of the girls in case of fire or illness.

Security is increased by screened or barred windows. Doors to remote or unused portions of a building are kept locked, as are outside doors. Doors to sleeping rooms are often locked during the day, thus keeping girls in the common rooms. At night, girls are locked in their rooms.

In appearance the newer structures closely resemble a well-kept small college campus, landscaped and set with attractive buildings distinguishable as living quarters, classrooms, gymnasium, and often a chapel. The interiors of the cottages also suggest college dormitories. It is only when security features are examined that marked differences appear.

Planning activities for many girls to account for all the hours spent in the cottage calls for ingenuity and skill. Simply locking girls in their sleeping rooms is condemned. Activities should be fitted into the general plan for rehabilitation. At the same time, good conduct and security are necessary for the operation of the program.

Training Schools for Boys—Quarters for boys tend to be more institutionalized than those of girls, although often not more so than college quarters and certainly less in many ways than military quarters.

Boys usually sleep in large dormitory rooms, usually with cots or double deck bunks set close together. The rooms tend to look very bare, in contrast to the colorful and livable effects achieved in many of the rooms of girls. Usually an attendant is in charge all night, to prevent any disorderliness or wandering around.

Living and dining rooms and sometimes a recreation room are provided, usually simply but adequately furnished. When the school has a number of cottages, each one usually has only a small serving kitchen; the food is cooked in a central kitchen and brought to the cottages to be served. Boys may have the task of serving, washing dishes, and mopping or sweeping the floors—perhaps after each meal.

As in the girls' quarters, every minute must be accounted for. Free time is filled in with radio or television programs, reading, crafts, or discussion groups. The boys are closely supervised at all times.

Weekends and Holidays—A special problem is presented by weekends and holidays. Usually, parents may visit the training school for some limited period during the weekend. In some schools, students may visit their parents over the major holidays. However, for various reasons, some boys and girls receive no visitors or are not permitted to leave the institution. A program must always be provided for them.

Cottage Personnel—The time spent in the cottage is usually regarded as especially significant for rehabilitation. In spite of scheduling and supervision, the boy or girl has more freedom than in school or at work and is thrown into close association with other students. A different set of personal qualities is revealed, and a less formal relationship with adults (the house parents and other cottage personnel) is often possible than in the formal program.

Cottage personnel and especially the cottage parents are extremely important. In institutions emphasizing treatment as opposed to punitive or custodial programs, they play an important part in each child's rehabilitative plan. Because they have, perhaps, the most intimate relationships with the students of any adult staff member, they are in a good position to have considerable influence both positive and negative over the students they supervise. Indeed, many observers rate them the key to the whole rehabilitative program.

Their crucial role in treatment programs, however, does not imply that house parents must have professional training as social workers or psychologists. They do need certain personal qualities and education to give understanding of human behavior. In a discussion of the qualities that house parents ideally should have, the Children's Bureau includes the following items: attitudes of genuine interest toward the child; sympathy, understanding, and respect; capacity to relate to the child; flexibility; toleration of deviant behavior without condoning it or repressing it punitively; emotional maturity and stability; ability to take hostility; alertness and sensitivity to group situations; moral integrity; acceptable physical appearance; imagination; understanding of the treatment philosophy; ability to make decisions, accept criticism, work under pressure, and follow directions.[23] They must be organizers, preferably skilled in group leadership; they should know when and how to use authority, finding a balance between overpermissiveness and domination. Graduation from college with a sequence in social science or its equivalent in education and experience are desirable.

Recent research suggests, however, that different types of workers are effective with different types of children.[24] For example, there is some evidence that workers who seek to establish close, friendly relationships with youths and want to help them work through emotional problems surrounding independence-dependence feelings or self-confidence are also most effective with youths from intact, middle class families who are verbal, impulsive, and anxious; or hostile and defensive. On the other hand, workers who typically maintain their social distance from youths, are interested mainly in behavior (and not emotional conflicts or feelings) and emphasize self-control and discipline as the best ways of preventing delinquency are most effective with anxious, moderately dependent youths who are seeking a surrogate parent.

TREATMENT PROGRAMS. As we indicated above there has been an efflorescence of techniques for treating delinquents since 1950. In addition to religious, educational, and work programs, which incidentally were regarded as treatment programs in the nineteenth century, there is a plethora of methods and techniques for accomplishing almost any treatment goal. For immature, impulsive, socially deprived children there is behavioral modification, which applies the insights of classical learning theory to the problems many students face in conforming to the simple but inexorable regimen of training schools. There is guided group interaction for those who can explore their innermost feelings

---

[23] *Institutions Serving Delinquent Children, Guides and Goals*, Children's Bureau Publication, No. 360, U. S. Government Printing Office, Washington, D. C., 1957, pp. 44–45.

[24] See Ted B. Palmer, "Matching Worker and Client in Corrections," *Social Work*, 18 (March, 1973), 95–103.

and inhibitions more easily with peers than with adults; there is transactional analysis for those who need to look at their more ineffective interaction patterns from a distinctive viewpoint; there is milieu therapy for those who need a totally supportive environment to master themselves; and there is a host of other programs as well.

The kind of treatment program that a particular institution develops depends very much upon the talents and training of its staff; the techniques that are currently in vogue; and the predispositions of its treatment staff. None of the techniques mentioned above has been proven effective in reorienting delinquents toward socially productive lives, although several have been evaluated outside of juvenile institutions (see Chapter 14). But it is clear that different treatment environments have a rather profound effect upon attitudes of their inmates and upon peer structures.

On the basis of an extensive series of studies on Michigan institutions for juveniles and youthful offenders, it has been established that in contrast to custodial institutions (1) treatment institutions generate favorable attitudes among their inmates toward the programs, the staff, and the institution as a whole; (2) those who are most intensely involved in the informal inmate social system in a treatment setting are also those who are most favorably disposed toward the institution; and (3) in treatment institutions inmate leaders tend to be more positively inclined toward both staff and institution than the inmate body as a whole.[25] All of this means that in treatment institutions the staff is much closer to the inmates; that they are able to mold their attitudes and behavior patterns more effectively; that inmates respond to humane treatment with appreciation; and that in such institutions inmates select as their leaders individuals who are most positive about the staff and institution.[26]

It has not been established yet that *rehabilitation* proceeds best where treatment staff and inmates are on good terms with one another. But certainly

[25] These conclusions were drawn from (1) Oscar Grusky, "Organizational Goals and the Behavior of Informal Leaders," *American Journal of Sociology*, 65 (July, 1959), 59–67; Bernard B. Berk, "Organizational Goals and Inmate Organization," *American Journal of Sociology*, 71 (March, 1966), 522–534. See also Lloyd E. Ohlin, *et al.*, "Radical Correctional Reform: A Case Study of the Massachusetts Youth Correctional System," *Harvard Educational Review*, 44 (February, 1974), 74–111; and Thomas G. Eynon and Jon E. Simpson, "The Boy's Perception of Himself in a State Training School for Delinquents," *Social Service Review*, 39 (March, 1965), 11–19. (2) Berk, *op. cit.* (3) David Street, Robert D. Vinter, and Charles Perrow, *Organization for Treatment*, Free Press, New York, 1966, Chapter 9.

[26] Recent research suggests that a similar pattern of mutually supportive relationships among staff and inmates can also be kindled in girls' institutions where a strict program is administered firmly but benevolently. See Raymond J. Ademek and Edward Z. Dager, "Social Structure, Identification and Change in a Treatment-Oriented Institution," *American Sociological Review*, 33 (December, 1968), 932–944.

it makes the experience of being locked up less difficult for all concerned, and insofar as rehabilitation does depend upon close, positive contact between staff and inmates, it may even have a lasting benefit for the inmates as well.

The Effectiveness of Treatment in Training Schools—There are at least three goals that training schools are generally expected to accomplish: the segregation of seriously delinquent children from the larger community; the preparation of delinquent children for a successful re-entry into the community; and the rehabilitation of delinquent children to the community. It is evident from our previous discussion that the more progressive institutions are having considerable success at modifying intensely antisocial attitudes toward more constructive social viewpoints. But their ability to prevent children from running away and their ability to insure a successful rehabilitation of children to the community are both open to serious question.

There is an inherent contradiction between maintaining close custody over children and the development of effective treatment programs for changing their antisocial attitudes.[27] Close custody inevitably means pervasive control over children within the institution and punitive attitudes toward defiance and nonconformity. Thus, if the first responsibility of an institution is to prevent internal disorders and escapes, it must assume a repressive posture vis-à-vis the children it contains. But as we have seen, a repressive, punitive stance destroys any opportunity for meaningful contact between staff and inmates and eliminates any possibility of staff members' influencing positively the attitudes and beliefs of the inmates. A repressive institution tends to create hostile, antisocial inmates. Accordingly, treatment institutions are notorious for their permissive custodial policies and for their inability to prevent runaways.

No careful research has been done on the question, but it is not unusual for a training school of sizable proportions, i.e., with 200 to 300 children, to have thirty or forty children a month flee during June, July, and August, or to have up to ten children escape in a single incident. People who reside near such institutions often feel considerable anxiety during the summer months because runaways regularly steal cars to make good their escape, or they break into nearby houses to hide or to get food and money. Unfortunately, there is no simple solution because the public desires both treatment institutions and secure institutions, and the two are not easily compatible.

The ability of an institution to rehabilitate its inmates, i.e., to enable them to adjust successfully in their communities after release, is also a difficult problem. There are several meanings that can be given to successful adjustment

27 See Richard McCleery, "Communication Patterns as Bases of Systems of Authority and Power," in *Theoretical Studies in Social Organization of the Prison*, Social Science Research Council, New York, 1960, pp. 49–77.

in the community. For example, a child might be counted a success if he simply avoids being returned to another correctional institution, regardless of his police record or social adjustment in the community. Or he might be counted a success only if he adopts a conventional style of life and avoids all indication of social maladjustment.

The solution is to use several criteria of success. Some institutions may be relatively effective in helping their inmates avoid further imprisonment but have relatively little effect on their ability to fashion meaningful lives in the community. Others may be effective in just an opposite manner. It would be well to know the differential successes of institutions along a graduated continuum of rehabilitation so that intelligent planning could be carried out.

Similarly, the definition of failure presents some difficulty. Some private institutions are able to eliminate those children who respond negatively to their treatment programs by returning them to court for reassignment. But most state institutions have little or no control over their admission policies and are obliged to keep nearly all the children sent to them regardless of their adjustment in the institution. Indeed, children who do not show good progress in such institutions tend to stay longer than those who do. Thus, institutions that can expel uncooperative children gain a certain advantage simply because many of these difficult children are also likely to fail (however defined) after release from the institution. The definition of failure, therefore, should take into account those children who do not complete the treatment program as well as those who do, if comparisons between state institutions and private institutions are to make any sense.[28]

The rehabilitative effectiveness of training schools is difficult to assess, furthermore, because so many other factors in addition to the school's treatment program affect the child's adjustment in the community. First, his own strengths and weaknesses play a major role in his ability to assume a new life in the community. Training schools tend to receive those children with the least personal resources, i.e., low I.Q. and limited social awareness, to adapt successfully to community life, and most treatment programs are powerless to change this fact. Second, the circumstances to which training school children return in the community are often inimical to their rehabilitation. Their families are often profoundly disorganized; most of their friends are delinquent; parents, teachers, neighbors, police, and judges are often bitterly hostile toward them; and there is little prospect for a stable social life for them anywhere. Thus, in the face of these adverse circumstances, the ability of training schools

[28] Paul Lerman, "Evaluative Studies of Institutions for Delinquents," *Social Work*, 13 (July, 1968), 55–64.

to rehabilitate children is severely limited, no matter how skillfully designed their treatment programs may be.

In order to assess training schools and their programs properly, therefore, it is important to measure these external factors, i.e., the social and psychological limitations of the children they receive and the quality of the family and community situations to which children return upon release, in order to measure *their* impact upon the rehabilitative potential of training school children. Few training schools have any degree of control over these circumstances and should not be held accountable for the limits they place on their rehabilitative success rate.

Very little research of this type has been carried out, and accordingly these remarks must be qualified by this fact. But the best evidence available suggests that about half of all training school children subsequently are imprisoned in a jail, training school, or adult institution.[29] Different institutions, however, exhibit different success rates. The Highfields Center in New Jersey was evaluated by H. Ashley Weeks, and his findings indicate that of the 229 boys sent by the court to Highfields between 1951 and 1954, 63 per cent successfully completed treatment and avoided subsequent imprisonment for at least eight months following release.[30] Using the same criterion of success Weeks found that 47 per cent of the 116 boys sent to Annandale, the state reformatory for boys, adjusted successfully after release. A recent analysis of Borstal graduates in Great Britain found that after ten years 63 per cent had recovered from crime, i.e., had assumed noncriminal careers.[31] But using a different criterion—subsequent reconviction—Alan Little discovered that only 44 per cent had achieved a successful post-release adjustment for a five-year period following discharge from a Borstal.[32]

None of these studies considered the differential quality of the inmates assigned to different kinds of institutions. When this factor is taken into account, some very interesting results appear. For example, Benson found that when the different kinds of inmates sent to Borstals and more traditional institutions in Great Britain are controlled for, Borstals are no more effective than traditional penal institutions.[33] Furthermore, after a comprehensive re-

29 *Task Force Report: Corrections*, p. 142.

30 H. Ashley Weeks, *Youthful Offenders at Highfields*, University of Michigan Press, Ann Arbor, 1958, p. 42.

31 Terrence Gibbens and J. Prince, "The Results of Borstal Training," in *Sociological Review*, Monograph No. 9 (1965), 230–239.

32 Alan Little, "Penal Theory, Reform and Borstal Practice," *British Journal of Criminology*, 3 (January, 1963), 257–275.

33 Sir George Benson, "Prediction Methods and Young Prisoners," *British Journal of Delinquency*, 9 (1959), 192–199.

view of seventy-nine studies of rehabilitative programs published between 1945 and 1967, Martinson found *little if any* empirical support for the following hypotheses: "A correctional facility running a truly rehabilitative program . . . will turn out more successful individuals than will a prison which merely leaves its inmates to rot" and "A truly successful rehabilitative institution is one where the inmate's whole environment is directed towards true correction rather than towards custody or punishment."[34] He concluded that "with few and isolated exceptions, the rehabilitative efforts that have been reported so far had no appreciable effect on recidivism."[35]

Martinson's pessimistic conclusions, however, must be tempered by the fact that few of the studies he and his colleagues reviewed sought to analyze the inmate populations into distinct personality types and examine the impact of different treatment programs on each type. When this is done, as in the Community Treatment Project in California, it is likely that some types of inmates will be found to benefit from certain types of treatment programs and not from others. Moreover, the studies cited by Martinson uniformly failed to consider adverse social and psychological factors affecting inmates but which rehabilitative programs were incapable of changing. It is entirely possible that evaluations of rehabilitative programs that take these factors into account will find more promising results.

THE PROBLEM OF PUNISHMENT. As in any grouping of children where rules are imposed, some of the boys and girls break the rules. Such behavior is common in public schools, community centers, churches, and other community groups. It may occur more often in the training school, for these are boys and girls who have been unable to conform to the laws and regulations of their communities and its institutions. Moreover, the training school imposes more rules than most other organizations because greater orderliness is expected.

In addition to cottage regulations there are rules governing the child wherever he goes in the institution. Some institutions may pride themselves on not having children march from one building to another with an attendant or two; but inquiry often reveals that when a child or children leave one building, the attendant there telephones to their destination to state that they have left the one building and should be at the other in a certain number of minutes. If they do not arrive, a search is begun. They are checked at numerous times during the day, unobtrusively, but nevertheless checked.

The constant surveillance creates serious tensions for some boys and

---

34 Robert Martinson, "What Works? Questions and Answers About Prison Reform," *The Public Interest*, No. 35 (Spring, 1974), 25, 33.

35 *Ibid.*, p. 25.

girls. They may deliberately break rules, start fights, run away, or occasionally attack a staff member.

Penalties—Violations of regulations are met in various ways. In a treatment-oriented school, an effort may be made to discover why a student rebels and to make some modifications in his program that will help him adjust better in the future. But when the institution is more traditional, the staff may simply punish the student in one of several ways without considering the motives of his behavior.

For breaking of minor regulations, privileges are often denied for a limited period as a penalty. Good behavior is rewarded by special privileges, awards, transfer to an honor cottage, temporary paroles, and eventually early release.

Disrespect or insubordination to staff is regarded as extremely serious. An impudent or refractory boy or girl usually is promptly removed from the group before disorderliness becomes general. In one boys' school a special officer (equivalent to a police officer in the community) makes the rounds and is called in case of any disturbance. The house parents and professional staff do not attempt to subdue or control a refractory student. This method places control in the hands of a burly man who can quickly remove a boy, and it also reduces the probability that the boy will become hostile to the house parent or staff member.

Institutions typically have some isolation rooms where a recalcitrant boy or girl may be placed. In modern institutions, these rooms may differ little from the usual residence room, except that they are sparsely furnished. In older institutions or those built under the domination of a punitive philosophy, the rooms may be little more than dungeons. In some old institutions they are located in the basement of a building, have little or no light, no furniture, and a heavy solid door with a small observation window through which an attendant may peer. Food may be reduced in quantity and may be very unsavory. Some institutions place a child in isolation only until he quiets down, acknowledges his unruliness, and promises not to repeat his offense; others may leave the child confined as punishment for many days or weeks. During his confinement he may be visited by the chaplain, social worker, or psychologist, and some effort may be made to get at the root of his problems. Where such services are provided, the place and conditions are usually more comfortable than when confinement is thought of as punishment.

A modern isolation unit observed by one of the authors in a boys' training school had well-lighted rooms, with an ample outside window and a small window in the door, all unbreakable by the inmate. An attendant was in the building at all times; the chaplain visited every day. The professional staff worked with the boy. The rooms were unfurnished. At night a mattress was placed in each room, but these were removed during the day as some boys relieved their tensions, anxieties, and boredom by tearing at the mattress. The boys were allowed, one at a time, to have frequent shower baths to reduce tensions. Some of the inside walls of this unit were painted pink.

Physical punishment is generally condemned and often is forbidden by state statutes. However, it continues in many forms and in many institutions, if not as a regular method of discipline then as a way of meeting crises or of dealing with especially obstreperous students. In a boys' training school with many rehabilitative aspects, the superintendent denied the use of physical punishment, but added that if a boy turned on a staff member, "we let him have it." Physical punishment is more likely to occur in boys' institutions than girls' because of the aggressiveness of boys and the differences in types of offenses that bring boys or girls to training schools.

The problem of defiance and unruliness in training schools should not be minimized. Among most boys and girls orderliness may be maintained by rewards for orderly living and denial of privileges for failure to observe regulations. But training schools receive very aggressive boys or girls who do not respond to these methods. Rather than have these few wreck the entire program, schools lock them up or severely punish them either in despair or in retaliation. Sometimes provision is made for their removal from the institution. Many states provide that unmanageable older boys or girls may be transferred to adult reformatories or prisons where close custody is part of the regular regimen. A few states provide psychiatric institutions for treating psychopathic children. But all too often the training school must cope with all the children committed to it.

RUNNING AWAY. One of the more serious problems facing institutions for delinquents today is the runaway. Frequent runaways tend to undermine public confidence in the institution no matter how effective its treatment programs may be overall. But if the institution attempts to deal forcefully with runaways, it confronts the danger of crippling its treatment programs. Most institutions face this dilemma by effecting a compromise. They take every reasonable precaution to discover and apprehend runaways, but they do not punish them severely when they are caught. The standard punishment for running away in one training school is one or two days in isolation and up to six weeks added time in the institution.

There are many reasons why children run from institutions. They may be fearful of the other children. They may rebel against a strict cottage supervisor. They may be homesick, not necessarily for their parents but for their clique or gang. Older boys or girls may become fearful of losing the interest of girl friend or boy friend. They may feel that other children have received privileges that they also deserved—perhaps a visit home. The program may be unstimulating and fail to hold the interest of the child. The student may be on the way to rehabilitation but unable as yet to accept responsibility for remaining in the school. Whatever their reason, however, running from the school often means further problems for both the child and the institution. Some children who make good their escape and avoid further trouble in the community may be allowed to remain at home if they are discovered. But most are simply returned from where they came to complete their assignment.

THE PREGNANT GIRL. Since one of the common problems of delinquent girls is their failure to control their sexual activities, it is inevitable that from time to time a girl who is pregnant is committed to the training school, or a girl already in residence becomes pregnant while on a visit home or in some community contact. Training schools make various provisions for the girl. An earlier practice of arranging for maternity confinements in the infirmary at the school is giving way to taking the girl to a community hospital at the time of confinement or to arranging for her transfer to a home for unmarried mothers. The training school makes arrangements ahead of time for the confinement and also for care of the baby.

It is no longer thought advisable for the baby to remain with the mother in the training school, even though it could be housed in a nursery. If relatives of the girl are not willing or suitable to take charge of the baby, a welfare agency steps into the picture. The baby may be cared for temporarily until the mother is released. In other cases, arrangements may be made for its adoption if the mother so desires or if she seems incapable of caring for the child. In all arrangements, the rights as well as the wishes of the mother must be observed, as some girls wish to keep the custody of their babies and to assume some responsibility for them after their release. Others look upon adoption as the best way out for them and the babies; and of course some girls have poor prospects of becoming dependable mothers able to support and care for their children.

What Lies Ahead?

Unquestionably, the future for juvenile training schools in America is clouded. As we have noted, there is a growing mood of revulsion for large-scale juvenile institutions among penologists, correctional officials, and juvenile judges, and in recent years the rate of institutionalization of juveniles has steadily dropped, although the arrest rate of juveniles has bounded ahead.

Between 1968 and 1970, for example, the rate of institutionalization declined nearly 10 per cent, and the number of children in training schools in the United States on June 30 declined from 45,200 in 1968 to 39,400 in 1970.[36]

Most of this decline represents the reluctance of juvenile judges to send any but the most seriously delinquent children to training schools. One result has been that many more delinquents than formerly are being diverted from large-scale institutions to group homes, YMCA's, foster homes, and independent placements (i.e., living alone). But another result has been that training schools are increasingly receiving just those children who are most difficult to treat and rehabilitate. There is a growing uneasiness among those who have committed themselves to treating juveniles in training schools that society will abandon all hope of rehabilitating such children and drift to a policy of simply segregating them from the community.

A return to the traditional policy of custodial segregation with little or no emphasis upon treatment, however, would be a cruel abandonment of such juveniles in institutions. Although the evidence suggests that few children in training schools are rehabilitated, *some are*. The state has a responsibility to those it incarcerates, and it must fulfill that responsibility. The state does not deny competent dental care to inmates simply because it is expensive and it does little lasting good to the majority of inmates. And it should not deny seriously delinquent children the best rehabilitative care available just because it is expensive and they are difficult to reach.

Moreover, the pervasive pessimism over the treatment of juveniles in institutions is to some extent unwarranted. Treatment institutions can and do bring about broad, positive changes in the children they receive. In addition we have learned how to match delinquents with particular emotional and ideological needs with adult workers who can effectively help them. As the techniques of identifying distinctive delinquent and worker patterns improve, and the matching of delinquent and worker becomes more precise, the success rate of treatment institutions should improve.

As we have seen, however, it is a mistake to use some variation of the recidivism rate as the ultimate measure of the effectiveness of a correctional institution. Many circumstances which are well beyond the capacity of any institution to change have a basic impact on the recidivism rate of its inmates. A better measure would be the changes it produces in its inmates while

[36] See U. S. Department of Health, Education, and Welfare publications: *Statistics on Public Institutions for Delinquent Children, 1968*, Office of Juvenile Delinquency and Youth Development, Washington, D. C., 1970, p. 1; and *Statistics on Public Institutions for Delinquent Children, 1970*, National Center for Social Statistics, Washington, D. C., 1971, p. 3.

in the institution. If it is successful in bringing about desired changes among its residents, it cannot be reasonably blamed if other circumstances in the community systematically nullify the gains it has achieved.

BIBLIOGRAPHY

ADAMS, STUART, "The Pico Project," in *The Sociology of Punishment and Correction*, Norman Johnston, *et al.*, eds., John Wiley & Sons, New York, 1970, pp. 548–561.

ADEMAK, RAYMOND J., AND EDWARD Z. DAGER, "Social Structure, Identification and Change in a Treatment-Oriented Institution," *American Sociological Review*, 33 (December, 1968), 932–944.

ASBURY, HERBERT, *The Gangs of New York*, Alfred A. Knopf, New York, 1927.

BENSON, SIR GEORGE, "Prediction Methods and Young Prisoners," *British Journal of Delinquency*, 9 (1959), 192–199.

BERK, BERNARD B., "Organizational Goals and Inmate Organization," *American Journal of Sociology*, 71 (March, 1966), 522–534.

EYNON, THOMAS G., AND JON E. SIMPSON, "The Boy's Perception of Himself in a State Training School for Delinquents," *Social Service Review*, 39 (March, 1965), 11–19.

GRUSKY, OSCAR, "Organizational Goals and the Behavior of Informal Leaders," *American Journal of Sociology*, 65 (July, 1959), 59–67.

LERMAN, PAUL, "Evaluative Studies of Institutions for Delinquents," *Social Work*, 23 (July, 1968), 55–64.

LITTLE, ALAN, "Penal Theory, Reform and Borstal Practice," *British Journal of Criminology*, 3 (January, 1963), 257–275.

MARTINSON, ROBERT, "What Works? Questions and Answers About Prison Reform," *The Public Interest*, No. 35 (Spring, 1974), 22–54.

MENNEL, ROBERT, *Thorns and Thistles*, University Press of New England, Hanover, N. H., 1973.

National Criminal Justice Information and Statistics Service, *Children in Custody*, U. S. Government Printing Office, Washington, D. C., 1974.

OHLIN, LLOYD E., ROBERT B. COATES, AND ALDEN D. MILLER, "Radical Correctional Reform: A Case Study of the Massachusetts Youth Correctional System," *Harvard Educational Review*, 44, No. 1 (February, 1974), 74–111.

PALMER, TED B., "Matching Worker and Client in Corrections," *Social Work*, 18 (March, 1973), 95–103.

President's Commission on Law Enforcement and Administration of Justice, *Task Force Report: Corrections*, U. S. Government Printing Office, Washington, D. C., 1967.

STREET, DAVID, ROBERT D. VINTER, AND CHARLES PERROW, *Organization for Treatment*, Free Press, New York, 1966.

WEEKS, H. ASHLEY, *Youthful Offenders at Highfields*, University of Michigan Press, Ann Arbor, 1958.

diversion:
an alternative

Diversion is not a new concept, although it has only recently come into vogue.[1] Diversion refers to policies and procedures that forestall the usual outcomes in criminal justice cases by channeling them to less formal and more supportive programs. Instead of committing a child to a training school, probation to a group home might be considered; or instead of filing a formal complaint in court a juvenile officer might elect to handle a child's case informally. Diversion, therefore, depends upon the existence of reasonable alternatives to more harsh dispositions, and it depends upon the willingness of juvenile authorities to utilize them.

But it is not a new practice. John Augustus practiced diversion when he invented probation as an alternative to jail in 1842, and the police and juvenile courts have been disposing of about half of their juvenile cases informally for a long time. And altogether only about 14 per cent of the juveniles that reach juvenile court are committed to a training school. But nevertheless diversion has become a compelling issue today because traditional training schools are exceedingly costly and criminogenic, and less punitive methods, e.g., probation, are relatively inexpensive and often more beneficial. Thus, little is lost and much is gained by radical nonintervention, i.e., by diverting children from

[1] See Robert L. Smith, "Diversion: New Label—Old Practice," in *New Approaches to Diversion and Treatment of Juvenile Offenders*, U. S. Department of Justice, Washington, D. C., 1973, pp. 39–56.

training schools and juvenile courts to programs that interrupt their lives and social milieus less drastically.[2]

The idea first gained currency when the President's Commission on Law Enforcement and Administration of Justice urged the establishment of locally based preventive agencies, i.e., youth service bureaus, to channel troublesome juveniles to community treatment programs before the intervention of the police and the courts became necessary.[3] The argument in favor of this proposal rested on two assumptions. First, local people, both lay and professional, were in a better position to provide effective preventive programs than state correctional officials, and at the same time participation in preventive programs would familiarize local residents with the problems of delinquents and the difficulties they face in the community. Second, being inducted into the criminal justice system often stigmatized juveniles so that they began to think of themselves as delinquent and act accordingly. More traditional methods of handling delinquents had been tried, and in light of their inability to curb delinquency, something new was needed.

Shortly thereafter many communities introduced youth service bureaus in a variety of forms.[4] Some communities used them as brokers between delinquent youths, the criminal justice system, and the community in the hope that effective solutions would result from tripartite negotiations. Others developed bureaus that aligned themselves against the police and the courts. In effect these agencies became child advocates against the traditional criminal justice system. But whatever their mission, it soon became clear that youth service bureaus were limited by the range of programs available to them, and under the impetus of generous offers of federal funds many states began to provide a variety of community-based programs for delinquents. Under the leadership of Dr. Jerome Miller (now in Illinois) Massachusetts was more aggressive than most and served as a model for others to follow.

Diversion in Massachusetts: A Model

In 1972 Miller closed all Massachusetts training schools and began to set up alternative programs for juveniles who came to the attention of the courts.

---

2 See Edwin E. Schur, *Radical Non-Intervention*, Prentice-Hall, Inc., Englewood Cliffs, N. J., 1973.

3 President's Commission on Law Enforcement and Administration of Justice, *Task Force Report: Juvenile Delinquency and Youth Crime*, U. S. Government Printing Office, Washington, D. C., 1967, p. 19–20.

4 John A. Seymour, "Youth Service Bureaus," *Law and Society Review*, 7 (Winter, 1972), 247–272.

These programs were characteristically small, involving no more than twenty or thirty juveniles in a single setting; they were locally based; and they made full use of volunteer, often nonprofessional help. Specifically, Miller established seventeen group homes scattered around the state. They were designed to function as therapeutic communities providing intensive counseling, group and family therapy, and educational as well as vocational programs. These homes were to become the principal means of caring for juveniles whose own homes were unsuitable. He set up a Homeward Bound Program on Cape Cod for first or second offenders consisting of a four-week intensive training program in survival techniques followed by a two-week solo experience in the wilderness. The aim was to give the youths confidence in their ability to provide for themselves, if necessary.

A Youth Advocate Program was inaugurated in which selected adults were asked to care for one or two youths in their own homes. They were to act as surrogate parents, seeking medical or legal help when needed, providing for the education and recreation of the children as required. A Parole Volunteer Program was established in which carefully selected and trained volunteers were assigned to juvenile parolees from more formal programs. The volunteer was expected to provide counseling and tutoring much as a concerned parent or older brother might. A Detained Youth Advocate Program was introduced in which a trained adult would counsel detained youths, their families, and probation officers to work out the most beneficial disposition of the juvenile. The aim was to provide alternatives to formal adjudication as a delinquent by the court and assignment to the Department of Youth Services. Finally, to care for those children who truly need intensive, secure treatment, Miller established secure units in detention homes scattered around the state and staffed them with psychiatric and social work personnel. In addition to these innovative programs, Miller made full use of more traditional facilities and programs like foster homes, Neighborhood Youth Corps, independent placements, and probation.

As might be expected in such a radical reorganization of the Department of Youth Services, there was considerable confusion.[5] Some group homes were found to be unacceptable, and the financing of these operations often bordered on chaos. But as the programs settled down, many of these problems were worked out.

Curiously enough, the aim of Miller's reorganization, i.e., the diversion of juveniles from the traditional criminal justice system, was to some extent

    [5] Lloyd Ohlin, *et al.*, "Radical Correctional Reform: A Case Study of the Massachusetts Youth Correctional System," *Harvard Educational Review*, 44 (February, 1974), 100–102.

subverted by the fact that many more children were being referred to the Department of Youth Services by the courts than previously. Many more juvenile judges were willing to refer mildly delinquent children to the Department when the institutions were closed, probably because they felt that the children would be dealt with humanely.

Many other states also initiated programs to divert juveniles from the criminal justice system. As we have already seen, California launched the Community Treatment Program and the probation subsidy program in the 1960's, and several states developed nonresidential programs providing group therapy, work, and educational programs to youths otherwise headed toward traditional training schools. Diversion has become the policy of a large number of juvenile judges and correctional officials throughout the nation, and there is little question that an increasing number of juveniles who formerly would have been sent to institutions will now be placed in community-based programs.

The Problems of Diversion

There are also dangers inherent in community-based programs. Most correctional programs experience problems as they develop, but these problems need not develop into fundamental flaws if they are confronted directly and honestly. Diversion is heir to the problems of both the courts and the training schools in that it must provide just and compassionate dispositions for the children it handles, and it must develop and maintain effective programs for these children. There are several reasons why these goals will be difficult to achieve. First, diversion by its very nature pushes the disposition of a juvenile's case back to an earlier stage in the adjudicatory process, i.e., from a juvenile judge to a probation officer, or from a juvenile officer to a youth advocate—that is, to a person whose experience and training are less than those of the person who formerly made such dispositions.[6]

Training and experience do not inevitably confer wisdom or compassion on those making such dispositions, but in the long run they probably help. As the novelty of diversion wears off and the idealism of its proponents wanes there is some danger that the quality of their decisions will deteriorate, and care must be taken that their errors in disposition do not reach scandalous proportions. If diversion as a policy is to maintain a favorable reputation among juveniles and the public at large, therefore, it should provide for an appeals process whereby juveniles dissatisfied with their disposition can request and receive a judicial review of key decisions in their case.

[6] See Paul Nejelski, "Diversion of Juvenile Offenders in the Criminal Justice System," in *New Approaches to Diversion and Treatment of Juvenile Offenders*, pp. 83–91.

The juvenile court, itself, was originally designed as a means of diverting juveniles from the more rigorous and punitive adult criminal justice system. But with the passage of time it has become an integral component in the punitive handling of delinquents. There is every likelihood that the forces that undermined the juvenile court will operate in the same fashion to undermine diversion and the programs it spawns, if the appropriate precautions are not taken.

Second, diversion implies a system of locally based treatment programs scattered throughout a state. The problems of administering such programs effectively in most states will be enormous—quite apart from such routine problems as financing their operations and providing for the recruitment of quality personnel. Programs designed to treat delinquent children inevitably face two difficulties. It is difficult to establish the long-term beneficial effects of such programs because delinquent children present a wide variety of personal and social handicaps that are difficult to remove; and the personnel involved in treating delinquent children typically lose enthusiasm and hope for their programs. Many of the young adults who staff community-based programs are genuinely committed to the children they are helping. But over the long run, the absence of evidence that the programs are effective together with the pressures that delinquent children exert on adults caring for them combine to dampen the enthusiasm of all but the most committed of workers. There is, in other words, a serious danger of demoralization among the staff of community-based programs. This danger is real enough in institutions, but in a loosely organized statewide system of small units, the likelihood is great that demoralization will lead to scandalous deviations from accepted practice. A persistent effort at quality control is essential, therefore, if the reputation of such programs is to remain untarnished. Training schools were the focus of expose after expose in the 1940's and 1950's, and we can be reasonably confident that community-based treatment programs will attract similar attention from the media if they are not careful to maintain high-quality programs in their widely scattered and diversified units.

Some Traditional Attempts at Diversion

As we have seen, diversion has been practiced by reformers for a long time—at least since the middle of the nineteenth century—and several of the techniques used earlier to protect juveniles from the harsher methods of handling delinquents have matured into effective, stable practices. In this section we shall examine two of these practices in detail.

FORESTRY CAMPS

Forestry camps, or work camps, have been used by several states since the 1940's to treat mildly delinquent boys, and in recent years their utilization has increased. In 1968, 4,881 children, mainly boys, were admitted to forestry camps, and by 1971 this figure had reached 5,666 for an increase of 16 per cent in just two years.[7]

ORIGINS OF FORESTRY CAMPS. The idea of forestry camps grew out of the experience of the 1930's with work camps administered by the Civilian Conservation Corps for unemployed nondelinquent youths. The C.C.C. was a federal program of work on public projects established during the depression to help stabilize unemployed youths by providing them outdoor conservation work in parks and on roads. Barracks were constructed across the country in areas where useful work programs could be developed. The center of the camp organization was work. A full complement of other services was provided, such as education, recreation, medical care, and religious services. The camps had a semi-military aspect, since many of the directors were reserve army officers. The boys were paid for their work, a portion going to their parental families on relief and a portion being saved for them for the day of their release.

The youth who entered these camps were not adjudicated delinquents and were not committed by the courts. The program was administered as a relief and welfare program. The program seemed to work well; boys responded to the opportunity to work in the outdoors, enter other activities, and earn money. They gained physical strength and learned to apply themselves to work, to live cooperatively, and to accept supervision.

With the entrance of the United States into World War II, the camps were no longer needed, as many of the youth were of draft age and others found employment in war production. The persistent question has remained, however: If work camps were accepted by unemployed youth and were beneficial to them, would they not also be of benefit to delinquent youth?

ORIGIN AND DEVELOPMENT OF CAMP MOVEMENT FOR DELINQUENTS. California took the first definite step toward forestry camps for delinquents, beginning with a short-lived county probation camp and moving on to a camp for transient boys, full development of county camps, and finally state camps.[8]

---

[7] See U. S. Department of Justice, *Children in Custody*, U. S. Government Printing Office, Washington, D. C., 1974, Table 1, p. 1; and U. S. Department of Health, Education, and Welfare, *Statistics on Public Institutions for Delinquent Children*, U. S. Government Printing Office, Washington, D. C., 1971, p. 3.

[8] This history of California camps is based primarily on the following sources: O. H. Close, "California Camps for Delinquents," *1945 Yearbook*, National Probation Association, New York, 1945, pp. 136–147; Allen F. Breed, "California Youth Authority Forestry Camp Program," *Federal Probation*, 17 (June, 1953), 37–43; Karl Holton, *California Youth Au-*

The first camp was established in 1927 in Riverside County, as a project of the probation office. Although it was regarded as successful it was terminated in 1932 because of lack of funds. The next venture was a forestry camp, opened in Los Angeles County in 1932 for the retention of transient boys who, without employment or the controls of family and home community, soon became delinquent. This camp later became one of twenty-eight county camps for youth on probation. The Youth Authority Act of 1941, as amended in 1943, established state camps as part of the total program of state training facilities for delinquents. The county camps continue and through the Youth Authority are provided with state funds; they are operated under the direction of the chief county probation officer.

The first state camp operated by the Youth Authority was opened in 1943 at Calaveras Big Trees Park with fifty boys transferred from county jails. These boys built a camp for 100 boys, using portable buildings transported from the Benecia State Guard Camp. The next step came in 1944, when the Youth Authority entered into an agreement with the U. S. Army for introduction of delinquent boys into production of war materials. Two camps of 150 boys each were opened at Benecia Arsenal and Stockton Ordnance Depot, to which boys were transferred from county jails. After the war ended, these camps were disbanded and the Youth Authority entered upon its present plan of forestry camps, operated cooperatively with the state Division of Forestry. In 1964, California operated four forestry camps and three subsidiary or spike camps.

The idea of work camps for boys caught on slowly. The Federal Bureau of Prisons operated the Natural Bridge Camp from 1944 until the mid-1960's, then discontinued this venture. Various states began experimenting with camps; by 1971, twenty-four states operated sixty-seven camps.[9] Since each camp houses only a small number of boys, the camp residents are only a small percentage of all institutionalized delinquent boys. However, interest is sufficient so that the Children's Bureau has issued a special guide for the planning and operation of work camps.[10]

ORGANIZATION OF FORESTRY CAMPS. Forestry camps are usually the joint responsibility of the state agency in charge of juvenile corrections and the state

thority, *Report of Program and Progress, 1943–1948*, California Youth Authority, Sacramento, California, 1949, pp. 92–99; articles in the *California Youth Authority Quarterly*; and *Biennial Reports* of the California Youth Authority.

9 *Children in Custody*, pp. 28–29, Table B-1.

10 George H. Weber, *Camps for Delinquent Boys, A Guide to Planning*, Children's Bureau Publication, No. 385, U. S. Government Printing Office, Washington, D. C., 1960. This pamphlet outlines acceptable standards and procedures.

agency in charge of forestry, conservation, or state parks. The camps seem to thrive in forested states, to the extent that most camps are referred to as forestry camps rather than work camps. However, in some states other types of public work are done by the boys. Since the boys carry out useful work (not "made" or contrived jobs), the forestry or conservation department pays an agreed-upon sum to the training school agency. The boys usually are paid a small sum for wages, channeled through the training school agency. Usually the boy may spend part of this money with the remainder being saved until he is released. The training school state agency operates the camps.

On the level of the individual camp, the work done by the boys is taught to them and supervised by employees of the forestry department. The correctional agency provides the camp administrator, his assistants, cooks, supervisors for the boys, and other staff. Although the center of the program is work, under the forestry or other appropriate department, the camp is part of the correctional facilities of the state.

The camps tend to develop in states with an integrated state agency in charge of a number of phases of correction. In some situations, boys are assigned to the camps directly from reception and diagnostic centers, when study of the boy and his record indicates that his chances of adjustment and rehabilitation will be better in a camp than in a training school. Such boys include those who would not profit from the vocational or academic programs at traditional training schools and those who would respond better to the freer atmosphere of the camp than to the greater regimentation of the training school. Other boys are transferred to the camps from training schools to which they were originally committed. These boys are nearing the time for release and need a gradual transition from the controls of the school to the freedom of the community. Conversely, boys who abuse the freedom of the camp may be returned to the training school. At their entrance to training, boys pass through the same reception center as all other delinquents; at the termination of their stay in camp, they share the same parole or aftercare services.

CHARACTERISTICS OF CAMPS. The camps are developed around the concept of rehabilitation more closely than are the training schools and are still in an experimental stage. The characteristics of the camps do not derive from traditional methods nor are they handicapped by outmoded buildings. The camps have been constructed or remodeled and organized with definite aims in mind calculated to aid the delinquent in adjustment to conventional roles.

1. Camps are small. The capacity of camps is purposely kept small in order to maintain an informal atmosphere. Many camps have no more than twenty-five or thirty-five boys, and few approach 100.
2. Camps are simple in structure. Especially when first established, many

camps resembled barracks. Some began in old camps of the Civilian Conservation Corps or other work or military camps. Although adequate, soundly constructed, and clean, they lacked many of the niceties of schools or cottages and hence required less in the way of regulations and restrictions in the way the boys lived.

3. The camps are work-centered. The work is constructive, needed work in public service, calculated to give the boy a sense of worth and usefulness. Most of the needed skills are quickly learned and immediately applied. There is no long delay between learning and use. For the most part the boys work in the open, up to eight hours a day, five days a week. Other parts of the program are scheduled for evening or weekends. The types of work bear a marked similarity from camp to camp, but with some variations. Forestry camps provide such work as operating a nursery for forest trees, replanting, clearing out underbrush, building fire lanes, constructing roads, and building camp sites for public use. In states without heavy forestation, the work may center in the development and care of state parks.

The criticism has been made that the boys in the camps are usually from cities and that the skills learned do not prepare them for any kind of city work. Camp administrations make no pretense of teaching the boys urban skills. They are intent upon teaching the boys to work effectively, to become accustomed to manual labor and cooperation, and to accept supervision. The experience of working steadily (holding a job) rather than specific skills is the objective.

4. A well-rounded program supplements the work. Since most of the youth in camps are aged sixteen or over and, therefore, are past the age of compulsory school attendance, school usually is made secondary. Often remedial training in one subject, such as reading or arithmetic, is provided.

In all camps the boys are encouraged to participate in hobby clubs, photographic classes, nature study clubs, and other informal means of expanding their horizons and learning indirectly. Active sports and quiet games are available. Arrangements are made for boys to attend church in the community, or a part-time chaplain comes to the camp. Medical service is secured from a community physician with return of the boy to the training school when serious illness or accident occurs.

5. Counseling. From the point of view of rehabilitation, the heart of the program is a close relationship between each youth and his immediate supervisor, often called a counselor to emphasize the type of relationship.[11] Each counselor works with a limited number of boys, perhaps no more than five to eight.

The relation of the counselor to his group of boys is not left to chance, but is structured. Each camp has its own method of assuring frequent contacts.

The counseling carried on in forestry camps makes no pretense of handling deep-seated problems. It is not individual therapy for severely mal-

---

[11] *Cedar Creek Youth Forest Camp*, Division of Children and Youth, Department of Institutions, State of Washington, Olympia, Washington, 1957; Allen F. Breed, "California Youth Authority Forestry Camp Program," *Federal Probation*, 17 (June, 1953), 37–43.

adjusted boys. The counseling deals with current personal and camp problems, attempts to give a boy insight, and provides some support to the boy as he changes his attitudes and conduct. Boys with serious emotional disturbance would be out of place in the usual camp; they can be helped only in special situations with professionally trained therapists.

SELECTION OF BOYS FOR CAMP. Boys are selected to meet certain qualifications found by experience to be necessary for successful adjustment to camp life. Usually, only older boys are selected, capable of performing a day's work at manual labor. In some states, even though the maximum age for commitment to training schools by the juvenile court is sixteen or eighteen, boys once in may be detained until age twenty-one if they seem to need prolonged training. In other states, older boys may be routed to training schools or camps from adult courts. When boys under sixteen are assigned to camps, they are usually separated from the older boys and have programs oriented toward education rather than work.

Another criterion is that the boy will probably respond to the full day of physical labor. First, this requires health and physical endurance; second, disinterest in academic advancement; and third, acceptance of manual labor as a worthwhile occupation. The boy must also be able to adjust to the conditions of camp life, which lack some of the comforts of a training school. The bathhouse may be separated from the dormitory without a covered passageway. Work may take the boy into the open in severely cold or wet weather.

The boys assigned tend to be "normal" late adolescent boys, capable of conforming and of accepting the responsibility of a job. However, they are not expected to adjust without help, which is given by work and camp supervisors, counselors, and other staff members.

The camps achieve some of their success because of the careful selection and also because they function in the shadow of the training school, to which boys may be transferred if they do not adjust in camp. The training school has no choice but to take them, and because it must accept all types, it has stricter regulations and closer custody than the camp.

REDUCTION OF ISOLATION. The isolation of camp life is often offset by planned contacts with the nearby community, which usually consists of villages or small cities. Under supervision, boys may be taken to see a motion picture (in addition to the showing of motion pictures in camp) or to attend some special function. Arrangements are sometimes made for boys to attend church in nearby communities, perhaps as guests of townspeople (although camps have their own religious services). Camp teams may play nearby high school teams, either at the camp or at the high school. In some camps, boys may visit their parents at home at intervals, and parents are encouraged to visit the boys in camp or are permitted to take them from the camp for a stated number of hours. Each type of contact has certain advantages for the boys, not only in giving variety but in teaching boys how one behaves in an orderly community, or how to compete with or accept defeat from an opposing team. Contacts with parents are designed to strengthen the family relationships.

REGULATION AND DISCIPLINE. Informality does not imply chaos. A pattern of work, recreation, classes, and household arrangments is established. However, there is less compulsion than in a training school for boys to participate in set activities. They are encouraged to have a well-rounded set of activities, but voluntary participation is sought as part of the treatment. Compulsion often means that upon release the boy will immediately avoid activities into which he was forced in the training school; voluntary participation gives an opportunity for the boy to build up a genuine interest which will carry over into his life after release. The choice of occupation is possible because supervision can be informal with a small number of boys in a limited number of buildings. Although supervision is inconspicuous, it is maintained.

Discipline is maintained through counseling, close contact wth adults, and, where necessary, denial of privileges. Usually, the camp has no isolation rooms, and in extreme cases, when disruption of the program is threatened by a boy, he is returned to the training school. In emergencies, it is sometimes necessary to lodge a boy temporarily in the county jail. Occasionally, a boy runs away. However, the runaway rate is lower than in training schools, a fact that may be attributed to the selection of boys, the closer tie to adults, and the greater interest of the program.

TIME IN CAMP. The length of time spent in camp is variable and depends upon the progress toward rehabilitation made by the boy. The average length of stay for all forestry camps is 6.6 months as compared to 8.7 months in state training schools. Several factors account for this: boys selected rarely include seriously malajusted boys; boys may already have spent some time in a training school before transfer; they may have been sent to the camp for only a few months before release on parole as a halfway measure to freedom.

EVALUATION. California noted that parole violation was lower for boys released from camp than for those released from correctional schools. In order to investigate whether the camp program was responsible, some boys eligible for the camp program were placed in training schools and others in camps—the placement being randomly made.[12] Fifteen months after release from camp or school, the recidivism rates of the two categories of boys were measured.

12 Chester F. Roberts, Jr., *The California Youth Conservation Camps and Their Wards*, Research Report, No. 43, State of California, Department of the Youth Authority, Sacramento, California, 1965; Martin J. Malof, *Forestry Camp Study: Comparison of Recidivism Rates of Camp-Eligible Boys Randomly Assigned to Camp and to Institutional Programs*, Research Report, No. 53, State of California, Department of the Youth Authority, Sacramento, California, 1967.

No significant difference was found. The research team was forced to conclude that differences in the correctional school and the camp programs did not affect the recidivism rate; camps had a lower rate than the total rate for training schools because of the types of boys assigned to the camps. When comparable boys were in the correctional schools, they also had lower rates than had the general run of boys. A consideration of the boys assigned to camps helps to make the situation clear.

Criteria for camp placement are age, sixteen years or older; medical and physical fitness; no need of specialized treatment services; no history of persistent escapes, arson, overt homosexuality, child molestation, forcible rape, homicide, or kleptomania; no history of prior negative psychiatric condition or assaultive behavior; unwanted in any other jurisdiction; sufficient intelligence to understand instructions regarding safety precautions, the use of tools and fire-fighting equipment; ability to be successful in close group living and working situations. In contrast the correctional schools receive boys with the many characteristics that make them ineligible for the camps.

The recidivism rate is only one measure of an institution's value, and not necessarily a very valid one. Many of the characteristics that may cause a boy to violate parole may have been built into him before the short term in the correctional institution. Also, he usually returns to the neighborhood and the family that gave him his first socialization. In adjusting to the neighborhood he may revert to the old patterns of behavior.

The recidivism rate—usually a violation of formal parole requirements—may not touch the heart of rehabilitation. The boy may have made progress toward acceptable attitudes and behavior, but not to the point of avoiding violation of parole.

The author of the California report lists five positive aspects of the California camps, which no doubt would apply to camps elsewhere.

1. The cost of operation of a camp, per boy, is less than operation of a correctional school, and the average length of stay is shorter, thus reducing the total cost per boy.
2. The boys perform useful and necessary work; if the state had to hire other workers, the cost would be above that when the camp boys are used.
3. The forestry camp boys learn to work and to perform useful functions.
4. The rate of recidivism is low, although no lower than when similarly selected boys are placed in correctional institutions.
5. There is general community acceptance of the camps.

The camps pose certain handicaps to rehabilitation. The boy rarely acquires any skills that he can use in an urban environment. He may so thoroughly adjust to the simplicity of camp life that initially adjustment to the complexities of urban life may be more difficult.

Another criticism concerns the possibility of exploitation of boys in the desire to further the work of the state forestry or conservation department with low-cost labor. However, the final control of the activities rests with the state agency for corrections, and treatment-oriented staff should effectively check any tendency toward exploitation.

Whatever the final conclusion as to the value of work camps, at present they seem to meet many requirements for rehabilitation, and their establishment is a growing movement in the United States.

PSYCHIATRIC TREATMENT CENTERS

Another movement in the treatment of juvenile delinquents is the establishment of special psychiatric centers for seriously maladjusted children. This movement serves a segment of the delinquent population not served elsewhere. Forestry camps and community-based programs treat minor delinquents who are able to live in a relatively free environment; psychiatric treatment centers remove seriously maladjusted delinquents who cannot fit into the regime of the training school, with the combination of restrictions and pressures that characterize most training schools.

NEED FOR PSYCHIATRIC TREATMENT CENTERS. When punishment was accepted as the means for reformation of delinquents, the child who did not fit into the pattern—who was emotionally disturbed, aggressive, defiant, unstable —was pressured or punished into submission or was placed in a dark isolation room sometimes for months at a time. With newer ideas of reformation and rehabilitation, the easing of repressions, and the use of more normal activities, delinquents who could not conform to the pattern acceptable to most inmates became conspicuous. They interfered with the carrying out of activities, induced other inmates to follow them into defiant acts, and seemed unable to improve their own conduct. In contrast, most inmates were able to conform either to save themselves trouble or because they were genuinely responsive to the staff and interested in the program.

These disturbers are neither completely psychotic nor feebleminded. Usually, the former can be placed in a mental hospital and the latter in a special school for mental defectives. The troublemakers and the nonconformers lie somewhere between the seriously afflicted children and the normally misbehaving inmates who are, however, capable of responding to the customary regime of the school.

ANNEX OF STATE TRAINING SCHOOLS FOR BOYS, GOSHEN, NEW YORK. This

New York special treatment facility cares for 100 boys at a time who fall into a "high risk" category when they are in the usual training school. They include:

> Chronic runaways and those runaways who can be considered a serious threat to the community, such as the arsonist or the aggressive sexual offender; those who are a serious threat to staff and other children in the institution because of explosiveness, aggressiveness, and assaultiveness; those who, because of their weakness, need protection from the peer group; those who need protection from themselves because of depression and suicidal ideation; and lastly, the group who can be described as acutely disturbed mentally and whose behavior is prepsychotic or borderline psychotic.[13]

From 1947 to 1962 the Annex operated in the former reception building of the New York City Reformatory, a grim prison-like building. In 1962, it moved into a new building, especially constructed for its needs. In the first years of the Annex close custody was emphasized, but since then the Annex has progressed into a highly developed therapeutic community. The complex is of the minimum security type, and many opportunities are made for off-grounds activities, such as working for nearby farmers, taking educational tours, entering into community recreational activities, and leaving the grounds for short periods of time with parents. These activities are all carefully planned and supervised.

The Annex receives boys under age sixteen from other training schools. It has the usual tasks of maintenance, care of the boys, and provision of activities to fill the week—some combination of school, work, recreation, and vocational training for each boy. The essence of the program lies in several features not usually found in training schools.

1. Small size of school, which makes it possible to have small activity groups —ten boys per group.
2. Intensive visual supervision. The boy is always under direct staff observation and supervision except when he is alone in his room. Much of this is on the part of the cottage staff, who usually come with an interest in the job and are then trained to understand personality development and to handle counseling. The relation of the boy to the cottage staff, teachers, and others in daily contact seems to be the most important one and hence has possibilities of becoming therapeutically important.
3. Totality of treatment effort achieved through the constant communication

---

[13] Joseph H. Kane, "An Institutional Program for the Seriously Disturbed Delinquent Boy," *Federal Probation*, 30 (1966), 37–44. The discussion of the Annex is based on this article, a number of unpublished reports from the 1950's and early 1960's, and publications of 1967 from the New York State Department of Social Services.

between program departments and administration, which makes it possible to consider individual boys and their needs.

Professional guidance of the staff and treatment of the boys is given by psychiatrists, psychologists, and social workers. The atmosphere of the institution is warm, understanding, but also demanding, as the boy is led to an understanding of himself and of the effect of his behavior on the way others react to him. Controls are at first applied from without, through counseling, denial of privileges, and if necessary detention. The goal is to enable the boy to control his own behavior.

PSYCHIATRIC TREATMENT PROGRAM, CALIFORNIA. California has authorized the establishment of special treatment units within each training school, the first two of which were opened in 1957–1958. The legislature passed an amendment to the Welfare and Institutions Code which provided that the Youth Authority should accept certain delinquent youth who formerly had been shunted from one type of institution to another without fitting into any. The amendment stated that the Authority should accept "a person committed to it . . . if he is a borderline psychotic or borderline mentally deficient case, if he is a sex deviate unless he is of a type whose presence in the community under parole supervision would present a menace to the public welfare, or if he suffers from a primary behavior disorder." The legislature authorized the establishment of a Psychiatric Treatment Unit in each training school, on a staggered basis, with the first two being opened at the Preston School of Industry for boys and the Los Guilucos School for girls. In these two units, various methods of treatment are being developed. Each unit is headed by a full-time psychiatrist and staffed by psychologists and social workers. Emphasis is on individual and group therapy. In the first year of operation, the treatment center at Preston School had eighty disturbed boys under treatment and the center at Los Guilucos School 100 disturbed girls.

PRIVATE PSYCHIATRIC TREATMENT CENTERS. Treatment centers in public correctional systems are relatively new. Somewhat more experience and experimentation have been achieved in privately supported institutions.

Exploratory and experimental treatment often comes more readily through private institutions than public. Less red tape and inertia are met in persuading an individual philanthropist, organization, or foundation that a new type of treatment is needed than in persuading a state legislature. A privately supported residential school for disturbed children (some of whom have been delinquent) is mentioned in Chapter 20 of this book—the Sonia Shankman Orthogenic School in Chicago. In this and other private schools the child is accepted as a patient not because he is delinquent but because he is emotionally disturbed. Delinquency is regarded as symptomatic of his basic maladjustment. Some children may be referred after an appearance before juvenile court. The private residential school, however, is not compelled to accept the child; on the basis of its own examination it determines whether the child can probably be helped by its psychiatric services.

The Danger of Overformalization

In this and preceding chapters we have traced the evolution of formal methods of handling juvenile delinquents. At first, as we have seen, wayward children were dealt with informally by parents, relatives, or neighbors. If necessary, they were treated as adults and subjected to adult punishments. But as civilization evolved, compassion replaced vengeance, and more humane, albeit more formal, methods for dealing with delinquents emerged. Today, we have a broad spectrum of alternatives for treating delinquents. All, or nearly all, are designed to help the juvenile overcome his difficulties and resume his place in his family and community. But with the broad range of programs and facilities now available to treat delinquent children, another problem has arisen that as yet has not been squarely confronted.

When the family and community can no longer cope with a child, and they relinquish their responsibilities to the juvenile court—or some other authority—not only do different people become responsible for the child, but the *quality* of their responsibility changes drastically as well. Parents and neighbors feel an obligation to care for children on a twenty-four-hour basis, every day of the year. With many parents these responsibilities come before all others. But when the child is assigned to a probation officer or a social worker, most often the responsibility of the worker is limited to his professional role, from 8 A.M. to 5 P.M. When the probation officer leaves his professional role, his obligations to the child cease. Someone else steps in but the fact remains that all too often *no one* has final responsibility for the child in the way that a parent does. Thus, when a child becomes a ward of the court, he enters a world of impersonal formal relations in which no one has ultimate responsibility for his welfare.

The result is that children's cases are not given the intensive concern they deserve, and all too often instead of focused treatment, the child is shuffled from one worker or treatment facility to another until someone rescues him from the impersonal labyrinth of the child welfare bureaucracy. The problem is especially acute when a child presents multiple problems that could be treated by two or more agencies. A delinquent boy who presents severe psychiatric symptoms might conceivably be treated by either a department of mental health or a juvenile correctional agency. It is not uncommon for such youngsters to bounce around between these agencies until they reach adulthood, or until they do something drastic—e.g., have a psychotic breakdown or commit a serious crime—that forces one of the agencies to assume final responsibility.

A graphic illustration of the confusion and irresponsibility inherent in a variety of independent formal programs to help dependent children is the case of Carmen, a ten-year-old girl who was taken to Bellevue Hospital in New York City early on December 31, 1973.[14] She was alone, frightened, and in considerable pain. A brief medical examination revealed that she had been repeatedly raped. Carmen's mother was being treated in Bellevue for cancer, and her father had deserted the family years before. In her mother's absence Carmen was being cared for by homemakers supplied by the Department of Social Services. On December 28, 1973, Carmen was raped by her older brother, Ishmael. Carmen immediately told the homemaker who did nothing and even neglected to report the fact to the next homemaker who came on duty that evening.

Ishmael had been treated by a wide variety of public agencies since he was thirteen, and although he had been in considerable trouble, no agency assumed responsibility, and he filtered back to the streets after each encounter with no restrictions.

When Carmen's condition was discovered at the hospital, a social worker filed a child-abuse report with the Special Services for Children branch of the Department of Social Services. But the agency refused to accept the report, stating that Carmen was already under the agency's care and that only a parent could abuse a child. The social worker next called the Society for the Prevention of Cruelty to Children, but they could do nothing for Carmen. As evening approached, the social worker returned to the Special Services for Children and the Bureau of Child Welfare, seeking someone to care for Carmen and her three younger brothers who were still at home with Ishmael. But everyone at these agencies was anxious to go home. It was New Year's Eve and their thoughts were elsewhere.

Carmen remained at Bellevue that night and New Year's Day, and finally on January 2, the social worker succeeded in getting a social worker from St. Mary of the Angels, a Catholic agency, to visit the apartment. She sought to persuade Ishmael to return to a private institution for children on Long Island but he fled the building. Finally, with the help of the Citizen's Committee for Children, the Bureau of Child Welfare was persuaded to accept Carmen as a child-abuse case. By now it was January 8, and on January 10,

[14] See John Corry, "About New York," New York Times, April 1, 1974, p. 28.

1974, the Bureau filed a charge against Ishmael in Family Court. As an abused child Carmen was eligible to receive psychiatric care, and shortly thereafter her mother was released from Bellevue and resumed care of Carmen.

If the social worker at Bellevue had not pushed the welfare agencies to come to Carmen's aid, the girl might have been forced to return to her mother's apartment on New Year's Eve and simply endure Ishmael's assaults. No one knows how many children are refused help in the same way, because it is inconvenient or bureaucratically awkward to come to their aid. It probably occurs more often than we would like to think.

BIBLIOGRAPHY

CARTER, ROBERT M., "The Diversion of Offenders," *Federal Probation*, 56 (December, 1972), 31–36.

KANE, JOSEPH H., "An Institutional Program for the Seriously Disturbed Delinquent Boy," *Federal Probation*, 30 (1966), 37–44.

OHLIN, LLOYD E., ed., *Prisoners in America*, Prentice-Hall, Inc., Englewood Cliffs, N. J., 1973.

SCHUR, EDWIN E., *Radical Non-Intervention*, Prentice-Hall, Inc., Englewood Cliffs, N. J., 1973.

SEYMOUR, JOHN, "Youth Service Bureaus," *Law and Society Review*, 7 (Winter, 1972), 247–272.

U. S. Department of Justice, *New Approaches to Diversion and Treatment of Juvenile Offenders*, U. S. Government Printing Office, Washington, D. C., 1973.

release, aftercare, and the delinquent's future chapter 22

The time that a delinquent boy or girl spends under supervision is a period of resocialization to enable him to make a better adjustment than previously to the community, usually the same one from which he came. In all probability the community and the family that receive him back are little changed. The child or young adolescent returns to the same school from which he was perhaps a chronic truant. The older adolescent finds his old gang waiting for him, with some other boys perhaps also returning from institutions. He finds the merchants, community center, church, parks unchanged. This is the community in which he became a delinquent. In the relatively few months spent in training school, has he gained a new perspective on his future and new strength to help him withstand the same pressures and pulls toward delinquency that he experienced before commitment?

Release

WHEN TO RELEASE

In some institutions the boy or girl is required to remain for a specified period of time, but in most the length of commitment is conditional upon the progress toward rehabilitation made by the student. Progress is sometimes measured in part by the acquisition of a certain number of merit points. In most institutions the student's adjustment is used as a measure of successful rehabilitation. None of these methods necessarily indicates the changes in attitude and goals which signify real, that is, inner, rehabilitation.

Institutions with satisfactory treatment services are in the best position to determine when a child is ready for release. When professional treatment personnel are on active duty at a training school, the original diagnosis may be followed by periodic checkups and eventually by a conference of the staff to determine whether the boy or girl is ready to re-enter the community.

The period of time for residence in the training school should not be set in advance. Some students are ready to return to the community within a few months, some not for a much longer period of time. It has previously been stated that the average time in training schools is slightly less than nine months. In individual schools, however, the average stay may be as low as six months or as high as two or more years. A short average stay does not necessarily mean that the school is especially successful in rehabilitation; it may simply indicate overcrowding and the premature eviction of students in order to make room for others awaiting entrance after court commitment. On the other hand, long terms do not always lead to rehabilitation; they may indicate failure to restore the boy or girl to the point where release seems justified, with final release as the youth reaches the age beyond which the school cannot hold him; or a judge may have specified a long term because the boy or girl has committed a serious offense. Most often, the longer a boy or girl remains in an institution, the more difficult his rehabilitation has been, and the less favorable his prognosis.

TEMPORARY RELEASE

Since many boys and girls are unable to adjust well after release, some schools have devised methods of trial release, either through granting a long furlough home or using some form of prerelease; if the young person misbehaves he can be returned to the training school with very little formality and later given another chance at outside adjustment.

Many schools have devised various ways in which to give students continuing contacts while in the school with their homes and with community life in general. These include periodic visits home, work under supervision in the community in which the school is located, or a final period for boys in a forestry camp where formal supervision is relaxed. Recreational contacts with the community are sometimes developed. These methods have several advantages: they prevent the youth from becoming so immured in the institution that he tends to forget what community living is like; they keep him aware of what the community expects in the way of good behavior; and they give him actual practice in work and in self-discipline under conditions where running away has few obstructions.

OBSTACLES TO ADJUSTMENT ON RELEASE

One of the major problems to good community adjustment after release is that little if anything has been done to modify family and neighborhood conditions. Rehabilitation of families when needed and preparation of the family for the return of the young person is theoretically regarded as a necessary part of the successful adjustment of the young person, but it is rarely carried out either because of lack of personnel for the intensive work which would be necessary or the failure of families to cooperate. Nevertheless, most children return to their families. Only a few are placed in foster homes or group homes.

For boys and girls in school, readjustment to school is a major problem. Chronic truancy has often been one of the facets of the delinquent behavior that led to commitment to the training school. Especially if the training school program has attempted to find the student's true level of ability and has adjusted his educational program to this, he may find it extremely difficult to step back into the traditional school pattern. Sometimes attempts are made to help him in this transition. The aftercare or parole officer may visit the school and talk with the principal and teacher or arrange a transfer to a different school where the student may make a fresh start. Many training schools release students toward the end of a school term or during the latter part of summer vacation so that they may re-enter school at the beginning of a term. Nevertheless, the boys and girls who entered the training school with a history of school maladjustment often slip back into their old habits of coming late to school, cutting classes, displaying aggressive behavior in school, or truanting.

The older boy or girl who does not wish to return to school faces the problem of finding employment. Aftercare officers usually try to help him secure employment, perhaps finding willing employers ahead of time and accompanying the youth for his first interview with the prospective employer. Many business concerns do not wish to employ someone who has been in the training school. Many young people are not able to accept the degree of industriousness, honesty, and cooperation required to hold a job. Case histories often show that a boy comes from training school filled with good intentions, accepts a job in good faith, but soon begins to pilfer or to come late to work or to find obviously false excuses not to come for a day or two at a time. Soon the boy is dismissed.

At all times, the pull of old companions and habits is very strong, even for the boys and girls who have determined while still in the training school to start a new life. Nondelinquent young people and their parents often refuse to associate with training school youth; church and community center groups may admit them with reluctance. The one group that will accept them is the old clique or gang. Here they may occupy a position of importance and are eagerly questioned about the training school.

Aftercare Supervision

Almost all released boys and girls are placed under aftercare supervision, which may be provided by the institution itself, by the state agency providing aftercare supervision for juvenile institutions, by the probation office of the court that committed the child, by various social agencies, or by volunteers. Each system has its supporters and each is adjusted to specific situations. The juvenile court without a probation officer is unable to accept the supervision of released boys and girls. When the juvenile institutions in a state individually provide aftercare for their students, a diversity of care and quality may exist within one state. When a state agency supervises, one officer may be assigned a wide territory and find it difficult to keep in close touch with his caseload. No one however seems to question the necessity of working closely with each child in his readjustment to the community.

Supervision of released boys and girls is a form of social work. Hence the officer should be a trained social worker; however, as with probation officers and social workers in training schools, many of them are not. They experience many of the same problems as probation officers—too many children to supervise, scattered over wide areas thus consuming much time in travel, and the association in the student's mind of aftercare with authority, the training school, police, and revocation of parole.

The Halfway House Program

The halfway house program, as its name implies, involves a residential center whose program bridges the gap between institutional life and complete freedom in the community. Halfway houses are incorporated into a number of public institutionalized programs, for example, as a transitional step between mental hospital and the community or adult prison and the community. A limited use of halfway houses is now made to serve the juvenile delinquent when he leaves the training school. The halfway house is especially useful for the care of delinquents who have no home to which to return or when the home conditions are unlikely to benefit the further adjustment of the juvenile.

Some of these boys and girls are still of school age; others are hopefully ready for employment; both types need some supervision to help them adjust to conventional community life, whether in school, work, recreational facility, or on the streets. The experience so far has pointed up certain cautions.

A publication of the Children's Bureau states that community relationships should rest on understanding of the program and willingness of the community to accept the resident into churches, recreational facilities, and educational institutions.[1] Preliminary work with the community and development of cooperation are desirable to avoid rejection of the residents of the halfway house. The implication is that the halfway houses are located in middle class neighborhoods, whereas the residents often are from lower status neighborhoods. Moreover training school students are unfamiliar to such neighborhoods, and parents and leaders fear the contact of delinquents with the youth of the neighborhood. Several projected halfway houses have been unable to open and a few forced to close because of the opposition of the community.

Since individual attention by the staff is of prime importance, the houses are planned to house a limited number of releasees—from ten to twenty-five. A total program is planned for the residents, built up around guidance and practical training for adjustment in school or on the job. Usually, residents are absent from the house only for school or work or other approved activities known to the staff. They are still under the control of the official correctional authorities.

The name of the house is important, and an attempt is made to avoid the use of halfway house, since this suggests that the residents are only halfway on the road to rehabilitation. They are assumed to be ready for re-entrance into the community, but in need of help in making the final step toward independent life. Since the time spent in the house is considered preparation for release to the community, it is usually short. The halfway house is not a long-term youth residence center. Release typically comes within a few weeks or months either via transfer to a conventional type of parole or in the form of outright discharge from the authority of the juvenile court.

Halfway houses are so new that final evaluation is not possible. After approximately a year of experience with three halfway houses operated by the Federal Bureau of Prisons for selected juvenile delinquents and delinquent youths, the Bureau announced that of a total of 174 youths and juveniles,

---

[1] *Halfway House Programs for Delinquent Youth*, Children's Bureau, U. S. Department of Health, Education, and Welfare, Washington, D. C., 1965; revised from Kenneth S. Carpenter, "Halfway Houses for Delinquent Youth," *Children*, 10 (1963), 224–229; a detailed description of a halfway house program is given in Frances McNeil, "A Halfway-house Program for Delinquents," *Crime and Delinquency*, 13 (1967), 538–544.

twenty, or 11 per cent, had to be returned to Federal institutions. Halfway houses are regarded as a promising part of the program of release from correctional institutions.

Failure on Release

Not all boys and girls released from training schools make good adjustments in the community. We have already seen that many young people enter the training school with a background of experience on probation or in training schools. These are youth who previously have failed to adjust on probation or parole, and have committed new delinquencies. In addition, among students released to aftercare, some will fail to adjust and will be returned as parole violators. An inspection of the annual reports of training schools shows as typical the following pattern: School A, 204 boys placed on parole, forty-two returned for parole violation; School B, 1,646 boys and girls released on parole, 488 returned from parole and nineteen recommitted; School C, 263 boys and girls released on parole, ninety-three returned for violation; School D, 330 boys and girls paroled, ninety returned as violators; and School E, 138 girls paroled, twenty-eight returned for violation. The ratio of students released to those returned for violation runs from about 3:1 to 5:1. This is the record for one year only; in succeeding years, additional boys and girls resume delinquency. Some annual reports note that individual students have been released twice during the year on parole and returned twice for violation.

Certainly failure on parole should not be regarded as entirely the fault of the institution. It cannot be expected to erase in a few months the effects of twelve to sixteen years of family and community disorganization. But parole failure does provide some indication of the seriousness of the problem facing institutions as they attempt to rehabilitate young people. It is a problem that will not be simply resolved.

The seriousness of the problem facing juvenile institutions, however, is no excuse for inadequate programs or ineffective staff. Both should be held to high performance standards. But it is all too easy to use the rate of parole failure as an index of performance without understanding the complexity of measuring effectiveness. Not infrequently an innovation in treatment is introduced, and its effects on parole success or failure used as the measure of its effectiveness. But comparisons of parole failure before and after the innovation are hazardous, because in addition to the specific changes introduced, the total system of handling delinquents is changed, institutional programs are revised, new training schools are opened, and new methods of parole are instituted. Also, a number of years should elapse in order to permit tracing the subsequent careers of released delinquents at least into adulthood. Some states have had rehabilitative programs for a sufficient period to merit such a study.

The Future of Juvenile Delinquents

What becomes of juvenile delinquents after they are beyond the legal age for the juvenile court and correctional institutions? Do they become criminals as adults? Are juvenile delinquents a potential threat to the community throughout their lives? In addition to limited studies that trace arrest records for a few years after release of delinquents from correctional schools, three extensive studies have been made, two of which compare delinquents with control groups. Adult outcomes other than continued crime are also noted. These studies pertain only to delinquents whose offenses have been sufficiently serious to bring them before the juvenile court and usually into the training school. In terms of the Behavior Continuum presented in Chapter 2 they are hard-core delinquents. The future of minor offenders placed on probation has already been reviewed in Chapter 19.

ONE THOUSAND DELINQUENT BOYS FIFTEEN YEARS LATER
(GLUECK STUDY I)

An intensive follow-up study of a thousand seriously delinquent boys during three five-year periods showed a marked decline in number of arrests and seriousness of offenses, but not the elimination of all crime. The Gluecks, who made the study, selected as their group boys who had been referred to the Judge Baker Foundation (a child-guidance clinic now called the Judge Baker Guidance Center) by the Boston Juvenile Court during the years 1917–1922. Each child was studied and recommendations were made to the court, but the Center did not enter into the treatment of the children. Eighty per cent of the children were seen only once by the Center; only 2.3 per cent were seen as many as three or more times. The recommendations concerned such things as where the boys should live, improvement of physical condition, type of supervision, education, industrial adjustments, disciplinary control, recreation, and need for further examination. Many of the recommendations were not carried out by the court.[2] These facts indicate that the cases were a run-of-the-mine series and not a selected group of boys who had received psychiatric therapy.

The description of the boys prior to referral to the Center coincides with descriptions of other delinquents brought to police and court attention: low

---

[2] The study is reported in two volumes: Sheldon and Eleanor Glueck, *One Thousand Juvenile Delinquents*, Harvard University Press, Cambridge, Massachusetts, 1934; *Juvenile Delinquents Grown Up*, The Commonwealth Fund, New York, 1940.

family income, low educational attainment of parents, large families in over-crowded living quarters, family disorganization, lack of affiliation by the boy with organized youth agencies, but affiliation with other delinquents in offenses. Of the thousand boys, two-thirds had been arrested prior to the "crucial arrest" that brought referral to the Center (and incidentally inclusion in the Glueck study). Most of the boys had had only one other arrest, but some had been arrested as many as five times. Two-thirds of the arrests were for forms of stealing; one-fifth were for petty statutory offenses against public peace, morals, or order; one-eighth for such distinctly juvenile offenses as waywardness, truancy, and malicious mischief; about 2 per cent were for assaults, and less than 1 per cent for sex offenses.

Since the Gluecks were interested in the degree to which the recommendations of the Center were carried out and the effect of these recommendations on future behavior, the first follow-up period was placed five years after the end of treatments as prescribed by the court. For boys whose treatment did not follow any of the recommendations, this time span was five years after court appearance; for the remainder it was about six years after court appearance, since the treatment period in the great majority of cases lasted less than a year. The later follow-up was made some ten years after the first, but was organized in such a way that data could be assembled for two five-year periods. Thus the entire study covers four periods: prior to the crucial arrest; the first five years after treatment ended; the second five years, and the third five years.

The average age of the boys was 13.5 years at the time of the crucial arrest, nineteen years at the end of the first follow-up period, twenty-four years at the end of the second, and twenty-nine years at the end of the final period. What are the trends of behavior during this period stretching from early childhood to young adulthood?

1. Trend toward nondelinquency. Table 20 summarizes some of the trends. Prior to the arrest that led to the referral, 37.4 per cent had not been arrested. The first five years after treatment saw one-fifth of the boys again in the nonarrest groups. In each follow-up period, the number without arrests increased, reaching 42.1 per cent in the nonarrest group approximately fifteen years after the crucial arrest. This group reached its peak of delinquency as measured by arrest at age 13.5 and steadily rejected delinquent behavior after that time.

2. Decline of unofficial delinquency. The Gluecks delved further into misconduct other than that shown by arrests and found a high percentage of "unofficial" delinquent and criminal acts, by which they mean acts for which the person might have been arrested but was not. The percentage of these incidents was very high (36.7 per cent) in the childhood period prior to the crucial arrest and no doubt signified acts regarded as trivial or as the

TABLE 20

Trends in Commission of Offenses, Percentage Distribution

	PRIOR TO CRUCIAL ARREST	AT TIME OF CRUCIAL ARREST	END OF FIRST FOLLOW-UP	END OF SECOND FOLLOW-UP	END OF THIRD FOLLOW-UP
Average age	Under 13.5	13.5	19.0	24.0	29.0
Approximate number*	1,000	1,000	941	877	846
Not arrested during period	37.4	0	20.2	33.9	42.1
Average number of arrests for those arrested	2.3	—	3.4	3.7	3.7
Crimes leading to arrest					
Against property	62.9	73.6	48.7	24.6	18.2
Against public welfare	21.7	5.6	22.2	30.3	22.5
Against person	2.5	1.6	4.4	7.3	6.8
Against chastity	0.3	0.9	1.6	2.4	2.6
Against family and children	0	0	0.5	1.6	3.3
Drunkenness	0	0	9.3	29.0	43.0
Drug-selling	0	0	0.1	0.3	0.6
Other†	12.6	18.3	13.2	4.5	3.0
Number of arrests	1,333	1,000	2,719	2,547	2,195

Based on material in Sheldon and Eleanor Glueck, *One Thousand Juvenile Delinquents,* Harvard University Press, Cambridge, Massachusetts, p. 100; and *Juvenile Delinquents Grown Up,* The Commonwealth Fund, New York, 1940, pp. 23, 43, 59, 309, 310, 311, 316, 317.

* The total number of cases decreased with each period due to deaths, failure to locate, or inability to secure information. The totals may also vary slightly from table to table, due to the last reason or because items are not equally applicable to all subjects.

† "Other," especially at the lower age periods, refers to such distinctly juvenile offenses as stubbornness, waywardness, disobedience, truancy, and malicious mischief.

normal misdeeds of childhood. In the follow-up periods, unofficial acts accounted for only 6 or 7 per cent of instances of misconduct.

3. Decrease of serious crimes. The pattern of offenses moved radically from serious to nonserious or noncriminal from the teen period to the adult period as judged by arrests. Offenses against property declined markedly; these comprised breaking and entering, larceny, pickpocketing, receiving stolen goods, forgery, and the like. Crimes against the person (assaults) increased but at all periods were a small proportion of the total. Crimes against chastity (lewdness, unnatural sexual acts) also increased, but again

were a small proportion of the total. Three crimes, against family and children (such as neglect or nonsupport), drunkenness, and drug-selling, not found among juveniles, appeared in early adulthood and increased. Drunkenness became a major reason for arrest by the last period studied, when the average age was twenty-nine years. Considered as a whole, arrests for the serious offense of stealing declined as did also those for the minor juvenile-type offenses under "other." The arrests that increased were dominated by drunkenness. When the Gluecks grouped offenses as serious or minor they found a general trend of decline for serious offenses and of increase for minor offenses.[3]

Some of the changes in offenses are linked with age. Many juvenile offenses are not regarded as serious among adults. Neglect of wife and children does not occur until after marriage, drunkenness becomes widespread only after the age for legal purchase of liquor, and drug-selling affects only a few juveniles. Within each category it is also probable that specific types of offenses rise or fall with advance into adulthood. From other evidence presented in earlier chapters we know that types of stealing change with age and that some types of sex offenses regarded as a serious threat to the young are not so regarded for adults.

The discussion above has dealt with arrests—with types of offenses—

TABLE 21

Changes in Behavior of Minor and Serious Delinquents
During Fifteen Years

NUMBER OF BOYS	TREND FROM FIRST TO THIRD PERIOD OF STUDY	PERCENTAGE
109	Nondelinquent throughout	13.3
88	Minor offenders throughout	10.8
226	Serious offenders throughout	27.6
162	From serious to minor	19.8
130	From serious to nondelinquent	15.9
63	From minor to nondelinquent	7.7
40	Erratic shifting about	4.9
818		100.0

Summarized from Sheldon and Eleanor Glueck, *Juvenile Delinquents Grown Up*, The Commonwealth Fund, New York, 1940, pp. 87–88. For the remainder of the boys, data were insufficient to trace a trend. Although "unofficial" offenses (no arrest) are included, 93 per cent of the evaluations of behavior are based on arrests.

[3] *Juvenile Delinquents Grown Up*, p. 317. Definitions of offenses are given on pp. 16, 77.

and not with the classification of the boys themselves, other than to show that the percentage arrested greatly decreased. For the boys themselves certain trends of conduct are clear. According to Table 21, 27.6 per cent of the original group may be thought of as "hard core" delinquents, who have been guilty of serious offenses throughout the fifteen years of study, from an average age of 13.5 years to an average of twenty-nine years. In addition, 10.8 per cent were minor offenders throughout. These high percentages support the contention that juvenile delinquents are the future criminals and troublemakers. However, for all other boys the record was much more optimistic: 13.3 per cent had no further record of delinquency after the crucial arrest, and 15.9 per cent of early serious offenders and 7.7 per cent of early minor offenders were nondelinquent by the third period study. In addition 19.8 per cent shifted from serious to minor offenses during the fifteen years.

Juvenile Delinquents Thirty Years Later

Another important study on the outcome of delinquency is a thirty-year follow-up study of a consecutive series of children referred to the St. Louis Municipal Psychiatric Clinic between 1924 and 1929. The 524 children, whose median age at first contact was thirteen years, came to the clinic because of a wide variety of problems; 37 per cent had had juvenile court referrals at the time they first came to the Clinic. Certain criteria were set up for inclusion in the study group: age under eighteen at first clinic contact; Caucasian race; I.Q. (Stanford Binet) not less than 80; referral because of problem behavior (not as part of school survey, for vocational advice, or the like).[4]

Since not all children interviewed at the Clinic were court cases, it was possible to compare the adult adjustment of the court cases with that of children referred for other reasons. In addition, a control group was selected that in childhood matched the Clinic group with respect to sex, race, and year of birth. The individuals were chosen from the same neighborhoods in which the Clinic patients lived. Children with I.Q. of less than 80 were excluded, as were children with behavior problems. The control group was randomly selected from public school records. A careful current checkup by records and interviews of Clinic cases and controls forms the basis for a series of reports.

The Clinic cases were classified according to the contacts they had had with court and police, as shown in Table 22. Group 1 with 37 per cent of Clinic cases is composed solely of children who had had an appearance before juvenile court prior to or at the time of the referral to the Clinic. They were typical

[4] Lee N. Robins and Patricia O'Neal, "Mortality, Mobility, and Crime: Problem Children Thirty Years Later," *American Sociological Review*, 23 (1958), 162–171.

TABLE 22

Police and Court Contacts of Clinic Clients and Control Group, St. Louis, Percentage Distribution

	TOTAL CLINIC GROUP	GROUP 1 JUVENILE COURT			GROUP 2 ANTISOCIAL BEHAVIOR			GROUP 3 NO ANTISOCIAL BEHAVIOR			GROUP 4 CONTROL GROUP		
		M	F	T	M	F	T	M	F	T	M	F	T
Juvenile court before Clinic	37	100	100	100	—	—	—	—	—	—	1	—	1*
Juvenile court only after Clinic	6	—	—	—	17	8	14	2	2	2	7	—	5
Juvenile police brushes only†	13	—	—	—	31	17	26	14	5	11	—	—	—
No juvenile police trouble	44	—	—	—	52	75	60	84	93	87	92	100	94
Total per cent	100	100	100	100	100	100	100	100	100	100	100	100	100
Number of Clinic cases	525	156	38	194	141	65	206	84	40	124	70	30	100

Lee N. Robins and Patricia O'Neal, "Mortality, Mobility, and Crime: Problem Children Thirty Years Later," American Sociological Review, 23 (1958), 165, headings modified.

* Juvenile court at any time, since control subjects did not attend Clinic.

† Arrests without court proceedings.

delinquents for whom it was thought the Clinic would be helpful. Group 2, with 39 per cent of Clinic cases, consisted of children whose behavior brought them into court after the Clinic referral or brought a brush with police, that is, arrest without a court hearing. Their conduct is considered in conflict with the mores but not sufficiently serious to be definitely delinquent. The children in Group 3, 24 per cent of the total, were referred to the Clinic because of behavior or neurotic problems not related to delinquency. Group 4, the control group, is virtually without behavior or emotional problems that the child and his family could not handle. The four groups may be thought of roughly as a continuum, with behavior ranging from seriously delinquent, through delinquent-type misbehavior, through other kinds of behavior problems, to nondelinquent and well adjusted.

Thirty years after the time to which the above classification refers, the four groups were classified according to adult arrests and imprisonment. Table 23 shows marked differences both in total percentage of arrested persons as well as in frequency of arrests in the four groups, with 60 per cent of group 1 (juvenile delinquents), 43 per cent of group 2, 20 per cent of group 3, and only 11 per cent of group 4 (nondelinquents) having had one or more non-traffic arrests as adults. Percentage of persons imprisoned followed the same trend.

TABLE 23

Relation of Childhood Behavior to Adult Arrests and Imprisonment, St. Louis, Percentage Distribution

ADULT ARRESTS	GROUP 1 JUVENILE COURT		GROUP 2 ANTISOCIAL BEHAVIOR		GROUP 3 NO ANTISOCIAL BEHAVIOR		GROUP 4 CONTROL GROUP	
Non-traffic arrests	60		43		20		11	
Three or more		38		20		9		3
One or two		22		23		11		8
Prison		28		13		6		1
No prison		32		30		14		10
Traffic only	2		4		3		5	
No arrests	38		53		77		84	
Total per cent	100		100		100		100	
Number	176		191		119		97	

Lee N. Robins and Patricia O'Neal, "Mortality, Mobility, and Crime: Problem Children Thirty Years Later," *American Sociological Review*, 23 (1958), 168. Numbers exclude those known to have died, been institutionalized (not in prison), or permanently out of St. Louis before age twenty-five. Title of table modified.

Comparison Between Glueck and St. Louis Studies

Both studies show a marked carry-over into adulthood of offenses on the part of juvenile delinquents. During the third five-year period of the Glueck study, 58 per cent of offenders were arrested; during the entire thirty years of the St. Louis study, 60 per cent of juvenile court cases were arrested. Since some of the Glueck cases were arrested at earlier periods but not in the third period, the total percentage arrested at some time would be greater than for the St. Louis cases; at the same time, the span covered by the Glueck study was shorter. It seems therefore that the delinquents in the Glueck study had a higher percentage arrested as adults than was true for the St. Louis delinquents. However, the difference might be due to different types of delinquents or to differences in police practices. Moreover, the St. Louis delinquents were about one-fourth girls, who had a lower proportion of adult arrests than did the boys.

The Glueck study shows a minority hard-core group of serious or minor offenders who persisted throughout the fifteen years of study; a slightly larger group, however, showed a gradual improvement in behavior with the passage of time. The St. Louis study shows that the more serious the childhood misconduct was, the more likely was the person to be arrested and arrested often in adulthood.

An important fact is that both the Glueck and the St. Louis studies show a minority of delinquents (13.3 per cent and 38 per cent) with no arrests at any time after the time of Center or Clinic referral.

General conclusions based on the two studies indicate that juvenile delinquency serious enough to bring arrests or court hearings leads to three outcomes in adulthood: a large minority of offenders continue into adulthood either at a serious or minor level of offense; another minority group conforms to the laws after early adolescence; and a larger group than either of these continues to commit offenses but with decreasing seriousness and frequency.

Five Hundred Delinquents Sixteen Years Later
(Glueck Study II)

When the Gluecks made their comparative study of 500 delinquent boys matched with 500 nondelinquent boys, they set the framework for follow-up studies.[5] The first follow-up survey of both groups of boys, not only in delinquency and crime but in many other aspects of life, covered the period up to age seventeen, the legal transition point from juvenile delinquent to adult

---

[5] Sheldon and Eleanor Glueck, *Unraveling Juvenile Delinquency*, Harvard University Press, Cambridge, Massachusetts, 1951.

criminal.[6] A second follow-up survey was made when the former delinquents and control subjects had reached age twenty-five, and a third follow-up when they had reached thirty-one. Since the boys were on the average fifteen years old at the time of the initial study, a span of sixteen years is covered by the follow-up studies.

The delinquents were boys who had been committed to a state training school in Massachusetts; the nondelinquents were matched with them as to residence in underprivileged areas, age, ethnic origin, and intelligence. The matching went so far as to select controls in numbers comparable to the delinquents according to the delinquency rates of specific neighborhoods.

As would be expected, the Gluecks were not able to follow all 1,000 boys into adulthood: some had died and others could not be located. The study is based on 438 delinquents and 442 nondelinquents who could be followed to age thirty-one.

The retrospective study of the 500 nondelinquents revealed that thirty-seven (7.4 per cent) had records as delinquents by age seventeen, some of which had been acquired before their selection as control boys, others in later teens. Fifteen were convicted for a single minor "juvenile type" offense and sixteen for one serious offense; six were convicted two or three times for serious offenses. Since this record covers all the years from early childhood up to seventeen years, and includes only a low percentage of the total group, the control group may still be accepted as essentially nondelinquent.

The delinquents had all been arrested prior to their seventeenth birthday—a necessary preliminary to their training school sentences. For many boys, arrests were almost a customary part of their lives: 41.3 per cent were arrested as often as once in six months and 35.2 per cent once in twelve months. The remainder, 23.5 per cent, averaged fewer arrests, but only 3.6 per cent were limited to one arrest in the total period.

Comparing the two groups one might say that nonarrests were the normal experience of the nondelinquents up to age seventeen, whereas frequent or occasional arrests were normal for the training school boys.[7] The delinquent group also had many convictions up to age seventeen, ranging from nineteen boys with only one conviction to fifty with eleven or more; the median number per boy was four convictions up to age seventeen.

The patterns of delinquency or nondelinquency established in adoles-

---

[6] Sheldon and Eleanor Glueck, *Delinquents and Nondelinquents in Perspective*, Harvard University Press, Cambridge, Massachusetts, 1968.

[7] *Ibid.*, pp. 49–50, 142–143, 149.

cence continued into adulthood. Between their seventeenth and twenty-fifth birthdays, forty-six of the nondelinquents had been convicted of crimes (9.2 per cent of the total group). This compares with 338 or 77.2 per cent of delinquents who were convicted during the age span seventeen to twenty-five.[8]

During the last age period, ages twenty-five to thirty-one, the nondelinquents had only sixteen convictions (equal to 3.6 per cent of the 442 who could be located on their thirty-first birthdays). In contrast, the delinquent group had 222 convictions or 51.3 of the total of 433 who remained in the study by age thirty-one. (Of the 438 in this group, five were incarcerated during the entire period and hence are not included in the total receiving convictions.)[9] The difference between delinquents and nondelinquents was still wide.

Among the delinquents, convictions decreased with age, as the above figures show for the three age groups, from 100 per cent for the period under age seventeen, to 77.2 per cent for the seventeen to twenty-five age period, to 51.3 per cent for the twenty-five to thirty-one age period. The nature of offenses also changed from one period to another. Before age seventeen, almost one-third of the delinquents were guilty of purely juvenile offenses, that is, offenses for which adults would not be arrested. Burglary and larceny, dominant at all times, decreased from the first (juvenile) period to the second, to the third. Robbery was most frequent in the second (first adult) period, lowest among juveniles, but still prominent in the third period. Among minor offenses, petty larceny, malicious mischief, and violation of probation or parole were highest in the juvenile period and then declined markedly. Other minor offenses had their peak in the age period seventeen to twenty-five: simple assault, offenses against public order, and violation of technical motor vehicle laws. Offenses involving drugs, drunkenness, and domestic relations were characteristic of both adult periods. In general serious offenders dropped from 59.6 per cent of the total number (438) of former delinquents in the first adult period to 28.9 per cent in the second adult period, whereas nonoffenders among former delinquents rose from 22.6 per cent to 48.2 per cent. Minor offenders showed little change, constituting 19.8 per cent at age seventeen to twenty-five and 22.9 per cent at age twenty-five to thirty-one.[10]

COMPARISONS, GLUECK STUDIES I AND II AND ST. LOUIS STUDY

So far as a comparison is possible between Glueck study I and Glueck study II, it indicates that in the same city of the same state (Boston, Massachu-

[8] *Ibid.*, pp. 148–149.
[9] *Ibid.*
[10] *Ibid.*, pp. 146, 151.

setts) the interval of about twenty years between the two studies made little difference in the trend of crime from the juvenile delinquency age up to about thirty years of age, either in percentage still experiencing arrests or in the types of crime. Almost half of the subjects in each study had avoided arrests during the age period of about twenty-five to thirty. For those still having arrests, serious crimes had been cut in half, and minor offenses had increased. Drunkenness had become more frequent as age increased.

The St. Louis study shows that at some time during the thirty-year follow-up 28 per cent of the former juvenile delinquents had served a prison sentence. It is not possible to compare this figure directly with the Glueck study II, but the following figures from that study are informative. In the seventeen to twenty-five age period, 354 offenders suffered 375 sentences to penal institutions (jail, house of correction, state farm, reformatory, prison). During the age period of twenty-five to thirty-one, 263 offenders received 158 sentences to penal institutions.[11] Since nonpenal dispositions are included in the same table, it is not possible to determine how many of the total number of offenders in each age span were never incarcerated and how many were imprisoned more than once. The table shows, however, the decrease in penal sentences from the first to the second age periods.

FUTURE OUTCOMES OTHER THAN CRIME

The seriousness of juvenile delinquency cannot be dismissed with the finding that many delinquents do not become adult criminals. Problems of adjustment other than crime beset many delinquents when they become adults.

ST. LOUIS STUDY. The St. Louis study shows that almost half of the juvenile court cases became alcoholics and one-fourth heavy drinkers. Among children who violated the mores but did not appear in court, one-fourth became alcoholics and more than one-third heavy drinkers. Among Clinic clients with no antisocial behavior, only 15 per cent became alcoholics and about one-fourth heavy drinkers. The control group of public school children had the startling record of no alcoholics, 2 per cent of probable alcoholics, and only 18 per cent heavy drinkers. Nondrinkers increased for the four groups from 28 per cent to 37 to 58 to 80. Thus high percentages of the court cases and the misbehaving noncourt cases used alcohol excessively as adults.[12]

Another portion of the St. Louis study relates childhood status with adult psychiatric status. Adults diagnosed as having no psychiatric diseases increased

[11] *Ibid.*, p. 150.

[12] Lee N. Robins, William M. Bates, and Patricia O'Neal, "Adult Drinking Patterns of Former Problem Children," dittoed, Department of Psychiatry and Neurology, Washington University School of Medicine, St. Louis, Missouri.

from 14 per cent among the former juvenile court cases to 60 per cent in the control group. The chief adult problem of the court cases was socio-pathic personality (37 per cent); an additional 14 per cent showed neurotic reactions. Socio-pathic personality is characterized by rebellion, belligerency, stealing, excessive use of alcohol, vagrancy, and irresponsibility—in other words, varied conduct that threatens society. The outcome for the group in conflict with the mores was chiefly neurotic reactions (30 per cent) and psychotic reactions (30 per cent). The children who came to the Clinic for nondelinquent neurotic problems as adults exhibited neurotic reactions in 37 per cent of the cases and psychotic reactions in 15 per cent. The controls had neurotic reactions diagnosed in 23 per cent of the cases.[13]

It is important to note that the lowest percentage of adults who exhibited neurotic reactions were the former court cases. Few of these definitely delinquent youth later developed psychotic reactions (6 per cent). Their chief difficulty, socio-pathic personality, seemed to be a continuation of their early delinquencies—chiefly thefts and destruction of property. Children who had been referred to the Clinic for truancy, incorrigibility, running away, and fighting were most likely to show psychotic reactions as adults. Sexual misbehavior, learning problems, and tantrums were associated with neurosis in adulthood. The associations between childhood misbehavior and adult maladjustment were not complete; however, the highest rates of well-adjusted adults came from among children whose troubles arose from fighting, common childish neurotic traits, tantrums, and sexual misbehavior. Thus, only in a general way was it possible to forecast the adult maladjustment from the childhood behavior.

The St. Louis study further shows that the Clinic clients who were court cases were much more likely to become divorced as adults than were any of the other groups. Fifty-seven per cent of court cases were divorced, 37 per cent of those guilty of violating the mores, 22 per cent of the nondelinquent problem group, and 12 per cent of the control cases.[14]

Direct lines of development from youth to adulthood are difficult to trace. Children and adolescents usually do not confine their misconduct to one type but range over a number of types. This is especially true of delinquencies carried out by groups of youth. A related cluster of delinquencies is the rule rather than one form only. Although adult offenders may limit their behavior to a narrow pattern, they also may be guilty of several, often related types. A

[13] Patricia O'Neal and Lee N. Robins, *American Journal of Psychiatry*, 114 (1958), 961–969. The diagnoses indicate personality set and do not imply commitment to a mental hospital.

[14] Lee N. Robins and Patricia O'Neal, "The Marital History of Former Problem Children," *Social Problems*, 5 (1958), 347–358.

given kind of juvenile delinquency may therefore be associated with more than one kind of adult behavior.

Nevertheless the evidence from the St. Louis study shows strong trends from certain types of childhood behavior—delinquent, neurotic, normal—to certain general patterns of adult behavior. The juvenile delinquents most frequently have serious criminal, socio-pathic, alcoholic, and marital problems when they become adults.

GLUECK STUDY II. Glueck study II compares the delinquent and nondelinquent groups on many of the same items upon which they were compared as teen-agers. The two groups are never completely different, either as adolescents or as adults, but decided differences are apparent at each stage. At the adult stage, the delinquent group differed from the nondelinquent in the following ways:

1. The delinquents married at a younger age; they had shorter courtships and more forced marriages; they were separated more often, more often married women of "poor character," had more children and more illegitimate children. The delinquents were more neglectful of their marital responsibilities. The marriages were within the conventional pattern for all marriages but tended to include characteristics that have been found to weaken marriages. As might be expected fewer families were cohesive.
2. The delinquents moved more often than nondelinquents, lived in poorer residential areas, had homes that were more poorly furnished and more overcrowded. The delinquents continued to live in much the same kind of surroundings they were in as children, whereas the nondelinquents had been able to make some improvements.
3. The work record of the delinquents was less favorable than that of the nondelinquents. The delinquents left school earlier and started to work at an earlier age. Their work status was lower, they had poorer work habits, more unemployment, and lower income. One-fifth of the delinquents became involved in illicit occupations, compared with a "handful" of the nondelinquents. Starting from approximately the same low economic status, the delinquents tended to remain there, whereas the nondelinquents made a reasonable but not spectacular improvement over their childhood and their parents' status.
4. The delinquents as adults spent less time at home than the nondelinquents although when at home the two groups engaged in much the same kind of recreation—radio, television, and light reading. Delinquents had more questionable friends and spent more time in cafes, taverns, barrooms, nightclubs, on street corners, and in gambling places. They spent more time in criminal activities.
5. The two groups differed little physically, but what difference existed favored the nondelinquents. Neuroticism, which had been more frequent among nondelinquents than delinquents during adolescence, in adulthood was

about the same. Delinquents more frequently were psychopathic and more often were poorly adjusted. They were more discontented with their lot in life, had unrealistic ambitions (e.g. to make a lot of money), and were less interested in improvement of their homes or of family status. They seemed more immature than the nondelinquents.[15]

The three studies indicate an interlocking in adulthood of personal characteristics and social attitudes and behavior patterns. This interlocking is true of both delinquents and nondelinquents. Since the control groups in both the St. Louis and the Glueck study II came from the same neighborhoods as the delinquents, the differences cannot be accounted for by gross social factors. Within the same social milieu, differences appear in innate physical, mental, and temperamental traits, in family relationships, and in peer group and community institutional contacts. In addition, for delinquents contacts with police, courts, and training schools have to be taken into account. Also, different types of delinquency may arise from different combinations of factors and lead to different future outcomes. The findings of the three studies are very important; they lay the groundwork for more detailed studies of the way in which the various factors that now seem related to the development of delinquency and crime are interrelated.

The Linkage of Juvenile Delinquency and Adult Crime

A study of the entire trend of delinquency and crime shows that juvenile court appearances reach a peak at ages fourteen to sixteen and that arrests as reported by the Federal Bureau of Investigation reach a peak at ages sixteen to eighteen. Many of these young people have only one arrest, court appearance, or short term of imprisonment. They do not, thereafter, continue in crime. Others more slowly adapt to conventional life. Some continue at whatever level of minor or serious criminal behavior they have achieved as juveniles.

Several reasons may account for the one official offense. The act may have been one that really was contrary to the personality set—the attitudes and moral standards—of the person and would perhaps not have been repeated even if arrest or court appearance had not followed. For some offenders, the arrest and court hearing may have given sufficient shock to turn the person back to conformity. Friends and family may have strongly disapproved of the misconduct but accepted the delinquent back and helped him to reaffiliate himself with conventional society. Various studies indicate that offenders who persist in misconduct or move toward continued criminal behavior more frequently come from disorganized areas and families than those whose foray into

15 These items have been drawn from Glueck and Glueck, *Delinquents and Nondelinquents in Perspective*, pp. 53–130, and regrouped.

crime is short-lived. We may surmise that only certain types of delinquents coming from certain types of backgrounds are likely to become adult criminals.

For complete understanding, another factor is important. What effect does a year or more spent in a training school or a few years in a prison have on the offender? Opportunities for re-education and personal rehabilitation differ radically from one institution to another. The months spent in some institutions may draw the offender into closer relationships with other offenders and build up permanent antisocial attitudes; in other institutions, lasting re-education and rehabilitation may be accomplished for some of the offenders.

BIBLIOGRAPHY

BATES, WILLIAM, LEE N. ROBINS, AND PATRICIA O'NEAL, "Prisons and the Problem Child," address given at the Midwest Sociological Society, 1960.*

CARPENTER, KENNETH S., "Halfway Houses for Delinquent Youth," *Children*, 10 (1963), 224–229.

CAVAN, RUTH SHONLE, ed., *Readings in Juvenile Delinquency*, Third Edition, J. B. Lippincott Company, Philadelphia, 1975, Chapter 12.

"Correction in the United States," *Crime and Delinquency*, 13 (1967), 97–112.

FRUM, HAROLD S., "Adult Criminal Offense Trends Following Juvenile Delinquency, *Journal of Criminal Law, Criminology and Police Science*, 49 (1958), 29–49.

GLUECK, SHELDON, AND GLUECK, ELEANOR, *Delinquents and Nondelinquents in Perspective*, Harvard University Press, Cambridge, Massachusetts, 1968.

———, *One Thousand Juvenile Delinquents*, Harvard University Press, Cambridge, Massachusetts, 1934.

———, *Juvenile Delinquents Grown Up*, The Commonwealth Fund, New York, 1940.

Halfway House Program for Delinquent Youth, Children's Bureau, U. S. Department of Health, Education, and Welfare, Washington, D. C., 1965.

MANELLA, FRANK L., "Aftercare Programs," *National Probation and Parole Association Journal*, 4 (1958), 74–80.

McNEIL, FRANCES, "A Halfway-house Program for Delinquents," *Crime and Delinquency*, 13 (1967), 538–544.

MICHAEL, CARMEN MILLER, "Follow-up Studies of Introverted Children, III, Relative Incidence of Criminal Behavior," *Journal of Criminal Law, Criminology and Police Science*, 47 (1956), 414–422.

National Advisory Commission on Criminal Justice Standards and Goals, *Corrections*, U. S. Government Printing Office, Washington, D. C., 1973, Chapter 12.

O'NEAL, PATRICIA, AND LEE N. ROBINS, "Childhood Patterns Predictive of Adult Schizophrenia: A Thirty-year Follow-up Study," *American Journal of Psychiatry*, 115 (1959), 385–391.

* Dittoed, Department of Psychiatry and Neurology, Washington University School of Medicine, St. Louis, Missouri.

————, "The Relation of Childhood Behavior Problems to Adult Psychiatric Status," *American Journal of Psychiatry*, 114 (1958), 961–969.

————, Jeanette Schaefer, John Bergmann, and Lee N. Robins, "A Psychiatric Evaluation of Adults Who Had Sexual Problems as Children: A Thirty-year Follow-up Study," *Human Organization*, 19 (Spring, 1960), 32–39.

Rappaport, Mazie F., "The Possibility of Help for the Child Returning from a State Training School," in Sheldon Glueck, ed., *The Problem of Delinquency*, Houghton Mifflin Company, Boston, 1959, pp. 947–955.

Robins, Lee N., *Deviant Children Grown Up*, Williams and Wilkins Co., Baltimore, 1966.

————, "Mental Illness and the Runaway: A Thirty-year Follow-up Study," *Human Organization*, 16, No. 4 (undated reprint), 11–15.

————, William M. Bates, and Patricia O'Neal, "Adult Drinking Patterns of Former Problem Children."*

————, and Patricia O'Neal, "The Adult Prognosis for Runaway Children," *American Journal of Orthopsychiatry*, 29 (1959), 752–761.

————, "The Marital History of Former Problem Children," *Social Problems*, 5 (1958), 347–358.

* Dittoed, Department of Psychiatry and Neurology, Washington University School of Medicine, St. Louis, Missouri.

index of names

index of subjects

Drug abuse, 19
Drug users, 148–153

East Side Disciples, 284
Ego-identity, 78–79, 134
Emotional maladjustment and delinquency, 89, 182
Empirical typologies, 141–142
Evaluation, of probation, 390–392
  of training school programs, 413–416

Failure of psychotherapy, 294–299
Father's attitudes and delinquency, 195–196
Forestry Camps, 428–435

Gang delinquencies, 116–117
Gang language, 126–127
Gang member, life history, 246–250
Gang roles, 159–160
  delinquency and, 11–12
Gangs, and the foundations, 284–285
  types of, 117–124
Gemeinschaft, 94–96
Genesis of a gang, 116–117
Gesellschaft, 94–96
Girl delinquency, 218
  family relationships and, 199
Girl delinquent, life history, 250–254
  lower class, 223–226
  middle class, 222–223
Gluecks' Socal Prediction Table, 294–298
Good boys in high delinquency areas, 135–136
Group therapy, 290–294

Halfway houses, 444–446
History of juvenile institutions, 396–400

Ideal typologies, 142–144
Immature Conformists, 88, 142, 165–166
Individual delinquent, 130–132
  life history of, 234–242
Informal gangs, 119–120
Intelligence and delinquency, 8, 177–181
Interpersonal maturity level, theory of, 86–91
Interpretive therapy, 288–289

Juvenile delinquency, in ancient Babylon, 2
  in ancient Rome, 4
  in Canada, 18–19
  defined, 1, 23–28
  drinking and, 50–53
  among the Eskimos, 19–20
  in Great Britain and Northern Ireland, 19–20
  in Japan, 19
  in Malaysia, 19

Juvenile delinquency (continued)
  mass media and, 10–11
  in medieval England, 4
  in Mexico, 20
  in modern America, 6
  in the Netherlands, 19
  in Poland, 19
  poverty and, 210–211
  race and, 9, 53–55
  recreation and, 16
  school and, 102–104
  social class and, 101–102, 108–112
  slums and, 17
  in Thailand, 19
Juvenile delinquents as adults, 447–460
Juvenile Court, and the Criminal Court, 363–365
  dispositions of juvenile cases, 378–381
  hearings and, 375–378
  judges of, 365–367
  kinds of, 358–362
  publicity for, 375–378
  reform of, 354–358
  screening of cases, 372–374
  social investigations in the, 374–375
  sources of referral, 371–372
  statistics related to, 55–57
  terminology of, 311–312
Juvenile officers, practices of, 325–326
  selection and training of, 323–325

Labeling theory, 82–84
Limitations of arrest data, 37–38

Male and female juvenile arrests, 44–45
Manipulators, 88, 143, 164–165
Mother dominant families, 205–208
Mother's attitudes and delinquency, 192–195

Neighborhood Youth Corps, 280–281
Neurotic delinquent, 76, 88

Organized gangs, 120–122
Overindulged child, 76–77

Parental discipline, 196
Police, discretion in handling delinquents, 317–320
  preventive programs of, 326–328
  relationships with the juvenile court, 328–329
  relationships with the school, 329–330
Probation, 382–392
Problems of post-release adjustment, 443–444
Psychiatric treatment centers, 435
Psychoanalysis, 289